Praise for *To the Bitter End*

"By far the fullest account to date of anti-Hitler plotting." —*Time*

"Gisevius is destined to be remembered as long as men esteem human freedom. . . . He simply tells the honest story of the fight waged by men of conscience against an evil despotism, and tells it with a vividness and felicity of style which places his work among the distinguished memoirs of history."
—*New York Herald Tribune Book Review*

"Gisevius unquestionably possessed the boldness and wit necessary for the dangerous game he played. When he left the safety of Switzerland and returned to Berlin in July 1944, he gambled his life as coolly as any submarine crewman or fighter pilot."
—*Saturday Review of Literature*

"[An] illuminating, highly readable account of a dark stretch of history."
—*New York Times Book Review*

To the
BITTER END

AN INSIDER'S ACCOUNT OF THE PLOT
TO KILL HITLER, 1933–1944

by HANS BERND GISEVIUS

*Translated from the German
by Richard and Clara Winston*

FOREWORD BY ALLEN DULLES
NEW INTRODUCTION BY PETER HOFFMANN

DA CAPO PRESS • NEW YORK

Library of Congress Cataloging-in-Publication Data

Gisevius, Hans Bernd, 1904–
    [Bis zum bittern Ende. English]
    To the bitter end: an insider's account of the plot to kill Hitler, 1933–1944 /
by Hans Bernd Gisevius; translated from the German by Richard and Clara
Winston.—1st Da Capo Press ed.
        p.   cm.
    Includes index.
    ISBN 0-306-80869-2 (alk. paper)
    1. Hitler, Adolf, 1889–1945—Assassination attempts. 2. Gisevius, Hans Bernd,
1904–   . 3. Anti-Nazi movement—Germany. 4. Germany—Politics and government—1933–1945. I. Title.
DD247.H5G5313   1998
943.086′ 092—dc21   98-8449
                                                                                          CIP

First Da Capo Press edition 1998

This Da Capo Press paperback edition of *To the Bitter End* is an unabridged
republication of the edition first published in Cambridge, Massachusetts in 1947,
here supplemented with a new introduction by Peter Hoffmann.

Originally published in German as *Bis zum bittern Ende* in 1946.

Published by Da Capo Press, Inc.
A Subsidiary of Plenum Publishing Corporation
233 Spring Street, New York, N.Y. 10013

To the Memory of

HANS OSTER

Who was killed on April 9, 1945
in the death camp
at Flossenburg

Introduction

Hans Bernd Gisevius, the son of a Prussian high-court judge, was born in Arnsberg in Westfalia, Germany on June 14, 1904 and died in Switzerland on February 23, 1974.[1] After attending high-school in Berlin, he became a student of law and received a doctorate in 1929. In the same year he joined the *Deutschnationale Volkspartei* (German National Peoples Party, DNVP), a rightist conservative party, and the *Stahlhelm* veterans' organization. When he was articling in the judicial system in Berlin, he also took part in the Right's campaign against the Young Plan, which rescheduled German reparation payments. His political activity resulted in his punitive transfer to Düsseldorf in May 1930, and in libel suits against him, with one brought by Chancellor Heinrich Brüning. Gisevius lost them all, although they provided him with prominence as well as notoriety: by the end of 1931 he had been elected to membership in the national council of the DNVP. In the autumn of 1931 Gisevius had formed under his leadership a young DNVP group (*Arbeitsgemeinschaft junger Deutschnationaler*) that involved itself in the party's internal struggles. He advocated cooperation with the *Nationalsozialistische Deutsche Arbeiterpartei* (National Socialist German Workers Party, NSDAP). In 1933 he was leader of the *Deutschnationaler Kampfring Westen* (German National Combat Ring West) in Düsseldorf-Ost and a member of the national executive board of the DNVP. But on June 11, 1933 the NSDAP daily newspaper *Völkischer*

Beobachter reported—on its front page under banner headlines—the sensational resignation of Dr. Gisevius and two other DNVP executive-board members, and quoted them for "their commitment to National Socialism" as the sole support of the German state.

In July 1933 Gisevius passed his second law examinations and in August he entered the Prussian civil service as an assessor in the Political Section of the Prussian Interior Ministry. He aspired to the position of chief of the Prussian *Geheime Staatspolizei* (Secret State Police, for short, *Gestapo*[2]), which soon became the national Secret State Police. He joined forces with the head of the executive department of the Prussian Secret State Police, Arthur Nebe, and intrigued with him against the successful candidate, Rudolf Diels, whom they denounced as a Communist. As a result, Diels was temporarily removed. When he returned after a short absence, he accused Gisevius of reactionary subversion and had a warrant issued for his arrest. Gisevius escaped through postings to positions without authority, such as observer at the trial of the *Reichstag* arsonist in Leipzig, and as a government counsellor in Münster and Potsdam.

Notwithstanding his application of November 15, 1933 to join the NSDAP[3]—two weeks *after* the *Gestapo* warrant for his arrest had been issued—Gisevius did not become a National Socialist. Whether or not he had made his application sincerely or for his own protection, there is no record to indicate that he later withdrew it. There was a moratorium for new memberships from May 1, 1933 to May 1, 1937[4], and since Gisevius was in some disgrace with the authorities, it was not likely that an exception would have been made for him. When the moratorium was lifted, his eligibility had not improved.

His attempt to crash the gates to power had failed; his career had become derailed. He was in and out of postings in the Prussian and Reich interior ministries, appearing as Berlin Police Chief Wolf Count von Helldorf's permanent deputy on the police staff for the 1936 Olympiad, only to be dismissed upon the intervention of Reinhard Heydrich, the new chief of the *Gestapo* and of the Security Police and SD.

The alternative to advancement within the National Socialist establishment appeared toward the end of the 1930s. At Hitler's announcement in November 1937 of his plans for war, both Field-marshal Werner von Blomberg, the War Minister, and General Werner Baron von Fritsch, the Commander-in-Chief of the Army, raised objections. By the end of January 1938 they had become tainted by scandal and were dismissed. During this crisis the conspiracy against Hitler began to form itself around the Chief of the General Staff of the Army, General Ludwig Beck, and the former Reich Prices Commissioner and Mayor of Leipzig, Carl Goerdeler. It included the chief of the *Abwehr* (military intelligence), Admiral Wilhelm Canaris; Canaris's right hand, Major Hans Oster; Helldorf; the former Reich Economics Minister Hjalmar Schacht; Nebe; and Berlin's Deputy Chief of Police, Fritz-Dietlof Count von der Schulenburg. Having made Oster's acquaintance, Gisevius attached himself to the conspirators. He specialized in observing the *Gestapo* and in using his connections to keep the conspirators informed and to help them plan a coup d'état. Oster and Gisevius were the most active conspirators.

Since the *Gestapo* had based the accusations against Fritsch on a false identification, Gisevius saw an opportunity to do battle against the agency that had rejected him and that he perhaps still hoped to head. Gisevius's ambition became a catalyst that helped to assemble the forces of the resistance movement that culminated in the abortive July 20, 1944 insurrection. By the late summer of 1938—after Beck had resigned in protest against Hitler's threat of war against Czechoslovakia, and after General Franz Halder had succeeded him as Chief of the General Staff—the conspiracy aimed at overthrowing Hitler. Oster and Schacht now referred Halder to Gisevius for matters concerning the deployment of the police in a coup d'état. The Berlin military district commander, General Erwin von Witzleben, employed Gisevius as a liaison between himself and the Oster group, and provided him with a cover name and an office on the pretext that he was sorting through family papers.

When war broke out, Oster arranged for Gisevius to be drafted into the *Abwehr*, and in 1940 installed him as an intelligence agent, disguised as a vice-consul, in the German consulate-general in Zurich, where he had no duties and no office. While there, he helped establish foreign contacts for the resistance. He worked for the *Abwehr*, and also collaborated first with British intelligence (who soon suspected him of being a double-agent), and from January 1943 (after the arrival of Allen W. Dulles in Bern as head of the Office of Strategic Services bureau there in the autumn of 1942) with American intelligence.[5] He helped to channel reports on SS atrocities into Hitler's leadership staff—onto the desk of the Chief of Armed Forces Supreme Command (OKW), Fieldmarshal Wilhelm Keitel—by disguising them as foreign intelligence material.[6] He risked his life with his double role, in the interest of ending the war and the crimes that were being committed under the cover of war.

During these years Gisevius persuaded Oster to use *Abwehr* money to establish a fund in Switzerland that would be available to a post-Hitler resistance government. In the autumn of 1942 Hans von Dohnanyi—with the aid of Oster, Canaris, Helmuth James Count von Moltke, and Dietrich Bonhoeffer—helped a number of Jews to escape to Switzerland. Gisevius withdrew from the fund $100,000 as partial compensation for the assets which the refugees had had to leave behind in Berlin, and as security against the émigrés becoming wards of the Swiss state, which the Swiss government demanded as a condition for granting the necessary entry visas. Gisevius got into difficulties with the OKW accounting section that supervised the financial transactions of the *Abwehr*, which was also a section of OKW. Some of Gisevius's appropriations from the fund had not followed prescribed procedure. The OKW accounting section investigated and found Oster, Gisevius, and others to be involved in unauthorized transactions. At the same time, the *Abwehr* chief in Bern, Commander Hans Meisner, had become suspicious of Gisevius's many contacts with enemy representatives in Switzerland, and accused Gisevius of collaboration with the enemy. The OKW accounting section demanded the repatriation of the fund in the summer of 1942. Gisevius at first resisted its repatriation, since his ability to use it had given him considerable status, but he relented toward the end of the summer of 1942.[7] He returned briefly to Germany in the summer of 1943, escaping just before he was to be arrested.

Gisevius continued in his double role in Switzerland until July 1944, receiving from *Abwehr* couriers information that he passed on to Allen Dulles, such as information on the development of what later became the V-1 and V-2 rockets and ballistic missiles, and, as Dulles wrote in recommending Gisevius as a witness for the Nuremburg War Crimes Trial, "clues which later helped toward the spotting of the German testing station at Peenemunde."[8]

On July 11, 1944, having been informed by his German contact in the conspiracy that the coup d'état was about to occur, Gisevius travelled to Berlin in order to participate in it. After it had failed, he went into hiding until he was able to escape to Switzerland on January 23, 1945, with the aid of a passport that belonged to Carl Deichmann, a brother of Helmuth James Count von Moltke's wife. The passport had been doctored through the offices of Dulles, and Georg Federer in the German Legation in Bern helped to provide the necessary visa.[9]

ii

Gisevius began his book in Germany in 1938 but completed most of it in Switzerland during the war. He continued writing it while helping Allen Dulles's assistant Mary Bancroft and her friends Mary Briner and Elizabeth Scott-Montagu prepare a translation, which was transmitted to OSS headquarters in Washington.[10] In fact, Dulles had initiated the translation as a method of unobtrusively but frequently debriefing Gisevius in the interest of American intelligence. But Gisevius was most anxious to have his book published as soon as possible, believing that it would launch him into the prominence that had eluded him in the years from 1929 to 1934, and again, through the failure of the coup d'état of

July 20, 1944. But, with the war over, he was now a *formerly* useful informant, and his attempts to gain an official or otherwise respectable position met with embarrassed or indifferent rejection by the beneficiaries of the information he had earlier transmitted.

To the Bitter End was first published in a German-language edition in Switzerland (1946) and in an English translation in Britain and in America (1947). The Swiss publishers had been reserved in light of rumors about Gisevius's association with the National Socialist dictatorship, but were eventually persuaded by testimonials from unimpeachable sources. The book was very successful in Switzerland and in Germany and was reprinted, with some revisions, several times. After Gisevius had testified at the Nuremberg War Crimes Trial in 1946, he was able to choose from among eight offers from American publishers.[11]

When I met Gisevius in Lausanne and St. Légier in Switzerland in 1971 and 1972, *To the Bitter End* had been subjected to criticism for 25 years. He said at once that he had written his book "in a subjective form, not as a book for historians."[12] Indeed, Gisevius had not intended to offer a memoir of life in Hitler's Third Reich, but rather a serious analysis of the National Socialist dictatorship and a history of the resistance to it. He had only thrown in the firsthand episodes to enliven the more serious aspects. He later made some changes, eliminated repetitious passages, and gave the text more of the appearance of a firsthand account. Although much of what he had related has been confirmed by other contemporary sources—often in crucial detail—the accuracy of numerous points has been disputed on the basis of other sources and of internal evidence.

The book begins with an account of the discovery of the burning of the *Reichstag* building, and of the arrest and prosecution of the alleged arsonist, the Dutch Communist Marinus van der Lubbe. In *To the Bitter End*, Gisevius indicted the National Socialist leaders (particularly Hermann Göring) of having masterminded the incendiary attack, as he had done as a witness at the Nuremberg War Crimes Trial in 1946.[13] He claimed in his book to give his description "from the author's experience," although he had only secondhand knowledge of the events.

In 1959 a researcher, Fritz Tobias, published a series of articles challenging Gisevius's version of the *Reichstag* fire in a number of points and concluding that Marinus van der Lubbe was indeed the sole arsonist. Tobias contended, *inter alia*, that Gisevius had sought successfully to associate himself with Hitler's National Socialists in June 1933; that he had aspired to head the *Gestapo*; that the Chief of the *Gestapo*, Rudold Diels, had not sent him as an observer to the trial of Marinus van der Lubbe; that he had not attended the proceedings except during their last few days in December 1933; that he was not competent to give a true account of the events of the night of February 27, 1933; and that—although in response to some of Tobias's allegations he had claimed to have studied the records of Marinus van der Lubbe's trial—he had offered a version of the events which differed from the findings of the court, and for which he had neither firsthand knowledge nor other evidence.

Gisevius immediately launched a series of articles of his own to affirm his account, and accused a former SA trooper, Heini Gewehr, a construction engineer, of having led the gang of SA arsonists who torched the *Reichstag* building. The real issue—which, however, the courts were not asked directly to judge—was Gisevius's suggestion that the National Socialists themselves had set fire to the *Reichstag*, and had blamed the arson on the Communists in order to justify repressive emergency decrees and the establishment of Hitler's dictatorship. When Tobias's work was published as a book in 1961, Gisevius obtained a court injunction in December 1961 forbidding further sales of the book. Beginning with a lower-court judgment in January 1962, the courts at every level decided in Tobias's favor. Gewehr brought suit against Gisevius. Ultimately, in 1966 the German Supreme Court decided against Gisevius. But Gewehr was ruined, having lost his position in the construction firm, and his health.[14]

In his original typescript version that he showed to Mary Bancroft in the spring of 1943, Gisevius had not offered an explanation to the mystery surrounding the burning of the *Reichstag*. When she asked him about it, he said he would have to talk over some points with Nebe first.[15]

Gisevius also relates, in his second chapter, that Ludwig Grauert, business manager of "the Employers' Association of Rhenish-Westphalian heavy industry," had used RM 500,000 slush-fund money, in collaboration with industrialist Fritz Thyssen, to "rescue Hitler from his financial catastrophe of 1932."[16] Grauert became undersecretary of state in Göring's Prussian Ministry of the Interior in 1933, and Gisevius describes himself as Grauert's protégé. His story must have come from Grauert. But, be it that Grauert had inaccurately told it, or that Gisevius imprecisely remembered it, the facts were not as he related them.

Grauert was, in fact, managing director of the employers' association of the iron and steel industry in the Ruhr district. In the autumn of 1930, after the large success of the NSDAP in the *Reichstag* elections of September 1930, and when Hitler was far from "financial catastrophe," Grauert arranged for a loan not to Hitler but to Otto Wagener, the former Chief of Staff of the SA, who had begun to work for the NSDAP Economic Policy Section in 1930. The loan was for the purpose of launching a Nazi newspaper, the *National-Zeitung*, in Essen in the Ruhr district. Wagener remembered the loan as amounting to 50,000 marks; Grauert remembered 100,000 marks.[17]

Gisevius's initial claim that in his book "all of it comes from the author's experience"[18] evidently merits some skepticism. The list of examples of revelations that are not based on Gisevius's own direct experience but on reports from others or on hearsay would be lengthy. Indeed, one may conclude that when he called his superior in the *Gestapo*, Rudolf Diels, "imaginative,"[19] the pot was calling the kettle black. During the war, when Gisevius worked in Zurich for the *Abwehr* while supplying Allen Dulles with military information, Dulles's intermediary, Mary Bancroft, asked him what he was sending his German superiors. Gisevius replied, "imaginative reports."[20]

iii

One of Gisevius's most grievous errors in judgment concerns Colonel Claus Count von Stauffenberg. Gisevius's description of Stauffenberg, the leader of the July 20, 1944 insurrection, reveals less about the colonel than about Gisevius's own political orientation, and about his resentment of a rival who did not seem to appreciate Gisevius's contribution to the resistance.

Gisevius met Stauffenberg for the first time in Berlin on July 12, 1944, eight days before the colonel's last assassination attempt against Hitler. Much of what Gisevius relates about Stauffenberg, however, came to him not mainly from his only conversation with Stauffenberg before July 15 and 20, 1944, but, as he himself relates, from conspirators such as General Friedrich Olbricht and General Ludwig Beck, and, most of all, from Canaris's successor as head of the *Abwehr*, Colonel Georg Hansen.[21] In view of Gisevius's own record as a transmitter of historical information for which he had displayed strong personal feelings, and in light of what is known about both Gisevius's alleged sources and Stauffenberg himself, Gisevius's account is at best questionable hearsay.

Gisevius disliked Stauffenberg. He sensed that this dynamic leader would be an obstacle to his own far-reaching ambitions and intrigues. In his book he mocked Stauffenberg as a presumptuous and ignorant amateur (p. 508): "As chief of staff to the commander of the home army he wanted me to 'inform' him about phases of the situation with which he was not acquainted. I came from Switzerland where all sorts of information was available. Would I give him my impressions?"

When Stauffenberg had joined the conspiracy in the late summer of 1943, he had begun quickly to take matters into his own hands, to organize and coordinate the preparations for Hitler's overthrow. In the matter of foreign contacts he relied on Helmuth James Count von Moltke, Adam von Trott zu Solz, and Otto John whom he knew, and who were able to travel abroad (to Turkey, Sweden, Switzerland, Spain), rather than on older diplomats such as Ulrich von Hassell or Friedrich Werner Count von der Schulenburg, the former ambassadors in Rome and Moscow respectively, who were no longer in a position to travel to neutral countries.[22] Stauffenberg must have been informed of Gisevius's background, and it cannot have inspired his confidence. Gisevius was understandably upset by Stauffenberg's attitude toward him. He had spent years establishing a usable contact for the resistance abroad, with the undertaking to Allen Dulles that every communication from General Ludwig Beck, the presumptive post-Hitler head of state, was coming only through Gisevius himself. He had revealed military information to Dulles in order to establish his own credibility, only to find that Stauffenberg seemed to regard him merely as an incidental source of background information.[23]

In his book Gisevius reduced Stauffenberg to a frustrated cripple[24]: "I sensed at once that this unfortunate man must renounce the hope of attracting masses of people to his cause. His effectiveness must henceforth be confined to small groups. It was as if a pitiless destiny had deliberately planned to thrust him into the rôle of a conspirator." He described Stauffenberg as rude and boorish, and judged that "consciously or unconsciously, he was trying to overcompensate for the inferiority feelings engendered by his mutilation." Gisevius considered Stauffenberg "a swashbuckler," "typical of the 'new' class of general staff officers: the kind of man best suited to Hitler's purposes—or to purposes of assassination" (which in the context must suggest a Nazi murderer), who "in the final analysis was fighting for the continuation of Nazi-militaristic 'legality.' "[25] And: "Stauffenberg was motivated by the impulsive passions of the disillusioned military man whose eyes had been opened by the defeat of German arms."[26] Stauffenberg "had shifted to the rebel side only after Stalingrad."[27] With patronizing insincerity, Gisevius—so he himself reports—personally expressed to Stauffenberg during their interview that night in

July his respect for Stauffenberg's courage to carry out the assassination.[28]

When he declares Stauffenberg "boorish," Gisevius's air of offended refined sentiments is not convincing in light of his insulting and inaccurate description of the man who dared to kill Hitler. Gisevius was not aware that throughout 1942 Stauffenberg had attempted, singlehandedly and against overwhelming odds, as a lowly major in the General Staff, to convince senior commanders on the eastern front to overthrow Hitler. Nor did Gisevius know Stauffenberg's inclination of taking the opposite side in any conversation for the sake of acting as *advocatus diaboli*.

There appears to have been a clash of views when Gisevius explained his anti-Communist and pro-American positions. Stauffenberg replied, according to Gisevius's account of the conversation —the only one that exists—that very likely it would be necessary to negotiate with the Soviet Union, since it was probably "too late for the West," and the Red Army would reach the gates of Berlin within a few weeks. If this is an accurate account of what Stauffenberg said, the basis of it was the fact that German forces were unable to halt the rapid advance of the Red Army, which was about to occupy east and central Germany. Numerous attempts of the resistance to arrange for a separate cease-fire had been rejected by the western powers, so that it was impossible for German forces to withdraw unilaterally without being thrown into chaos by the pursuing enemy. There was no alternative to negotiating with, or surrendering to, the Soviet Union as well as to the western powers.

But Gisevius himself believed, as he told Beck the next day, that the western powers had no inclination at all to treat with any German government, and, according to Gisevius, Stauffenberg had not said that he sought to negotiate *only* with the Soviet Union.[29] In fact, it is not clear from Gisevius's account what exactly Stauffenberg had said. Gisevius describes his own summary of what Stauffenberg said as "only an approximation of what he said, for he contradicted himself in the same breath."[30]

There are two other sources by which one may gauge Gisevius's account. Firstly, Allen Dulles was convinced of the necessity to offer assurances to the German and German-occupied peoples that America would prevent the Soviet Union from "imposing their brand of domination on Europe," and, soon after his arrival in Bern, he had urged his government, in a dispatch dated December 6, 1942, to implement the necessary policies.[31] This was his view *before* he met Gisevius in January 1943. Gisevius took the same position and sought to convince him that America must defeat not only Nazi Germany but the Bolshevik world revolution as well, and that therefore America needed to conclude a separate peace with Germany after the resistance had overthrown Hitler. Secondly, there is a memorandum that Gisevius left behind for Dulles in Zurich before travelling to Berlin on July 11, 1944. Herein Gisevius advocated—before he had ever met Stauffenberg—an arrangement to have western Germany occupied by the western powers, and here he claimed, before Stauffenberg had allegedly suggested it, that many Germans believed their country could come to an arrangement with Russia if Germany accepted a Bolshevik government.[32] The implicit threat to the western powers' postwar position is obvious. These views were part of the basis on which Gisevius and Dulles collaborated.

After Gisevius had escaped to Switzerland, he reiterated and apparently expanded his predictions and warnings. They are reflected in Dulles's January and February 1945 cables to Washington, in which Dulles sought to induce his government to offer terms to German military leaders who surrendered in one or all of the western theaters of war. Dulles was already pursuing a secret contact with the German Supreme Commander West, Fieldmarshal Gerd von Rundstedt, and he had established such a contact with the German Supreme Commander Southwest, Fieldmarshal Albert Kesselring in Italy.[33]

It appears, therefore, that the conclusions Gisevius claimed to have drawn from his conversation with Stauffenberg were views

he had held before he had ever met Stauffenberg, and which co-
incided with those of Dulles.

Finally, there is a further dimension to the immediate rift between Stauffenberg and Gisevius: the latter's personal ambition
strongly suggested that he must have a role in the dispositions of
the western powers for Germany. If these dispositions were made
as he suggested them to Dulles, Gisevius would gain standing. It
was really too late for all of this since Germany could now only
surrender unconditionally, and the victorious powers would see no
need to honor any commitments. But Gisevius tried desperately to
stay in the game. He had told Mary Bancroft just before leaving
Zurich in July 1944 that he claimed for himself the position of
foreign minister in the future German government.[34] When he
mentioned the question of a post-coup position for himself to
Stauffenberg, the colonel had not said anything but had merely
smiled.[35]

In a report for Dulles in February 1945, Gisevius went even
further. He claimed that the resistance conspiracy of July 1944
had planned, immediately following upon a successful coup d'état,
to put in place a directory of five that was to hold all executive
power. Three days afterward, a cabinet was to have been formed
under the authority of the new head of state, General Ludwig
Beck. There were to be a chancellor, a vice-chancellor, and ministers of the interior, economics, justice, cultural affairs, finance, foreign affairs, and war. But all civil executive authority was to be
turned over to Gisevius.[36]

To the end of his life Gisevius believed that Stauffenberg had
been "left-leaning," mostly under the influence of the Social-
Democrat Julius Leber. He believed this equally about several others such as Fritz-Dietlof Count von der Schulenburg.[37] Perhaps,
having lived abroad for so long, and with his background as a
right-wing die-hard conservative in the *Deutschnationale Volkspartei* and in the *Stahlhelm*, Gisevius was hypersensitive to any
hints of an association with socialist forces.

As the political animal Gisevius was, he evidently misread Stauffenberg's idealistic views. He sensed in Stauffenberg the hidden agenda of the Secret Germany of the disciples of Stefan George and thought that this involved "the continuation of Nazi-militaristic legality.'"[38] Stauffenberg, for his part, understood Gisevius's potential for mischief when he threatened, no doubt in jest, to have the book that later became *To the Bitter End* suppressed.[39]

iv

What Gisevius's book does offer—beyond the more or less accurate outlines of certain key episodes in the twelve years of the National Socialist dictatorship in Germany—is an authentic atmosphere, a firsthand flavor of life in that dictatorship, and of life at a rather high level. Gisevius has obviously overblown the substance and importance of the interviews he managed to have with eminent persons. But his account of the conspiracy to overthrow Hitler is important because it is, to a large extent, a rare firsthand account, detailed, and chronologically close to the events, although it is colored by Gisevius's flamboyance and resentments.

A substantial amount of the contents of *To the Bitter End* is valuable and, on the whole, not necessarily less reliable than other autobiographical works. The reader needs to approach the book critically, and to keep in mind whether or not Gisevius was describing his own personal experiences or those of others, and was thus depending on other firsthand witnesses, or on hearsay, or on official correspondence, or on newspapers and the radio. A researcher wishing to use this book as a primary source would in any case have to look for corroboration in other primary sources before accepting anything as fact. Indeed, a good number of Gisevius's accounts of episodes may be confirmed by reference to the diaries of the former German ambassador to Rome, Ulrich von Hassell, or of an officer in the *Abwehr*, Helmuth Groscurth, or the wartime account of Otto John.[40]

Whatever the weight of Gisevius's ambitions and career orientation, his commitment to destroying Hitler is undeniable, and it led him to take extraordinary risks with his life. Still, questions remain. For example, it is unclear why Gisevius erected a monument for his friend Nebe and made excuses for Nebe's function as commander of *Einsatzgruppe B,* which was responsible for the murder of more than 100,000 Jews in Russia. Did Gisevius really believe that his friend Nebe was not responsible for mass murder? Did Gisevius really lack the knowledge of what the *Einsatzgruppen* had done?[41]

In the end the reader must decide for himself whether this is the book of an aspiring statesman unjustly frustrated in his righteous ambition, or the work of someone whose personality clashed with his ambition.

PETER HOFFMANN
Montreal
February 1998

Peter Hoffmann, William Kingsford Professor of History at McGill University in Canada, is the author of the acclaimed The History of the German Resistance 1933–1944, Hitler's Personal Security, *and* Stauffenberg: A Family History, 1905–1944.

NOTES

1. This biographical sketch is based mainly on Gisevius's own book (*To the Bitter End*, Houghton Mifflin Company, Boston, 1947); on his testimony at the Nuremberg War Crimes Trial (*Der Prozess gegen die Hauptkriegsverbrecher vor dem internationalen Militärgerichtshof Nürnberg 14. November 1945–1. Oktober 1946*, vol. XII, Sekretariat des Gerichtshofs, Nürnberg, 1947); on Allen W. Dulles's postwar accounts (Allen Welsh Dulles Papers, Firestone Library, Princeton, N.J.); on Dulles's cables from Bern in the National Archives; and on Allen Welsh Dulles, *Germany's Underground*, Macmillan, New York, 1947. The most important sources for Gisevius's biography besides his own book are his extended testimony during the Nuremberg War Crimes Trial; his personnel file in the Berlin Document Center; his papers in the Archiv für Zeitgeschichte in the Eidgenössische Technische Hochschule in Zurich; the records of the German Foreign Office, particularly the files of the legation in Bern; the records of the American Office of Strategic Services (now in the National Archives in College Park, Maryland); and my interviews with Gisevius in 1971 and 1972. Numerous works dealing with wartime intelligence and resistance contain references to Gisevius. See also Rudolf Diels, *Lucifer ante portas*, Deutsche Verlags-Anstalt, Stuttgart, 1950, *passim* and p. 342; Susanne Strässer, "Hans Bernd Gisevius—Ein Oppositioneller auf Außenposten,'" in Klemens von Klemperer, Enrico Syring, Rainer Zitelmann, eds., *"Für Deutschland." Die Männer des 20. Juli*, Ullstein, Frankfurt/M.-Berlin, pp. 56–70.

2. Gisevius, *End*, pp. 133–138.

3. Hans-Bernd Gisevius, Aufnahme-Erklärung, Berlin, November 15, 1933, BDC Parteikanzlei-Korrespondenz.

4. Hans Volz, *Daten der Geschichte der NSDAP*, A. G. Ploetz, Berlin, Leipzig 1943, p. 54.

5. Dulles to Justice Robert Jackson, March 27, 1946, Library of Congress, R. H. Jackson Papers, Box 102, file "Gisevius, Hans Bernd"; Anthony Cave Brown, *The Last Hero: Wild Bill Donovan*, Vintage Books, New York, 1982, pp. 288, 290.

6. *Prozess* XII, pp. 292–293.

7. Winfried Meyer, *Unternehmen Sieben. Eine Rettungsaktion für vom Holocaust Bedrohte aus dem Amt Ausland/Abwehr im Oberkommando der Wehrmacht*, Hain, Frankfurt am Main, 1993, pp. 322, 325–329, 332.

8. Dulles to Justice Robert Jackson, March 27, 1946, Library of Congress, R. H. Jackson Papers, Box 102, file "Gisevius, Hans Bernd."

9. Hans Bernd Gisevius, *Wo ist Nebe? Erinnerungen an Hitlers Reichskriminaldirektor*, Droemer, Zurich, 1966, *passim*; Gisevius's dedication in Federer's copy of the German edition of *To the Bitter End*; author's interview with Federer, March 29, 1977; Dulles to Donovan, January 28, 1945, OSS records, National Archives, Washington, D.C.

10. Cf. Mary Bancroft, *Autobiography of a Spy*, William Morrow and Company, Inc., New York, 1983, pp. 164–170; Mary Bancroft papers.

11. Mary Bancroft, "The Story of a Book," typescript, n.p., n.d. [ca. 1946/47], Mary Bancroft papers.

12. Author's interview with Gisevius, August 4, 1971.

13. Gisevius, *End*, pp. 69, 73–75; *Prozess* XII, pp. 190, 277.
14. Landgericht Hamburg, Urteil (Judgment), January 17, 1962; information from Fritz Tobias, February 10, 1998.
15. Bancroft, "Story."
16. Gisevius, *End*, p. 38.
17. Henry Ashby Turner, Jr., *German Big Business and the Rise of Hitler*, Oxford University Press, New York, Oxford, 1985, p. 147. Gisevius's book is not in Turner's bibliography; Turner discounts it as a source on this matter. Turner to the author, January 11, 1998. There is no evidence to support the story as Gisevius told it. Fritz Thyssen, *I Paid Hitler*, Hodder and Stoughton, New York, 1941, mentions neither the episode nor even the name of Grauert.
18. Gisevius, *End*, p. vii.
19. Ibid., p. 41.
20. Mary Bancroft papers; interviews with M. Bancroft, December 16, 1980, March 16, 1985.
21. Gisevius said this in a letter to Dr. Ferdinand Sauerbruch on April 1, 1947 in which he encouraged the famous surgeon to publish his reminiscences about Stauffenberg, particularly, as he had told Gisevius, that Stauffenberg was physically unsuited for his role as assassin and coup-d'état leader. According to Gisevius's letter, Sauerbruch based this on his observation of Stauffenberg when Stauffenberg recovered in Sauerbruch's hospital from the wounds he had sustained in Tunisia. In his reply to Gisevius, Sauerbruch mentioned only "long observation" upon which he based his view of Stauffenberg. Copies of both letters are in the author's possession, the originals are presumably in the Gisevius Papers. In fact, Stauffenberg did not recover in Sauerbruch's hospital, the Charité in Berlin, but in the First General Military Hospital in Munich; Peter Hoffmann, *Stauffenberg, A Family History, 1905–1944*, Cambridge University Press, Cambridge, New York, Melbourne, 1995, pp. 181–185, 187, 190. In 1972 Gisevius named Hansen as his main source for his views on Stauffenberg, and additionally Olbricht, Beck, and Goerdeler: interview with the author, September 8, 1972.
22. Hoffmann, *Stauffenberg*, pp. 213–224.
23. Gisevius, interview, September 8, 1972.
24. Gisevius, *End*, p. 507.
25. Ibid., pp. 508, 510–511.
26. Ibid., p. 510.
27. Ibid., p. 512.
28. Ibid., p. 510.
29. Ibid., p. 518.
30. Ibid., p. 509.
31. Allen Welsh Dulles, *From Hitler's Doorstep: The Wartime Intelligence Reports of Allen Dulles, 1942–1945*, Neal H. Petersen, ed., Pennsylvania State University Press, University Park, Pennsylvania, 1996, p. 25.
32. H[ans] B[ernd] G[isevius], Memorandum for A[llen] W[elsh] D[ulles], typed, n.p., July 1944, Mary Bancroft papers.
33. *Foreign Relations of the United States. Diplomatic Papers. The Conferences at Malta and Yalta 1945*, United States Government Printing Office, Washington, 1955, p.

957; Dulles to Donovan No. 4077, January 25, 1945, OSS records, National Archives, College Park, Maryland.

34. Bancroft to Dulles [May 11, July 11, 1944], Mary Bancroft papers.
35. Interview, August 4, 1971.
36. H[ans] B[ernd] Gisevius, Bericht [to Mary Bancroft for Allen Dulles], typed, [Zurich], February 1945, Princeton University Library, Allen W. Dulles Papers, Box 20, p. 31. There is a more subdued reference to this proposed arrangement in the first German edition of Gisevius's book (*Bis zum bittern Ende*, Fretz & Wasmuth, Zurich, 1946, vol. II, pp. 304–305, 325); it is part of numerous passages that are omitted in the English edition.
37. Interview, August 4, 1971.
38. Gisevius, *End*, p. 511; author's interview with Gisevius, August 4, 1971; Gisevius in interview with Joachim Fest [1971]; Hoffmann, *Stauffenberg*, pp. 243–247, 293–295, and *passim*.
39. Interview, August 4, 1971.
40. *Die Hassell-Tagebücher 1938–1944. Aufzeichnungen vom Andern Deutschland*, expanded ed., Siedler Verlag, Berlin, 1988; Helmuth Groscurth, *Tagebücher eines Abwehroffiziers 1938–1940*, eds. Helmut Krausnick and Harold C. Deutsch, Deutsche Verlags-Anstalt, Stuttgart, 1970; Otto John, "Some Facts and Aspects of the Plot against Hitler," typed, London, 1948, Institut für Zeitgeschichte (Munich), Slg John; Otto John, "Zum Jahrestag der Verschwörung gegen Hitler—20. Juli 1944," *Wochenpost*, July 18, 1947, pp. 4–6.
41. Gisevius, *Nebe*, pp. 240–253; cf. Raul Hilberg, *The Destruction of the European Jews*, revised and definitive edition, Holmes & Meier, New York, London, 1985, p. 1,214.

Preface

THIS BOOK is not intended as a history of the Third Reich. The author has selected a few prominent incidents out of the confusion of contemporaneous events and has attempted to use these as points through which to trace the broad curves of the historical process.

The account is not drawn from hearsay; all of it comes from the author's experience. At the age of twenty-nine, when the Brown dictatorship was initiated, I intended to make a career of the civil service; the circumstances of the times plunged me at once into the midst of the revolutionary turbulence. I was buffeted on all sides by the mounting waves and many times came close to going under. Now I believe that the time has come when, for the sake of my dead friends and for my own sake, I ought to set down the most important experiences and impressions of this period.

I have no wish to apologize either for my approach or for my present point of view. There are some who are proud of having kept aloof from the rapid changes of these past twelve years, who have learned nothing new during those cataclysmic years, and who now would like to take up again the attitudes and habits that were so suddenly interrupted. I have learned a good many important things. Those years have provided a discipline without which I should probably have clung to many errors and prejudices. On the other hand, I am not ashamed to declare frankly that I formerly stood on the Right, and that, in spite of all unsavory experiences, I have not abandoned my conservative point of view.

From 1929 on, it became more and more apparent that the leaders of our Left and Center Parties were incapable of holding the masses in line. It seemed quite reasonable to hope that the rising flood could be stemmed by the Right and safely guided into evolutionary channels. In any case, the attempt had to be made; otherwise the plunge into the Brown Revolution would be inevitable. Conservatism is not synonymous with social reaction or retrogression. The circle of 'young Rightists' (the last militant representatives of whom we shall meet again among the tragic victims of July 20, 1944, twelve years later) considered themselves far more progressive and European-minded than the clique of parliamentary leaders who governed from 1918 to 1929. The latter group consisted almost entirely of persons who had facilely made the shift from the Kaiser's Germany to the allegedly 'new' republican system. The faces might not have been all the same, but the mentality of imperial Germany was everywhere in evidence.

The fact that our *Stahlhelm* and our German nationalists did not succeed in carrying out the mission that had fallen to their lot is no argument against our experiment. But it is an indication that we were gravely deficient in real inner conviction and in the will to resist. The tragedy of German history before 1933 was not that so many Germans swung to the Right; the real tragedy consisted in the fact that for more than fifty years there had been no real conservatives on the Right. Government circles under Kaiser Wilhelm who later, after the First World War, became imperial nationalists, had only a spurious conservative outlook to offer. It is they who were most to blame for the general feeling in Germany that conservatism was irreconcilable with social progress and democracy.

But let us not deceive ourselves. Both German liberalism and German Marxism must bear a considerable measure of guilt for the disaster of Nazism. More than any other intellectual movement of the nineteenth century, liberalism, with its overemphasis upon individualism, contributed greatly to the dissolution of religious and ethical principles. Similarly, liberalism's mechanistic idea of centralization helped to obstruct any step toward a healthy kind of federalism. The speed with which centralism can deteriorate into extreme nationalism is something that we Europeans, who have felt the worst blows of nationalism, have experienced not only in Germany but in the rest of Europe.

As far as Marxism is concerned, the slogans of 'the dictatorship of the proletariat' and 'the mobilization of the masses' also gave a fateful turn to the whole subsequent course of history. When the younger generation vigorously rejected political institutions which shaped, not a living democracy, but a caricature of democracy, they were impelled by motives deeper than political immaturity.

The things that were swept away in 1933 were by no means *all* good or worthy of being preserved. Not every politician whose constituency turned against him can plume himself on the soundness of his former policies because the Nazi régime turned out to be so dreadful. It would hardly be of any use to bring about a restoration of those who perpetually insist that they were in the right. History has proved that all of us Germans were so terribly in the wrong that it simply won't do to pillory only registered members of the National Socialist Party and the SS, or to condemn as pro-fascist everyone who stood on the Right before 1933. We must fight our way forward to new forms of life, over ground pitted with graves and ruins. In so doing, the more thoroughly we free ourselves from the spell of the immediate past — but also from the specters of the more distant past! — the more clearly and resolutely we shall perceive that we must begin again at the beginning. We must realize that not only have our institutions become heaps of rubble, but their yellowed mortgages are also worthless; no matter what forces and traditions of the nineteenth century underlie these deeds, they are now no more than scraps of paper.

The occupation powers have allowed the Communists, who were the most consistent opponents of the German political system that prevailed between 1918 and 1933, a significant share in the work of reconstruction. This policy implies that the powers do not consider open opposition to the principles, customs, and legal codes of the Weimar Republic a damning fault. One can have opposed the Weimar Republic and still be entitled to work for the establishment of a real democracy — which the German people have not yet been privileged to experience. Therefore, I hope that after this period of utter ideological confusion on the part of the Right, new conservative forces will in time arise. In a true democracy, the groupings that spring up out of party politics cannot be limited to the strict Center. Precisely because ours is a revolutionary age, there is a real need within Germany for sincere advocates of a new legitimacy, for a courageous anti-collectivism and a supra-national point of view. Such a conservative movement must not only put nationalism far behind it, but must have the intellectual alertness to draw the significant lessons from the downfall of all three German empires of the past: the Hitler dictatorship, the Bismarckian reign, and the Prussia of Frederick the Great.

So much for my political philosophy. In the following chapters I shall give an account of my principles and my activities during the sway of the Brown millennialists. It must be noted that this book was not written after the battle. The basic structure and content were set down by 1941. The cuts I have made in the first version were dictated only by the consideration that the German people today no longer need a detailed demonstration of the criminality of those who led them into the abyss. And, on the other hand, certain additions were necessary because the Black Terror had since silenced certain of my friends and comrades who otherwise would have completed the story with their own recitals.

This applies particularly to the second part, which will cover the period from Munich to July 20, 1944. Since so many important witnesses and almost all the secret collections of documents have been destroyed, I feel it my duty to enlarge on matters which may be of interest to future historians as well as to our wearied contemporaries. For historians will one day try to discover why no one was on hand to avert the catastrophe in time.

H. B. G.

Contents

Foreword

HANS BERND GISEVIUS is one of the few survivors of the group of Germans who actively plotted to do away with Hitler. In the early days of the conspiracy he was at the center of activities in Berlin. Then he became one of the foreign envoys of the conspirators, and that is how I came to know him in Switzerland.

We met there early in 1943. I was then in charge of the work in Switzerland of the Office of Strategic Services and attached to the American Legation in Bern. Gisevius was ostensibly a German Vice-Consul in Zurich. In reality, he belonged to a small circle of men in the German counter-intelligence service, the *Abwehr*, who, under Admiral Wilhelm Canaris and General Hans Oster, were working against the Nazis. Our first secret conference took place in January of 1943, after I had taken careful soundings about the man I was to meet. Sources I trusted thoroughly had told me in strict confidence of the work he was doing, and that he was the one person in Switzerland who could tell me the inside story of the German underground.

He did that, and much more. As soon as mutual confidence was established Gisevius let me into the secret of the conspiracy, led by General Beck and Carl Friedrich Goerdeler.

Even before I met him Gisevius had completed roughly one half of his present book. It is interesting to note that he had done this writing before the German defeat was apparent, in fact, when Germany was riding roughshod over Europe. After I had known him a few months he gave me the bulky German manuscript and asked my help in getting it translated, as even in those days he was looking forward to the time when he could make available to the English-reading world the story of what went on behind the scenes of Nazi Germany. Also, he wished the manuscript to be in safe hands in the event that he did not live to finish it.

Gisevius's philosophy can be summed up in a few words. To him, a victory for Hitler meant the end of Christian civilization, and of Western culture in Europe and possibly in the world. He proposed to do his bit to prevent it, and felt that in doing so he was only carrying out his duty as a German. Quite rightly, he did not consider that he was working against his country; he felt he was working for it. But he wanted the Allies to hurry, to destroy Hitler before all the foundations on which a better Germany could be built had been demolished. He wanted to prevent Hitler from carrying on the fight 'to the bitter end.'

This was not to be, but not because Gisevius and his fellow conspirators lacked courage or the determination to risk everything in the attempt. Fate had ruled that Hitler was to carry on until Germany was in ruins.

It is hard to say whether or not it is better that the plot should have failed. If Hitler had been killed German resistance would have collapsed and the war would have ended in 1944. But possibly the crimes of the Nazis were so great that nothing short of total destruction could have sufficed, despite the cost to the Allies and the loss to Germany of a group of men who are sorely needed now in the task of German reconstruction. At least one thing is clear. We have the evidence that there were some Germans who were willing to make the attempt to do away with Hitler and his régime, even though they received no encouragement from Hitler's enemies, and even though it was clear that if their effort was successful it would mean the total military defeat of Germany.

When Gisevius left Switzerland on July 11, 1944, to join in the final phases of the last plot, he took his life in his hands. The Gestapo had been trying to get him for a long while, and when the plot failed I hardly expected to see him again. Through underground channels he finally succeeded in getting word out to us that he was safe and in hiding in Berlin, and after careful preparation we were able to find a way to get through to him false papers, on which he traveled unmolested to the Swiss frontier. Thus he was able to write the last dramatic chapters of his book, and to add another touch of drama to a life already crammed with adventure.

In April, 1946, Gisevius appeared as a witness at the Nuremberg Trials, and during three days on the witness stand confronted Goering and his cohorts with damning evidence to add to the accumulated record of their crimes. In the course of his cross-examination of Gisevius, Mr. Justice Jackson described him as 'the one representative of democratic forces in Germany to take this stand to tell his story.'

It is in this book that he really tells his story. It is one of deep human interest and of historical importance — the inside story of what went on within Germany among those who plotted against the Nazis.

ALLEN W. DULLES

New York, 1947

Part One

FROM THE REICHSTAG FIRE TO THE FRITSCH CRISIS

I

The Reichstag Fire

THE ACT

LATE IN THE EVENING of February 27, 1933, the building that
housed the German Reichstag suddenly went up in flames.

Was it the Reichstag alone? Was not all Berlin on fire?

No, not yet. Our cities were not yet smoking ruins. The fiery
tempest, the infernal hurricane, had not yet roared down upon unfortunate men; the blasting heat had not yet seared them. The time
was still to come when they would go about perpetually blackened
with soot. The time was not yet when they would rush in fear and
trembling into the cellars as soon as the siren howled. Nor were they
yet scrambling distractedly out of their concrete caves and sighing with
relief because there were 'only' fires, because they were lucky, and it
was 'only' the neighboring quarter of town in which the flames raged.

As yet it was only the prelude.

In normal times arson — and in the case of the Reichstag it was
obviously arson — is considered a particularly heinous crime. For its
effect upon men is deeper and more lasting than any of the other
capital crimes. There is always something uncanny about a huge fire,
particularly a nocturnal one. It is so elemental a thing that at first
no one bothers to wonder what criminal hand ignited the flame. Once
fire dominates the stage and lures a terrified audience to watch its
grim drama, individual actors are reduced to insignificance.

Even when a murder remains unsolved, the act is always associated
with some murderer who will never be able to wash the blood-guilt

3

from his hands. The very basest of crimes are bound up in men's minds with the idea of some unfortunate, erring human being or some incurable pervert. In all such criminal acts the presence of the agent, of some fanatical or degenerate person, is the significant factor. Who he is and what he wanted, whether he was prompted by lust, avarice, or drunkenness, need or desperation — these are the questions the criminologist must answer. But the usual criminal act does not in itself exercise an elemental fascination over men's minds. Since the main interest is in the agent behind it, the immediate effect of the crime upon the rest of society is always blurred and mitigated.

This applies to all crimes except arson. In the presence of a sea of leaping flames, the idea of human agency vanishes. It is the elemental power of fire that grips the imagination, not the thought of some audacious incendiary. Anyone who has seen a proud building crumble before the fury of unchecked flames — anyone, that is, whose appreciation of such a sight has not been dulled by long immersion in the purgatory of all Europe — will know what a magical effect a conflagration has upon the minds and imaginations of the spectators. Fire burns deep into the soul. Involuntarily the spectator thinks of it as a vast and dreadful portent.

And so it was on that cold February night, when the fire engines suddenly began roaring up from all quarters of the city and crowds of people thronged to the burning Reichstag. The masses were seized by overpowering emotions. Wherever the incendiaries and their accomplices might be lurking, whoever they might be, they had to be given credit for one thing: they knew how to move the masses.

They had a real flair for the sensational.

The symbolism of the event was clear to all. Was it only the Reichstag that was burning? It was far more than that. In the midst of political changes whose effects were already visible everywhere, the flames leaping into the night sky of the German capital signaled the revolution that was about to begin.

German parliamentarianism had crumbled inwardly long ago; now its outer shell was collapsing. Of the constitution that had been so solemnly adopted in the National Theater in Weimar in 1919, little more than a sham parliament remained, a parliament that convened simply to carry out noisy demonstrations. Democracy had been done to death long before — had been going downhill since March, 1930, when the Social Democrats overthrew their own chancellor and, with him, the last parliamentary government in Germany. The two following 'executive cabinets' under Bruening established the fatal trend toward government by emergency decrees. Thus the deputies of the Left and Center voted their own extinction.

The Brown usurpers, who had just come to power in the guise of a 'legal' nationalist Opposition, were the last people to object to this trend. They were not interested in tiresome discussion of alternatives nor in impartial estimates of causes. They were not interested in renewing or restoring anything. They wanted revolution. To them the Reichstag building was no more than the 'gossip club' of a democracy which they had sworn to destroy.

In consequence, the greedy flames were a double symbol. They did more than eliminate a useless parliament building. While the fire consumed the desolate home of the 1918 Republic, it also illumined the beginnings of a new order of things.

Everywhere the old order was falling, and its relics bore a strong resemblance to the split and blackened pillars in the assembly hall of the Reichstag. They still stood, but they no longer supported anything. Amid the turbulence of the changing government, frightful forces burst violently into life like a long-dormant volcano. They broke irresistibly through the crust of the old order as though the elements themselves were directly in league with them.

And the dramatization of this by the flames of the burning Reichstag made a greater impression on the people than any of the urgent police reports.

It must be said that the official statements of the police yielded little information, in spite of their verboseness. The statements mentioned the arrest of a Dutch Communist and of the chief of the Communist fraction in the Reichstag; both men were said to have taken part in a conspiracy to burn the Reichstag. Later on, three Bulgarian agents of the Third International were added to the roster.

But the successive official statements appeared so beautifully vague that the public began to wonder whether the investigation was being pursued along the straight and narrow path. Why had it turned out that the arrested persons, who allegedly had been caught *flagrante delicto,* balked so at making real confessions? Why, after days, weeks, and months, did the story of what exactly had taken place in the Reichstag building on the night of the fire continue to be quite hazy? And yet in the beginning, all the details dovetailed so nicely that it sounded almost like a case out of a textbook of criminology.

Let us follow, in slow motion as it were, the course of events as the police and the court reconstructed it.

That Monday evening, shortly after nine o'clock, a certain divinity student was going home. His way led past the west side of the Reichstag building. At that hour of the night, whenever there was no evening session going on in the Reichstag, the street was always sparsely illuminated. The Reichstag building stood silent and dark on the quite deserted Koenigsplatz.

It was so quiet that the young man could hear the echo of his own footsteps. No wonder that he was startled by the sudden splintering of a window-pane. For a moment he paused. He heard again the sound of shattering glass.

Naturally he turned around to see what was happening. His eyes had already accommodated to the dim light and he saw, before one of the windows on the first floor of the Reichstag building, a dark, moving figure. The figure floated like a ghost past the glow of a tiny fire.

The student was standing quite close to the west side of the building, close to where the ramp led out into the large esplanade. He, therefore, had to look almost straight up, but he had an excellent view of the windows directly in front of him. He could distinctly make out the upper part of the man's, presumably the burglar's, body. At the same time a tiny light flickered. The student considered whether the man was trying to get into the building or whether he was climbing out by this highly suspicious route. In any case he instantly suspected that something was amiss. He ran along the ramp to call a policeman. And by good fortune he came across a patrolman at the north end of the ramp. He called breathlessly to the officer and told him what he had just seen. Then he gave the bewildered policeman a shove to start him off, and the policeman ran toward the west side of the building.

The divinity student now considered that he had done enough in the way of civic duty and quietly continued on his way home. Nevertheless, with his characteristic precision he took out his watch and noted the time. After all, one never could tell. It was 9.05 P.M.

Meanwhile, the policeman — Patrolman Buvert, who was at that time making his usual rounds — ran around the Reichstag building to the spot the student had indicated. He also saw the broken window and, inside the building, a glow of fire. He discussed the matter with the man beside him. What man? Buvert took it for granted that his companion was the student who had called him. Instead he suddenly noted, to his surprise, that the person who had come up was not the same man. Buvert later described him as young, about twenty-two years old, wearing a dark coat and high black top-boots.

These two were unexpectedly joined by a third person, a writer named Thaler. Thaler had been walking along the south side of the building when he also heard the sound of shattering glass; but he was somewhat more curious than the divinity student. Halfway along the ramp, he climbed up on the railing. From there he saw two persons entering through the broken window. One of them stood upright, the other was somewhat stooped. Thaler, too, had run for a policeman; he remembered having encountered a patrolman near Portal 2 a few minutes before. He found the policeman standing by the ramp with the other young man at his side. Thaler, convinced that this incident was going to prove fairly important, also noted the time. It was 9.10 P.M.

As the three men stood there, they witnessed a weird phenomenon. On the ground floor a flickering light suddenly appeared and swished mysteriously back and forth. For a moment it would illuminate one window, then sweep swiftly past to another. It moved so fast and so far that the three men on the ramp began to run to keep up with it. When the strange intruder inside the building paused for a moment, Thaler was the first to regain his wits. Excitedly he called out to the policeman to shoot.

Buvert did shoot — and the ghost immediately vanished.

Meanwhile, two couples had come walking down the Koenigsplatz. From a considerable distance they noticed the glow of fire in the ground floor of the Reichstag. They, too, promptly ran toward the ramp and were in time to witness the first huge tongues of flame which now began leaping upward on all sides. The massive window curtains were burning. Patrolman Buvert sent them off to ring a fire alarm, telling them to hurry.

The couples set out willingly enough and gave the fire alarm at the first signal box they came to, which was at the porter's lodge in the near-by Engineers' Building. The time the fire alarm was given was 9.14 P.M.

Within four minutes the first fire brigade was at the scene. A minute later another fire engine arrived. This one had been summoned by a patrolling policeman who had come running when he heard Buvert's shot. He and another policeman who had also heard the shot now joined the growing group of spectators around Buvert.

Buvert sent one of the policemen off to speak to Wendt, the night doorman at Portal 5 of the Reichstag. At first Wendt refused to believe the policeman's shouts and rushed out on the ramp without hat or coat to see for himself. Then, having seen the fire, he hurried back to his post and at once warned all the Reichstag personnel he could reach by telephone.

Finally Buvert got a message through to his own police precinct. He asked a soldier who had joined the group to run over to the station house. The soldier set out. But curiously enough, in his stead it was the unknown young man in the dark coat and the high black boots who arrived at the station house. He spoke to Police-Lieutenant Lateit. Eagerly, Lateit took his report and at once rushed out. The young man again departed — alas, forever! In the general confusion it had occurred to no one to ask him his name.

According to the police blotter, the time was 9.15.

By 9.17 Lieutenant Lateit and his police car arrived at the scene of the fire. His first act was to send back for considerable reinforcements. Then he checked up with Buvert to find out whether the fire alarm had been given. He then ordered the patrolman to remain by the ramp and to shoot at once if the incendiary again appeared. He himself raced off to the nearest portal in order to gain entrance to the interior of the building. He found Portals 2 and 3 locked, but Portal 5 was open. Lateit, accompanied by the building superintendent, Scranowitz, and a number of policemen, hastened into the building which by now was filled with smoke.

The time was 9.20 P.M.

The vast staircases and galleries lay swathed in gloom. But these latest intruders did not take the time to fumble around for light switches. They ran straight ahead in the direction where, they presumed, the fire had been started. That was, as well as they could reckon, at the end of the main lobby where the spacious Reichstag restaurant was situated. The window through which the man had entered must be there; in any case, it was there that curtains and portières were in flames.

But when they reached the middle of the hall, by the memorial to the old emperor, they paused. On their left, through the glass door, they could see the glow of flames. On both sides of this door, which separated the hall from the narrower corridor that went around the assembly hall, the flames were leaping high. Both the portières and the wooden paneling were burning. And as they looked, a curious object caught fire. The police-lieutenant went up to it and saw that it was a folded man's overcoat.

Lateit and his companions hurried on a few steps farther, to the door that led into the Reichstag assembly hall. He wrenched open the door. And what a sight met his eyes! Opposite, at the other end of the room, rose a huge, unbroken pillar of flame. Straight and steady as a candle, the flame almost resembled a giant organ pipe a yard wide and several yards tall. There did not appear to be any other sources of fire. The lieutenant justifiably assumed that the hall could certainly be saved.

At the same time this pillar of flame was clear evidence of incendiarism. Lateit drew his revolver and ordered his subordinates to do the same. Then he hurried back to make his first report to his station. He left his men and the superintendent at the building, ordering them to keep a sharp lookout.

On the way out Lateit encountered the first of the firemen. He blurted out something about incendiarism, reached his car, and sped away. He must have broken a number of speed records; for according to the police blotter he was back in his station house near the Brandenburg Gate at 9.25 P.M.

Meanwhile, Superintendent Scranowitz had turned on the electric lights in the assembly hall and the lobby. Then he raced over to the restaurant for a moment. He was met by a vast sheet of flame. In the hall every one of the huge curtains was burning. Several small fires were even springing up out of the carpet that ran down the middle corridor, but Scranowitz was able to trample these out easily. He then glanced hastily into the assembly hall. The room no longer seemed salvageable; every nook and corner was on fire. The single column of flame that Lateit had observed had spread enormously. Scranowitz slammed the door and turned to look for other places that were on fire. He and the policeman with him hastened first to Bismarck Hall and then to the south portal.

All along the corridor they saw nothing but burning sofas and leather chairs. Nothing else. But then one of the patrolmen suddenly caught sight of a human figure. Breathing hard, a man came running toward them, apparently from the rear of the assembly hall. His appearance was dreadful and somehow madly daredevil. He was naked to the waist; he wore only trousers and shoes. The bare upper part of his body was dripping with sweat; his long hair hung in a confused tangle over his sweat-streaked face. When they shouted at him, the man crouched in terror. Obviously he had not heard anyone approaching.

He surrendered at once. Obediently, he held his hands in the air. Without moving, with an air of indifference, he allowed himself to be searched. He looked numbly on as the police removed a penknife and a passport from his trousers' pocket. He did not speak until Scranowitz shouted at him, demanding to know why he had done this. Then, in guttural, foreign-sounding speech he mumbled, 'Protest! Protest!'

By 9.30 P.M. the incendiary was sitting in the police station and the personal data on him were being recorded. His name was Marinus van der Lubbe; he was a native of Holland.

One of the first personages to arrive at the scene was the Prussian minister of the interior, Hermann Goering.

Goering's official residence was on Unter den Linden, only a few steps from the Reichstag, of which he was president. By chance, pure chance, in spite of the fact that the election campaign was nearing its climax, Goering was not speaking at any meetings on that particular Monday night. He was sitting at his desk working — all of his secretaries could testify to this — when he received the dramatic news that the Reichstag was on fire. He rushed at once to his car and drove to the burning building, where he was given a brief report on the situation by Fire Chief Gempp. Gempp informed him that the general fire alarm had been ordered; fire engines were now opposing the fire on all sides. Goering appeared chiefly interested in the fate of the Reichstag's extensive library and its precious tapestries. It was outside his province, he informed Gempp, to make any suggestions on how to fight the fire. 'I am not the fire chief; this is your responsibility.'

Shortly afterward the Reich chancellor arrived. Adolf Hitler had been dining with Joseph Goebbels when the startling news reached him. How fortunate it was that he also was not scheduled to speak at a campaign meeting that night, and that his loquacious propaganda chief was equally at leisure! The Fuehrer, surrounded by a group of cabinet ministers and other officials, stared fixedly at the fire. Obviously this master of auto-suggestion was extremely moved by the spectacle. As the minutes passed his excitement grew. Speaking passionately, he conferred upon Goering extraordinary police powers.

That same night the notorious emergency decrees of February 28, 1933, were promulgated. They were expressly described as emergency decrees 'for the protection of nation and state' against 'Communist assaults.' But soon their reach was to be considerably expanded.

The Social Democrats found that out the same day. On the basis of the new decrees, Goering at once banned their entire press. They had the consolation of not being alone in their misery for long. All the other parties were soon to be smashed with the same arbitrary power. At that time the Left still had a chance to protest at election meetings, and there were still newspapers run by the democratic Center which would print these protests. At that time there was still considerable opportunity for the people to vent their resentment in the coming Reichstag elections. But later on the opportunity to protest narrowed down: people could send written complaints to the various ministries, petitions which would be tossed into the waste-basket or would land their authors in a concentration camp. The emergency decrees had the effect of annihilating all judicial check on governmental acts.

Who could have suspected, reading the text of the emergency decrees which appeared in the newspapers the morning after the historic fire, that those few brief ordinances would legalize the revolution? But so it was. Jews and Christians, members of the *Stahlhelm* and the Freemasons, Centrists and German Nationalists, glee clubs and consumers' organizations — all of them would in time become unduly cognizant of this new police power. The leaping flames on the Koenigsplatz had given a specious justification to the launching of a reign of terror against a nation of sixty million souls.

THE SUSPECTS

NATURALLY, in order to do a thorough job of ditching the existing constitution, the Nazis had to prove that a 'Communist assault' had been attempted. It was the business of the police to demonstrate this, and they began to work feverishly on their task that very night.

They based their first zealous efforts, naturally enough, on the information they could get out of the Dutchman. But the interrogation of Lubbe was not proving very fruitful. He had been taken directly to police headquarters on the Alexanderplatz, where he remained throughout the night. He sat with his naked torso wrapped in a blanket and patiently listened to his questioners.

The first interrogation lasted for hours. It turned out to be less a criminal inquiry than an excited talkfest. At times there were thirty or forty police officers standing around the criminal. These policemen were joined by dozens of other inquisitive persons, all of whom wanted to catch a glimpse of this mad incendiary. All the bustle and excitement was not very conducive to the progress of the investigation. Lubbe appeared quite pleased with the stir he was causing. He revealed a certain relish in his rôle and a tendency to pose as a second Herostratus.

Lubbe was a Communist. That much he admitted from the first. On the other hand, he stubbornly refused to say anything about who had employed him, or who had assisted him in carrying out his incendiary work. He claimed that he alone had set the whole vast structure on fire.

The police decided that it was quite impossible for the fire to be the work of a single man. Therefore, the political police, who were under Goering's command, that night arrested every deputy and functionary of the Communist Party of Germany whom they could lay their hands on. They worked from lists that had been carefully prepared in advance.

Meanwhile, a special commission of the criminal police was tracing every possible clue. Any hint that might lead to the discovery of Lubbe's accomplices was carefully investigated. Remarkably enough, they twice stumbled across references to the chairman of the Communist Reichstag fraction, Torgler.

A Reichstag employee in charge of the deputies' cloakroom made his report early that night. According to his statement, at the time he closed his cloakroom at eight o'clock, Torgler was still in the deserted Reichstag building.

A few hours afterward, three other witnesses appeared, witnesses whose position and statements made them extremely important. Two of them were Nazi deputies, Karwahne and Frey; the other was a chief of the Austrian Nazi cell organization. The two deputies had been showing their Austrian guest through the building. They passed through the second mezzanine where the budget committee held its sessions and where a number of interesting paintings depicting the history of popular representation were displayed. Adjoining this hall was a large room with tables, easy-chairs, and telephone booths. In this comparatively quiet part of the building many deputies used to receive visitors. Members of the Communist fraction, whose rooms also adjoined this one, were particularly fond of holding conferences here.

According to the testimony of the three Nazis, they ran across Torgler in this room. The Nazis reported that his appearance was very different from usual; he seemed remarkably pale and excited. He was sitting with several mysterious persons. Karwahne himself had been a member of the Communist Party for a long time before he joined Hitler's Party. He had known Torgler personally for years. Naturally enough, he was familiar with the type of person in whose company Torgler was ordinarily to be found. For this reason he was all the more struck that afternoon by the slovenly appearance of Torgler's companions. He described one of them as looking like a Polish migrant laborer, with a truculent expression, a broad, flat nose, and dark, piercing eyes.

The police eagerly seized upon this statement. They immediately confronted the three witnesses with Lubbe. Karwahne looked carefully at the Dutchman, and at once declared that this man Lubbe had been one of the Communist deputy's visitors.

Karwahne's companions were less positive. One of them expressly stated that the Dutchman possibly was taller than any of the persons he had seen that afternoon. But Karwahne's certainty that he had seen Lubbe with Torgler outweighed the doubts of the others.

The following morning Torgler gave himself up. He had heard about the fire the same evening it had broken out, and had even driven over to the burning Reichstag. But though he had tried to make use of his parliamentary pass, he had not succeeded in getting very close to the scene. Afterwards he conferred with some of his Party friends in a well-known Communist rendezvous. Late that night, when the morning papers were hawked through the streets, stressing the astonishing premature announcement that he was under suspicion, he decided that it would be prudent to spend the night at the home of a comrade, a Communist district leader.

Early in the morning his host's doorbell rang. The district leader was being taken under arrest in the course of the general round-up. The two policemen actually glanced into the living room, where Torgler was resting on the couch. Seeing him get up, sleepy and half-dressed, they accepted the quickwitted landlady's introduction that he was a visiting relative from out of town and let the man alone.

Torgler dressed at leisure and calmly drank his morning coffee. He gave his comrade's wife a hundred-mark note and a package of coffee he had bought the evening before, and asked her to deliver the money and coffee to his wife. He intended to surrender to the police, he told her.

On his way to the police station he made several telephone calls. Among others, he telephoned a Communist editor, a close friend of his, to inform him of his intention to confront and disprove the charges against him. On the editor's advice, he then got in touch with a Social Democratic attorney, in order to have someone to back him up when he surrendered. Then, with his customary propriety, he telephoned the chief of the political police to announce that he was coming. Finally he called his dismayed wife.

To anyone reading the testimony, this final telephone call sounds utterly grotesque. This class-conscious Communist protests his innocence with the indignation of a schoolboy accused of cheating. 'Don't cry, mama, everything will be cleared up' — such was the simple good faith of this elegant parliamentarian of the Red Front.

A few minutes later in the Alexanderplatz a door closed behind

him. The police thrust the Communist leader into a cell without
overmuch fuss.

After Torgler's arrest the investigation ground to a halt and for a
long time did not proceed a step further.

Evidence piled up absolving the Reichstag staff of any charge of
negligence; in fact the staff had been prepared for almost every
possible contingency. Their regulations insured that the building was
kept under permanent guard. Visitors could enter the building only
when they had given previous notice in writing, and then the visitors
were always accompanied by one of the attendants. Records were
kept of all visitors who entered and left. All regular occupants of the
building had to show their passes at the entrances, and this showing
of passes had never degenerated into a mere matter of form. In fact all
the security regulations had been carefully checked over during recent
months, after the theft of a valuable document from the archives.

In interims when no sessions were being held, these regulations
remained in force. In fact the precautions were redoubled, for by
eight o'clock the deputies' entrance, Portal 2, was closed. After eight,
Portal 5 alone remained unlocked, and here there was always a night
doorman on guard. Except between the hours of eight and ten another
attendant in addition to the night doorman was on guard at Portal 5.

But even during those two hours there was no slackening of the
watch. An inspector made the round of all the rooms, completing his
circuit toward nine o'clock. At eight, nine, and ten o'clock a mailman
emptied the mailbox near the post office in the gallery. From ten
o'clock on the regular rounds of inspection began, and the correct
execution of these rounds was governed by a time-clock whose accuracy was above reproof. It is evident that the Reichstag staff was
very careful.

Nevertheless, the best of regulations are worthless if they are not
obeyed. Consequently, the police checked up with extreme care to
determine whether there had been any deviation from the routine
during the period in question. They found not the slightest breach
of regulations. The time-clocks proved that the rounds had been made
on time. The register of visitors was in perfect order. The guards and

inspectors had come to work on time and had been relieved precisely according to plan. The inspector had made his usual round; the mailman had passed through the gallery at 8.55 P.M.

All this detailed investigating only contrived to make the whole affair more mysterious. Obviously, several incendiaries must have been at work. Where had they come from? Where had they gone? Even if they had consisted only of a small group of four or five men, someone must surely have seen them.

The possibility did exist, of course, that the incendiaries had slipped into the building after eight o'clock. But the inspector and the other guards declared that by night every step in the empty edifice could be heard from one wing to the other. Had all the guards suddenly become deaf and blind?

In the first stages of investigation the detective is frequently confronted by a host of clues. The most impossible people offer the most improbable testimony. Once the attention of the public has been aroused, the investigator is showered with accusations and denunciations of the most unlikely people by other people. A quarrel among housewives about the use of the laundry, a high grocery bill, the latest poker game on the commuter's train, and especially the memory of the detective story in the latest Sunday magazine section, spring to life again in undreamed-of, fantastic forms just as soon as the public is asked to help solve an important crime.

In the Reichstag case, then, the police did not suffer from lack of information. They received sheaves of affidavits, and in the beginning many of these appeared to be of value. But real elements of drama did not crop up until the three Bulgarian Communists were caught in the toils of the law. The noteworthy feature in the arrest of these men was the significant part played by pure chance. The police officials were not even on their track; they did not suspect the existence of the three aliens. The overjoyed captors were certainly as surprised as their unhappy captives.

A waiter in the Bayernhof Restaurant on the Potsdamerstrasse had been studying the proclamations in the Berlin papers. Along with pictures of Lubbe was the generous announcement that twenty thousand marks reward would be paid for the capture of the Dutchman's accomplices.

The restaurant in which this waiter worked was frequented by National Socialists. For this reason it had struck him as odd, as far back as 1932, that now and then a group of foreigners should appear in what was virtually a Nazi Party headquarters — foreigners whose whole appearance and manner was that of Bolshevists. The waiter finally concluded that the men came to the Bayernhof precisely because they felt safest among the Nazis — in the lion's den, so to speak.

On the evening of March 3, as soon as the first photographs of Lubbe appeared, the waiter again thought of these patrons. It seemed to him that he recognized Lubbe as one of the group. He showed the picture to several of his fellow waiters and asked them whether they did not recognize the incendiary. They admitted that there was a certain resemblance, but they were unwilling to take the responsibility of making a statement to the police. Our informant refused to be put off. He insisted that Lubbe and the group of foreigners had come into the café on the very afternoon before the fire. On March 7, after having given himself ample time to think the matter over, he presented a formal affidavit to the police.

The police instructed him to report at once should the suspicious patrons reappear. The investigators were in luck. Only two days later the waiter telephoned the police. Three foreigners, two of whom he knew well, were again at his table.

The rest took place swiftly and according to plan. The three aliens suddenly became aware that they were under observation from the next table. They were on the point of leaving when a burly man came up to them, flashed his badge, and asked them for their identity papers. Two of the men appeared quite unconcerned. Calmly, they handed over their passports, which were quite in order, and issued in the names of Doctor Hediger and Henry Panef. The third diner made for the door, but he had underestimated the thoroughness of the Prussian police. The revolving door spun around several times, but the would-be fugitive found himself in a treadmill. On both sides police were waiting.

The police entered a cab with their captives and drove off to head-quarters. On the way one of the aliens thrust his hand into one of his pockets and then stuffed something under the seat of the taxi. One of the keen-eyed detectives observed what he was doing, but pretended not to notice. After the arrested men were out of the car, he searched under the seat and found a crumpled leaflet, a proclamation by the executive committee of the Communist International dated March 3. At the least, this little visiting card was a valuable proof of the prisoners' activities. Anyone who had in his possession such a document less than a week after it had been printed in Moscow must also have excellent means of communication with the Bolshevists.

It was soon discovered that the passports were forged. They had come from a Communist passport-counterfeiting ring which had been broken up only a few days earlier. At the time the ring's head-quarters was raided, quantities of mats and rubber stamps from every nation in the world had been confiscated. Now the police had two first-rate specimens of the counterfeiting the ring had been doing. In reality no such persons as Doctor Hediger or Herr Panef existed; they were creations of the counterfeiters' laboratory. When the two men were directly confronted with this evidence, they made no attempt to deny it. They readily admitted that they were Bulgarian *émigrés*. One of the three even gave his right name, a name that was to become world-famous. The three aliens were: Blagoy Poppoff, Vassil Taneff — and Georgi Dimitroff.

At once the whole investigation took a new lease on life. The police were convinced that at last they were on the right track.

The three Bulgarians proved to be remarkable individuals. Not the least remarkable was the number of previous convictions which they admitted. Dimitroff, for example, had been sentenced as an anarchist once to twenty and another time to twelve years at hard labor. Taneff and Poppoff had in the past each received sentences of twelve and a half years. It was because of these convictions that they had fled Bulgaria and made their way, through a series of amazing adventures, to the safety of Russia. There they attended the school for *émigrés.* Then they had set out for Germany where they were acting as 'transmission belts' for the Communist propaganda apparatus, smuggling literature via Germany into their native Bulgaria. This much they had confessed to — although not until the police, after days of work, had confuted each of the falsehoods with which they attempted to cover up their past and present conduct.

Certainly little credence could be given to their protestations that they were not at all in touch with the German Communists. In fact, the police concluded, their vigorous denials only made it the more probable that they had been collaborating closely with the Communist Party of Germany and were consequently somehow involved in the Reichstag fire. Since they had been arrested originally because of their alleged acquaintance with Lubbe, why should they not have had a hand in the incendiary work? In fact, why should the Communists have not deliberately employed a number of foreigners to carry out the crime? If that had been their course, Torgler would then have been the only German liaison agent whose assistance would have been necessary — and since Torgler was a Reichstag deputy, it would have been easy for him to help.

This hypothesis was strengthened by the discovery of a map of Berlin, with the Reichstag marked in red pencil, in Dimitroff's pocket. Moreover, it was discovered that Dimitroff was renting several apartments simultaneously. In addition, the waiter's suspicions were confirmed by other witnesses. As soon as the news of the Bulgarians' arrest got around, a swarm of witnesses appeared who all claimed to have seen Torgler and the three Bulgarians consorting with Lubbe.

Nevertheless, one fact remained unexplained — and that the chief problem. None of these witnesses was able to show in what specific manner any of the accused men had actually participated in the act of setting fire to the Reichstag. The men had been observed together in restaurants; they had been seen conversing in one of the Reichstag lounges; they had been seen carrying mysterious boxes, chatting in elevators, whispering in the lobby or lurking suspiciously in front of the Reichstag, or rushing out of the building even more suspiciously. In short, they had been encountered in every possible situation — but during the one interval that really counted, no one at all so much as glimpsed them. All the evidence was circumstantial.

And yet there was one proof in the hands of the police which should have made it childishly easy for them to solve all the puzzles. After all, they had Lubbe. Not only had he been caught *flagrante delicto,* but he made no attempt to deny his guilt. He did not even keep silence. At times he babbled away at great length. And yet he opened to his inquisitors none of the secrets locked in him. No one was able to do anything with this skeleton key that had fallen by chance, stupidity, or intention into the hands of the police. Everyone was able to look through the keyhole — police, examining judges, court, lawyers, medical experts, the press, and the world public. But what good were key and keyhole if they did not know the proper twist?

There was the rub. Lubbe's accomplices had been clever and experienced locksmiths.

MARINUS VAN DER LUBBE

LET US FIND OUT a little more about this Dutchman.

We left him a few hours after the deed, still sitting half-naked, wrapped in a blanket at police headquarters. His statement indicated that he was an active Communist, if not an anarchist. He claimed that he had committed his crime on his own impulse and quite independently. At the time nothing more could be got out of him. In the meantime, however, a good deal more information about him was collected. At least the external events of his chaotic life can be set down with some degree of assurance.

Marinus van der Lubbe grew up in poor circumstances. We do not know much about the milieu in which he was born; but the few facts on hand are sufficient to paint a picture of painful poverty of body and soul. His father, an alcoholic, owned a small retail store which brought in very little income. The family was unable to hold together in the face of destitution and adversity. Marinus, born in

1909, was still quite young when his parents separated. The father departed; the mother kept the children. Compelled to toil incessantly in order to feed them, she died relatively young from overwork.

Marinus proved to be the most difficult of her children. In his early youth he was given to wild religious enthusiasms. Later on, lacking paternal discipline and the authority of a decent home, he grew into a thoroughgoing lout. He kept up in school and was an average pupil, but his extracurricular activities soon became so wild that he was placed under guardianship.

When he was finally released from school and guardianship, he was instructed to learn the mason's trade, but he showed no inclination to become a serious apprentice mason. He worked as a butcher and as an errand boy, temporarily went in for raising bulbs, and finally tried his hand at trade. But he was never able to stay long at any one occupation; he simply drifted from one job to the next, always unreliable, lazy, and refractory.

For some reason his fellow workers assumed that he was not 'all there.' One time a group of rough comrades on a construction job played a nasty trick on him. They pushed an empty bag of lime upon his head, and a few bits of lime dust got into his eye. A hasty operation barely saved his sight; but his eyes were permanently affected and from that time on he received a small sickness pension.

At the age of sixteen Lubbe had become a member of the Communist Party. He eagerly attended meetings and parades and made his first attempts at street-corner speaking. At the age of nineteen we find him acting as chairman at a public demonstration of the Young Communist League. He rented a warehouse in Leyden as a meeting hall for the Young Communists of the city. He organized discussion groups and proved himself an effective speaker.

All of his acquaintances of that period described him as dreadfully self-righteous, a trait that led to many conflicts within the Party. These conflicts were all the more intense because Lubbe, with his inability to think straight, did not himself know what he wanted. Some of his friends called him a genuine Communist who was loyal to the Party; others accused him of anarchistic-syndicalistic deviations. He continued to waver back and forth; with each swing of the pendulum he either left the Party or re-entered it until, at the age of twenty-two, he finally turned his back on the Communist Party for good and all. By this time he was already well known throughout the town of Leyden as the author or editor of many Communist leaflets, school newspapers, factory sheets, and anti-militaristic pamphlets.

He was no more than twenty when he first gave rein to his wanderlust. He drifted clear across Belgium and northern France, either begging his way or taking occasional jobs. At one time, in partnership with another Dutch Young Communist, he organized what he called a workers' sporting tour to the Soviet Union. In this enterprise he showed great business ability. He had a postcard printed, which showed a photograph of himself and his companion; on each of the four margins were explanatory texts in a different language. He sold these postcards in order to raise funds for his tour. In actual fact he raised a good deal of money, but before they were ready to start, he quarreled with his companion, and the upshot was that Lubbe set out alone.

It was on this journey that he passed through Berlin for the first time — in April, 1931 — and spent ten days in a flophouse. When he reached the Russian border he discovered that the Russians would allow no one to cross the border without an entrance permit. Disappointed, he drifted back home, stopping nowhere for any length of time. In Gronau, however, he was locked up for a few days for peddling without a license.

At home he spent the remainder of the winter months hunting around for some new enterprise. He still longed to get to the Elysian Fields of the Soviet Union. And, in fact, in the spring of 1932 he tried his luck once more, and was again turned back at the border. They would not admit him into paradise. Not only that, but he was arrested and jailed for a time, and then ungraciously sent back.

To add to his troubles, when he returned he was arrested by the Dutch police. During his absence he had been sentenced to two and a half months imprisonment because, a few days before his departure, he had led a demonstration against the Leyden Relief Office. In prison he practiced his own form of Communist activity by indulging in a little individual action — a private hunger strike. He was successful — after eleven days he was sent to the hospital.

After his release, on January 28, 1933 (two days before Hitler took power in Germany), he turned his back on his native land. Prompted by some obscure urge, he set out once more for Germany. By the middle of February he was close to Berlin, and on the eighteenth of that fateful month he spent the night in the public lodgings at Glindow, near Potsdam. He was at this time twenty-four years old.

Now we must pause a moment for breath. For now there remain but ten days before the Reichstag will go up in flames.

But in those ten days the whole picture changes fundamentally. Up to now we have watched a vagabond of no particular importance, out of sorts with himself and the world, and unusual only in his precocity and, perhaps, in his unmistakable urge to win recognition.

That was all; but soon it was to change. Within a few days Marinus van der Lubbe was to become a part of revolutionary history.

That February night and the following nights in Berlin, when he drifted around from one flophouse to another, are wrapped in mystery and obscurity for us. And the transition appears equally obscure and mysterious, the sudden leap, within so short a span of time, from vacuous vagabondage to Herostratian prominence. What must have gone on in his mind during those obscure days when the specter of revolution was haunting Germany?

In those exciting weeks before the crucial Reichstag elections there was a tremendous inner turbulence within Germany. The country seethed and hissed. We can well suspect that the Dutch vagabond was caught up in the tumult.

Nevertheless we would like to know more. Above all we want to learn why Marinus van der Lubbe, this unfortunate human being, this stranger in the country — why he of all people was chosen to cast the fatal firebrand.

On Saturday, February 26, Lubbe entered a store and bought — a box of matches. Then he went into two other stores asking for coal-tinder. By that he meant a combustible material composed of sawdust and raw naphthalene used by Berlin housewives to start their coal fires.

In the afternoon we find Lubbe in Neukölln. After dark he went to the relief office, a plain wooden barracks in front of which he had been loitering for the past few days. Through an open window he tossed a few sticks of burning coal-tinder. It did no damage. He threw others up to the roof, but they were extinguished by the newly fallen snow.

Lubbe did not wait to see the results. He ran off, hurried into the subway and rode to the Alexanderplatz. His goal was the town hall, and then the Schloss. As he passed through the Koenigstrasse, he happened to spy a half-opened cellar window. Just for good luck he tossed a few of his tinder sticks through the window. They started a fire, but made such a stench that the inhabitants were awakened by the smell and put out the fire before it got very far.

Meanwhile, Lubbe reached the Schloss. It was just eight o'clock, and by this time pitch-dark. A large scaffolding stood near one of the entrances to the Schloss. Lubbe swung himself up on this scaffolding and clambered up to the roof. There he crossed from the west to the south side of the Schloss, looking for a likely place to start his fire. He found nothing at all inflammable. Finally he dropped the remainder of his package of tinder down an open ventilator. It fell on a window-sill and started a small fire which was immediately noticed by the fire guards and put out before it could do any damage. Lubbe, of course, had meanwhile climbed down the scaffolding and vanished into the darkness. Apparently he decided that he had 'fooled around' enough for the day; he spent the night in the public lodgings in the Alexandrinerstrasse. Sunday he again drifted idly around Berlin; in Spandau he watched a Nazi parade for a while.

And now we come to that historic Monday, February 27, 1933. It was just one month since Hitler had become chancellor of the German Reich.

Shortly before eight o'clock in the morning Lubbe left the flophouse where he had spent the night. In Muellerstrasse he purchased more coal-tinder. He asked for four packages and specified the brand he wanted: the kind 'with a red flame' on the wrapper. Around two o'clock he was wandering around in the vicinity of the Reichstag; in any case, an office clerk claimed to have met him at the northeast corner of the building. Afterward, according to his own statement, he drifted over to the eastern part of the city. He returned to the Reichstag shortly before nine o'clock.

We have seen what happened then. The question that presents itself is this: Did Lubbe, in the fifteen minutes that passed between the time he was observed climbing in through the window and the time he ran into the arms of the policeman, really succeed in setting the Reichstag on fire?

If we were to take his word for it, he did. For he rushed madly from room to room, tossing his tinder sticks at random into every nook and corner, and was on his way out, intending to make his escape, when he was caught by the police.

Unquestionably there is much that is correct in the foregoing description of his activities. There were clear traces of his wild dashes hither and thither through the Reichstag building. And indeed, to cite the words of the judicial decision, 'it would not have been possible for this man to have described the complicated wanderings of that night again and again in the same fashion if it were all the product of his invention and his imagination.' Nevertheless, this self-accusation does not answer for all the gaps in the story.

Against Lubbe's declaration that he was the sole incendiary stood a united front of experts. Fire inspectors and court chemists agreed that the work must necessarily have been done by a considerable number of persons. There was no other explanation possible for the number of centers of fire and the speed with which the flames spread. A few sticks of tinder could not possibly have set the Reichstag afire. Everyone agreed that the incendiary work must have been done by a group, and that this group must have used some highly inflammable fluid.

But why were the criminals not found? It is worth noting how quickly the conduct of the investigation was turned over to a punctilious justice of the supreme court. Soon afterward the chief state prosecutor intervened. In both cases the men in question were high judicial officials who had been in office for decades and who could not be accused of having been 'co-ordinated' within a few months. It could not be said even of the officials of the Reich ministry of justice, who were in charge of the indictment, that at that stage of the game they were taking their orders from the propaganda ministry. Minister of Justice Guertner was not a Nazi. Yet these officials could not clarify the facts in the case. They became firmly convinced that the four Communists were the only possible accomplices Lubbe could have had and they placed their entire hopes upon the trial itself to prove this theory.

This is the crucial point: that Lubbe was tried, not before some arbitrary tribunal, but before men who were all federal justices under the Republic, all appointed long before 1933. Lawyers, psychiatrists, experts on fires, and the world press were all invited to help solve the mystery, or at least to be present while it was being solved.

Since that time we have come to know the Nazi practices only too well. We know how many involuntary 'suicides' cropped up in those first months of the Third Reich. Why, then, did the Nazis not choose this simpler method of disposing of the Reichstag incendiary? Why, in the case of this Dutchman, did they not skirt all unpleasantness? For instead they went to great trouble to create a special law retroactively providing the death penalty for Lubbe's crime, and then they arranged a forensic spectacle.

Looking backward we may wonder at the incomprehensible zeal that led them to stage a months-long trial of the Reichstag incendiary. We must realize that this sort of 'legal' murder was a favorite Nazi trick. *Adolphe Légalité,* as he was at times sarcastically called, was starting out on his thousand-years reign by tasting the joys of a show-trial. All his opponents ended by dying, but all who were in the least prominent first had to submit to the farce of a judicial verdict. It sounded better; it placated the more naïve among his subjects. And it was upon these naïve people that, in the final analysis, he depended

— at first as voters to be herded to the polls and later on as cannon fodder.

At this first show-trial the hard-boiled puppet-masters could operate the more boldly because they were employing judges and prosecuting attorneys who had not yet become suspicious. These good officials of the Republic believed everything the police laid before them without question; they were so enamored of jurisprudence that they did not even notice that a travesty of justice was being put over. Nevertheless, at times it seemed as if the propaganda artists of the Wilhelmstrasse were momentarily relaxing their tight grip on the reins. There were a number of painful incidents that had not been foreseen. Everybody noticed that something was going wrong. Either the script was poor or the stars were playing their parts badly; either the supporting cast was not quite convincing enough or the audience was reacting poorly — or else the whole play was about something else entirely.

THE TRIAL

ALMOST SEVEN MONTHS to the day after the Reichstag fire, on September 21, 1933, the justices in their scarlet robes entered the great hall of the Leipzig supreme court.

The room was far too small to hold all the spectators who had come from distant lands to hear the mystery of the fire solved. Since everyone was convinced that a judicial murder was about to take place, the world press was, so to speak, eager to attend to try the case on its own hook.

For quite a while, however, there was nothing sensational at all about this sensational Leipzig trial.

That sort of thing is always embarrassing when there have been so many grandiose preliminary announcements. In this case it was particularly bad. For the curiosity-seekers of the world will forgive anything except being deprived of the promised and expected revelations. In the beginning the spectators sat tensely in their seats, and the reporters from the whole world alertly watched developments. But nothing happened; there were no incidents of any interest, and the mystery was not cleared up. Slowly, like a heavy, viscous liquid, the stream of witnesses and experts flowed by. Everyone said the piece he was expected to say; none of the witnesses made any lasting impression. The trial proved unexpectedly boring as it dragged on for a full three months. Whenever the faintest hint of drama began to develop, the unemotional presiding judge hastily poured on his soothing oil and the drowsing audience sank back into apathy.

Meanwhile, the chief defendant was silent. Not a word could be got out of him. He played dead. This sullen silence seemed to be a protest. And more, day after day the mystery of it grew and became more tormenting. The Lubbe who had drifted from Glindow into the capital of Germany on that winter morning was definitely not mentally unfit. The psychiatrists had one and all pronounced him responsible for his actions. But the Lubbe who, scarcely half a year later, sat in the dock was no longer a self-conscious person and certainly not a cunning quick-change artist. He gave the impression of a burnt-out candle-end. Anyone who saw this shrunken heap of clothes will never forget the utter wretchedness of it. Crouching before us was an indefinable living creature, bowed down and so hunched up that his head literally hung between his legs. Ghastly pale, numb, insensible, he showed scarcely any emotion. At most, now and then an insane smile flashed across his expressionless face.

The strange defendant indifferently suffered himself to be led in and out; he rose when the presiding judge called out his name, and he occasionally stammered a yes or no. But that was all. For the most part he did not respond when he was spoken to; he did not move when he was poked or nudged. Nothing affected him; he reacted to nothing. Once, when Count Helldorf sharply ordered him to lift up his head, he started and for a brief moment actually raised his head. That incident was an unexpected bit of diversion for the unhappy audience whose lethargy almost equaled his.

The endless hearing of witnesses only brought confusion upon the criminal aspects of the case. If we except the professional liars — I mean the SA group leaders and the new chief of police — the remarkable fact is that the witnesses were by no means all bribed. Their testimony was too diverse and artless for it to have been framed. Most of them were, in fact, quite genuine. They were typical witnesses such as appear in every court. None of these clerks, housewives, waiters, bartenders, chauffeurs, and elevator boys would casually have wanted to perjure himself. They firmly imagined that they had seen with their own eyes the things to which they volubly testified. They did not want to obscure; they wanted to help illuminate the case. They wanted the guilty to suffer their just punishment — but by that very desire they confused the issue and helped the true criminals to hide successfully.

Presiding Judge Buenger was an aged, honorable man who in civil life was undoubtedly a model grandfather. But he was not the sort of man to conduct a sensational trial. It was obvious that he was interested in justice, but that he also wanted everything peaceful and quiet. He was upset by the turmoil that had suddenly descended upon his sober and estimable supreme court. And he took his revenge for the turbulence in the palace of justice by demonstrating how cleverly a jurist who is tired of life can smother the leaping flames of curiosity by throwing on them the dust of documents.

Whenever the political background of the trial was exposed or when random questions momentarily revealed the shadows of Lubbe's accomplices, Buenger hastily extinguished the sparks. Above all, whenever Dimitroff landed one of his clever, impudent sallies, the disarming, monotonous, old-man's voice was heard to say: 'We shall now take a brief recess.'

Under such circumstances, can we blame the defendant Dimitroff for itching to do something in this propagandistic vacuum, to introduce a little life into the proceedings?

He did not thrust himself forward. The rôle fell to him quite naturally. The other defendants were of no use. Torgler trembled; Taneff and Poppoff did not speak a word of German; Lubbe was stubbornly silent. Dimitroff's unique opportunity virtually fell into his lap. And he revealed himself as a Bolshevist activist of considerable stature. It was unfortunate that the presiding judge always cut him off so quickly, so that he had to follow most of the proceedings from outside the courtroom. Inexorably, he was ordered out at the slightest show of effrontery.

Nevertheless, Dimitroff succeeded in making himself the chief personality of the trial. He could indulge in such an extravagance with all the greater pleasure because his position was comparatively secure. He was able to prove definitely that he had been in Munich, not Berlin, on the day of the fire. He could not possibly have dined in the Bayernhof with Lubbe at noon or helped the Dutchman fire the Reichstag at night. In vain the prosecutors presented one unsavory witness after the other who claimed that the three Bulgarians were in the conspiracy with Torgler and Lubbe. Everyone in the hall of justice would have believed Dimitroff capable of every imaginable crime against civil order, but he simply could not be blamed for the Reichstag fire.

Consequently, Dimitroff felt certain of a verdict of not guilty and was therefore able to lay about him recklessly. He did so with wit and penetration. A whisper passed through the courtroom whenever he rose to speak. At the very first preliminary hearing he permitted no doubt of his opinions. 'I am a friend of the Soviet Union and proud to belong to the Party of Stalin,' he declared, and he adhered to this line throughout the trial itself.

'Why do you think you are here?' the naïve presiding justice asked him. 'I am here to defend Communism and myself,' Dimitroff retorted from the dock. And from then on this emissary of the Comintern consistently kept to his rôle of doing propaganda work. Not for a moment did Dimitroff forget that he was a political prisoner. The charge of arson in itself was something he shrugged away, just as he dismissed his previous convictions. 'I have heard that they've condemned me to death in Bulgaria; I haven't inquired further into the matter because I am not interested,' he remarked with a careless wave of his hand.

This incorrigible character behaved according to his own conception of the case. As he himself once expressed it: 'I am not the debtor here, but the creditor. . . . I am a political defendant, and I am defending myself politically. . . . I am here not only to listen to charges, but to defend Dimitroff.'

This last remark caused him to be put out of the courtroom once more. It was high time. For he was already fumbling his way dangerously close to the heart of the matter. 'Is it possible that the incendiaries entered the Reichstag through the underground tunnel?' he asked inquisitively, and he continued to repeat his embarrassing question.

Goering came. And the trial was turned into a tribunal.

The minister of the interior had had a costume made especially for this scene. Never before and never afterward did any of his multitudinous photographs show him wearing it. But it was perfectly suitable for this particular day. A loud brown hunting jacket, knee breeches, high brown boots — his very appearance was calculated to flout the dignity of the highest German court.

And then Goering cut loose. He shouted. His voice broke with excitement. With one hand he gestured wildly; with the perfumed handkerchief in his other hand he wiped the perspiration from his brow.

First he waxed satiric: 'In the Brown Book the wild assertion is made that my friend Goebbels suggested to me the plan for burning the Reichstag and that I then joyfully executed that plan. It is also asserted that I watched the fire — wrapped, I believe, in a blue toga. By some mischance they forgot to add that I fiddled like Nero at the burning of Rome.'

Then he thundered: 'The Brown Book is a filthy inflammatory rag that I will destroy wherever I find it. We need not pay any attention to that idiotic investigation; it would only serve to pervert our own conceptions of justice.'

Then he ranted that he had taught the police the forgotten art of shooting straight. 'I take the responsibility. If anybody is shot, it is I who have shot him!'

At last the minister of the interior quite lost control of himself —

because of Dimitroff's insolence, of course. To give the reader some sense of the atmosphere, some picture of the unforgettable expressions on the three faces — Dimitroff's full of scorn, Goering's contorted with rage, Presiding Judge Buenger's pale with fright — it is only necessary to cite the stenographic record.

Dimitroff: 'I ask this: what did the minister do on February 28 and during the next few days to make sure that the police, in investigating Lubbe's travels from Berlin to Henningsdorf and his stay in the lodgings there, would uncover the names of the two persons Lubbe became acquainted with in those lodgings? This might have helped to reveal his accomplices.'

Goering: 'I myself am not a detective; I am the minister responsible for the over-all direction of the work. For me, therefore, it was not so important to lay hands on the individual scoundrel as to determine the Party, the criminal ideology, that was behind it.'

Dimitroff: 'Is the minister aware that this criminal ideology rules one sixth of the world, namely, the Soviet Union?'

Goering: 'I am aware, for one thing, that the Russians pay in bills of exchange, and I would like it better were I aware that these bills of exchange were being honored.' [The following morning the amazed newspaper public read the following official announcement: 'In connection with false reports and tendentious distortions of Prime Minister Goering's statement at the Reichstag fire trial, it is stated that the Soviet government has always punctually fulfilled its commitments in Germany.']

Dimitroff: 'This political ideology rules the Soviet Union, the greatest and best country in the world, with which Germany maintains economic and diplomatic relations. Because of the industrial orders of the Soviet Union hundreds of thousands of German workingmen have been given work. Isn't that well known?'

Goering: 'I'll tell you what is well known to the German people. The German people know very well that you are behaving shamelessly here, that you came here to set the Reichstag on fire. To my mind you're a crook who belongs on the gallows.'

Presiding Judge Buenger: 'Dimitroff, I have told you again and again that you must not preach any Communist propaganda here. The witness's outburst is quite natural. I strictly forbid you such propagandizing. Your only business here is to ask questions of fact.'

Dimitroff: 'I am quite content with the minister's reply.'

Goering: 'Get out, you scoundrel, get out!'

Dimitroff: 'Are you afraid of my questions, Herr Goering?'

Goering: 'Get out of here, you crook!'

Dimitroff (while being dragged out amid a great uproar): 'Are you afraid, Herr Goering? . . . Are you afraid? . . . Are you afraid, Herr Goering? . . . '

What a wretched figure Torgler cut in comparison to this!

We must remember that Torgler was not just some rank-and-file Communist who was picked up in the streets. Next to Thaelmann he was probably the best-known leader of the German Communist Party, and he had risen in the ranks of that Party to become chairman of the Reichstag fraction. In that capacity he had delivered the most bloodthirsty speeches, had brought up the wildest motions. It was true that he had never quite thrown off the ways of a somewhat dandyish clerk in a retail clothing shop; but among the bourgeois parliamentarians of the Reichstag he had the aura of a resolute soldier on the barricades.

And now he sat pale and nervous in the prisoners' dock. Would he take this opportunity to make a last ringing statement of his political beliefs? Would he cry one last Communist slogan before this remarkable forum? Would he at least say where, in his opinion, the incendiaries should be sought?

Not a bit of it. A petty bourgeois sat trembling for his life. 'Don't cry, mama, everything will be cleared up' — this pathetic cry could still be read in his frightened face. Certainly, everything would be cleared up — but when? Well, right now, before the highest court of this wicked Nazi government. And what would be cleared up? Well, the fact that, while playing a little with fire, he had in reality not the slightest intention of putting this bourgeois-parliamentary social order to the torch. After all, he wouldn't want to bring the whole structure down on his head — it was too congenial to him.

A hundred-mark note and a pound of coffee for mama, and for himself a Nazi lawyer with good connections in the Gestapo — that was how Torgler the revolutionary edged his way out of politics at the very hour when his movement was being attacked most viciously. Standing up for principles and fighting, being beaten to death — he preferred to leave such heroics to those unfortunate followers of his who honestly believed in all those militant proletarian virtues which hundreds upon hundreds of similar petty-bourgeois Torglers had preached to them for ten years and more.

Torgler proved to be so harmless that the court simply let him loose. Even the Brown hangmen, who, God knows, were not particularly concerned about a few corpses more or less, did not bother to kill him. For a short time they locked him up in a concentration camp. Then they released him and he swiftly took cover among the anonymous millions of Berlin.

One wonders whether, with their infallible instinct for all baseness and corruption, the Nazis sensed that some day they would find a use for this remarkable Red chieftain. For some time they let him go; then they fetched him out of obscurity. In the winter of 1939-40, when the loudspeakers in the German trenches blared across to the Maginot Line, it was Torgler who wrote the Communist speeches intended to convert the French to defeatism. And a year later, when Heydrich made his fateful entrance into Prague, there was an adviser on his staff to assist him in duping the Czech workers; the Black gangster hoped to reconcile the Czechs to his reign of terror by higher wages and socialistic promises. The name of this SS leader had been invented a few days earlier and was inscribed on his false passport. But anyone looking at him would recognize — Torgler.

Along with the three Bulgarians, Torgler was also exonerated, and justly. They could not very well pass a death sentence on the basis of the federal prosecutor's judicially unprecedented claim that even if nothing definite could be proved against the Communist deputy, he must nevertheless have been involved in the fire 'in some manner.'

Thus, on December 23, 1933, when the curtain went up for the final act of this great trial, Marinus van der Lubbe stood alone in the court to hear his sentence of death.

The judges declared the confessed and convicted arsonist to be one
of several incendiaries; but they made no attempt to define who his
accomplices were. They candidly admitted that the origin of the fire
remained a mystery to them.

Lubbe stood apathetically in the dock, listening to the legal opinion
and the sentence. He did not move a muscle. It was as if he had
already left this world.

As the representatives of the press hastened out of the courtroom to
cable their last messages from Leipzig, Lubbe was led away. No one
had time to cast another glance at him. Everyone was tired of him.
And so he disappeared from the hall of justice as silently and unosten-
tatiously as, less than a year before, he had stolen out of the flophouse
in Glindow and into the history of the world.

He had only a few days of life remaining. With Christmas scarcely
over, he was sent to the scaffold.

Would he talk, would he reveal what he must know, on the last
night? The judges kept this possibility in mind. They issued orders
to the ministry of justice to postpone the execution of the sentence
should Lubbe offer to talk. But this precaution was unnecessary. Lubbe
did not open his mouth, not even when he took the final steps up to
the block. A few murmured formulas, and the guillotine mercilessly
cut in two the keeper of the mystery.

2

Gestapo

L UBBE HAD KILLED HIMSELF by silence. But those who silenced
him to prevent him from revealing his secret were themselves
unable to keep their mouths shut.

Before I go into the background of this first Brown show-trial, I
must devote a few lines to the matter of my qualifications — to explaining how I have come by my knowledge of the affair. As I have
asked my readers to follow the destiny of the Reichstag incendiary
through a Germany shaken by revolutionary passions, so I must also
ask them to follow my personal destiny. For — largely involuntarily
— I was plunged into the midst of this significant segment of revolutionary history.

I must begin with the alarming confession that my professional
career started — in the Gestapo. This sounds worse than it really was.
In the first place, it was not Herr Himmler's Gestapo, and at the time
the name *Gestapo* was not yet current; and in the second place I
entered the organization in the course of a virtually normal professional career.

In July, 1933, I passed my assessor's examination, the second state
examination in law. I then reported for duty in the Prussian government. It was the custom for newly appointed assessors to begin their
careers as assistants to the political police. Therefore, obtaining such
an appointment required no special effort on my part. Moreover, it
was my fortune, good or bad, to have stuck in the memory of the
person who was at that time Goering's closest collaborator in the
Prussian ministry of the interior, Under-Secretary Grauert. Grauert

remembered me because in 1929, when I was a junior barrister, I had been banished from Duesseldorf in punishment for my political activities. At the time the affair had been something of a sensation.

Grauert had been business manager of the Employers' Association of Rhenish-Westphalian heavy industry. In that capacity he became notorious for ruthless strike-breaking. How the socialistic Nazis could take up such a person seemed highly problematical. But Grauert was cunning enough to recognize the way the wind was blowing. Grauert, together with Fritz Thyssen, plunged into a desperate financial venture. There were at the time ample funds at hand for combating strikes; the captains of industry were very generous when it was a matter of attacking the unions. Without even consulting the committee in charge of such matters, Grauert and Thyssen took from these funds — which were under Grauert's control — five hundred thousand marks. They used the money to rescue Hitler from his financial catastrophe of 1932.

This was the sort of aid that was highly tangible. For this reason Grauert could feel that he had taken out the best sort of insurance with the leaders of the Third Reich. But there was another factor. Goering was the broker in this deal, and that fact gave him a considerable advantage over Gregor Strasser, who was also angling for the favor of heavy industry, in the competition for the future post of minister of the interior. This advantage was not the least of the reasons that impelled Strasser, several months later, to give up the race. Thus Goering had a double reason for being grateful to heavy industry, and after the Nazis took power he made Grauert his under-secretary.

Grauert was rather matter-of-fact with me when I reported to him for service in the Prussian government. And I, for my part, had no special requests to make of him. Nevertheless, he thought he was giving me a good chance for advancement when he suggested that I earn my spurs in the newly founded secret police, the *Geheime Staatspolizei.* In addition to sending me there he gave me a personal recommendation to my new chief.

Unfortunately, he neglected to inquire of Ministerial Councilor Diels whether the Gestapo needed a new man, and I soon discovered that in this newly established branch of the government neither the patronage of an under-secretary nor a ministerial order made the slightest impression. The new secret police was run in the revolutionary tradition. The young Gestapo chief was not eager to permit the ministry to which he was theoretically subordinate to look too closely into his practices. Anyone who came bearing a recommendation from the ministry was miscalculating sadly.

I had heard in my student days of Rudolf Diels, who was at the time exactly thirty-three years old.

When I began my studies in Marburg, he was just finishing his courses there. His reputation was on the shady side; the students consequently built up legends about him. Member of a highly popular students' *Korps*, he established records in the consumption of beer. Involved affairs with women were a regular thing with him, and he earned the admiration of all die-hard beer-guzzlers by the power of his jaws: at the end of bacchanals he would bite beer-glasses into pieces.

In his official life Diels continued to distinguish himself by munching glass. He was placed as a young assessor in the political police force and contrived to make Severing, the Social Democratic minister, think so highly of him that he was called into the ministry and placed in the political bureau. This was, one would think, a highly embarrassing situation for a member of a feudal students' *Korps*. The *Korps* were at that time being cried down as nests of reaction, and certainly it was not the custom of their membership to supply recruits for the Social Democratic political police force. Consequently, Diels was considered a renegade by his fellows. He was called an opportunist and his former associates avoided him.

Diels was undoubtedly very clever, but he was also dangerously unstable; for all his boldness he never quite went the limit; and although his prime motive was the urge to acquire power, no matter how unscrupulously, he wasted his substance on alcohol and women. In spite of all his unscrupulous ambition, he never became a Fouché because he lacked the conscious self-discipline that his cold-blooded model had so overwhelmingly possessed. And in spite of his unabashed

insolence he never was able to match Talleyrand, though this later
became his secret wish.

From 1931 on, when the Brown flood began to rise inexorably, the
turncoat *Korps* student began to worry. Had he not staked his career
on the wrong horse? He realized clearly that his former associates
could be placated only by concrete and considerable penance. Since
he had never been one to be troubled by an overnice conscience, he
began turning over official police documents and information to the
Nationalist Opposition. At first he betrayed the government in whose
employ he was to the *Stahlhelm*, and later, when the Nazis began
winning great victories in the elections, to the Brown House.

In the middle of 1932, Diels distinguished himself by an historic
perjury. The new chancellor, von Papen, was in a quandary; he needed
some strong pretext for deposing the socialistic cabinet of Prussia.
Diels offered to testify before the federal court that his superiors were
doing things dangerous to the common welfare. He testified that he
had been personally present when Severing's secretary suggested making a regular fighting alliance with Torgler, the chairman of the
Communist fraction.

A few days afterward Braun and Severing were thrown out of office
in Prussia and the chief witness emerged as master of the battlefield,
with the post of assistant minister. But he was not long to enjoy his
first great advance. What good was Papen's favor to him if General
Schleicher were about to take over? Of what use was the 'socialistic
general's' good will if the wicked Nazis were about to take over?
Diels had to risk his neck in more and more dangerous escapades to
make people forget his political past.

Fearful things were in the air. Goering — Goering, of all people —
was to be minister of police. Goering, with his intimate connections
in the old student *Korps*. Since it could not be prevented, Diels had
to find some other way to avoid being bounced; and almost as soon as
Goering was settled in his ministerial seat, we find Diels taking his
place at his side as an experienced adviser in police matters. And now
this nimble turncoat had really to think hard. If he did not manage to
win his new chief's confidence at the very beginning, it would be all

up with him. Diels was acquainted with the character of his new employers. They were brutal, and they could take no jokes from those whom they had once fought or who had once betrayed them.

What if Goering should happen to look up the records of the days when the Nazis were struggling for power? What if he should recognize with fatal frequency the unmistakable handwriting of his protégé among the multitude of cases against Nazis? What, for example, would happen if Goering should find out that Diels, who now heartily reviled the Marxists, had been responsible for the publication of the notorious Roehm letters? I refer to an incriminating correspondence which the Prussian government had made public, a correspondence in which the chief of the SA frankly revealed his homosexual inclinations.

No wonder Diels had to perform some extraordinary gyrations in order to worm his way into Goering's favor and to hold on to it. Nevertheless, in the country of the blind the one-eyed man is king; among the Red or Pink police functionaries the Nazis had inherited, the former Marburg *Korps* student was temporarily the most useful person around. Goering, the all-powerful minister of the interior, needed someone who knew his way around in the police department and could initiate him into the department's habits. Above all, he needed someone who could show him how to use the untapped resources of the police organization for purposes of blackmail. The new czar of all the Prussians was already on the lookout for opportunity to launch a juicy piratical expedition; and his primitive instinct for thievery led him to suspect that Diels, this renegade who was trembling for his life, would prove a willing tool. Goering had been living for years by borrowing from Fritz Thyssen; he needed money badly, and Diels was desperately eager to help him out.

Those first waves of arrests which the minister undertook at the suggestion of his upright adviser undoubtedly created a good deal of public stir. But the SA too had done pretty well at locking people up. The wonderful scandals that the imaginative Diels reconstructed out of his police records about the petty bribery and corruption among former officials were, no doubt, a source of glee to the Brown press.

But they did not satisfy Goering's aspirations. The Nazis were at the time accusing their predecessors, who now were penned in concentration camps, of every crime under the sun. The novelty of it was visibly growing stale. After those first tempestuous weeks, who cared in the least whether some small Republican functionary had or had not dipped his fingers into the public pie? Goering decided that his young man ought to busy himself with more important matters, even if these were technically not quite in the line of his professional duties. Thus, for example, he sent Diels off to see the directors of the Berlin Stock Exchange. Diels introduced himself impudently and made it clear to the directors that he expected his orders to be obeyed. Then he brashly named the stock he wanted to fall one day and to rise the next.

In the truest sense of the word, Diels *bought* his way into a position of indispensability under Goering — though the purchase price was certainly not his own money or his own blood. From the very beginning he recognized the true nature of Goering's tremendous urge for power. With his innate craftiness, Diels perceived that Goering was determined to let as few people as possible share his power. Goering had no intention of letting even such close collaborators as Kurt Daluege, the ministerial director in the police department, or Under-Secretary Grauert, know all his business.

The young police councilor skillfully worked on Goering at his most vulnerable spot. Within a few months he convinced his chief that the only way really to keep down every variety of enemy of the state was by the establishment of a special secret police — and, of course, a police force that would be free of any judicial or ministerial control.

All Germany pricked up its ears when, in June, 1933, Goering issued his famous decree by which the political police were reorganized and formed into a tightly knit independent authority. Everyone in Germany thought: at last the new state power is wresting control from the Party. But at bottom Goering was guided by wholly personal considerations. The best proof of this is that he did not appoint as head of the newly created Gestapo some tried and tested old official, or an SA or SS leader, though high posts in the police force had hitherto been reserved to them. Goering chose Diels!

In order to make sure of the independence of his new department, Goering placed it in a building specially confiscated for the purpose. On the Prinz Albrechtstrasse, not far from his magnificently reconstructed palace, he spotted a suitable group of buildings. It had previously been occupied by a school of arts and crafts. The political police swiftly discovered that during the Weimar period the school had been a center of wild doings. The Brown newspapers reported that Communists had wormed their way in among the art students and used to organize sexual orgies during the annual winter festival.

Such outrageous practices could not go unpunished. Diels took steps. And soon, in those halls devoted to study of the arts, where the only loud sounds had been the music of dances held twice each winter, the first Gestapo men set about their business. And within a few days the first screams of agony were heard.

It was at this building, which then meant no more to me than it did to most Germans, that I presented myself in August, 1933.

At first I thought that the extremely cool reception given to me was due to the character of the guards at the entrance. For not only was I not welcomed; I was simply not admitted. Doorkeepers are always stern folk. But these were no ordinary doorkeepers. Ferocious SA or SS thugs with a pistol in each pocket of their breeches and another in their belt, and with wicked-looking night sticks lying ready to hand, barred my way into the newly founded Gestapo paradise. These men were the dregs of the Berlin SA, the very lowest of the low; for at that time there were far more profitable occupations for any 'old fighter' who had any talents whatsoever. Only the scum of the SA was allocated to the wretched job of guarding the door of the new palace of the Gestapo.

Thanks to my appointment, I considered myself already a member of this highly interesting department, and I was therefore utterly amazed at the rude reception. But I thought I understood it at first.

Never, in all my time in the Third Reich, did I wear a uniform. At that time everybody was running around in new brown or black costumes. Well, I told myself, these fellows think I'm a civilian, and worse yet, a bureaucrat; naturally they have no conception of what a ministerial order means and they can scarcely be expected to understand that their Gestapo is merely a subdivision of the ministry of the interior. Nevertheless, I applied myself to the task of persuasion. In spite of all my efforts they not only refused to admit me, but I barely saved my beautiful ministerial papers from being torn up.

I tried once, twice, four times, six times. But strangely, though there were different doorkeepers each time, they were all forbidding. At last, after three days of trying to storm the door, I resorted to the telephone.

Again I tried and tried — once, twice, twenty times. But I never got further than the Gestapo chief's secretary's secretary. One time Diels had just gone out, another time he was in a conference, or eating, or sleeping, and so on. At last I realized what was going on: it was the old army game. Rudolf Diels simply did not want to let me in. But why? I had not the slightest idea, but I immediately changed my tactics. If this man Diels was unwilling to be pleasant about it, I should have to exert pressure.

For a moment I considered complaining to Grauert. But I gave up the idea; it didn't seem right to use my heaviest cannon right away. Moreover, it was dangerous. It might antagonize Diels still more, and Grauert might even refuse to help out. I knew the oily syndic well enough to realize that he would not want to get into any political difficulties on my account. Moreover, at that time Grauert was still something of a demi-god; a newly appointed assessor, even one who was on a personal footing with him, did not burst into his office without thinking the matter over once or twice. Therefore I decided to go ahead on my own.

By the use of a little cunning and the assistance of a driver of a police delivery truck, I got into the building through the back door, and a few minutes later I entered Diels's office. I flashed my ministerial order, gloated over his amazement, and enjoyed the sight of his fury.

My triumphant expression and his fierce one told the same fact: I was 'inside.'

If I had been at all wise, my sole thought from then on would have been to get out again as fast as possible. But I unfortunately acted in just the opposite way.

I listened to my new chief's hypocritical welcome: how glad he was to meet me at last and how could I have delayed so long in reporting to him; what unfortunate misunderstanding had made the doormen and secretaries behave so incomprehensibly? He would do his best to make my new life here as pleasant as possible. Then he passed me on to one of his department heads. I was, after all, a beginner, he observed; since I had had no previous experience I would have to work my way into the activities of an office; he couldn't possibly entrust a whole bureau to me at this point. Therefore, I was to report to the head of the executive section who was an experienced criminologist.

I realized at once that Diels was interested in keeping me from learning too much about the affairs of the organization.

On the other hand, the Gestapo was at that time still in process of formation; nothing was as yet settled. Out of the hopeless confusion a sensible leadership might have constructed a reasonable administrative department. The higher officials who had been assigned to this department were by no means all Nazis. For the most part they were young professional civil service officers who felt ashamed at having been placed in this den of thieves. If they had obtained any support from their chief — who knows whether they might not have reduced the chaotic stronghold into an asylum of public order? But Diels's chief criterion for the quality of his collaborators was that they did not surpass him in age or experience. He had, moreover, a conscious motive in picking men who were not good Nazis — none of his subordinates would then enjoy the full confidence of the Party. In time they were all eliminated as 'unreliable.'

The principal duty of all these unfortunate young men was to sanction infractions of the law — the vigilante actions of the Party or the SA — by issuing warrants or confiscation orders. There was really very little that a new man could learn.

Therefore, I had reason to be glad that I was being assigned to one of the older officials — no matter what thoughts Diels may have had in the back of his head.

NEBE

I HASTENED up two flights of stairs to the office where *Regierungsrat und Kriminalrat* Nebe was just getting settled. He looked suspiciously at me.

This man Arthur Nebe whom I now met for the first time was still a believer. Why should I not openly declare this? In the first place, at that time a vast number of Germans believed in Hitler as a knight without stain and without reproach; most Germans were convinced of the purity of his aims. In the second place, their enthusiasm for the new ideals was by no means the product of a general psychosis. Nebe himself was an excellent example of a rational pro-Nazi attitude. Formerly chief of criminal affairs in the office of the Berlin police commissioner, Nebe had ample cause for feeling that the dubious characters of his old superiors had driven him into the Opposition.

In the First World War Nebe had risen from the ranks to become an army officer. Afterward he had devoted himself to criminal work. In time he became one of the most respected detectives in his department. But as the years passed, he saw crime constantly on the increase; he saw indifference, corruption, and political maneuverings corroding the entire police force. Since that time the evil twins, Himmler and Heydrich, have taught us how shamelessly police power can be debased to support unimaginable terror. In the light of what we subsequently learned, pre-Hitler abuses may well seem utterly innocuous. But at the time they were felt as disgraceful enough.

National Socialism took to its bosom the discontented and disappointed people of all political factions. The Brown agitators were masters at exploiting both general and particular dissatisfaction. Nebe was one of their victims. But he was soon to find that his new superiors treated the law far more cavalierly than their imperfect predecessors had ever dared to do.

In the days when I first met him, Nebe was experiencing his first disillusionments. A short time before, he had been transferred to the Gestapo; but it was no part of anyone's intention to have him use his extraordinary technical abilities to help organize the new department. Nor was he, of course, to interfere in any way with political decisions on higher levels. Nebe was supposed to see that Diels's orders were carried out by the executive organs of the Gestapo without the slightest friction. Nebe was soon promoted to *Oberregierungsrat* (chief government councilor), but he was nonetheless ill at ease in this new environment.

It was because of these recent experiences that Nebe gave me a look of such penetrating skepticism and suspicion. It was clear that he was strongly prejudiced against me.

Why should he be? Diels had prepared his subordinate well for my reception. He had tersely informed Nebe that he was sending him a 'reactionary,' a *Stahlhelm* adherent, whom he had unfortunately not been able to keep out of the department. Nebe was ordered to 'take care of' me — if necessary with the assistance of Karl Ernst, the Berlin SA group leader.

'Take care of' was equivalent to 'finish off.' And 'finish off' was equivalent to 'liquidate.' Nowadays I need not describe what that meant.

Diels's unequivocal recommendation led to my becoming fast friends with my superior. Our friendship endured many a tempest and lasted almost to the end of the Gestapist millennium — until Nebe's tragic fate caught up with him. But it still seems to me that his reaction against Nazism was due less to the influence of our friendship than it was to the persistent twinges of his conscience.

Since Nebe had gone into the Gestapo, his inner conflicts never quieted. And now my appearing before him involved a fresh torment. Once more his two selves dueled within his soul. On the one hand there was his sense of justice and decency; on the other hand his faith in the purity and higher vision of his superiors. When Diels ordered him to do something, was it not his duty to obey blindly? For did not Goering speak through Diels, and through Goering, the Fuehrer?

How easy it is to smile contemptuously at such considerations nowadays! And later on Nebe himself shook his head and could not understand how he could have been in doubt. For today everyone knows to what a pass those merciless monsters have led the German people. And their greatest crime consists, perhaps, in their selling the souls of sixty million persons to the devil. But in those days, when the *danse macabre* was just beginning, these issues were not yet perfectly clear. In those days there were many men who believed with fervent hearts and a noble passion in the new form of socialism which was now allegedly being realized in Germany, in the surmounting of the class-state and the elimination of the rule of Junkers and industrial magnates, and in a just redistribution of goods.

It is precisely because I never believed in the Brown promises of salvation that it is important for me to say all this. Nebe paid dearly for his mistaken faith — first in bitter disappointments and terrible qualms of conscience, then by accepting the nerve-racking suspense of underground work, and finally by suffering the cruelest tortures and death on the gallows. I think everyone may well respect such a man.

I struggled hard and resolutely to win Nebe's confidence.

In the first place, I did not avoid him; in spite of his evident hostility, I stuck so close to him that he simply could not get rid of me. This method may sound somewhat tactless, but by it I succeeded in time in making our personal tie more important than political considerations. And since by chance our apartments were fairly near each other, I persuaded my good-natured superior to call for me in his police car in the mornings and to take me home at night.

That was more important than it may sound today. Automobiles were often my guardian angels in the Third Reich. The one talent I developed to the point of mastery within the thousand-year epoch just past was that of securing automobile rides. Often I was so overzealous in my planning that two or three cars would be waiting in front of my door. I am firmly convinced that this trick saved my life a number of times. When, for example, at critical periods a succession of automobiles would roll up to my door — the official car of the Berlin chief of police, a minister's limousine, the Reichsbank president's car, or an official Gestapo vehicle, the spies around the next corner were put off the track for a time. To their primitive point of view, any man who had command over so many stately and official cars could not possibly be an enemy of the state, no matter how suspicious his behavior might otherwise seem.

I continued my struggle for Nebe and with Nebe in another way. I spoke directly to him about all the things that I felt were causing him constant inner torment. Nebe was far too reticent to bring up his doubts about the latest Gestapo practices. He was still wavering, still hoping, still refusing to believe the evidence of his reason and his sense of justice. I may perhaps have influenced his feelings to some degree by my remarks; but he was visibly alarmed at my openness in talking about such things.

I may add that during all those years my habit of candidly expressing my opinion seems to have horrified people and convinced them that I was a paid Gestapo *provocateur*. Under certain circumstances nothing can serve so well to dispel suspicion as unexpected candor.

The point where I could let my candor operate on Nebe was not difficult to find. For the present, criticism of the lofty ideals of the movement and the personality of heroic Teutons like Hitler and Goering was to his mind sheer heresy. He had even persuaded himself, for the sake of the grandeur of this new age, to overlook the hundreds of shiftless carpetbaggers who thronged around every Party headquarters. But his loyalty had a sharp limit wherever the Brown canaille interfered in his private territory — the police.

The person who personified this evil most thoroughly was naturally Diels. And since Nebe could conceive of wickedness only in terms of the Marxist Party state (the Weimar Republic) which had just recently been defeated, he came to the incredible but inevitable conclusion that Diels, who was now chief of the Gestapo, was in reality a Communist in disguise.

He had evidence for this. Did not the fact that Diels permitted the worst type of SA excesses, and that he allowed the Gestapo to commit untold crimes under his nose, if not directly on his orders, lead directly to the conclusion that he was secretly in league with the Moscovites? In any case, he was evidently trying to play into the hands of all those elements in the Nazi movement who were trying to sow dissension or to raise doubts about the sterling purity of the movement.

I could never take seriously this fantastic theory. Diels seemed to me so corrupt and unsteady a personality that I could not ascribe to him any such grandiose rôle. Nevertheless, from morning to night I adduced fresh arguments to strengthen Nebe's suspicions. After all, it was a matter of utter indifference to me whether the Gestapo chief was condemned as a Brown or a Red Bolshevist. What I wanted was to bring about his fall as swiftly as possible.

And as a matter of fact it was not very difficult to collect plenty of evidence. For we were living in a den of murderers in which we did not even dare step ten or twenty feet across the hall to wash our hands without telephoning a colleague beforehand and informing him of our intention to embark on so perilous an expedition. Not for a moment was anyone's life secure. Nebe, of all persons, Nebe the Nazi, the old fighter who had the best of connections, forcibly impressed this on me morning, noon, and night. His own opinion of his illustrious department was quite clear. As a matter of principle he entered and left by the rear staircase, with his hand always resting on the cocked pistol in his pocket. And again and again he angrily reprimanded me for incautiously coming upstairs near the banister — which could be seen more easily from above — instead of stealing up along the wall, where a shot from above could not easily reach me.

It was so usual for members of the Gestapo to arrest one another that we scarcely took notice of such incidents unless we happened to come across a more detailed example of such an arrest — by way of the hospital or the morgue. I shall never forget the remarkable precautions we found it necessary to take. By far the wittiest idea was that of the detective who had worked out a special process for shielding himself from arrest. He always carried in his pocket a warrant for arrest made out in his own name. This worldly-wise colleague of ours was quite convinced that some day the SA would come to 'fetch' him, in spite of his prestige as a Gestapo officer. Then, his idea was, he would whip out his warrant and declare that he had been arrested long ago. He counted on gaining at least two minutes by this trick, and that would be enough time for him to make use of his gun and vanish around the next corner.

INTRIGUES

BEFORE TWO MONTHS were up, the gradual *rapprochement* between Nebe and me bore its first fruit. Nebe started dropping hints to Daluege about Diels and I tried to see what I could do with Grauert.

Diels began to find the going hard. We had a number of willing assistants; even some Nazis helped because they began to be afraid of the consequences of their own excesses. In fact, the whole hierarchy as high as Hitler himself were beginning to fear that radicalism was leading them to brutalities that could not be controlled and would bring them to a fall. Even Goering did not feel quite easy about this Gestapo he had created. In the federal ministry of the interior his rival, Frick, was waiting for his opportunity [1]; and in the palace of the Reich president the generals were talking things over with Hindenburg.

At the end of September, Diels was removed from office with the lightning swiftness common to all Nazi actions. The Gestapo chief was assigned to the post of assistant police commissioner of Berlin; but he sensed that his career was in a bad way and thought it better to

---

[1] Goering's position as minister of the interior of Prussia was insecure because Frick wanted to incorporate the Prussian ministry of the interior into the Reich ministry of the interior. Frick ultimately succeeded in this, since the general Nazi policy was — theoretically, at any rate — administrative centralization. (*The translators.*)

flee to Czechoslovakia on a false passport. Nebe and I, who had persistently intrigued for his removal, breathed easier.

Diels did not remain long in disgrace. From his retreat in Bohemia he threatened embarrassing revelations and asked a high price for keeping his mouth shut. By the end of October he moved in again, into his old post as chief of the Gestapo. At the same time the Gestapo was removed from the sphere of the ministry of the interior and placed directly under Goering in his capacity as minister-president of Prussia.

I can still see Nebe collapsing into his chair when he returned from the ministry and told me the bad news. My immediate reaction was to decide that I must not sleep at home that night. I hid out in a hotel, and that was fortunate, for the hangmen were already out looking for me. But since ordinary SA men rather than trained detectives were sent out, they happily did not even come to disturb my parents' sleep. Instead, they bothered the new tenants of the apartment from which we had moved several weeks earlier.

The following morning I stole into the ministry of the interior by a back entrance and, with a telephoned introduction from Nebe, went to see Ministerial Director Kurt Daluege. In spite of the previous day's order, Daluege was still Diels's superior, for he was nominally the chief of the entire police force. He was, therefore, the most logical person for me to apply to. Nebe assisted me, and there was a stupid idiot by the name of Hall also present. I recall that because Hall was shaking like a leaf. Hall feared the worst for himself and his chief. In his cowardly terror, he was convinced that with Diels's return the Last Judgment was going to descend on all the conspirators who had been behind that short-lived ministerial order which deposed Diels. And, of course, it suddenly occurred to him that I must be the chief victim, since I had persuaded 'our general' — he meant Daluege — to make this misstep. (Daluege held the title of general of the police.)

The embarrassing situation did not last for very long. While Hall was still scolding me and at the same time — cleverly playing upon our apprehension — suggesting that we call a conference and that, when Diels appeared, Nebe and I grab him and throw him out of Daluege's third-story window — the door opened and Daluege's secretary entered. She informed us that a Gestapo agent was waiting outside and wished to arrest me — in the office of the chief of police, of all places!

Daluege did not flare up to defend me — far from it. In fact, the spark of courage that remained in him seemed to go out. Nevertheless, he was generous enough to show me how to escape through an emergency exit. I slipped one flight downstairs to Grauert's office. Grauert was not one to get excited easily. Nevertheless, he was somewhat indignant. But everything would soon be straightened out, he said; I had better go home and take it easy for a while. I kept urging him to do something, and simply refused to leave. At last he consented to telephone Goering in my presence. Goering pretended to be outraged at such a thing and ordered a stringent investigation. It is still pending.

But the temporary result was that I returned to the Gestapo Headquarters three days later and was greeted cordially by Diels. 'My dear fellow, what a dreadful misunderstanding! I knew nothing about it; it was simply a piece of arrogance on the part of the SA. You're my very best adviser!' And he wished me the best of luck in my future work.

Goering had not, of course, intervened for my sake. The crude truth was that he still harbored a grudge against Diels and had used this occurrence to remind the Gestapo chief that he had been in disgrace only recently and was not immune from correction for all time to come.

It was with mingled feelings that I recommenced my career in the Prinz Albrechtstrasse. An obscure presentiment warned me that it could not last very long — and in fact it was over within two months.

But those few weeks were enough for me to find out a good deal about Lubbe.

Diels was, of course, furious with me. And I, for my part, did not feel any too happy. Our mutual dissatisfaction made it necessary to make some changes in my assignment. My kindly disposed chief suggested that by now I was very well acquainted with the work and need not go on making the stations from one bureau to the next as an assistant recorder. Since I was evidently highly talented and capable, he was going to assign me to an especially honorable task. He had picked me to be an observer at the Leipzig trial.

At that time the trial of Lubbe had been going on for a month. There was certainly little more to see than the lengthy newspaper accounts described. And Diels had emphasized the word 'observer'; I was to have nothing at all to do with the internal conduct of the trial, or with the police investigation of the act and the agent, and certainly I was to have no connection with the special commission that was employed by the chief federal prosecutor for obtaining witnesses or supplying technical and legal advice. In point of fact I had nothing to do but sit in boredom among the spectators. Nevertheless, I eagerly accepted — partly, I admit, out of curiosity, and partly because it seemed a convenient method of getting out of the way and waiting to see how long Diels would survive in his contested position. For sooner or later this bird of ill omen had to go.

The reader may wonder at my saying I was curious. Would not a member of Goering's secret police, even if he were not exactly a favorite son, have known by November, 1933, what the story of the Reichstag fire really was?

Believe it or not, I am convinced that not five out of a hundred Gestapo men had any exact conception of what had happened on the night of the fire. We bureaucrats must have been envied by outsiders for being in the know. But any visitor who happened to overhear our whispered discussions in the dark corridors of the building on the Prinz Albrechtstrasse would at once have realized how literally in the dark we were. We would tell each other in whispers about the latest atrocities, and naturally the Reichstag fire was an important topic for such gossip. But no matter how often our guesses and suspicions turned in a single direction, we never succeeded in getting hold of any tangible evidence or even obtaining any idea where such evidence might be lurking.

We might, of course, have asked the detectives who were employed on the case; after all, we talked to them almost every day. But we would have received either no answer or definitely not the right one. For certain questions caused certain persons' lips to shut tight and to remain shut.

On the other matters the personnel of the Gestapo were certainly not overreserved. But a veil of silence lay over everything that had the slightest connection with the Reichstag fire. Anyone who ventured to touch upon this improper theme received a frightened or suspicious, a cunning or malicious look. I can vividly recall that several times I felt a distinct nervousness when I succeeded in getting across a pointed allusion. And to this day I ought to feel gratitude toward a certain detective, certainly one of the craftiest and most unscrupulous fellows in the department, who plucked my sleeve familiarly one day and remarked casually that he didn't want to interfere in my private life, but that my interest in the Reichstag fire struck him as quite out of place.

What definitely was calculated to arouse suspicion was the way the normally loquacious Diels turned closemouthed over this. Ordinarily he was ready enough with his brash comments on everything imaginable. But in the matter of the Reichstag fire he kept his mouth as discreetly shut as if Goering in person were at his elbow.

As a matter of fact, it was not particularly hard for him to keep quiet, for interest in the Reichstag fire had lapsed for many months, if not from the very first weeks in March. The reader may wonder at this, but it is quite typical of the atmosphere in the newly formed Gestapo. In those exciting months the Nazi movement was marching on the double from co-ordination to totality; it was arrogantly swilling the wine of power and merrily plunging into excesses. The Reichstag fire had been followed by weeks and months of untrammeled rejoicing, of jubilant demonstrations, of scrambling for positions, of trials for bribery and corruption, of raids, arrests, persecutions of Jews. Who still cared that the Reichstag had gone up in flames at the end of February?

When Diels sent me off to Leipzig at the beginning of November, he was not giving me a chance to participate in one of the more colorful events of contemporary history; from a Gestapist point of view he was condemning me to fearful boredom.

However, my chief did not suspect that I had already peeked in at the door.

I mean that literally. For during the days when the trial was just beginning, I had had a curious experience. Directly across the hall from me was *Kriminalrat* Geissel's room. Geissel was a sluggard of stature who had the additional characteristic of extreme talkativeness. He always poured out his cornucopia of true atrocity stories whenever I paid him a visit under the pretext of wanting to learn something about the higher mysteries of criminology. Officially he was a *Kriminalrat* 'for special purposes,' which meant that he did everything, or rather nothing.

The door to this master detective's room was literally wide open all day long. He always welcomed any visitors, inquirers, or colleagues who drifted in and kept him from his work. Consequently, it naturally attracted my attention when, one fine day, this hospitable door was tightly shut and Geissel, opening it carefully on a crack, informed me that he was sorry, but he was dreadfully busy. What could be going on?

The suspense grew when Geissel's urgent business continued through the next day and the next.

Naturally I called Nebe's attention to my discovery. But Nebe merely mumbled something to himself. And when I informed him that I had caught a glimpse through the crack in the door of a strange SA man inside who was busy helping Geissel paste scraps of paper to a sheet of cardboard, Nebe actually became angry. Although I had repeatedly asked Nebe to make a good detective out of me, we always quarreled whenever I did a little digging on my own for purposes of practice.

There was another subject that Nebe did not like to hear about. He sternly advised me to abstain from my detective work for a while. He thought I was going in for far too risky a business when I kept on trying to find out what was the story of that strange letter which had been the subject of a large number of excited telephone calls to Leipzig.

Now and then I had dealings with our deputy chief, a man named Volk, whose intelligence was not impressive and whose fondness for bathos was immense. He was not especially suited to be a representative of Diels and was soon transferred to the position of public prosecutor in the people's court, where his declamatory style stood him in good stead. Around this time there had been set up in Volk's room an apparatus which evoked amazement and respect from everyone. It was a new invention which made it impossible to tap telephone conversations; the invention distorted or 'scrambled' the sounds at one end and unscrambled them at the other. Significantly enough, the telephone line to the supreme court at Leipzig was the one chosen to test out this new apparatus. The sensation lasted only a short time, as a matter of fact. Then the monster was removed because it made too much noise. In any case, someone had come to the brilliant conclusion that no one would dare to eavesdrop on the Gestapo's secret conversations.

In those days, when the scrambler was such a novelty that everyone wanted to listen in when it was being used, there were a great many telephone calls to Leipzig, and strangely enough no one objected to having listeners. The conversation all revolved around the same subject. Volk would telephone wishing to know whether 'the letter' had arrived. Or he insisted that 'the letter' must be sent to Berlin at once by special courier. Or he ranted about how slow the mail delivery was in Leipzig. Or he swore that 'that letter' must, absolutely must, be found. Or he issued orders that every office that had had anything to do with it must make a thorough search. Finally he shouted in fury into the telephone that 'the letter, the letter,' and again 'the letter,' must arrive by the following morning at the latest.

What a terribly important letter this must be? What was all the excitement about? Before long I had gathered that the letter in question was an official communication from a lower court near Berlin to the supreme court at Leipzig.

All this nervous excitement about the letter lasted only a few days. Then the waves died down; smiling faces appeared once more; and the incident was over. Obviously the letter had been found, and presumably it was now in Berlin.

When I reported this observation to Nebe, he merely frowned and said he wanted no part of my amateur detective work.

On the other hand, Nebe raised no objections when I brought him another piece of information a few days later.

Assessor Sch . . ., another of those unfortunates who had been transferred into the Gestapo by the kindness of someone in the ministry of the interior, came to me one day fuming with indignation. This time that fellow Diels was really going too far, he burst out; it was getting to be past endurance. That morning Assessor Sch . . . had met the chief in a department store. They had exchanged a few words, and then Diels had genially remarked that he was just about to buy a new green hunting jacket. He had none and he intended to take a trip to the woods one of these days; this time it was someone really prominent who was going to be 'finished off.'

In this case no dangerous state secrets were involved. This seemed a private affair of Diels, that outright scoundrel. Consequently, Nebe was fearfully indignant; he was eager to participate in our investigations as to the potential victim of Diels's little hunting party. It was evident that the person in question must be really prominent if the Gestapo chief were going to take a personal hand in the murder. Ordinary killings were turned over to the SA; Karl Ernst's group headquarters had a magical attraction for 'suicides' and the coroners knew at once what it was about when they were called in to certify that so-and-so had undertaken the usual high-jump from the top of a flight of stairs. It must be someone really important to have such lofty assistance in departing this life, and to have it take place under the open sky instead of in some tiny room.

Beginners that we were, we thought that this incident would be the best sort of opportunity for tripping Diels up. For days we were on the trail of this case — not because we deluded ourselves with the hope of being able to save the unfortunate unknown from being murdered; but because we modestly thought we might at least bring his murderer to justice.

For the time being we could only watch and wait to see whether any noteworthy suicides or hunting accidents took place in the next few days. Nebe had a clear plan in mind of what procedure we should next follow.

In those days the revolutionization of the society had already progressed so far that murders had virtually been incorporated within the system of officialdom. There were, of course, the reckless killings on the part of the SA, which always caused a great deal of trouble, since they necessitated at the very least an involved sham investigation. But there were also what were called 'concessionary corpses' which were not subject to police investigation at all because the killers had been pardoned by the higher authorities before the crime was committed. There were many amnesty decrees in those days which provided pardons for crimes committed 'in excess of zeal for the sake of the National Socialist Revolution.' One of these decrees contained the remarkable provision that in certain cases no judicial investigation should be undertaken. However, in each such case Hitler or his plenipotentiary, Goering, had to sign personally a special order. Diels had improved on this technique and had extorted signatures from his chief for future and still-unspecified murders.

Nebe quite rightly interpreted this as a clever device for putting the blame directly upon Goering and Hitler. Consequently, we thought we had a good chance to make Diels pay for his cynicism.

If we had known at the time what the true situation was, we should have cherished no illusions. But we did not learn all the facts until much later.

Once again it was Diels himself who talked out of school. One evening over drinks he expansively recounted that they had liquidated Aly Hoehler.

Hoehler was a well-known Communist thug — by no means an idealistic Communist, but a convict with a long record, a notorious pimp who had killed the author of the Nazi hymn, Horst Wessel, who

was also a pimp. The killing was not at all a political one; Hoehler
shot him, not because he was a prominent Nazi but because he was
a rival in the trade. The two had quarreled over the same prostitute.

Such is the temper of revolutionary times that this fact did not stand
in the way of Horst Wessel's apotheosis. He became a national saint,
a kind of group leader in Valhalla. His portrait was plastered on
every kiosk, and since he himself could no longer appear at public
demonstrations his mother and his sister were sent from town to town.
About a year later, however, in spite of the two ladies' photogenic
value, they vanished into obscurity and the whole Horst Wessel legend
was carefully buried. Hoehler had escaped with a life sentence to the
penitentiary. Now the Nazis wanted to put him out of the way.

That was no easy matter because the ministry of justice still had
certain scruples about turning its prisoners over to the SA. Later on,
murderously combing out the prisons became a regular Gestapo sport.
Although the judges of the Third Reich could certainly not be accused
of exercising excessive clemency, the Gestapists nevertheless 'revised'
their sentences in their own fashion. Some lower official would sanction the 'revision' and — if the asocial person in question were not
needed for forced labor — the case quickly ended in a mass grave. I
know of several cases in which Hitler, on the basis of a three-line
item in a newspaper, dropped the word that condemned a man to
death. The unfortunate magistrates never knew whether it might not
be an act of kindness to a defendant to pass a death sentence, which
at least gave him some hope of commutation, or to sentence him to
a long prison term only to have the Gestapo alter the verdict.

In those early days, however, this procedure was not yet regular
and would have attracted attention. Consequently, in the case of
Hoehler, Diels used the trick of getting the convict out on a writ, for
the purpose of a Gestapo investigation. Naturally, once they had him
they could kill him in any SA barracks. To cover it up they decided
to 'finish him off' while he was being transported from place to place.

For this purpose Diels, together with Karl Ernst and members of
Ernst's staff, took a long drive out into the country. Everything worked
out harmoniously, as was to be expected. According to the testimony

of numerous witnesses, the automobile in which Hoehler was being moved had a breakdown. During the stop the convict made the usual attempt to escape. In order to avoid any unnecessary fuss, the Gestapo men buried the fugitive on the spot in the beautiful Mecklenburg Forest.

The reason Diels talked about this story is highly significant. A few weeks afterward a group of people hunting mushrooms in that vicinity had come across a corpse. The naïve local newspapers had played up the case until the higher authorities cracked down and forbade further publication of news about it. At first the horrified mushroom-seekers had seen a solitary hand projecting out of the ground; presumably the body had not been buried deep enough and wild boars had been rooting up around it. The police of the vicinity were at once alarmed; and in that rural neighborhood the matter naturally gave rise to a good deal of talk. Nor did the Party headquarters of the vicinity succeed in stopping the gossip by assuring the local populace that the dead man had been an unusually clever suicide! In fact the whispering swelled in volume and the Gestapo chief was put to the trouble of answering a number of highly unpleasant telephone calls.

Diels did not conceal his annoyance. After all, he remarked, he couldn't attend to the burial of the corpses in addition to everything else; that wasn't his responsibility. There you were; this was one more example of how unreliable those SA braggarts were when it came to the simplest technical duty. The fools couldn't even finish a man off properly. Why, Pigface — that was the nickname for one of the most vicious louts on Karl Ernst's staff — had missed twice when he tried to shoot Hoehler. And afterward Pigface had practically broken down. The only one with any guts in the whole business had been Aly Hoehler. When they stopped the car by the side of the road and started walking Hoehler into the woods, he, Diels, had asked Hoehler what he thought was going to happen now. Hoehler had merely smiled and said he guessed they were going to 'pop him off.'

We might well have spared ourselves the days of wondering who was to be the victim of Diels's hunting expedition. For he had disarmed us completely by his free talk; we couldn't possibly incriminate him with the higher authorities for the sake of an Aly Hoehler. To use a technical expression which, a year later, was officially introduced into German legal terminology, the Nazis regarded the death of such a man as 'in accord with the law of the land.'

Nevertheless, our alertness was not in vain. We were on the lookout for some unfortunate unknown. What we ran across was the body of someone who was linked up with the Reichstag incendiaries.

RALL

HOW DID THIS COME ABOUT? It was very simple. We had been on the alert, waiting to hear when, how, and where the next corpse would 'turn up.'

May I ask the reader not to misunderstand this expression. It sounds flippant and very ugly, but there is great profundity in the vigor and vividness of the phrase. In those early days of the Revolution, dead men frequently rose to accuse their murderers. We might almost speak of an uncanny inner compulsion that made the corpses of those first years of Nazidom turn up again and again, whether they had been deposited in the depths of a reservoir, in the deepest woods, or in a crowded mass grave. The diabolic frequency of such incidents so troubled our noble revolutionaries that in the end they consigned all their victims to the fire. After the thirtieth of June, 1934, the dead were never buried; they were shipped at once to the nearest crematorium.

To go back a bit — in those first days after Diels's brash remark in the department store, we kept our ears to the ground. For a while we heard nothing at all, and we were on the point of believing that Diels had simply been boasting. Then, as so often happens, pure chance came to our aid. I have mentioned that Nebe had formerly served in the Berlin police commissioner's office. Naturally he still had a good many friends there, and one day a detective told him the story of an incident that, to the ears of a police official, sounded monstrous.

A few days before, a corpse had been found in the vicinity of Berlin. It had been buried only seven or eight inches deep in a cultivated field, and a peasant had uncovered it while plowing. The homicide bureau was at once called in, since the case gave every sign of being one of assault and robbery.

The case in itself, though horrible enough, did not strike the Berlin homicide bureau as unusual. But within a few hours an unpleasant fact was revealed. The fingerprint office quickly identified the dead man. His name was Rall; he was a criminal with several previous convictions whose portrait adorned the rogues' gallery. According to the police records he was at the moment a prisoner on remand to the Neuruppin court. However, upon telephoning Neuruppin the police learned that, on the request of the Gestapo, he had been transferred for a few days to the Berlin police headquarters for purposes of investigation. From the point of view of the police, the corpse was at that moment officially 'sitting' in the Berlin police lock-up.

Nebe grabbed at this scandal. We were familiar enough with SA killings, but at the time the murder of a prisoner whom the ministry of justice had temporarily turned over to the Gestapo was not yet customary. We did not yet know anything about Hoehler, and so we had no suspicion that we were dealing with a common practice of the Gestapo.

Nebe inquired around, and at last got a rise out of Geissel — our colleague who had been so busy pasting bits of paper. When Geissel heard that the body of a certain Rall had been found, he jumped as if he had been bitten by a tarantula. Then we knew whom we had to work on, and it was not long before we pieced the whole story together.

In point of fact Rall had been brought to Berlin on orders from the Gestapo and subjected to a detailed cross-examination. The hearing had taken place in Geissel's room. After it was over, the prisoner was taken out of the police lock-up by night, stripped of all his clothes except his shirt, and driven out of the city. The car stopped at what seemed to be a favorable spot. The rest of the story was eloquently told to me by one of the murderers, a man named Reineking, who later ended in a concentration camp for knowing too much and talking too loosely. Near a small forest they saw an open field, and near-by there was a bench. They forced Rall to sit down on this bench, and then they choked him to death. According to Reineking's story, it took ages before their victim died; at any rate, the murderers felt that each minute was an hour.

They then left the body sitting on the bench and set about digging a grave in the field. But imagine their horror when they suddenly heard a noise, turned around, and saw their 'corpse' running away. The sight of this dead man racing along in the bright moonlight, his shirt fluttering behind him, was terrifying even to these hard-boiled SA killers.

But the murderers' dread that they would be discovered outweighed their terror. They rushed after the corpse, and this time really choked him to death. Then they hastily buried him. We can easily believe Reineking when he reported that he and his accomplice were very uneasy when they were called to account about the matter by the following noon.

There are certain impressions one never forgets. This description of Rall's murder is one of those for me. Although, in later days, I heard thousands of more horrible tales, this ghostly scene repeatedly rises before my eyes: the automobile roaring through the countryside, the moonlit night, the man in the shirt, the dead man sitting on the bench, the running corpse — I use the word because that is how Reineking expressed himself — and last of all, that hasty, inadequate burial: the ghastliness of the whole story is so vivid and significant that I feel it a chronicler's duty to recount it in narrating the history of the Reichstag fire.

But what was Rall's crime? Why had the Gestapo questioned him all day long and then murdered him expeditiously that same night? To anticipate our story: his tale was nothing to shake the world. We had all imagined the course of events much as he described it. But Rall supplied the proof.

Rall, a prisoner on a burglary charge, had one day appeared voluntarily before the examining magistrate of the Neuruppin lower court and made a statement about the Reichstag fire. The magistrate incorporated this statement into that 'letter' to the Leipzig court which had caused such a stir in the offices of the Gestapo. We shall see later why Rall 'talked,' but for the present let us consider his information.

Rall himself was no very pleasant character. An habitual criminal, he lived on by grace of that mistaken clemency which frees notorious criminals after they have served their sentence, although their next felony can be predicted with mathematical exactitude. In 1932, after having completed a long term in prison, Rall grasped the tempo of the times. His asocial instinct led him to recognize that the whole public order was in dissolution. Rall, the criminal, scented revolution. Without more ado he joined the SA.

In those turbulent months no one in the SA inquired about social origins. Children of the people; unknowns who had hitherto lived on the other side of the tracks of life; Communists whose quick conversion won them high praise — all were heartily welcomed into the SA. Temporary delinquents and hardened criminals were taken to the bosom of the Movement, and these *Volksgenossen* would begin their new and purified way of life to the thunderous trumpet blasts of Goebbels's propaganda or to frenetic, revivalistic applause in the *Sportspalast*. Such persons were in fact more sought after than the ordinary solid citizen; for they had the virtue of possessing hard fists. And there were still a good many recalcitrants among their fellow countrymen who had to have the fact of their wonderful good fortune pounded into them.

Rall plunged at once into the sort of turmoil that was entirely suited to his character. He was welcomed jubilantly and swiftly made a place for himself. Within a few weeks he traveled the usual SA-man's course — I mean that of the professional thug who received a small 'donation' for his unselfish Party work and a sackful of tinkling promises.

So Rall went around smearing Brown inscriptions on walls and tearing down the election posters of the other parties. He took part in the propaganda marches in which he along with his comrades had to roar until their voices were hoarse: 'Germany, awake . . . Jews to the stake . . .' or 'Heil Hitler . . .' Every evening he tested his biceps at the bloody brawls that were part of the routine of every public meeting. In short, he 'fought' and was soon promoted to membership in the so-called 'staff guard.'

The staff guard was the élite formed of the most savage daredevils. These thugs were, of course, paid somewhat better for the effectiveness of their fists and the toughness of their consciences than were the poor wretches who imagined that the future Reich could be built by conscientious toil for the cause.

Not the least of the functions of these cadres was the creation of 'incidents.'

At that time the Nazi Movement lived on incidents. As is well known, the year 1932 produced a number of grave defeats for National Socialism. At times the Brown tide seemed to be distinctly on the ebb. The Nazi leaders saw that something had to be done. If the masses would no longer throng to their victory demonstrations, a series of which were held whenever some local elections gave the Nazis a majority, then the credulous populace would have to be gathered in by some other kind of demonstration, say that of mourning. For that purpose Goebbels used the brawls and stabbings that took place among the lowest rabble of the streets to give rise to Nazi heroes.

But what could be done if there were no victims ready at hand? Necessity knows no law — if there were none, some would be provided. About half of those 'comrades who were shot by the Red Front and the reactionaries' are probably, to this day, continuing their tussles in Valhalla along with Horst Wessel. These victims were, for example, informers whom the Communists had sent into the ranks of the SA and who then, having been found out and stabbed in the back, were given a pompous swastika funeral. Or else they were Brown fellow fighters who, to employ the terminology of the thirtieth of June, were shot down by their own snipers 'by accident.'

Nebe stubbornly insisted that such 'accidents' were planned beforehand, with details of time and place, at district headquarters. I have never obtained any proof of this. Nevertheless, I did find a document in my safe in the ministry of the interior — it had been left there by an oversight — which contained the testimony of numerous witnesses to the effect that the killing of SA Storm Leader Maikowsky and two unfortunate police patrolmen in February, 1933, had been done by the Nazis themselves and not by the Reds. Numberless wholly innocent Marxists had to pay with their lives in atonement for that murder. The testimony of the hearings had been borrowed by the Gestapo from the ministry of justice 'for brief inspection.' That was the usual process by which incriminating documents were made to disappear from the archives of the ministry of justice.

There were various kinds of incidents that these SA thugs were required to stage, and some of them were a good deal more innocuous and even had their humorous side.

One of these popular amusements was setting fire to the advertising columns [1] that dot Berlin. The columns would shoot flames high into the night. It was a wonderful sight to see; the masses would stand around gaping, the fire engines would be called, the police would growl, and by a little clever handling a resounding riot could be worked up. What could make Herr Goebbels happier than a scene that ended in the police's going into action with their night sticks?

As a matter of fact, when these first pillars of fire became the fashion in 1932, a good deal might have been learned. If the police had investigated a little more energetically, if they had examined the question of why these advertising columns burned so brightly, who knows but that they might not have got on the track of something more important than these pre-election carousals?

Instead, squads of police were sent out to guard Berlin's advertising columns, those symbols of a democratic freedom of opinion that had long since been beaten into extinction. Or, instead of whole squads, plainclothesmen were stationed near the columns to watch whether anyone busied himself about the posters just before a fire.

[1] In Berlin and other European cities round pillars are the equivalent of American billboards. (*The translators.*)

Since it was no simple matter to set fire to such a thick mass of paper — layers of posters pasted on top of each other — the police imagined that by patience and alertness they would eventually lay hands on the pyromaniacs. But the higher the records of incidents piled up, the lower was their score of results.

Even if the police had succeeded in finding out what technical magic the firebugs employed, they would not have solved their problem. For the incendiaries were using a highly inflammable fluid which could be so mixed that it would take one or two hours to burst into spontaneous combustion. All that was needed was for someone to spray the liquid against the column unobserved. And who could detect the one mischief-maker with a small canister concealed in his briefcase among hundreds of innocent passers-by?

This was the element of novelty, the point at which Rall's story began to be interesting. His other tales about the life and doings of an SA staff guard had no unusual features. He talked about the activities of his mobile detachment, about brawls, riots, and beatings administered, the way an old soldier might reminisce about the rules of the drill ground. However, Rall afterward realized the significance of those first attempts at incendiarism — afterward, because at the time he and his comrades only wanted to introduce a bit of diversion into the nightly round of disorderly conduct.

From that point on his narrative flowed rapidly. The convict reported vividly how one evening at the end of February — in the meanwhile the Third Reich had dawned — he was ordered to report to Brigade Leader Karl Ernst. At that time Ernst was still subordinate to Count Helldorf, who headed the Berlin SA group. However, for the delicate mission in question Ernst was considered more suitable than his superior. This was quite true, for Ernst, who had grown up in the streets of Berlin, had an incomparably better command of down-to-earth language and rough-and-ready abilities than the radical SA count. Helldorf really hankered to be taken back into society and to return to the feudal customs of his forefathers.

Ten-men strong — we can see from the fact that he was among this ten what a tried and tested Nazi champion Rall was considered to be — they were told to report to Karl Ernst. Ernst began the conference by giving them a piece of his mind. That was a routine procedure among the Brown mercenaries. It was necessary to show a thorough command of the jargon of vituperation to be considered 'really hot.' The power of a man's voice might not give proof of his superior mental equipment, but it showed that he could be forceful in practical arguments.

But then the brigade leader suddenly shifted ground; he became very pleasant, very human, almost paternal — to the extent that his thirty years permitted. They were now, he said, going to 'turn a trick' that was really going to 'be something,' and these boys had been chosen to take part in it. In the near future they were going to deliver an annihilating blow to the Marxists. Everything was prepared. All that was lacking was a pretext; it was to be their business to make one. As everybody knew, the Communists wanted to burn all Germany to a cinder. All they, the Nazis, would do was to start a fire in the Reichstag, that stinking gossip factory. Afterward they would say that the Communists were responsible.

The police? They need not worry at all about them. If it were possible, they would like to fool the police as well as everyone else. But if necessary they would guide the investigation into the proper channels. As far as that was concerned, the 'Doctor' — that is, Goebbels — had already discussed the matter thoroughly with Goering.

The conference ended with the appointment of a sort of bandit chieftain. Karl Ernst intended merely to direct operations; the brigade leader considered himself too important to take actual command of the shock troop. And thus it was that Storm Leader Heini Gewehr, a twenty-five-year-old ne'er-do-well, was ordered to demonstrate, in an historic hour, his loyalty, his obedience, and his pyrotechnic abilities.

No dress rehearsal took place. Instead, the men went through a blueprint performance.

Sketches of the Reichstag building were spread out on a table, and on paper the incendiaries marched along behind Heini Gewehr. Heini

Gewehr actually went through the building, accompanied by Karl Ernst. Ernst was a Reichstag deputy and could therefore show a visitor through the building without difficulty. Since they had no intention of astounding the fire department by the artistry of their work, their tour did not have to be intensive. They planned to set their fires thoroughly, but without wasting any time, and were therefore interested in closely inspecting only those rooms which were easily accessible and which contained a good deal of highly inflammable material. These were the Reichstag restaurant, the galleries, and above all the assembly hall with its wooden paneling. If that hall didn't burn like dry tinder, their names were not Karl Ernst and Heini Gewehr.

During the days preceding the gala performance the paper rehearsal was gone over several times. The men had plenty of time to study their task, since as a precautionary measure they had been deprived of leaves and kept locked up in their barracks so that there would be no unlooked-for blabbing.

The rehearsals were, as a matter of fact, necessary. There were a number of matters that could not be left to the last minute. Who, for example, was to stand guard? Who would meanwhile spray the incendiary fluid? Who could run fastest and would therefore take over the restaurant or the galleries? And who on the other hand could enjoy the pleasures of deliberately setting fire to the assembly hall? Who would be the two unfortunates who would be left out of it, who would have to stand outside the Reichstag building and watch from the street to see that everything went according to plan?

At the time Rall also gathered that there was to be a counterplot, in addition to their visit to the building; something was to go on with which they had nothing to do. But what was meant by that, how the two separate actions were to supplement one another, what additional 'trick' Karl Ernst or Doctor Goebbels intended to 'turn' — that was something that no one bothered to indicate to Rall or his comrades. And when they timidly ventured to ask, the ten men who considered themselves the heroes of the day were promptly put in their place. Karl Ernst snarled, 'Shut your traps!'

Whereupon they kept their questions to themselves and abandoned all further investigations of the higher strategy.

On the day of the fire they set out late in the afternoon.

Their first stop was a drugstore in the north of the city. The druggist was an old Party comrade, a devoted SA man. He was also an expert at his profession. And this evening he, too, was 'really hot.'

He turned over to them a quantity of liquid that was far less than they had reckoned on. Each of them received a square vessel of the precious fluid. It was small enough to be stowed away in the kind of large knapsacks that are used for carrying newspapers. The men were somewhat surprised; they could scarcely believe that this would be enough. But the druggist must know.

Toward six o'clock they drove up to the Reichstag president's palace, which lay opposite the main structure and was connected with it by an underground passage. There were so many cars around the palace that their arrival attracted no attention, nor did anyone notice the odd-looking briefcases. Whether the doorman was in on the game or whether he had been called away by some higher official at that moment, Rall could not say.

The squad descended at once into the cellar. There they had to wait a considerable time. Apparently they were to start on some prearranged signal. Perhaps someone outside had to make sure that the coast was clear. Or perhaps they were waiting for a report that the other 'trick' was functioning. In any case, Karl Ernst suddenly came thumping down the stairs. Heini Gewehr reported that everything was in order, and with a few friendly curses the brigade leader dismissed them.

From that point on everything moved like the wind. They raced through the notorious underground tunnel. 'Raced' is perhaps a bit misleading, for naturally they avoided making any unnecessary noise. On the other hand, they had not bothered to remove their heavy SA boots. Nor had they taken any other precautions, such as exchanging their SA outfits for some anonymous civilian clothes. They had not even troubled to conceal their identity papers.

There was a good reason for this. For days before the ground had been spied out in advance and, as far as it was possible to calculate, they would not be likely to meet anyone in the silent and deserted edifice. But if any of their three groups — one group of four men for the assembly hall and two groups of two men each for the restaurant and the galleries — should chance to meet with someone, they would be taken for harmless messengers on their way to the room of the National Socialist fraction. But if they got involved in any unpleasant arguments, they had orders to shoot at once. That was better than risking discovery. And afterward, after the wicked Communists had set fire to the Reichstag, it might well augment Nazi dramatics or emphasize the ruthlessness of the Reds if a few innocent bystanders had lost their lives.

But everything went like clockwork. I am almost ashamed to write it down: this is the end of Rall's story.

No chance visitors rushed down the hall shouting alarms. No guards called the police. No whistles pierced the air; no shots were fired. Nor were there any complications afterward. Nothing happened except that the three columns did the work assigned to them and then, after about ten minutes, met again in the tunnel.

It was all over. For the rest — see the morning newspapers.

When they returned to Karl Ernst and saluted stiffly, they were not 'cussed out' this time. Instead, they heard words of highest praise. Once again they were admonished to keep their traps shut and — and this was the main thing for Rall — they were given to understand that they would be well rewarded.

But that was just where the trouble began for Rall. The fool actually believed that the bonus would be paid. When, instead, he was expelled from the SA a few months later (he claimed that it was because his bosses were too 'hoity-toity,' but the real reason was that his previous record was a little too grim even for a member of the staff guard), Rall decided that he would have to find another way to obtain his hard-earned bonus. He based his hopes on the cumbersomeness of justice, which could not be completely co-ordinated overnight. And he was right: there were still judges who were ready to give him a hearing. . . .

But there were also Dielses who were ready to order his execution.

THE INCENDIARIES

WAS RALL LYING?

Not at all. Everything he said was, in itself, wholly credible. And even if we should be inclined to doubt one point or another, his former SA leaders vouched for his truthfulness when they came to the fatal conclusion that he had to be 'finished off.'

Let us for the moment leave aside the whole question of Lubbe and concern ourselves with the incendiary act alone. None of the facts run counter to the above description. On the contrary, all the experts testified in court, on the basis of their own deductions, that it could have been done in no other way. Rall, therefore, revealed nothing, he uncovered no secrets; fundamentally he merely confirmed what everyone thought. His chief contribution was that, instead of the imaginary Communists, he named the concrete Nazis by their real names.

We must, however, check up to ascertain whether he did not incriminate the wrong persons or conceal the names of one or another of the right persons. We miss Helldorf, who was often accused, or Daluege, who certainly ought to have been in on the plot. Goebbels was mentioned with suspicious brevity in Rall's account, and Goering's rôle was not touched on. Yet the world persisted for twelve years in the opinion that without Goering there would have been no Reichstag fire.

But it is precisely these omissions in his recital that authenticate Rall's tale. The 'Doctor' was in on it; the matter of the police had been discussed with Goering — these two slim allusions he wove into his story. And certainly neither Karl Ernst nor Heini Gewehr, let alone Goebbels or Goering, would have confided any more than that to Rall.

The whole action must be conceived as an extremely elementary and primitive undertaking. It would be quite false to picture a band of perfectionists sitting down together and racking their brains to invent a dramatic stroke of propaganda for the crucial Reichstag elections. Rather, the Reich propaganda minister thought up an incident that would provide a neat song-hit for the election bandwagon, discussed the affair with his colleague Goering, and then turned the whole filthy business over to the lower functionaries, as was only proper. It was the business of the latter to look around and find the criminals best suited to the job, men who were rash and unscrupulous enough to lend themselves to such dirty work.

Rall merely followed orders — no more. Rall knew only as much as he had to know. Therefore, he could only blab about the aspects of the plot in which he himself had taken part. He could also, of course, give the names of his accomplices and did so; but I never was able to lay my hands on the list.

In any case, what would it matter now? Karl Ernst, Heini Gewehr — and so far as I know Pigface was also one of them; we don't need much imagination to picture the rest of them. No police will ever come to 'fetch' them because they have since all died. Most of them did not survive the thirtieth of June. The last to go was Heini Gewehr. He fell in the East — while serving as a police officer.

Rall's rather primitive confession was sufficient, so to speak, to loosen the bonds of propriety which had restrained all talk about the Reichstag fire. After a few drinks Ernst or Diels or Geissel would recapitulate their memories of the night of the fire. The untimely discovery of Rall's body broke the seal of silence which had been placed on the case. Consequently, Nebe and I received enough hints to put together a fairly exact sketch of the more obscure aspects of the fire. A harmless, casual question or two put to other participants rounded out the picture for us.

The sensational element for us — and we had a hard time convincing ourselves that it was true — was that Goebbels, not Goering, was the real Reichstag incendiary. It was Goebbels who first thought of it. Goebbels had held the preliminary conferences with Karl Ernst. Goebbels had approved the choice of the squad. Goebbels had indicated the rooms where the fire would get the best foothold. Goebbels had 'facilitated' the execution of the business by giving his sanction to the shooting-down of any chance witnesses.

Goebbels had guaranteed that no one would conduct a search in the group headquarters or in the palace of the Reichstag president. Goebbels had promised that any action against the SA men would be denounced as a libelous attack on the Nazi Movement itself. Goebbels had originated the plan of not merely accusing the Communists, but of generously turning over the problem of solving the crime to the police.

Goebbels had clearly perceived the value of muzzling the entire Left press as a device for concealing the truth. Goebbels had therefore vigorously urged the proclamation of the vicious emergency decrees. It was this point that Goebbels had discussed at length with Goering. In the course of this discussion Goebbels had mysteriously hinted that the Fuehrer was aware that something dramatic and thorough had to take place — perhaps an attempted assassination, perhaps a fire — but that Hitler wished to be surprised.

And Goebbels had then taken the responsibility for 'preparing' the Fuehrer for the game, laying the ground for Hitler's outburst of fury on the night of the fire. Let us remember that Hitler was dining with Goebbels when he was startled by the news of the fire!

Goering had simply given his consent to the whole plot. The Reich propaganda minister's proposal appealed to him; he particularly liked the fact that virtually no participation would be required of him. He was perfectly willing to place the palace and the underground tunnel at their disposal, but if Goebbels and Karl Ernst wanted to do the rest, to turn the trick by themselves, so much the better for him. That way was far safer: he need only wait to see Hitler's or Hindenburg's reaction. Naturally Goebbels could depend on Goering's willingness to seize the slightest and most fantastic pretext to strike out at the Marxists. Goering did, of course, have some part to play. He took the precaution of talking the matter over with Diels and dropping a few hints to Daluege. But for the rest he merely let the affair run its course.

Helldorf had no part at all. This SA group leader was enjoying champagne and caviar in a luxurious night club when the sirens began howling and the word was passed around that the Reichstag was on fire. Accompanied by his SA comrade, von Arnim, the rector of the Technical High School, Helldorf went out into the street and convinced himself that the sky was indeed blood-red. The two men debated whether they ought to drive to the scene. But learning that the fire engines had already arrived, and that the Fuehrer, Goebbels, Goering, and Papen were also on the spot, Helldorf decided to return to his good food and his *tête-à-tête*.

I heard Helldorf give this account of the scene repeatedly. It was widely believed that he must have participated as one of the leaders in the affair — this impression arose from the incident of Lubbe's momentary reaction at the trial when Helldorf sharply ordered him to raise his head. To my mind this was a mere bit of drama whose significance was greatly magnified. Unlike the other SA leaders who testified before the Leipzig court, Helldorf moved in these lofty circles with complete social ease. Men like Heines, the SA group leader and police chief of Breslau, would have been incapable of the nonchalance with which Count Helldorf, in response to the question of whether he had ever seen Lubbe before, condescendingly ordered the Dutchman: 'Lift up your head for once.' All the other SA toughs who killed every day without the slightest compunction were in agony every time they had to appear before the court and the throng of foreign correspondents. Their discomfort was plainly visible, and they stood rigidly at attention while they poured out their perjuries. Such men would never have ventured to address Lubbe that way in the solemn atmosphere of the court.

The key question still remains: How did Lubbe become involved in the diabolic business? We already know that this poor fellow was not needed to set the Reichstag on fire. We did not need Rall to certify to this obvious fact. On the other hand, Lubbe could not very well have stood around in a corner until the flames were shooting high.

The first fact that we determined with certainty was that the performance would have been given even without Lubbe. The date, the incendiaries, the inflammable fluid were all prepared down to the last detail before this blunderer into world history put in his appearance.

Naturally, he was eagerly welcomed. It is hard to say, however, whether Goebbels did not have occasion later on to curse the chance that made him stumble across Lubbe. For the original plan had envisioned nothing more than a crude swindle, a raw piece of election propaganda. Basically it was, originally, merely a matter of burning to the ground a building with ugly associations for the Nazis. An absurd act whose immediate effect was to disconcert the Opposition, followed by a reign of terror that would silence all doubters — such was ever the Nazi logic.

This crude plan was rudely disturbed when Lubbe made his bid to become a second Herostratus. Goebbels, of course, would not have been Goebbels if his perverted imagination had failed to reach out at once to grasp at this unfortunate Dutchman. What an obvious and splendid stroke of propaganda the man afforded! Not only would they accuse his Communist fellows; they would also produce a living, and moreover an alien, Bolshevist caught *flagrante delicto.* Then, according to the plan, as soon as they had posted the man's picture in placards all over town, he would be hanged in an outburst of public fury. Lynch justice, the Americans called it. What could go wrong with such a plan?

But things did go wrong — the cunning Goebbels had not foreseen two possibilities. In the first place, Lubbe's arrest introduced a complication which would not have been present if there had simply been a conflagration and the police had found no incendiary. For now the formalities had to be observed; there had to be hearings, investigations, indictments, and ultimately a trial. And the more involved these public activities became, the more the swindle was imperiled. Moreover — and this is the second feature that the propaganda minister overlooked — Goebbels's imagination was not the only one that set to work. The spark ignited another mind — Hitler, too, let his imagination work on the alien hobo who provided so picturesque a subject for the impending tribunal.

It does not matter whether Hitler knew or suspected anything before the fire; for the moment the flames leaped into the night sky, the moment the populace thronged to the scene and Lubbe's wretched

figure stepped out of the burning building, the Fuehrer was no longer
the man he had been half an hour before. Hitler himself was en-
chanted; as in all dramatic moments he became the victim of his
capacity for self-hypnosis. From that moment on, all he could think
of was the great show-trial in which he, who was so fond of making
revelations, would be able to say all manner of things to an astonished
world.

Although the original plan was thus fundamentally altered by the
inclusion of the Dutchman, the synchronization of the incendiary work
with Lubbe's gymnastic feat in climbing through the window was a
masterly stroke.

How was this managed?

As we have seen, Rall knew merely that 'something' else was to be
going on; what that something else was or how it was to be worked he
could not say. Of the squad, Heini Gewehr alone had been acquainted
with the details of the matter.

The contrapuntal action was conducted by Karl Ernst, who was
thus in charge of both the real and the sham incendiarism. Ernst
waited until Lubbe had arrived at the scene and was already creeping
about the Reichstag before he turned the real firebugs loose. At that
point the stratagem could scarcely fail. The boldness of the trick consisted in their concealing from Lubbe the fact that he had a number
of busy assistants at work at the same time.

But what if Lubbe had funked it at the last moment? That had to
be considered. Would the game have been up in that event? Not at
all. For then the Reichstag would simply have burned without the
aid of this newcomer. They would be able to 'catch' Lubbe in any
case — if not in the act, then while trying to escape. They had primed
him so that he would readily have fitted into either version of the
story. They therefore thought it unnecessary to waste words; why
disappoint the Dutchman by explaining the reason he had to be so
punctual? Why let him know that for all his ridiculous fire-lighters
and his nimbleness at climbing, it was not he alone who was going
to create an historic Reichstag fire. And obviously it was still less
advisable to inform the thugs of the staff guard that their function was
no more than that of stage hands.

Lubbe, however, far surpassed what they had expected of him; he proved himself a true artist on the great stage.

All our reservations about the practicability of running two simultaneous plots, all our dozens of ifs and buts, must in the end come down to one prime question — Where did the Nazis pick up the man and what means did they use to fit him for his part?

It is at this point that the story is interrupted by those painful lacunae which Nebe and I kept trying for so long to fill. Everything up to now has sounded quite credible, but now we come to an element of the improbable, to an explanation that satisfies me no more than it would any other reasonable man.

For one day Lubbe was suddenly there, simply there. The Nazis picked him up somewhere after he tried to fire the palace — just where is not clear.

According to one version, it was Diels who brought the Dutchman to their attention. Since Lubbe had shuffled across the footlights just as the curtain was about to rise on the Nazis' fiery spectacle, Goering's crafty policeman scented a splendid opportunity and handed the arrested incendiary over to the SA. Diels later denied this, and that in itself would tend to corroborate the hypothesis. On the other hand, I have my doubts about the theory because at that time the Gestapo had not yet been founded. It seems to me questionable whether at that time Diels, in his post in the ministry of the interior, had sufficiently good connections with Berlin police headquarters to be able to put over such a neat bit of gangsterism.

According to the other version, a number of SA men picked up Lubbe. These men were unemployed who had met Lubbe in the public flophouse and become interested in him because of his vague, confused Communistic threats. They had therefore spied on him; SA men who had nothing better to do made a habit of such informal espionage. Apparently they had some premonition of their later function as auxiliary police and liked to practice. And, of course, they played at being policemen in a manner that corresponded to their low milieu and their limited intelligence: they trailed after men of their own sort and made 'official reports.'

In this way Lubbe, after his first attempts at incendiarism, fell into the clutches of some SA storm troopers. They gave him a thorough beating and were on the point of turning him over to the regular police. But the SA group headquarters intervened and he was released. . . .

The reader may take his pick of these two versions. Both of them are somehow unsatisfactory. For the fact that Joseph Goebbels should have come across Lubbe just at the time the Reich propaganda chief was planning to set the Reichstag afire seems utterly grotesque. At best we can say that it is one of those puzzles that confound our rational minds, but that reality is fond of posing every now and then.

Whatever the case, let us say that one day Goebbels 'had' Lubbe. What did they do with him?

To put it briefly: they beat him, they doped him, they hypnotized him.

The beating is easy to imagine. No doubt the doping and hypnotizing were done with the same cool, technical attitude with which the inflammable liquid was compounded. If we are to believe the story of one of the participants, Karl Ernst and his comrades considered that their real achievement was to have directed Lubbe's attention toward the Reichstag — he was already on an incendiary tour, but he might have ended up anywhere — and then to have restrained him for three days until everything was ready for the gala performance.

They had to make sure that Lubbe did not get out of their sight. But they also encouraged him in the delusion that he was in good Communist company. Up to the time he went to the scaffold, or rather — since they actually murdered him ten months before his execution — up to the time his consciousness was completely blacked out, they did not permit him to know how he was being used as a tool to murder all those of his own faith. The Herostratian attitude he quickly assumed was therefore genuine, and the cry of 'Protest! Protest!' which he uttered when he was captured in the burning Reichstag, was also genuine — to the extent that we can speak of genuine behavior in a hypnotized man.

But in all that followed — Lubbe in jail, Lubbe in court, Lubbe in the spotlight of world publicity — he was no longer the same woolly-minded failure whose anarchistic impulses had been intensified by suggestion. He was an empty husk whose pitiful, numbed insanity and defenseless reversion to an animal existence gave evidence of the deadly effects of a chemical formula.

3

The Frenzy of the Masses

GLEICHSCHALTUNG

THE REAL NATIONAL SOCIALIST REVOLUTION broke out in full earnest by June, 1933. Everything that had happened before that time, including the Reichstag fire, was only the prelude.

On January 30, 1933, President von Hindenburg asked the leader of the strongest Opposition Party of that date, Adolf Hitler, to form a government of 'national renewal.' We all remember vividly the sharp struggles that preceded that event. From the superficial point of view, the problem revolved around the notorious question of legality. Old Hindenburg was unwilling to violate the constitution which he had taken an oath to defend. Although he had allowed his advisers to convince him that the tortuous domestic politics of Germany could be straightened out only by a temporary dictatorship, he wanted to act in as constitutional a fashion as possible; he hated to do anything outright illegal.

Perhaps Hindenburg's only thought was to satisfy the forms. But it is possible that a degree of wisdom was contained in this stubborn adherence to legality. The old man may have had a premonition of the danger of shaking the last pillars of the existing order. It might have seemed more sensible to him to prop the crumbling dikes rather than to let the surging floods sweep away all that had been in the past. Hindenburg wanted 'renewal'; Hitler meant revolution. That was the reason the two could not agree for so many years. And that was why the suspicious president of the Reich tried to rein in his new chancellor even after he had reached that historic crossroads of January 30, 1933. Hindenburg thought that the elastic Article 48 of the Weimar Constitution, which in the past two years had already served Bruening as the basis for a host of emergency decrees, would permit Hitler to exercise the necessary dictatorial powers; but at the same time the article would set a limit that could not be crossed. To make sure, the Reich president reserved the ultimate decisions for himself.

Hindenburg at that time was already too old still to be ambitious; too tired to want to cling to his office. And certainly he was much too experienced to seek adventures. He had no need to strain for further power and fame. On the other hand, if a dictatorship were in fact inevitable, he preferred to have it accomplished by a *coup d'état* on the part of the president rather than by a revolt by the tribune of the people.

On the other hand, Hitler would obviously not be content with such a curtailment of power. A minority government which had to ask Hindenburg's sanction for emergency decrees in each individual case would have to proceed all the more cautiously because it could never be sure of the president's attitude. Hitler, therefore, decided to dissolve the Reichstag at once in order to secure a dependable parliamentary majority.

His companions in the coalition government — Hugenberg, Papen, and Seldte — had nothing to gain by an election and were not at all warm to the idea. But Hitler bought their consent by giving his word of honor that, notwithstanding the expected Nazi victory in the election, he would undertake no changes of cabinet for four years. He was to keep this promise, although after his own fashion. There were no resignations in the government of the Third Reich.

In the month-long election campaign that followed, the whole repertoire of National Socialist methods for influencing public opinion was reviewed for the first time. Hence the anticlimax was all the greater when the Nazis did not even obtain a simple parliamentary majority, much less the two-thirds majority in conjunction with the German Nationalist bloc which they needed to carry through their planned changes in the constitution. Support from the Center Party remained indispensable, in spite of the fact that the parliamentary arithmetic was helped out by the arrest of the entire Communist fraction.

Nevertheless, on March 21 Hitler passed the first stage of his activity as chancellor. Cleverly calculating the value of the gesture, he convoked the newly elected Reichstag to the tomb of Frederick the Great. He knew that such a demonstration would touch all patriotic Germans to the heart. Wisely, the orator mentioned nothing of his intention soon to furl the black-white-and-red flags, nor did he state that this would be the last time, except for the funeral next year of the old field marshal, that he would permit a member of the clergy to participate in an act of state. Emphatically Hitler declared his devotion to all the traditional forces that help maintain the state. Standing in the venerable church, he took Christianity expressly under the protection of the government and of himself personally. Then, still under the spell of this solemn dedication, the Reichstag was persuaded to pass a law transferring all its powers to the cabinet for a period of four years.

By that fateful act the Reichstag not only eliminated itself from the government, but also limited the powers of the president. Hindenburg could still sign decrees, but he could scarcely obstruct his chancellor any longer. On that day in Potsdam Hitler successfully made a snatch at absolute power.

Looking back we may say without reservation that this first phase of the Revolution cost relatively few lives. Until the day of the election there were, of course, innumerable brawls and street battles. But these scarcely went beyond what had come to be the usual thing during the past few years. Meetings of the Republican *Reichsbanner* continued to be held, as did Communist demonstrations. Hoersing and Thaelmann spoke in the Sportspalast; the police, with exemplary impartiality, supervised the demonstrators as they marched in and out. Meetings of the other Opposition parties were also virtually undisturbed. It was not until the last week before the elections, shortly after the Reichstag fire, that the waves of turbulence rose higher. But in comparison to what came later, it was all quite mild.

With the Reichstag out of the way, the ministers of the cabinet of 'national renewal' set to work at once. The temperament and the previous lives of the Nazis naturally stamped their work with a special character. But the German Nationalists, the 'black-white-and-reds,' also labored each according to their nature.

Hugenberg, for example, converted his ministry into a model beehive. He worked indefatigably, reading all messages, drafting ordinances, correcting all reports down to the last comma. Now and then his master of ceremonies admitted a ministerial secretary or some similar official; men from his own entourage were almost never allowed to see him. This kind of self-imprisonment was very well suited to the natural tendencies of the leader of the German Nationalist Party. Now minister of economy and food, he had a good time playing hide-and-seek with the revolutionary currents. He relied on Hitler's promise that his ministry would be untouched no matter what the result of the elections, and deluded himself in the belief that his whole political party could be pastured by the Nazis in some national preserve. Since, however, the SA were not the sort to observe the game laws, Hugenberg learned one fine day that the party he headed had been annihilated, and not very gently at that.

Seldte, the *Stahlhelm* leader, lacking the zeal and earnestness of the Prussian Hugenberg, took things easy from the beginning. His proud title of minister of labor did not prevent him from working as little as possible. He had more important business than social politics. By means of friendly letters, personal chats, and, above all, by extended absences from his office, he managed to shake off all those members of the *Stahlhelm* who applied to him for help — for they were no better off than their Nationalist comrades. Utterly without principle, Seldte betrayed his old fellows one after the other. First Duesterberg fell; then this or that district leader of the *Stahlhelm;* finally the whole organization broke up. The former leader alone remained, now proudly decked out in the uniform of an SA *Obergruppenfuehrer.*

Papen was too much a man of the world to emulate Hugenberg and build up a little monastery for himself. He was also too ambitious to be content with a political sinecure with title and salary, like

Seldte. In the coalition government Papen suddenly manifested an appetite for ministerial work as overwhelming as his lust for political power. He set up a huge office and had letterheads printed with the imposing designation: 'Deputy of the Reich Chancellor.' Under this title he pretended that his office was an adjustment bureau for Nationalist petitioners.

This great bluffer entered upon a program of furious labor, or rather made his unsuspecting and unfortunate collaborators toil endlessly covering reams of paper and gathering up bundles of documents. Soon rumors went the rounds of government circles that Papen was gathering 'evidence.' As soon as darkness fell, he would steal across the street to the Reich president's home, where, however, Oscar von Hindenburg and Meissner were on the lookout to protect the old man from Papen's troublesome visits. At times Papen also crawled to Goering with his sheaves of paper. Each time Goering promised a stringent investigation and then passed the documents on to the state police, where they were so securely wrapped up in red tape that they would never again be opened to all eternity.

Franz von Papen demonstrated to his amazed contemporaries how a vice-chancellor with countless documents and petitions of protest under his arm can turn the trick of doing nothing at all, but can let his own collaborators, one and all, be murdered. Nevertheless, Papen did at least know what was going on, while Hugenberg sealed himself in his bureaucratic ampoule and Seldte debonairly looked on at what was happening.

In the meantime, under the direction of the ministers who counted — Goering, Frick, and Goebbels, and under pressure from the Nazi movement throughout the country, the second phase of the National Socialist seizure of power was being initiated.

During the months of April and May, 1933, there took place a reconstruction of the entire organization of the state which was as thorough as any revolutionary could desire. All the highest provincial officials, almost all the state governors, and all the police chiefs were changed. Scarcely a single mayor was left in office. Countless district prefects were dismissed. In the ministries, too, the important secretaries were changed. There were shake-ups in the police force from top to bottom. The new rulers well knew that the police formed the nuclear center of their new government. Overnight the Gestapo was created; new heads were appointed for the security police and the criminal police; and orders were issued to the bewildered policemen to shoot at the drop of a hat and to make arrests without thinking twice about it.

The Nazis did not confine their attentions to the central authorities; they were at least as diligent in the provinces. And they concerned themselves not only with town authorities, but with villages and economic organizations. It is, of course, always a tendency of new brooms to sweep clean; but this activity could scarcely be termed a mere vigorous sweeping. The most obscure corners were visited by this sudden Nazi urge for cleanliness. Indictments piled up; temporary arrests were the order of the day. Almost anyone who had administered a post that paid a decent salary was suspected of being a swindler. Or he was declared to be an adherent of the previous 'system,' which was sufficient reason for replacing him by a Brown commissar. The first act of the new appointee was to rummage through all the files and correspondence in order to find some grounds for his rather arbitrary assumption of the office. He inevitably discovered that his expelled predecessor had committed outrageous malfeasances and at once publicized these in long columns in the local newspaper.

Although this crude procedure did free a considerable number of posts for Nazi occupation, it was by far insufficient to provide for the large demand. In spite of the new commissioners' zeal in tracking down abuses, not everything in the German Fatherland was corrupt. Most of the indictments that were hastily handed out had to be withdrawn very quickly. Moreover, the federal government soon put a ban on the superabundant listing of frauds and embezzlements; for only a few months of such publications were sufficient to convince horrified foreign countries that Germany must have been a den of thieves. For good or ill the Party had to find more plausible grounds

for installing its members in the various minor posts throughout
Germany.

In revolutionary times a good slogan can work wonders. And
once again the right word appeared at the right time. The word was
Gleichschaltung — 'co-ordination.' Heaven only knows who first
invented the expression. Probably it cropped up by pure chance. But
once the spark of this watchword was thrown among the people, it
spread like wildfire through the country. All the Party offices were
startled into activity by it; all the job-hunters of Germany became
ecstatic. Things were being 'co-ordinated.'

And, lo and behold! this sport was all the more entertaining because
the country was suddenly swarming with technical experts in all fields.
For every office, for every imaginable government job, an old Party
comrade was on the spot, ready and eager to offer his talents to the
service of people and Fuehrer. It was astonishing how many undis-
covered or unrecognized abilities there were riding on the co-ordination
bandwagon. All these unselfish persons lined up at district Party
headquarters or in front of the ministries; they all flocked to the
kill whenever the scalp of a 'Weimar adherent' was about to fall.
Whether the man in question was a mayor or a theater director, a
state commissioner for the Christian labor fraternities or the general
director of a municipal power plant, a member of a High Consistory
or a newspaper editorial writer — in every case there were dozens of
brilliant minds who had been diligently preparing themselves for
years to hold that particular post.

After a very short time Goering had to issue a stern decree forbidding this frantic chase after sinecures. For it had gone beyond
all bounds. No one could any longer make anything out of the
sheaves of accusations of corruption which piled up in the most unlikely offices. Indescribable confusion was wrought by the mob of
newly hatched state commissioners who governed without the slightest
semblance of order and without the least understanding of their
tasks. The Prussian prime minister made no bones about revoking
orders originating in their offices. But for all the indignation of the

ministerial bureaucrats, for all the crossness on the part of the minister himself, Goering did not win out. For a full year the whirligig of passing officeholders continued, each man in his turn trying to push the others from his fat prebend.

In those months from April to June, 1933, a process took place in Germany which has been repeated in the history of all revolutions. One group of revolutionaries traditionally grab power. They occupy the most important positions and usually create a few new offices in order to make places for those among the victors who particularly merit reward. But otherwise, the leaders of the movement are at this point entirely taken up with realizing their ideological aims. Nevertheless, before they know it, that first shift of personnel, in which they themselves shot to the top, becomes a boiling maelstrom of change; all their adherents have been impatiently waiting to be taken care of. Revolutionary overturns never stop at a change of personnel in the leading positions. They inevitably bring about a complete transposition of classes. The ruling class is dispossessed and the dispossessed advance to fill their place. We might almost say that this sociologic process is the classic indication that what is going on is real revolution and not merely some reform movement.

For this reason the great revisions that began in 1933 are not particularly remarkable for the impudence with which newcomers, most of whom were utterly without professional training, took over all the better-paid offices. The remarkable thing was the speed with which the Nazis profited directly by the shifts. No other party had so insisted on the necessity for an incorruptible professional civil service. Nevertheless, no sooner had the Nazis tasted victory than they set up a veritable wholesale business in Party-membership books. The law, promulgated in the first upsurge of enthusiasm, for 'the restoration of the professional civil service' became in the hands of its authors a notorious and feared exceptional law directed specifically against the civil-service class.

How can we explain this wave of cynicism? A more or less materialistic point of view regards revolutions as the undesirable but inevitable consequences of a great economic and social crisis. Others maintain that the prime element is not the disruption of national finances or private budgets, but the devaluation of all those ideas of religion, justice, and morals which had hitherto been considered precious. The overturn of 1933 certainly seems to be an example of the latter case. Nevertheless, it cannot be denied that in the post-war years the Brown tide rose exactly in proportion to the growing economic disintegration of Germany as a result of the lost war, the inflation, and the approaching world-wide depression. In 1932, Hitler could pound so loudly upon the doors of the Reich president's palace only because six million desperate and hungry unemployed were also thundering their appeal for work.

This army of millions did not disappear overnight merely because the leader of the National Socialist Party had become chancellor. It took years before the problem of unemployment was finally solved. And as long as the widespread distress persisted, just so long the revolutionary pressure had to continue. It did not matter that for Hitler himself, as he so often said in the early months, the Revolution ended with his personal seizure of power. For his ardent followers the Revolution really began only then. The real creditors of the Brown Revolution, the disinherited and the dispossessed, presented their bill.

But the new government could not at once take care of all these unemployed, let alone satisfy all the demands which had been stimulated by the Nazis' extravagant pre-election promises. The unemployed wage-workers could only be drawn gradually into the accelerating process of production; the horde of white-collar workers had to be patient for just as long.

But there was one group which was unwilling to wait and whose members could not be dismissed bluntly and sent back to their old places of work. These were those close followers who had accompanied Adolf Hitler on his rise. They had not fought for the Movement in order now to be thrust back into their old misery, or at best to their old routines. Every one of them, somehow and somewhere, wanted something, and something better and finer than he had had. Granted that the Fuehrer had said in every election speech that he was making no promises. Had they not at the same time been promised a minature kingdom in every storm troop headquarters, at every Party meeting? Were all these great and small aspirations which they had been storing up for years to dissolve away into nothingness? Were they to be left out now, of all times, when the National Socialist Party was in possession of the whole state power? Had all those beautiful promises which had spurred them on to ever more and more sacrifices — had all those promises been no more than fraud and deception?

It was at that time that a new magic formula appeared in conjunction with the slogan of *Gleichschaltung*. Suddenly everybody everywhere was talking about *alte Kaempfer* — the 'old fighters.' It is still possible to trace the development of this concept in the months between April and June, 1933. From a sociological point of view it meant nothing more nor less than office-seekers. The real 'old fighters' had acquired jobs in the initial shift of top personnel. Their only thought then was to set to work. But the dynamics of their own Movement taught them that they had not come to political power as 'chiefs.' They had been installed as hired managers. All their noble ideals of leadership, achievement, and integrity vanished into thin air. Such might have been their functions in the Party program. But the victory had not been won by idealists intent on carrying out every iota of the Party program. The compact majority had won the decisive victory, and now these excited, brawling masses wanted to collect.

There were the SA rowdies tried in a thousand scuffles, the indefatigable attenders of meetings, the vagabond unemployed who pasted stickers at night and incited riots by day, the hoarse-voiced barkers at propaganda parades, the distributors of leaflets, the loyal toters of collection-boxes, and last but not least, the faithful payers of dues. In short, all those who had helped to win the struggle — and who was going to examine their records and determine whether they had participated out of sincere enthusiasm or out of frivolity? — now wanted to be paid off. They did not all want to be ministers or under-secretaries. But they had the feeling that there ought to be a place for them somewhere, now that the whole vast area of Germany belonged to their Movement.

If from the very beginning Hitler had resisted the greedy pressure from office-seekers of all varieties, he might have dammed the flood which within a few years undermined his administration and completely corrupted public life. If he had resisted, he might slowly have converted to National Socialism a well-trained and uncorrupted civil service. Instead, he made installment payments to the Movement. In the beginning he contented himself with appointing district leaders to the offices of provincial administrative presidents or state governors and making police chiefs of the SA and SS group leaders. But what was sauce for the district leader was sauce for the section chief. And what a group leader can get, a brigade leader deserves. The road to paying positions was open to all.

The resulting course of development took place in the crudest possible fashion. The higher dignitaries, who had been swamped in debts, soon were receiving incomes of far more than two thousand marks a month. The sub-leaders, who were still in debt, observed and envied this. The obvious envy on the one side, the natural sense of shame on the other, led the top leaders to choose the only solution that presented itself to their simple mode of thinking: the state ought to pay. Since the state could not very well, or would not, make outright contributions, the payments would have to be made by means of sinecures.

The higher-salaried positions were the first to fall. Municipal jobs were far more attractive than federal positions because they were so much better paid. Most of the mayorships and aldermanships changed hands more than once in the first two years of the Nazi régime; some of them had three or four incumbents, and as each new man entered the office the former officeholder was granted the highest possible pension.

The first victims of this practice were the professional civil-service workers. But their fate was not the worst of it. What was worst was the total blinding of the new rulers. Holding office, they mutually convinced each other that they had the qualifications for holding office, so that in time they seriously believed that they could undertake and accomplish anything. The novelty of having power lured them into making wilder and wilder demands — the logical development of which led them to the final step, the bold attempt at totality.

The intoxication with power is a complex theme. We must see the drive toward totality in connection with the whole course of German history. True, there was outright seizure of all the important posts in government, but this factor has its antithesis. The Nazi Revolution can only be truthfully pictured as a complicated pattern involving consent as well as force.

Our contemporaries have often and justly smiled at the adverbs 'spontaneously' and 'voluntarily,' words which soon became clichés of all Nazi journalism. At the same time it would be wrong to see only force and domination in those first months of National Socialism. There was, to be sure, a tremendous amount of bitterness and distrust, and frequently open revolt appeared. But there was at least an equal amount of enthusiasm and devotion, not to say fanaticism. Seldom had a nation so readily surrendered all its rights and liberties as did ours in those first hopeful, intoxicated months of the new millennium.

There was a long history behind the welcome the Germans gave to the Nazis' radical program. The lost war, continual unrest, the inflation, grave evidences of cultural decay, unemployment to an extent hitherto thought impossible — all these things and a great deal more preyed upon the souls of sixty million people.

And then it suddenly appeared that the pressure was relaxing. All distress of mind was to be cast off; all misery of body was to be exchanged for work, bread, and a good livelihood. And this new day dawned amid blasts of trumpets and the boom of drums, to the melody of gay marches, the cheering of jubilant crowds, and the blaring of countless loudspeakers.

Few persons had the hardihood to stand up against such an experience. Even the doubters were sucked into the torrent of joy and hope. The stirring slogans, the new rhythm, the colloquial language, the gay and youthful songs, the optimism, and the passionate promises of the Nazi Movement — how the excited people were carried away by them! After all the Germans had gone through, they simply could no longer resist the impetus.

And consequently it was not just individuals who went over to National Socialism. The masses as such were set in motion. In a mob everyone remains himself and yet can do nothing but push and shout, and be pushed and outshouted, until at last the crush dissolves and each person, an individual once more, with battered hat and hoarse voice, plods wearily and thirstily home. So it was: everyone, whatever his name, whatever his nature, men and women, old and young, luke-warm and enthusiasts, opportunists, defeated opponents and rough-and-tough SA men — all were forged into a molten mass of human beings capable of reacting only as a mass.

No one considered that these millions of willing-unwilling drops of humanity constituted a flood danger. And all of them, as individuals, were thinking only of themselves. They wanted simply to be in on the great events, to link themselves up with history before it was too late. But as a mass they created a new will and forced events in fresh directions. Moreover, it was this sudden, obscure pressure from below in the victorious movement that lent fresh courage to the new rulers, that strengthened their own drives and inspired them with the ultimate audacity they needed to go all out.

Abruptly men's spirits changed. A wild national jubilation broke out. Banners, garlands, testimonials, laudatory telegrams, worshipful orations, changes of street names, became as commonplace as parades and demonstrations. Victory celebrations, community appeals, followed one another in rapid-fire succession. The glorious sensation of a new fraternity overwhelmed all groups and classes. Professor and waitress, laborer and industrialist, servant girl and trader, clerks, peasants, soldiers, and government workers — all of them suddenly learned what seemed to be the greatest discovery of the century — that they were comrades of one race, 'Volksgenossen.' Above all, youth, youth was getting its due. The dreary past was forgotten, even the oppressive present was hardly noticed in view of the transcendent future of this new, this Third Reich, which was at last being established.

No wonder that the popular rejoicing verged on the ecstatic.

Serenity vanished; all rational thinking, all inner restraint, were abandoned. In the end there remained nothing but black and white, good and evil; the whole world was divided into rascals and heroes, the past and the eternal, centuries of ignorance and a thousand years of salvation. Everything ran to superlatives.

If, today, a radio program consisting of phonograph records from those days were played, I rather think that our people would not believe their ears. They would be unwilling to believe that they had listened to so much trash and had themselves participated in such raucousness, such singing, such idiocies. But in those days we were on the eve of a revolution. The surging flood was just gathering. Day after day the people sang and marched themselves into ever-madder states of intoxication; and naturally the loudest singers and the hardiest marchers were in demand.

This state of affairs accounts for the swift thrusting aside of the Nationalist members of the coalition. They could not keep up with the tempo of the marches and the volume of the shouting. Their highly intellectual essays and their simple-minded boasting that they, too, had had their share in the great victory were drowned out by the shouts of the Brown Shirts. In the midst of all the commotion of victory the hypnotized masses did not even hear them. Almost overnight they found themselves an entirely subsidiary group and were fortunate if they were able to reach the shelter of the Party or the SA as *'Maerzgefallene'* — the name given to those hordes of sudden converts who joined the Nazis in March, 1933.

Was the snub given to the Nationalists due only to base ingratitude on the part of the leader of the National Socialist Party? Not at all. The people themselves in those exciting weeks wanted their wild celebrations to go on without complication; they had no patience with bickerings and jealousies inside the coalition. Now, when the glorious victory had come, who cared about calculating the share of credit that accrued to the Brown or the 'black-white-red' victors?

With utter disregard for the sober triumvirate of Hugenberg, Papen, and Seldte, the people thronged to the 'non-partisan' victory demonstrations of the Nazi Party. And the Party cleverly utilized these

affairs to establish its right to exclusiveness. National Socialism not
only got drunk at its own victory celebrations; it found that the
demonstrations helped it to pull itself up by its own bootstraps.

Men make history, but it is the masses who make revolutions. Only
the interacting impulses described above, only the irrational turbulence in the souls of the people, can explain the total *Gleichschaltung*
that took place in that summer of 1933. It was accomplished by
vigorous thrusts from the Party, but it was also voluntary and spontaneous. People worked themselves up into a wholly unwonted revolutionary excitement, and in their irrational and malleable mood they
helped to swell the power of the revolutionaries.

Once the broad masses had been thrown off balance, the further
course of the Nazi Movement became inevitable. Since no one wanted
to be last, all rushed to be first. This meant that everyone rushed up
and asked to be co-ordinated; all were so anxious to fall into line that
they yielded themselves up utterly to the greedy revolutionaries. Clubs,
publishing houses, business firms, suddenly threw open their doors to
Nazis. Every manager wanted to have his SA man, every half-Aryan
business wanted two SA men. The rage for taking on a few 'old
fighters' as quickly as possible was manifested by the most unpolitical
organizations, even by church congregations.

Then there began the great process of individual *Gleichschaltung*.
Not one of these zealots would confess to another whether his principal motive was idealism or opportunism. But all of them understood
that they could no longer hang back. And in order to stress their enthusiasm, they went on mouthing the same revolutionary slogans for
months. They made sure to remember the names of their district
leaders; they noted the insignia of rank of all their neighborhood
SA leaders, and they tried their best to obtain a membership book with
a low number, or lower than the neighbor's, at any rate.

Membership books were no longer cheap. The Party made sure that
its election debts were paid back twice and threefold. Necessity had
made the Nazis ingenious. The treasurers of the Nazi Movement were
very shrewd at extracting impressive tolls from the late-comers. Noth-

ing was omitted: entrance fee, retroactive dues, sponsorship, special contribution for the Reich treasury, extra dues for the district, voluntary subsidy for the local group, extra gift for the propaganda fund, tithes for the SA, fund for promoting membership in the SS, registration fee for air-raid defense, cash payment for insignia, small price of membership book to cover costs of printing, an obligatory permanent subscription to the *Voelkischer Beobachter*, two extra levies for SA men in need, four tickets of admission for the next demonstration for the member's personal use and another dozen or so which must be disposed of.

Rarely at any time did so much money change hands so freely as in those first jubilant and hopeful months of the Revolution. No one knew what all these sacrifices were for; and after a while the levies certainly got on the nerves of the solid middle-class citizens who loved things to be orderly. Someone in the neighborhood was said to have been 'taken away' recently. When he returned, he loudly assured everyone, without being asked, that he had been treated splendidly. But he was carrying one arm in a sling and his face looked strangely swollen.

In the innermost recesses of his heart everyone wondered whether, if he failed to insure himself by being overgenerous, he could be sure of his nearest and dearest neighbor. Had not everyone, at some time or other, quarreled with the concierge or told off the coal man? Didn't you at one time throw out an impudent messenger boy or angrily refuse another advance to your shop clerk? When, how . . . ? Painfully, the conscience of every *Volksgenosse* labored. For a revolution has an extraordinary memory; it presents accounts long since forgotten, and it exacts retribution not only for historical debts, but for extremely personal ones. Consequently, all the unfortunates whose political reliability had not yet been vouched for by their house porter or block captain suffered from nightmares.

That was why everyone was in such a hurry. Undoubtedly many were motivated by real enthusiasm. But there were cunning opportunists who scurried into the Party, the SA, or the SS. The really shrewd ones grabbed some administrative post in one of the myriad new organizations such as the air-raid defense or the winter relief. All agreed that insignia on your sleeve were good, but a uniform was even better.

Before long people in plain civilian dress were a rare exception in the streets of the cities. They were either stared at as foreigners or considered suspect. Everyone wore brown. A full year was to pass before this horde of brown uniforms vanished — and then it disappeared overnight and quite completely, as the first shots of June 30, 1934, rang out.

The SA must be given the credit for helping along the spontaneous *Gleichschaltung* mania. Wherever an individual had not quite decided about his voluntary desires, the storm troopers bluntly put a stop to all hesitation. Their methods were very crude, and for that reason all the more effective. For example, the novel Hitler salute — raised arm and *Heil Hitler!* — was impressed upon the populace with extraordinary speed. Alongside of every marching SA column — and SA columns were marching everywhere in those days — a few strong-armed storm troopers followed on the sidewalk and slapped the face of every bystander who did not salute the column. The storm troopers' behavior in all other matters was of the same order.

Even staunch individualists decided that it was the better part of valor, under these circumstances, to give in temporarily. In conversations among themselves they spoke contemptuously of the unprincipled cowards around them, and emphasized that they themselves were, of course, merely going through the forms. But what was the difference? In time the most obstinate reactionaries and the reddest Red-Fronters got used to their brown exteriors, and no amount of mental reservations detracted from the external victory of the Movement. All opposition disappeared from the surface. The great political parties dissolved, unions and employers' associations were eliminated, all the lodges and most of the leagues and clubs ceased to exist — in short, the slate was wiped clean all along the line.

We must not imagine that there was a plan operating behind this violent procedure. On the contrary, everything was utterly chaotic. Once again the same inexorable inner dynamics was driving the victorious movement on and on. The impetus could no longer be checked; it was not to be stopped until the whole of our national life was reduced to one undifferentiated level.

Everything was in process of dissolution. Undoubtedly there were a good many bases that were taken by force, but many more were simply surrendered. The advancing ranks of Nazis encountered only fleeing wraiths. The hollowness of the existing system, the weakness of the dozens of parties, the fragility of clubs and associations, are best demonstrated by the fact that there was scarcely any group that seriously offered to defend itself. Who was there to fight? The so-called middle class ran away from the terror; the remnants of the Marxists manifested no greater courage. Wherever the Brown Front moved forward, it ran into no determined resistance. It thrust ahead into empty space.

A gigantic vacuum suddenly opened up before the victorious Movement. How was it to be filled? The Nazis did not know; they could not solve the problem at the moment. For the present they draped a brown cloth over the gap and bragged about the totality they had achieved.

THE VIOLENCE OF REVOLUTION

BY JUNE, 1933, the totality was universal. By this time there no longer existed any kind of organized opposition. The German people were utterly 'co-ordinated.'

Just as partial power, once seized, had quite imperceptibly and of its own accord extended into total power, so there now took place an equally involuntary, equally inevitable step. Germany entered a new — or shall I rather say the first real? — phase of its revolution. We cannot exactly fix the beginning of this development, but we can demonstrate that it was in full swing in June and July, 1933.

A revolution comes about when the existing authorities fail to perform their function. Traditional concepts of justice and order are shaken. People cease to know what they ought to do. Everyone feels that he ought to do something; everyone understands that a great turning-point has been reached; but no one has a name for it. And because no ideas present themselves at the right time, because no tangible order of things is left, the only force for order that remains at the moment is violence. Violence takes over the offices of government; violence rules in all administration; violence penetrates deep into private life; violence supersedes justice; violence establishes new laws; violence becomes the all-powerful sovereign.

In the midst of an historic process of disintegration a great popular leader may succeed in gripping all power in his own hands. But this power is vain unless he creates a new sort of legality. Otherwise the unleashed forces cannot be stopped at all, and sweeping revolution is inevitable.

Adolf Hitler knew this very well. He wanted above all to control the rampant forces. Therefore, he at first thought only in terms of a radical seizure of power. At times he gave that process the name of revolution, but he never really meant it. For revolution frightened him. As soon as he attained power, he implored his followers to put an end to the revolutionary turbulence. It seems strange to us today when we read this constant leitmotif in the speeches he made that first summer of his rule. Passionately the newly appointed chancellor opposed the idea of a permanent revolution. Instead, he rejoiced that — for the first time in world history — his 'revolutionary' achievements were to be stabilized so that they would last forever. Hitler was jousting with invisible demons when he defiantly proclaimed that this time the leaders of the victorious movement would survive their own revolution.

But this determination did not go farther than oratory. More and more he permitted himself to belie his unhappy foreknowledge. He himself enthroned the fundamental principle of all revolutions: violence. And thereby, against his will, he corroborated the theory that a revolution which is not reined in while there is still time cannot be held back at all.

But why was violence necessary? Have we not said that the *Gleichschaltung* was accomplished by a kind of involuntary volunteering?

The simplest explanation, of course, is merely to point out the character of the new rulers. Seldom in recent times has such an assembly of similarly minded politicians existed. The dominant trait of all of them was brutality. Goering, Goebbels, Himmler, Heydrich, Roehm, Streicher — to name only these few — thought and felt only in terms of violence. Those who did not know how to manipulate violence — Frick, for example — did not rise. The experts at violence shot to the top.

How easily naked violence is learned and practiced! We can observe this even more in the sub-leaders than in Hitler. We have seen how, within a few weeks, the Party leaders and sub-leaders found themselves in positions of power beyond their wildest dreams. What were men of such a type, who had been deep in debts or had been eking out a bare petty-bourgeois existence and who had suddenly risen to the position of ministers, under-secretaries, governors, provincial presidents, police chiefs, aldermen, mayors, and so on — what were such men to do with all their power? They had no professional training. They knew nothing about law. They did not trust the professional officialdom who worked under them. What could they do but extemporize? They simply dictated, in the firm conviction that their subjects would obey.

And they made a wonderful discovery. They found that their clumsy method worked splendidly because diligent clerks and indefatigable bureaucrats could not be liquidated. The decrees that they thickly mouthed over their evening drinks appeared, in polished phrases, on their desks for signature by noon next day. Rude orders were transformed into spick-and-span ordinances. Rough curses read like intelligent textual commentaries on the civil code.

Thus, to mention only this example, the cabinet and the Reichstag continued to exist, although they no longer served any function beyond that of yea-saying. In the popular phrase of the time, the Reichstag was a very expensive glee club, since all the lordly deputies had to do was to sing the two national anthems.

It is certainly enticing to trace all the various impulses to violence to their hidden sources in revolutionary psychology; but it is perhaps more important to indicate the other compulsions to which these Nazi leaders were subject. In the final analysis they were overwhelmed not only by their own inadequacy, but by the stuff of revolution itself. They could not escape the dynamism that forced them onward. They remained the slaves of the incalculable will of the masses, the will which had chosen them to serve it.

And that is the other reason why National Socialism was dragged into the whirlpool of its own revolutionary violence. Undoubtedly the Nazi leader was one of the world's supreme movers of men. He ignited passions; he molded men's thoughts and feelings. Nevertheless, he was not master of himself. Besides the leader of men there was another Adolf Hitler: the organizer who thrashed about in the meshes of his own organization.

Within the space of a few years this Hitler had conjured out of the ground one of the biggest organizations in the world. Successful, vigorous, eager to act, it stood behind him and thrust against him with all its weight, with all its tremendous dynamism. It was not opposition from outside, but the contradictory internal forces that pressed for a test of power. These forces could not bear to stand still; they wanted something, anything, to happen. They continually impelled the Movement forward to fresh involuntary actions.

There is an uncanny logic in this dramatic development. Hitler's own revolutionary children could no longer be checked. First, they conquered power. By means of power they achieved totality. Soon they tasted the pleasures of arbitrary rule. And then, swiftly, they plunged into excess — and thereby into the midst of the Revolution.

Foremost among the children of the Revolution were the storm troopers. They were the incarnation of the Revolution.

The SA was founded originally by Hitler to fight terror with terror. It arose during those post-war years when Germany was already, or perhaps it would be more accurate to say still, in a revolutionary ferment. We might call it the last eddies of the Spartacus wave of

1918. The Red pressure gave rise to the Brown counter pressure, and the outward form of the latter took the name of storm troops.

For fifteen months Adolf Hitler let the SA run things. It was only natural that the storm troopers should feel themselves the real victors. But now they wanted to taste the full fruits of their triumph.

For years they had filled themselves with their own bloodthirsty songs of hatred. At all their 'storm' meetings the dream of their revolutionary vengeance, the so-called 'night of the long knives,' had been painted for them in glowing colors. Is it any wonder that these starvelings — morally degenerate from years of unemployment, roused to fever-pitch by countless speeches at innumerable meetings, their 'heroism' proved in a hundred brawls — should now begin to live and to react in their own fashion? Fundamentally, this private army of the SA put into practice after the seizure of power only what Joseph Goebbels had persuaded them would be their merited glory as the Brown nobility of the Third Reich. This extraordinary fraternity took in all those who came to it voluntarily, and knocked down all who resisted.

The ancient and eternally new intoxication that comes from possession of power proved as heady as ever. The SA, in accord with the Party platform, though with very little deliberation, had been appointed an auxiliary police force. Very well, then it would really play the part of a police force. To be sure, Goering might have had his own conception of this decree. He may very well have imagined that by the side of every two heavily armed police patrolmen there would stand an SA man equipped with a white armband. But he had misjudged the ruffians of the SA. Before long they were leaving the policeman behind at headquarters and roaming the streets alone in search of 'enemies of the state.'

The SA conducted large-scale raids. The SA searched houses and offices. The SA made confiscations. The SA conducted hearings of witnesses. The SA imprisoned. In brief, the SA established itself as a permanent auxiliary police force and laughed at the administrative and judicial principles which dated from the days of the 'system,' of the Weimar Republic. The worst feature of all, so far as the helpless government authorities were concerned, was that the SA would not release its prey. Woe to the unfortunate who was caught in the clutches of the storm troops.

At this time there arose the 'bunkers,' those dreadful private jails of the SA. It was the duty of every good SA unit to have at least one of these. 'Taking away' unfortunate persons became a customary right of the SA. The efficiency of a leader was judged by the number of his prisoners, and the reputation of an SA tough depended on the strength of arm with which he conducted a prisoner's 'education.' The Movement could no longer offer the attraction of *Saalschlachten,* those rousing brawls that had so often taken place at Nazi meetings before the seizure of power. Nevertheless, the 'battle' continued; the difference was that beatings were handed out for the purpose of feeling the reality of power.

The first opponent, of course, was Communism; but it was in reality only the first. Once the strong-armed heroes had been appointed auxiliary policemen in defense of their imperiled government, a reign of terror in the streets began which had nothing to do with the struggle against Bolshevism.

The sort of violence that went on in our large cities in those first months during and after the struggle for totality is almost beyond belief. The beast in men was let loose with a vengeance; the basest instincts came to the fore. Blindly the old fighters and the newer and newest fighters struck out against the enemy.

The enemy was first alleged, as we have noted, to be Communism. Then it was — somewhat more generally — Marxism. Later the limits were extended — reaction. And — always — it was the Jew. But names meant nothing at all. All had their turn, of course — the men of the Red Front, the Social Democratic functionaries, others whose political color was not brown, and the Jews. But as the SA developed its taste for sadism, the concept of 'enemy of the state' was extended to unpleasant neighbors, the club treasurer, to the troublesome landlord and the impolite creditor. People who had never harmed anyone were horribly abused. Innocents who had been picked up by chance were beaten half to death.

All these excesses are typical mass orgasms, familiar in all times of revolutionary turbulence. It was the unleashed masses who howled, plundered, tortured, and killed in those days. The best proof of that is the fact that within a few months the enormously expanded SA consisted, at least a third of it, of former adherents of the old parties of the Left. It is well known that in June and July of 1933 there were some SA units which were almost entirely Communist. The popular phrase for them was 'Beefsteak Nazis' — Brown on the outside, Red inside. These noble fellows were by no means any gentler with folk of their own kind. They were even worse.

In that first decisive year more cases of manslaughter were presented before Reich Minister of Justice Guertner than his office had previously dealt with in a whole decade. He was compelled, no matter what he may privately have thought, to pardon all those outrages as committed 'in excess of zeal for the National Socialist Revolution.' It was these officially sanctioned bestialities of the first months that later emboldened the sadists of the concentration camps. The generalized brutalization that extended far beyond the realm of the Gestapo toward the end of the Revolution were the inescapable consequence of that early practice of condoning the Brown violence.

For a long time people tended to imagine that Hitler knew nothing about the outrages of that summer of 1933. Hitler, of course, knew far more than he permitted any of his intimates to guess. He had, as we have noted, a clear perception of what it would mean to give violence its head. But he felt that he had to throw some bones to his followers. He treated his Party comrades with a laxity unusual to him. If they persistently importuned, he let them have their way. He waited to see whether things would not fall into line of themselves. He called this procedure 'letting a situation mature.' He recognized that at the moment he could not fight the waves of the storm and so he simply let himself and his affairs drift. For the present he chose to be neutral. Goering would in any case contrive to put a stop to the wildest abuses.

Hermann Goering was certainly not one to be prim. He had no objections whatsoever to political killings, no more than did Hitler. On the other hand, Goering had no liking for the rabble. He had just changed his SA duds for that series of colorful and fantastic uniforms, each more magnificent than the last, for which he later became famous. In his imagination he was already building Karinhall. He dreamed of his future rôle as that of a Nordic Renaissance tyrant. Such a man despises mass excesses. He did not want the reek of blood from the streets to penetrate into his perfumed wardrobes. To Goering's mind, even in the Third Reich the masses must be kept under the knout.

We have noted that his lust for power was such that he could not endure to have others reigning beside him. If one wanted to make Goering do something, it was beside the point to tell him that such-and-such atrocities had taken place. That did not move him. But if one told him that one of his assistants had wanted to intervene in a case, but that all appeals made in the name of the mighty minister-president of Prussia had been in vain, then Goering flew into a rage and roared: 'Arrest them! Arrest them! Arrest them!'

But unfortunately the storm troopers were highly averse to being arrested. They preferred to do all the arresting themselves. As soon as the police attempted to fetch anyone from the SA bunkers, there. were nasty fights.

Goering had a brilliant idea. Disguised in civilian clothes and accompanied only by two armed police captains, he personally visited the Hedemannstrasse, where one of the most notorious bunkers was located. Fearful stories were told of this private prison, and documents on it were piled high in the minister-president's office.

We must picture the scene: Goering standing on the street corner and personally convincing himself that frightful screams could be heard hundreds of yards away. He did not dare to enter the bunker. But he found a characteristic solution. During the next few days he sent for the entire SA staff of the Hedemannstrasse bunker, and for another squad from the General Papestrasse. Having assembled the boldest killers of the entire Berlin SA, he appointed this picked group of scoundrels to be his 'field police.' He decorated them with prominent police shields and conferred upon them unlimited police powers — particularly within the storm troops themselves. They were instructed to lash out ruthlessly against their fellows.

Goering calculated well. It did not matter in the least to these toughs whom they beat to death or why. For them the principal thing was that they filled their bunkers every night. Before long the field police were dreaded by the entire Movement. After their fashion they actually did restore a degree of 'order.' And the whole concept had the additional unexpected advantage that in time they eliminated each other. Hardly any of the original group survived the mutual killings, and those who did were later — after the first two years, when times grew quieter — locked up for criminal offenses.

At this time Goering issued a so-called 'protective custody' decree. Tens of thousands were confined in prisons, bunkers, or camps without having the slightest idea why they were there. Even the wardens and camp commanders had no idea why the prisoners had been turned in. The decree attempted to regulate the novel system of depriving men of their liberty in order to protect them against their own wicked impulses.

The SA, however, was far from pleased at such interference with their hard-earned revolutionary rights. There was open growling about Goering's 'treachery.' And in those days an SA group leader was virtually a demi-god. He was considerably more important than any government minister; he was the real ruler in the provinces. Ministerial decrees could not make him blink an eye, and he was not going to permit anyone in Berlin, not even the minister who controlled the police force, to butt in on his territory.

By October the conflict had come to such a head that Goering was given a sound lesson by the SA. For the solemn opening session of the council of state Goering was planning a pretentious festival, with flags, garlands, parades, bands, and so on. To crown a day of pageantry, Goering himself was to ride in a gala coach from the Wilhelmstrasse to the State Opera House, escorted in front and behind by gallant and splendid squadrons of mounted police.

But the SA had other ideas. It considered all this pomp not sufficiently socialistic. It therefore complained to the Fuehrer about Goering's showy plans, and Roehm ordered his group leaders in the council of state not to take part in the festival.

This was a fearful blow to Goering, for it struck directly against his enormous vanity. Not to risk public insult he revised his entire program. Then he sent a formal note to Roehm, inviting him and Himmler to be the two chief persons of the day.

Nevertheless, Goering still had to swallow a piece of raw effrontery. A rather jagged police parade took place on the festival day. In conclusion an SA brigade was to march past. But the brigade's band did not play a note; the men sauntered by in slovenly formation, and promenaded with an air of utter indifference past the Prussian minister-president.

Karl Ernst had planned this taunt, but undoubtedly Roehm had approved it. The meaning was clear enough. It was a threat that could not be misunderstood: the commander of the revolutionary troops was issuing a warning to the head of the police force. Roehm was publicly demonstrating what small respect he and his whole SA had for the so-called state authority.

And Goering? For the present there was nothing for him to do but 'take' this insult. But he meditated revenge. He would pay Roehm back, twice and thrice over.

It is time to find out what sort of man is this Ernst Roehm whom even a Goering must treat respectfully.

The general picture of the chief of staff of the storm troops has long been a distorted one. That is not surprising. For Roehm was not one of the political leaders of the Nazi Party. His name really came before the public for the first time when his homosexual inclinations became generally known. And, in fact, the SA under his leadership became a veritable nest of homosexuality. He also quite quickly acquired the reputation of being a modern bandit chieftain. Because he stood behind his SA even in its vilest excesses, he was widely feared as the commander-in-chief of a gang of desperadoes.

When he began, Roehm was no more than an earnest officer who felt that the disastrous outcome of the war made it his duty to enter 'politics.' The politics he engaged in were of the only sort that nationalistic army officers could conceive. He concealed arms; he led around by the nose the commissioners of the Entente Control Commission; he set up a novel system for the clandestine training of troops, and was always Johnny-on-the-spot whenever a *Putsch* was in prospect.

It was this latter trait that led the Munich Reichswehr officer to tie up with Hitler, or, rather, led Hitler to tie up with him. For at that time Captain Roehm was a good deal more of a personage than was the unimportant chairman of an unimportant club in an unimportant suburb of Munich. Although the two were utterly unlike in background and character, they became real friends. Their friendship was full of stormy quarrels, separations and reconciliations, but it survived all crises. It even led to so close an intimacy that Roehm was one of the few persons in Adolf Hitler's life who was permitted to address the Fuehrer with the familiar *'du.'*

There is, however, no ground for deducing from Roehm's homosexuality a relation with the Fuehrer which did not exist. Roehm, as his candid letters prove, discovered his erotic perversion at a time when the mutual friendship was already firmly established. The extremely strong attraction between the two men must be attributed to one of those mysteries of human relationships, in which basically different natures are so often drawn together. It is sufficient to say that the two felt a bond of fate between them, and in the truest sense of historical irony it can be asserted that death alone could part them.

This close link appears all the more remarkable because Hitler and his chief of staff differed on one of the most vital points of politics. They could not agree on the tasks of the SA. Hitler wanted a kind of legal Party bodyguard, a group of men who knew how to swing chairs and throw beer mugs. But Roehm, since 1918, had lived only for the dream of a new people's army. All his zeal was devoted to this goal and the most daring means appeared to him precisely the right ones for his purpose. He was firmly convinced that he could transform his undisciplined SA squadrons into cadres for the army of the future.

Roehm was so hipped upon this idea that he could consider no alternative. He did not listen when Hitler tried to slow down his forward march. Phrases about *Realpolitik* merely annoyed him. Primitive and uncomplicated, possessing the temperament of a soldier-of-fortune, Roehm preferred to lash out at once at opponents and knock them down. It was for this reason that he placed such emphasis upon the practice of terrorism by his SA. Roehm had never paid any attention to the prison records held by so many of his SA men. And during the period of struggle for power the Fuehrer had never inquired about that. Why should he, now that his Party was in power, worry about the fearful number of criminal convictions that the various federal bureaus now reported to him? Nor did it in the least matter to Roehm who of his men had recently been a Communist or anything else. The chief thing for him was to build his storm troops into an enormous striking force. Roehm's idea was simple and logical: the sooner he took advantage of the first upsurge after the seizure of power to hack a path through the jungle of laws and the mazes of foreign policy, the sooner would his revolutionary army become the German army of the future.

Roehm imagined in all seriousness that his SA would swallow up the regular army. In place of the reactionary officers he already envisioned Heines, Karl Ernst, Heydenbeck, and Hayn as commanding generals. He quite openly apportioned the most important army corps among his fellows, and these prospective generals at once distributed the lower commands to their fellow rowdies. It sometimes happened that an SA brigade leader would pay a friendly visit to the commander of a corps to pick up a few hints about his future work. Karl Ernst would talk freely over his beer about the composition of his future general staff.

'The SA remains Germany's fate.' By an historic chance, these were Roehm's last words to the public, spoken only a few days before his violent death. That was his firm conviction, and it was his stubbornness in clinging to this belief that led to his downfall. The faster revolutionaries sail toward their goal, the sooner and the more surely they must be wrecked by it. Their secret strength and their terrible error consist in trying to compress into the space of a few years policies that must take decades to mature. By so doing they set up a tremendous, an incredible pressure. Nothing seems able to resist them; they are able to set the machine going at top speed in no time at all. But suddenly the boiler bursts and the world experiences an explosion of unimaginable magnitude.

Roehm's political career would probably have lasted a good deal longer if the Fuehrer had opened a few relief valves in time. But Hitler could not make up his mind to do this. He undoubtedly saw the threatening peril; but the power manifested by the racing machine had too great an allure for him. His SA was the great engine of the National Revolution; was he to make it sit quiet or was he to let it tear along till it went smash? Hitler simply could not make up his mind to either course. Faced with the conflict between his revolutionary feelings and his political intelligence, he took the easy way out and simply let things drift.

It was solely Hitler's deliberate renunciation of leadership, and not any similarity in sexuality or any legendary *Putsch,* that led to the unhappy fate of his chief of staff.

It was all very well for Roehm to dismiss angrily the considerations of *Realpolitik,* or to make fun of government officials and their laws. Roehm was not a bureaucratic minister; he held no office in the Reich government. His sole function was to whip up his revolutionary soldiers.

But Hitler, on the other hand, had to consider everything from innumerable angles. As yet he did not possess unlimited power over budgets and laws, life and death, war and peace. He was still the chancellor of a coalition government. The cabinet still came to decisions; there were still diplomatic protests and even sometimes open resistance to counter. Above all, the aged field marshal loomed behind him. Hindenburg had raised a threatening finger over the excesses in the struggle with the churches. There was always the possibility that someone might whisper other nasty stories into Hindenburg's ear. Hitler did not want to run this danger. Hindenburg was an authority of weight. The regular army stood unitedly behind him. Why should the Fuehrer unnecessarily incur the old president's hostility?

Hitler realized fully that absolute power in the government would be his if he could avoid the manifold temptations to act prematurely. At the latest the power would fall into his lap when Hindenburg died, and then there would still be time to settle with all his hated enemies. For then he would hold the one weapon that still gave him qualms: the soldiers' oath of loyalty to the president. Roehm wanted to act at once; Hitler had to wait. From the contradiction arose the internal frictions of the first year.

So far the new chancellor had had no 'successes.' For the present he was governing solely by dint of promises and false starts. Unemployment continued to exist on a broad scale, for the economic depression would not disappear simply on command. In the money market new sources of funds were appearing very slowly and hesitantly. Trust and distrust were hanging in the balance. Everything was still in the theoretic stage. Not even the personnel changes in political offices could be put through overnight.

The situation in the realm of foreign policy looked worst of all. The alarm of various foreign countries refused to be soothed. Although the 'peace speech' of May, 1933, had won Hitler a little breathing spell, the first gallant essay to carry out one of the planks on foreign policy in the program resulted in a decisive defeat. In Austria, after noisy but premature fanfares, the trumpets and drums had to be hastily silenced. What would happen if the Opposition struck back? What would happen if the Western Powers looked a little closer into the planned rearmament, or if a great Jewish boycott against anti-Semitic Germany were organized?

Such questions could not trouble a simple cut-throat such as Roehm was. But they were of the utmost concern to a chancellor who wanted to make world history. Moreover, Hitler was equally troubled by the numerous problems that arose out of 'totality.' Should he be content with the simple *Gleichschaltung* of the whole population?

Or should he allow the states, communes, and social organizations a degree of limited constitutional freedom? In general, how was he to decide between an 'elastic' constitution and an undisguised dictatorship? And what was he to do with the so-called Nazi *Weltanschauung*? During the period of the struggle for power Hitler had made use of Rosenberg's pompous philosophical system only to a limited extent. He had repeatedly disavowed Rosenberg's anti-Christian digressions. Was he now to permit the opening of a grand struggle against the Church?

If Hitler had not been concerned about such questions, there were at that time a good many other factors to bring them unpleasantly to mind. There was, above all, the bourgeoisie. We know very well that the bourgeoisie was no awe-inspiring force. Nevertheless, it was a factor that could not be omitted from consideration. Large sections of the working class were in any case skeptical. The chancellor certainly did not wish to alienate by careless phrases or clumsy acts those segments of the population who would traditionally support the state. There was simply no sense, at this point, in his maneuvering them into open opposition.

Caution was particularly necessary in regard to economic matters. No matter how Hitler despised individual economists, he could not, for all his daring plans, do without them. Private enterprise was heartily damned on all sides, but the success of the new government depended on getting private enterprise in motion again. Once the wheels were turning and the factory chimneys smoking, the noble ideal of industrial socialism might be introduced. But until then measures for creating more employment were more important than socialistic dogmas of salvation. Though it was a bitter draft to swallow, Nazism had nevertheless to seek the support of the very groups which it later intended ruthlessly to subdue.

Hitler took occasion now and then to placate the sensitive — but easily reassured — bourgeoisie by a few deprecating phrases about 'unfortunate abuses' committed 'in excess of zeal for the National Socialist Revolution.' In one case after another he promised an immediate liquidation of radicalism in the Nazi ranks. And the Fuehrer found that the legend that the notorious 'wild men,' the Roehms, Schirachs, Leys, and Streichers, were being allowed enough rope to hang themselves, was a very useful tale. These men were, the interpretation ran, being consciously permitted to rampage while the 'statesmen,' the 'conservative' Goering and the 'government official' Frick, together with their bourgeois ministerial assistants, were getting a firm grip on the state machinery.

Such, in general, was the situation in the summer of 1933. We can see that in many respects it had already reached high tension. Nevertheless, Hitler accomplished a great deal: he was making time pass. He concealed his intentions so that everyone pondered where he was headed. With whom would he move and against whom? With the Party against the SA and the SS? Or *vice versa*? With Goering and Frick against the 'wild men'? Or with such resolute men of action as Roehm, Streicher, Ley, and the fanatical Goebbels against the government bureaucrats? With the 'moderates' — that is, with Schwerin, Neurath, Schacht, Guertner, and Papen — against the Party-liners? Or would he back Feder and Rosenberg against the despicable reactionaries? With the 'old fighters' against the generals? Or with the Reichswehr against all his pretorian guards? With whom, against whom? — these were the questions that occupied all these Brown tribunes of the people during the latter half of 1933.

And Hitler did not answer their questions. Only once, at a secret conference in the war ministry, attended by all the generals and SA group leaders, Hitler for the first time hinted darkly of his resolve to rule, if necessary, against the Party or the SA.

THE SCENT OF BLOOD

FROM THE SPRING OF 1934 on, events mounted inexorably toward an explosion.

On April 1, 1934, Goering appointed Heinrich Himmler, Reich leader of the SS, as chief of the Prussian *Geheime Staatspolizei* (Gestapo). Superficially this appointment meant no more than that Diels, a man considered politically untrustworthy, was replaced by a member of the Movement. Nevertheless, the event constituted a decisive turn in the affairs of the Revolution. For on that day an alliance was sealed which meant the end of Ernst Roehm.

Up to this time Goering had anxiously guarded the secret of his power, the control of the police force in Prussia. With sure instinct for the nature of power he had secured that control on January 30, 1933, and he had not let it out of his hands for one moment since. At the beginning of the new year he had amiably relinquished the other, the purely administrative branches of his ministry of the interior, to devote himself to his hunting and theatrical interests. But he guarded his executive power over the police all the more closely. The Gestapo was his pampered child, for he knew only too well that it held the key to his power. The Fuehrer enjoyed reading his spicy and highly dramatized secret reports.

By this time the aura of terror surrounding the word 'Gestapo' had grown to immense proportions. Moreover, Goering had already discovered how much blackmail and outright confiscation could be covered by the use of so mysterious and sinister an instrument. Consequently, when Frick attempted to snatch up the whole of the Prussian ministry of the interior, he found the most desirable portion of the booty slipping through his fingers. Goering quickly incorporated the Gestapo and the regular police into his minister-presidency. Organizationally this was an absurdity, but in an era of power politics it was the best kind of life insurance.

It was, therefore, incomprehensible that Goering should suddenly give up his favorite domain, and give it up, moreover, to an open rival. For Himmler, who was already police chief in Bavaria, thereby became the most powerful police officer in the Third Reich. It certainly did not affect the situation that Goering was formally retaining the over-all direction of the Gestapo. Himmler unquestionably now held the real power.

Since Goering was not generally inclined to yield power to anyone, the natural question is: What did he get out of it?

What possible ties were there between Goering and Himmler?
Their natures differed fundamentally. The ostentatious, megalomaniac
air-force general and the unprepossessing, colorless SS leader had
nothing at all in common. There could not even be a question of the
attraction of opposites, in fact, there seemed to be every likelihood
that drab Heinrich and magnificent Hermann would be deadly
enemies. But where there is no love, hate can be the stronger bond.
And when two weak men fear a strong man, they can kill him the
more easily if they work together.

We have already seen that Goering had every reason to distrust
and dislike his rival, Roehm. The newly hatched Gestapo chief was
also at odds with the chief of staff.

Himmler was the Reich leader of the SS. His élite guards were the
special police of the Movement. Nevertheless, they did not constitute
an independent section of the Party. They remained a part of the SA,
and Roehm was their commander-in-chief; consequently, Himmler
had to obey Roehm's every command. This, in itself, was bitter for
the ambitious Himmler. His position as chief of the 'Black Corps'
was made all the more difficult because Roehm backed his SA unconditionally against all comers. Roehm, the straightforward blackguard,
did not even attempt to understand the complicated inspirations of
his SS subordinate. He made fun of Himmler's religious cultism and
his exaggerated racism. Deliberately, Roehm kept down the numbers
of the SS. Any SA *Obergruppenfuehrer* who chose to let fly at the
Black columns was covered by the chief of staff, no matter how
vehemently and frequently the Reich leader of the SS protested.

The SA looked upon both Himmler and Goering as traitors: the
minister as much because of his luxurious mode of life as because of his
constant interference with the SA's revolutionary practices, and the
Black SS man because his wiliness and falseness was written all over his
face, and because he so priggishly disassociated himself from the excesses
of the Brown storm troopers. If it came to a test of force, it might
very well happen that Himmler would fall overnight, and Goering
would be showily pensioned off with a few impressive titles and flashy
uniforms.

The balance of power was a precarious one. It did not at all follow that Goering and Himmler by joining forces could outflank their enemy and deal defeat to both Roehm and his entire SA. There was always Hitler to think about. His fits of rage were feared by all; he was in every respect incalculable and fickle.

It was, therefore, necessary for the pair to steer Hitler into a position where he would be left with no choice. And then they must reckon with his mental state at the time they would be set to strike. Only by exercising extreme psychological precautions could they possibly hope for success. They did not dare a direct revolt against the Fuehrer's authority. It was sometimes possible to conceal a fact or two from Hitler. Occasionally he could be confronted with a *fait accompli.* If necessary an order of his could be 'extended.' But never could anyone openly oppose his will. That he would not stand for. What good, then, would it do Goering and Himmler to strike against their rival unless they had first made sure of Hitler? Consequently, the conspirators' diabolic calculation ran as follows: they themselves would gladly deal the fatal blow, and they would make sure it struck home; but first Hitler must solemnly take the responsibility for the murderous command.

At the same time Roehm and his comrades were not idle. They also sensed the gathering thunderclouds, although they did not, apparently, look for treachery in their own ranks. Rather, they suspected that the wicked industrialists, the priests, or the reactionaries might conspire with the generals against them. At the same time they were pressing for a quick decision. They wanted to conquer the Reichswehr, to take it over while their revolutionary tempo still afforded them irresistible momentum. As they had done so often in the past years, they thought they would be able to carry Hitler along with them in spite of his hesitancy.

But the generals of the Reichswehr feared precisely this. And therefore they, too, were in a hurry. They were determined to make good use of the time Hindenburg still had to live in order, with the help of the old president, to prevail upon the wavering chancellor to cut short the aspirations of Roehm's SA. Generals Blomberg and Reichenau were the chief actors behind the scenes in this little plot.

At the same time other fires were being stirred up by those well-mannered nationalistic circles which were gradually beginning to be terrified by their own revolutionary courage. They were coming to the conclusion that it was at last time to restore order. Their risqué election slogan, 'with Hitler against the National Socialist Party,' was being whispered around everywhere; and the less that this optimistic sentiment was borne out by Hitler's words and acts, the harder these sensitive and temperamental bourgeois clung to Hindenburg. These little braveries on the part of the Nationalists in turn worried the Nazi Party functionaries.

Thus, the problem had many aspects beyond the machinations of Goering and Himmler. From all sides pressures crowded in upon Hitler. And Hitler, caught in a painful dilemma between his emotional reactions and his reason, was being hustled toward a blunt decision. But how was he to decide? With whom, for whom, and against whom must he act?

Meanwhile, the SA itself was giving trouble. The SA men no longer knew what to do with themselves. Hitler had permitted Roehm to increase the numbers of his private army by millions within a few months. Naturally, in such a vast and disorganized mass of men an orderly system of duties could not be maintained. A selected few, those with the loudest voices or the hardest fists, were able to run the show. And it was these men who kept the intimidated populace in a permanent state of terror by their incredible crimes, and who thereby thoroughly discredited their innocuous comrades who formed the vast majority of the SA.

The SA of the period of struggle for power was probably the only one among the Nazi groups in which the phrases about socialism had struck roots. The Party itself, even during the times when it was growing most rapidly, had never been anything but a movement of the decaying middle class. But among the storm troopers socialistic aspirations were of considerable importance. The SA succeeded in doing what the organized Party had done to a very limited extent only — in penetrating into the great mass of the disinherited proletariat. The ruthlessness and aggressiveness of the SA attracted those young and vital segments of the population who in all the turmoil and confusion of a century had not yet found their hoped-for place in society. They were filled with passion, with bold fancies, with covetousness, but also with pious idealism, devotion, and a readiness to make sacrifices. This dawning Reich which was to last a thousand years would be — were they not daily assured of this? — a socialistic kingdom. Very well, then. Even if the new Party plutocracy forgot this, even if a Goering should prove himself a traitor to this ideal, the SA would hold high the tattered banner of socialism. But the new reality that confronted them was anything but socialistic. The laboring class was not to learn the full extent of this sad fact until years later, when they had long since obtained work and wages, but found that their standard of living was dropping precipitately. Instead of too little they later had far too much work, and in addition to being overstrained physically, they were degraded to a commodity and moved from one place to another without being asked.

But in the summer of 1934 the dream of socialism still meant something. And the Nazi Movement now suffered from the deliberate vagueness that the Party had practiced in all its agitation. For the favorite trick of the Nazis had been to permit everyone to conceive of his socialism in different terms. To one the word meant 'commonweal'; to the second, 'thousand-mark limit on incomes'; to the third, 'smashing interest-slavery'; to others, 'industrial democracy'; to still others, 'liquidation of the department stores'; to more, 'expropriation of the expropriators'; and to most people, 'work and bread.' How fine it would have been if, at such a critical moment, the SA had served as a filter to clarify this chaos of ideas! But for clarification more was needed than a vague, indefinite impulse, an 'anti-capitalistic nostalgia.' Something visible and tangible was needed, and the Nazis were totally unable to make any kind of part-payment on their new order.

Is it any wonder, then, that the restless spirits in the SA pushed in the opposite direction, in the direction of more and more disorder? The excesses of that first year of the Revolution must, to a large extent, be attributed to negative *Ab*-reaction of socialization complexes. Frequently enough these excesses were wholly primitive upsurges that followed inevitably from the social and intellectual predicament of the SA of that time. But the fault lay with the top leadership, who had dangled the socialistic bait, and in frustrating the misguided masses of the SA had turned them into anarchistic rebels.

The depravity and inadequacy of the SA leadership, together with the inward planlessness of this socialistic army of millions, gave rise to conditions of utter chaos in the summer of 1934. The unleashed impulses of an uncontrolled mass movement broke through the last restraints of order and decency.

Although it was incumbent upon Hitler, as chancellor of the Reich, to minimize the dreadful things that had, after all, occurred under his leadership and for which he was therefore responsible, he nevertheless sketched a very vivid picture in his well-known speech of July 13, 1934. He spoke openly of the 'gravest abuses' on the part of 'groups of terrorists especially sworn in under the name of staff guards.'

These conditions had not suddenly burst upon Hitler's consciousness. He had obviously long been familiar with them. On the morning of June 30, 1934, he described them in the form of an order to the newly appointed chief of staff, Lutze. The order read:

> . . . I require every SA leader, as well as every political leader, to be aware that his behavior and his bearing must set an example. I require SA leaders as well as political leaders who damage their prestige by their conduct in public to be expelled at once from the Party and the SA. In particular I insist that the SA leader be a model of simplicity and not of ostentation. I do not desire SA leaders to give or to attend expensive banquets. . . .
>
> Millions of our *Volksgenossen* still lack the barest necessities of life. They are not envious of those to whom fortune has been kinder. But it is unworthy of a National Socialist to increase the distance between want and good fortune, which is already vast enough. . . .
>
> I particularly forbid funds of the Party or the public to be used

for festival dinners and similar purposes. It is irresponsible to hold carousals with money that has, in part, been accumulated from the pennies of our poorest citizens. The luxurious staff headquarters in Berlin in which, as has recently been determined, as much as thirty thousand marks were spent on banquets every month, must be dissolved at once. . . .

I forbid all SA leaders to give any so-called diplomatic dinners. . . . I do not wish SA leaders to make official trips in expensive limousines or touring cars, or to use official funds for procuring such vehicles. . . . SA leaders or political chiefs who get drunk in public are unworthy to be leaders of their people. The very fact that carping criticism has been prohibited places an obligation on all to exhibit exemplary personal behavior. Mistakes can always be forgiven, but not bad conduct. SA leaders, therefore, who behave unworthily before the public, who engage in brawls or instigate excesses, are to be removed at once without any consideration.

. . . I expect all SA leaders to assist in keeping the SA a clean and pure organization.

I particularly desire it to be possible for every mother to give her son to the SA, the Party, or the Hitler Youth without fear that he may be ethically or morally corrupted in those organizations.

I therefore desire all SA leaders to keep the closest watch and see to it that all violations of Paragraph 175 are punished by immediate expulsion. I want the SA leaders to be men and not ridiculous puppies.

Had any leader ever passed a more incisive judgment upon the subordinates that he himself appointed? Had any German chancellor ever revealed more dreadful violations of the public order and security which were entrusted to his hands?

But Hitler not only accused. He went to the bottom of these excesses and trenchantly analyzed the sociological and psychological make-up of the trouble-makers of that first year of Revolution.

This group of destructive elements is formed of those revolutionaries whose former relation to the state was shattered by the events of 1918; they became uprooted and thereby lost altogether all sympathy with any ordered human society. They became revolutionaries

who favored revolution for its own sake and desired to see revolution established as a permanent condition. . . . Among the numerous
documents which it has been my duty to read during the past week
I have discovered a diary containing the notes of a man who, in
1918, was thrown into the path of resistance to the laws and who
now lives in a world in which law in itself seems to be a provoca-
tion to resistance. It is an alarming document — an unbroken tale
of conspiracy and continual plotting. It gives one an insight into
the mentality of men who, without realizing it, have found in
nihilism their ultimate confession of faith. Incapable of any true
co-operation, with a desire to attack all order, filled with hatred
against any authority, their unrest and disquietude can find satisfaction only in some conspiratorial activity of the mind, in perpetually
plotting the disintegration of whatever the set-up of the moment
happens to be. . . . This group of pathological enemies of the state
is dangerous; it represents a reservoir of those ready to co-operate
in every attempt at revolt, at least just for so long as a new order
does not begin to crystallize out of the state of chaotic confusion.

It would be a misconception to think that the SA alone was tearing
along at top speed. Undoubtedly it gave the impetus to the rest; it
was the boiler in which was stored high-compression steam formed of
unrestrained passions, unleashed desires, and disappointed yearnings.
But there were other motivating forces which propelled the Revolution
forward all along the line. In the spring of 1934 all the radical
elements in the Nazi Movement gathered their forces to strike afresh.
Anti-Semitism, which had somewhat died down, was given a violent
new impulse. The struggle against 'disguised Marxists' or 'Weimar adherents' was also intensified. The anti-Church program burst out in
full force. The Hitler Youth launched a campaign against their resisting parents. In particular, what was called 'reaction' was fiercely
assaulted.

It was at this time that the Nuremberg satrap, Streicher, reached the
apex of his career. The notorious ritual-murder issue of his *Stuermer*
was published, significantly enough, during those months. For weeks
this disgraceful calumny was circulated in editions of millions, and it
was not until it had penetrated into every class in the public schools

that the chancellor decided to ban it. Even then, he capped the false-hoods by asserting that the sheet was banned because it contained 'mockery of Christian symbols.'

Similar incendiary rags appeared overnight. And anti-Christian polemics flooded the country. All of these pamphlets followed the same method: that of sensationalism. Some revealed vicious Jewish machinations or produced obscene commentaries on Old Testament stories; some dealt with the Freemasons or invented stories of current reactionary conspiracies. But what force they all had depended on their style, which was a mixture of frantic incendiary agitation and hothouse pornography. All of these wild brochures with their flashy format disappeared 'in time,' not because the police clamped down on the agitators, but simply because no one was interested any longer in reading the trash. But at that time they were considered a new discovery, and anyone who objected to that sort of agitational literature was considered prudish, superannuated, and, at the very least, a bourgeois reactionary.

This latter charge was the most serious, for it was at this time that the Nazis started their first great campaign against those very bourgeois circles which had helped them take power. A flood of press attacks and 'educational' lectures began, all of which dealt with the same subject: the struggle against reaction. Once more the enemy was on the Right — and the real conservatives were rather glad to hear this, for to them the Brown collectivism was farther left than the Left.

It is a matter of history that revolutions exert their greatest fanaticism against their last enemy. Now the last obstacle that National Socialism had to overcome before the attainment of power came, not from Communism or from what was called the 'system,' but from that bourgeois group who had backed Papen and the Nationalist electoral bloc. The bourgeoisie was therefore the 'last' enemy.

The bourgeois camp, meanwhile, had recovered a little from the shock they had received from the Revolution. After almost a full year of irresolution these circles suddenly took heart. They began emphasizing the part the black-white-red groups had played in the 'National

Revolution.' They called to mind Hitler's solemn promises that he would protect Christianity and preserve old traditions. More and more they opposed the continually increasing moral terrorism. They began openly disapproving excesses and encroachments on the rights of peaceful citizens.

It is necessary for us to recall that at that time there still remained certain bases for a Nationalist-Bourgeois Opposition. For example, the *Stahlhelm* had not been destroyed. Seldte, the leader of the *Stahlhelm,* had long since written off his league, but his betrayed followers did not know this as yet. Still putting trust in their spineless leader, they voiced their criticism of the régime openly. The consequences followed swiftly. Hair-raising examples of brutality were daily reported from all parts of the country. The Stahlhelmers tried to defend themselves, and bloody battles resulted between SA and *Stahlhelm* men. The SA always had the advantage because they could call in the police, which were commanded by their own SA leaders, to protect them against these new 'enemies of the state.' Nevertheless, a sort of organized bourgeois *fronde* did operate for a while and make things difficult for the revolutionaries.

At one time, by a kind of poetic justice, the *Stahlhelm* leader, Seldte himself, was nearly killed. Under the leadership of the police chief, the SA in Magdeburg went on the warpath. Minister Seldte was given a few punches which made him speedily take to his car and head for distant parts while the blood-stained members of his entourage were abandoned to take the rest of the punishment. I happen to remember this incident, which took place in the middle of June, 1934, because I tried to use my position in the ministry of the interior to intervene. Naturally, I got nowhere. And why should I have tried? When I mentioned the matter to Seldte personally he appeared to be already completely consoled. Proudly he informed me that the Fuehrer had just sent him a telegram congratulating him on his birthday. That seemed far more important to him than a few blows.

But the rest of the Stahlhelmers were not so cowardly as their leader, and that was true also of the other Nationalist groups. It is not going too far to assert that in that summer of 1934 the bourgeosie was solidly

united in opposition to the excesses of the Revolution and that they
were awaiting only the signal to strike out. (I include in this category
the greater part of the working class and use the word 'bourgeoisie'
only in contrast to the rootless, proletarianized masses formed out of
all groups of the population.) Those circles who in this particular
phase of the Revolution's history may be called 'conservative' were
moving closer to one another. They had no intention of starting a
Putsch, nor did they look forward to the prospect of finding someone
strong enough to replace Hitler and his government. But they were
insisting that the state's authority be reasserted. They wanted the unchecked reign of terror to be stopped.

Pressure creates counter-pressure; in that summer of the Revolution
the pressure was rising so swiftly that the boiler must, inevitably, soon
burst.

Joseph Goebbels would not have been the evil spirit of the National
Socialist Revolution if he had failed, at this critical moment, to con-
coct some new deviltry. Just then, when the task of the moment was
to calm and to divert the masses, Goebbels gave them several vigorous
shoves. He stirred up the coals, he incited, cast suspicion, mocked,
libeled, hurled invective. He set going a two-months-long campaign
against the 'alarmists and criticasters, the rumor-mongers and idlers,
the saboteurs and agitators.'

It is necessary to repeat this fine list of words one by one, for they
provide a good index of the popular temper. Alarmists, criticasters,
rumor-mongers, idlers, saboteurs, agitators — that is rather a much of
a muchness, even taking into account Goebbels's rhetorical habits. Of
course, every speaker at public meetings and every shock-troop agitator
insisted that scarcely one per cent of the population belonged to this
repulsive clique of enemies of the state. But there was little difference
between them and that one or two per cent who regularly voted
against the government at elections. For their benefit a whole noisy
election campaign took place; they were thundered at as if they were
at least eighty out of every hundred; and in point of fact more than
half the population felt that these speeches, these streams of invective,

applied to them. Then, when the votes were counted, each would look in amazement at his neighbor and wonder which of the two of them had had the originality of mind to be a despicable one-per-center.

We should have to reread the *Voelkischer Beobachter* or the provincial newspapers of the Party to recall what a torrent of words poured over the people during those weeks. No smallest market-place in the smallest village was spared. At every meeting accusations, incitements, and invectives rained down on the meek audience. All these allusions, of course, were to the absentees, which was why those present applauded so frenziedly. Nevertheless, when the peaceful citizens read the report of the meeting in the newspaper on the following morning, a shiver ran down their spines, for they realized then that this hail of vituperation was, at bottom, directed at them. Was it not they who were the Christians and monarchists, the reactionaries, Freemasons, Jew-lovers, and disguised Marxists? Everyone felt himself accused. But not everyone was intimidated. In fact, this vast and lengthy campaign of conversion achieved in the end the very opposite of what it had intended.

But worse was yet to come. If Joseph Goebbels was orating, Franz von Papen could not keep quiet. This elegant gentleman decided that those sultry weeks before the thunderstorm provided the best possible opportunity to storm the barricades of destiny.

On June 17, 1934, in Marburg-on-the-Lahn, von Papen ascended the podium to deliver one of his famous intellectual speeches. He spoke before a group of university students and was rewarded by thunderous applause when he said openly what all decent Germans were feeling, all who were not in the grip of mass hysteria.

> It is time to come together in brotherly love and respect for our fellow countrymen [*Volksgenossen*], to silence the doctrinaire fanatics and put an end to the meddling with the serious work of serious men. . . .
>
> The domination of a single Party in place of the system of many parties, which has justly vanished, seems to me from the historical point of view a transitory phase which is justified only so long as

it is necessary to safeguard the Revolution and organize the selection of governmental personnel. . . . But no nation can afford an eternal revolt from below if that nation wishes to continue to exist as an historical entity. At some time the Movement must come to an end; at some time a firm social structure must arise and must be maintained by an incorruptible judiciary and an uncontested state authority. Permanent dynamism cannot shape anything lasting. Germany must not be a flashing meteor of which none can say where it will come to a stop.

Most of what Papen said in his speech was true, but to those in the know it sounded like the rattling of a prayer-wheel. For the man was merely repeating mindlessly the dictation of someone else. Edgar Jung had composed the speech for him and had read it aloud to his friends about a week before. Presumably the police knew the whole oration more thoroughly than did the impassioned orator who so aroused the enthusiasm of the Marburg students. And since Goebbels immediately clamped down on any publicity, the only ones who were affected by the speech were those very students. The German people were not permitted to hear a word of what their vice-chancellor had said.

Edgar Jung was arrested by the Gestapo. And the Marburg speech, far from accomplishing its purpose, merely accelerated the crisis. Goebbels swiftly struck back, in a speech four days later, at the 'little circle of critics who work in the dark, trying to tamper with the necessary work of construction. . . . These people will not stop the progress of the century. We will trample them down as we march forward.'

In revolutionary times a single, unimpressive word can set loose a political avalanche. That was what the word *Gleichschaltung* had done in the beginning. That was what happened now with the slogan of a second revolution, which Goebbels hurled into Papen's face. Goebbels shouted and everyone repeated the cry. The Party press publicized the phrase in a hundred variations; the radio proclaimed it, the public speakers roared it. And the revolutionary SA was stirred to its depths. It was the ideal audience for such a battle-cry, with its stimulus and its promise.

Afterward no one was able to say when it was that Roehm had picked up this cue from the Reich propaganda chief. But whenever it was, during those weeks of inner turmoil Roehm, the confused revolutionary, seized at the promise that the 'reactionaries' would be trampled down. The chief of staff became more bloodthirsty than ever before. Most of his close friends in the Party felt ill at ease when he began ranting about the heads that had to fall or ominously remarking that it had taken several years of the French Revolution before the guillotine really got started.

What in the world was going on? What fresh demon of revolution had taken possession of them all?

What in fact had taken place was a profound psychological disorganization in which the only idea that occurred to them all was more revolution. They had gone through one revolution. In their appalling simple-mindedness they held on to this one panacea, hoping to quell all opposition by means of it and at last to realize their thousand-and-one unfulfilled individual desires.

A tremendous sense of muddle and insecurity prevailed. Throughout Germany the phrase about the second revolution lurked like a mysterious flame, now flaring high, now smoking thickly. And wherever it was spoken, all those who had not yet been displaced from their accustomed paths felt a paralyzing uncertainty. The revolutionaries themselves became uneasy. There was something in the sultry air, and a flood of probable and wildly fantastic rumors spilled out over the intimidated populace. Insane tales were fondly believed. Everyone whispered and peddled fresh rumors.

Apparently everyone saw ghosts as well. Among those to whom the bogy man in person appeared were Goering, Himmler, Roehm, and Karl Ernst. All of a sudden these ill-sorted comrades in fear became extremely concerned with the question of whether assassins had been hired to murder them and who these killers might be. Significantly enough, they did not search for suspicious Jews, Marxists, or reactionaries. Old hands at intrigue that they were, they looked for their deadly enemies in their own ranks.

It was this atmosphere that conferred such importance upon two ridiculous incidents which in peaceful times would not have caused the slightest stir. Yet now we cannot think of them except as essential parts of the drama of June 30. As the plot thickened, some poor devil in Berlin threw a hand-grenade fuse from the rafters of a building on Unter den Linden. The fuse exploded harmlessly; there was a bit of a stir, which quickly faded out in the noise of the streets. The foolish part-time worker who had been cleaning up the garret of the building was not trying to kill anyone. He was, to be sure, a Communist, and now, being in bad humor about something, he tossed into the street this fuse that he had been wanting to get rid of for years. His act was simply intended as a demonstration. And within a few days the police solved the mystery.

Nevertheless, the two or three days that it took them to clarify the case were sufficient to start a whole series of rumors about assassinations. First it was said that the frightful bomb-plot had been laid against several dozen of the Party leaders. For, of course, during the hour before and after the incident a large number of flashy Mercedes limousines had raced down the avenue, and none of the big-shots wanted to forfeit the precious notoriety of claiming that he had just escaped being killed by an infernal machine. Finally, however, the *Obergruppenfuehrer* of the Berlin SA won the race among the many claimants to this distinction. He had in fact been seen at the intersection not five minutes before the explosion, and Karl Ernst, clever child of the Berlin streets, was not one to miss blowing his trumpet. Ernst was smart enough to give the right twist to the story. Himmler, he asserted, had tried to assassinate him. Yes, that was the way it had been: the Reich leader of the SS had personally made an attempt on the life of the Berlin SA hero.

The whole fraud was quickly exposed, as we have said. But during that brief period there was so much whispering, so much winking and nodding of heads, that traces of suspicion remained. And by that time the methods of the police had become so refined that it was easy for the augurs to read confirmations of their own suspicions into the official police reports.

It did not seem at all improbable that Himmler should be trying to kill Karl Ernst. On the other hand, Himmler's informers who had been sent into the Berlin group headquarters had frequent occasion to report that Karl Ernst had sworn up and down that he would 'get that black Jesuit.' Was it not a case of each accusing the other of his own ugly intention? In any case Himmler had his own chance to be convinced that the minions of the SA were lying in wait for him.

To look for proof is to find it. The grand occasion was that morning in Karinhall when Goering, amid incredible pomp, interred the mortal remains of his first wife.

Everyone who counted was there — ministers of the Reich, diplomats, Party leaders, and the generals as well. Even Hitler came. The ceremony was about to begin; *Gauleiter* Kube was struggling for the last time to memorize his greeting to 'Germany's noblest lady' who had died two years before — as is well known she was Swedish by nationality — when Heinrich Himmler put in an appearance. He was white, trembling, excited. Hastily, he drew Goering aside; Goering spoke to Hitler; and before the astonished eyes of all these guests a stormy council of war took place. Himmler demanded that forty Communists be shot at once. On the way to Schorfheide he had been shot at; the bullet had passed right through the windshield of his car. 'Providence' alone had saved his life, he said.

A few hours later, amid roars of laughter, Daluege told me about this incident. Daluege was soon to become Himmler's highest and most obedient chief of police. But at this time he could still afford to make fun of Himmler, with whom he was on terms of closest intimacy and whom he could not endure. With the pious mien of a conscientious official, Daluege offered to get to the bottom of this attempted assassination.

I took the opportunity to obtain the original report of Daluege's investigation. It serves as a valuable supplement to the events of June 30. For on that day two SA brigade leaders died, allegedly for the attempt on Himmler's life. Himmler had them shot in spite of Daluege's findings, which he had had ample opportunity to study. The report had definitely established that the hole in the windshield could not have been caused by a bullet, but must have been made by a stone thrown up by the wheels of another car that had passed Himmler's at a speed of more than sixty-five miles per hour!

The same Himmler who first wanted to slaughter forty Communists at random later picked out, equally at random, two SA leaders who probably had committed every other imaginable outrage except that of shooting at Himmler. Once unnerved, Himmler's first impulse was to take revenge as quickly as possible. He wanted the world to know how dearly an attack on him would have to be paid for. But at the same time this unpleasant affair fitted beautifully into his preparations for the thirtieth of June. It was with cold calculation that he, therefore, blamed the attempted assassination on the SA. It was a splendid opportunity to demonstrate to Hitler and Goering how far Karl Ernst, Heines, and Roehm would dare to go.

Meanwhile, Hitler wavered. He wavered whenever he thought of Hindenburg. He suspected that the old man was on the watch, but he knew that if he acted prudently there would be no need to fear the president much longer. Still cloudy was the question of whether his own succession to the presidency would go through without a hitch. That depended on the army. But what would happen if the army should again choose a field marshal, say old Mackensen, for the head of the state?

Hitler wavered whenever he considered the army. Could he bend it to his will, as Roehm kept urging? Or should he throw Roehm to the dogs as a sacrifice to the army?

He wavered when he thought about the men behind the army. Could he rely on the black-white-red Nationalists, or was that reactionary clique agitating against him? Should he let the remnants of the bourgeoisie alone, or must he liquidate those last centers of resistance?

He wavered when he thought of Goering, of Himmler, of Goebbels, Ley, Hess, and all the myriad other little Hitlers who surrounded him.

If Adolf Hitler at this point, scarcely one and a half years after his seizure of power, had possessed a few allies within the country, the threatening catastrophe might have been averted. For then he could have employed the black-white-red groups, the Stahlhelmers, the bourgeois, or the churches as supporting troops in a campaign against radicalism. He might have re-established some kind of political equilibrium by playing off the adherents of state authority against the Party fanatics. But since in his passion to achieve totalitarian power he had thrust away all the others, he was backed only by his revolutionaries.

And the revolutionaries were pushing forward impatiently. The bankrupts were confessing old sins and making new demands. The idealists were waving yellowed programs and devising new plans. The zealots were recalling old promises and proclaiming new glories. The boors were talking about the virtues of austerity and demanding uniforms with gold braid. The candidates for pensions babbled enthusiastically about the thousand years of plenty to come and grabbed what they could in ten months. The gamblers hypocritically played the peacemakers and speculated on all the powder kegs in Europe. But all of them had one sovereign cure which they hoped would bring them closer to their confused and ill-understood goals. That cure was a 'second revolution.' In April, May, and June the Tribune of the People must have felt that the imp had been let out of the bottle.

There he stood, 'our Leader'; his voice drowned the clamor of his retinue; even while he was menaced by their insane demands, he was cheered by the silly, credulous masses. What was he to do now? What rock was he to climb to escape the sweeping tide which his own sorcery had created? We need not look far for an answer to our questions. It is interesting to note what he himself afterward admitted about these last weeks: 'The danger and the tension that bore down upon everyone had gradually become unendurable.' These words make clear not only what happened, but the fact that it had to happen.

There is no need to introduce unnecessary complications in analyzing what led up to June 30. It is manifestly false to attribute the events to reactionary uprisings or treason on the part of Roehm, the chief of staff, or the fact that the SA was a hotbed of perversion. Fundamentally the reason was very simple indeed: the old magic formulas had ceased to work. Adolf Hitler could no longer command the demons he had called up.

All he could do now was shoot at them.

4

June 30, 1934

GESTAPO POLITICS

THE DAYS IMMEDIATELY PRECEDING the fatal one were dreadful enough. Tension was at the highest pitch. The tormenting uncertainty was harder to bear than the excessive heat and humidity. No one knew what was going to happen next and everyone felt that something fearful was in the air.

I remember that period so vividly because at the time I occupied a very advanced observation post. The year 1933 had not ended without also putting an end to my brief but exciting career in the Gestapo. Diels, of course, had kept his eye on me; after the incident of his dismissal and reinstatement, I had made no attempt to conceal my opposition to him and his methods. Diels cold-bloodedly decided that it was time to get rid of me. And I for my part was so foolish as to accelerate my own removal by taking a vacation at Christmas-time. When an acute crisis is in progress, one should never go on vacation. Being on the spot affords a certain power; often it is enough to save one's life. That, at any rate, is an axiom for revolutionary times. Vacations should be taken only in so-called 'dead' periods — and then they should be stretched out as long as possible. For it is as much of an art to lie low at the proper time as it is to be on hand during a dangerous crisis.

But in December, 1933, I lacked experience in this sort of revolutionary technique. While in the country I received a surprising New Year's greeting which looked, outwardly, like a quite ordinary business

133

letter. I unsuspectingly opened it and read that I was transferred to a remote provincial office, a tiny sub-prefecture in East Prussia, where I would presumably receive 'further training.'

I rushed into the next train and arrived in Berlin just in time. Diels had done his work very slyly. He had postponed his revenge until Christmas because he assumed that Under-Secretary Grauert would also be on vacation. Grauert was well aware of my conflict with Diels and had observed it with a certain degree of benevolence. I felt sure that he would not abandon me without a struggle. At the time Grauert's deputy was a certain ministerial director who was politically indebted to Diels. During the Christmas lull these two had concocted the plot by which I was virtually exiled to East Prussia.

As chance would have it, I was able to reach Grauert in Berlin. I managed to convince him that this maneuver was by no means directed against me alone, and that the best retort would be to re-establish me in Berlin. I could not, of course, remain in the Gestapo any longer; but I felt sure I would fit into the ministry of the interior very well.

Reluctantly, Grauert agreed. He recalled that a young assistant was needed to straighten out all the vagrant items that had been repeatedly misdirected to the ministry of the interior since the separation of the Gestapo from the ministry at the end of October. All such matters had to be redirected to the competent authority, which was Goering's ministry of state. Grauert thought I would do very well for such a job; I should, after all, be staying in the field with which I was already familiar. In order that I should not engage in any policy-making on my own hook, he made me subordinate to a particularly watchful ministerial director. Moreover, he emphasized that I could show my gratitude for this kindness by being in the future less obtrusive and, above all, by keeping a close check on my tongue.

Naturally I agreed. Grauert, after all, could forbid me to take any action with regard to the documents that came into my hands, but with the best will in the world he could not prevent my reading all these denunciations, complaints, or petitions before I passed them on to the Gestapo. Nor was there any way for the Gestapists to check up if I left the originals untouched and made a few copies for my own use.

There were a tremendous number of complaints directed to the wrong address in the powerless ministry of the interior. For during that first year of the Revolution a great many indignant citizens labored under the delusion that a conscientious police force actually existed and that 'if the Fuehrer knew' or 'if Goering should find out,' action would certainly be taken.

The outcome of this appointment was a delicious little farce. As soon as Diels heard that I had departed only to reappear in the ministry of the interior, he struck back. Somehow his instinct told him that even in so subordinate a post I might cause trouble for him. In any case he did not like the idea of my continuing to be so close to Grauert or Daluege. For although Goering had placed the Gestapo directly under his minister-presidency, he was also, in his capacity as minister of the interior, head of the rest of the police force. And in this latter capacity Grauert and Daluege served as his deputies. The result of this administrative nonsense was that Diels lived in constant fear that Goering's friend Grauert, or Daluege who already stood high in the SS hierarchy, might find any number of pretexts and roundabout ways to interfere with Gestapo affairs and supplant him.

I was somewhat amused to find that I became the subject of a correspondence that Goering conducted with himself, for in his capacity as Prussian minister-president he signed an order to himself as minister of the interior demanding that I be removed from the ministry of the interior. Diels, of course, had drawn up this order and laid it before his chief for signature.

The obvious method would have been for Goering simply to have telephoned his subordinate, Grauert, in order to transmit such an order to him. But perhaps Diels thought a letter would be more effective. Or perhaps he was loyal to the good old bureaucratic principle: why do anything simply when it can be done in a complicated fashion? In any case, three or four such letters arrived in succession from the ministry of state, but Grauert, on the advice of Daluege, did not carry out the order. Daluege could not forgive Diels his reinstatement in the Gestapo, and both he and Grauert wanted to talk the matter over with Goering personally before they did Diels the favor of removing me.

But even at that time it had already become extremely difficult for an executive secretary or an SS group leader to secure an interview with 'Iron Hermann.' It was precisely this fact that I was gambling on. I knew that Frick was on the point of incorporating the Prussian ministry of the interior into the Reich ministry of the interior. If I could only succeed in holding on for a brief period, until Frick replaced Goering, I should be safe for the time. For at this time Frick was an outright opponent of the Gestapo. He had followed my quarrel with Diels and I did not think it likely that he would let me be shelved.

In revolutionary times a great many things that are ordinarily possible are impossible, but the converse is also true. And so, in spite of Goering's definite objections to me, I succeeded in holding out for three months. In April, 1934, Frick took over the Prussian ministry of the interior — very much against Goering's will; up to the last moment Goering had tried to prevent this diminution of his power.

Frick, who at that time was past sixty, was unquestionably a thoroughgoing Nazi and a loyal disciple of his Brown master. But at the same time he did not attempt to deny his background as a civil servant. He was a bureaucrat, and thought that even during a revolution everything could take place in a lawful and orderly fashion. Frick thought in legal terms, and sincerely believed that the circle could be squared; that is, that at the proper time terrorists would voluntarily cease to practice terror. In any case, he was not one of those who believed that the dictatorship must necessarily be founded upon murder and blackmail. Therefore, he had no objection to my informing him about such excesses upon the part of the Gestapo as came to my knowledge. On the contrary, he wanted to be kept informed and actually supported me in carrying out a novel idea.

As Prussian minister of the interior, Frick was subordinate to Goering, the minister-president, and had to follow the latter's instructions.

As Reich minister of the interior, however, he had the power to issue orders to all the various state governments, and consequently to Goering as well. I exploited this situation of overlapping authority by taking those valuable and significant documents which I was not permitted to work on in the Prussian ministry of the interior and driving a few blocks away to the Reich ministry of the interior. There I had the documents copied, and laid them before Frick. Frick would demand explanations from the Gestapo. Goering fumed. But what could he do about it? On the other hand, Frick liked this procedure so well that he expanded the staff to take care of such matters and at the same time gave me an appointment in the Reich ministry of the interior.

This facilitated my work. From then on no one could make the accusation — which was quite valid — that I was suppressing or intercepting documents of the Prussian ministry of the interior. After all, I could not divide myself into two halves, and my minister was in both cases Frick. Grauert and his colleague in the Reich ministry of the interior, the self-important Under-Secretary Pfundtner, protested repeatedly because in these important matters I enjoyed virtually a personal monopoly on reports to Frick. Nevertheless, I achieved my purpose completely. Frick was pleased because, in contrast to the timidity of his two under-secretaries, he had found someone who would supply him with the necessary documents and the necessary vigorous drafts of ministerial orders.

During that time, however, a radical change took place which hardly eased my difficult predicament. My feud with Diels had to be brought to a premature halt. For while I was sniping at my enemies, our little battle was taken over by two more portentous figures than ourselves. I could very well venture combat with Diels, the unsteady playboy who, conscious of being a bourgeois renegade, had a good many inhibitions holding him back from foul play. But as soon as Himmler and Heydrich entered the arena I should have prudently withdrawn.

Unfortunately, on that first of April, 1934, when Diels at last left the

Gestapo for good, I did not understand that the hour had struck. I realized it only very gradually, and I did not grasp the full situation until after the thirtieth of June.

Part of the reason for my ignorance was that Frick, in order to provide me with a certain status — since I had never belonged to the Party, the SA, the SS, or any of the other Brown organizations — had transferred me into Daluege's police department. At that time the struggle was still raging over who was to be the chief of police in Germany — Himmler or Daluege. Daluege was Frick's favorite; Daluege was well liked by Hitler; Goering had appointed him general of the police and, to Himmler's great annoyance, Daluege also occupied the second-highest rank in the SS. Since Daluege had the additional honor of being *oberste Polizeifuehrer* [1] in the Reich and in Prussia, there were very good grounds for assuming that he might succeed in blocking the Gestapo from achieving total power in the Reich.

Kurt Daluege was by nature no Gestapist, nor did he ever become one, although he richly earned the gallows for his behavior in many other matters. I had the opportunity to follow his career closely for about two years, from the middle of 1933 to the middle of 1935, and honesty forces me to say that he had his good points. His reputation was for a long time worse than his behavior. I might put it that he was not the type of an utterly lost soul, but rather the model of one utterly corrupted. Stupid, immeasurably vain, but on the other hand neither hungry for power nor steeped in falsehood, his first reaction was usually decent, never malicious. If one took instant advantage of this reaction — if, for example, one had taken the precaution of bringing documents for signature — he often let himself be persuaded to take steps that required amazing courage. It was only when he had a chance to make calculations that he became a scoundrel. For if

[1] Literally, 'supreme police leader' — an SS title and a position carrying a great deal of power, since the SS was employed as an auxiliary police force and gradually came to be the principal police power in Germany. Later, the SS, through its *Sicherheitsdienst* (SD), controlled all the German police forces, including the Gestapo. Although the Gestapo was, strictly speaking, only the secret state police of Prussia, the name was generally applied to all the police organizations created after 1933. (*The translators.*)

he were given time to consider what his Fuehrer really thought, or what Goebbels might reply, or whether Goering agreed, or how Himmler would behave, or whether his own action might endanger his position — then hope was lost.

Incidentally, it was Daluege who first called my attention to the Black menace. He knew these birds very well. Diels he hated, but he feared Heydrich. 'You will end by using Beelzebub to drive out the Devil,' he warned Nebe and me when we refused to slacken our struggle against Diels. He had hoped for a while to check the SS invasion of the police force — though he himself was so high an SS officer — by persuading certain of the bourgeois ministers to act. Only after he realized how utterly inadequate these ministers were did he capitulate. But then he went the whole hog; as weak men do in such cases, he abased himself in submissiveness.

But who was this Heydrich, whom Daluege feared?

When Daluege first mentioned the name to me, early in 1934, it meant nothing at all to me. Himmler had become a subject of gossip, although this agricultural college graduate with his pince-nez was scarcely taken too seriously. He was still obscured by the shadow of Roehm, and his hundred thousand SS men did not carry much weight when compared to the millions in the SA. But Heydrich was almost totally unknown in the upper circles. Who cared about the misdemeanors committed by Himmler's deputy police chief in Bavaria when, in Prussia, countless infamies took place daily? The SD (*Sicherheitsdienst*), or security service of the Reich leader of the SS, as Heydrich's private army of cut-throat Party stool pigeons loftily called itself, made its first bloody and public appearance on June 30.

Because so little was known about Heydrich, I did not take him seriously. Today I know only too well who and what Heydrich was. It was not only an inferiority complex or his intense guilt feelings that led him to persist in maintaining his incognito. His criminal craftiness automatically showed him the darkest and most roundabout ways to attain his goals, and he preferred to enjoy his feats of terrorism in secret. Heydrich did not want to be recognized for what he was.

My first encounter with Heydrich — though I did not meet him personally until two months after June 30 — was amazingly mild. I was sitting at my desk in the ministry of the interior — this was some time in mid-February, 1934 — when my door flew open. A *Sturmbannfuehrer*[1] of the SS entered with a diabolic grin on his face. He was a greasy-looking bird, quite true to type, but as it turned out he was not nearly so bad as he looked. He invited me, in Heydrich's name, to attend an important conference at Lichterfelde, in the barracks of the *Leibstandarte,* or bodyguard brigade of the SS. We had better hurry, he burst out; the car was waiting outside.

Naturally I thought my last hour had struck. I suspected that this was a new trick on the part of Diels, who had once before sent a fearsome SS man after me. What was I to do in this ticklish situation? I tried calling Daluege, but was unable to reach him. I didn't think it would help matters any simply to refuse, so I decided to accept the inevitable.

But before I went up before the Judgment Seat, I wanted to inform at least one sympathetic soul. I therefore assured this deputy of hell that I should be delighted to attend on time, but that I had an important conference at Prinz Albrechtstrasse. Would he kindly pick me up there in an hour? Then I rushed off to see Nebe. Nebe was not at all surprised; he thought it was quite all right. He had also been invited, he said; we should do best to go together.

At that time Lichterfelde meant nothing to us; we had no suspicion that in a few months the place would resound with the dreadful salvos of firing squads. But even though we had no such premonitions, our reception was impressive enough. There was the usual vigorous clicking of heels; adjutants zealously passed us from one door to the next, and then a high-ranking SS leader stood stiffly before us and greeted us as if we were famous guests of honor. Afterward Nebe informed me that he was Sepp Dietrich, who later became general-issimo of the *Waffen-SS* (the 'SS in Arms'). We could scarcely believe our ears when Dietrich, in his friendly Bavarian dialect, congratulated us in the names of Reich Leader Himmler and Group Leader Heydrich

[1] In rank equivalent to a major in the army. (*The translators.*)

for so stoutly leading the fight against corruption in the state and the Party. As we all knew, he said, Himmler detested the excesses of the SA. Above all, he could no longer put up with the rampant sins of the Gestapo. Would we please set forth in writing, here in this SS barracks, all our grievances. Naturally everything would be held in strictest confidence. Himmler wanted to use this material as the basis for a personal appeal to Hitler.

For a long time I hoped that the bombs of the war years would spare the remarkable document we composed on that day, and that I should be able to find it again. What amazing, naïve good faith we had! I should like to have published that brief but suggestive outline of the activities of the Gestapo during its first year. Not only did we record any number of instances of extortion, torture, and killing, but we actually hinted cautiously what we knew about the Reichstag fire.

It is still utterly inexplicable to me that Nebe and I survived such blatant indiscretion.

My purpose in recounting this story is certainly not to indicate that Himmler and Heydrich were, after all, decent men. Quite the contrary. It was always a favorite SS tactic to appear in the guise of respectable citizens and to condemn vigorously all excesses, lies, or infringements of the law. Himmler, when talking to a small group, sounded like the stoutest crusader for decency, cleanliness, and justice. It was all histrionics, of course. Count Helldorf used to say that Himmler was the greatest actor of his time, even greater than Goering. That is why he has come off so well in so many memoirs by men whose hatred for Gestapo methods is undeniable.

Heydrich was not so accomplished a hypocrite as his 'ardently beloved' SS leader. But although Heydrich preferred brutal, straightforward struggle with his foes, he was nevertheless the real ideologist of the SS. In addition to being the great practitioner of terrorism, Heydrich never wearied of teaching his men what he called the bylaws of applied terror. One of his slogans, as pithy as it is primitive, was: 'Pass the buck.'

When Heydrich oppressed — he did so for reasons of discipline. When Heydrich blackmailed — he did so in the name of socialism.

When Heydrich tortured — it was to purify the victim. When Heydrich murdered — he acted in the interests of justice.

To be German meant, to Heydrich, to be a cold-blooded, inexorable terrorist. And he was dedicated above all else to being a good German.

As far as I was concerned, the change of cast within the Gestapo made no essential difference. Whether my opponent was Diels or Heydrich, the struggle was the same — except that Heydrich, with his peculiarly murderous bent, was even more dangerous.

An additional difficulty for me was that Nebe began daily plaguing me with lamentations. He wanted to break clear of it all. Heydrich was reluctant to release him because of his long experience in detective work. Frick, nevertheless, called him to take a post in the ministry of the interior, and in the early part of 1935 Nebe was able to return to purely criminological work. He was instructed to establish a Reich criminal office which was to be quite independent of the Gestapo. Naturally Frick had definite intentions in the back of his mind. And who knows whether this new authority of Nebe's might not some day have become a bastion from which the Gestapo could have been combated and defeated. But, unfortunately, in the middle of 1936 Himmler became police chief of the entire Reich and thereby Heydrich once more became Nebe's superior.

However, I do not want to anticipate. I have not as yet mentioned another path that I opened up about the same time, and one which was of considerable significance. During the stormy period of my troubles with Diels, I had made the acquaintance of a staff officer in the war ministry, with whom I soon became closely associated. This man was Hans Oster, who later became a general, and who has an important part to play in this story. At that time he was occupied with setting up the war ministry's counter-intelligence organization, which was to function both as the secret service and the secret police of the army. This organization was known for short as the *Abwehr*.

From 1933 to 1938 we all placed the most extensive hopes on this organization, which had such extraordinary potential powers. And in the later years, even though we worked under more difficult conditions, we still thought that the *Abwehr* would eventually prove the long arm of the lever that would overturn the structure of the Gestapo. For in the first place a secret service had the capacity for finding out practically everything worth knowing in a 'legal' fashion, and it would be able to assemble evidence without arousing suspicion. Moreover, such evidence also afforded the possibility of 'legal' action. And thirdly, although the men in black suspected the *Abwehr* of underground activity, they were chary of laying hands on members of the army.

The reader will see, from my later discussion of the Fritsch crisis and of the subsequent events of the war, that the *Abwehr* did in fact have enormous potentialities. These were not exploited to the full, but nevertheless more was done than is generally believed. Retrospectively, however, any pride we might feel in what was accomplished is outweighed by the shameful manner in which the generals spoiled so many daring efforts. Oster had been the moving spirit behind this underground use of the *Abwehr,* and when he departed the entire organization broke up. When in June, 1943, Himmler succeeded in deposing Oster, this practically sealed the fate of Oster's chief, the much-maligned Admiral Canaris. Scarcely half a year after, the *Abwehr* became a section of the SS.

When Oster entered the *Abwehr,* he was an unimportant major. When our friendship began in 1933-34, the situation was not at all clear. Nevertheless, we could already see the first signs of that alarming development which ended in the subjugation of the generals to the dictatorship of the SS. I do not mean to criticize Oster when I say that at first he refused to see what was bound to happen. He was too much a soldier of the old school, too thoroughly convinced of the honorableness of the top army officers, to believe that the once-proud and self-sufficient German army could ever be degraded to a section of a revolutionary party.

It may be that he did not realize the danger to the army until the shots of June 30 rang out. But however that may be, it is to Oster's eternal credit that he recognized the despicable character of the Gestapo men from the very beginning and had begun fighting the

whole scoundrelly crew — even while Diels still reigned — more resolutely and tenaciously than any other member of the army.

In this preview of June 30 I shall confine myself to noting that it
was Oster who helped me make my first connections with the war
ministry. We often met at night before the entrance to the ministry's
offices in the Bendlerstrasse and I would hand him a plump envelope
full of documents. The choicest bits would then find their way to the
chief of the *Wehrmachtsamt* or to War Minister von Blomberg. Many
of the documents were never returned; they remained with Oster in
'protective custody.'

I must add that I had, of course, no intention of jealously hoarding
those highly significant documents which I was amassing in the
ministry of the interior. As far as possible, I always tried to secure
publicity for them in the other ministries, for I went on hoping that
one or another of the bourgeois ministers would get up enough courage
to do something about these facts.

Gradually, by perseverance and despite a good deal of opposition,
my original tiny little office expanded into something like a small department of the political police. With the political balance of power
what it was, there was little prospect that my office could actively
intervene to remedy abuses, although here and there I was able to do
something. My position, however, was especially favorable for accu-
mulating, sifting, and evaluating material on significant aspects of
'inside' politics. Since Frick was generally considered to be an energetic person who might on occasion oppose gangsterism, all sorts of
pathetic persons turned trustfully to him. This was particularly true
of provincial administrative presidents, who were compelled to look
on helplessly while terrorism raged throughout their territories. As a
result, the 'evidence' that flowed into my office mounted sky-high.

Obviously, my personal position was not altogether enviable. On
the other hand, I occupied a valuable observation post and would not
have willingly abandoned it, for I did not want to be guilty of the
cowardly evasion of responsibility that characterized so many of the
middle class. If, in those first ominous fifteen months of the Brown

dictatorship, there had been more people 'in the know,' or if more of those who knew had made use of their knowledge, perhaps the thirtieth of June might have turned out differently. Perhaps the Nazis would have met their end then and not ten bitter years later.

THE BLOOD PURGE

FROM THE BEGINNING OF JUNE on, the inner tension became unbearable. It was something almost physical in its quality. But it was impossible to make any sense out of the utter confusion, and above all we could not guess who would take the initiative.

I myself, I must admit, had a very poor conception of the situation. A few days before June 30, I had a meeting with Oster to exchange opinions and a few documents. For prudence' sake we rowed out into the middle of Lake Schlachten for our little confab. At the time Hitler was preparing to address the SA at its conference in Wiessee. I predicted that he would take this occasion to change sides once again and effect a reconciliation with Roehm. This in turn would signify the end of Goering and Himmler, and would inevitably hasten the decisive conflict with the army.

There is a peculiar twist to this matter of the SA group leaders' conference in Wiessee. We had all known for some time that Adolf Hitler had personally issued the invitation to the later 'putschists' to attend this conference. Hitler, too, had selected the place of meeting. Apparently this was an overture of friendship toward Roehm who in a sulk had retired to Wiessee to take the cure. At the same time there were rumors that Roehm was to be deposed and replaced by Lutze.

When I relayed this interesting rumor to my superiors, my 'gossip-mongering' was rudely received. Under-Secretary Grauert indignantly refused to believe that Roehm's position was in any way shaken, and did not want even to hear rumors about it. Daluege, on the other hand, who certainly would have known the truth, burst into lengthy explanations intended to prove that the Fuehrer would never desert

Roehm. In his innocence Daluege was not even astounded when, in the middle of the week, he received a telephone call from Karl Ernst, who excitedly informed him that all sorts of idiotic rumors were flying around Berlin to the effect that the SA was planning a *Putsch*. Daluege merely asked me to tell Frick of Ernst's desire to submit a declaration of loyalty to the minister of the interior.

This actually took place. It was a unique scene, and highly indicative of the temper of the time: an SA group leader solemnly assured the Reich minister of police that he was definitely not planning a revolt.

Even the haughty Roehm seemed to be growing uneasy. At any rate, he sent word to General von Fritsch that he hoped his conflicts with the army could be settled on a friendly basis; he planned to pay a call on the general as soon as he returned from his furlough. There is every reason to believe that neither Ernst nor Roehm was being dishonest and evasive. On the contrary, both sensed something in the air and wanted to anticipate false accusations. The two men were destined to be more surprised at the charge that they were plotting a *Putsch* than was their poor 'betrayed' Fuehrer.

To make the confusion complete, in the last week of June, Rudolf Hess put in his oar. He delivered an address over the radio which, apparently, meant everything to everyone. Afterward it was asserted that he had pronounced a 'last warning.' As a matter of fact, he did speak against continual revolutions 'in the manner of the annual revolutions of certain foreign republics.' That might have been considered an allusion to Roehm, who had served for a time as a lieutenant colonel in the Bolivian army. On the other hand, Hess also said: 'Perhaps Adolf Hitler will some day consider it necessary once again to hasten events by revolutionary methods. We stand ready to obey his command, confident that he will call upon his old revolutionaries.' Was that the language of a man who wished to pacify certain belligerent spirits among his followers?

Saturday, June 30, 1934

I CAN ONLY DESCRIBE THIS DAY in a fragmentary manner, as I experienced it. But that was enough for me — enough for the rest of my life.

Contrary to my usual habits, I went to work early. A deep restlessness had kept me awake the night before, and I felt impelled to get to the ministry as soon as possible. There was a sense of urgency in the air; it was necessary to be on the alert.

For three days the national police had been under emergency orders. Twice the alarm had been rescinded late in the afternoon, but on the eve of June 30 it was permitted to stand. Moreover, Nebe had been ordered to report at once to Goering. What for? Was he to guard Goering, as he had done so often before? Why? From whom? After all, an official in the ministry was not a private detective, and the police squadron in the palace ought to have been protection enough for Goering.

Nebe had promised to telephone me at night to let me know what was going on, but he had failed to call. Therefore, either he must have stayed at the palace or been sent off to a special meeting. My curiosity about this made me all the more eager to speak to him, and I felt sure that I should find him at the ministry that morning.

I had not yet got to my desk when Daluege telephoned me to come to him at once. I ran over to his office and found him in a fit of depression. Daluege, chief of the Prussian police and head of the police division of the federal ministry of the interior, wanted to know whether I had any news. When I said I had none, he assured me that he was equally ignorant. Then he began to rant. Was he not the commander-in-chief of the national police (these were camouflaged police troops who were later openly incorporated into the army)? Nevertheless, Goering had thrice proclaimed a state of emergency over his head, and without letting him know a thing about it! Daluege was furious; he swore that he was going to see Goering at once to complain. As one 'old fighter' to another he was going to give Goering a piece of his mind.

I could well understand his excitement, and I was malicious enough to press him to carry out his resolution. But he was still declaiming when the telephone rang and he was ordered to report to Goering at once. This was shortly after nine o'clock. Within the hour he returned, his face chalk-white. He had received an explanation; the national police had been alarmed because an SA revolt was to take place that night and Goering had been ordered by the Fuehrer to put it down. Roehm had been deposed, he said; several of the higher-ranking SA leaders had been shot and others were to follow. In brief, there was going to be a bloody purge within the SA.

We rushed to Grauert's office. The under-secretary had just arrived, suspecting nothing. As soon as we had informed Grauert, he and Daluege reported to Frick. I went along, although I was not admitted to see Frick. But I was close enough to witness an amazing scene: a few minutes later the minister of the interior of the Reich rushed downstairs, accompanied by his under-secretary, and set out to see Goering. At Goering's palace he was to find that a good many things had been going on in Berlin and Munich of which a minister of police should have been aware. At the same time he would be told that all these things were not in his province. For the duration of the present 'action' the Fuehrer had transferred all police power to Goering and Himmler.

Daluege and I returned to our offices. While we sat there talking utter nonsense, I was called to the telephone. The administrative president of Potsdam wished to inform me that according to a report from the local magistrate General von Schleicher and his wife had been shot that morning in their home in Neubabelsberg by persons unknown. The magistrate had taken possession of the bodies and instituted an immediate investigation.

I rushed back to Daluege with this bit of news. Daluege had not heard anything about it from Goering. The murder had probably not been committed at the time he had spoken with Goering. Consequently, it did not occur to us to connect this incident with the Roehm affair. I was called to the telephone once more. This time it was the local magistrate himself. He repeated his report and added that he had just learned that both General von Schleicher and his wife had been shot on orders from the Gestapo. He had been forbidden to conduct any investigation. But now he wanted to know what to do with the bodies.

Now Daluege and I realized what was what. The killings had started.

Daluege sent me down to Grauert's office with this news. Grauert had just returned from Goering's palace, and when I began excitedly pouring out my news, he calmly waved it away as if the murder of a former chancellor of Germany were the most natural thing in the world. He had heard all about it from Goering, he said. Schleicher had taken part in the *Putsch*; he had tried to defend himself when being arrested and had been shot, together with his wife. In any case, Grauert added, these two were not the only victims. Among others he named Heines, von Heydebreck, Hayn, Schneidhuber, Ritter von Krausser. Roehm, too, was supposed to be dead. Karl Ernst was going to be shot, but had not yet been caught. That gallows-bird had been one of the arch-conspirators, Grauert said.

I asked just where and how the revolt had taken place. Grauert could tell me little about that. He murmured something about Wiessee and Munich. That was all he knew, he said. Then he started on a fulsome eulogy of Goering. It was true, of course, that Grauert's admiration for Goering was of long standing; he had no reservations where Goering was concerned. But I distinctly heard another note behind all this praise: Grauert was obviously overjoyed that he himself was not on the list of victims. I must admit that at the moment I had precisely the same feeling. I still had no suspicion that the shooting was just beginning and that it was to go on for no less than two days more. I was being a bit hasty in thinking that I was out of danger.

Obviously Grauert considered the Schleicher affair finished. In any case, he had no intention of letting it trouble his weekend. He would not give me any definite answer to my inquiry about the bodies. The Gestapo would take care of that. He again gave me a friendly warning to watch my loose tongue and dismissed me.

I returned to Daluege and told him what news I had gathered from Grauert. Daluege was astonishingly calm about the list of victims, although many of them were old comrades of his. He mentioned some more names to add to the list of those who had been shot.

By now the whole affair was really beginning to puzzle us. Just what was happening? They even seemed to be after Gregor Strasser — an old Party comrade had just made a dramatic appeal to Daluege to help save Strasser. What a strange *Putsch* it must be, in which Roehm, Schleicher, and Strasser were working together! Moreover, according to the police radio messages that kept pouring in, almost every one of the higher-ranking SA leaders had been arrested. The traitors seemed to be suspiciously numerous.

We decided to scout for news. I suggested that we go to Goering's palace, where I hoped I would meet Nebe. I thought he would be able to tell me what was going on. Moreover, I had the feeling that I should be a good deal safer there than in my office or at home. It was better to go into the lion's den in the company of someone like Daluege than to run around alone. And Goering's palace was the last place in which anyone would be likely to look for me.

We drove the few hundred yards from the ministry on Unter den Linden to the Leipzigerplatz without noticing any signs of excitement. Berlin at this time was utterly unsuspecting. The streets were crowded, although we noticed the absence of the usual horde of SA uniforms. But the Leipzigerplatz was closely guarded by troops of the national police, and crowds were watching them, open-mouthed, wondering what was going on. We made our way through the narrow gate that led to Goering's palace, which was not visible from the street, fortunately, for as we turned the corner we were confronted by an array of machine guns pointing down at us from every corner of the roofs and balconies. The yard was swarming with police. Were it not for the gravity of the moment, the contrast this made with peaceable Berlin would have struck me as wholly comic.

As I followed Daluege through the succession of guards and climbed the few steps to the huge lobby, I felt as if I could scarcely breathe. An evil atmosphere of haste, nervousness, tension, and above all of bloodshed, seemed to strike me in the face. Everyone's expression betrayed the awareness that something dreadful was going on.

Nervous adjutants were coming and going. Self-important messengers came running up bearing fat confidential envelopes. Small groups stood around waiting uneasily or talking earnestly. Not a loud word was to be heard. Everyone whispered as if he were in a morgue.

Fortunately I ran into Nebe at once. We greeted each other with the technique of communication that had gradually developed between us — a handshake and a silent raising of eyebrows. Neither of us knew what to say or what to ask. At last I began with the most unimportant subject and inquired what he had been doing all day yesterday. 'Oh,' he said, 'nothing special. I was told there was to be an attempt at assassinating Goering and I was ordered to accompany him. He simply went around shopping with his wife. But I had to spend the night in the palace. And this morning, well . . .' Again he looked at me significantly. Then he quite casually asked me whether I had seen Papen drive off as I came in. I said I had not. What had Papen been doing here? 'Oh,' Nebe said, with the same emphatic casualness, 'this morning *Oberregierungsrat* von Bose was shot in the waiting room of Papen's office. The vice-chancellor himself is under house arrest. Two armed SS men are parading as a guard of honor in front of his official residence.'

We quietly took a seat in a corner of the room. A few yards away sat an SA group leader, his chin quivering, his teeth chattering audibly, his whole frame shrunken in terror. 'What's wrong with him?' I asked. Nebe informed me that he had had to arrest the man awhile ago. The poor fellow had been summoned by telephone. As soon as he arrived, Goering had informed him that he was a homosexual swine and would be shot at once.

A few feet farther on, no less wretched, sat SA *Obergruppenfuehrer* Kasche. He had been picked up on the street and dragged into the palace, just as a precaution. By now he had an inkling of what he was in for. But the man was lucky. He was overlooked, perhaps because of the very fact of his being there in that den of murderers. In the afternoon he disappeared into some overcrowded dungeon, and from there was shipped to a concentration camp for a few weeks. A month later he was back in office and enjoying all his former privileges. In the end he became an ambassador of the Greater German Reich in the Balkans.

Nebe now began reciting the names of the more important victims, so far as he had heard of them. He began with Roehm and ended with Karl Ernst and the latter's group staff. Among the latter was Gehrt, a veteran of the last war, for whom we felt particularly sorry. We knew very well that every one of those toughs deserved death twice and thrice over for the atrocities they had committed in the course of the Revolution. Nevertheless, it was revolting to think of their meeting punishment in such a manner.

Servants in livery came around offering sandwiches to the 'guests.' We refused. We had lost all appetite.

Suddenly loud shouting reached us from the adjoining room. This room was Goering's study, and here the execution committee was meeting. Now and then couriers from the Gestapo rushed into and out of this room, slips of white paper in their hands. Through the door we could see Goering, Himmler, Heydrich, and little Pilli Koerner, under-secretary to Goering in his capacity as minister-president. We could see them conferring, but naturally we could not hear what was being said. Occasionally, however, we could catch a muffled sound: 'Away!' or 'Aha!' or 'Shoot him!' For the most part we heard nothing but raucous laughter. The whole crew of them seemed to be in the best humor.

Goering radiated cheerful complacency. It was easy to see that he was in his element. He swaggered about the room, his long hair waving, in a white military tunic and blue-gray military trousers, with high black boots that reached over his fat knees. There goes Puss-in-Boots, I thought suddenly. The epithet seemed appropriate, not so much because of the spiteful, catlike attitude of the man as because there was something puffed-up, counterfeit, and ridiculous about him.

But to continue — we suddenly heard loud shouting. A police major, his face flaming, rushed out of the room, and behind him came Goering's hoarse, booming voice: 'Shoot them . . . take a whole company . . . shoot them . . . shoot them at once!' The written word cannot reproduce the undisguised blood lust, fury, vicious vengefulness, and, at the same time, the fear, the pure funk, that the scene revealed.

Everyone sensed that someone had escaped who was high on the list, someone without whom the day's bag would seem valueless to Goering.

At first we took it for granted that the one in question must be Roehm or Karl Ernst. But then we heard Goering shouting again. Once more he began pacing back and forth in his gilded cage, and five or six times we heard him cry in a voice hoarse with rage: 'Paul, of all people . . . Paul, of all people . . . Paul . . .' Then we realized that he must mean Paul Schulz, Gregor Strasser's closest associate.

I had met Schulz not two weeks before. At the time I did not know him, though I knew of him that he had worked unsuccessfully with Strasser up to 1932 trying to clean some of the worst filth out of the Nazi Party. When I heard that the Gestapo was on the heels of Strasser and Schulz, I felt it my duty to warn him. At the appointed time I jumped into his car and we drove around for a while until we were certain we had shaken off any would-be informers. Then we dropped in at an outlying open-air café. I told Schulz all I knew. He received my news quite calmly. He did not doubt that Himmler was anxious to do him in, but he hoped to get word to the Fuehrer and obtain a kind of exemption. Hitler occasionally issued such instructions to the Gestapo — ordering that So-and-So must not be murdered.

Schulz flatly rejected the suggestion that he and Strasser take flight. It was hopeless, he thought. He was prepared for at least ten years of dictatorship and did not think he could live out his life in exile for so long a time. He reasoned that National Socialism would hold on to power by brute force, and his logic made a deep impression upon me. At that time I still believed that Christian Europe would quell the reign of terror a good deal sooner. But Schulz knew his fellow Party members better than I did, and he was only too well aware of that cowardliness on the part of the middle class which had helped the terrorists to take power.

Goering's henchmen had, of course, set out to get Schulz early that morning. In fact they had thought they already had him. But all the while Schulz was sitting peacefully in his apartment, knowing nothing of the slaughter that was going on all around him. The police had picked up the wrong person. The mistake was not discovered until they reached headquarters, which was why Goering was in such a fury.

Some ten years later, when we unexpectedly ran across one another in Zurich, Schulz told me what had actually happened.

Long before Hitler took power a *roman à clef* dealing with Schulz's adventurous past had been published. The hero of this novel bore the name Wolfgang Scholz — a slight variation on the real name. The result was that the keen detectives of the Gestapo had not been hounding Schulz at all, but some unfortunate person by the name of Wolfgang Scholz who happened to be listed in the telephone directory. Satisfied with their own perspicacity, the Gestapo detectives overlooked the fact that this Scholz differed in every particular from Schulz.

It was this Wolfgang Scholz who had been arrested that morning as a dangerous and seditious criminal. But Scholz vigorously defended himself at the interrogation; he swore up and down that he was not and never had been a Brown 'hero of the nation,' a Reichstag deputy, or a friend of Hitler's. *Mirabile dictu,* they believed him at last. His was one of the exceptional cases in which Himmler's henchmen even attempted an identification. Consequently he was not shot. However, as punishment for being implicated in the case — even though through no fault of his own — he was given six months in concentration camp.

Goering's rage is understandable. By now, he felt sure, Schulz would have made good his escape. And he one of their chief targets!

Some hours later, in the late afternoon, Heydrich reconsidered the matter. He tried his luck and, wonder of wonders, the unsuspecting Schulz was found at home. Five tough Gestapo men with drawn guns invaded his apartment. At first Schulz was able to bluff them. Although he had no knowledge of what had gone before, Schulz had the presence of mind to insist that there was some mistake. But this gained him just a little time — which the thugs employed in collecting a little plunder. They even took a portable typewriter. Then they decided to get down to business. They thrust their victim into an automobile and set off at a wild pace.

After a brief halt at the Gestapo headquarters in Potsdam, they drove swiftly out of the city and stopped near the thickest woods beyond Potsdam. We can well imagine the rest. The Gestapo men staged one of their famous attempts at escape. They pushed Schulz out of the car and started shooting. But in their excitement they aimed poorly. Paul Schulz got a good start and really did try to escape. With several bullets in his abdomen, he ran for his life. A wild pursuit through dense woods followed. The pursuers continued shooting, but in the end they lost the trail.

Schulz lay unconscious for some time. Later he made his way painfully to a small town, rented a car, and drove by himself to the home of some friends! These friends concealed him and sent for a doctor. He was operated on in secret and then sent to a hospital under an assumed name.

When Hitler at last heard about it, he pretended fierce indignation. Had they wanted to harm his good friend Schulz? Frightful! What a misunderstanding! The Fuehrer sent greetings and ordered his personal physician to tend this precious patient. With unexampled generosity he expressly extended his protection to Schulz — and three weeks later he 'pardoned' the man (who had never been tried, let alone sentenced for anything) to banishment for life. He informed his dear friend that if he did not get out of Germany within ten days, he would no longer be able to guarantee his safety. . . .

Daluege joined us. He had heard enough, and we decided to leave. In the car he told me his impressions. With his customary simple-mindedness, he had swallowed the official account. I heard all about mutiny, revolt, homosexuality, embezzlement, and, above all, about the magnificent alertness of the latest descendant of Sherlock Holmes, Heinrich Himmler. 'I always said Himmler was a great man.' Daluege generously overlooked the numerous times he had described the SS chief as an imp of Satan because Himmler was trying to replace him as federal chief of police.

We returned to the ministry of the interior. But what was the use of working on our outdated documents when, a few blocks away, the slate was being wiped clean. We decided to wait and see what the morrow would bring in the way of new material for our useless files.

Instead we paid a visit to the propaganda ministry, where Goering was to issue a statement to the press. When we got there we found, crowded into the room, the élite of our Nazified press. I examined the faces of our editorial writers. Those faces were unquestionably more revealing than their paeans of the morning would be. They expressed an unpleasant mixture of curiosity, shamefacedness, malice, and genuine horror.

The bourgeois minister of labor, Seldte, was among those present. Goering intended to speak with him afterward. We wondered why. Had a number of *Stahlhelm* leaders been shot? This proved not to be the case. Goering merely wished to give Seldte the pleasant news that Schragmueller, the police chief of Magdeburg who had recently given Seldte such a beating, was already on the way to the crematorium. It was of no importance at all that Seldte's former political ally, Lieutenant-Colonel Duesterberg, had been shipped off to Dachau to receive the humane treatment for which the place was famous.

Goering arrived, in one of his full-dress uniforms. Once again he did not walk; he strutted up to the platform with slow, mincing steps. He began the session with a long, impressive pause, leaning forward slightly, his chin propped in his hand, and rolling his eyes as if he feared his own revelations. There seemed no doubt that he had been studying this pose at home before he came.

His explanation was something of a bouillabaisse. He talked about a Roehm revolt, degenerate homosexuality, unrest throughout the country, reactionaries, high treason, sedition, second revolution, stern judgment, the Fuehrer's mercy. Schleicher had conspired with a foreign power. When arrested, 'he attempted to make a sudden assault' and 'unfortunately lost his life.' Nothing was said about Strasser or about the incident in Papen's office.

About the same time Hitler's emotional order of the day was issued from Munich. In it Hitler castigated the moral and political degeneracy of his top SA leaders. We therefore need not trouble ourselves about Goering's vivid portrayal of events. One phrase of Goering's was, however, noteworthy: 'I took occasion to extend my orders.' Goering meant that he had liquidated not only the seditious SA leaders, but that, on his own responsibility, he had fired a few shots at the 'perpetually discontented relics of the past.'

At the moment no one paid special attention to this remark. The newspapermen assumed that this was Goering's explanation for Schleicher's murder. Those few who knew of the incident thought of von Bose. No one there suspected how many victims this 'extension of orders' would claim by Monday night.

We had a hasty bite to eat in the restaurant at the ministry of the interior. While we were there we heard that the Fuehrer had taken a plane from Munich an hour ago. He was expected shortly at Tempelhof airport. His arrival ought certainly to be worth seeing.

The entire airport was surrounded by heavily armed SS men. In addition several companies of the air force were posted here and there. The plane was delayed, and Goering seized the opportunity to deliver an oration to his air force soldiers. These men were at that time serving as a camouflaged group. Their uniforms were quite unfamiliar to most of the populace. Goering abruptly decided to hold a kind of dedicatory ceremony.

The soldiers in their gray-blue uniforms stood in the shadow of the long hangars. Goering stood pompously before them, in the full consciousness of his power, and babbled to them — on this of all days — about loyalty and comradeship in a soldier's life. They might be proud, he said, that on so memorable a day as this he was raising them to the status of official troops. Everyone felt that this ridiculous and unrealistic scene was being improvised simply to kill time. There were no spotlights, no photographers and microphones. The speech, to which no one listened, faded quietly away into the twilight.

Daluege and I met with Nebe. He informed us that Gregor Strasser was dead. Allegedly he had committed suicide. We were outraged, and would have been more so had we known of the cowardly and treacherous manner in which he was murdered. An eye-witness told me about it some days later. Strasser had been taken to the Gestapo prison around noon. By that time some hundred arrested SA leaders were crowded together in one big room. These men had no idea why they had been arrested, nor did they know about the shootings that were going on in Munich and at Lichterfelde in Berlin. They were therefore inclined to look at the situation in its most humorous light, a mood which is common when people are arrested *en masse*. They cheered Strasser when he was brought in as a new comrade in misery.

Some hours passed and there was a great deal of coming and going. Then an SS man came to the door and called out Strasser. The man who had formerly been next in importance to Adolf Hitler in the Nazi Party was to be moved to an individual cell. No one thought anything of it as Strasser walked slowly out of the room. But scarcely a minute later they heard the crack of a pistol.

The SS man had shot the unsuspecting Strasser from behind and hit his main artery. A great stream of blood had spurted against the wall of the tiny cell. Apparently Strasser did not die at once. A prisoner in the adjoining cell heard him thrashing about on the cot for nearly an hour. No one paid any attention to him. At last the prisoner heard loud footsteps in the corridor and orders being shouted. The guards clicked their heels. And the prisoner recognized Heydrich's voice saying: 'Isn't he dead yet? Let the swine bleed to death.'

The bloodstain on the wall of the cell remained for weeks. It was the pride of the SS squadron, a kind of museum piece. These cut-throats showed it to all the terrified inmates and boasted that it was the blood of a famous man, Gregor Strasser. It was only after he had received numerous complaints that Heydrich ordered the bloodstains to be cleaned.

While Nebe and I were pacing back and forth at the airport, we saw a small Junkers plane land. First three SS men got out. They were followed by Karl Ernst, whose hands were bound. Ernst seemed to be in fine fettle. He almost skipped from the plane to the waiting car. And he smiled at everyone around, as if to emphasize that he considered this arrest a fine joke.

His droll temper did not last long. They carted him off to Lichter-felde at once, and before he knew what was happening he was placed against the wall. There was ample reason for such a hurry. The night editions of the newspapers were already headlining the official communiqué to the effect that seven SA group leaders had been shot, and Karl Ernst, whom we had just seen arrive, headed the list.

We asked where the plane had come from. Bremen, we were told. 'So that's it,' we said. For we at once realized the full truth about the so-called SA *Putsch*. Up to now, amid all the contradictory stories about treason and sedition, we had believed that Roehm's clique had prepared a few 'vigorous 'arguments to help convince Adolf Hitler at the conference in Wiessee. That sort of insolence perfectly accorded with their mentality. Now we had evidence that Karl Ernst, who was accused of being second to Roehm in the plot, had been preparing for his 'mutiny' by taking a vacation. And, as we later found out, he had in fact spent the day seeing the sights of the city and later attending a reception held in his honor by the good citizens of Bremen. Around three o'clock, when the banquet in the Ratskeller ended, an excited SA man came running up to Ernst and warned him to clear out: there was trouble in the air and he was being hunted. Ernst laughed and returned to his hotel, where the Gestapo men were waiting for him.

Even at this point the Berlin group leader did not realize that his life was at stake. He became offensive, and a heated argument followed. Prisoner though he was, he demanded that they let him get in touch with his group staff in Berlin. And the Gestapo officials were actually so intimidated that they permitted him to telephone; but to his astonishment no one answered. Apparently the line had been blocked. This gave Ernst pause for the first time. He hastily tried to get Wiessee. The chief of staff would straighten matters out in short order, he assured his captors. But here, too, he could not get his connection. Then Ernst gave up; he permitted the men to tie him up and lead him off.

Nevertheless, he remained outwardly nonchalant. He offered consolation to his companions, who had been arrested with him. What could possibly happen to him, a chief group leader, councilor of state, Reichstag deputy, and friend to Roehm? It was because of this failure to understand the situation that he smiled so confidently when he stepped out of the plane at Tempelhof. The charge of treason seemed so utterly weird that he imagined he would be able to refute it at the first hearing. Even as the command for his execution rang out he cried, 'Heil Hitler.' In the brief hour between the time he

emerged from the plane at Tempelhof and the time he was shot at
Lichterfelde, he had been unable to conceive what was taking place.
All he could imagine was that Goering had started a reactionary revolt
against Hitler, and he felt sure that Roehm and his Fuehrer would
win out in the end. In that faith he gladly died.

The plane from Munich was announced. In a moment we saw it,
looming swiftly larger against the background of a blood-red sky, a
piece of theatricality that no one had staged. The plane roared down
to a landing and rolled toward us. Commands rang out. An honor
guard presented arms. Goering, Himmler, Koerner, Frick, Daluege,
and some twenty police officers went up to the plane. Then the door
opened and Adolf Hitler was the first to step out.

His appearance was 'unique,' to use the favorite word of Nazi com-
mentators. A brown shirt, black bow tie, dark-brown leather jacket,
high black army boots — all dark tones. He wore no hat; his face
was pale, unshaven, sleepless, at once gaunt and puffed. Under the
forelock pasted against his forehead his eyes stared dully. Nevertheless, he did not impress me as wretched, nor did he awaken sympathy,
as his appearance might well have done. I felt quite indifferent to
him. It was clear that the murders of his friends had cost him no
effort at all. He had felt nothing; he had merely acted out his rage.

First Hitler silently shook hands with everyone within reach. Nebe
and I, who had taken the precaution of standing some distance away,
heard amid the silence the repeated monotonous sound of clicking
heels. Meanwhile, the other members of his entourage got out of the
plane: Brueckner, Schaub, Sepp Dietrich, and the rest. All of them
showed grave faces. At last a diabolic, grinning caricature of a face
appeared: Goebbels.

Hitler walked slowly and laboriously past the guard of honor as if
he were wading through sloshing mud. He seemed to be moving with
such an effort that we felt he might bog down at any moment.

On the way to the fleet of cars, which stood several hundred yards
away, Hitler stopped to converse with Goering and Himmler. Apparently he could not wait a few minutes until he reached the

chancellery. He listened attentively as the two made their report, though he must have been in constant telephone communication with them all day.

From one of his pockets Himmler took a long, tattered list. Hitler read it through, while Goering and Himmler whispered incessantly into his ear. We could see Hitler's finger moving slowly down the sheet of paper. Now and then it paused for a moment at one of the names. At such times the two conspirators whispered even more excitedly. Suddenly Hitler tossed his head. There was so much violent emotion, so much anger in the gesture, that everyone noticed it. Nebe and I cast significant glances at one another. Undoubtedly, we thought, they were now informing him of Strasser's 'suicide.'

Finally they moved on, Hitler in the lead, followed by Goering and Himmler. Hitler was still walking with the same sluggish tread. By contrast the two blood-drenched scoundrels at his side seemed all the more lively. Both Goering and Himmler, for all the bulkiness of the one and the drabness of the other, seemed cut out of the same cloth today. Both manifested the same self-importance, loquacity, officiousness, and the same sense of guilt. Without a sound, the rest of the procession followed at a discreet distance. Everyone behaved with an abashed deference, as if he had been permitted to touch the hem of world history or to carry the blood-streaked train that dragged behind this unholy triumvirate.

Nebe and I brought up the rear. We did not say a word, but we kept nudging one another, for both of us were impressed by the ghastly quality of this funeral procession. Nebe, the former Nazi, was on the verge of tears. I felt more like laughing. The bathos of the scene, the woebegone expressions, the combination of violent fantasy and grim reality, the gratuitously blood-red sky, like a scene out of Wagner — it was really too much for me. The mockery reached its climax when suddenly, from a group of laborers who were working on top of a hangar, someone shouted loudly: 'Bravo, Adolf!'

It was anything but usual to call Hitler by his first name. Goering might be Hermann and Goebbels Joe, but Hitler — he was simply 'the Fuehrer.' Gods and the sons of gods were not addressed with such rude familiarity. But in spite of the oppressive solemnity of this particular occasion here was someone who did not stand at attention and cry 'Heil!' but in simple joviality called out the Fuehrer's first name. Hitler and his entourage pretended not to hear.

But before their automobile started, the same brash voice cut through the sentimentality of the evening once more with its impudent 'Bravo, Adolf!'

There is little more to say about the rest of the evening. The cup was full for the day. All I recall is that late in the evening I met Oster in a small restaurant and we exchanged notes. I found to my amazement that the officials of the war ministry had no idea of the extent of the executions. Oster did not know what his chiefs intended to do about the murder of General Schleicher and his innocent wife. But he suspected that Blomberg and Reichenau were so happy to be rid of Roehm that they were willing to pay a certain price for their relief.

Oster reassured me that there would certainly be an aftermath. But he did not feel too sure of his ground; Heydrich might still be in the saddle on the morrow. At that time we were naïve enough to imagine that the gruesome purge was already over, that by tomorrow a reckoning could be drawn up. We took it for granted that those Gestapists who had literally gone hog-wild with their pistols would be made to answer for it.

By eleven o'clock at night I was back in the ministry of the interior. At Daluege's request I accompanied him in another call on Grauert. We remained with the under-secretary for about an hour, gave him a superficial report of what we had seen, and then returned to our offices. On the way Daluege declared that he intended to spend the night there in case he should be needed in a hurry. He suggested that I do the same. At that moment nothing was more welcome to me than such a pretext for spending the night under police protection. I still did not feel any too easy, even though I thought it was all over.

I sat up for a long time with Daluege and his adjutant. It took quite a while for our excitement to die down and for our overwrought nerves to realize how weary they were. Daluege had set up a comfortable sleeping place in his office. I had made no such preparations. So much the better, I thought; I would not need to sleep in my own room. Who knew whether someone with unpleasant intentions might not come looking for me during the night? I should be all the safer in one of the many offices along the corridor.

Before I went to sleep, I went over the day's events once more with Daluege's adjutant, a fine fellow. In conclusion I remarked that it was indicative of a great sense of duty on Daluege's part for him to spend the night in his office. 'What's that?' this most loyal of adjutants snapped at me — 'sense of duty, sense of duty?' He gripped my arm, tears of rage in his eyes. 'He's scared stiff, that's what he is. That's why he won't go home . . .'

I must admit that I thought Daluege's behavior this evening not at all unreasonable. I myself was not the police chief of Prussia nor the head of the police department in the federal ministry of the interior, nor was I an SS group leader, but I concurred with Daluege that on days like this there was no sense in challenging fate. I rested better in a strange office on a battered old plush sofa whose style was reminiscent of a past but more peaceful century than I should have done at home upon the softest down. It was very comforting to know that my present location could not be found in the telephone book.

Sunday

THIS DAY struck me as even more dreadful than had Saturday. For Sunday was the day of dawning realization.

The day before we had been overwhelmed by the succession of events. We had tried to keep up with them, but we had actually been merely stowing them away in our memories quite mechanically, without really thinking about them. We were then still incapable of thinking through to the ultimate meaning of all the horrors. Numbly we had registered the fact: So-and-So has been shot, murdered, arrested. We even knew who were the chief actors behind this peculiar

Putsch. But we had no perspective from which to judge the events; we were still unable to see the wood for the trees.

That one tempestuous night was sufficient to settle our spinning minds and to sharpen our dulled senses. We awoke to the grim understanding of what had taken place. The day before, a great many things had been mysterious; on Sunday we understood them. That was why this Sunday was so dreadful and oppressive to us from the first moment. On Saturday we might still have been fooled into giving some credence to such labels as 'treason,' 'mutiny,' or a *Putsch.* But on Sunday we realized that hate, ruthlessness, and pure wantonness were holding sway. Sunday was the day of mass killings.

Precisely because the day was one of understanding, of analyzing the meaning of facts, I can no longer describe it accurately, with all the events in their proper chronological succession. I can no longer say when I learned of this particular shooting or that assassination, or whether a conversation took place in the morning or at night. There remain in my memory of my own activities only a few scattered snapshots. For the most part I must confine my description to the objective facts which I amassed in the course of the day or later on, without reference to my personal experiences.

It would be pointless, at this late date, to reproduce the list of murders that Nebe and I drew up in the course of the day. Two incidents will suffice to show the kind of stories of rampant brutality and icy callousness that we heard all day long.

Heines, the SA leader, had a tubercular brother who was convalescing in the Silesian mountains. Apparently it would have been too much of an effort to take him all the way to Lichterfelde. The executioners found it more convenient to have him attempt to escape in the mountains; thus the Heines brothers were wiped out. Some weeks later Frick received a letter from Heines's aged mother, written in a clumsy hand. The mother pleaded that this last of her sons be released from 'protective custody.' He was, she wrote, her sole remaining bread-winner; moreover, he was sick. An investigation was made. It developed that by some oversight the mother had been sent the ashes of only one of her sons. The second cardboard box was promptly dispatched.

Old President von Kahr had dared, before Hitler's farcical *Putsch* of 1923, to express the opinion that Hitler had been trying to blackmail him. When Hitler waved a revolver under his nose and cried passionately that 'the morrow will see us victors or dead,' Kahr had calmly said, 'Be careful, Herr Hitler, you might shoot me.' Obviously such a 'traitor' could not be given the privilege of an honorable death. Therefore, he was beaten till he died and his body thrown into the peat bogs near Dachau.

My own list contained some sixty names. Hitler, in the accounting he later gave, admitted seventy-seven, and in addition the victims of 'acts of violence which had no connection with this action.' He alleged that these latter cases would be taken care of by the regular courts, but every single one of the murderers was later pardoned. Some thirteen murders fall into this category. Thus, according to Hitler himself, my own list lacked thirty names. How many more should there have been in reality?

Throughout the course of that Sunday we asked ourselves this question repeatedly. It was well known that there had been thousands of arrests. Rumor put the numbers of victims far more generously. For it was no easy matter for anyone to emerge from one of the SS bunkers. Consequently, a number of persons were reported dead who shamefacedly returned a few weeks later, with their hair cut short in jailbird fashion, and hastily assured everyone without being asked that they had been extremely well treated.

To judge by hearsay, on that Sunday there were at least a hundred executions at Lichterfelde alone. Undoubtedly this is an exaggeration; probably there were no more than forty. Even that many means a salvo about every quarter hour. For the people who lived in the vicinity of the barracks the sound of the shooting was an uninterrupted series of shocks. Frick's adjutant, who lived in the neighborhood, informed me that around noon he had had to take his wife to stay with relatives in the city; she had been unable to endure the continual shooting and screaming.

More and more such tales were recounted that day. In general I recall that in contrast to the day before, people began to talk quite

freely on Sunday. The numbed horror of the first day had been overcome. Naturally, nothing was said that was really to the point. The
truth about the *Putsch,* homosexuality, and the reactionary conspiracy
were left strictly alone. But there was a great deal of talk that tacked
cautiously close to the essentials. The shootings at the Lichterfelde
barracks, who had been arrested, who had been found dead, and who
surprisingly had turned up alive — such matters were avidly discussed.
Everyone felt the need to say something. But people's faces revealed
far more than their careful words. In everyone's eyes on that bloody
July 1 sheer horror could be read.

I saw Frick five or six times during Sunday, and he did not conceal
his horror at the way in which Goering and Himmler had run amok.
I recall particularly a long walk that Frick and I took around his
lovely garden. We discussed a variety of new cases that had come to
our knowledge in the course of the day. Somehow our talk turned
once more to Strasser. By a deliberately indiscreet remark I let Frick
know how I felt about this strange 'suicide.' And suddenly this icy,
unemotional person began talking heatedly. He called murder by its
proper name. Strasser had been involved in no sort of treason at all,
he said; Goering and Himmler had simply seized the opportunity to
get rid of one of their deadly foes.

One word led to another, and soon we were right in the middle of
the problem of the Gestapo and Himmler. We said just about everything there was to say about the matter. I don't know exactly when it
was that Frick spoke out to Hitler, but I do know that at some time
in the course of the day he did say: 'My Fuehrer, if you don't proceed
at once against Himmler and his SS as you have against Roehm and
his SA, all you will have done is to have called in Beelzebub to
drive out the Devil.'

Hitler, however, was in no mood to listen to such counsel. He had
slept well and recovered sufficiently to receive guests for tea in the
chancellery garden. There were ladies present and the inevitable
Goebbels children, as well as all the other usual appurtenances that
make touching snapshots.

Had I not seen it with my own eyes I would not have believed in the reality of this garden tea party, for even while it was going on a great many 'traitors' were being butchered. But I happened to have accompanied Daluege to the chancellery, where he was hoping to meet Himmler. I had to wait outside for a rather long time, but I was rewarded with a vivid description of how nice the tea party had been. The Fuehrer and his guests were apparently having a lovely Sunday.

While waiting I had an unexpected opportunity to see Hitler. He left the garden to appear at that famous window where he received ovations; the Berlin Nazi Party section had drummed up a sizable mob for the purpose of cheering the Fuehrer. Returning, he had to cross the inner court where I was waiting. Besides myself there were only two officers from his bodyguard standing around. I hastily slunk behind them, so that when he passed, the two SS men were about two paces from him and I some six more away. We saluted in the customary fashion, just as dozens of servants or bystanders must have done during this short passage of his from chancellery to garden. But instead of simply passing by, Hitler stood still. Just as if our mark of respect were something special, he raised his hand in greeting and his body froze into immobility. For a moment he stood in the same pose which the mob outside had admired a few minutes before. Then, surprisingly, he shook hands with the SS men. As if that were still not enough, he repeated his solemn salute in the same pose of immobility.

He was treating the two men as if they were an entire regiment drawn up on the parade ground, I thought. But to my dismay this little ceremony was not yet over. He saw me standing a few steps behind the SS men, and although I already felt that I had had quite enough of a share in his two stiff-armed salutes, he seemed to think that I ought to partake of the blessing also. He took a step to one side, so that I was no longer concealed by the SS men, raised his hand in salute once more, and remained again in the same rigid position for about ten seconds. As he stood there without moving a muscle, he looked intensely at me, as if I were a crowd of at least a hundred thousand of his worshipful subjects. Since I was only one man, I had the distinctly unpleasant feeling that I would sink into the ground under the weight of this Caesarean gaze. Involuntarily the thought flashed through my mind: Can he read minds? I wondered when I was going to be shot. But he had no evil intent. Apparently he was concerned only with enjoying his pose, while I in my ingratitude breathed a sigh of relief as soon as he returned to his tea party.

I mention this trivial incident only because it illustrated to me how overwrought Hitler actually was that day. In his inner insecurity he took refuge in pose, which had always been his strongest armor.

Hitler had never been cheerful, relaxed, easy-going, or spontaneous; as a son of the gods he had always been above such human frailties. But on that day, more than ever, there was literally a physical aura of the possessed and the fated about him. On that day he seemed to be, more than ever, pure volition. No matter how tight his grip on himself, he could not help betraying this. On June 30 he was thrust forward by the combined impetus of tyrannical volition and daemonic compulsion.

Goering took it much more easily. Whenever I saw him on that Sunday I had the feeling that none of it really touched him. He had an infantile ability to devote himself completely to the occupation of the moment, whether it was a banquet, the donning of a new resplendent uniform, or his wedding celebration, to which thousands of guests had been invited. Whatever the occasion, his frank and primitive childishness permitted him to wade through blood without losing a whit of his chubby, complacent epicureanism. All the other killers were visibly nervous, but Goering beamed with pleasure because now no one could contest his claim to being 'Iron Hermann.' His competitors, Roehm and Strasser, were dead; Goering was so delighted by this fact that he did not even reflect that he was the murderer.

We have somewhat anticipated in our description of events, and have left the German people in ignorance of all that had happened. The only public references had been brief official communiqués announcing that Lutze had been installed as chief of staff and that the

Schleichers and seven mutinous SA leaders had been shot. On Sunday morning Goering's address to the representatives of the press was published. But twelve hours passed before Joseph Goebbels stepped before the microphone. His was the task of revealing the details of the 'action.' Goebbels launched into an heroic tale of epic proportions, but in spite of the dramatic material at his command, his tale fell flat. The lies he concocted this time were unusually feeble.

When we examine it closely, we find that the description of the *Putsch* given by Hitler's propaganda minister is a tissue of contradictions. On the one hand he lauded the Fuehrer's foresight. Hitler had known all about it in advance, and at the proper moment he took steps. 'In a brief period of unimaginable nervous tension and incredible physical strain, by resolute, courageous, and hard-hitting deeds,' he provided his nation with 'a shining example of energy and loyalty.' Loyalty, no less! Goebbels went on to describe how Hitler had been visiting Essen and how he had inspected the labor camps in West Germany 'in order to present an outward impression of absolute calm and to give no warning to the traitors.' On the other hand, the plan 'for a thorough purge was worked out.' The Fuehrer personally directed the accomplishment of the purge.

Strangely enough, the chief conspirators appeared to have slept through their dangerous uprising. As Goebbels described it, these mutineers were slumbering peacefully in their beds when they were arrested at seven o'clock in the morning at their headquarters in Wiessee. Roehm, still sleepy, 'submitted to arrest without a word and offered no resistance.' 'In Heines's room, directly across from Roehm's, a shameless sight was to be seen. Heines lay in bed with a homosexual boy. The repulsive scene which took place when Heines and his boy were arrested cannot be described.'

But the whole business was not at all a matter of a lightning surprise assault. According to Goebbels's story, Wagner, Bavarian minister of the interior, had on his own initiative deprived Group Leaders Schneidhuber and Schmidt of Munich of their command over the SA. He did so after the SA formations 'had been convoked that night by their top leaders, who had issued the mendacious slogan: "The

Fuehrer is against us! The Reichswehr is against us! Into the streets!" ' Wagner heard about it, went to the spot and brusquely told the SA men to go home. And these vicious rebels, strangely enough, obeyed the command without a word of protest.

Schneidhuber and Schmidt were, of course, arrested. From Goebbels we heard for the first time that the Fuehrer was personally present at their arrest. 'The Fuehrer had them brought before him and personally ripped the epaulettes from their SA uniforms.' The question remains: What in the world were these conspirators and all their accomplices doing from midnight until dawn? It would seem as if they had sat over their mugs of beer while their troops were quietly sent home. Nor did it occur to any of them to warn their commander-in-chief in Wiessee, scarcely an hour's ride by car from Munich, that the game was up. All in all it seemed to have been a badly bungled uprising.

The rest of Goebbels's speech was equally disappointing. He did not give any indication of how many persons had been arrested or shot, although this was precisely what everyone was waiting breathlessly to hear from some official source. Nor did he even name names. On the other hand, he elaborated on some aspects which he would have done better to play down. For example, he recounted how 'a number of the SA leaders who took part in the mutiny were haled out of their trains at the main railroad station at Munich!' Armed conspirators quietly preparing for their revolt by sitting in the club car of their trains and walking into the arms of the police on their arrival are rare indeed. During such desperate undertakings the plotters are usually to be found at the head of their troops.

That Sunday night the news of Roehm's shooting was finally released. Why, we wondered, had the fact been concealed for an entire day? The only explanation we could find was that the murderers had to overcome a certain amount of embarrassment and guilt. Were they recalling all the many pledges of friendship and comradeship that had been exchanged between Hitler and Roehm? Had someone happened to remind them of Hitler's New Year's greeting to Roehm?

How unfortunate it was that this little note could not have been burned in the crematorium, along with Roehm's body! In the interest of historical irony we must quote it:

> At the close of this first year of the National Socialist Revolution I feel moved, my dear Ernst Roehm, to thank you for the lasting services you have rendered to the National Socialist Movement and to the German people. I wish to assure you of how grateful I am to destiny that I may call such men as yourself my friends and companions in struggle. In cordial friendship and grateful appreciation I remain,
>
> Yours
>
> Adolf Hitler

On the Fuehrer's orders the last shots were fired on the morning of July 2 at seven o'clock. One of the most horrifying dramas in modern history was over. The curtain fell — an iron curtain behind which the actors hid themselves from the amazed audience.

Shortly after I settled down in my office on Monday morning, the official in charge of the police radio system came to see me. He handed me a message which did not actually concern us; it was a note sent up to the ministry of the interior by mistake. The message read:

> From the Prussian minister-president and the chief of the secret state police [Gestapo].
>
> To all subordinate police stations: All documents concerning the action of the last two days are to be burned, on orders from above. A report on the execution of this order is to be made at once.

The police official looked inquiringly at me. 'Are we also to burn all our teletype messages?' In his hand he held a sheaf of small white slips of paper. 'Of course, they must be destroyed at once,' I replied. I rudely snatched the bundle of notes out of his hand.

As soon as he was out of the door, I locked them in my safe.

AFTERMATH

A WORD BY WAY OF POSTSCRIPT as to the position of the army after June 30.

Hitler alleged that by his action he intended to 'depoliticalize' the army. The generals were foolish enough to believe him. They dreamed of a glorious future in which they would be permitted to build up their army without interference from the Nazi Party. Hitler, of course, had no intention of permitting them to do this. He simply went about the business of achieving control of the army more skillfully than the blunt Roehm had done. For Hitler understood how the gold-braided Prussians had to be treated. The generals were still powerful. For this reason Hitler considered it necessary to enter the war ministry by the back door, rather than to take it by frontal assault, as Roehm had wished to do.

Hitler knew very well what Roehm wanted. That was precisely why it took him so long to make up his mind to stop Roehm. For his friend was really trying to fulfill his Fuehrer's innermost wishes. Roehm wanted a people's army. So did Hitler. Roehm wanted to get the reactionary generals under his thumb. So did Hitler. Roehm demanded that the soldiers think and act in a far more brutal fashion than that to which they had been trained. That was Hitler's desire, too. Roehm was contemptuous of the bureaucracy; he made fun of the economists and wanted to put the Nazi Party above the state. All these aims undoubtedly were in greater harmony with Hitler's than were Goering's aims.

And in point of fact, almost as soon as Roehm was dead, Hitler proclaimed that the Party was in command of the state. A few months later he took the venturesome step of creating a people's army. And a short time after that he smashed the generals' idea of a relatively small but efficient professional army. He inflated the army to such an extent that it became, as a vast mass of humanity, automatically a section of the Revolutionary Party. From that time on, Hitler went on announcing for years, with a perfectly straight face, that in the whole nation the army was 'the sole bearer of arms.' But at the same time Himmler's forces were excepted. Less than four years later, Himmler was in command of several well-equipped SS army corps. Thus, with the help of the SS the army put an end to its rival, the SA — only to find that it had nurtured the SS killers who were to strangle it.

For it must be remembered that the leadership of the army had contributed a great deal, behind the scenes, to the slaughter of the SA. The army leaders had incited Goering and Himmler to act. They had repeatedly urged Hitler to do something about Roehm's janissaries. But when the time came for action, they did nothing. They remained passive and did not seize the unique opportunity to influence German affairs in an evolutionary direction. When the collision occurred, they began to fear their own courage.

Blomberg was naïve, Reichenau crafty, and both conceived of themselves as miniature Machiavellis. A year afterward Reichenau, with folded arms and a significant raising of the eyebrows, told me confidentially that it had really not been a simple matter to 'work' things on June 30 so that the affair presented the surface appearance of a 'pure Party matter.' He made this admission to me because I had wandered into his office in the mistaken hope that the men in the war ministry would come to a timely realization of how dangerous Himmler and his Gestapo were. At the time I merely looked dumbfoundedly at him; I had not dreamed I should ever encounter so much political craftiness on the part of any member of the war ministry. Now, of course, I know very well what part he played in reality. He never was more than a pawn upon the political chessboard. In the long view, the army gained nothing at all on June 30. And in human terms the leaders of that army lost everything overnight. By their silence before the fact of rampant lawlessness they became accomplices to the butchery.

5

Bloodless Revolution

THE 'RESPECTABLE' REVOLUTION

A MONG ALL THE TURBULENT YEARS through which we have
passed I have always felt that 1936 and 1937 were the worst.
Throughout 1933 and 1934 the impetus of the Revolution still held.
Events followed one another in rapid succession; everything was in
flux; people were in a state of continuous excitement. Before the
eyes of all of us there were enacted tragedies and farces such as our
fathers and grandfathers would never have thought possible. Even
the daily newspapers, in spite of their thorough Nazification, supplied
enough valid information to keep the soberest of citizens in a state
of tension. Moreover, rumor-mongering flourished. Nobody could say
where the whisperers got their information, but there was always
'something to' their stories. The grapevine circulated news so fast that
not even the most modern rotary presses of the Party publications
could keep pace. Even though foreign newspapers were banned almost
without exception, access to world and German opinion was not yet all
shut off. For the time being the radio remained unhampered by the
Gestapo. Now and then forbidden books or leaflets appeared. They
were read greedily, and the harder the Nazis hunted for such literature,
the more swiftly it changed hands, thus being read by more and more
people. In short, whether activated by official or unofficial propaganda,
by radio or rumors, the overstimulated imaginations of the people
were busy continually.

This state of mass excitement lasted through 1935. It can best be measured by the frequent 'agitational speeches' and 'press campaigns' which the Party conducted for the purpose of converting grumbling or recalcitrant sections of the nation. In the course of these campaigns Joseph Goebbels occasionally had a new idea — not new in terms of content, of course, for since the seizure of power he had carefully suppressed anything like a new intellectual concept — but new in the method of presentation.

For example, it was during these two years that the full possibilities of political pornography were first recognized. Those were the halcyon days of Julius Streicher. The majority of the people turned away in disgust from the creations of the Streicher clique; the stories were too obviously the effluvia of sick brains. But how could such 'literature' be kept out of the family when the children brought this enlightened reading matter home from their social evenings at the Hitler Youth Organization? Here was another instance of the total cynicism of the Nazis. In 1933 they had conducted a 'campaign against filth and literary trash' and had wiped out that whole class of innocent popular literature which dealt with the adventures of Sioux Indians and master detectives. Now they replaced it with worse trash in which the chief rôles were played by lascivious Jews and immoral nuns. In 1935 the Party encouraged teachers to set their classes themes based on the obscene headlines in the *Stuermer*.

By 1936 the storm had abated somewhat. Dullness and a dulled acceptance of existing conditions followed. The Movement ceased to be a violent current sweeping everything along with it. Since the last dikes had been broken through, the waters had spread out a great distance. But they no longer dug such deep channels. They poured out over the countryside and sank into the ground, and gradually the whole land was turned into a morass. In time every group, every branch of culture and economy was invaded by the Party. But there was no longer any real drive. After 1935 it was no longer the force of conversion that won battles. Violent Nazification no longer took place. Force of habit proved sufficient to hold the fort. It is a familiar psychological process. People simply got used to the new régime. The new songs and oaths became common property. No one thought anything of it when he raised his hand in the Hitler salute and murmured his obligatory 'Heil.'

In the social realm as well the gears began to mesh. The thugs put on more resplendent uniforms; the professional revolutionaries manicured their fingernails. On the other hand, so-called 'good society' proved eager enough to accept the brash intruders. In the first place it was good life insurance, and in the second place it was good business. Mutual compliments were the order of the day. The revolutionaries remarked that they had never expected society to be so pleasant and easy-going. The remnants of past society marveled at the good taste and good manners of the new rulers.

This change in attitude was not restricted solely to Germans. Even skeptical foreigners decided that it was time to take these Nazi intruders seriously. François Poncet, unquestionably the greatest cynic among the foreign diplomats, continued to produce his incisive *bon mots*. Nevertheless, his feelings about the Nazis became more temperate, and in time he even came to like the targets of his mockery. He began using to the full his gift for brilliant reporting to cloak the fact of revolution. The other diplomats accredited to Hitler's government also became accustomed to the quieter note of the times.

The British in particular became thoroughly tired of their ambassador's attitude of everlasting disapproval. Since the city of London no longer wanted to hear the word 'revolution,' Sir Nevile Henderson was sent to the city of Berlin. For the longest time he chivalrously repaid the courtesy with which he was taken into German society by taking no notice of the subterranean currents. His business was to make peace with the Revolution, but he preferred not even to acknowledge that anything like a revolution was taking place. His book, *Failure of a Mission*, is sad testimony to this. It testified, moreover, not only to Henderson's own political stupidity, but to that alarming attitude which was becoming universal.

People were simply sick and tired of staring revolution in the face. Instead of recognizing the historical inevitability they preferred to escape to an ivory tower of historical philosophy, a philosophy of the 'As if.' They and their governments pretended that the Terror now lay in the past, and that the longed-for lasting peace and comfortable life were at last beginning. Since they were neither willing nor able to combat the Revolution, they pretended that it was already over.

What was taking place at that time in Germany and the world was an historical process as uncanny as it is familiar. All those who bore any political responsibility closed their eyes. The Revolution, be it noted, did not fall asleep, but it put to sleep everyone who stepped into its magic circle.

In their political content the years 1936 and 1937 may perhaps best be compared with the most flourishing years of the Weimar Republic, the years 1924 to 1929. By that time the immediate shock of the inflation was over. The abortive uprisings of 1923 had resulted in the collapse of the Right and Left Oppositions. Ample funds from abroad poured into the country and this money brought with it a security and calm. The people craved peace of mind above all, but they were eager to work hard. Everybody was enjoying a sham prosperity. Everybody was borrowing money from everybody else without giving thought to the evil day of repayment.

In those days a person who raised his voice in criticism was not, to be sure, shipped off to the concentration camp, nor was he removed from office. Nevertheless, he was ostracized by the democratic forces. How dare anyone indulge in such 'negative oppositionalism'! Things were 'working out,' weren't they?

Things were 'working out' in the same way in 1936 and 1937. Naturally the people grumbled now and then. Weren't the Nazis going too far? Why wouldn't they let the churches alone? Must they go on forever torturing the Jews? Wasn't the government wasting too much money? Were all those huge new buildings necessary? Did every top bureaucrat have to have two palaces rather than one? Were cannon really more important than butter? Above all, did the Nazis have to chalk up a new coup in foreign policy every single year? Those were but a few of the questions that troubled the minds of the people.

At the same time all such objections were raised in the general

atmosphere of joviality and optimism. People asked them only because they wanted to throw a bone to their own consciences. It was
just as well, they felt, not to appear altogether taken in; the times
were so uneven that no one could say definitely how it all might
ultimately end. Nevertheless, there was no sense in being excessively
gloomy. After all, you couldn't really 'do' anything about it. You
might just as well swallow the situation whole, without troubling
your head too much about it. After all, things were working out.
Hitler 'was simply lucky.' It was 'going to last at least fifty years.'

In point of fact I often found it necessary to ask myself during those
two years whether things were not working out, after all. For Hitler
was daily demonstrating that, in spite of the wildest financial experiments and the most perilous adventures in foreign politics, as well as
the gravest signs of inner disintegration, the régime could be maintained for an amazingly long time by force and violence alone. The
elasticity of an economy, an administration, and of the mental and
physical constitution of a nation is almost inconceivable. It can be
strained to the utmost for years on end before it will break.

We know now, of course, after the fact, that Germany and Europe
could not have survived forever under the burden that Hitler imposed.
We have learned that in the political realm abuses are all ultimately
punished. But it takes extraordinarily long for the breach to become
apparent. As long as dictatorships can produce 'successes' and conceal
abuses, they remain armored against opposition. The masses will not
desert them. The hangover does not begin until the financial or
economic crisis can no longer be averted, or when a lost war leaves
behind nothing but a heap of ruins. But by then it is usually too late.
The dictators vanish and the people must pay the bill.

Throughout 1936 and 1937 Hitler's technique of letting situations
mature once more proved successful. He continually avoided publishing his decisions until all opportunity for debate was over and there
remained nothing for anyone to do but to sanction a *fait accompli.*
Such, for example, were his tactics when he appointed Himmler as
chief of all the police forces in 1936, or when he removed Schacht

from the ministry of economy in 1937. Both events were of the type calculated to stun the public. But they did not take place overnight. The nation was prepared for the changes for months in advance. When they finally took place, they were looked upon as little more than purely administrative measures and not as fundamental realignments. For these two events were in fact profoundly significant; they foreshadowed the whole of the future development. Himmler was now able to extend his reign of terror unopposed; and simultaneously, in the economic sphere, all economic brakes were removed. There was now no longer anything or anyone to prevent a precipitate plunge into a collectivistic economy.

Although 1936 and 1937 were the quiet years of the Revolution, they contained many portents of more painful days to come. During those years the inevitable crisis was preparing which was to terminate in the catastrophe of war. Could that catastrophe have been averted? We must definitely answer: Yes. But to avert it those who still had power to stop the Revolution had to summon up the requisite understanding and resolution. Those people were the military leaders, the generals.

But the generals did not want to do anything. And that indifference was to my mind the most discouraging feature of those years of habituation. Instead of resisting in time, the generals let themselves be pushed step by step toward the precipice. Though they themselves were not active members of the Nazi Party, and were in fact either suspicious of or hostile toward the Party, their very passivity supplied the Nazis with a tremendous momentum.

I can best demonstrate this by continuing the story of my pilgrimage through the Third Reich in the period after June 30, 1934. I had opportunity to observe from many sides how the forces of revolution and evolution were heading for an inevitable collision. For years, however, it was possible to hope that when the clash came, the Black gangsters would be beaten back before they were able to seize all the crucial posts.

For the time being I remained in the Reich ministry of the interior. In addition to my ordinary work I was charged with the task of closing the books on the events of June 30. Significantly enough, even the oldest Nazi Party members were unwilling to touch this extremely delicate material. The innumerable petitions, inquiries, disputes with life insurance companies, and demands for compensation — all consequences of the mass killings of June 30 — were embarrassing to everyone, and dangerous as well. But I felt that such shameful documents were, under the circumstances, more useful in my hands than in the wastebaskets at Gestapo headquarters. Although, unfortunately, my chief function consisted in filing away these pitiful pleas for help, I felt that eventually they might be of use to historians of the Hitler millennium. As a matter of fact, they remained safe for some ten years, but ultimately they fell into the hands of the Gestapo — after the thorough raids that followed the attempted assassination of Hitler on July 20, 1944.

It would undoubtedly lead too far afield were I to discuss the history of the Gestapo in detail, the story, that is, of how this greedy Moloch grew to its later dimensions. For the Gestapo, too, did not spring full-blown into being. It would be worth devoting a special study to the problem of how much blind confidence and leniency, how many innocent legal paragraphs, organizational rulings, and budgetary appropriations went into the nurturing of such a bureaucratic monster.

But I must emphasize once more that up to 1936, in contrast to the later years of the dictatorship, no unified federal police power existed. Police power rested primarily with the separate states. The federal minister of the interior could make requests to the states, but he had no real control over the execution of his orders. In practice Frick was dependent upon the good will of the various satraps, most of whom enjoyed greater favor at the chancellery than did Frick himself.

Right at the start of the Nazi régime an internal struggle raged over who was to exercise the chief police power. There was no doubt that whoever eventually won would occupy a decisive position. By April, 1934, Goering was out of the running. From then on, his only hope was that he might regain his lost influence over the war ministry. Himmler pursued his goal with cold-blooded tenacity. Undoubtedly he alone among his rivals perceived clearly what vast possibilities were open to him. But Frick still stood in his way. Stubbornly Frick blocked his young rival from entering the ministry of the interior. And Hitler looked on with spiteful satisfaction, for the Fuehrer never permitted any one of his underlings to taste the temptations of too much power. Whenever two of his men fought, his own strength was reinforced.

There are few things that can be said in Himmler's favor. But he must be given credit for one quality: he was a sly fox, never at a loss to find roundabout ways where the direct path was blocked. If he did not succeed at once in accomplishing his whole purpose, he bided his time, but eventually he reached his goal. If Hitler would not make him minister of police, Himmler simply gathered up the strings of police power that were in the hands of the myriad little Hitlers.

After he had taken the leap from Bavaria to the Prinz Albrecht-strasse, Himmler literally set out to conquer the villages. He traveled to Lippe, Anhalt, Oldenburg, Hesse, Braunschweig, Mecklenburg; he visited all the tiniest provincial governments that boasted a relative independence. After a snappy SS parade he would return to his head-quarters with a new title, that of 'political police commander' of the place in question.

This title was a new acquisition not only for Himmler; it was wholly without precedent. Equally novel, in so far as the law was concerned, were the powers that the SS leader arrogated to himself. It was the business of the Reich minister of the interior to lay down the general principles governing the activities of the political police. The various provincial ministries were responsible for carrying out these instructions. There was no place for Himmler in this system — officially. But what could Frick do? He would be opposing the general program of Nazi centralization if he declared that Himmler, as a Bavarian, had no business operating in the various provincial centers. And in any case Himmler repeatedly gave assurance that he had no intention of acting on his own; he intended, he claimed, merely to carry out the orders of the provincial governments. And these, after all, were subordinate to the minister of the interior.

The significance of this procedure can be understood fully only by those who lived in Germany during those times. It will scarcely be believed today, but Germany was still something of a constitutional state. The Gestapo Terror did not rage unchecked. Now and then the Reich minister of the interior could right a wrong. More often than is generally realized he could save persons or organizations from harm. This came about from the fact that such matters as bans on newspapers, the dissolution of clubs, and changes in the regulations regarding 'protective custody' were federal concerns. Consequently, if Himmler wished to organize some large-scale affair, such as a general raid against Jews, Freemasons, or the Church, he had to get in touch with Frick beforehand. There existed certain enclaves in the midst of the Black Terror, to which the persecuted could flee. Himmler's powers were largely local. More than once, clever 'enemies of the state' were able to put this peculiar sort of extraterritoriality to good use. Himmler distinctly did not like to make any requests of Frick; he would rather abandon temporarily whatever unpleasant business he had in mind.

On the other hand, Frick was hesitant about engaging in disputes with the local state governments once those authorities had acted. The technique of the *fait accompli* was as prevalent in Nazi domestic affairs as it was in foreign politics. For example, if the Gestapo in Bavaria had issued a highly questionable decree, a good deal of tugging back and forth was necessary before it could be rescinded. The side that had the most perseverance generally won, and the Black Gestapists were incontestably experts at playing 'possum when faced with annoying inquiries. Consequently, if Himmler succeeded in having the majority of the states adopt the same measure simultaneously, Frick would generally overlook it. Formally speaking, Frick had a right to protest to the Fuehrer. But in practice Himmler had the greater weight on his side and could simply file away the complaints from the Reich ministry of the interior.

Frick sat idle for a while and merely watched this struggle. He sat idle too long; by the time he had decided to act, Himmler had conquered half the German states. Then Frick forbade all further raids for the time being. He instructed the state governments that in the future no new appointments could be made without his consent. As minister of the interior he was empowered to do this.

In the guerrilla warfare between Frick and Himmler that followed this step — a war often fought by the most grotesque means — Himmler emerged the victor. Since Frick would not let him acquire any more government appointments, Himmler abandoned this particular stratagem. Instead he went to the finance ministers of the various states and requested subsidies for his concentration camps. Heretofore, he pointed out, the SS in its great-heartedness had been maintaining these camps out of its own funds. Now they wanted to do something for the inmates, Himmler said; from now on he hoped it would not be necessary to keep the poor fellows under such wretched conditions. It was intended to construct a sanitation system in those institutions which would astound the world. But that took money, of course — lots of it.

If the finance ministers paid up — in compensation they received a share of the income from the confiscated properties of the 'enemies of the state' — Himmler went one step farther. Was it possible, he urged, to guarantee the life and security of the prisoners in protective custody when there were so few guards to watch over them? Obviously not. Himmler did not mention that he reckoned on five SS men to protect every inmate of a concentration camp.

The finance ministers paid — and Himmler built up his Gestapo.

DUEL WITH HEYDRICH

TO THE EXTENT OF MY POWERS I strove to put a check on the growth and prosperity of the Gestapo. In the long run nothing much came of the effort — certainly not nearly so much as I had hoped for throughout the whole of an extremely tense year.

My chief opponent during that time was SS Chief Werner Best, who was later to become the Reich commissioner for Denmark. Best was chief of the organizational section in Heydrich's security service (SD); Best's section was particularly important during the early years of the Nazi régime when he had to dig up funds from somewhere to supply the constantly mounting demand. Moreover, his lord and master, with his diabolically clever understanding of the middle-class state of mind, employed Best wherever it was necessary to pour oil on troubled waters.

Best was always sent forth when the necessity arose of expressing regret for a new wave of arrests or of explaining away one of the multitudinous 'unfortunate accidents' that occurred in the course of the Gestapo's work. In general it was his business to placate aroused bourgeois consciences. Best always pretended to be boiling with rage. Often his eyes filled with crocodile tears of indignation. At each of these visits of condolence he would give vent to a number of mysterious hints to the effect that now the cup was overflowing, now something was really going to be done about it. One day he would claim that Himmler was at last going to take care of Heydrich. Another time Heydrich's overstrained conscience could no longer endure the brutal character of his superior. Or else Himmler and Heydrich together were going to send all of their roughnecks to the gallows. In short, everything would undoubtedly be cleared up once and for all, provided that in this last case you, Herr So-and-So, withdraw that troublesome complaint. When on such occasions Best quite incidentally broke into one of his radiant smiles, no ministerial councilor or army colonel was able to resist such sincerity and goodness of heart.

Up to the very last there were Germans who considered Best a decent fellow, an unfortunate innocent who had fallen in with bad company and now could no longer help himself and must run with the wolves. For my part, I always considered him one of the worst of the crew, precisely because he behaved in a fashion so disarmingly decent. It was Best who composed the notorious Boxheimer document, the first draft of the decrees which later made possible the Reign of Terror.

Naturally, Best also tried to pass on to me his sugar-coated pill. But since I was daily doing my best to warn others against him, he did not get very far. Best resented this. In consequence, after my big row with Heydrich we never saw each other again, although he continued to play the part of a moderate up to the last, so that his name was actually included by some credulous persons in lists they drew up of the potential Opposition.

The blowout which finally ended my relations with Heydrich was due to a puncture precisely where I expected to find my greatest strength and support. The traitor was in the war ministry.

From the very beginning I had realized that Frick and Daluege could be of only limited value in the struggle against the growing Gestapo terrorism. Daluege's only real motive in the matter was his hope of supplanting Himmler. Frick, with his bureaucratic temperament, found himself paralyzed as soon as the Gestapo illegalities were codified into a few dozen new sections of the law. At the same time they were not prepared to give up without any fight at all. The question was, who would be willing or able to lend them some backbone.

In searching for that person or persons I blundered into several wrong berths. I tried the bourgeois ministries, of course. I had entry to Neurath's foreign ministry because the minister daily received at least three diplomatic protests — a foreigner would have been beaten half to death, or illegal smuggling into Austria by the Nazis was going strong, or the Gestapo had instigated another border incident somewhere. I worked on Guertner's ministry of justice as long as my handling of the complicated affairs resulting from June 30 afforded me a pretext. In Schacht's ministry I found that economic raids and plundering expeditions were, refreshingly, called by their proper names. But no other minister would risk teaming up with Schacht on any issue. Wherever I knocked, I found the lower officials in the ministries wringing their hands in despair. But none of the ministers had any serious intention of doing anything. All of them were peering toward the Bendlerstrasse to see whether the army was going to come to their aid.

It was therefore more than an *idée fixe* of my own to feel that the attitudes of Blomberg, Reichenau, Fritsch, and Raeder were crucial. Should the generals pound on the table, Frick was in luck. Unquestionably Hitler would have listened to them. During that first half-year after June 30, Himmler and Heydrich were so insecure and there was such widespread indignation against Heydrich, especially in the highest Party circles, that it would have taken very little to overthrow the Gestapo. The worst of it was that Blomberg could not be moved by moralistic arguments. Murders of Jews, attacks on the churches, physical brutality, arbitrary imprisonment — all these things he considered mere incidentals to the Nazi domestic policies. He was not going to permit any politics at all in Hitler's army.

Consequently, the war minister had to be approached on the basis of *formal* malfeasances; our quarrel had to be represented as a bureaucratic disagreement. This was quite possible, since Blomberg insisted that as a federal minister he would have dealings only with the federal authorities. Thus he got into the habit of discussing all questions pertaining to the political police with Frick. Himmler was left out in the cold. Moreover, once Blomberg began his conversations with Frick about all these delicate matters, one word was likely to lead to another. In a short time the personnel of both ministries began to conduct an exchange of opinions and documents.

Our aim was to put sufficient evidence on Gestapo gangsterism into the hands of the generals. And for a time we succeeded. The material that our indefatigable Oster put on the desks of his superiors, Blomberg and Reichenau, was read by them with avid interest. For a time I was sending virtually every important item that came my way to the war ministry for a twenty-four-hour stay. But the two generals adroitly managed to evade the responsibility of conclusions or decisions; 'officially' they took no notice of all this evidence.

I can best make clear what I was trying to achieve by describing what I was unable to prevent.

Himmler succeeded in persuading Reichenau and Blomberg that, since he already controlled the political police in two thirds of the Reich, they would do better to deal directly with him instead of wasting time by routing their complaints and inquiries through Frick. Naturally Himmler was lavish with assurances of loyal co-operation, and hinted that he and the generals might line up together in a little tug-of-war against the Nazi Party. Promises were cheap!

Himmler won his point. The result of that fateful interview was that Frick, whom the Black gangsters found such a troublesome busybody, was brushed aside. Moreover, by the same stroke the SS solved some of its financial difficulties. In those early years of rearmament the generals were being treated opulently. Money was no object in the Bendlerstrasse. For the sake of smooth collaboration between army and SS, the generals were quite willing to put in a good word for Himmler with the minister of finance. After all, hadn't Himmler demonstrated that he, too, was a lover of order? And the Gestapo, of course, was willing to reward the generals for this assistance by devoting its forces to counter-espionage work.

As the first token of the era of good will, the chief of the *Abwehr* was dismissed. He was replaced by Naval Captain Canaris, a man who was craftier than Himmler and Heydrich put together. He was, Oster whispered hopefully to me, an officer who was absolutely reliable and to whom I could safely talk with entire freedom. Naturally I made it my business to pay him a call as soon as possible — and that was where I came to grief.

Canaris was in fact extremely understanding. From the time of that very first meeting he never abused my confidences. Toward me he always acted more uprightly than I had any right to expect. But I did not know at the time how limited his powers were; his hands were tied by the orders he had been given when he assumed his office. My chief mistake, however, consisted in assuming that the others in his office were of his own complexion; I reckoned without Major Bamler, who was present at our talk and who was a staunch Nazi and a stool pigeon. Bamler felt it incumbent upon him to report my discourse to Heydrich that same day. Heydrich felt that he had heard enough. He called me up, and there was a heated exchange. When we both slammed the receivers down on the hooks, our connection was broken once and for all. But before I reproduce this telephone conversation, I had best say a word or two about my brief personal relationships with this gangster.

Our first meeting was bizarre, as were all my experiences with Heydrich. The campaign against the Freemasons was the fad of the moment, and the Gestapo men had laid it on thick by assembling symbols and ritualistic books from the lodges they had raided. Since I have never been a Freemason, I was unable to tell which of the objects on exhibition were plain forgeries and which, if any, of them were authentic. In any case, no charnel house could have made a more gruesome impression than this jumble of weird sorcerer's materials. According to Heydrich's interpretation, the black arts of the darkest Dark Ages had been nothing but sweetness and light by comparison with present-day Freemasonry.

Somehow, for some reason, I had been invited to attend this chamber of horrors. Perhaps Heydrich had felt that it could not very well be avoided. Or perhaps he hoped that the psychological torture of it would have a certain pedagogic effect upon me.

I was quite grateful for this personal introduction into the Nazi wonderland. In return I tried to be on my best behavior. But when Himmler invited us to his rooms and became involved in a philosophical discussion of his Teutonic cults, it was too much for me. I could not refrain from making a few strong remarks about the 'German Christians.' I made fun of the dogmas they were proclaiming, although this peculiar sort of 'Christianity' was enjoying Nazi protection. The Nazis were interested in pretending, at the time, that they merely desired certain reforms in Christian dogma. The time 'was not yet ripe' for Rosenberg's new mythology.

'The time is not yet ripe' — this was Himmler's own expression, and with that as a justification he characteristically admitted that I was right on every count. Yes, he agreed that the German Christians were all hypocrites or fanatics. And certainly the old Germanic rites they proposed were ridiculous. Yes, that was the whole trouble — the Nazis had not tried to replace the Christian rites by something new. But in one respect I was hopelessly wrong, Himmler continued. I imagined that Christianity could be revived, while in reality that utopian doctrine was as good as done for.

On this question we got into a heated argument. For at this time I was still very young and inexperienced. My mistake lay, not in admitting myself an adherent of the Protestant Church and a friend of Niemoeller — since Himmler knew that anyway — but in thinking that speaking plainly for once would be useful. Since then I have realized that the character of these revolutionaries was such that it was impossible to debate with them.

Heydrich, who took a lively part in the discussion, paced energetically back and forth in the room. He never quite finished making his point, and as we were taking our leave he ran after me to get in a final word. Tapping me on the shoulder he said with a grin: 'Just you wait. You'll see the day, ten years from now, when Adolf Hitler will occupy precisely the same position in Germany that Jesus Christ has now.'

To be candid, the most striking thing about this prophecy was the glad news that according to such an eminent authority I was going to survive the next ten years. However, I soon had reason to doubt whether I could really count on surviving. For the frankness of our first conversation did not necessarily mean that the sword had been sheathed.

I certainly would not make it a rule that the underground Opposition should inform its opponents of its intentions. On the other hand, the last twelve years have taught me that it is necessary to stand by one's opinion frankly and fearlessly from the moment the true state of affairs is recognized by the opponent. Once you have exposed yourself, there is no harm at all in talking out of turn. In fact, by so doing you frequently may disarm your opponent. For another thing, he no longer has to set spies on your heels — which has its advantages under certain circumstances.

A man like Heydrich, who prized the roundabout ways and would commit murder only from ambush, was bewildered by candor. He did not quite know how to defend himself against open opposition. As a result, he sometimes acted against his normal impulses. As far as I was concerned, that is, he let me run loose.

Naturally Heydrich spied on me. He questioned his Gestapo officers, for example, to find out whether 'that reactionary Gisevius' had helped any members of the *Stahlhelm* or other enemies of the state during the few months he worked in the Gestapo. He kept account of how often

I was seen in Niemoeller's church. He sent his spies into the ministry of economy to find out when and in whose company I had visited Schacht. Any decrees of the ministry of the interior on which I had worked were carefully scrutinized, and my telephone conversations were diligently tapped. All the information he gathered he filed away in a dossier. The fact that this evidence was never used while Heydrich was alive is due, in my opinion, to the fact that our hostility was too well known.

This needs some explanation. During the past twelve years there have been so many cases of the Gestapo's torturing its victims to death that a fact of considerable psychological interest has been consistently overlooked. Thousands and even hundreds of thousands of 'enemies of the state' were imprisoned, and most of these unfortunates ended their lives, after fearful torments, in the crematoria of the concentration camps. *For those diabolic institutions were set up for Germans;* it was not until the war began that they were used for foreigners. But after the thirtieth of June we will find scarcely one well-known name among the victims. In the camps it was the nameless heroes who died, the more obscure fighters in the great revolutionary war who had covertly resisted the Nazis or overtly committed sabotage.

The Gestapo had a distinct aversion to doing away with so-called prominent persons. Everyone whose name was fairly well known either was taken care of in 'legal' fashion by the courts or else was plagued with petty persecutions and obstructed in his work until he resigned of his own accord and withdrew. Such well-known 'enemies of the state' were eliminated in a bloodless fashion. They were the victims of a conspiracy of silence; the press was forbidden to mention their names and they were prevented from making any public appearances. Every contact with them was likely to have evil consequences for their rash friends or acquaintances.

As a result, throughout the course of the Nazi régime, members of the Opposition lived on. They would confide privately that they could not understand why they had not been arrested or murdered long ago. The reason for this hands-off policy on the part of Himmler and

Heydrich was the trouble they ran into after June 30. A number of their victims of that date had not been on the official death list as drawn up by Hitler and Goering. Himmler had learned to his dismay that the Fuehrer resented all but the 'legal' murders. The SS chief drew the logical conclusion. News of his various infamies ordinarily would not come to the attention of ministers, generals, or other troublesome inquirers unless the persons in question were well known and important. Consequently, such persons Himmler was content merely to quarantine. This could best be done by arresting, beating, and killing the more obscure members of their followings. This apparent paradox made his reign of terror all the more frightful; it made the behavior of the Gestapo the more wanton, the more inexplicable. Meanwhile, Himmler enjoyed a reputation for generosity and tolerance among the gullible. The proof of this was the fact that he let acknowledged opponents of the Nazi system run around loose.

It was only after July 20, 1944, that Himmler dropped his mask. From then on, the necessity no longer existed to tolerate certain people for the sake of propaganda. Since the Opposition had come out in the open, he could counter it with the frankest sort of terrorism. It was then that he made a clean sweep.

In my conversation with Canaris I had said no more than what I had often told Himmler and Heydrich to their faces: that all matters pertaining to the federal police should be routed through the ministry of the interior and all requests should be made to Frick. But Heydrich was furious because I had tried to sway Canaris my way, when his function was to further a reconciliation and institute collaboration between the war ministry and the Gestapo.

The following day Heydrich's telephone call came to me out of a clear sky. Since I knew nothing of Major Bamler's talebearing, I was amazed when Heydrich ironically declared that he had observed with the greatest interest my 'expedition to the war ministry.' However, I replied composedly that it was a pity that he had not been present, since reports of such conversations were liable to be grave distortions of what was actually said.

That was too much for him. 'I know perfectly well what you're up to and what you're aiming at,' he said. 'You want to be my successor.'

'But my dear Herr Group Leader, you overestimate me. You know quite well that I am not even a member of the Party or the SS.'

'Oh yes, oh yes, I know with whom I'm dealing. I know a great deal more than you suspect. Please take note of the fact that I can see my deadly enemies to the grave.'

'I've never doubted that, Herr Heydrich. But I am extremely grateful to you for your openness. I shall not neglect to inform my minister of it.'

'You can go ahead and do it.'

'I shall go ahead and do it.'

'Thank you.'

'You're welcome.'

I may be mistaken, but I am quite convinced that this brief telephone conversation helped me to survive the next few eventful years. For naturally I at once ran off to Daluege and Frick with the story. Both of them were outraged, and one of them challenged Heydrich. Meanwhile, I took a month's vacation, partly because I cherished the delusion that Heydrich might calm down and partly because I somehow was hoping for 'the miracle' — that Heydrich might die of appendicitis or, still better, that the whole Nazi business would be swept away overnight. I was also curious to see whether, when I returned, I should be admitted to the ministry or handed a transfer.

None of the changes I had imagined took place. There had been no miracle. On the other hand, I had not been banished. Frick seemed determined to hold on to me. But it was obvious that Heydrich was only waiting for his chance to strike. I took the precaution of passing the word around that I expected to be transferred very soon. I wanted Heydrich to feel that I wasn't worth battling about. But Heydrich did not fall for this bait. He continued hectoring Frick.

I was unseated at last when, on my suggestion, Frick prepared to take energetic action on the question of 'protective custody.' I considered this question a favorable starting-point from which to attack the Gestapo on a 'legal' basis. If we could succeed in depriving the Gestapo of the right to arrest without any judicial check, we should be removing one of its most venomous fangs.

In the spring of 1935 there were still a good many ministers and officials who felt that the whole apparatus of justice had been unhinged and that a strong attempt must be made to bring order to the absolutist and arbitrary state of affairs. With this in mind, a new law was drafted. It decreed the right of prisoners in protective custody to make complaints to the courts and provided for subordination of the local branches of the Gestapo to the local governors.

At the last moment Frick lost his nerve. He could not quite bring himself to take the initiative, and turned to Goering. He asked Goering to set a good example by beginning in Prussia. Goering placed the law on the agenda of the Prussian ministerial council. Himmler was invited to attend the cabinet meeting at which the law was to be discussed. This, by the way, was quite unusual — Heinrich Himmler possessed very little influence at that time!

Himmler came to the meeting in a fury. A few days before, he had received a strongly worded communication from Frick, which I had drafted. I had cited a particularly crass example on which to hang a discussion of the whole problem of protective custody.

The case concerned a lawyer who had been arrested for acting in behalf of the widow of former Ministerial Director Klausener, one of the 'suicides' of June 30. His widow had tried to collect payment on his insurance policies, which amounted to declaring that her husband's suicide had been involuntary, I went to a great deal of trouble to illuminate every imaginable aspect of the unfortunate lawyer's case; and I did not omit from my discussion the SS squad, without whose visit Klausener would probably have bethought himself twice before ending his own life.

This document was not sent directly to Himmler, but was transmitted to him through the chancellery. Frick hoped that so bald an example of the Gestapo's shamelessness would make an impression upon Hitler. Naturally Himmler was infuriated. He was particularly offended by the ironical tone of my little paper. He had promptly

gone off to a meeting of the *Reichsleiter* and read the document aloud.
Were such expressions customary in correspondence between high
Party officials? he demanded. The noble company all agreed that they
were not, and Frick was reproved. Encouraged by this support,
Himmler decided to push his advantage. He would not consent to
the proposed law unless I were removed from the ministry of the
interior.

At the cabinet meeting there was a good deal of angry bickering.
Goering also voiced strong objections to me, whereupon Frick innocently pointed out that he had not taken me into his ministry originally, but had simply inherited me from Goering himself. As in all
such dealings among ministers, nothing concrete came of all the
discussion. The law against protective custody was not adopted, and
I was not dismissed.

While this ministerial council was going on, I sat all unsuspecting in
my office. It was from Herbert Goering, who worked as an assistant
in the ministry of economics, that I finally heard the story. Herbert
Goering was a good and helpful friend to me during all those difficult
years. He bore up well under the curse of being a cousin to 'Iron
Hermann.' Never a Nazi — although Himmler 'honored' him with
an SS uniform in 1933 — he skillfully worked to keep his family out
of the coming catastrophe. He proved particularly loyal toward
Schacht. When the majority of our captains of industry capitulated in
fear and trembling to Hermann Goering, the new star, the director of
'Four-Year Plan,' Herbert did not desert Schacht, whom Hitler already
held under suspicion and whom Himmler was persecuting.

It was to Herbert Goering that I owed my first meeting with
Schacht. In the fall of 1934, shortly after Schacht had taken over
the ministry of economics, Herbert visited me one morning on urgent
business. Schacht and Himmler were about as friendly as cat and dog.
Schacht made no effort to restrain his sharp tongue, and naturally his
remarks came to the ears of the Gestapo. Himmler, of course, resolved
to take revenge and began gathering evidence against his opponent.
Schacht was afraid that the Gestapo might have placed a microphone

in his home in order to record even the remarks he made to his family circle. Since I had in time become something of an expert on Gestapo techniques and was frequently consulted in such matters, he sent Herbert Goering to me to find out whether and how he could cover himself.

The next day I reported at the home of Hitler's minister of economics, accompanied by a microphone expert whom I had borrowed from the federal postal administration. We went through the whole apartment, room by room, Schacht adding spice to our work by his sardonic comments on contemporary history. And, in fact, we found a good deal more than we were looking for. The Gestapo in its thoroughness had not only built a microphone into the telephone, but had also employed one of the servants as a spy to watch over all the habits of this minister who was considered an enemy of the state. The servant had been so lazy that she had simply plumped down the listening apparatus in her own room, where it was discovered quite easily.

In the brief discussion that Schacht and I had at this first meeting, our fundamental differences came to light. We disagreed in our judgment of what program should be followed by the bourgeois Opposition. I argued that if an economic crisis, with a consequent political crisis, were inevitable, the proper tactic would be to bring the crisis about as swiftly and deliberately as possible. 'Start the inflation yourself; then you will at least have the initiative. Then it will be you and not the others who set the time of the collapse, and therefore you and the generals will be able to take the necessary steps before you find that the reins have quite slipped out of your hands.' I remember vividly what Schacht answered: 'The difference between us is that you really desire the disaster and I do not want it.'

At that time Schacht was still firmly convinced that he, in conjunction with Neurath, Guertner, Schwerin, and Seldte, could win over War Minister Blomberg and impose a more moderate program. It was not until the Fritsch crisis that he realized how mistaken he was.

But to return to my personal affairs. Herbert Goering dropped in to see me and told me that Schacht had just come from a meeting of the Prussian ministerial council. There had been an unpleasant debate about me, he said, but the matter had not turned out too badly. Schacht wished to congratulate me on my transfer to the provinces in the capacity of a sub-prefect.

I was somewhat disconcerted. Although Herbert Goering and Schacht apparently regarded this appointment as a promotion, which technically it was, I had an idea that it was nothing of the kind. Frick and Daluege agreed with me; they suggested that it was high time I disappeared.

The question was, Where was I to go? If I left government service and became one of the anonymous masses, I should no longer have any defense against Heydrich's killers. At the same time, to submit to my transfer to the provinces under such poor auspices seemed a highly dangerous thing to do. I therefore worked out, in collaboration with Nebe, a plan whereby I should be transferred to the Prussian criminal office. This office was at that time still a section of the Berlin police department.

The Berlin chief of police, Admiral von Levetzow, was friendly to me and agreed. But no sooner had my transfer gone through than he was removed from his office and replaced by Count Helldorf. The meaning of this was clear: the police department, which had long been condemned as bureaucratic and reactionary, was going to be thoroughly Nazified.

Helldorf at once received a request from the Berlin *Gauleitung* of the Party to dismiss me. But luck was on my side. Daluege talked with Helldorf and pointed out that under the existing conditions to transfer me to the provinces would be the equivalent of a death sentence. It was absolutely necessary, for the time being, for me to remain under the eyes of the ministry. Helldorf agreed. This decision may have been made easier for him because, as a member of the SA, he was bitterly hostile to Himmler's and Heydrich's ambitions. But whatever his reasons, I am eternally grateful to him for his behavior. Had Helldorf been stubborn about the matter, it would have been all up with me.

My new job had unexpectedly favorable aspects. On the one hand,

Helldorf took the view that I was still a member of the ministry of the interior and had merely been assigned an office in the police department (my ostensible task was to work on the plans for a federal criminal office). On the other hand, the ministry of the interior insisted that I was no longer a member of its organization, and that Helldorf was my sole superior. The advantage of this for me was that for a time no one paid any attention at all to me.

Some months passed in this serene fashion. Then, early in January, 1936, Helldorf sent for me. The Olympic Games were soon to begin. An independent command of the Berlin police was to be set up, and Helldorf was thinking of me to head this squad. It sounded like a tempting and interesting occupation. The Nazis had dedicated their entire foreign policy to winning over foreign nations, and these Olympic Games were to be a gigantic propaganda campaign. Since things were quiet, I could well hope that this new assignment might provide me with excellent camouflage for the next half-year.

But I was sadly mistaken; my troubles were about to begin again.

I suggested to Helldorf that we go to Garmisch for the Winter Olympics in order to make preliminary studies of the police problems we should encounter. This was little more than a pretext, for of course the techniques of international pickpockets could be studied much more intelligently in Berlin, and the traffic on the tiny streets of Garmisch provided no parallel to the traffic problems we should encounter in Berlin. But I simply wanted to go.

This competition among the athletes of the whole world was as brilliant as any I had ever attended. But it was difficult for me to enjoy the sports. The Nazis had always been expert at conducting celebrations — and unfortunately there were many foreigners who saw only the amazingly efficient organization, the pomp and circumstance, the splendid illumination. They allowed themselves to be deceived as to the true nature of the Third Reich. If only they had looked a little more sharply behind the façade! Garmisch was not far from Dachau!

But most of the visitors wanted to see only the pleasant side of the picture. Many of them returned home 'converted.' It was quite infuriating to read their enthusiastic writings, in which they blithely corroborated the claim of the dictators that the Nazis were behaving in a very mannerly fashion; that in Germany — in contrast to the democratic nations — 'order' prevailed and that they had nowhere found any evidence of an Opposition. As if the Nazis would have let the world see the invisible Germany!

It had not occurred to me that Heydrich would also be wanting to enjoy the winter air. Naturally he noticed me at once, and the fierce glance he shot at me boded ill. Even before I returned to Berlin, he had written a letter to Helldorf.

Berlin, February 17, 1936

Dear Count Helldorf:

I have learned that Government Councilor Gisevius of the criminal police office has been charged with certain tasks under your direction with regard to police preparations for the Olympic Games. I consider it necessary to call your attention to the fact that Gisevius, during his term of office in the federal and Prussian ministry of the interior, continually interfered with the work of the secret state police [Gestapo], so that the relationship between him and us was a most unpleasant one. I fear that his participation in police preparations for the Olympic Games would certainly not promote collaboration with the secret state police at this time, and I therefore ask you to consider whether Gisevius cannot be replaced by some other suitable official.

Heil Hitler!

Yours

HEYDRICH

Helldorf sent for me at once and handed this letter to me. He was somewhat disturbed, for he had no wish to quarrel with Heydrich on my account. Nebe, too, who was invited to confer with us, looked worried. Both of them felt that matter was very grave. However, I pretended nonchalance and declared to Helldorf that I considered this letter the greatest distinction I had received in my whole official career.

My hour had struck in any case. In April, 1936, Himmler reached his goal: Hitler appointed him chief of all the police forces in Germany. That same day a letter from the ministry of the interior arrived dismissing me from the police department.

BANISHMENT

IT WAS NOT EASY to find another refuge. Everyone was very pleasant, but all doors remained closed. For a short time I considered quitting government service altogether, but it appeared extremely inadvisable. Only by remaining in the service could I continue my efforts. At that time I still hoped that some day the generals would launch a decisive blow against the Gestapo. Until then, to belong to government service provided a certain amount of insurance against my being quietly liquidated. Superiors tend to take note of it when one of their subordinates doesn't show up for work some day. If he remains away two whole days without some excuse, they inquire about his health. Consequently, news of my arrest would have got around. It would have been reported to the ministry, and the ministry might very well have asked the Gestapo where I was. If I judged Heydrich aright, he was eager to avoid any kind of stir. Therefore, for good or ill, I decided to remain in the ministry and risk being banished to the provinces.

After prolonged debate I was finally assigned to the government in Muenster, Westphalia. I did not consider this so bad, since I was already acquainted there with a sympathetic person, *Oberpraesident* Ferdinand Freiherrn von Luenink, with whom I had had more than one heretical conversation. I had known this clever and distinguished man for many years and knew that he would help me to the best of his ability.

A devout Catholic, Luenink was an 'anti' through and through. However, he foresaw that the Nazis would go on ruling for a long time because he correctly recognized from the start the passivity of the Western Powers. For this reason Luenink, former chairman of the Westphalian chamber of agriculture, felt that he owed it to the peasants of his province to stay at his post as long as possible. A good administrator could help his people a great deal in the small difficulties of ordinary living; he was in a position to protect them against all sorts of chicanery. I know many cases where such magistrates and mayors were literally implored, on behalf of this really good cause, to make the sacrifice of joining the Party. It would be a bitter injustice to make these people pay for their Nazi Party membership. In any case, most of them were dismissed or transferred for being untrustworthy after a year or two of public activity.

Luenink was such a case. Although he might well have retired to his estate, he held on. He did not retreat before the Brown onslaught until 1938. In all probability he was able to remain so long only because there were three district leaders quarreling for his post in the province of Westphalia. After his retirement he went on being as active as possible. He kept in close touch with the Resistance Movement until, after July 20, 1944, he suffered the tragic fate of so many sincere men. Fearless and loyal to the last, he died on the gallows.

On this first journey into the unknown, my partner in the sleeping compartment of the train proved to be one of the cleverest district leaders Hitler had ever had. He was Erich Koch, satrap of East Prussia and later of the Ukraine. Koch was really a devil of a fellow. A first-rate demagogue, a bold adventurer, at home in the highest and the lowest walks of life, he towered above his fellow leaders. He had a vigorous imagination and was always ready to pass on — in whispers and under the seal of absolute secrecy — utterly fantastic stories.

He had established the Erich Koch Institute and cheerfully watered the stock again and again, whenever he needed money for his palaces or similar amusements. And there was the Indian maharajah whom Koch was trying to persuade to place his legendary treasures in gold at the disposal of the Reichsbank, at no interest. And there was that air cavalcade shortly before Mussolini's invasion of Abyssinia which was to bring the diamonds of the Negus 'home to the Reich.' Koch befriended dozens of equivocal persons. There was the alchemist escaped from prison who was permitted to drum up support for his project of making gold; the man set up shop in Koenigsberg, the seat of Koch's domain. There was the notorious swindler who went about selling shares in the alluring 'island in the Amazon River.' There were the Rumanian Jews with whom the anti-Semitic *Gauleiter* conducted peculiar transactions in grain. Much to the annoyance of his bitter enemy, Darré, minister of food, Koch paid for the grain several times over. And then there was that horde of bankrupt entrepreneurs, pathetic inventors, and insolent plunderers who operated under Koch's protection and smuggled the most fantastic industrial projects into the official program of the Four-Year Plan.

To some extent even Koch's most harebrained schemes were based on a shrewd insight into the character of his master. For, as this really original fellow once admitted to Schacht, most of the district leaders or ministers made the mistake of boring the chancellor, whenever they were admitted to his presence, with dry statistics or deadly earnest proposals. As Koch looked at it, that was the worst sort of psychology. It was necessary to provide the Fuehrer with something novel at every interview, something extravagant, exorbitant, and impressive. It was like having a huge magic box, Koch said. The proposal had to be wrapped up and hidden in twenty different colored boxes and in twice as many precious little secret compartments. Then the Fuehrer's interest would be aroused, and once that was done the game was as good as won.

Koch was hard-boiled, but he was also something more. Under a well-regulated and responsible government this undoubtedly talented man, who had begun his career as a railroad worker, might have done a great deal of good. But the inevitable result of his being able to do as he pleased was that he devoted his versatile talents to swindling. By the time he was assigned to the Ukraine in 1941, he had become a megalomaniac.

As I have said, I met this archetype of the 'old fighter' in the sleeping compartment. I had known him for some time because he was an enemy of Himmler's. His name occupied a prominent place on Himmler's black list; consequently, a certain comradeship in peril united us. Moreover, it was astonishing how openly one could exchange views with him. Apparently my habit of talking bluntly about Nazi conditions somehow stimulated him.

During that ride through the night Koch did not rest until he had consumed the entire stock of alcohol in the sleeper. His loquaciousness increased proportionately; so did the truthfulness of his talk. At last our conversation got around to HIM. We had started by talking about the thirtieth of June. Then we discussed whether and in what fashion the next series of killings would take place. I put the obvious question: When, I asked, did Koch think his turn would come?

Koch responded to my question with admirable objectivity. He had not the slightest doubt that his hour would soon strike. They would be coming for him any day now, he said. And by 'they' he did not mean only Himmler's henchmen; he was also thinking of the Fuehrer. For he suddenly nudged me roughly and whispered into my ear: 'Believe me, he will kill them all, one after the other. I know the perfidy of the Hapsburgs.' He was so pleased with this *bon mot* that he repeated it twice.

Somewhat disconcerted by so much candor, I tried to find something consoling to say. I shall never forget Koch's reaction. I carried his thought a little further and observed that Hitler would in all probability suffer the same end. But Koch shook his head and stared at me with glazed eyes. Passionately he contradicted me. I began to worry about my cursed audacity as his voice rose louder and louder. But his outburst was not directed against me. It was difficult to tell whether he spoke more in rage or in admiration; one moment he babbled drunkenly, the next his voice broke with excitement. Again and again he repeated, 'Gisevius, the man has done it. . . . Mark my words, Gisevius, the man has done it — the man has become a legend . . .'

Muenster at that time was the capital of the flourishing province of Westphalia, the seat of a prefecture, the headquarters of the commander of a military district, the city of Bishop von Galen who was famed for his martial courage. The Brown Revolution had by-passed this vestige of the Middle Ages; it was more concerned with the adjacent industrial districts. There, money was in profusion; there the masses surged. Muenster, with its lovely old patrician houses and ancient colonnades, dozed through the thunder of the Revolution like a sleeping beauty.

What is my most lasting memory of the year I spent in Muenster? I confess without shame: it is of the table in the café where I sat regularly with a small group of friends. At noon and in the evening by half-past five at the latest we dyed-in-the-wool bureaucrats had our sessions.

I don't mean to give the impression that our little club was a collection of superannuated old gentlemen. Even the most decorous of them were pretty spry. They were, every one of them, officials of the old school in the best sense; they possessed a great deal of knowledge and experience and were qualified to occupy much higher and more responsible positions. But they were not in favor; they had not been timely about getting themselves a Party membership; and as a result they had no future. These unfortunate government officials, who all had families to care for, were quite literally in a hopeless situation.

That was the chief lesson that I learned by observation at Muenster. Merely 'being against it' did not help; the most ardent desires and the best will in the world were insufficient. I myself was young, unmarried, and eager to act; in a thousand-and-one individual cases I attempted to apply my so-called 'good' principles. With what result? My activities led to a few experiences that at the time seemed dangerous and in retrospect appear almost comical. No more.

If anyone should claim that it would have been possible for a government official or for any other member of the terrorized masses to practice sabotage for ten years without being caught, I should insist that it was impossible. My experience during that single year taught me that much. It was in clear recognition of my powerlessness that I turned my back on Muenster and looked around for some 'higher' sphere of activity, where I felt I could be more effective. Had I not done so, my zeal would soon have trickled away, or else the Gestapo would have undertaken to squeeze it out of me.

In a system of terrorism organized to the ultimate degree it is not possible to sabotage successfully from below. *Only intrigue from above offers any prospect of success.*

Even then, some propitious starting-point is necessary. If the oppositionist does not find any such firm initial ground (and the greater the terrorism, the slenderer is the individual's chance of finding any), then there is nothing to do but resign oneself to the paralyzing consciousness of utter helplessness, to the dreary knowledge that it is hopeless, and in fact suicidal, to attempt to swim against the stream. Then one must wait and wait and wait, until the mass jubilation has been converted into mass agony. And then — then it is time to pronounce the bitter words, 'Too late.'

I had another reason for not regretting the year of banishment in Muenster. It was a very good place for me to observe the internal development of the Revolution, for although all the important decisions were made in Berlin, their effects were unquestionably felt most intensely in the provinces. It was easy to see that our allegedly highly centralized *Fuehrerstaat* had already begun to break up into dozens of satrapies and scores of tiny duchies. Each of the Nazi governors interpreted the law according to his own sweet will. These men succeeded in disrupting all local governments to an incredible extent and completely ruining the finances of those governments. What kept the state apparatus going — unfortunately — was the indefatigable devotion to duty of the despised bureaucrats.

The more they labored, the more they were mocked at public meetings. But the fact that the administrative machinery of the Third Reich continued to run up to the beginning of the war, and did not break down even under the complications of a war economy, is certainly not due to the toil of the Nazi heads of state. All the spade work was done by those numberless anonymous officials who attended the mass demonstrations with the utmost reluctance, but who unwearyingly went on performing their monotonous tasks.

What a pity it is that this infinite capacity for work, this readiness to take pains, was misused for such obnoxious purposes instead of being used to further constructive and peaceful works! But the tremendous impulse of the revolutionary machinery started them off in the wrong direction. The terrible and mysterious dynamism of the Movement did not drive these unfortunates forward; it wrenched them backward into the Nazi chaos.

It was during this period in Muenster that I learned many significant facts about the disintegration of the state executive power. My teacher was Administrative President Schmid, who governed what was considered a particularly difficult district. Probably for this reason he was allowed to remain in office, although he was *persona non grata* with the Nazi Party.

As soon as I arrived at the scene of my banishment, I tried to get in touch with the commanding general of the area. Luenink and Schmid helped me; and I needed help, for it was not a simple matter at all. Nevertheless, I managed to get several opportunities to expatiate to General von Kluge on my views on the latest political developments — without being shown the door.

Both the position and the influence of such a commanding general meant far more in those days than can be realized now. Since that time we have been subjected to rampant inflation in the generals' market. But in 1936 and 1937, and even during the two following years, a military district commander was a little king in his territory. He was equal in rank to the federal governors and in power he might have been — I stress the 'might' — far superior to the Nazi rabble. For not only did he command hundreds of thousands of heavily armed men, but the hopes of millions of decent citizens in his area were pinned on him. He was looked upon as the sole refuge, the one 'strong man' who could act if the reign of terror became absolutely unbearable.

My unexpected success in having Kluge grant me a hearing led Schmid and me into an adventure that might easily have turned out very ill indeed. We decided that for the present nothing could be done in Berlin; it would, therefore, be best to continue our revelations of what was going on in Nazidom in Muenster or Duesseldorf. We picked on Schacht to be our chief mouthpiece.

Schacht, for his part, was eager to have a talk with some of the generals. In Berlin he could not; all the uniformed gentlemen with the exception of Beck considered a meeting with him too compromising. The only way for Schacht to arrange a talk with the commander-in-chief, General von Fritsch, was through an intermediary. Kluge was known to be very friendly with Fritsch. Therefore, Schacht welcomed our suggestion of a meeting with Kluge.

It may sound like a very simple matter for a government minister, an army commander, and an administrative president to get together. But not in revolutionary Germany. For weeks I had to shuttle back and forth between Muenster, Duesseldorf, and Berlin before I finally got all parties to agree on a time and place of meeting. Each of the men wanted to prepare an alibi; each had to arrange some official journey as a pretext. General von Kluge was the most cautious of the three.

At long last it was arranged. We agreed to meet in a small Westphalian hotel near Hamm on Monday, February 1, 1937. I had worked out the final details with Schacht on the previous Wednesday. I was to meet him at the railroad station in Hamm at a certain time and conduct him from there. No telephone calls or letters were to be exchanged, no matter what befell.

On Friday I talked with Kluge. The general had begun to worry a great deal about the whole business. He wanted to come, oh yes, but he didn't like the idea of meeting in broad daylight in a public place. I was somewhat irritated; it had been Kluge all along who had refused to consider the obvious rendezvous, either in his or Schmid's home. After a lengthy discussion we finally agreed to meet for supper at Schmid's official residence in Duesseldorf. On Saturday I informed Schmid of this change of program. Since no telephone calls or letters were permitted, there was no possibility of informing Schacht in time. I would have to take the train to Hanover on Monday morning, find Schacht on the train, and ask him to go on through to Elberfeld, where Schmid would pick us up in his car.

I arrived at Hanover punctually to take the train from Berlin, and between Hanover and Hamm I walked up and down that train a dozen times. But there was no sign of Schacht. I could not imagine what had happened. Had he fallen ill suddenly, or missed the train?

In Hamm the train stopped for five minutes. I raced back and forth from the platform to the station entrance and back to the train.

But this last hope proved vain; Schacht was nowhere in sight. Breath-lessly, I hurried to the stationmaster and asked permission to use his office telephone to get in touch with the administrative president in Dusseldorf; it was very urgent, I said, and concerned a guest who had not arrived on the train. I succeeded in reaching Schmid's home, but Schmid had already left for Elberfeld; as far as Frau Schmid knew, no one had canceled his appointment.

I jumped into the train just as it was starting. Two uneasy hours later I was shaking hands with Schmid at the Elberfeld station.

Schmid was an old hand at the game of politics and adept at disen-tangling himself from complicated situations, but in this case he had no idea what to do. If he knew Kluge, he said, the general would be furious with both of us. We spent two tormenting hours at Schmid's office, expecting every minute that our tension would be relieved by a telephone call from Schacht telling us that he had taken the wrong train and would arrive shortly. We waited in vain. At last, in spite of our agreement not to use the telephone, we begged Frau Schmid to do the telephoning for us. She called Schacht's office to ask whether the minister could be seen in Berlin on the following morning. She received the baffling reply that Schacht was not in Berlin; he had left early that day for an unknown destination. This made my missing him on the train or in Hamm all the more inexplicable. I vividly imagined him standing on the station platform, all alone, his collar turned up and his lips set bitterly.

Meanwhile, the hands of the clock moved relentlessly toward half-past seven. I felt utterly crushed, and Schmid, too, could not conceal his nervousness. Then the time came: Fate in the form of the com-manding general approached with lithe, youthful steps.

Schmid sprang to his feet hospitably. 'You'll have to pass the evening somehow; I guess you had better tell us about your expe-riences,' he flung at me. To this day I can see the general pausing stiffly in the doorway; with a glance he had sized up the situation. For a second I was afraid he would turn on his heel and have me con-scripted on the morrow. But instead he condescended to listen to me — listen, that is, to the babble by which I attempted to make a con-

fusing situation even more confusing. Schmid, meanwhile, lent splendid assistance by murmuring repeatedly that the case was absolutely
mysterious, simply incomprehensible. I went on and on, talking as
fast as I could, describing my every movement, explaining that Schacht
had left Berlin but had not arrived; that he might still arrive unannounced; that he might have changed his mind about the railroad and
traveled by car; that . . .

'Now wait a minute,' Kluge interrupted commandingly. 'Let us
think over all the possibilities.'

Then I knew I had been successful. The ice was broken; instead
of feeling righteously indignant, Kluge was ready for a peaceable chat.
We considered even the vaguest possibilities. Then the talk switched
to Frau Schmid's excellent cooking. And two hours later, by the time
Kluge resignedly took out his watch and observed that it was now
half-past nine and Schacht certainly would no longer be showing up,
we had got so far that he could scarcely revert to chagrin.

The rest of the conversation consisted of a series of anecdotes about
various abuses on the part of the Nazis, for Schmid was malicious
enough to lead me on, and I told one story after another. When Kluge
at last decided it was time to go, he patted my shoulder jovially and
said, 'Since you live in Muenster you must come along in my car.
Then you can tell me a few more of your stories.'

And so it went throughout the two-hour ride. Kluge was very
cordial as he bade me good-bye. He thanked me in a very friendly
fashion. Then he shook both my hands.

'I don't doubt that all the stories you've told were accurate . . .'
Pause.

'But nevertheless I don't believe you.'

The following morning when I got to my office, feeling distinctly
overtired, I found a letter waiting for me. The handwriting seemed
quite familiar. Eagerly I ripped open the envelope and took out three
small white sheets of memorandum paper such as I had seen lying in
a box on Schacht's desk. Two of them were blank; on the middle one
was written — without date, salutation, or signature: 'I must go to

Dortmund on business tonight. I will, therefore, meet you by your train from Muenster in the station at Hamm at twelve o'clock.'

What had happened (as I found out from Schacht on the following day) was that Schacht had waited for me at the station in Hamm. Not finding me, he telephoned my office at Muenster, but of course I was not there. He assumed that Schmid was on his way to the rendezvous. Therefore, he had taken the next train back.

Since Schacht had waited at the station, I felt that I owed him an explanation. Although it was not easy for me to take time off repeatedly from my work, I took the train for Berlin that same night. As I was standing on the railroad platform in Hamm, waiting for the connecting train, the stationmaster approached me. It was the man who had kindly allowed me to use his telephone to call Duesseldorf. Consequently, he had heard me talk about my failure to meet my visitor on the train.

'Did you meet your visitor, after all?' he asked me.

I said I had not.

Since I had a feeling that the man was quite straight — he was the solid government-official type and probably a dyed-in-the-wool enemy of the state — I went on chatting with him. One word led to another, and suddenly he came out with his latest piece of news. 'You know,' he said, 'we had important visitors yesterday? There must have been an important conference taking place. Herr Schacht waited for half an hour on the platform. Apparently he had missed someone, for afterward he went away by himself. At first I could scarcely believe it was the minister in person. One of the porters told me and I went up to the platform to see. I recognized him by his high collar. He was standing at the cafeteria counter having a bite to eat.'

For a moment I stared open-mouthed at the man.

'But you yourself got me the telephone connection and heard me talk to the administrative president's office at Duesseldorf about a visitor I failed to meet. You must have noticed from the way we talked that the guest was an important one. You mean to tell me you stood there listening and didn't think to ask whether I was looking for Schacht?'

The stationmaster smiled. 'Well, you see, sir, we railroad officials are discreet. How could I be sure Schacht would be pleased if I called your attention to the fact that he was here?'

This reply struck me as so idiotic that I was on the point of screaming at the man.

'You see,' this stout-hearted 'enemy of the state,' continued, 'downstairs in the waiting room, surrounded by a lot of lieutenants, was the Reich leader of the SS — Himmler.'

Schacht was inclined to think that we might spare ourselves any more such nerve-racking experiences. I ought to return to Berlin. The difficulty was to find some way to manage it. As a government official I was still unable to find any ministry that would take me in. Finally, through Schacht's intercession, I was able to locate an understanding business manager in Bremen, Franz Stapelfeld, who 'engaged' me as his representative in Berlin on the express condition that I was not to deduce from my contract that I had any 'right to work.' The ministry of the interior granted me leave to take employment in private industry for a year. Thus I escaped temporarily from the bureaucratic treadmill. I was given a free hand to devote myself to my principal avocation.

Unfortunately, the details were not fully worked out by the end of April, so that I still had to find a way to escape participating in the obligatory May first celebration. One of my chief sports under the Nazi régime was the dodging of the public receptions, parades, or other demonstrations; and I made out tolerably well; except for two voluntary visits to the performances of what Adolf Hitler called his Reichstag, I evaded all such public occasions.

But in May, 1937, in Muenster I had a close call. The members of our lunch and dinner clique followed my doings with appreciative suspense as I struggled to escape from the net. Late in the afternoon of April 30 the tide turned: I contrived to have myself sent to Berlin that same night, on urgent business.

In my extremity it had occurred to me to transmit a long-pending dispute over the shutting-down of a creamery to — the wrong authority. I was at the time working on questions of price control and the first essays at rationing. Goering's Four Year Plan had just been exalted to the status of a semi-ministry. For lack of anything more sensible to do, the employees of this new organization took up the most absurd matters in order to demonstrate that they had some bureaucratic *raison d'être*. I therefore proposed that they reopen this creamery which the Nazis had closed because of rancor against the owners. I had a resounding success. Ordinarily these employees of Goering were far from philanthropic, but the question of this creamery awakened their noblest impulses. They were all the more interested in the dispute because by no imaginable interpretation of their function did they have anything to do with the milk business. Before long such a muddle of conflicting authorities had arisen among the milk producers, the ministry of agriculture, the Four Year Plan, our local authorities and the Nazi Party that I was sent off to Berlin to clear up the misunderstandings and to explain how the matter had ever been delegated to the Four Year Plan Authority.

I mention this little matter because I want to take this opportunity to remark upon a curious phenomenon. Even in the years before the outbreak of the war, a goodly number of cylinders missed in the Nazi economic machine, and each time Hitler got himself out of the difficulty in an extremely primitive manner. He launched into the usual fit of rage; some scapegoat was punished; and a Nazi quack received a 'special assignment.' The first thing this 'strong man' did was to create a sort of super-authority, which simply added one more 'bureau' to the swollen staff of economic bureaucrats. And every time things somehow 'worked out.'

For years it was Goerdeler's fate to personify economic rationality and inexorable logic; for years his rationality and logic, his figures and prognoses, were repeatedly contradicted by the impossible 'successes' of the new methods. Again and again the arithmetic employed by Hitler's chief economic expert, Goering, proved to be not wholly insane. I am referring to that excited argument between Goering and the skeptical Schacht in 1935 in the course of which Goering had pounded his fists on the table and exclaimed: 'And I tell you, if the Fuehrer wishes it, then two times two is five!'

The truth of the matter was that the Nazis were able to go on for a long time robbing Peter to pay Paul. The vast area of Germany and Europe offered, for years, almost inexhaustible opportunities for sheer plunder. But even without the bombings the German nation would one day have faced an unparalleled financial and economic catastrophe.

Early in January, 1938, I was finally shifted to Berlin. The future content of my shadow existence concerned chiefly that great crisis which I shall describe in the next chapter. This Fritsch crisis — to give a name to that moral and political collapse which started on February 4, 1938 — is the classic story of the Third Reich. One must be acquainted with it to understand the history of our confused times. The Fritsch crisis is an allegory that clarifies many events prior to it and casts light upon the whole opaque stream of subsequent history.

During the 'quiet' years of 1936 and 1937, everyone could sense the increasing tensions within Germany. The fateful question upon which not only the recovery of German freedom, but war or peace for the world, depended was: How would the generals act? Those generals held every imaginable honor; they had been supplied with all the implements of power. Would they resolutely attempt to hold back the Revolution, or would they lead the masses of men and material that had been entrusted to them into the turbulent Nazi current? That alternative existed then; it is not merely a matter of historical retrospect. If ever a situation was alarmingly clear, it was so during those years. The Revolution was, so to speak, crouching, but preparing to spring up with renewed vigor. Anyone who looked sharply (instead of simply closing both eyes) could not help seeing what the future inevitably held.

In the economic sphere the machinery of rearmament, which was now running at full speed, was kept going at the expense of all other production. A significant cut in the standard of living could not be avoided in the long run. The value of the currency had again become wholly fictitious; but this time inflation was furthered, not by the printing presses but by the misleading assertion that money did not matter. *Raubbau* — the practice of exhausting the soil — staved off any shortage of raw materials for the time being; but at the same time it limited mobility in the sphere of foreign policy and left, as the only possible avenue for securing new sources of raw materials — the path of war.

In the intellectual sphere, the brutal Nazification of public opinion, the increasing harshness of the anti-Semitic laws, and the tenacious struggle with the Church, all had the same aim: the undermining of all traditional views of justice, morals, and faith. The struggle for power was deliberately transferred to the intellectual sphere. The education of youth was removed as far as possible from the parental home; young Germany was educated in those Nazi institutions for producing an undifferentiated mass — the so-called *Ordensburgen.* The 'breeding' of men of the master race began. Day after day the masses were fed the Nazi poison in sweet and bitter pills; day after day they were made to swallow the slogan of the new morality: 'Might makes right.'

Almost inevitably this violent seizure of the spiritual realms, which had previously been under the protection of school, church, and home, brought about a perverse mass psychosis. In the end the proletarianized masses must seek release from their predicament in war, in undisguised campaigns of conquest and plunder; they were forced by the Nazis to escape from economic and psychic nihilism into predatory activity, into snatching at the wealth of all their neighbors.

It is against such a background that the Reign of Terror becomes comprehensible. The utter demolition of conscience and good conduct, the regimentation of occupations and of intellectual life, the suppression of personal concerns and of all outstanding personalities — these things were not being done in the name of 'order,' 'discipline,' 'duty,' or 'socialism.' The Revolution had been exalted into an end in itself, and the terror was clearing a bloody path for it.

Throughout 1936 and 1937, Hitler maintained a careful pretense of being a reconciler and peacemaker. Nevertheless, from 1936 on, it was obvious that his uncontrollable will and the undisciplined dynamism of his Nazi Movement would drive him into war. Therefore, all persons who desired peace, decency, morality, and justice could not sit idly by and wait; they had to take the responsibility for action; they had to put a halt to the Revolution.

But what group was in a position to turn the course of events by courageous action? To ask the question is to answer it. It took some years before the 'authoritarian' system of government which existed in 1933 was extended into an absolutist totalitarianism in which the Gestapo alone possessed state power. The process did not really begin until 1936 and culminated two years later in the Fritsch crisis of February, 1938.

It must not be thought that the turbulent masses who were oscillating between one extreme and the other provided the backing for this intensification of autocratic rule. The masses were already groaning loudly enough under the SS terror. Nor is Heinrich Himmler the one to blame, for he was not yet Germany's omnipotent commander of the police forces. It was in reality our top army leadership which nurtured this fateful development. Standing by their oath of allegiance, whose inner meaning they horribly mistook, they shielded all the constitutional breaches that their Fuehrer repeatedly committed.

Undoubtedly a small group of generals were at heart earnestly troubled. These men were conscious of a tremendous responsibility; they felt that no command from above, no matter how unequivocal, could erase their responsibility. In fact there was only a minute group of army officers who were, in 'principle,' co-conspirators in the Nazi Terror. Most of the officers' corps remained 'neutral,' both inwardly and outwardly. They were part of that irresponsible group of human beings who always seek a secure life without cares and are allured by the prospect of a career. By their excess of passivity our generals, willy-nilly, consciously or unconsciously, became profiteering participants in the Nazi Revolution. The cases of Blomberg and Fritsch were to show how ill-prepared they were to act, how disastrous had been their policy of splendid isolation.

The Church alone spoke out frankly. By contrast with the timidity of the army officers, the courage of the clergy stands out all the more. Perhaps I should qualify that statement: it was not the Church as such that fought, for as an organization the Church was swathed in a thousand bureaucratic ifs and buts.

In the history of the Nazi struggle against the Church, the name of Martin Niemoeller must always take first place. Hitler hated him and considered him *the* opponent in the Church. The Fuehrer made Niemoeller his private prisoner. Many persons have testified to the fury that would distort the tyrant's face whenever he heard the name of the intrepid pastor of Dahlem. This fact alone is sufficient to explain why German churchgoers, both Protestant and Catholic, looked upon Niemoeller as their hero.

Niemoeller had to fight in two directions at once. First of all there were the Nazis. His passionate quarrel with them has become part of history. On the other hand, he had to defend himself against those very people who stood closest to him and whose mode of reasoning was most akin to his. These people were the 'patriots,' those good Christians whose ideology stemmed from the days when 'throne and altar,' were one. They suffered most strongly from the chronic disease of German Protestantism, its unfortunate tendency to support faithfully any sort of government. They still tended to do so even when the Hitler dictatorship had become a grotesque mockery of all genuine authority. Because of this, they were strongly moved by Niemoeller's anti-Nazi pleadings. But why must the man always be so incautious? Weren't things really 'working out' at times, even with regard to the Church? It was necessary for Niemoeller to give this attitude serious consideration, for he encountered it daily in his closest associates. He became familiar with a thousand variations of the 'patriot' mentality. It is a bitter experience to find oneself at the decisive moment surrounded by hesitant, questioning, and frowning friends, or to be totally deserted by them.

The Nazis wanted to lock Christianity into a ghetto, and many Christians believed it was their duty to accept this isolation gladly. Niemoeller knew that it must not be accepted. He saw that the true path of the Protestant Church led straight into an area that had been a kind of *zone interdite* for German Protestants until 1933. That straight and narrow path led directly to 'politics.'

It may be that even for Niemoeller this transition from unpolitical to political struggle was arrived at by unconscious rather than conscious processes. The public justifications for all his actions had to be religious. But those political propositions for which he has so stalwartly fought since his return to freedom must have been present in his mind even in 1933 and 1934. His stern rejection of National Socialism was in essence pure politics. The people who listened to him in his pulpit perfectly understood the practical conclusions implicit in his sermons. Hitler and Himmler knew this very well. They did not give a damn about religious questions. They knew perfectly that they were fighting Niemoeller on their exclusively political plane. For this reason his arrest in the middle of 1937 had a significance that went far beyond the conflict with the Church. To my mind, Niemoeller's incarceration removed the last personality around whom any sort of civilian revolt movement might have gathered.

From the day the dictatorship began, the practicality of individual actions had seemed highly dubious, but a popular movement from below had seemed quite possible. For a time a general strike or other action by the disbanded labor unions appeared quite likely, but this likelihood turned out to be wrong. Thereupon, the resisters all turned their eyes to the Church. Would the Church succeed in rallying its masses against the revolutionary masses? I still think Niemoeller was right in believing that the chance was worth the full devotion of his whole personality. Unfortunately, however, the number of his true adherents was too small. The Protestant Church was unable to maintain its initial impetus. There were too many ecclesiastics who tried to compromise. At last, by arresting Niemoeller after they had succeeded in isolating him, the Nazis quelled the last chance for a real popular opposition movement.

This meant a radical change in the situation within Germany. From that point on, only a revolt from above could succeed. The 'sole bearers of arms in the nation' looked on idly as this enslavement of the nation took place. They 'kept out' of the struggle. The consequence was that after Niemoeller's elimination they alone were capable of reforming the situation. The question was, Would the generals ever understand that by refraining from action they had not 'neutralized' themselves? They had, in fact, brought down upon themselves an awful responsibility.

By the end of 1937 the lines were clearly drawn. On the one side stood the forces of evolution, devoted to the preservation of state authority, to tradition, to a policy of wait and see. These were the soldiers in their field-gray uniforms. On the other side pranced the revolutionary groups, untamable, without tradition, proponents of violent change. These were the Black troops of the SS. Both sides were propelled toward their destinies by the same inescapable impulse: both had either to act or to be destroyed by not acting. As long as Himmler's reign of terror could rage unchecked, there could be no order or quiet within Germany, and no peace with Germany; but as long as there existed within Germany powers which might some day rise up against the tyranny of the Gestapo, those powers constituted a check upon revolutionary expansion at home and abroad. One of the two had to break — either the rule by force and violence of the SS or the top leadership of the army.

The decision involved not only the fate of the SS, or of the German army, or of Adolf Hitler. The game that was being played had as stakes the future of Germany and of Europe.

The phrase 'Fritsch crisis' is an awkward and undescriptive title for the story we are about to tell. The simple facts of the case are not the things that shock us, although the nature of those facts was unique in German military history. That terrible human and political catastrophe which had been creeping upon us from 1936 on, and which broke with such fearsome force in 1938, was not at all something out of the blue. More than once its arrival was announced to the top leaders of the army, and in particular to Fritsch himself; but the commander-in-chief of the army did not want to hear about it; he did not want to act. His sole desire was to obey his orders; and therefore, within two brief months, Fritsch not only ruined his own career, but cast away his army's unique chance to free Germany from the Nazi yoke and to protect us all from the approaching calamity of the war.

A plethora of contradictory explanations of his 'case' has been and will be offered. Every imaginable 'reasonable' interpretation has been suggested; but in the final analysis it was all quite plain and uncomplicated. A crisis was approaching. The storm mounted to a *crescendo*, and those who should have heard and seen stubbornly closed their ears and eyes. That, in fine, is all there was to it. What happened was that one fine day the herald of revolutionary change knocked on the doors of the Third Reich, and he did not knock at the entrance to the Brown House in Munich, or at Goering's Karinhall, or Hitler's resplendent chancellery. It was at the sober portal of the ministry of war that he chose to make his fateful entrance.

6

The Fritsch-Blomberg Crisis

January 12, 1938

T HE BERLIN EVENING PAPERS headlined the news that General Field
Marshal von Blomberg had been married that afternoon to Fraulein
Erna Gruhn. Adolf Hitler and Hermann Goering were witnesses at
the wedding. In spite of the prominent headlines there was little
comment in the press beyond a few polite lines of congratulation. No
details of the wedding were given, and nothing was said about the
origins of the happy bride. This reticence on the part of the press
was something noteworthy, for in the Third Reich festive occasions
were always celebrated with a vengeance. Still, since the bridegroom
was the minister of war, it was possible that he had forbidden extensive
publicity. Perhaps, it was suggested, this incident indicated a trend
back to the traditional Prussian modesty and decorum.

With unusual speed and suspicious persistency rumors flew around
about the first lady of the German army. Some rumors alleged that
Blomberg had married his private secretary. Some persons had looked
up the Berlin Directory and found the name of a Frau Gruhn, a
masseuse who lived in the suburb of Neukoelln. Those who wished
to be kind put it that the field marshal had married a child of the
common people; the unkind wrinkled their noses and called it a
mésalliance. A large majority of the rumor-mongers insisted that the
new *Frau Feldmarschall* had had a distinctly unsavory past, and they
elaborated on this; but no one pretended to have any facts.

219

January 20, 1938

IN THE EVENING, before going to bed, a Berlin police inspector's wife told her husband the latest bit of gossip. It concerned the recent marriage of General Field Marshal von Blomberg. As it happened, her husband was employed in the population registry office. It would be easy for him to check up on that story, he thought; and the following morning he looked through his vast files. He gaped, then rushed to the desk of his immediate superior. The superior went to see the director, who went to see the assistant police chief, who went to the chief of police. By eleven o'clock in the morning a preliminary report lay on Count Helldorf's desk. Toward one o'clock an additional report followed it: the copy of a dossier that had been hurriedly dug up out of the inactive criminal court files.

That same day someone telephoned the commander-in-chief of the army. The caller would not give his name or state his business. When Fritsch's adjutant refused to connect him with the general, the anonymous caller lost his temper. He snarled into the telephone: 'Then tell the general that Field Marshal von Blomberg has married a whore.' With that he hung up. The adjutant gaped at the silent telephone. He reported the call to Fritsch, who conferred with the chief of the general staff, General Ludwig Beck. A good deal of head-shaking, meditating, and discreet inquiry followed, but no one knew the lady.

Count Helldorf, the chief of police, studied the documents before him. The dry legal language defined the wife of the general field marshal as a prostitute. Erna Gruhn's mother had run a brothel disguised as a massage salon. She had been convicted for this offense, and the dossier was proof that her daughter, too, had been unlucky enough not to escape the law. There was also a record of Erna Gruhn's having posed for pornographic pictures which had been obscene enough to sell tremendously. The section of the Berlin police for the suppression of immoral pictures had swiftly put an end to the brisk trade in these pictures, and Erna had been haled into court.

She pleaded that her lover, who had posed with her for those highly indelicate snapshots, had skipped out in 1933 and that she had received only sixty marks for her 'assistance.' This plea induced the court to impose a mild sentence.

Helldorf was flabbergasted. What was he to do with this information? By rights, of course, he should report it to his superior, the chief of all the German police forces, Heinrich Himmler. At the same time Helldorf realized the implications of such a step. If Himmler received those documents in their present state, and if, moreover, he was the first to see them, he would at last possess the weapon he needed to strike the decisive blow against the army. He would be able to blackmail the war minister. Blomberg, who was in any case popularly known as the 'rubber lion,' would henceforth be nothing but a pliant tool in the hands of the Gestapo.

At last Helldorf made the difficult decision to violate Gestapo orders rather than involve Blomberg, and with him the whole army, in a terrible scandal. This behavior on the part of Helldorf was all the more courageous since he had only recently got into trouble for a similar breach of discipline. As chief of police he had come across undeniable proofs that Funk, the under-secretary in the ministry of propaganda, was prey to the same weakness that had allegedly been the reason for the executions of Roehm and Karl Ernst. Helldorf had passed this material on to Funk's superior, Propaganda Minister Goebbels. Some time later Goebbels had returned the documents with a note to the effect that it was unfortunate, but that there was nothing to be done about it. In such a case, Goebbels said, the only thing that could be done was to arrange an automobile accident, and that would be no way to treat an 'old fighter' like Funk.

The affair was almost forgotten when Goering proposed that Funk take over Schacht's office as minister of economics. Hitler at first refused. There was something wrong with Funk, he said; the man was a homosexual. Goering, of course, knew that 'there was something wrong,' but how did Hitler come to know about it? There was a hasty investigation, and it came out that Goebbels had confidentially conferred with Hitler about Helldorf's information. Goering and

Himmler were furious; they looked upon the matter as a serious in-
cursion upon their special privileges. They considered that they alone
had the right to decide whether incriminating material was to be
passed on to the Fuehrer. Himmler called Helldorf on the carpet and
warned him against a repetition of his indiscretion.

Helldorf went to see Blomberg's closest associate, General Keitel.
As delicately as possible, he explained the contents of the dossier.
Keitel was not very helpful. All he could think of was that the frightful story had to be — suppressed. Helldorf would not agree. He objected, quite justly, that any such procedure was impossible for three
sound reasons. In the first place, too large a circle of police officials
knew the story by now. In the second place, there was so much talk
going the rounds of Berlin that suppression was no longer possible;
and in the third place, the thing itself was not something that could
be forgiven and forgotten.

Keitel was finally forced to concede that Helldorf was right, but he
could not muster up enough courage to make a soldierly decision in
the matter. He declared that he wanted to have nothing to do with
the whole affair; that it did not lie within his competence; and he
sent the chief of police to see Hermann Goering.

For good or ill, Helldorf had to pack up his dossier once more.
Now he was being asked to carry the bomb with its lighted fuse to
the very place where the most spectacular explosion would be welcomed, for Keitel must certainly know that Goering wanted to be
Blomberg's successor, and that Heinrich Himmler's most ardent wish
was to make the SS which he commanded a fourth branch of the
armed forces.

Karinhall, Goering's magnificent home
Saturday, January 22

GOERING DID NOT LIKE his weekends disturbed. He admitted his
visitor ungraciously and asked abruptly what he wanted. His annoyance increased when Helldorf began an involved preamble to the
effect that he had come in connection with the marriage of General

Field Marshal von Blomberg. Goering cut him off short and snapped, 'Well, what's it about?'

Helldorf briefly narrated the facts in the case. Goering paced nervously back and forth while the chief of police talked. Finally he went to the window, threw open one of the casements, and took a deep breath. Then he sighed heavily. 'This is the last straw,' he said.

Helldorf knew very well that Goering was an excellent actor. Once upon a time, in 1933, before the Axis had been forged, Goering had infuriated Mussolini by his acting. At a gala dinner in the Palazzo Venezia he had suddenly improvised a special performance, to the scandalized amusement of the other guests. Goering had mimicked with remarkable fidelity the manner of the Holy Father, who had just received him. In Rome this was something altogether too risqué.

This time, however, Goering did not seem to be acting; apparently he was really shocked. Evidence of that was that he began talking quite freely about the matter and contributed a few crumbs of information about the history of the marriage. He mentioned, for example, that Blomberg had informed him and the Fuehrer beforehand that the lady he intended to marry had 'a past.' With his well-known greatness of spirit the Fuehrer had nevertheless given his approval to the marriage. Goering also said some other things. We will return to them later.

Sunday, January 23

HIMMLER, HEYDRICH, AND GOERING had a conference in Karinhall.

Monday, January 24

GOERING REPORTED TO THE FUEHRER, who had just returned to Berlin from Munich. There was the usual fit of crying and storming — inevitable in all such cases. After a time Hitler recovered his composure. Blomberg must get a divorce at once. Or, better still, let him contest the validity of the marriage on grounds of gross deception. In this way they could keep that Gruhn woman from running around using his name and title for the rest of her life. In the meanwhile, the Fuehrer ordered, his field marshal was not to be permitted to enter the chancellery, nor to continue wearing his uniform. Goering dutifully agreed, but his predatory instinct warned him of danger. What if the marriage were actually annulled? Then the scandal might be hushed up, and who could say whether in the end Blomberg might not remain? It was quite possible that the Fuehrer, after his indignation had raged itself out, might graciously forgive the repentant sinner. Then nothing would have changed. Goering imagined that he had nearly reached his goal, and he decided to strike while the iron was hot. He himself set off to see Blomberg and to convey Hitler's orders to him in the form he considered appropriate.

Blomberg's staff of adjutants were on edge. As it was, they had had enough trouble during the past week. After all, a field marshal does not marry every day, and when before had a field marshal's wedding been so secret, so hasty, so shamefaced? It was all confusing enough; and now, after a succession of excited telephone calls, Goering was announced: something must be wrong.

Goering entered Blomberg's office. What did he say? How much did he say? Did he bark out the entire contents of the dossiers? Or did he merely hint at the secret? Did he flatly repeat the Fuehrer's demand that the marriage be annulled? Or did he rather talk a great deal about the scandal, less about the divorce, and not at all about the possibility of annulment?

The adjutants, burning with curiosity, stopped work and tried to catch a word or two through the closed door. When Goering left, one of them quietly opened the door of Blomberg's office a crack. He saw the hale and hearty field marshal staggering, a broken man, to his private rooms behind the office.

Goering drove straight back to the chancellery. He did not dare lose any time, for the question of succession was being discussed. According to rank, the commander-in-chief of the army, Colonel-General von Fritsch, was the logical person. Hitler was in fact seriously considering making Fritsch his new minister of war. Fritsch was a first-class soldier; he was loyal; the troops would go through fire for him. There were a great many arguments in favor of such an unpolitical solution of the difficulty. Hitler was all too familiar with Goering's aspirations to be Blomberg's successor. That was all the more reason for him to refuse to grant such a dangerous increase of power to his crown prince. Indecisively, the Fuehrer paced up and down in his rooms. Now and then he spoke with his chief adjutant, but he conspicuously steered clear of asking the advice of any of the top army leaders.

Goering and Himmler entered. At first they shyly stammered a few earnest sentences about their complete loyalty and obedience, and then they suddenly waxed enthusiastic about the unstained honor of the army. Hitler glanced at them in amazement, wondering what they were getting at. Gradually, Goering and Himmler got around to the point. They reminded their Fuehrer of the Fritsch dossier of 1935. Oh yes, Hitler remembered. He listened to a review of the events of that year.

We shall have to glance backward for a moment at the year 1935. At that time there happened to be no reactionaries or Marxists to persecute. The Jews were also being granted a breathing spell. The Nazis were not yet ready to attack the Church. The Gestapo was virtually unemployed. For lack of anything better to do, the Gestapo men instituted a homosexual hunt. A number of truly fantastic incidents within the Hitler Youth provided the immediate pretext for this action. But when had the Gestapo ever stopped at reasonable measures? This time as well, instead of administering a mild purgative the Gestapo went in for a purge — and thereby founded a flourishing new branch of its business.

Sexual crimes are the province of the ordinary criminal police force in all the police departments in the world, for by no stretch of the imagination can these be considered to have any connection with politics, but the Prinz Albrechtstrasse was convinced that homosexuality was a particularly heinous political crime. Behind this conviction lay the perception that a hunt for homosexuals offered the Gestapo tremendous new possibilities of extending its system of protective custody. Someone who was neither a Jew nor a Marxist nor a

Bolshevist, who had not even stolen a silver spoon or been reckless about his telephone conversations, could always be accused of a violation of Paragraph 175. That always drew blood.

For months Himmler and Heydrich played this new game to the limit, and with wonderful success. The concentration camps filled swiftly. The special courts handed down verdicts on an assembly-line basis. Then one of the Gestapo men had a diabolic inspiration. It was well known, he urged, that violators of Paragraph 175 were generally involved in a great many other breaches of the law. They were particularly given to blackmail. There were a large number of young delinquents who were willing to offer themselves for immoral purposes in return for hard cash, but there were perhaps a greater number of scoundrels who afterward pounced upon these poor devils and their rich patrons and hounded them until they had extorted their last cent. The courts habitually imposed long sentences on such parasites.

Suppose that the Gestapo looked around for such degenerate black-mailers in the prisons and penitentiaries? They might well have a good many tales to tell. It was through this chance suggestion that Hans Schmidt, fairy, pimp, and blackmailer of parts, entered the SS examining room. As a boy this good-for-nothing had been sent to the reformatory. Almost as soon as he was discharged from that, he was sent to prison. Two more prison terms followed. Finally, he went up to the penitentiary as an almost hopeless recidivist. His crime was always the same: he spied on homosexuals and then blackmailed them.

This habitual criminal was about twenty-eight years old when he fell into the clutches of the Gestapo. Schmidt dictated his memoirs to the examining officer. He named one person after the other as his 'customers.' Among them were a good many ordinary respectable citizens and quite a number of prominent persons, including, of course, a well-known under-secretary in the ministry of propaganda. The examining officer knew that the latter possessed a kind of safe-conduct from the very highest authority, so he merely noted the man's name and title without asking for details.

He pricked up his ears, however, at the mention of another name. The convict talked about someone called 'von Frisch' or 'von Fritsch.'

Who else could he mean but that notorious arch-reactionary, the commander-in-chief of the army, whom the SS had been trying vainly for so long to 'get something on'? The Gestapo official wrote down everything the blackmailer told him about this excellent customer, from whom he had extorted thousands of marks.

It seemed that one winter evening toward the end of 1935, Schmidt had been lurking in the dimly lit lobby of the Wannsee railroad station in Berlin. His hunting ground was the vicinity of the public toilet, because experience had taught him that profitable connections were most frequently made in such places. While he waited, a medium-sized, rather elderly gentleman with a monocle, dressed in a short jacket with a fur collar, and carrying a cane with a silver knob, came along in the midst of a group of army officers. The gentleman excused himself and entered the washroom. He came out in a moment, accompanied by a well-known fairy named Bavarian Joe. Along the length of the station ran a narrow, dark alley. Several hundred yards away was the scaffolding of a new building that was going up. Schmidt crept along behind the two men until they vanished among the foundation walls.

When they came out again, Schmidt waited until Bavarian Joe had been paid off. Then he hurried after the monocled gentleman and confronted him. The gentleman nearly fainted from fright, for the blackmailer told him that he was a detective and had just been watching his shameful behavior. The usual song and dance followed; the question at issue was not the fact of bribery, but the amount. The elderly gentleman groaned and moaned. He tried to buy himself off as cheaply as possible. First he emptied his purse, then his wallet. But the sum was still too small, and so they rode together to the gentleman's apartment, somewhere in East Lichterfelde. There the gentleman had the blackmailer wait outside for a few moments. He went into his apartment and returned with several hundred-mark bills. Since Schmidt still was not satisfied, they agreed on a meeting-place for the day after the next.

Of course, the convict insisted the next time and the time after that he was still unsatisfied. Plead as he might that he was unable to pay any more, the gentleman, who had meanwhile given his name as von Frisch, could not escape Schmidt's clutches. When the extortion had been repeated for the fourth time, 'Detective' Schmidt suddenly turned up with a colleague who, it appeared, was also involved in the case. Once again the victim could do nothing but pay, but the crime, now that it involved the services of two detectives, had become considerably more serious and more expensive; also, it seemed, Christmas was just around the corner.

A meeting was arranged for the following noon in the station restaurant of the East Lichterfelde railroad station. All three arrived punctually. First they drank several light beers. Apparently they washed them down with a good many whiskies; in any case, the proprietress of the restaurant remembered this peculiar beer-party for years afterward. Later Herr von F. went across the street to the Deutsche Bank. When he returned he handed the two detectives several thousand-mark bills.

This went on and on until, one fine day, Schmidt was sent to the penitentiary for another crime. Shortly afterward the Gestapo had summoned him. His memory of the events was therefore still quite fresh.

The Gestapo official finished his interrogation and had the convict sign the stenogram. Then he hurried to Heydrich's office. Heydrich rushed joyfully off to Himmler, who was delighted, and went directly to see Goering. 'Iron Hermann' rubbed his hands with pleasure and hastened to the Fuehrer.

Adolf Hitler read the remarkable document, but to Goering's dismay he tossed it angrily aside. He did not want to hear about such 'filth,' he said. Moreover, he gave orders for the record to be burned at once.

Reluctantly, Goering and Himmler obeyed. The record was destroyed — by Heydrich and after Heydrich's manner.

1935, 1936, 1937

ADOLF HITLER, in his unexampled generosity, promoted General von Fritsch to a colonel-general. He conferred upon the new colonel-general the Party insignia in gold. He presented him with a portrait of himself bearing a special dedication to the commander-in-chief.

We return to the turbulent days at the end of January, 1938.

There was a great deal of bustling in the Gestapo building. The surprising order had come from the chancellery that the Fritsch dossier, which had been destroyed in 1935, was to be reconstructed. In less than two hours Heydrich, the miracle-worker, had conjured those burned papers out of their ashes. They looked extremely well preserved, and, remarkably enough, their number had expanded considerably. Additional sheets had been inserted at the point where the dossier was broken off in 1935. A few errors had crept in, but none of them serious enough to disturb great minds. One or two statements, it seemed, had been written down by the hearing officers 'from memory' and therefore lacked signatures or contained a few wrong dates. Nevertheless, the dossier reached the chancellor quite punctually.

Hitler read it through once more, and this time it struck him as more credible. After the Blomberg scandal he considered anything possible.

Goering and Himmler kept after him.

Blomberg declared that he was ready to leave the country for a time. To make this decision easier for him, Goering had taken the precaution of sending the war minister a thick wad of foreign-exchange notes. Hitler thereupon ordered that the field marshal remain in exile from German soil for a full year.

Shortly before his departure, Blomberg went to see the Fuehrer, in spite of the express order that he must not set foot in the chancellery. There was a touching parting scene. It was Blomberg's turn to weep. By the time he left Hitler, the Fuehrer had half-forgiven him.

The marshal decided to make his first stops at Rome and Capri. Hitler sent a letter to Mussolini by special courier informing the Duce why Blomberg had had to be dismissed. He added a request to the Italian dictator to supply a police guard for his former war minister to protect Blomberg against possible insults.

Meanwhile, Morals Case II was running *its* course. Hitler decided to send for Fritsch. When Fritsch entered Hitler's study, he found Goering in attendance on the Fuehrer. The scene became a tribunal. Hitler informed Fritsch of the contents of the dossier. The commander-in-chief of the army indignantly repudiated the charge, but his denial made no impression on Hitler: Goering and Himmler had already carefully coached him that homosexuals always lied. Fritsch gave his leader and commander his word of honor that the whole business had no connection with him. His efforts were in vain. Without a word, Adolf Hitler went to the nearest door. He opened it, and a young man of .twenty-eight entered — Schmidt. The young man paused in the doorway, pointed dramatically at the man in the general's uniform, and said: 'That's the man.' Fritsch was flabbergasted. His face turned beet-red; he breathed heavily; and several times his shoulders twitched nervously. Hitler considered this behavior proof of his guilt.

After a moment Fritsch regained control of himself. He suggested the possibility of a confusion of persons. His phrase was something like 'The gentleman must be mistaken.' Hitler took this polite form of expression for another token of the general's guilt. Fritsch continued to rack his brains. Suddenly an inspiration came to him. Some time ago he had undertaken to provide board and lodging for a boy of the Hitler Youth. When the boy turned out to be a cheat and petty pilferer, Fritsch had boxed his ears and turned him out. Perhaps that was the source of this insane charge; the boy may have decided to slander him for revenge. Fritsch, however, was highly inarticulate and vague in describing this supposition. So there had been another intrigue with a Hitler Youth, the Fuehrer thought. By now Hitler was absolutely convinced of the general's guilt. Thereupon he demanded that the commander-in-chief resign his office at once. In return for the resignation he would be willing to cover up the incident and dismiss Fritsch with full honors, but Fritsch refused. He insisted that the accusation was mad and demanded a judicial investigation. Goering would not agree to this. The case was clear as day, he maintained.

Hitler postponed a decision. For the present Fritsch was ordered on leave.

Next Hitler sent for the chief of the general staff, General Beck, who was now the senior officer on duty. Goering was present, of course, and showed signs of extreme excitement, although he did not behave quite so nervously as his Fuehrer, who twisted about in his chair and was dripping with perspiration. In an inquisitorial tone Hitler asked his chief of the general staff when and where he had last lent money to Colonel-General von Fritsch. Fritsch, it seemed, had no account at the bank in East Lichterfelde. And since the dossier distinctly recorded that the victim of the blackmail had obtained money in that bank, Hitler suspected that the money was in Beck's account and that Beck had given Fritsch the right to use his checkbook freely. Beck had no suspicion of his Fuehrer's talent for refined detective work; he indignantly denied ever having lent money to Fritsch.

It was only after this denial that Beck learned what had been happening with Fritsch and Blomberg. Naturally he was horrified. In the name of the army he energetically demanded that the entire matter be clarified. His position was that Blomberg's lapse was so vile that he had automatically excluded himself from the army, but as far as Fritsch was concerned, the dignity and prestige of the army required a thoroughgoing investigation.

Beck noticed that Hitler did not at all like this clear distinction between the cases of Blomberg and of Fritsch. He noticed Goering's irritation when he supported Fritsch's demand for an investigation by a military tribunal. He was informed that the question was in any case to be settled on a friendly basis between Fritsch and Goering on the morrow.

Beck went directly to see Fritsch. The two men discussed what procedure would be best, and agreed that an immediate judicial investigation should be set in motion.

Meanwhile, Hitler sent for the Reich minister of justice. He told

Guertner about Blomberg's dismissal and Fritsch's enforced leave. Then he asked Guertner to examine the Fritsch dossier carefully and to make a report directly to him. Guertner read the document. This was not the first time he had dealt with such matters, and he knew only too well the quality of evidence supplied by the Gestapo. This case was unquestionably clear as day. Since a charge was being made against the commander-in-chief of the army, the tribunal competent to undertake the trial was a federal military court, but since Hitler had expressly asked him for an opinion, Guertner came to the astonishing conclusion that he must conduct an investigation on his own and deliver a kind of preliminary judicial decision. Therefore, he took his personal secretary along and, more or less incognito, started a grand jury investigation.

Overnight Beck decided that it might be better if he took a personal hand in the affair. He somehow felt doubtful that Fritsch would insist upon his rights with sufficient vigor. Therefore, in order to anticipate Fritsch, he called on Goering early in the morning. He was admitted to Goering's presence at once. But he learned to his astonishment that the planned conference between Goering and Fritsch had been called off. Goering had changed his mind; he had decided that he could not possibly discuss matters with a person who was in such odium. Instead, Fritsch was at the moment being subjected to an examination at Gestapo headquarters. During the heated conversation Goering was notified that another visitor was waiting. Beck noticed that the adjutants wished to conceal this visitor's name and presence from him. At the end of the interview, he was deliberately led out through another door, instead of through the door by which he had entered. He could not refrain from walking back a few steps and glancing into the reception room. He saw Minister of Justice Guertner standing there, nervous and ill at ease.

It seemed that Hitler had telephoned Fritsch and ordered him to go to the Gestapo headquarters at once in order to clear up the charges against him, and Fritsch actually went. As he strode down the long corridors of the Prinz Albrechtstrasse, he caught brief glimpses of suspicious figures hidden in dark corners. A number of homosexual boys had been picked up by the Gestapo men and given this opportunity to see Fritsch. Later they would 'recognize' the general as one of their 'customers.'

In the examination room an SS lieutenant received him. The SS man refused to be impressed by Fritsch's rank or title. On the contrary, he gave a splendid performance of the hard-boiled detective who had before him a virtually convicted criminal and was merely urging him to confess for the sake of form. The hearing was transcribed on phonograph records, and Himmler, Heydrich, and Goering made much of it. They cited a number of phrases that the lieutenant had impudently spoken to Fritsch's face and emphasized that the general had not once pounded his fist on the table in fury. Because Fritsch practiced exaggerated patience and silently put up with incredible insults, his opponents felt that his guilt was absolutely sealed.

January 26

WHEN I RETURNED early in the morning from a trip West, I found an urgent message from Schacht to come at once to the Reichsbank. Schacht led me directly into the room back of his office. There he whispered excitedly to me that he had heard a mad rumor, but had given his word not to say anything about it. In any case he had received only vague hints. He urged me to hurry to Helldorf and talk to him about Blomberg.

I took his car and drove to Alexanderplatz. On the way I decided that I had better look in on Nebe before speaking to Helldorf. Since Nebe's office was also in police headquarters, no time would be lost, and if there were real trouble afoot, Nebe would probably know something.

As soon as I entered Nebe's office, he looked at me in that significant manner of his. Then he took a small file under his arm and went out into the hall with me. We went up the stairs and around corners and paused in one of the remote hallways of the complicated building. There followed the usual warnings about keeping my mouth shut, deadly peril, Gestapo, and so on.

I pulled the papers out of his hand and glanced impatiently through them. They contained his report on the Blomberg affair. The central section for the suppression of immoral pictures and writing, which was under him, had assembled its material on the field marshal's wife. I saw five piquant photographs, and I had to admit that they were anything but decent. But Nebe had added his bit. Although the case was now six days old, Nebe was the first to think of examining the register of arrest warrants. Now he had added fingerprints to the collection of photographs, for the name of Erna Gruhn had even made its appearance in the register of arrest warrants. The warrant had been issued, not for a crime against morality, but for a suspected theft which, however, had never been proved. Out of malice or great foresight, the police had never troubled to remove the record after she was cleared of the charge. I must admit that the sight of those curves and whorls fazed me most of all. Fingerprints are common enough in police work, and they all look pretty much alike to the careless examination, but the fingerprints of a real field marshal's wife were something I had never dreamed I should see if I lived the full thousand years of Hitler's Reich.

I left Nebe and went to see Helldorf. The police chief gave me a hasty summary of what had happened. I then returned to Schacht and told him what I knew. We both agreed that I ought to look in at the war ministry right away. By chance I met Oster in the lobby, and he took me upstairs to see Canaris, who admitted me at once. This was quite remarkable in itself; for at least a year the admiral had consistently avoided meeting me. Before I could say a word, Canaris burst out: 'Isn't this all dreadful?' He was much disturbed. These intense reactions of his always impressed me, for as chief of the secret service he might well have become more immune than other officers to such unpleasant affairs. Canaris listened attentively to my account of the details. Significantly enough, at this late stage of the scandal he had received only hints as to the nature of Erna Gruhn's past.

In the course of our conversation, Canaris casually dropped the remark, 'There's supposed to be something wrong with Fritsch too.' He said no more because that was all he knew — he did not even know that for the past two days Fritsch had been suspended from office.

From this point on, we worked like mad. Oster and I agreed on a definite course of action. Our first effort was to find out what the Fritsch business was about. Schacht was a minister of the Reich, Canaris the chief of military intelligence. It would seem that in such positions these two ought to be able to find out things. How far from the truth this glib supposition was! Being a minister meant no more than relative security against being spied on too brashly. By their passivity the ministers had completely excluded themselves from participation in crucial decisions. They had no right at all to any political information. Incredible as it sounds, the chief of military intelligence had even less claim to information on domestic events. In 1935, Blomberg and Reichenau had accepted the fateful division of spheres of interest between the army and the SS. Since then the 'unpolitical' army had maintained no political information service. It was allowed to engage only in military espionage. It was only after the bitter experiences of the Fritsch crisis that Canaris decided that this state of affairs could not continue. He, therefore, deliberately encouraged his subordinates to work on information outside their appointed realm; it was the only way he could guard the generals against being tricked once more by the Gestapo. After the Fritsch crisis, Oster set up his own secret service, so that the men in the war ministry would learn in good time what plots were being devised in the triangle formed by the chancellery, Karinhall, and the Gestapo.

The only member of the Opposition who was in a position to find out anything definite about the Fritsch case was Nebe, whose work placed him in close contact with the Gestapo. His federal criminal office was a part of Heydrich's security office *(Sicherheitsamt)*. Helldorf might have helped, but Heydrich and Himmler had found what he had done with the Blomberg dossier. After that second act of disobedience, they were not likely to tell Helldorf anything. Most of the work fell upon Nebe, who had the opportunity to poke around in Himmler's and Heydrich's anterooms. Fortunately, the adjutants of the Black twins were not at all close-mouthed.

At such tense periods, whenever my telephone rang and I heard when I lifted the receiver an unrecognizable voice uttering grunting sounds, I knew that the call came from Nebe. Even the best microphone could make nothing out of those weird noises of his, but to me they meant that something special was in the air. I would then hurry outside and go to a certain corner, where his car would be parked. At a near-by shop window my friend would be standing, watching the reflection in the glass to make sure that no one was spying on him from across the street. I would drift innocently past him, and he would follow inconspicuously. At last he would catch up and we would stroll along together.

My meetings with Oster, Goerdeler, or Schacht, to mention only these three, were carried on with similar caution. This, be it noted, was only in the early part of 1938. Nevertheless, we already felt it unwise to be seen together in public. We made it a principle to telephone only from public telephones and to use aliases for such calls. For years the doormen and chauffeurs of the Reichsbank and of *Wehrmacht* headquarters did not know my right name. This was a real burden, for to maintain a disguise for any considerable period of time takes more discipline than is generally realized. How great a temptation it often is to hasten matters by telephoning from one's private telephone! But a disguise that has been exposed is a thousand times worse than none at all.

Oster decided to take a risky step. He sent for one of Blomberg's adjutants, a young captain, and questioned him. When the captain proved not unwilling to talk, Oster brought me in. Then I launched into a kind of official interrogation. I started with the question of when the Gruhn woman had first appeared and went on to ask about the field marshal's habits. Unfortunately, the captain could not tell us how Blomberg had chanced to meet his present wife. What we wanted to know, of course, was whether it was by pure chance that this woman had crossed Blomberg's path. It was hard to determine, for it appeared that many nights he would leave his car and disappear into the turmoil of the streets for hours.

We also heard a little more about the wedding. It had not, ap parently, been a very happy affair. There had been, of course, no church ceremony. And the civil rites were performed with suspicious haste. Ordinarily anyone who wanted to get married in the Third Reich had to present dozens of documents: police records of residence, genealogies, and so on. But this time all such formalities had been waived! In just this one case!

The wedding had taken place on Goering's birthday. In the morning Blomberg had sent his adjutant to Goering with a present. The rather naïve young captain had been somewhat surprised at the manner in which Goering took him aside and inquired with obvious nervousness about the program of the wedding ceremony, which was set for that afternoon. Apparently there was something about the matter that was highly embarrassing to Goering.

The top army leaders who were in Berlin at the time kept in close touch with one another, and soon realized that General Keitel was working out a special plot of his own at the chancellery. The first decision the group of generals came to was that Fritsch must not, under any circumstances, continue going to Gestapo headquarters. Beck transmitted this request to Fritsch. He learned, in the course of his interview with the commander-in-chief, that Fritsch was still obsessed by the idea that there was something he had to 'clarify.' Apparently the general believed that not only he, but also Hitler and Goering, were the victims of a dreadful mistake; and that these two would, therefore, help him clear the matter up. That was the only reason he had consented to be interrogated at the Prinz Albrechtstrasse, Fritsch said.

It occurred neither to Fritsch nor to any of the other generals to look around for other support, and yet at that time there still existed a cabinet in which bourgeois ministers were in the majority. There was, moreover, a good deal of secret opposition in the rest of Germany. What the generals needed was the courage to risk publicity, in spite of the tremendous embarrassment that the Blomberg affair involved and in spite of the fact that the Fritsch case was at this time so mysterious. Instead, the generals obediently submitted to Hitler's order that the two affairs be kept secret. Didn't they realize, or didn't they want to admit, that now everything was at stake for them?

Our uncertainty became all the more painful when we learned that Raeder had visited the Fuehrer in order to suggest that it would certainly attract attention if a Fritsch scandal were made public right on top of the Blomberg scandal. Such a peculiar duplication of events would certainly cause talk, Raeder said, especially since the Gestapo had had a hand in both affairs. We heard that Hitler had made no reply, but had merely handed the admiral the Fritsch dossier.

When I speak of 'we' in those days of the crisis, I mean only Schacht, Goerdeler, Nebe, and myself among the civilians — and Helldorf also — and Beck, Canaris, and Oster in the war ministry. Our mood of depression can best be gauged by the phrase we repeated to one another almost every time we met: 'Now it's come.' For years we had seen it coming — a grand *coup de main* by the SS against the war ministry. The fact in itself did not surprise us. What completely baffled us were the concomitant circumstances. Why, at this particular juncture, did both the war minister and the commander-in-chief of the army have to be involved in scandals? The two most important leaders of the army had been deposed, and there appeared to be no one to jump into the breach.

From the very beginning we saw the broader meaning of the events quite clearly. It did not really matter what was the real story in the cases of Blomberg and Fritsch. The important fact was that the SS was getting ready for the decisive blow against the army. Even at that time we saw and declared quite openly that this bloodless *coup d'état* meant *war*.

We therefore saw only one course open. Counter-action must be taken, and at once. The army would have to beat the Gestapo to the draw. Schacht went to see Raeder and explained why something had to be done. The admiral was generally in agreement. But — he was sorry — unfortunately he could do nothing. The affair did not lie within his competence. Schacht also tried Rundstedt, but was coldly received. The Berlin commander haughtily replied that he would know what to do if and when he chose to act.

Goerdeler, of course, promptly set up headquarters in Berlin. Since his dismissal from the office of price administrator in 1936, Goerdeler had devoted his whole time to traveling up and down Germany trying to arouse people. Years later, when the presiding judge of the people's court charged that he was a 'traveling salesman of the defeatism,' we had to admit that the sanguinary Freisler had lifted the correct phrase out of his Nazi vocabulary. Throughout all those years Goerdeler had one noble, besetting passion: he wanted to admonish, to warn, and, if possible, to act. He saw the catastrophe coming and tried, with all the energy of his powerful personality, to hurl back the horror of a Hitler war. But who listened to him?

Months before, he had predicted to Fritsch exactly what was going to happen. At that time the colonel-general had been loath to believe that any attack on him was planned. Now Goerdeler again tried, through the mediation of Beck, to talk to Fritsch. But Fritsch would not see him. He then went to see Guertner. A great deal might depend on Guertner's report — which he had not yet sent to Hitler. If the minister of justice would join with the generals, so that a drive against the Gestapo could be launched from two sides at once, the affair might turn out well after all; but Guertner refused to stir. He behaved with his usual passivity. He saw the situation quite clearly and would even mournfully contribute a story or two of his own to prove that things were even worse than anyone imagined, but he could not bring himself to act, and by his resignation he reinforced the stand of all the other timid souls.

Nebe kept busy trying to uncover the preliminary intrigue behind the Blomberg and the Fritsch cases. Helldorf, too, was working along these lines, but more and more we were forced to recognize that the top leaders of the army were going to shirk this unique opportunity to act. Goerdeler and I tried some of the commanding generals in the provinces, but we found to our dismay that they had not even heard of the events in Berlin.

Meanwhile, behind the scenes there raged a fierce battle for the succession to the fallen leaders. Goering considered himself the chief favorite. Reichenau, too, who was at this time the local commander in Munich, received hints of the way the wind was blowing, and sud-

denly found that he had urgent business in Berlin. Himmler lurked
in the background. He would be content if, at the end of the crisis,
his SS were installed as a fourth branch of the army. Hitler vacillated
among the various candidates. This was not surprising, for up to
now he had always been careful not to give Goering too much power.

At last Nebe picked up some information. It was not much, but it
was the key to everything. He had heard, he told me, that the 'case'
of Fritsch was a matter of confused identities. Heydrich and Himmler
knew this, he said, but had taken every imaginable measure to cover
up the fact. We discussed at length how we should proceed in order
not to endanger any of the officials who had betrayed this secret, for it
was obvious that Heydrich would run amok if he discovered that
someone in his own organization had played him false.

I got in touch with Oster at once. He informed Canaris early in
the morning, and Canaris saw to it that Beck and Keitel were told.
I myself went to the war ministry and dictated a memorandum. I
emphasized that it is the obligation of every police officer to proceed
with the greatest caution in dealing with charges or denunciations of
homosexuality. I pointed out that in this particular sphere perjury
for purposes of extortion was extremely common. For that reason a
precise check-up on all allegations was always indispensable. In this
way I beat about the bush and, without mentioning details, suggested
a host of questions arising from the case that pointed to the possibility
of mistaken identities.

Canaris at once passed my statement on to Beck and Raeder, and
within the next few days it was placed in the hands of other interested
generals.

Meanwhile, the conferences in the chancellery were growing more
and more hectic. Hitler stormed and raged and waxed insulting to the
army officers present. The officers energetically insisted that a military tribunal be convoked to try the case of Fritsch. Goering and
Himmler objected vehemently. They insisted that there was nothing
to clear up and that the generals merely wanted to postpone a decision by clouding the issue with judicial sophistries.

Blomberg had left for his honeymoon without handing in his resignation. Consequently, Hitler must have been undecided up to the time Blomberg departed. Apparently the generals' uncompromising attitude decided him: the field marshal had to go. A courier was sent to Capri to obtain the war minister's resignation. The choice of courier fell upon Oster, since he was one of the few persons in the war ministry who knew anything about this scandal. He found the new bridegroom given up to the enjoyment of connubial happiness and apparently quite forgetful of his former conceptions of morality and class status.

February 3

ANOTHER OF HITLER'S HISTORIC SATURDAYS. Oster had returned by plane. Now the stage was set. The radio stations asked their listeners to stay tuned in for an important special announcement. Then the inevitable march music began. But we waited for two hours for the announcement, spending our time guessing who was to be war minister and who commander-in-chief of the army.

What followed was one of Hitler's masterpieces of camouflage and craft. First we heard that Foreign Minister von Neurath had resigned and Ribbentrop had been appointed his successor. Neurath was consoled with the presidency of a privy council which was created specially for the purpose (and which never convened). Some ten ministers were listed who had been appointed to this new council. Then it was announced that a number of ambassadors had been retired. Only after all this did we at last hear that Blomberg had resigned his post as war minister. The commander-in-chief of the army, it was added, had also asked to be relieved of his duties for reasons of health. General von Brauchitsch, commander of the East Prussian army group, had been appointed to succeed Fritsch, while Hitler himself was taking the post of war minister. The war ministry as an independent ministry was being dissolved. General Keitel was appointed as Hitler's permanent representative on the newly formed *Oberkommando der Wehrmacht* (OKW).[1]

[1] Supreme command of the armed forces.

Goering also received a consolation prize for not being given the war ministry. Hitler gave him the title of general field marshal, thus promoting him to the highest ranking army officer. As commander of the air force, Goering, curiously enough, now ranked higher than the heads of the army and navy.

As if this were not enough, a general transfer of posts among army commanders was announced. About a dozen commanding generals were forced to retire because they had offended the Nazi Party. In addition, a whole series of changes in the ministry of economics was announced. Most of these were insignificant, but Funk, who had long been designated for the post, was finally appointed Schacht's successor.

This dramatic special announcement produced the impression that these happenings were merely one of those broad shifts in personnel that occur now and then in every government. The brief official commentaries stressed this point of view; they instructed the German public that the purpose of these many changes was a tighter organization of the government machinery under the unified leadership of Adolf Hitler. Nothing was said, of course, of the fact that the head of the National Socialist Party had secured, by a bloodless *coup d'état,* sole command over the army. Nor was there any mention of the scandals in which Blomberg and Fritsch were involved.

Nevertheless, we few initiates were amazed at Hitler's effrontery. What cynicism to dismiss Fritsch for homosexual misdemeanors that were entirely unproved on the same day that he appointed a notorious homosexual, Funk, to the office of a cabinet minister!

February 4, 1938

THIS IS AN HISTORIC DATE. On that day the revolutionary changes that had been announced the night before were finally ratified.

At ten o'clock in the morning the cabinet met — a rare enough event in itself. The ministers had no conception of how highly Hitler was honoring them by calling this meeting, for it was the last meeting of the cabinet in the Third Reich. The Fuehrer reported on the events of the past few weeks. This report took about half an hour.

Then the ministers silently took their leave. In the evening the bewildered participants read in the newspapers that they had approved Hitler's measures and offered him their congratulations.

Next the commanding generals of the army were called to the chancellery. Hitler, still in a state of extreme excitement, roared at them; his speech was at once menacing and imploring. First he described the case of Blomberg; remarkably enough, he let the field marshal off very easily. He stuck to the old version about Erna Gruhn's being a 'lady with a past,' and said not a word about her being a prostitute. But, he added, by the exercise of no amount of broadmindedness was it possible for him to accept this marriage.

After this prelude the Fuehrer launched into a detailed exposition of the Fritsch case. In order to imagine the effect of this speech, it must be remembered that the majority of the générals present had not yet heard so much as a rumor about the whole story. Now, from the lips of the chief of state, they heard a garish detective novel. Every smallest detail was mentioned; threateningly, the orator waved the dossiers that lay before him and read aloud a few extracts from them. He behaved like a prosecuting attorney addressing the jury, and his persuasiveness had its effect. Kluge later told me that as he was going out one of the generals with whom he was friendly tapped him on the shoulder and whispered into his ear: 'After hearing him talk I could almost believe it.'

The generals had, however, won at least one point. Hitler announced that a military tribunal was to be convoked to investigate the Fritsch case.

Goering and Himmler did everything in their power to obstruct the convoking of the military tribunal, but under pressure from the new commander-in-chief, Brauchitsch, Hitler at last kept his word and issued the directive for the court to convene. But there was still another hurdle to be crossed: the appointment of the examining magistrate. After twenty-four hours of tugging back and forth, the magistrate was at last named — a member of the National Socialist Party.

Meanwhile, we were insistent that excitement over Fritsch should not make us forget the Blomberg case. We wanted to know what part the Gestapo had played in this extremely odd marriage. How could Blomberg have married this woman without someone's informing him in time about her previous life? What had Goering and Hitler known about this 'lady with a past'?

Suddenly we learned that a mysterious unknown was involved in the marital history of Erna Gruhn. Acquaintances of friends of friends passed on the story that a clerk in a certain Berlin firm had taken passage for South America with suspicious haste. Apparently his voyage was not entirely voluntary. After a time we found out all the details, which were later confirmed by Helldorf who had heard the story directly from Goering.

It seemed that one fine day, about three months before his marriage, Blomberg had come to see Goering to ask his advice in a confidential matter. The war minister informed Goering that he was having an affair with a girl of the people. He wanted Goering to tell him whether there was any objection. Goering replied that in the Third Reich, especially in such matters, every minister could do just as he pleased. When the field marshal alluded to his high position, Goering told him not to worry; such social prejudices were scarcely good form in the present day.

After some time the infatuated Blomberg came to see him again. This time he asked whether there would be any objection to his marrying his 'affair.' As he had said, she was a person of the lower classes and, moreover, a 'lady with a past.' Goering frowned briefly, but the frown was at once superseded by the expression of a kindly well-wisher. He promised the aspiring suitor that he would put in a good word with the Fuehrer for him, and he did in fact secure a dispensation from the Fuehrer. As Hitler later put it, the phrase 'lady with a past' had given him the idea of 'a woman who had been divorced several times and perhaps had also passed through several hands in other ways.'

Some time afterward Blomberg again came to see Goering. This time he was completely broken up. With tears in his eyes he told his plaint. It seemed that his future bride had a lover with whom she still maintained a close 'friendship.' The field marshal asked Goering whether he could help him put his rival to flight. Goering frowned this time as well, but again he played the part of well-wisher — of 'friend,' as he put it to Helldorf. The two discussed what would be the quietest way to settle this embarrassing situation. Astonishingly enough — probably out of consideration for the chivalrous notions of the field marshal — Goering did not suggest a suicide in concentration camp. Instead, he proposed that Erna's beloved be banished across the high seas.

No sooner said than done. Goering sent for the man and informed him that his cabin on shipboard was already reserved and that his new home in South America was waiting for him. The lover was sensible enough not to object. He took the ticket and money and hastily said good-bye to his sweetheart; but before he left, he paid a second call on Goering: he felt obliged, he said, to warn Goering about Blomberg's prospective wife; Erna Gruhn was a woman of highly questionable character. With that off his chest, the lover departed.

This story made the fateful marriage more mysterious than ever. Apparently, not only must Blomberg have known a great deal about his lady's past, but Goering and Hitler also could not have been entirely ignorant. Goering, at any rate, must have known precisely what sort of adventure Blomberg was plunging into. Why had he not warned him? Why had he not forcibly restrained him? Why had he not at least refused to assist in removing the lover? Above all, why had he been willing to be a witness at the wedding? Moreover, Hitler had been the other witness at the wedding. Was it possible that he had known nothing at all about the banished lover? As head of state, would he have cared to compromise himself in this manner if he had known the full story?

The Fritsch investigation continued.

After a long struggle, on about the eighth day of the hearings the convict Schmidt communicated some details. In response to close questioning, he named the street and house in East Lichterfelde into which Fritsch had allegedly gone in order to get the money. This basic testimony should, of course, have been obtained during the first hearings in 1935.

The obvious thought occurred to the examining magistrate to make an on-the-spot check. That was the simplest way to find out whether Schmidt's allegations were true. Hitler had, as a matter of fact, issued orders that such investigations were to be conducted only with the assistance of the Gestapo, but the examining magistrate had somehow got the idea that it might be necessary to anticipate the Gestapo if he hoped to learn anything at all. Therefore, accompanied by another magistrate, Doctor Sack, he set out for Lichterfelde early in the morning. He left instructions at his office to telephone the Gestapo and inform them of his errand only after he and his companion had reached the scene. Thus he contrived to obey the letter of Hitler's orders.

The two magistrates visited the house Schmidt had mentioned. They found no sign that anyone was or had been living there who fitted Schmidt's description. However, they decided to look around the vicinity a bit. They did not have far to seek. In the very next house they found a door marked plainly with a very interesting name: von Frisch.

A housekeeper opened the door. She expressed her regret that the gentleman could not receive them: he was in bed and very sick, but she readily gave them what data she possessed. It seemed that the man was a retired Captain von Frisch who had been living on his pension in East Lichterfelde for several decades. Through a crack in the door the magistrates caught a brief glimpse of the sick-room. As far as they could tell — the man was, after all, lying in bed — von Frisch conformed pretty well to Schmidt's description. They also looked around the hallway and saw the green hat, the short jacket with the fur collar, and the cane with the silver knob which were described in Schmidt's statement.

As the two were taking their leave, they noticed that the housekeeper was a little put out by their visit. She shook her head and asked what was wrong this time. 'This time?' the amazed visitors asked. 'Yes,' the housekeeper replied; she added that some Gestapo officers had been there only a few weeks ago. By chance she recalled the exact date. It was January 15. The two magistrates could scarcely believe their ears. The fifteenth of January — it was impossible, for that unpleasant scene in the chancellery, when Hitler had confronted General Fritsch with his accuser, had taken place on January 24; but the housekeeper insisted that she was right about the date.

The following day the two magistrates went to Lichterfelde once again, intending to interrogate the man, no matter how sick he was, but alas, when they arrived at the apartment Captain Frisch was no longer there. The night before the Gestapo had arrested him and taken him away.

There began a breathless struggle for the dying von Frisch. Brauchitsch, Keitel, Guertner, Goering, Himmler, Heydrich, and dozens of satellites raced around the chancellery in a state of feverish excitement. Everyone felt that the affair was reaching a dramatic climax, for the nth time we idiots imagined that the Gestapo had gone too far and that at last the generals would take action. Nothing at all, however, came out of all this frenzied negotiating. Hitler was, of course, compelled to make a decision, but as usually happened in such cases he made an empty gesture of compromise. The Gestapo had to surrender the retired captain, but the military court did not get him. Instead, he was handed over to the minister of justice who had him placed in federal detention headquarters. There, on the following day, the hotly disputed interrogation took place. Captain von Frisch confessed to having been the unfortunate victim of blackmail. He corroborated Schmidt's story down to the smallest detail. Then he died.

Frisch's statement produced a whirl of confusion in Goering's home at Karinhall and in the chancellery. The generals demanded that Fritsch be re-established at once. Hitler raged, Goering roared. The only ones who kept their heads were Himmler and Heydrich. They realized that their only hope now lay in sheer impudence. Boldly they pretended that nothing at all had happened. They flatly denied that the Gestapo had visited Frisch in Lichterfelde on January 15. The housekeeper was lying, they insisted. The explanation they offered was so wild that it was almost credible. There had, they said, been two separate cases; by chance Schmidt had blackmailed both a von Frisch and a von Fritsch. To support this assertion, they haled Schmidt out of the Gestapo cellar at Prinz Albrechtstrasse. Schmidt readily declared that there had indeed been two different cases, and that his part in both had been exactly the same.

We tried repeatedly to persuade the new commander-in-chief of the army, von Brauchitsch, to take immediate action, but Brauchitsch stalled: first the military tribunal had to pronounce its verdict; then, he assured us solemnly, he would act.

Meanwhile, it was rumored that Fritsch wanted to challenge Himmler to a duel. We heard that Fritsch was taking target practice at home. Everyone hoped something would come of it. We joyfully pictured Himmler as the target.

The investigation continued, and produced new sensations. The examining magistrate went to the bank located near the railroad station at East Lichterfelde. He found that Captain von Frisch had had an account there and that the sums named by the blackmailer had been withdrawn from the account. He also found out something else of significance. The Gestapo had anticipated him there too. On January 15, Gestapo officials had examined all the records of the von Frisch account.

Now there could no longer be any doubt. The housekeeper had not lied. The Gestapo was convicted of having framed the whole case against Fritsch. Himmler had knowingly tricked Hitler into taking action against Fritsch. We took heart again. Perhaps Brauchitsch had not been altogether wrong with his dilatory tactics. Now the Gestapo was really unmasked. Now even the most gullible general must perceive the nature of the intrigue that had supplied Hitler with a pretext for his *coup d'état*.

Nebe learned that when Fritsch had gone to Cairo in December for his vacation, two Gestapo officers had followed him to spy on him. This was proof enough that the Gestapo had been trying to get 'evidence' on Fritsch for some time. While this sort of thing became routine later on, in those early days it was something novel for the

Gestapo to spy on the commander-in-chief of the army. When this story came out, Heydrich insisted that he was not the originator of this reconnoitering expedition to Cairo. He had, he asserted, merely passed on orders, and quite reluctantly. But what else could he do? Goering had asked him to send the men. How the name of Goering kept cropping up! The chain of events seemed very strange indeed. In January, when Hitler had wanted to make Fritsch war minister, Goering had felt obliged to remind the Fuehrer of the 'burned' dossier dating from 1935. Yet this same Goering had placed spies on the trail of Fritsch in December.

Around this time, it will be remembered, Goering was disposing of Erna Gruhn's lover. He therefore knew that Blomberg was pretty much done for. All he needed to complete the picture was to push Blomberg into the idiocy of marrying the woman — preferably with Hitler as one of the witnesses at the ceremony. Then Blomberg would have to go and the road to the war ministry would be clear. But — Fritsch would also have to be dealt with by then. To accomplish that, Goering needed some powerful evidence against Fritsch. Apparently he had not felt too secure about the validity of the evidence in the 1935 dossier. For this reason he had sent the two spies to Cairo to watch the unsuspecting Fritsch. Unfortunately for his purposes, the two spies reported that Fritsch had behaved like the perfect gentleman he was.

During this time, Schacht was reappointed as president of the Reichsbank. Twice he refused to accept the appointment because the conditions he had set (they dealt with the amount of credit the Reichsbank was to extend to the treasury) had not been fulfilled. The third time he rejected the appointment in a personal message to Hitler. The Fuehrer knew, he wrote, that Schacht often had his own opinions and often criticized the government openly. Since these were the same misdeeds for which Fritsch had been dismissed, he wished to inform Hitler that he would accept the reappointment only on condition that he would be protected against libelous charges similar to those that were now being made against the former commander-in·

chief. The following day he received final confirmation of the appointment. Hitler protested to him that he was harboring some unfortunate misconceptions. If he really knew all the details of the Fritsch case, he would look upon it in a different light.

Schacht used his reappointment as a pretext for seeing Brauchitsch, but as soon as Brauchitsch realized that Schacht wanted to discuss the Fritsch case, he refused to continue the conversation. Was this a bad sign? we wondered. Or was Brauchitsch merely practicing extreme discretion?

After weeks of postponement, Hitler finally appointed the other members of the military tribunal. The composition of this tribunal was a matter that had given us grave concern, for the charges against Fritsch had already receded into the background. It was obvious that he would be cleared; the chief question now was whether the court would look into the circumstances behind this remarkable case.

Adolf Hitler made matters very easy for himself. As judges he appointed the present commander-in-chief of the army, Brauchitsch; the commander-in-chief of the navy, Admiral Raeder; and two judges of the federal supreme court. With his invariable formal correctness, he appointed the highest-ranking officer in Germany as presiding judge of the court — General Field Marshal Hermann Goering. In regard to these appointments Hitler appended the explanation that Goering was particularly well suited to conduct this delicate affair since he was already very well acquainted with it. Unquestionably his familiarity with the material would help him to bear more easily the burden of judicial objectivity!

We tried to persuade Fritsch that this epoch-making trial gave him the chance to play the part, not of the accused, but of the inexorable accuser. He had, we pointed out, a better opportunity to speak out than did the judges. It was up to him to call a certain witness whom Goering would not be likely to invite. In fact, we suggested, it would be best for Fritsch to take the bull by the horns; he could refuse to accept Goering on grounds that the field marshal was implicated in the case. Hitler would find it difficult to reject this charge. At the least it would be clear from the beginning what Fritsch conceived Goering's part to be in this obscure affair.

Since, after all that had taken place, we did not feel we could put much trust in Fritsch's resolution, we also tried to work on Brauchitsch and Raeder. Again we pointed out that in this unique trial their business was to do more than clear the honor of a colonel-general of the army. If they showed just a spark of courage, we said, they would free all of Germany from the clutches of the Gestapo. This time Himmler and Heydrich could not escape if — but only if — that pair of criminals were challenged. To expose the entire frame-up, only a few facts had to be laid bare. All the two commanders had to do was to ask a few questions with military precision. I hastily drafted a list of questions which was given to Brauchitsch and Raeder on the eve of the trial. Beck and Canaris made an effort to explain each of the questions orally to them.

March 11

THE MILITARY TRIBUNAL was to convene early in the morning. All of us waited tensely. At Gestapo headquarters, too, there was great suspense. Toward noon one of our observers returned in haste. Something must be wrong, he said. During the trial an adjutant from the chancellery had suddenly appeared, and immediately thereafter the tribunal had adjourned *sine die*. Goering, Brauchitsch, and Raeder had sped directly to the Fuehrer.

What now?

The following morning we read all about it in the newspapers. Overnight Hitler had marched into Austria. No comment is necessary. Under such circumstances there was no time for a military tribunal, of course. Soldiers on duty had to report; retired colonel-generals would have to wait. Moreover, the army could not bother about domestic scandals at this time; there was too much tension abroad. Every decent officer had his eyes on the frontiers rather than on trivial Gestapo cases.

It would seem that a move like the occupation of Austria would be of sufficient gravity to be discussed beforehand with Brauchitsch and Raeder, for it was obvious to all that Austrian Chancellor Schuschnigg's call for a plebiscite had merely provided a welcome superficial pretext for Hitler's action, but Hitler was very clever; he was shrewd enough to know the best way to launch a political diversionary project. What psychological effectiveness there was to that trick of summoning the unsuspecting commanders, Brauchitsch and Raeder, away from the trial under such dramatic circumstances! By his first military *Blitz* Hitler not only caught the foreign powers off guard, but completely surprised his own generals.

The propaganda machine went into action; Goebbels announced that reasons of foreign policy made it necessary for Hitler to hold a popular referendum on the Austrian *Anschluss*. Now was the time for all good Germans, whether or not they were Nazis, to show perfect good faith. Who at such a time would dare to raise the banner of domestic opposition? The internal crisis that had raged before and after February 4 was forgotten — now the Fuehrer was the uncontested victor. Had he not really 'pulled it off' this time? Neither England, France, Italy, nor the Little Entente had declared war; and how generous he had been in giving a share of the Party's glory to the army! Flowers rained down on the victorious troops. Wasn't the Fritsch case worth a Mass in Saint Stephen's Cathedral?

March 17

AFTER A WEEK'S INTERVAL the military tribunal met again. The proceedings limped slowly along. Dozens of insignificant witnesses were called to testify, and all of them stated that Fritsch had never behaved in a blameworthy manner. Fritsch, who by now was certain of being cleared, was unwilling to make trouble. The real subject of the trial — the rôle of the Gestapo — was not mentioned.

It slipped into the business of the court three times, however. One of the judges asked the Gestapo official on the stand whether it was true that he had visited von Frisch's apartment on January 15.

The official answered that he had. He also admitted that at the same time the Gestapo had confiscated the bank records of Captain von Frisch's account, but, he testified, they had not had time to read them through.

Another judge asked whether it was true that General von Fritsch had been spied on in Cairo. The Gestapo official lied boldly; no such spying had taken place, he asserted. Thereupon Goering interrupted him and warned: 'You had better say: not to your knowledge.'

Schmidt was asked whether he had been influenced or threatened by any members of the Gestapo before he appeared on the stand. Yes, he said, SS *Oberfuehrer* Meisinger had warned him only the night before that if he did not stand by his former statements he would find himself on his way to heaven on the morrow. Meisinger, questioned about this, admitted having used this phrase. But his intention, he said, had been merely to give Schmidt 'a drastic warning to tell the truth.'

The trial: second day

NO ONE REQUESTED that Himmler and Heydrich be invited to testify. Apparently the generals were so considerate that they wanted to spare them the necessity of perjury.

Schmidt followed instructions and lied. Captain von Frisch had not been Fritsch, he insisted, nor had Fritsch been Frisch. He could not explain how it had happened that all the confusion about Fritsch and Frisch had arisen, nor how he chanced to have met them at precisely the same places under precisely the same circumstances, but he was certain that he had met Fritsch just as he had described in his original statement.

Goering followed the usual Nazi conventions and roared at the blackmailer. In vain. Schmidt kept his mind on Meisinger's warning. Then Goering tried cajoling the convict. He appealed to his criminal's pride: Schmidt must not pretend to be more stupid than he was. In vain. Schmidt was still thinking of the prospects of his finding himself 'on his way to heaven.' Goering then made a few slips of the tongue. Now, he said, the time had come to speak frankly. He, Goering, had also threatened Schmidt with shooting if he did not stand by his statements, but he had not really meant it that way. In order to dispel any possible fears in the heart of this star witness he, Goering, would now solemnly retract his previous threat. This, too, was in vain. Schmidt knew the Gestapo only too well and he wanted to go on living for a while.

Then Goering's patience gave out. He snarled at the witness that he had better stop lying. If he confessed the truth now, he would not be harmed. Field Marshal Goering gave the convict his word, there, where so many high dignitaries of the army could hear him, that nothing would happen to him if he admitted that he had falsely accused General von Fritsch. By this time Schmidt was completely bewildered; he no longer knew what was going on and confessed that, after all, Frisch had been Frisch and only Frisch. Goering was so delighted at this confession that he completely forgot to inquire how the embarrassing misunderstanding had arisen in the first place.

The defense's speech followed. Fritsch, speaking in his own behalf, said not a word about the real issue. He limited himself to a discussion of the charges which had already been disproved. The verdict of not guilty followed immediately, and the trial was closed.

Now, we said to ourselves, the time had come. The Gestapo had been convicted, as far as everyone in the know was concerned. The generals could no longer maintain an attitude of lofty detachment. Now they had to act. Perhaps, however, Hitler would at once rehabilitate Fritsch. By dismissing Himmler, or at least Heydrich, the Fuehrer might be able to appease the wrath of the generals and keep them from taking action. Such a step might forestall further looking into the scandal and any detection of Goering's dubious rôle.

The verdict had been pronounced around noon. Early in the afternoon I talked to Nebe, and my friend's weary resignation spelled the end of all my hopes. He had just come from the trial and had been deeply depressed by Fritsch's refusal to speak out. 'You'll see, they won't do a thing,' he said to me. I tried to oppose his pessimism, but he had been watching Brauchitsch and Raeder at close quarters for two days, and his observations determined his view of them — for years to come.

What followed were days of disputing at the chancellery. It was rumored that Brauchitsch was putting forward very energetic demands. We waited in suspense for the results.

A week passed. Then came the long-awaited news. The German official news agency (DNB) reported that the Fuehrer had sent a telegram to Colonel-General Freiherr von Fritsch congratulating him on his recovery of health. That was not all. Brauchitsch was able to chalk up an additional 'success.' On his urging, Goering ordered a disciplinary trial of the Gestapo official who had admitted in court to having visited von Frisch's apartment on January 15. It must be noted that there was no hint of a trial against the Gestapo for concealing, on January 20, when the dossier was shown to the Fuehrer, the information it had obtained on January 15. Charges were leveled only against this poor devil of a minor official for having made such an awkward admission!

Nevertheless, there still remained a chance of getting somewhere, for this minor official could not possibly have acted on his own initiative. Who had given him his instructions? Who had been clairvoyant enough in the middle of January to foresee that the Fritsch case would come up again by the end of the month? It was quite evident that this disciplinary case provided a rope by which all the Gestapo criminals could be hanged, one after the other, but it was necessary for someone earnestly to want to hang them. Brauchitsch would have to insist on a close investigation; he would have to keep a sharp lookout for any chicaneries. Because he did not do so, the whole affair came to nothing.

The ministerial councilor who had been entrusted with the disciplinary investigation very swiftly touched the core of the whole ugly affair, but he instantly perceived that he was dealing with dangerously explosive material. Consequently, he procrastinated for days during his interrogation of the Gestapo official. He succeeded in enacting a classic model of judicial delay. And why not? The ministerial coun-

cilor quite rightly decided that it was not his vocation to make earth-
shaking revelations. If the army wanted to find out anything, let it
ask. Brauchitsch, however, asked no questions at all. Once or twice
we made an attempt to point out to him the significance of this disciplinary investigation, which he himself had urged. We even informed him confidentially that the official in charge of it was only
waiting to be asked a few concrete questions, but our efforts were in
vain.

During those weeks of anxious waiting I finally decided to take a
reckless step. I went to see Brauchitsch myself. Since I could not
make a direct appointment with him and wanted to avoid official
mediation, I simplified matters by one night buttonholing him in his
hotel after dinner. The commander-in-chief was, contrary to my expectations, quite genial. When I told him I wanted to talk with him,
he accompanied me to a small room off the lobby. There we sat close
together and chatted in whispers.

It was fortunate, I think, that Himmler had no microphones at
hand, for I soon became aware that my interlocutor's mood was one
of indignation, whereupon I dropped all my inhibitions and began
releasing all the venom I had stored up for years against the Gestapo.
I passionately insisted that the criminal band in Prinz Albrechtstrasse
must be broken up at once. Brauchitsch did not contest this; he
merely expressed doubts as to the best procedure to follow. Thereupon
I offered my concrete proposals.

I had by this time gained some insight into the psychology of these
high military officers. I knew that they wanted to do whatever they
considered to be inevitable in the most legalistic fashion possible.
Consequently, I tried to prove to Brauchitsch that no one was asking
him to conduct a *coup d'état* or even to perform an act of disloyalty
toward Hitler. A state of emergency plainly existed, I said, and immediate measures would have to be taken in order to prevent further
attacks upon leading officers of the army. Afterward there would be
no trouble at all finding ample proof of the criminality of the Gestapo
and of its plans to undermine the *Wehrmacht*. I gave him my personal
promise that a few hours after he acted, I would supply all the

evidence he needed from the Gestapo files. There would be no lack of legal grounds for his action, I assured him.

As far as I could see, the general was pleased by my plain speaking. No one, it seemed, had as yet put my 'legality theory' to him in quite so definite a form. At any rate, he clapped his thigh several times with enthusiasm as I rattled off quite extemporaneously a list of dozens of sound warrants that could be used to arrest the whole Gestapo crew, from the most minor henchman right up to Himmler, Heydrich, and Goering. I kept insisting that the whole action need not be conceived in political terms at all. The Gestapo, I said, was a criminal organization. As soon as the courts had a mandate to examine the untold number of Gestapo crimes, no German would question the justice of such an action by the military. Moreover, the cases of Blomberg and Fritsch still remained as pivots; both cases illustrated a deliberate Gestapo attack on the army.

I did not fail to point out to the commander-in-chief what a scurrilous part Goering had played in both these intrigues. Goering, I emphasized, was more dangerous to public welfare than any of the others. Brauchitsch would not agree, however. He assured me that his private thoughts about the field marshal were not different from mine, but, he said, it would be unwise to overstep oneself in the contemplated action. It would be better for the army to try to hitch Goering to its own wagon.

We sat together for some two hours. I talked myself into a pitch of excitement and tried to show Brauchitsch that any more hesitancy would be disastrous. We civilians had done a great deal in regard to the Fritsch affair, I pointed out. We had a right to expect that our efforts would be rewarded — especially since the generals had been promising us continually for over a month that they were going to take action. Before long the psychological strain on the civilians would prove overwhelming, I said, and they would be unable to stand up under it. It was all very well for the soldiers in their unpolitical 'splendid isolation'; their uniforms would protect them for a while against the Nazi reign of terror. They did not have to submit to Party inquisitions into their beliefs or to the daily spying of the

Gestapo. This Fritsch case, however, was a foretaste of what they might expect in the future, but, I argued, the past four years had left its trace on the civilians. All hope of a radical change in conditions was ebbing away. No wonder that some of those who had held firm up to now were beginning to grow weary. There was a growing tendency to make peace with the system, if not inwardly at least in external matters, and once the army lost its backing among the officials, the intellectuals and the economists, then it — and all the rest of Germany — would be utterly at the mercy of the Nazi Party's insatiable lust for power.

Two details of this conversation have stuck particularly fast in my memory. The first was Brauchitsch's careless reference to the Fuehrer as 'that fellow.' The second indication of his disrespect for Hitler came about when I referred to the fact that Hitler, consciously or unconsciously, was heading toward war. If someone did not put an end to the reign of terror very soon, I said, the catastrophe of a second world war would be unavoidable. At the word 'war' Brauchitsch raised his fingers to his temples and made an unmistakable gesture to indicate his opinion that the Fuehrer was not altogether sane.

How often I thought of that gesture during the years that followed! But that evening I was naïve enough to believe that the words and gestures of an army commander-in-chief could be taken at face value. I left Brauchitsch that night firmly convinced that the man was going to act.

In the Reichstag elections and in the plebiscite on Austria, Hitler had his greatest electoral triumph.

Goerdeler, the indomitable Goerdeler, succeeded in getting an interview with the reluctant and uneasy Brauchitsch. As he had done so often before, Goerdeler energetically depicted the internal and external situation, concluding with the statement that some action had to be taken. In his analysis Goerdeler never forgot to point out the imminence of war and to explain, at the same time, by what means an honorable peace could be assured. The first prerequisite for a purging of internal and foreign affairs, he said, was the liquidation of the Gestapo.

In spite of his frequent disappointments, Goerdeler never gave up hope. His cool, logical mind simply could not grasp that a general's 'yes' had already become almost a 'no' by the time the door closed behind him. This time he was filled with particular optimism, for Brauchitsch had not only agreed to every word he said, but had shown signs of visible emotion at the end. In parting he had virtually sworn to act soon. Goerdeler was bubbling with enthusiasm. There was no doubt about it now, he said; it was only a question of time. I was somewhat more skeptical, but my hopes, too, ran high.

Brauchitsch had said that he needed one more tiny item of proof in regard to the Fritsch scandal. He wanted evidence that Goering must have known about the Gestapo man's investigation of von Frisch's home on January 15. Hearing about this, I volunteered to explain the matter, and Goerdeler wrote a letter to the commander-in-chief suggesting that he give me an immediate appointment. The following morning, when Oster personally delivered this letter to Brauchitsch, the commander-in-chief went into a fit of rage and declared he absolutely would not see me. In our initial dismay we assumed that I must again have done something wrong or spoken out of turn. But Oster soon learned from Brauchitsch's adjutant that the commander-in-chief had nothing special against me; he had simply declared that he would never receive Goerdeler again for the rest of his life.

It turned out that Brauchitsch had received a letter that morning which was causing all the trouble. A relative had informed him that he had heard from somebody who knew somebody who had heard from somebody that another somebody had heard a dreadful story. Goerdeler, it seemed, had been in London for a brief stay recently. While there he had hinted to some persons that a general clean-up might soon take place within Germany. It was alleged, by way of this string of somebodies, that he had referred to Brauchitsch as the man who was going to do the cleaning-up.

Goerdeler, who was on his way to South Germany, was hurriedly recalled. His amazement at this sudden turn of events can well be imagined. He discussed the affair with Beck and General Thomas. Both reported that Brauchitsch was in a fury and wanted to hand the matter over to — the Gestapo! Thereupon Goerdeler insisted that Brauchitsch see him personally, and when the commander-in-chief refused to accept any explanations, Goerdeler anticipated him by proposing that the case should be submitted to an official investigation.

Naturally, we all flatly asserted that there was no truth at all in the story, but whether or not there was any truth in it, what bewildered us most was Brauchitsch's behavior. Two days before he had been so impressed by his conversation with Goerdeler that he had piously declared: 'God grant that I act soon.' Now he was so outraged that he wanted to report this trivial incident at once. In fact, he did run to the Fuehrer with the story, but Hitler, unpredictable as always, gave him the reception he deserved. It was just nonsense, Hitler said; just another typical example of the kind of silly gossip that had become commonplace during the past few years.

For us this incident completely unmasked the quality of Brauchitsch's brave resolution, for even if the charge had been true, what would it have mattered? It would have meant merely that Goerdeler had talked a little prematurely about an action that we were all waiting for and that Brauchitsch had promised again and again to begin. This hero in gold braid had been leading us astray for months. He permitted the civilians to gather evidence for his purposes at the risk of their lives, and when the time came to speak out boldly, he ran whimpering to the Fuehrer — and betrayed one of his principal assistants. At the same time he placed extraordinary trust in the decency of the man he had callously exposed. Apparently he was convinced that Goerdeler would prefer to go quietly to concentration camp rather than report the piously seditious sentiments with which the commander-in-chief of the army had been stringing him along.

The following days and weeks were filled with countless conferences, hasty automobile trips, fruitless journeys to generals in other cities, turbulent rumors and the usual alarms. We heard that the Gestapo was on the trail of every one of us in turn; we heard that they were merely waiting for a favorable opportunity to liquidate us all.

I tried to persuade Helldorf that it might be safest for us to launch a counter-attack against Goering. After all, the entire intrigue could be traced to him, and it was becoming more and more evident that the generals' tactics of concentrating on Himmler and Heydrich were utterly wrong, for those two cut-throats repeatedly dodged behind the broad back of their fellow conspirator. If Goering fell, he would necessarily carry the Gestapo down to ruin with him. On the other hand, the Gestapists would hold the field as long as the originator of the conspiracy remained as powerful as ever.

But how and where could we strike at Goering? It was possible only by approaching Hitler directly. Since the generals could not get up enough courage to do that, someone else would have to. Helldorf declared himself willing to take the risk. He had a certain right to speak out, since it was through him that the Blomberg scandal had come to a head, and he was equally well informed about the Fritsch affair. Why could he not simply go to Hitler and inform him about the chronological course of both sensations? Perhaps Hitler would then recognize how shamelessly he had been deceived by his 'loyalest paladin,' Goering; perhaps he would see that Goering had deliberately involved him in the embarrassment of being a witness at Blomberg's wedding and had forced upon him that disgusting scene in which he confronted Fritsch with the convict, Schmidt.

It was obvious, however, that such a step on the part of the Berlin police chief would have no prospects of success unless the generals took action immediately afterward. Through Oster we informed Brauchitsch of our intention. Brauchitsch gave us a typical answer. Helldorf could do whatever he thought right, but he, the commander-in-chief, had his own plans and would pursue them. The army stood in need of no support, and particularly not from a high-ranking member of the Nazi Party.

I may have given the impression that during all these weeks of nervous tension we were exclusively concerned with the Fritsch case. Far from it. Unquestionably the trial of Colonel-General von Fritsch was a matter of great moment, for in it the conflict between the army and the SS, and thus between evolution and revolution, came to a head, but the trial of Martin Niemoeller was, fundamentally, of far more profound importance. It revealed with merciless clarity the daemonic tendency of Nazi secularization. Criminal entanglements such as the Blomberg-Fritsch scandals dealt with are possible only when the leaders of a state have already cynically broken with traditional faiths and have set about deliberately undermining the religious foundations of a national community.

Some nine months before, the Nazis had at last ventured to lay hands on Niemoeller, who was so popular that they simply could not unobtrusively put him behind bars in a concentration camp. Consequently, by July, 1937, no other course remained open to the Nazis but that of 'legal' liquidation; that is, they decided to use their Nazified judicial system rather than the Gestapo. This dangerous enemy was haled before a Nazi special court.

The trial had been repeatedly postponed, but at last it was begun. According to all reports, the indictment rested on very shaky grounds. Niemoeller was undaunted. He not only defended himself, but attacked his accusers. His unusual behavior as defendant had made such a deep impression upon the judges that his exoneration seemed almost certain.

Now we were awaiting the verdict, which was to be handed down in the morning. I visited Helldorf at his home quite early the next morning and asked him to hurry to his office and use his connections to find out what the Gestapo intended to do. I then returned to my home to await Helldorf's telephone call. How well I knew this painful waiting for something to happen! It is that, more than anything else, that tries the nerves most of all in such mad times. Anyone who is engaged in underground work should try to keep active incessantly, instead of being compelled to wait and see whether and how the crucial decisions will be made.

By a series of circumlocutions I was informed of the verdict. Practically, it was not guilty; in any case, Niemoeller was to be released at once, but 'the doctors had unfortunately decided to transfer the patient to a near-by sanatorium.' That meant to me: the concentration camp of Sachsenhausen.

I now had to wait for one more call, this one from Doctor Koch, Niemoeller's splendid defense attorney, whose qualifications for his task were of the very highest: he himself had spent a long time in a Gestapo bunker for venturing — in 1935 — to introduce a writ of equity protesting the expropriation of a Jewish industrialist.

I waited until nearly two o'clock before Koch called. His voice sounded thoroughly weary, which did not surprise me. Since he was afraid to tell me anything definite over the telephone, we agreed to meet for lunch at a near-by restaurant. Koch had no idea that Niemoeller's fate had been sealed for hours. I need not describe his feelings when I told him about Helldorf's telephone call. We choked down our lunch. Then I set out for the Fuerstenhof Hotel. Koch had other business, and it devolved upon me to break the news to Frau Niemoeller. I found her waiting in the hotel lobby, her eyes fixed nervously on the front entrance. She had been too excited to wait upstairs alone. As I entered, she came rushing toward me. I accompanied her back to Dahlem.

It might have consoled us slightly had we known at the time what a ferocious outburst had occurred at the chancellery. Hitler foamed with rage; he screamed and shouted that he was sick and tired of the judiciary. He threatened to send not only Niemoeller but the entire court to concentration camp. The federal minister of justice stammered his usual phrases about the independence and inviolability of the judges, but this time he had less luck than ever with his liberalistic arguments. Nevertheless, he succeeded in preserving the judges from an expedition to Sachsenhausen, but for Niemoeller, despite the exonerating verdict, there was no mercy. Hitler declared that the pastor would 'do time until he's blue in the face.'

I sat up late that night, talking with Frau Niemoeller and a small group of friends at the Dahlem parsonage. For the following morning I had an appointment with Beck. He instantly grasped the significance of this act of vengeance against Niemoeller.

Niemoeller was a former U-boat captain. The army chiefs were unquestionably obligated to demand that the shameful order be revoked.

The very fact that the generals and admirals had failed to receive any satisfaction in the Fritsch case would make it all the more likely that Hitler would meet them halfway if they requested that Niemoeller be freed.

Then it came. An official DNB communiqué reported the 'final' result. In a cordial letter in his own hand the Fuehrer conferred upon Colonel-General Freiherr von Fritsch the dignity of honorary commander of his old regiment, and Fritsch — accepted.

All the Gestapo officials who had played a part in the affair were promoted one or several grades. The only exception was the man who had made that awkward statement in court.

Herr von Brauchitsch evidently decided that if others could marry, there was no reason why he should not make a stab at it, and there was no time like the present for courting. He had met the lady of his heart many times before, but now that he was commander-in-chief of the army the path of love proved smoother; the lady condescended to give him her hand for his third marriage. Brauchitsch moved into a magnificently renovated villa with his newly wedded wife, and our Fuehrer, with his inimitable generosity, facilitated the marriage by handing Brauchitsch a princely check with which he was able to portion off his second wife.

Some time later the commanding generals of the army met for a conference. When Hitler had last convoked these gentlemen, he had announced that Fritsch was guilty of homosexual misdemeanors. There was a consensus of opinion that the Fuehrer himself must recant this slander before the same group. Hitler talked at length about Austria. He talked even longer — this in the summer of 1938! — about the coming war against Czechoslovakia. With all this, he let fall a few words about the Fritsch case. The whole affair had turned out to be a regrettable mistake, he said. Fortunately, thanks to Goering's splendid work in getting to the bottom of the matter, the truth had come to light at last. Schmidt, the convict, had been duly punished for his dreadful lies; he, Hitler, had personally ordered that the man be shot 'without more ado.' There was not a word against Himmler, not a word against Heydrich, not a word against the

Gestapo as such in the whole speech. On the contrary, Hitler praised the police forces for having performed excellent work, by and large. To err was human, he said.

It is interesting to speculate why Hitler had had Schmidt shot. For a real rehabilitation of Fritsch, other men would have had to pay for their crimes — above all, the Gestapo blackguards. But Hitler did not intend to punish anyone. He was merely avenging himself because he, the omniscient Fuehrer, had been so thoroughly taken in by the convict. Obviously someone had to pay.

January 25, 1939

A CONFIDENTIAL RADIO MESSAGE from a border post to the army high command reported that former Field Marshal von Blomberg, returning from abroad, had crossed the German frontier. The year of atonement was over. In the meantime, pictures of Blomberg had been removed from all officers' clubs. His name was silently stricken from all army registers. The former field marshal and his wife settled down to private life in lovely Wiessee.

September, 1939

WHEN HITLER'S WAR at last broke out, Fritsch was, of course, not given an assignment. For Fritsch's soldier's temperament, this was a terrible blow. The general set out in his car and drove along behind his regiment. Deliberately, he sought and found death on the battlefield. A Polish bullet struck him so fortuitously that he bled to death within a few minutes.

Hitler ordered a state funeral, which took place in Berlin. As Hitler's representative, Goering stepped before the bier and with a vain, complacent gesture raised his marshal's staff. Some words were engraved in the heavy gold of this ornate, diamond-studded bit of paraphernalia. There was a dedication and the date Goering had received the title of field marshal.

The date on the staff with which Goering saluted Fritsch in the Fuehrer's name for the last time was — February 4, 1938.

7

The Magic and the Vicious Circles

L OOKING BACK on the history of the Third Reich we note that the outbreak of the war in 1939 marks the mid-point of the twelve years. This is a superficial observation, to be sure, but it indicates the vital caesura in the line of the great drama.

War is always of fateful significance to authoritarian governments. To resort to arms, to try for all or nothing, is usually the last chance for usurpers. Beyond yawns the abyss. Hitler, too, sensed this on September 1, 1939. He knew well that there was no longer any turning back for him. However, if we wished to describe truthfully the story of this turning-point in world history, we should have to avoid equating the superficial outbreak of the war with the real beginning of hostilities. We must look farther back, to the seizure of Prague, for it preluded the invasion of Poland, and even farther back than that, to 'Munich,' for that prepared the cynical rape of Czechoslovakia. It was at Munich that the war really began. From September, 1938, on we were in the midst of it. The Western Powers, however, refused to recognize the beginning of this *drôle de guerre;* indeed, they did not come out of their trance of self-deception until the swastika was waving over Paris.

If we were to inquire, however, at what point the waters of the Brown Revolution were so augmented that they overflowed their banks, we should have to look back to the Fritsch crisis. With the events of January and February, 1938, the Nazi seizure of power within Germany was completed. The last area of resistance, the army, was thoroughly *gleichgeschaltet* and the revolutionaries were able to

266

operate unchecked. Up to the Fritsch crisis and the invasion of Austria, the world might well have hoped for the famous 'miracle,' for an assassination, a revolt, a swing toward 'evolution.' But from then on, the rest of the world should no longer have depended on any *fronde* within Germany to force a shift toward democracy. From then on, any assault against Nazism had to be made from outside Germany; without such an assault there was no hope that the sorely pressed Opposition would ever escape the Nazi prison.

The reader may well ask why it has been necessary for us to describe the unsavory Blomberg-Fritsch affair in such detail. Certainly the whole business offends against good taste, but yet it is essential to an understanding of all that followed. The story is above all one of complete moral disintegration on the part of those whose responsibility it was to uphold decency and public order, not to speak of world peace.

In the Fritsch crisis another Lubbe turned up to start the ball of history rolling. The symbolism remained consistent; in this case he did not play with fire, but practiced a repulsive and pathological form of sexual blackmail. In all other respects Schmidt was the same sort of petty criminal with the same sort of stupid history. He was taken up with the same enthusiasm as a heaven-sent tool, and, when they were finished with him, the puppet-masters cast him on the scrap heap with the same indifference. The circle was closed. Another circle — the Nazi encirclement of the German people — was also closed.

Events moved swiftly and logically from the Nazis' first great crime, the Reichstag fire, to the execution of the convict who had inadvertently brought about the destruction of the German army's independence. Nevertheless, a mystery remains. Although the facts are all at hand, we nevertheless find ourselves asking: But how was it all possible?

In spite of all the attempts at explanation that have been made during the past twelve years, a completely cogent answer is not yet forthcoming, for guilty or not, the enslavement of some eighty million people within a mere six years remains a unique historical phenomenon. It cannot be dismissed with a few generalizations about politics.

On the other hand, I balk at calling Hitler a great magician, although there is no doubt that he possessed considerable talent for hypnotic suggestion. I refuse to weave legends about his innumerable satraps, for these men were not even heroic gangsters. Their practices manifest no special ingenuity or criminal talent. They were simply unusually crude and brutal.

In general I have always considered it a mistake to seek too avidly for what was 'behind it.' The various techniques of the Nazis were always crude and primitive. Their 'reasonable' adversaries were always so disconcerted largely because they could not conceive of so much baseness, so much unrestraint, and so much barbarism all rolled into one. Again and again they racked their brains trying to imagine what 'really' lay behind Hitler's peculiar behavior. How often the world wondered at the speed with which the Nazi lightning struck — and yet the usurper and his clique were merely taking advantage of the period that his opponents devoted to civilized reflection.

It is sobering, indeed, to consider how elementary were the means by which Hitler achieved total control of the nation during the first six years, but we must not overlook the remarkable fact that always, at the proper moment, the proper cue appeared. In each case the pretext was of such a nature that it enabled the dictator to 'intervene' with a show of great moral indignation, and to 'restore' order. If no Lubbe were at hand, there was sure to be some bungler of a monk who was not familiar with the regulations regarding foreign exchange and so provided the sensational pretext for the persecution of the Church. If there were no Jewish assassin to supply justification for fresh pogroms, there was sure to be a blackmailer whose dirty story outraged the Fuehrer. Every time there were an ample number of honest people who hastily agreed that, yes, there was something rotten here, the affair was very mysterious, the embarrassing incident must at least be 'investigated.'

We cannot help thinking of Andersen's lovely fairy tale of 'The Emperor's New Clothes,' transposed into diabolical terms. Goebbels or the Gestapists would find some stupid puppet and clothe his physical and psychic emptiness with a fantastic Nazi garb of lies.

One would expect every normal person to call the swindle by its proper name. But instead all of them — ministers of justice, judges, bishops, industrial notables, and generals — would busily contribute their piece to the fantastic tale. Each was unwilling to expose himself by blurting out that he thought there was nothing 'behind it,' and therefore everyone gravely went into a discussion of the case. They debated, they tried to explain, they advanced arguments, they adduced testimony for the defense, they weighed the pros and cons, they held court — until in the end they could not admit, without utterly exposing themselves, that they had been the dupes of an impertinent hocus-pocus.

It would appear that, with the aid of a host of obscure persons and mysterious things, a kind of magic circle — that is the best name I can find for it — was nevertheless drawn around all those people who, by virtue of their office, their intelligence, their conscience, or their ordinary egotism, should have reacted. Had these men merely said out loud what they really thought, the whole chimera would have been blasted to nothingness, but like the chicken on the chalkline, they all stared in fascination at the novel and showy 'pretext.' There is indeed no doubt that this pretext was the one unique and original element in each situation: the Blomberg-Fritsch crisis is typical of that. The time was ripe, the hand was poised for the move against the army — and against Austria, and yet Hitler himself was no doubt more surprised than anybody else at the actual form of the solution.

I should not use this rather daring metaphor of a magic circle were it not for an auxiliary fact. As soon as the German people were 'encircled,' which meant also the encirclement of the Nazis themselves, there followed incessant attempts to break out of the circle. We shall soon see how many such attempts there were, but none of the participants, neither the narrow clique of Nazis, nor their opportunist accomplices, nor the skeptical fellow travelers, least of all the generals were able to escape the treadmill. From 1938 on, they all turned endlessly in a vicious circle.

No one can say that Hitler's dynamic foreign policy lacked variety. It proceeded by leaps and bounds; it kept the world watching with bated breath. Fundamentally, Hitler was constantly fumbling for a weak spot, now in the East, now in the West, now North, now South. He was constantly trying to find a way out of the encirclement into which he had, in his megalomania, brought himself. Certainly the other nations did not encircle him. For years, with a generosity that amounted to rashness, they endeavored to give him as much freedom of movement as possible, but Hitler inflamed himself with a thousand self-concocted delusions; he cast himself into an abyss of guilt; he himself threw out slanders and threats in all directions, until even the most cordial of his neighbors were alarmed and looked to protect themselves against this eternal trouble-maker.

Why did he not content himself with his triumph at Munich? Why at least did he not quiet down after Prague? Why, after the victory parade in Warsaw, did he not accept with good grace the reprieve offered him by the 'phony' war? Why, after the fall of Paris in 1940, did he not make every effort to come to an agreement with the Western Powers, even at the price of sacrifices? Why did he not make use of the wealth of imports that Russia, in its reluctance to go to war, was willing to supply? Why, on top of it all, did he have to declare war on America? It is hard to see in these acts of war any kind of preconceived plan or broad strategy. At the time Hitler leaped from success to success, and later from defeat to defeat, but when we look back on the whole turbulent epoch, we see that it was merely a matter of rotating faster and faster in a vicious circle.

The same was true of the German oppositionists. Once caught in the circle, they were unable to find their way out. Again and again they entangled themselves in their own arguments. One time they clung to the 'lesser evil'; then they wanted 'to avert something worse'; then they waited for the 'proper time.' Or else — so they imagined — the 'others' were unwilling to act; or — so they alleged — they themselves could do nothing. Sometimes they were loath to break their own oath of allegiance, or they feared the stigma of having dealt a 'stab in the back.' Finally, when they had run out of reasons and could no longer evade the issue, they groaned that now it was too late; that in the meantime we had all become 'collectively' guilty and there was nothing left for us Germans but to win the war or be ruined.

Yet, if there were no one within Germany capable of breaking this vicious circle, could not help have come from outside Germany? Who can say whether an encouraging word from the Western Powers would not have opened a breach? Certainly the German Opposition cried out for help often enough. It was all in vain, for by that time the Churchill-Roosevelt-Stalin coalition could not abate their demand for 'unconditional surrender.' They were determined that this time they would not again leave a German army 'unbeaten in the field.' They had sworn to close the iron ring tighter and tighter, month by month, until the Nazi force was utterly spent.

The German Opposition could understand the reason for this policy very well, indeed. The only remaining question was: Would not the chaos of Germany infect all of Europe? Certainly the Allies also considered this question, but could they trust any Germans at all? Was there not a trick behind the proposed shift in government? First, those Germans set half of Europe on fire, and then, when they can no longer extinguish the flames, they plead for a pact with their erstwhile enemy.

'There you are; Hitler was right after all,' the German generals reply. 'The enemy wants to exterminate us; that's why we must go on fighting.'

So it was. All the politics of this Second World War moved in a vicious circle. There was no alternative other than the frightful catastrophe that indeed took place.

Perhaps the war policies of the 'enemy' contained many mistakes; perhaps he failed for a long time to make a prompt response to the situation or interpret events properly; perhaps the Allies also could not escape their own vicious circle; but today there is no salvation for the Germans unless they recognize that it was they who first enclosed themselves in that magic circle, unless they recognize their past guilt and their present need for atonement.

Part Two

FROM MUNICH TO JULY 20, 1944

I

War in the Offing
May, 1938, to September, 1939

BECK'S RESIGNATION

WE MUST UNDERSTAND the deeper consequences of the Fritsch crisis in order to see how the crisis in foreign politics reached its apex in the fall of 1938; and we must understand the real meaning of Munich in 1938 and of Prague in 1939 if we are to know why the Second World War developed directly and with lightning swiftness out of those two events.

The February crisis of 1938 brought about a great shift in the balance of forces within Revolutionary Germany. The army leadership let slip a unique and last opportunity to swing the country into evolutionary paths. From the time of the Fritsch crisis, Hitler ceased to fear the generals. They might grumble occasionally, but their empty gestures did not alter the fact that their army had been degraded to a virtual section of the Nazi Party. The sinister figure of Himmler thrust itself powerfully forward. From that time on, Black Heinrich was the uncontested chief of police over all Germans, including the soldiers. His death's-head bands had originally been founded as garrisons for the concentration camps; now they expanded into splendidly equipped armies which were always ready to take Hitler and all his generals under their unequivocal 'protection.'

This eventful change, however, did not take place on the very night of February 3 to 4. As in all of Hitler's historical dramas, there was a loud explosion which fixed the attention of his contemporaries, while the real changes came about through gradual and almost imperceptible means. Neither the sensational resignations of Blomberg and Fritsch, nor the promotion of Goering to the rank of field marshal, nor the appointment of Ribbentrop as foreign minister, were the essential features of the change. Far more significant was the speed with which these external shifts were embodied in internal institutions. The change of personnel seemed to signify a new political attitude — and not inside Germany alone. The outrageous dénouement of the Fritsch crisis was simply accepted, as though it were quite in the revolutionary order of things. The coup resulted on one side in a tremendous swelling of the sense of power possessed by the triumvirate, Goering, Himmler, and Ribbentrop; and simultaneously reduced our once so self-assured generals to a state of depressed resignation, for they were now lackeys who took orders.

In the ordinary course of events, times of war or imminent war produce a shift in political power in favor of the military. In 1938 we experienced just the reverse. The army was deposed and the right to decide the question of war and peace was taken over by the usurper. It may be that the generals at first were unwilling to recognize Hitler's war policy for what it was. During the early stages they were no less surprised by his 'blitzes' than the statesmen of the invaded nations, but it was excusable that the latter should place some trust in the basic principles of morality and should rely on solemn sworn international agreements being honored. Our generals, however, had had experience enough to have taught them, nay compelled them, to be skeptical. They could no longer hide behind their sense of protocol, their dullness at apprehending the truth, or their oath of allegiance, after Hitler had cynically demonstrated to them again and again that it was preposterous to count on his truthfulness or loyalty.

Anyone who handles explosive materials is duty bound to exercise more than ordinary caution. The rearmament of Germany placed in the hands of our generals a species of dynamite which, if handled carelessly, could blow up not only their own country, but the rest of Europe. From 1934 on, these 'sole bearers of arms in the nation' had by their passivity abetted the growth of Nazi totalitarianism. Now they had to take the consequences. They could no longer plead that they were not men of politics. It was incumbent upon them, first of all, to recognize Hitler's dangerous game for what it was. They should have seen that Hitler, led on by his dilettante ideas of foreign policy or by pure lust for adventure, was encouraging war.

And by 1938 any war meant world war.

One man understood this: General Ludwig Beck, the chief of the German general staff, and therefore he voluntarily resigned his post. This decision should have been a warning signal to all the others, for Beck was by general agreement considered the supreme intellect among the generals. He was a man of great ability who had risen to his high position by virtue of his indubitable excellence. To the members of the general staff he represented the true heir of the traditions of Moltke and Schlieffen. He set extremely high standards for his subordinates. He looked upon the general staff, not as an élite corps of military technicians, but as the conscience of the army. Consequently, every thinking officer could not help reflecting upon the significance of the step when such a man as Beck resigned at so critical a juncture.

Hitler could not have been altogether averse to Beck's resignation. Months before, at the time of Fritsch's dismissal, the Fuehrer had considered appointing a new chief of staff. He had had some unpleasant brushes with Beck during those weeks of the Fritsch crisis. He suspected that Beck, if only because of his position, had become the leader of the *fronde* of generals, and Beck was equally in disfavor with Brauchitsch; the two men had quarreled bitterly about the Fritsch affair.

In the Third Reich it was customary for the dictator alone to decide on the time and propriety of resignations. In June, 1938, he felt that the situation was too tense for the army to be subjected to another shock; and the resignation of the chief of the general staff would be

likely to have unpleasant reverberations abroad. Consequently, the
new army chief, Brauchitsch, was ordered to persuade Beck to stay.

Beck, however, remained adamant. For years he had harbored the
hope that 'National Socialism will grind itself to pieces against the
flinty good qualities of the German people.' So long as Fritsch remained in office there was some ground for this hope. Beck, like
everyone else, had looked upon Fritsch as a 'strong man.' He had
never doubted that some day the colonel-general would intervene, that
he would never permit any 'adventures' abroad. Now Fritsch had
fallen, and the fable of a purely defensive rearmament was smashed
to smithereens on the day Austria was brought by force into the Nazi
totalitarian system. For years Hitler had claimed that all he desired
was an army strong enough to command respect and thereby to bring
about a pacific revision of the Versailles Treaty. Now this claim had
been proved a lie. Evidently Hitler was not at all interested in a new
European balance of power. He was rushing Germany into a war.

Beck recalled once more that fateful hour on August 2, 1934, after
the death of Hindenburg. That night the Berlin garrison, deeply
moved by the passing of the old president, had been called out to the
Koenigsplatz to take the oath of allegiance by torchlight to the new
head of the state. The significance of this act for the fate of Germany
and of Europe cannot be overestimated. Hitler forced the stupefied
officers' corps to swear loyalty 'unto death' — which in fact meant
unto physical and moral suicide. Once again the dictator behaved
with exemplary 'legality.' The constitution of the Reich provided
that upon the death of a president the chancellor was to become
acting head of state until a new election could be held. Therefore,
interpreted literally, the rôle of chief of the army also passed automatically to Hitler. Hitler availed himself of this 'right' by ordering
the troops to swear allegiance to him, but the officers did not notice,
until they had already raised their hands to take the oath, that the
formula was a completely novel one; it specified explicitly allegiance
to the person of Hitler himself. As they stood there repeating the
formula which was being read aloud to them, they had no opportunity to grasp the full and fateful significance of the *coup d'état*

that was concealed in this simple act, for they were binding themselves to blind obedience to Hitler, and in the future they would be able to free themselves only at the cost of breaking their oath.

This surprise coup, for which Blomberg must be blamed, had shaken Beck deeply at the time it happened. On the way home from the Koenigsplatz he had confided to one of his comrades: 'This has been one of the most fateful moments of my life.' And so it proved to be. To the last hours of his life, up to July 20, 1944, Beck brooded about this incident. Again and again he referred to the matter in conversations with me. He was tormented by the question of whether and how he could have reacted differently to such a wholly unexpected stratagem.

It now seemed to Beck that the time had come to break with Hitler once and for all. The external pretext was remarkable in itself. At the beginning of June a conference of the commanding generals took place on the army proving grounds at Jueterbog, and Hitler, though barely mentioning Fritsch, had spoken openly about Czechoslovakia as his next target.

Immediately after this speech Beck sent his adjutant to see Brauchitsch to request an interview on a matter of urgent importance. He intended to demand a clarification of Brauchitsch's stand on this amazing announcement, but the commander-in-chief refused to enter into a discussion with his chief of staff. With great deliberation, he got into his car and informed Beck through the adjutant that he was taking a short furlough and would be at Beck's disposal after his return.

Beck took this incident as a pretext for handing in his resignation. He objected strongly to Hitler's having announced his bellicose intentions without previously consulting with his chief of the general staff. At the same time he composed a detailed memorandum showing why he considered that a war, even a so-called *Blitzkrieg,* would be a disaster for Germany and for all of Europe. For good or ill, Brauchitsch had to give this memorandum to Hitler. Both of them were outraged. Such an action on Beck's part was tantamount to open revolt. On the other hand, both agreed that he must be persuaded to withdraw his memorandum, even at the price of his continuing in office for a time. *Quod non est in actis, non est in mundo,* at that time the war was strictly a forbidden subject. Even though Hitler had talked prematurely at the conference, it remained the generals' duty to preserve a decent silence, instead of composing heretical memoranda.

Beck's action in handing in his resignation was far from a purely negative gesture of protest. He felt that the time had come at last to cease the perpetual retreat of ministers and generals. Otherwise, the Nazi aggrandizement of power could continue without check. Since the generals had failed so miserably in the Fritsch crisis, it was now up to them to provide a good example of firmness and principle. Beck hoped to carry along others of his comrades who were in agreement with him. His intention was to give the signal for a general defection from Hitler. Possibly Hitler would counter the blow; possibly his counter-attack would be a bloody one; but that risk had to be taken. At the very least, Beck hoped to alarm other nations, which seemed to have been lulled into a hypnotic sleep.

In his search for politicians who would be likely to join in his action, Beck naturally thought of Schacht first of all. Since the Fritsch crisis there had been no doubt at all about Schacht's oppositional stand. Moreover, his name carried greater weight inside and outside of Germany than did those of the other bourgeois ministers — although it would have been very pleasant, of course, if Neurath, Guertner, or Schwerin could have summoned up the resolution to take a similar step.

During June Beck conferred repeatedly with Schacht. These conversations were always arranged by Oster and me — a clumsy and roundabout business which was necessary because the Gestapo was already extremely suspicious. As a result, however, I observed the negotiations at close quarters and was able to express my opinion freely to both Schacht and Beck.

A highly complex situation soon developed. I was for Schacht's but against Beck's resignation. Oster held exactly the opposite

opinion: he wanted Beck to resign and Schacht to stay. This disagreement between us, the liaison men, was typical of the difficult problem
that faced the German Opposition. I had been urging Schacht to
resign for years. He had long since been virtually superseded by
Goering, whom he had foolishly helped to install as head of the
Four-Year Plan Authority. What sense was there in his holding on
to a position which no longer had any real validity or power? He
was burdened with the title of office, but could no longer direct the
chief business of his office: the guidance of currency policy. Nevertheless, the president of the Reichsbank felt that he had taken over a
great responsibility and that it was his duty to the people to try to
fulfill it.

Oster wanted Schacht to remain in office because he had observed
what a weight Schacht's name carried in the *Wehrmacht*. A casual
reference to someone in high office or in a high Party position who
supported one's own proposals made far more of an impression on
the generals than the most cogent arguments. They respected the
title of minister of the Reich. Although Schacht was suspect at the
moment, one could never know whether that political prestidigitator,
Hitler, might not some day spirit him up again to the height of
favorite. Oster supported Beck's resigning because he thought it
would make a lasting impression upon the generals.

The same arguments applied in reverse, of course, to the chief of
the general staff. All the bourgeois ministers and department secretaries were constantly looking toward the Bendlerstrasse to see
whether *the* general had yet put in his appearance. It would be disastrous from the viewpoint of the civilians, I felt, if such a man as
Beck voluntarily relinquished what power he had.

This was essentially the same old problem of whether or not to
'stay in,' a problem which occupied us throughout the years of Nazism.
Once we had discovered somewhere a trustworthy and courageous
man and had cautiously established relations with him, it was discouraging to see him step out of the picture, no matter how admirable
were the reasons for his resignation. Every key position that was left
open was immediately occupied by an adherent of the Nazi system.

How could we ever hope to bring about a change in régime if every important position was voluntarily abandoned to the Nazis?

This time, however, our dispute appeared to be pointless. Beck consoled us with the assurance that his successor would in many respects be an improvement upon himself. In his militant opposition to the system, he said, his prospective successor was easily as determined as he himself; also the new man would have the advantage of not being under suspicion as Beck was because of his firm stand during the Fritsch crisis. Consequently he, far better than Beck, could prepare a counter-blow.

Goerdeler, who repeatedly conferred with Beck about this matter, confirmed Beck's view. Eternal optimist that he was, Goerdeler sang the praises of this new man of iron resolution. The man was already one of Beck's closest collaborators, General Franz Halder.

Unfortunately, Beck ended by neutralizing most of the effect of his resignation. With exaggerated aristocratic sensitivity, he resigned without making any fuss about it. He bade good-bye only to his closest associates. Hitler, on the pretext that the foreign situation was already tense enough, refused to permit publication of his resignation, and Beck did not argue with this decision. Thus, the German people heard not a word about the significant action of their chief of the general staff. Only after the triumphal termination of the crisis over the Sudetenland was there a casual announcement that for months another general had been chief of staff.

From this time on, there were many instances of this sly method of covering up embarrassing occurrences. It was soon developed into a polished technique. First came the *fait accompli,* then weeks or months of apparently baseless rumors, and finally the announcement of a stroke which had taken place so long ago that its immediate effect could no longer be felt. It was an altogether cynical and effective process which, applied in the realm of foreign policy, time and again enabled the Nazis to outstrip the democracies.

This trick has a bearing on the question of political responsibility. The cordon of silence was one of the Nazis' most dangerous weapons.

There was no way of bringing important political issues to the attention of the public. During the past twelve years we were forced, by countless tragic individual cases, to draw the conclusion that such-and-such a protest or such-and-such a resignation was altogether senseless because it was converted into an empty gesture by the Nazi technique of smothering the action in a blanket of silence. When brave men took unusual risks, no one heard about it either at home or abroad. The Gestapo took care of the practical consequences of such admirable examples of intrepidity and principle, which consequences were of a nature to discourage rather than to embolden.

Later on I repeatedly asked Beck why he did not insist more energetically upon public announcement of his action. He did not deny that he had made a mistake, but he had never been one to thrust his own personality into the foreground. At that time he was still so deeply immersed in the traditions of the Prussian officers' corps that he wished to avoid even the faintest semblance of an attack upon the authority of the state. It was only with the passage of years that he outgrew these limitations. Only someone who understands how much tradition meant to this noble man can properly appreciate the inward change that took place between the time he quietly resigned and the time he became a convinced and active 'traitor.'

HALDER'S SETBACK THEORY

A FEW WEEKS PASSED. Then Halder let his voice be heard. Beck had informed his successor that in all delicate questions he need not hesitate to turn to Oster. As chance would have it, Halder was already acquainted with Oster. Anyone familiar with the German military machinery knows how difficult it was for like-minded officers to come into contact with one another unless they happened to be of the same rank. In the German army direct relationships existed only between superiors and their own subordinates. Private relationships between senior and junior officers were strictly tabu. It was, therefore, all the more remarkable that General Halder, the new chief of staff, approached Lieutenant-Colonel Oster.

In their very first conversation Halder spoke with amazing candor. This might partly have been because of the subject matter of their discussion, for even in the middle of the summer of 1938 scarcely any of the higher officers, much less the subordinate officers, knew anything about the more intimate details of the Fritsch crisis. It had been bruited about that there had been a terrible scandal, but the army was generally in ignorance of the deeper interrelationships. Either because they justly felt ashamed of their failure or because they took very literally the rule of silence that Hitler had prudently imposed, the top generals had staunchly seconded the Nazi efforts to hush up the story. As a result, even a highly placed officer like Halder could feel fortunate in having found an informant who knew so much and who was altogether reliable.

Halder discussed with Oster the multitude of puzzles that the Fritsch case had presented. Naturally, Oster did not conceal his indignation at the army's having muffed so precious an opportunity. From this point the conversation turned quite of itself into the desired channels, and Oster left with the same impression as Beck had had — that Halder seriously intended to make up for past neglect.

At that time, in midsummer of 1938, it was no longer possible to strike out against the Gestapo overnight. The pretext was wanting, and Halder saw no immediate opportunity for creating one. On the other hand, he was playing with the idea of letting events proceed until he was driven to the step of taking the chancellery — which was only two short blocks from the Bendlerstrasse — under his military 'protection.' For was not Hitler heading toward war? The final proof of this had not yet arrived, it was true, but perhaps before the year was out, the army leadership would be in a position to take more thorough action than it could have done at the beginning of the year — to act, at least, under more favorable conditions. Although the generals had hesitated to take the offensive against terrorism, the Nazi assaults on the Church, the persecutions of the Jews, and the methods of the Gestapo, they were nevertheless in an authoritative position where war was in question. They needed merely to adopt a purely defensive stand against Hitler's war-mongering. If only they cried, 'So far and no farther,' the Fuehrer would be stopped dead in his tracks.

It was well known that protests did not bother the dictator. In the existing situation the generals could show their earnestness only by flashing their weapons. But would war actually come, or was Hitler merely bluffing? Unlike most of the other generals, Halder perceived that Hitler was bent on starting a war. He believed this, but he had no proof, for all the measures which he as chief of the general staff had been ordered to take might possibly be in reality what they were alleged to be; that is, they might be no more than the ordinary precautions that were taken by all nations against potential opponents during diplomatic crises. Even the mobilization orders that were issued during those months could be interpreted according to the official explanation: that Hitler was merely threatening and that he would never push a step farther than the Western Powers were willing to retreat.

Because of this confusion, Halder was all the more dependent upon the accuracy of his political information. He wanted to know in time what was going on among Hitler, Goering, and Himmler; for it was in the Wilhelmstrasse, Karinhall, and Prinz Albrechtstrasse that the real war-mongers sat — not in the offices of the general staff. Goering's part, however, still remained vague. The commander of the *Luftwaffe* was not anxious to risk his new toy prematurely. There was no doubt that the vain field marshal was dreaming of military laurels; but he was evidently worried that he might be asked to strike his first blows before he was quite ready.

Halder was obviously reluctant to request Canaris to supply him with political information. He knew what Canaris's views were, for he had spoken quite openly with the chief of counter-intelligence. Nevertheless, he preferred not to expose himself entirely to the sharp-eyed admiral. Moreover, the *Abwehr* had been expressly ordered not to set up its own political intelligence service. Halder, therefore, preferred to conspire with Oster and not to inquire too closely where Oster obtained his information.

In retrospect it might be thought that Halder wanted to leave himself an avenue of escape and therefore shunned too direct an understanding with Canaris, a man who was, after all, of his age and rank. I am inclined to think, however, that he was not motivated by any such petty considerations until a year later, after the outbreak of the war.

The chief of staff went a step farther. In one of their earliest conversations he surprised Oster by asking what technical and political preparations for a *coup d'état* had been undertaken. Nothing had in fact been done. During the Fritsch crisis we had never been able to come to agreements which would permit us to go ahead and outline definite plans of any sort. In answer to Halder's question, therefore, Oster made general references to those prominent politicians who he considered were among the most confirmed oppositionists. Of the civilians, he named at once Schacht and Goerdeler. In reality, there were very few others who could be depended upon at that time.

Significantly, Halder refused to get in touch with Goerdeler at all, although Beck had specially recommended him. Goerdeler did not meet the chief of staff until a year later, when affairs had progressed much farther; but Halder was very eager to arrange a meeting with Schacht. Schacht was a cabinet minister; for all the fact that he was under suspicion, a meeting with him could not be labeled out of hand as treason. Oster had, therefore, been right when he insisted that Schacht was of more importance in the government than out of it.

The meeting had to be arranged with great care; for Halder was not bold enough simply to telephone Schacht's ministry and announce that he wished to pay an inaugural visit. The conference had to take place secretly, and under such circumstances that the two participants would not have to beat about the bush, with each waiting for the other to broach the dangerous topic.

Halder had suggested a meeting at some neutral place. I advised Schacht against this. It seemed to me psychologically important to make things clear right from the start. I wanted the high army officer to come to the civilian! It represented a sort of additional appropriateness for Halder to come to Schacht's apartment. This may sound a little like the overniceties of diplomatic protocol, but after all we had been through we felt that it was absolutely necessary.

One night after dark Halder came to see Schacht. Their conversation lasted for several hours, so that Schacht was not able to inform me about it until late the following morning, by which time I had received a brief summary from Oster, to whom Halder had talked. Apparently Halder had not resorted to evasions, but had driven right to the heart of the matter. He had bluntly asked Schacht whether he was prepared to take over the administration in case Hitler pursued his course to the point of war and made a violent overthrow of his régime unavoidable.

In retrospect I find it necessary to emphasize that little phrase, 'in case.' This condition proved to be far more elastic than it had sounded in the beginning. Later on, there was occasion after occasion when this man Halder was willing to venture a first step without daring to take the second. But at the time it seemed to be agreed that Hitler was to be deposed by force.

A few days later, Halder asked me to see him. Schacht and Oster had referred him to me for further details on the problem of using the police in case of revolt. Since I was neither a minister nor an army officer, it might well have seemed somewhat unusual for a chief of staff to talk with me. The fact that Halder dismissed such prudent considerations seemed to me a sure proof that he was in earnest.

At that time Halder was not yet living in that luxurious villa in Grunewald which was soon assigned to him for his official residence. Hitler knew how to make life pleasanter for his high army officers by showing them such little attentions. Except for Beck and Canaris, who never moved from the apartments which corresponded with the more modest style of life of former times, all of the gentlemen in gold braid proved wonderfully adaptable to social improvement. As soon as each reached a more highly salaried rank, he obtained a more magnificent dwelling. They changed their habits of life almost as swiftly as they shifted from their traditional principles. I recall how Oster used to evaluate how far a given officer would go along the road of rebellion by studying these apparently trivial externalities. The scale of each officer's domestic arrangements, the number of his official automobiles, and the size of the estates he had received as presents enabled one to predict with almost mathematical precision the degree of his courage.

When I rang the doorbell of Halder's apartment, the master of the house himself opened the door. Even a chief of staff could not be sure of the reliability of his servants. He avoided the usual polite phrases and allusive circumlocutions and plunged directly *in medias res*. For several hours we talked with what was to me such singular frankness that I involuntarily thought: 'Isn't this man *the* general?'

In personal and political acquaintanceships it is a good rule to trust one's first impression. The first impression is really decisive. Somehow, one is forced to return to it again and again. This rule held true in my experience with Halder, although for a time I fought against acknowledging the fact. My astonishment was boundless on meeting him, for before me sat a colorless, bespectacled schoolmaster, his hair combed back, with somewhat taut features in an inexpressive face. Had it not been for his uniform I should have taken him for a kindly disposed, stolid philistine. At that time I did not yet know that Halder was accustomed to lay a handkerchief on his knee whenever he crossed his legs — so as not to crease his red general's stripe. I did not know it, but it was the kind of act I would have expected of him. The whole impression he gave was that of the so-called 'little man.' 'Hitler has picked out an obedient functionary,' I thought to myself, and I could not understand how others could consider him determined and eager to act.

I soon began, however, to doubt my first impression — just as so many other persons were to do after me. For suddenly this apparently stolid man came alive — not so much in his gestures as in the acerbity of his words. Suddenly he was all fire and fury. I had heard a good many angry words about the Fuehrer, but I cannot recall having heard before or since so eloquent an outburst of stored-up hatred as Halder produced.

'Oh no, I know him . . .' Halder interrupted me several times in his rather pedantic manner; but it was like balm to my skeptical soul, for he never interrupted in order to call a halt to my disrespectful remarks. On the contrary, he was eager to show me that I was being much too moderate and naïve in my estimate of Hitler. I had deliberately restrained myself, so that my argument was that Hitler was being driven into war by the dynamics of his own revolution. Knowing the oath-complex of the generals as I did, I had deliberately left it an open question whether the dictator actually wanted war or was being carried along by the current, but Halder would not agree to this. He held that 'this madman,' 'this criminal,' was consciously steering Germany into war, possibly because of his 'sexually pathological constitution' which created in him the desire to see blood flow. 'A blood-sucker' — this was the term the chief of staff used to describe the chief of state, and he offered as proof of his contention the events of June 30 and the countless murders in the concentration camps.

We found it quite easy to come to an agreement on basic matters. Halder certainly seemed determined to put an end to the Nazi reign of terror. But when? It was on this question that our views parted. I knew very well what a diabolically clever system of espionage Heydrich had created, but at the same time I felt it my duty to warn Halder against taking the magnified view of the power of the Gestapo which was then prevalent. In the final analysis the omnipotence of the SS extended only to the areas from which the generals retreated. If they only had the will, they could still prove Himmler vulnerable even at this late stage. Handled properly, the majority of the police forces could be won over. The greater part of our security police consisted of staunch former soldiers who hated the Gestapo practices. The criminal police force was also composed primarily of officials who had seen long service and whose consciences suffered daily when they were requested to perform acts of arbitrariness and injustice.

Our starting-point had to be there. I repeated to Halder the proposals I had framed at the time of the Fritsch crisis — that the Nazi bureaucracy be attacked from the criminal rather than the political angle. As I had done in February, I suggested that controversial political proclamations be altogether eschewed and that the *coup d'état* be justified instead by a few dozen examples of outrageous acts on the part of the Gestapo.

The generals feared above all the specter of post-positive criticism of the legality of their intervention. Consequently, the army had to be maneuvered into a position where its sole task would appear to be that of restoring order. If possible the head of the state, to whom it had sworn fealty, must be kept out of the affair. That would scarcely be feasible if the issue were made political, but it was quite possible if we took the line of justice and morality. How could the officers and soldiers demur if they were ordered to take action against such practices as murder, deprivation of liberty, extortion, and corruption, and if the criminals, once arrested, were handed over to the regular courts of justice? And how, on the other hand, could Hitler continue his reign of terror once his most reliable terrorists were behind bars? If only the judges and prosecuting attorneys were permitted three days of freedom of speech, or rather freedom of movement, we would see the disappearance of that 'popular will' which was allegedly urging the usurper into warlike acts.

I again advanced the proposition that a few hours after the occupation of the Gestapo headquarters would suffice for me to secure as much evidence as was desired — enough evidence to convince even the most scrupulous of the military men that their interference was perfectly legal and justified.

It sounds rather strange today that this question of incriminating evidence should have come up at all. Since that time Buchenwald and Belsen have become matters of public knowledge, and millions of other crimes have been revealed at the Nuremberg Trials. The proof has long since been supplied; but it would be a gross distortion of the truth to assert that all these Nazi crimes were known beyond doubt in 1938. In the first place, they multiplied with the passage of the years. The outbreak of the war gave the Gestapo a welcome pretext for accelerating the tempo of its savage activities. Moreover, the Gestapo was protected by the more stringent laws of wartime and was able to exploit cynically the 'patriotic' duty of German citizens to keep secrets. In the war period Himmler's inquisitors made up for all the orgies they had missed since June 30, 1934.

In the second place, during the first five years there were a great many people who simply refused to hear about the Nazi atrocities or, worse, refused to believe them. Millions of Germans played hide-and-seek with themselves. They made-believe, and it was extremely difficult to convince them because their assertive state of ignorance was in fact just that, for they never took the trouble to look beneath the surface. These extremely 'proper' citizens were content with the information that was 'officially' given to them, and it was these gullible, opportunistic, and cowardly people who had to be convinced by facts. Halder, it was true, no longer needed to be convinced. Nevertheless, he wanted 'proofs.' A good dossier seemed to him more important than a bomb.

We had observed a similar mentality operating during the Fritsch crisis. It will be remembered that Brauchitsch, for example, had wanted 'proofs' of Goering's intrigues. This request had more to it than the desire to procrastinate. To this day I am not certain whether the imminent action was stalled because of our inability to supply formal legal evidence of Goering's part in the plot, or because of that fatal 'indiscretion' charged to Goerdeler, which had so frightened this intrepid commander-in-chief of the German army.

The great question was: How could we obtain such evidence beforehand? For years examination or transcription of archives had been banned. The safes and filing cases in all the ministries were closely guarded by the Gestapo, and indiscretions were fatal. Everyone was afraid to pass on information in a coherent manner which would betray himself as the middleman. We were in a position to set down in writing a general picture of the situation, and to indicate what we knew must be locked in the secret ministerial files or in the Gestapo records, but it would be impossible to produce those documents until we were able to search for them without the certainty of being shot.

Fundamentally, Halder and I did not disagree about the technique of a revolt. We did differ, however, on several questions of policy — the question, for example, of whether Goering could or should be played off against Hitler and Himmler. This problem had arisen during the Fritsch crisis also, when Brauchitsch was toying with such a plan. Halder thought of it anew. For my part, I insisted that any commerce with Goering would be equivalent to signing a pact with the Devil.

However, our sharpest difference was the question of timing. We both recognized the approaching situation as inevitable — but should it be deliberately induced or allowed to mature of itself? Halder was in favor of waiting. He insisted upon what I later came to call his setback theory. For long, painful years our generals and, unfortunately, considerable sections of the rest of the Opposition, operated on this theory, so that it is necessary to give a full accounting of it.

According to Halder, in 1938 Hitler still had such strong support among the common people that there was little prospect of overthrowing him successfully. The great danger was that any attempted *coup d'état* would result in the exact opposite of what was intended — that the Nazis would be more firmly seated in the saddle than ever. The soldiers, Halder argued, were as unreliable for our purposes as any other group in the population. They owed everything to the dictator; they constantly cheered him as their hero. It would take a succession of bad experiences to enlighten the army. What was needed was a setback, such as no propaganda tricks could dissimulate, to induce the army to co-operate with an uprising against Hitler.

When would such a setback take place? The system of terrorism was by then so firmly established that no event on the domestic scene would be likely to have much influence. At best, such an event must come from without; the setback had to be in the realm of foreign policy. Once the tension in foreign affairs had mounted to the breaking point, the Western Powers would no longer hold back even from a declaration of war. Then, according to Halder, the moment for action would have come. Until then — I am still quoting Halder — the only thing for true patriots to do was to set their teeth, to get ready, and to keep under cover. Even at that time there was an obvious flaw in this thesis: once a Second World War actually started, it might be too late to utilize the long-awaited 'setback.' Would there then still be time for a peaceful readjustment? Was it possible to switch the vast and complex war machinery on and off so easily? It seemed a rash assumption that the British and French would show benevolent understanding of our plans for getting rid of Hitler by means of a declaration of war. It seemed far more likely that they would prefer to deliver a few quick, hard blows and put an end to these German trouble-makers once and for all.

Such, in any case, was the way I argued, and I must admit that my predictions were very much mistaken. I could, of course, not even imagine such a thing as the 'phony' war, nor was I aware of how unarmed the Western Powers were. Moreover, I had no idea how tremendously the Western nations overestimated the extent of our own rearmament. Like everyone else, I imagined that a declaration of war would be followed by immediate bombings of the Ruhr or a grand offensive against the Rhineland. Halder, as a matter of fact, made the same assumptions. He expected that any thrust against our unarmed western flank would prove successful. This seemed to me all the more reason for immediate intervention. If Halder took Hitler's war-mongering seriously, he ought to be eager to stop the Nazi leader at once, before irreparable harm was done.

I had little luck, however, with these arguments. Halder preferred to stand the risk of bombings rather than, as he conceived it, precipitate a civil war within the army. Perhaps a few rough blows would prove the lesser evil, he declared. Until the people were given tangible evidence that Hitler wanted war in bloody earnest, they would not snap out of their state of permanent intoxication. At the present time, the chief of staff thought, the overwhelming majority of the workers and soldiers stood behind Hitler. If he called upon them, they would support his régime, with arms in hand, if need be.

Several times Halder referred to his four or five sons-in-law, all of whom were serving in the army as captains. Their attitude, he believed was fairly representative of the temper of the corps of officers; and that temper, he insisted, was pro-Hitler. The attitude of the generals was irrelevant; the decisive factor in any projected *coup d'état* would be the attitude of the lower officers, because they had the closest contact with the bulk of the soldiery and, therefore, with the broad masses of the people.

I was extremely disconcerted. This method of gauging the temper of the times by noting the viewpoint of the lower officers was something entirely new for me. I remarked — and my comment was not taken very graciously — that as a rule the generals counted a good deal more than did the young officers, and that in my opinion the latter would undoubtedly obey the orders of their superiors. If there was any doubt of that, then obviously the army's sense of discipline and confidence in leadership had seriously deteriorated, and if that were true, I said, it was all the more reason to act as quickly as possible, since it indicated that the Nazis had already gone very far in breaking down the morale of the army. All my persuasion was in vain. I could not overcome Halder's fears. He no longer had confidence in his troops and wanted to have his 'setback' before he took action.

In retrospect we may find a certain piquant similarity between this attitude on the part of the German chief of staff and the attitude among certain Allied military leaders. The French generalissimo followed virtually the same line of reasoning when he evaded battle and tried to treat the declaration of war as a more or less necessary evil to accomplish the removal of Hitler without struggle. Gamelin's *drôle de guerre* was a kind of comradely gesture of aid to his colleague, Halder, so that the latter could organize a *drôle de révolution*. But instead of begetting a 'phony' revolution, the 'phony' war turned into a real war.

If Halder was chary about placing confidence in his soldiers, he was certainly bold in some of his other conclusions — far bolder than seemed proper for a man in his position. His imagination was so bold that he was inhibited from doing anything at all. He felt that even more was necessary than the sheer physical shock of a declaration of war by the Western Powers. Even at that juncture, he warned me, he could not take open action. For he was too much intimidated by recollections of the 'stab-in-the-back' legend. This was the legend, invented by German military writers and eagerly taken up by the Nazis, that the German army had been 'unbeaten in the field' in the First World War, and had been defeated solely because of the break-

down on the home front. The civilians, it was alleged, had stabbed
the glorious German army in the back when it was on the point of
winning total victory. This distortion of history encouraged the
people to place more trust in the Nazi and Nationalist militarists.

Halder was afraid of promoting a Hitler legend. He feared to
stand before the people as an individual or as the representative of a
class who had brought about the Titan's fall. Such a situation, he
said, would be intolerable for the army. First the dictator must suffer
a fatal 'accident.' The best thing to do would be to blow up the
Fuehrer's train a few days after the declaration of war, and then to
spread the report that Hitler had been killed by an enemy air attack.

More than once during the past years professionals and amateurs
indulged in such wish-dreams — but that did not mean that they
would take part in a bomb plot. Usually such ideas were advanced
after lengthy debates when despairing oppositionists felt themselves
at the end of their rope. After 1938 especially, when the crisis of
war was coming closer and closer, they racked their brains to find
something that they could do by themselves or in conjunction with
others. Even the boldest imagination could not envisage a successful
popular uprising, and a daring individual action seemed even more
impossible. As a result, all these conversations ended in the suggestion — somewhat jestingly advanced, but nevertheless accurate — that
Hitler was so well guarded that the only solution lay in a bomb attack.

On the lips of the chief of the general staff, however, this proposal
had a very different sound, for Halder had at his disposal both prerequisites for a genuine *coup d'état*. In the first place, he commanded
the army — and certainly a part of the soldiery would obey his
orders. In the second place, he always had access to the person of
the Fuehrer. If he himself did not want to fire the shot, he could
certainly find a few officers who would be quite ready to commit
assassination.

The frequency with which Halder returned to this idea of an
anonymous bomb attack and his ingenious outlines of the various
possibilities were proof that he had carefully considered what he was
saying, and the very fact that he had thought out such a method of

assassination alarmed me. Hundreds of thousands of wretched victims
of the Terror might brood over such plans, but it was to be expected
that a general would disdain such circuitous methods; it was to be
expected, above all, that he would openly stand by an act which his
intelligence and his conscience made mandatory for him.

As a result of the bloody events of June 30, 1934, the soldiers had
become the 'sole bearers of arms in the nation.' For years they had
accepted the various comforts that pertained to this rôle. By as early
as 1938 they would look back upon personal careers that had proved
brilliant beyond their expectations. They knew what faith the mass
of the people placed in them. The men, who were ready to stake their
lives in a battle with foreign enemies, should have confronted the
despoilers at home with equal courage. It was unseemly for them to
commit a necessary deed only to dodge taking the responsibility for it.
The prospects were poor if they insisted on beginning a *coup d'état*
with a fabulous historical lie.

Late that same night I got in touch with Oster. Loyal fellow that
he was, he was hurt by my sharp condemnation of Halder's timidity,
but the following morning he was all smiles again. The chief of staff
had ordered him to co-operate with me in preparing an outline of all
police measures to be taken in the event of a *coup d'état*.

We were approaching the first of the few serious attempts at a
coup d'état in the Third Reich.

WITZLEBEN IS WON OVER

THERE WAS A GROUP of anti-Nazis of my age, who had entered government service at about the same time as myself, who now tended
to give serious thought to the many advantages a title would bring
them. I do not mean advantages only in the personal sense. Many of
these young men insisted that it was vitally important to occupy
so-called key positions, or in any case posts which afforded some protection and some opportunity to observe the workings of the state

machinery. Such posts were, naturally, the ones rather high in the bureaucratic hierarchy. No one ever objected when army officers were promoted regularly to higher and higher ranks. In the civil service, of course, promotions were less systematized and more a matter of politics. Nevertheless, these men were entirely sincere in posing the question of whether they should not press forward for their advancement. All of us, after all, wanted to acquire 'influence.' Experience had taught us that the generals were impressed only by those civilians whose titles had the ring of importance.

I can scarcely blame my fellow officials for feeling this way. During the years 1936 to 1939 the end of the Nazi régime certainly did not appear to be in sight. For the married men it was very difficult to decline promotions which carried financial increases. On the other hand, the price of advancement was almost inevitably membership in the Party, the SA or the SS, or some other kind of intellectual tribute. Very few were able to retain their principles in this psychological stress.

For my part, I always considered it worth while to remain in the civil service, but I deliberately avoided promotions. I never advanced beyond the lowest ranks in the service. The more a man became outwardly involved in the system, the more difficult it was for him to keep himself untainted inwardly by it. With each promotion there was increasing temptation to content oneself with mildly advocating an 'evolutionary' course. From 1937 on, it was my lot to witness many cases in which people whose courage we had esteemed left our ranks. Even if the later course of the Revolution drove them back to us, their defection had left its stamp.

One of the favorite justifications for these tactics of 'staying in' was that an individual by himself could do nothing; he was powerless and had to wait; everything depended on the generals. This argument was, to be sure, quite true. The key to successful revolt was in the hands of the generals from 1937 on. They alone had the technical prerequisites for driving a breach into the government's defenses. Although good sense dictated a period of waiting, it was profoundly discouraging to see, in that interval, how each man went his own way.

If the civilian *fronde* had increased during those 'quiet' years, that fact would certainly have made a deep impression on the generals.

We 'civilians' were also convinced that any *Putsch* must be prepared thoroughly beforehand. We were not advocating a swift and sudden stroke. We as well as Halder were acutely aware of the importance of timing. The great difference between us was that we were unwilling to make the outbreak of a war an essential condition of our preparations. We maintained that a tremendous eruption, such as every war is, carried with it too many imponderables. It was something that could not be stopped as easily as it was started. However, there seemed to be a possibility that a compromise might be found between these two viewpoints. Suppose that we agreed to let things drift to the point of actual war, and that Halder for his part pledged himself to attempt the *coup d'état* as soon as Hitler irrevocably and irrefutably issued marching orders?

It was on this basis that Schacht and I tried to come to an agreement with the chief of staff. Diplomatic tension was growing worse and worse. We were becoming impatient. Schacht made an appointment through Oster to pay Halder a return visit, and I made up my mind to go along. Whether Halder was pleased by this presumption, I shall not attempt to say, but we did not care what our host thought about that. We did not mind demonstrating that we civilians did not jump simply when he cracked the whip, but responded on our own to the needs of the situation.

The interview was a stormy one. From the very beginning there was a certain mood of dishonesty. Schacht and I had the distinct feeling that Halder was not so brave as he had been a few weeks ago. For some reason he was looking for a line of retreat. 'Whom the gods wish to destroy . . .' Had Hitler's heady oratory already made him mad? Or had the Tempter dangled the bait of 'strategic considerations'? We did not know. But it was clear that the chief of staff was trying to convince us that everything might turn out well after all, that the Western Powers might present Hitler with a free ticket to the East.

Today I know that Halder had a premonition of something which

we innocents smiled at as another of Ribbentrop's mad fancies:
'Munich.' In consideration of this his change was not so reprehensible
— except that his exposition did not stop at this, but included violent
and unexpected denunciations of British policy.

It is, to be sure, difficult for us to extol British policy toward
Germany. We have learned much about the fatal rôle that Wilhelm
II played in the tragic fiasco of Anglo-German relations, and we
Germans must largely blame ourselves for Anglo-German rivalry.
Nevertheless, clumsy and semi-megalomaniac newcomers though we
were to the arena of imperialism, it is regrettable that the British did
not adopt a somewhat wiser policy toward us. If anyone, however,
and especially a German chief of the general staff, felt the need to
reproach the British in the summer of 1938, his complaint should
have been directed at their incomprehensible and unforgivable
patience with Hitler. Evidently, there was something queer about
Halder.

Fortunately, it was at least possible to discuss concrete details with
him. He continued to assert that he was determined at all costs to
prevent war. He gave us an extremely pessimistic — and in retrospect
exaggerated — description of our unpreparedness. He called the tanks
that were then being used by the army 'traveling coffins.' Obviously,
he had no conception of how incomparably worse prepared the other
side was; for he counted on the Western Powers' being willing and
able to launch an immediate and effective counter-blow.

The most important outcome of the conversation was that Halder
gave us some reassurance on the question which was our principal
concern. The *coup d'état* was now scheduled to take place in the brief
breathing spell between Hitler's final order for the troops to march
and the first exchange of shots. Our plans, of course, absolutely
depended upon the dictator's not taking us by surprise with his *Blitz*.

'No,' Halder assured us, 'there's no chance of his tricking me. I've
arranged the plans in such a way that I cannot help having three days'
warning before any action is taken; moreover, the final order must be
issued directly to me at least twenty-four hours beforehand.'

We were still saddled with the painful question of whether Halder was really in earnest. When Schacht attempted to dispute the wisdom of waiting till the last moment by arguing that sooner or later even Englishmen of Chamberlain's ilk would have had enough, Halder replied tartly: 'Herr Minister, that remark might be interpreted as an invitation to the British.' It was evident that he did not want to be pressed in any way and hoped to withhold his consent until the very end.

From then on, we were tormented by the suspicion that this uniformed dialectician was unreliable. Although he had given us so many assurances, although he had committed himself so thoroughly and, in a sense, put himself in our power, we still felt that we had to be on our guard. In any case we must take precautions, so that we would be in a position to remind him of his promises when the time came. We would do best to let his fellow generals push him forward.

Around the middle of August I went to Duesseldorf to pay a visit to Administrative President Schmid, one of our most reliable advisers on the 'inside.' In his complex territory he had a splendid opportunity to survey the general situation and above all the situation in food, which was often critical. He also had an excellent insight into other aspects of the productive process, such as the frequent shortages of raw materials or labor. Schmid was particularly skilled at reading the barometer of public sentiment.

Although in 1938 we could no longer hope for a popular revolt from below — Gestapo rule had become too formidable by then — the factor of public morale was still vitally important. In such eras, what exactly does morale imply? We must not confuse it with simple whims or with the frequent expressions of satisfaction or discontent. There were periods of extreme crisis and want in the Third Reich, in the midst of which the morale of the public was good. On the other hand, the masses frequently reacted badly to diplomatic successes or improvements in conditions. It all hung on the willingness on the part of the public to 'go along.' Unfortunately this willingness was often present, although it might not be manifested in noisy demonstrations. It was present far more often than is admitted today by those who were 'against it' from the beginning.

Let us remember that Hitler was not towed through his crises only by the registered membership of the Nazi Party, by the state functionaries, or by the soldiers. Somehow, he was borne along by the collective unconscious of the masses. This is the deeper significance of the idea that it was 'working out,' of which I have spoken earlier. Psychologists must take note of this if they want to find a fairly adequate answer to the tormenting question of why this usurper who never possessed a democratic majority was nevertheless the executor of an imaginary popular will.

In discussing such psychological conditions we must be all the more forthright because it is so easy to fall into the practice of 'myth-making' once more. It is quite erroneous to play off groups of the population against one another by asserting that certain occupational groups, say the workers, suffered most from the reign of terror or proved least malleable under its blows. The responsibility, and hence the blame, is greater for those whose education and propertied status more easily enabled them to make a reasonable judgment of the situation, and who nevertheless played traitor to their better knowledge and their traditional duties; but when we speak of sociologic susceptibility to the germ of Nazism, it would constitute a serious distortion of history to claim now that the broad masses of the people were more immune than they actually were at the time. To assert this is to overlook a dearly bought historical lesson: that the so-called 'little man' has played a decisive and alarming rôle in this mass age of ours.

Everyone, from top to bottom, from unskilled worker, foreman, taxi-driver, tailor, or waiter to the white-collar clerk, the university professors, and business managers, from landed proprietors down to the peasants and the agricultural laborers — all of them were a part of that great contingent of semi-voluntary, semi-involuntary camp-followers who were caught up in the mighty current of revolution. No occupational group can be excepted.

On my visit to Duesseldorf two observations were forced upon me.

The first was that everyone who was connected with industry was contented — not only the business men, but the workers and clerical forces, who were receiving high wages. Things were 'working out.' My second observation was that no one gave much thought to the growing diplomatic tension. Partial mobilization? Well, what of it? Hitler was merely bluffing. He was too sharp a political intriguer to permit an actual war to start!

'Hitler wants peace . . .' 'Hitler is only threatening . . .' We can smile sadly today at the memory of those assurances that we heard again and again from Goebbels in the hot summer of 1938. The very fact that this was the official propaganda line gave us our great chance, for even to mention the word 'war' was equivalent to treason. Even the most fanatical Party members frankly expressed their conviction that their millennial Reich would not last twelve months if war were declared. All remembered the horrors of the First World War; they feared these perils to the marrow of their bones. The people, exhausted by the turbulence of revolution, sincerely longed for peace and quiet. Everyone realized that war was a deadly serious matter. War meant bread cards, starvation rations, and intensified terrorism. War meant hundreds of thousands of lives, not to mention air raids. War meant a headlong plunge into the abyss. In 1938 such things were simply inconceivable. In spite of Hitler's triumphant emergence from the Fritsch crisis, in spite of his amazing success in annexing Austria, the fear of war still far outweighed all loyalty to the Nazi Party and to the Fuehrer.

Let us keep in mind this imponderable factor of public morale while we try to comprehend the grim significance of the dramatic events of the next few months. During those crucial months that preceded his triumph at Munich, Hitler had strayed farther than ever before from the tenor of public opinion. The people no longer understood him. During the twelve years of his reign people often speculated on the possibility of his being insane, but never was it so frequent a topic of conversation as in those days, whenever the bare possibility of a war was mentioned. War would be sure proof of his madness — consequently, both possibilities were rejected.

The key generals took much the same view. I found this out in the course of a short, extemporized trip to Muenster. General Hans von Kluge, who was still commander of the sixth military district, had heard of my presence in Duesseldorf. He was so eager to see me that, to save me time, he sent his private automobile to fetch me and bring me back. In view of his usual caution and of my own insignificant status, that was a good indication of his shakiness. He was willing to stake rather high in order to obtain information.

Kluge had, in fact, no more than an inkling of the meaning of certain military measures he had been required to take in line of duty. That points up how skillfully camouflaged these maneuvers were, so that the middle and lower brackets of the officers' corps could not be certain what was taking place. In the course of our conversation he conceded that certain of these measures could, depending on the slant of the observer, be interpreted as something more serious than feints designed to implement diplomatic pressure.

Nevertheless, he clung to his conviction that a war was inconceivable from an economic or military point of view. Above all, he insisted, a war was psychologically unthinkable. If it came to that, he expected popular uprisings and mutinies among the troops. Even more emphatically than Halder had done, Kluge asserted that we were completely unprepared for war. He ought to know, he said, what wide gaps there were in the supplies of arms, munitions, and trained lower officers. He thought that Hitler's speech at Jueterbog, the speech which had precipitated Beck's resignation, had been intended merely as another of the Fuehrer's diversionary tricks — combined with some of his customary boasting.

Late that same evening I met a well-known industrialist at President Schmid's home. It was easy for me to see that both gentlemen were far better informed on military-political questions than was their military district commander. I mention this incident only to demonstrate once again the hardly credible fact that in 1938 none of the leading generals wanted war. Indeed — although this sounds even more improbable — most of them did not even believe in the possibility of war. These sensible strategists considered the mere idea of war such madness that — and this was their fatal error — they were sure a sharp politician like Hitler would know enough not to bring down such a patent disaster upon himself and Germany.

Almost a full year later, Kluge still refused to believe in the earnestness of Hitler's war-mongering. The triumphs at Munich and Prague completely deceived him. Nevertheless, my insistent prophecies troubled him. As I shook hands with him for the last time on this earth, he bade me good-bye with a whimsical melancholy unusual in so high-ranking a general. 'Well,' he said, 'see you again in a mass grave.'

Witzleben was cut of another cloth. Sobered by our conversation with Halder, Schacht and I kept pressing Oster until he established contact with the commander of the Berlin military district. As chance would have it Erwin von Witzleben, who was subsequently promoted to field marshal, had also been Oster's chief for a time. That made the situation easier for my indefatigable friend. How otherwise could he have approached a commanding general?

At the time of the Fritsch crisis, Witzleben had been recovering from an illness in a Dresden sanatorium. Now he learned the real background of that affair for the first time. He also heard further details about the planned war against Czechoslovakia. Both stories aroused his indignation.

Witzleben was a refreshingly uncomplicated man. He had no bent for that kind of political finesse so dear to a bureaucratic general such as Halder. The Berlin commander was a typical front-line general who had his heart in the right place. Probably not too well read and certainly not inclined toward the fine arts, he was nevertheless a man firmly rooted in the chivalric traditions of the old Prussian officers' corps. He liked country life and was a passionate hunter; there was nothing of the schoolmaster about him, as there was about our chief of staff. Oster had only to hint at the delicate matter at hand. Witzleben understood at once and placed himself unconditionally at our disposal.

There was, however, one point that Witzleben, too, wanted clarified beforehand. Would it actually come to a war? Or were the diplomatic disturbances that were being played up by Goebbels just the usual stage thunder? Were not the Western Powers actually aiming at something else entirely? Was some crucial shift taking place behind the scenes about which the initiates had been whispering for so long? Would Hitler be given a clear channel to the East?

Since the very beginning of rearmament, the army men had been instructed that there was a secret agreement with England and France under which Germany was to defend Europe against Bolshevism. Whether this 'defense' was to be offensive or defensive was not discussed. But after every diplomatic bout that Hitler had won against the advice of the suspicious generals (the re-establishment of conscription, the reoccupation of the Rhineland, the silent tolerance and then the open recognition of the German air force, the Anglo-German naval agreement, the annexation of Austria) — after each of these 'peaceful' achievements, Hitler had dropped a whole series of mysterious hints. What was the present situation? Would there really be a war because of the Sudetenland? That was what Witzleben wanted to know.

Shortly after he put these questions to Oster, I met with him to discuss a number of police matters. I proposed that he have a talk with Schacht, since Schacht was in the best position to know what the British intended to do. The general found this suggestion very opportune, since he wanted in any case to leave the handling of political affairs to Schacht. What was finest about Witzleben — at that time and in the later years — was that he manifested no political ambitions for himself. He deliberately restricted himself to the military realm. He never got himself involved in the political jealousies and intrigues which were the constant, and perhaps inevitable, concomitant of all our plans for *coups d'état*.

We arranged for a quiet afternoon at Schacht's country home northeast of Berlin. At Witzleben's request, the commander of his Potsdam division, General von Brockdorff, accompanied him. Witzleben intended to charge von Brockdorff with the execution of the military action in Berlin itself. The very fact that the three of us

so openly went to visit Schacht was proof that Witzleben was not
given to that exaggerated caution which was to cause us so much
trouble later on.

It was a joy to see how quickly the two generals came to an agreement with the minister. Here was another instance of the great authority Schacht possessed at that time among the higher army officers.
There was good reason for this. Where else could the generals obtain
trustworthy diplomatic information? Certainly not from the Nazified
press or from Ribbentrop's foreign ministry. Unfortunately for
Schacht, he was unable to anticipate Munich, and he lost considerable
prestige when his predictions proved false. The clairvoyant Fuehrer
turned out to be a wiser politician than Schacht. Witzleben and Brockdorff were carried along by Schacht's enthusiasm. They agreed that
they must do everything in their power to prevent the disaster of a
war that fall. When we parted, Witzleben pledged his word. With
or without Halder, on orders from above or against the orders of his
own military superiors — he was ready to go the limit.

INVOLVED PREPARATIONS

I WAS ABLE to set to work at once. Now we had to think out the
coup d'état down to the most minor technical details. At Witzleben's
suggestion, we worked out a scheme of division of labor. Brockdorff
would take care of the military arrangements, while I made plans for
the necessary police measures. We put aside all political questions.
Schacht was charged with drawing up a list of political administrators.
This last seemed to us to be the least of our worries. We reckoned
on the balance of power's remaining with the military for a time.
There would be a transition period of a few days during which the
state of siege would continue, and only then would power be handed
over to the civilians. What persons were to compose the new cabinet
would be settled after Hitler and the Nazis were safely out of the
way. There was still a sufficient reserve of well-known statesmen

and officials to fall back on. Later on, too, we should have been better advised to concentrate on the technical details of the revolt instead of manufacturing trouble for ourselves by setting up hotly contested lists of future ministers.

Nevertheless, there were two political matters that had to be settled at once. First of all, we had to write a proclamation explaining the why of the revolt. The slogans were obvious: against the war, for justice and freedom of conscience. In the second place, we had to answer the difficult question of whether we wanted to collaborate with certain Nazi groups. In specific terms, this meant — as usual — did we want to deal with Goering?

Somehow Goering had found favor with the generals. Although they did not consider him one of their own, they had some amazing misconceptions of his moral and political character. They could not get it out of their heads that they ought to use this 'conservative' middleman as a 'buffer' between the Party and the army. In any case, they felt, Goering was too popular for them to thrust him roughly aside.

But what would collaboration with Goering have meant? Germany and the world would have had to contend with a diluted and therefore all the more diabolical Nazi system for decades to come. There was no doubt that Goering was unscrupulous enough to order the dissolution of the Nazi Party without a second thought, but never again would he 'intervene on the side of justice,' as he was now allegedly doing. The end-result would have been a continuation of all the totalitarian practices, under a somewhat more plutocratic guise. German militarism would have changed its skin once more, from brown to field-gray.

I have often racked my brains trying to decide why so many persons among the bourgeoisie and the officers' corps were infatuated with Goering. Was it because this jovial monster pretended to be such a fool? That may be. The Nordified Renaissance tyrant strutted about in one of his multitudinous uniforms and seemed to be encouraging the observer not to take him more seriously than he took himself. It was as if he were deliberately caricaturing himself. In this respect he was pleasantly different from the other revolutionists, who were without an ounce of humor.

A good caricaturist stresses the essential features of his subject with a few incisive strokes. Goering, the buffoon, must have known beforehand exactly what typical characteristics he could distort grotesquely without arousing repugnance, for he wanted to have people laugh with him. He was clever enough, or intuitive enough, to create precisely the sort of effect that would make people fall in love with the amiable target of their mockery. Or should we say, not mockery but self-contempt?

Goering was the Falstaff of our mass epoch. His peculiar trick consisted in magnifying on a gigantic scale a characteristic phenomenon of our epoch. The Wilhelmine bourgeoisie, who lacked all resolution, faith, and profundity, found in this pompous, boastful, power-mad, bloodthirsty man all those traits of character with which they were familiar in their own selves. They saw their dilettantism represented in his possession of a hundred offices and titles; their own escape into make-believe from the poverty of reality; their own elevation of trash to the status of fine art; their own superficiality which so soon became a menace to the commonweal; their own degenerate externalization, brutalization, and corruption of the old military traditions.

Goering's popularity was thus a kind of alibi. By caricaturing all these traits, he assuaged the consciences of all those who did not behave quite so madly and excessively as Goering himself, although they were all given to the same inanities. Our Wilhelmine bourgeoisie applauded the bemedaled field marshal as if he were a clown — but in reality they cynically recognized in him a symbolic figure. These pseudo-bourgeois were playing with revolution, but basically, they did not want any part of it. That was why this jovial fat man suited them so well. His perpetual gormandizing seemed to confirm anew every day their conviction that, really, there was no need to take it all too seriously. Who can say how much longer the people would have endured Hitler by himself, with his death's-head guard? But the addition of Goering with his gala theatricals, his magnificence, and his banquets — of Goering surrounded by the élite of the generals in gold braid — that somehow took the edge off the knife. Goering created that deceptive atmosphere of nonchalance through which a doomed class had once pranced to the guillotine.

Goering had to go. This was something we had to insist upon from the beginning, for we wanted to get rid of the Nazi system itself. Therefore, we could not come to any agreements with one of its most prominent representatives, whether Number 2 or Number 3. The danger consisted precisely in Goering's popularity. He might be welcomed enthusiastically as the 'savior' in a difficult situation — and welcomed not only in Germany.

On the other hand, we hit on a rather clever stratagem in connection with the problem of Hitler — though during this early period we did not discuss that problem in too great detail. In preparing for a revolt it is always well to start out by assuming the worst possible circumstances. We thought it wise to reckon on the contingency of one or several crucial persons' making their escape. What should we do then if they gathered their forces for a counter-blow? Especially if Hitler were not gagged at once, he might incite grave confusion and qualms of conscience among the troops. We decided that it would be best to issue a clear and unequivocal military slogan, and at the same time to obscure the political situation as far as possible. We must create a situation in which the bewildered soldiers would sooner obey the orders of their superiors than radio proclamations. So many confused reports and rumors would have to be started that the disconcerted Nazis would not know what to think and would therefore content themselves with obeying the military regulations.

At that time the people were unwilling to believe that Hitler himself wanted a war The real war-mongers were considered to be Himmler and perhaps even Goering. It therefore seemed an obviously sound idea to use their own successful propaganda against those two chief plotters of June 30, 1934. We would claim that we had just discovered that these two were planning a *coup d'état* in the hope that they would be able to confront the vacillating Fuehrer and the reluctant ministers with an actual war situation.

People believed Himmler capable of any crime, including an attack upon Hitler or the army leadership. Invoking the army to protect its supreme commander against an SS plot was therefore not so fantastic. In fact, it was almost credible. Should the orders be framed along such lines, the overwhelming majority of the officers would not ask too many questions; they would act at once. They were not being asked to break their oath of allegiance. As a matter of fact, the soldiers were only waiting for such a signal to settle scores with the Black rabble of the SS.

This line had numerous advantages. How was Himmler going to disprove the assertion that he contemplated an SS *Putsch*? It would cost him precious time to convince the public of the contrary, and in the meanwhile the most important Nazis would be arrested without too much trouble. All that would be required was to issue a public summons for all leaders of the Party and the SS to report at once to the nearest army headquarters or else be subject to prosecution as participants in the SS *Putsch*. Unquestionably the majority would have reported at once, with a thousand assurances of loyalty; they would have behaved with the same cowardliness, the same air of 'innocence,' that even the most notorious SS generals adopted in 1945 when they exchanged their werewolves' pelts for lambskins and meekly reported at the Allied assembly points.

Energetic action and simultaneous stirring-up of confusion — that would be the first act. With the *Putsch* organized in such a fashion, we could afford the risk that Hitler might escape the first dragnet. If necessary we should have to pretend that he was utterly unsuspecting, completely in ignorance of the projected SS revolt. Such a story would be perfectly in consonance with the general attitude of the Germans at that time. For the masses still persistently refused to attribute the responsibility for corruption and for the Gestapo atrocities to Hitler. They considered him disgracefully 'betrayed' by his subordinate leaders. 'If the Fuehrer only knew . . .' This foolish exclamation was still to be heard. It was a great help in avoiding the consequences of serious and independent thought.

What was to be done with Hitler in the end was another question entirely. My views on this point differed considerably from those of almost all my friends. Most of them wished to take the dictator alive in order to try him in a court. These men preferred to take their chances with the many incalculables that are involved in every political trial rather than sin against the forms of strict legality. Others thought it would be better to have Hitler declared insane. They were already on the lookout for psychiatric testimony to this effect. They, of course, were absolutely opposed to any attempt on his life. In reply to all the legal, political, or religious scruples, I held that tyrannicide had always been looked upon as a moral commandment. There was far too much at stake in a *coup d'état*; rebels could not afford the moral luxury of giving their main enemy even the smallest opening by which to escape and possibly launch a counter-attack.

I am not, be it noted, speaking of a violent overthrow of government such as may now and then occur in the course of social crisis. Not every attempt at a *coup d'état* can be judged by the same ethical standards. I am speaking of a situation in domestic and foreign politics which already was rife with murder and injustice, which was moving toward the blood-bath of a war. At stake was much more than the peace and security of one single country. The interests of millions of innocent people were more imperative than the requirements of justice — requirements which the tyrant himself had unfailingly violated.

The only antidote for poison is another poison.

In our preparatory work it soon turned out that some problems were easier to solve than we had imagined, and many were more difficult. We soon saw that it would not be a formidable task to make the multitudinous shifts in personnel which would insure our control over the state apparatus. This rather surprised us. We found that we had been subtly victimized by Goebbels's reiterated propaganda that chaos would follow the overthrow of the Nazis. Upon examination we found that it would be necessary merely to replace a few chief men in the various ministries and the apparatus would continue to run smoothly on the momentum characteristic of all bureaucracies. That

was one drawback to the leader principle. The subordinate government employees were accustomed to obey orders. Replace their
superiors and they would be highly unlikely to undertake immediate
resistance. In their alarm most of them would prefer to wait and see
what the outcome would be.

A close study of the personnel situation in the provinces convinced
us that a temporary replacement from the existing body of officials
could be found for every federal governor, local chief executive, and
administrative president. Even within the police force there were
sufficient well-trained officials whom we knew were reliable. These
men could certainly jump into the breach. Afterward, of course, a
thorough revision of personnel would have to be undertaken, but that
would be a matter for the coming government to take care of. The
task of the generals must be restricted to transfer of the government
to a new central political power. Anything else, and especially any
attempt to influence the selection of ministerial and provincial personnel, would look suspiciously like a military dictatorship. And we
wanted above all to avoid giving such an impression.

There was no need to worry unduly over the Nazi infiltration and
infection of the civil service. The system of spies and informers was
very closely woven; not so the network of Nazi government functionaries. Up to the very end there were considerable gaps in that,
in spite of the increased pace of Nazification in later years. This distinction between inner Nazification and outer supervision of the
officials has never been properly appreciated. In order to retain control, Heydrich's security service had only to occupy a few key positions. The 'importance' of the post often lay in its superficial pettiness.
For example, in order for Heydrich to keep an eye on the course of
affairs in some provincial office employing several hundred persons,
he would need scarcely a dozen alert registrars or stenographers, and
perhaps one or two higher officials in addition, to take care of ideological matters. At once, the other ninety-five per cent of the office
employees, whether they were 'decent' men, opportunists, coerced
Party members, or outright Nazis, became the quarries of an anonymous terror. They were all the more intimidated for not knowing

exactly who were the informers. Consequently, they tended to imagine the unknown security service men in each of their fellow workers and to scent a microphone at every telephone.

The strategy of the military action gave us far more to think about. Where this was concerned, we had not realized the complexity of our task. For the rest of my life I shall hear ringing in my ears Goerdeler's emphatic phrase that the generals must 'act.' Since those first efforts at planning in the latter part of the summer of 1938, I became much more circumspect in using the word 'act.' In trying to plan everything that was involved in that simple word, I became convinced that very little indeed could be accomplished by a simple military command.

It is worth while going into this matter in some detail, for the essential complex of problems remained the same from 1938 to 1944. I have complained repeatedly of how difficult it was to extract a courageous decision from the generals, but in all fairness I must indicate the multiple difficulties that even the bravest general had to overcome.

Let us assume that the general who has decided to 'act' is a military district commander. His reputation, let us say, is so unblemished that the populace places high hopes in him. Let us assume also that this man is the real master of his soldiers, which certainly was not true in all cases. The officers' corps had been so greatly expanded that it was utterly heterogeneous. Moreover, the conjunction of the army and the quite independent air force had created a series of novel problems.

How many troops would this general have at his disposal? At best no more than two divisions that could be used as a striking force; the myriad special formations were only very loosely under his command. Two divisions were not going to accomplish a 'march on Berlin.' Employed by the government, two well-motorized divisions would work wonders in quelling a revolt, but for rebels trying to seize power they would scarcely suffice to conquer a province — unless the overwhelming majority of the population joined in the rebellion and formed a militia that would take over lines of communication and government centers. Such co-operation could scarcely be expected in 1938. Neither the Right nor the Left had been able to sprinkle partisans throughout the land. There was nothing like a civil-war situation, any more than there was a great strike movement in the offing. For the present, then, any general who chose to act was pretty much thrown on his own resources. At most he could hope that the spark would leap to some of his fellow generals — and that depended largely upon the success he achieved during the first few hours of his rebellion.

In this age of the airplane and the radio, moreover, not more than twelve hours would pass before the threatened rulers would strike back. Presumably the counter-blow might be launched even before the two divisions could unite their forces. The various sections of each division were scattered throughout the area of an extensive military district. In view of the strict centralization of command, the mobilization of divisions could not escape the notice of the general's superior, the army group commander, or his neighbor, the commander of the air force in the military district. Simply the issue of live munitions would arouse suspicion, and what reply would the general make to their inquiries? Once the top army leadership was alarmed, it would not take too much presence of mind for the chancellery to depose the mutinous general and his entire staff. A number of new troop leaders could be sent by plane to the critical spot, and certainly some of the lower officers would obey the new commanders rather than the old ones.

It was often objected that even a defeated local revolt meant something; that it would be a signal. Undoubtedly such an 'act' would have created a great stir both within Germany and abroad; but a defeat inside Germany would be disastrous, and would produce a mistaken impression in other countries. The Gestapo would seize on any attempt at rebellion as a pretext for a terrible purge. At the same time the outside world might decide that such definite symptoms of dissolution within Germany justified it in continuing the policy of wait-and-see. An isolated action would, in the end, do more harm than good. Success was possible only if a large number of generals rebelled at the same time, or if the military chiefs were part of the conspiracy. If the latter should close their eyes, or, better still, if they should issue the crucial order, the greatest danger that a military uprising could face would be avoided: the danger of a counter-command.

There is a single alternative to the above analysis. We took this alternative into consideration in forming our plans. If it were not some provincial general who acted, but the commander of the Berlin military district, and if he succeeded in seizing not only the main Nazi Party and government headquarters, but the war ministry as well, he could prevent the issuance of a counter-command for at least the first ten hours. His problem would then be to present the hesitant or confused provincial generals with a *fait accompli.*

If the general were bold, if he reduced his precautionary measures to an absolute minimum, he would have to silence in his first lightning stroke the radio transmitters, the entire public telephone system, and the teletype network of the various ministries. At one blow he would have to occupy the central headquarters of the federal police and the Berlin police. This feat was complicated by the fact that the Gestapo, the criminal police, and the security police all occupied their own buildings and possessed their own communication systems; but not until these preliminaries had been completed could the general proceed to the main purpose of the action — the occupation of the chancellery and of the most important ministries. The element of surprise was decisive; otherwise the project of making wholesale arrests would peter out in useless and time-consuming searches — because the most important birds would already have flown.

Then it was essential that the surprised provincial generals should join the revolt. Not all of them would have done this. Nevertheless, with the proper groundwork laid, there was a reasonable prospect of success. The appeal to these generals must be accompanied by concrete suggestions or orders. The very first telegram (there would have to be a separate one for each military district) would have to specify what offices should be occupied, what persons should be arrested immediately, and what indispensable regulations should be proclaimed under martial law. We could not, after all, expect the provincial generals to pull such orders out of their hats when we had had to spend weeks discussing the value and feasibility of each one.

It is easy to see that taking action was not so easy. That is why, after these first experiences, we concentrated entirely on trying to recruit generals who commanded really large forces. It would have been futile to expect action from some department head in the war ministry or some member of one of the many special staffs, merely because he wore the red stripes of a general. Some of these generals had less actual power of command than a lieutenant.

In 1938, Witzleben found in General von Brockdorff an associate who would go along with him up to the hilt. His Potsdam division was considered a model one. It was often used for parades, but experts maintained that it would do far better as the spearhead of a *coup d'état*. Witzleben had resolved to be prepared for both a *coup d'état* from 'above' and a mutiny from 'below.' He repeatedly assured Halder that his preparations were purely for an action that would be ordered ultimately by the commander-in-chief of the army or by the chief of the general staff. Nevertheless, Witzleben never lost sight of the second possibility — that he might have to by-pass the two of them. He had not forgotten Brauchitsch's shabby behavior during the Fritsch crisis, and he suspected that Halder was not of the stuff of which heroes are made. He would have been perfectly content to place them behind bars during the crucial hours should that be necessary. At times I had the impression that he rather chuckled over the prospect of being forced to use his revolver against the corrupt Brauschitsch. In any case, he had reserved the momentous interview with the commander-in-chief — the announcement that the *Putsch* was about to begin — for himself personally.

As the crisis approached, it became more urgent that I should have an office that could be sealed against the eyes and ears of the Gestapo. Witzleben, with his characteristic fearlessness, found a place for me in his military district headquarters. He supplied me with false identity papers and assigned me a large reception room which adjoined his own private office. He took the precaution of locking the door to this room from the inside; anyone who wanted to reach me would have to pass his desk. His adjutant was informed, with a wink, that I was a close relative of the general's and was arranging the family papers. Whenever the general went on a trip, I was left in sole charge of the key to his safe.

There I sat and studied the map of Berlin or the organization of the federal police. Nebe kept me supplied with material. Oster borrowed our carefully hoarded collection of documents from the hiding-places of the counter-intelligence division (*Abwehr*). It was in the course of this work that we realized how cannily the Nazi *Ordensburgen,* the SS schools, the concentration camps with their bands of death's-head guards, and the garrisons of the *Waffen-SS* (the SS-in-arms) were distributed throughout the entire territory of the Reich. Not even the war ministry possessed exact lists of them. Very quietly the SS had set up heavily armed units in all key positions.

MUNICH

AT THIS POINT I shall discontinue the mode of description I have been using. Who has the power to convey with the detail and drama it deserves that segment of the Nazi Revolution which is commonly called the Munich crisis? For that was one of the most decisive moments of the Hitler dictatorship — and it marked the real beginning of the Second World War.

We still lack perspective. We are not yet able to grasp fully the tragedy that was enacted in Munich in September, 1938. There are numerous contradictory accounts. Many memoirs, notes, and documents are still awaiting publication. Above all, intense conflicting feelings hinder all of us from depicting objectively the course, the motives, and the effects of the events at Munich. Estimates vary

according to the national allegiance of the observer. I am still seized
with fury when I think of how it all might have turned out differently
— and how in fact it did turn out. Therefore, it will be better if I
presume to draw only the broad outlines of those furious times.

'Incidents' in the Sudetenland mounted. The Goebbels-controlled
press raged and the radio shrieked at the frightened population with
the vehemence that was later to become all too familiar. This propagandistic prelude to *Blitzkrieg,* the methodical aggravation of alleged
or staged incidents, was still something new. First brawls and riots
broke out, then shootings and assassinations; then came uprisings, and
finally a mass flight of our *Volksdeutsche* from the persecution of the
'Hussites,' the 'Czech bandits,' or the 'Bolshevists.' The propaganda
ministry was not yet alternating its alarming reports with sudden
peace rumors. The result was that the agitated populace, who above
all did not want war, began to show grave discontent. That was the
only occasion in the whole twelve years of the Nazi régime that such
manifestations were seen.

The excitement passed to England and France. They countered
German mobilization measures by calling up reserves and taking their
stand on the Maginot Line. Reports of these moves made a profound
impression on the Germans. Such unnerving news could not yet be
suppressed; listening to foreign radio stations was not yet punishable
by death. But the Western Powers frittered away the effects of their
firmness; sensational articles supporting Hitler appeared in the British
press. The German generals were completely bewildered by these
mixed reactions.

The same lack of clarity prevailed in regard to the diplomatic
negotiations. Hitler distrusted the reports of his 'incompetent' diplomats and sent out special emissaries on his own to determine the 'true'
mood of the Western Powers. In contrast to the later crises, the
German diplomats still held their ground and unanimously warned
Hitler not to go too far. Canaris carried his secret reports, all of
which were of the same tenor, from Keitel to Ribbentrop, from the
chancellery to Brauchitsch or Raeder. Wherever we 'Westerners'

sensed a weak spot in the *fronde* of generals, we at once advanced our expert opinion that this time the British and French would certainly go as far as war.

We went even further and informed the British government in unequivocal terms of Hitler's true intentions and of our own plans for a revolt.

There was far too much at stake for us to keep our secrets to ourselves. War and peace, the triumph or the fall of the dictator, hung in the balance. We could no longer be concerned about Germany alone; in our thoughts was the fate of all Europe. Since May we had repeatedly advised London that while Hitler talked only of the Sudeten Germans, in reality he was determined to conquer all of Czechoslovakia. In September another such report was conveyed to London. By September 5 the British government must have known definitely what importance was attached to its standing fast. As the crisis approached its climax, a last emissary flew across the Channel to inform the British of our plans for a *coup d'état*. This time even Halder was informed of the mission.

We felt so sure of ourselves that, after years of feeling out, I at last talked plainly with Count Helldorf. And Helldorf declared himself ready to go along with us. The speed with which we took control of the regular police was of the greatest moment for our action in Berlin. The technical knowledge and commanding position of the Berlin police chief would be of invaluable aid to us in this respect. Moreover, the collaboration of so highly placed an SA leader would serve to confuse the situation further. It would lend a great deal more credibility to our story of an SS *Putsch* headed by Himmler. Nevertheless, I was somewhat cautious with Helldorf and did not lay all our cards on the table. I said nothing at all about Witzleben, for example.

There were so many buildings to be occupied that we had considerable trouble deciding which ones must be seized at once and which could be left until a little later. Daily, Nebe brought in new material on SS hiding-places. Each time we had to decide where the enemy's greatest strength lay. We soon discovered that except for the main buildings of the Gestapo in the Prinz Albrechtstrasse and the Wilhelmstrasse, the various Gestapo headquarters were really quite innocuous. Heydrich had camouflaged his organization very well. We had to admire the skill with which he had set up a system of SS strong points to cover each of the police precincts.

One afternoon General von Brockdorff and I met Frau Struenck — we shall learn more of this 'little lady' later on — at a suburban railroad station. She drove the two of us, harmless sightseers that we were, through the German capital in her handsome automobile. It turned out to be quite an extensive tour. We had to drive in circles around each of the pertinent groups of buildings in order to spot possible escapes through gardens and neighboring structures. Brockdorff wrote steadily and calculated the minimum number of troops necessary. The concentration camp of Sachsenhausen, the radio station at Koenigswusterhausen, and the barracks of the guards regiment at Lichterfelde would require an unusually large number of soldiers, we discovered. Once and for all, we learned the lesson that without the co-operation of the security police a *Putsch* in Berlin was almost impossible. Without the police we should have to divide our army forces into too many small units.

Meanwhile, we were all waiting tensely for the impending Party meeting at Nuremberg. Would Hitler finally show his colors? Everyone had a different answer to offer. We heard that Hitler himself was undecided; that he was vacillating and meditating what course to take. A feverish air of suspense reigned in the special diplomatic train that went to Nuremberg. Every word that François Poncet or Sir Nevile Henderson dropped was picked up by invisible listeners.

In his perplexity, Hitler turned to the Nazi masses. He tried to find in them the backing that his ministers and generals would no longer give. Meanwhile, the nervous tension was almost unbearable for us. We feared precisely what others were hoping for: that Hitler, who was never at a loss for excuses, would find some way to retreat. He himself apparently saw that he had ventured too far, but there was no help for it now; he had to cut the Gordian knot; and so he made the most dangerous statement a dictator can make; he declared that the Sudetenland must return to the Reich, 'no matter what.'

Immediately thereafter a series of bloody outbreaks occurred in various places in the Sudetenland. The Prague government responded by imposing martial law. We, fools that we were, thought the time had now come. Now the Western Powers would certainly come publicly to the aid of the Czechs; the Nazis would retort by breaking diplomatic relations between Germany and Czechoslovakia; and this in turn would lead to an Anglo-French threat of war. Once that came, the lines would be clearly drawn. Even a Brauchitsch would then be forced to see, and we would strike out, 'no matter what.'

Hitler finally decided to issue mobilization orders and set a deadline for the meeting of his demands. Now at last the mask had fallen. No one continued to talk of 'bluff' or 'secret agreements' with the Western Powers. The machinery of mobilization began moving; more and more persons were necessarily initiated into the military secrets. The obscurantist tactics with which Hitler had deceived the generals and diplomats for months were now to no avail. The reputation of Hitler as a 'peace chancellor' vanished, and this was a psychological event of prime importance.

The reaction to these mobilization orders was something we had never expected. The political innocents lost their heads; the opportunists were overcome by panic; even the Nazis were frightened out of their wits. Suddenly we had all we could do to save ourselves from our friends who ran about wringing their hands and imploring *the* general to come out and save them. People who had been quiet for years suddenly turned up. Many of those who turned to us were so sincere in their opposition that we hated to have to lie to them, but in those days we pretended to be the loyalest of the loyal.

Then, on the morning of September 15 there came a report which at first we were unable to believe. But to our horror we found that it was true: Chamberlain was flying to Berchtesgaden. We were struck dumb at first, but finally we agreed on our 'line': that it was merely a tactical gesture. The British must be temporizing in order to 'pass the ball' to our generals. They wanted to show Hitler as glaringly in the wrong. In such situations it is the worst possible course to give way to despair or fear. Therefore, we continued our preparations as energetically as ever. We worked on the assumption that the air of Europe would at last be cleared by this conversation in Berchtesgaden. In all seriousness we imagined that the chief danger for us lay in the possibility that not Chamberlain but Hitler might back down.

Since the dictator had always suffered a nervous breakdown before each of his important acts, we had prepared ourselves for this possibility. In the past there had always been someone with strong nerves, a Neurath or a Himmler, to intervene and steer the Fuehrer through his crisis. This time we wanted to take advantage of the chance that Hitler might be temporarily incapacitated. We wanted to make use of the confusion by striking a forceful blow. If only Chamberlain would not give Hitler too good a scare . . .

We soon realized, however, to our dismay that Chamberlain had not come to utter a last warning. The British government wanted to resume negotiations. Once more we of the 'pro-West' party had been proved fools, but the international tension did not diminish. There was more confusion than ever; it was almost impossible to sift the truth from the mass of contradictory rumors. Unexpectedly, Hitler let his secret mobilization continue. The press propaganda campaign was not turned off. Konrad Henlein founded his illegal Sudeten German free corps. That was a typical Hitlerian reaction to Chamberlain's weakness. Nevertheless, Daladier and Bonnet hastened to London. They accepted the general outlines of the Nazi ultimatum. The only questions at issue in the horse trade were the very rawest bits of blackmail and a matter of a few dates. Hitler had won, and we bowed our heads in despair. To all appearances it was all up with our revolt.

Then, just at this dramatic moment, the Poles struck the Czechs in the back with their claims on Teschen. This act of folly revealed with great force the terrible rifts that cut across the continent of Europe, but the Nazis rejoiced; Hitler had been right.

We expected the worst from Chamberlain's second trip to Germany, and we could scarcely believe our ears at the strange reports that came from Godesberg. Chamberlain sat sulking across the Rhine;

the two parted lovers of Europe could not come together. Soon the mad rumors were confirmed: *Hitler had retracted the proposals he himself had made at Berchtesgaden and was now making new demands, such monstrous demands that they would certainly be too much even for Chamberlain.* We felt a tremendous sense of relief. Impatiently, we counted the hours, feeling sure that the negotiations would now be broken off and the prime minister would return to London.

As the news got around, a wave of disappointment, indignation, and panic spread through Germany. Never before had the Germans spoken so freely and vituperatively. Strangers talked to one another on the streets. The fearful shock could be read plainly in people's faces. This time Hitler had really gone too far. Even Brauchitsch mumbled grim threats. Hitler suddenly became insecure. He himself felt that he had really brought the structure down this time. Within a few hours, Goebbels was required to drum up a huge demonstration at the Sportspalast. Hitler made an impassioned speech. Cleverly he diverted attention from his extravagant demands by personifying all the objective points of dispute. 'Benes or I . . .' Morally he disgraced himself with the statement: 'We don't want any Czechs.' Everyone felt that this hysteric had overreached himself. The crisis was reaching its climax, and the people were fast losing confidence in 'their Fuehrer.'

The reaction of Paris and London, however, was exactly the reverse of what it should have been. The Western Powers made new offers. Instead of exploiting Hitler's nervousness by forcefully following up their advantage, they tried to reward Hitler's 'good will' by a diplomatic gratuity. Sir Horace Wilson was sent to Germany as a British dove of peace.

Thereupon the dictator pulled himself together. He paid his opponents for their remarkable patience by reverting to his original declaration that his troops would march on September 30. Both reactions were typical of the man: the nervous collapse and the recovery. Both were psychologically predictable, and both should have been remembered, for they were to be repeated a year later.

For our part, we got set for the final spurt. We kept our own intelligence service on emergency status. Since Hitler and Ribbentrop were not publishing their diplomatic information, we had to keep ourselves informed by our own efforts. We had to let Brauchitsch and Halder know exactly what was happening, for the fateful question was whether the dictator would be able to put over his *Blitz* in the brief but crucial moment before we could act. We had our spies everywhere — in the war ministry, the police headquarters, the ministry of the interior, and especially in the foreign office. All the various threads came together in Oster's office; there we had our co-ordination center and from there we would press the alarm button.

For the first and the last time in this life I nearly quarreled with Oster because of his increasing pessimism. When he declared that the Western Powers would yield, I told him he deserved a post in the propaganda ministry. Unfortunately, he knew better than I. Into his hands poured a series of copies of memoranda made by Goering's 'research department,' which had charge of decoding and of tapping telephone conversations. Masaryk, the Czech ambassador in London, was telephoning his London news on wires that ran through Germany; and Masaryk was not only well informed but unfortunately extremely indiscreet during those dreadful hours.

Hitler, feeling strengthened in his stand, ordered a grand parade of troops through Berlin for the afternoon of September 27. This parade was intended as diplomatic intimidation and as internal propaganda. Witzleben was furious about this theatrical gesture; he would have liked best to march his men right into the chancellery, but as it turned out we could have desired nothing better, for never had soldiers been treated so badly in Berlin as they were on that day. In the workers' quarters clenched fists were raised against them; in the center of the city people turned conspicuously away. Hitler stood for a while on his 'historic' balcony, but when the people of Berlin did not cheer him and when they continued to glare irritably at the parade, the Fuehrer retired. From behind the curtain he stared down at the apathetic populace. He took his fury out on Goebbels, snapped: 'I can't lead a war with such a people.' And the propaganda chief placated: 'No, my Fuehrer, I saw for myself down there. These people still need intensive enlightenment.'

Nevertheless, Hitler signed his answer rejecting Chamberlain's offer to negotiate, and the British special envoy flew back that same night. Although Hitler had had his way on all points, he stubbornly insisted on his insulting demand that the territory already promised to him must be handed over punctually on September 30. Oster received a copy of his defiant letter late that night, and on the morning of September 28 I took the copy to Witzleben. Witzleben went to Halder with it. Now at last the chief of staff had his desired, unequivocal 'proof' that Hitler was not bluffing, that he wanted war.

Tears of indignation ran down Halder's cheeks. Bold rebel that he was, he was amazed that Hitler could have played him so false as not to inform him of his real plans. Witzleben insisted that now it was time to take action. He persuaded Halder to go to see Brauchitsch. After a while Halder returned to say that he had good news: Brauchitsch was also outraged and would probably take a part in the *Putsch*. Thereupon Witzleben picked up the telephone on Halder's desk and called Brauchitsch. He said openly that everything was ready. He literally pleaded with the commander-in-chief of the army to issue the liberating order. Brauchitsch did not say either yes or no. He would reserve his decision until after his return from the chancellery, he said; he was going there directly to demand an explanation. While Brauchitsch set out for the Wilhelmstrasse, Witzleben rushed back to his military district headquarters. 'Gisevius, the time has come!' he told me excitedly.

Meanwhile, Chamberlain, startled out of his sleep by Hitler's letter of reply, had called on his ambassador in Rome for help. Toward ten o'clock in the morning the ambassador had an audience with Mussolini and implored him to arrange another meeting. That was all that was needed, he said; the contesting parties had agreed on almost everything.

Count Ciano attempted to telephone Ribbentrop, but was not connected with him because the foreign minister was in conference with Hitler. Ciano repeated his call, this time to the German chancellery; but in vain — Ribbentrop would not answer. Then Mussolini personally called his Berlin ambassador, Attolico. 'This is the Duce, do you hear?' He vigorously seconded the British proposal to resume negotiations and in a voice breaking with excitement instructed his ambassador that he absolutely must get to see Hitler. 'Tell him what I've told you. Hurry, hurry!'

Attolico did hurry, first to the foreign office and then to the chancellery. He arrived at the chancellery shortly after eleven. He saw a horde of bewildered people standing around helplessly — ministers, department secretaries, army officers, adjutants, servants. All were in a state of sheer funk. Attolico found a Hitler who no longer knew what to do. The 'moderates,' with Neurath and Brauchitsch at their head, were busy 'moderating' their leader once more. At first Hitler resisted hysterically. Finally he agreed to Mussolini's intercession.

Meanwhile we waited and waited. We could not understand why neither Brauchitsch nor Halder sent word. The minutes passed into hours of unutterable suspense; and then the sensational report crashed down upon our heads. The impossible had happened. Chamberlain and Daladier were flying to Munich.

Our revolt was done for.

For a few hours I went on imagining that we could revolt anyway. But Witzleben soon demonstrated to me that the troops would never revolt against the victorious Fuehrer.

A few days later, Schacht, Oster, and I sat around Witzleben's fireplace and tossed our lovely plans and projects into the fire. We spent the rest of the evening meditating, not on Hitler's triumph, but on the calamity that had befallen Europe.

I prefer not to speak of what followed; for I should have to describe the feelings that swept us when we read the news during the next few days. The Parisians cheered Daladier wildly on his return. A similar scene took place at Croydon Airport. And Chamberlain waved a scrap of paper in the air, and held it up for the people to see the signatures . . .

Peace in our time?

Let us put it a bit more realistically. Chamberlain saved Hitler.

GLASSBREAKERS' HOLIDAY

DURING THE DAYS of the Munich crisis there was one of our friends
who raged about like a wild beast, beating his head against the bars
of a cage; but all doors remained closed to him — in the OKW, in the
Reichsbank, in all the ministries where he had reliable acquaintances.
We had not let Goerdeler into our secret.

That was really not very kind of us. We knew Goerdeler and we
thought well of him. If our plans had come to anything, we should
have drawn him in at the moment we struck; but unfortunately we
felt that Goerdeler's finest virtue was also his gravest weakness. The
passion for justice burned so fiercely in him that he forgot all moderation. He preached and preached and preached, until the people on
whom he was dependent lost all patience with him. Moeover, he
always wanted to make political agreements in advance. Usually
that policy produced nothing more than a grand coalition of rumors.

Precisely because this time we were resolved to go the limit, we believed we could get along without Goerdeler's ardor. In addition,
neither Halder nor Witzleben was personally acquainted with him.
They thought it would be risky to meet a person so suspect at the
very moment when affairs were approaching a climax. Later on, however, we told him all our plans, and he shared in our profound
despondency.

It was at this time that Goerdeler wrote his letter to a well-known
American statesman. The words make sad reading today:

> . . . A magnificent opportunity has been missed. The German
> people did not want war; the army would have done anything to
> avoid it. Only Hitler, Himmler, and Ribbentrop were for war. They
> were gravely troubled by increasing domestic difficulties. On the
> other hand, they insisted to the army that England and France were
> neither willing nor able to protect Czechoslovakia. No one in
> Germany would believe them, but they were right. . . .
>
> If England and France had taken the risk of declaring war, Hitler
> would never have used force; then he would have made a fool of

himself and not, as is now the case, the better elements of my
nation. . . .

You can hardly conceive the despair that both people and army
feel about the brutal, insane, and terroristic dictator and his henchmen. . . .

The Munich agreement was just sheer capitulation by France and
England to bombastic charlatans. . . .

The end of the German people's sufferings under brutal tyranny
and medieval practices has been postponed for a long time to
come. . . .

By refusing to take a small risk, Chamberlain has made a war inevitable. Both the British and the French nations will now have to
defend their freedom with arms in hand. . . .

If ever he had been a spokesman of the German Opposition,
Goerdeler was that in this letter. Indeed, we can well say that he
spoke for the majority of the German people. More clearly than anyone else at the time he realized that the torture of an entire nation
would now go on for a long time to come, for Hitler, being what he
was, could not help exploiting to the full this victory which had
been so inexplicably handed to him.

The dictator, from now on, did not need to care a button about the
Opposition. Its political weight could mean nothing. The persistent
'carpers,' 'know-it-alls,' 'Westerners,' with their bourgeois mentality,
had been exposed as fools by one of their own sort, the Birmingham
'plutocrat,' Chamberlain. Never again would the dictator permit his
wavering ministers and generals to interfere with his plans. Overnight the Opposition had been reduced from a class which Hitler had
to placate, intellectually and politically, to a small group of grumblers
on whom Himmler's Gestapo could operate at will.

The more clearly this logic presented itself to Goerdeler, the more
he felt drawn to the idea of emigration. He debated with himself and
others whether he ought not to emigrate to America in order 'to proclaim to all the truth that men must be ready to use arms to defend
their ideals of justice, Christianity, and humanity.'

During the last twelve years all of us considered this prospect time and again, and time and again we came to the conclusion that we had to remain. We did not condemn those who had left after 1933. Most of them had had no choice; they went into exile to save their lives. Every one of us would have done the same to escape the Gestapo; but so long as the possibility of choice remained for us, we were restrained by the lessons of the past. Never in history had exiles ever brought about political changes in their native lands. Had we any reason to expect that it would be different this time? On the contrary, the worse the terror raged in Germany, the more improbable it became that exiles could exert influence — if only because they could not keep up with the tempestuous revolutionary tempo.

All of us, of both Right and Left, were depressed by the speed with which the exiles lost contact with their homeland. From outside we received schoolmasterly and often arrogant instruction, but no advice that could really have been helpful to us. Threats also came from outside, but no authoritative words that could have saved the nation from the abyss. None of the many newspapers and pamphlets that were printed by exiles and smuggled into Germany for wide distribution there — none of them had any lasting effect. This was true also of the most rousing radio addresses. The statesmen also in foreign countries were increasingly alienated by the exiles. The exiles were and remained isolated at home and abroad.

Therefore, we felt that we could leave only if we were ready to give up the struggle, but how did we have the right to do that? Was it the world's business to restore order, justice, and decency in Germany by a more or less sanguinary intervention, or was it not first of all the business of the Germans themselves? It struck us as a parody of all natural concepts of responsibility and morality for those who did not like tyranny to withdraw from the battle, saying *en passant* to the British, the Americans, or the French that unfortunately it was now up to them to issue forth and shed their blood for freedom.

It is important for me to testify that we stuck it out deliberately, for I belonged to a group of men who, during all those years, could have found a new field of activity and influence outside of Germany.

But we did not want to sit comfortably in some neutral place and look on from outside while the dire decisions were being made at home. We wanted to stay in, to be in on the decisions, to force a change for the better by our own exertions. So long as we saw the slightest prospect for a violent overthrow of the government, so long as we had the slightest hope of building a *fronde,* we wanted to stay and fight. Exile is a bitter and tragic fate; it is never a political action station.

They were sorely disappointed who had looked upon Munich as opening an era of world brotherhood. A scant ten days after the signing of the Munich agreement, on October 9, 1938, Hitler delivered his incendiary speech at Saarbruecken. At first foreign newspaper readers thought that gross errors in translation must have crept into the reported speech; Hitler's oratorical flights seemed otherwise wholly inexplicable. The dictator behaved as if he had just received the greatest defeat in his life. He particularly inveighed against Churchill who had warned the House of Commons not to indulge in false hopes; and Churchill at this time was merely a member of the Opposition and had no post in the British government! But for years Hitler had realized that Churchill was his chief antagonist. The Fuehrer always sensed whom he must hate and whom combat.

Hitler talked himself into a frenzy, and did not omit a barbed allusion to certain statesmen armed with umbrellas whose penchant for travel did not always serve the cause of European peace — as the German prince of peace understood the word. Chamberlain was ill rewarded for his compliancy.

Why was Hitler so angry in spite of the fact that he had just pocketed one of the neatest victories in diplomatic history? Many people in Britain and France asked themselves this question, but few found the answer. They were still prey to that enervating indecision which had plagued them for years. Since 1933 they had watched the phenomenon of revolution without knowing quite what they ought to do about it; and all the time they went on hoping vaguely that they would be spared the necessity for doing anything.

It is incorrect to present the history of Europe between 1933 and

1938 as if there were two groups from the very beginning: those who were 'for' and those who were 'against.' Let us not stupefy ourselves with such simplistic formulas. Undoubtedly there were some Europeans who were never lured by the siren song of National Socialism and who consistently stuck to their opposition, but during the first period of the Revolution the majority were on both sides at once, both for and against; and this ambivalence on the part of our chief statesmen, their constant vacillation between arguments and counter-arguments, explains to some extent the world-wide paralysis during the time that Hitler was rearming Germany.

Possibly Hitler owed a goodly number of his 'successes' — the successes with which he paved the way to his inferno — to his notorious surprise tactics, but it cannot be asserted that the statesmen of Europe simply let the torrent of revolution surge where it would until their alarmed peoples forced them to intervene. The statesmen were not so short-sighted or light-minded as all that. If it had been a question only of Hitler and his brazen methods, they would have struck back sooner and harder; but in the final analysis the reason for their inaction was the necessary consequence of a general distaste for existing conditions.

The Western Powers were half willing to admit of their own accord that the order established at Versailles was functioning miserably. They wondered — rightly — whether they would not have done better to have made a few concessions to Stresemann or Bruening, instead of being forced to make concessions and confessions to this upstart agitator. On the one hand the Western Powers were fairly sure that the forces of revolution could not bring about a better and more stable order. On the other hand they were terrified by the prospect of what would happen when the crumbling dikes of their own orders finally broke.

Hitler intuitively took advantage of this ambivalence. His trick consisted in appealing to the guilty consciences of those whom he intended to surprise by sudden assault. The real secret of this shaker of the world was nothing 'magical'; it was based upon the indecisiveness of all Europeans. They had come of themselves to the fatal conclusion that things could not go on as they were, but they did not know what next to look for. Hitler's character was fundamentally easy to label: he was simply the prototype of a fanatic enmeshed in his own delusions; but the discontented statesmen of the world projected their own contradictions into Hitler for so long that at last they magnified him into a kind of superman or super-devil.

Another shock followed the Saarbruecken speech and shattered the last illusions of 'peace in our time.' Revolutionaries are never content with part payments, no matter how high the sum. Anyone who tries to do business with them soon learns that they cannot be satisfied; either he pays until he is completely stripped, or he is forced to bear the brunt of his associates' moral and material bankruptcy. On November 9, 1938, Hitler gave an unequivocal lesson to all those who up to then had not realized this ugly fact.

By sheer stupid chance, a few days before November 9 some shots had been fired in the German Embassy in Paris. A young diplomat — who incidentally was anything but a Nazi — was fatally wounded by a Jewish hothead. Curiously enough, the world has never learned exactly why this senseless assassination was attempted, although the ostensible reason given was the maltreatment of Jews in Upper Silesia. After the occupation of France, however, the Nazis failed to stage their usual show-trial. This omission is a good ground for assuming that even a Goebbels was unable to derive anything of propagandistic value out of this 'assault by world Judaism.'

The diplomat's death, however, served Hitler very handily. Having been robbed of his Czechoslovak war, the dictator sensed a perfect opportunity to keep whipped-up revolutionary passions from cooling. Before the judicial investigation could be completed, and even before the unfortunate embassy secretary had breathed his last, the Nazi fury descended upon the Jews throughout the country.

The word 'pogrom' is not strong enough to describe what happened everywhere in Germany. Not a Jewish home remained undemolished, not a Jewish business unplundered, not a synagogue unburned. In less than twenty-four hours the howling mob destroyed a vast amount of property, and like wild dogs hounded the owners. Anyone who experienced those terrible hours will never forget them, not even those who have lived to see the ruins all around us today. The unleashed rabble was possessed by a senseless destructive fury; nothing at all frangible survived. Incited to a pitch of insanity, the mob vented its emotion on defenseless people. Like hunted creatures the terrified victims fled through the streets. Their haste was surpassed only by the speed with which thieving pimps and prostitutes fled to their hideouts with stolen furs, jewelry, and other 'Jewish' objects of value.

To the credit of the people it must be said that the overwhelming majority had no part in this hideous affair. They watched the horrid scenes with repugnance, shame, and sorrow, not unmixed with evil premonitions. Where possible they avoided the mobs, and at last an 'outburst of popular rage' that was quite genuine turned against the Party. The Nazi instigators of the riots stopped them abruptly and with significant haste began cleaning up. The burned-out ruins of the synagogues remained standing for some time. The temper of the people was not yet 'ripe' for these to be totally razed. Heaping insult on injury, the Jews were then fined a billion marks for 'creating a public nuisance.' Thus the appropriation of Jewish property, which had been going on since the beginning of the Nazi régime, was now done officially and on a sweeping scale.

In comparison to later events, this pogrom might be considered moderate. Nevertheless, it has its special place in the course of the Revolution. Previously, excesses against the Jews had been committed by overzealous local Party functionaries, with or without the permission of the police, but this time the general orders and the specific directives were issued from above. The destructive fury was instigated by the Party and protected by the state. The police and the fire department received strict instructions to interfere only when 'Aryan' places in the vicinity were also endangered.

Although Himmler and Heydrich also signed the orders, there was no doubt at the time — and it has since been proved — that the Fuehrer himself inaugurated these frightful and portentous excesses.

The significance of this 'glassbreakers' week,' as it was popularly called, cannot be overestimated. The reaction abroad was unmistakable — which was fortunate or unfortunate, according to one's point of view. After the week of pogroms the world could no longer harbor any doubts as to the ultimate aims of the Nazi Movement. Death and destruction were now being visited on the Jews, but it was clear that very soon indeed all the other accounts would be settled which Hitler had drawn up with such care in *Mein Kampf*. For fifteen years his platform had been written down in black and white for the world to see, but the world did not choose to look.

The conclusions that were forced upon every thinking German were grim and depressing indeed. Not a single general had had the impulse to bring out his troops and see to the clearing of the streets. The top army leadership had played deaf and blind. The meaning of this is clear. Everyone had long since given up hope that the cabinet would ever do anything. From whom could decent Germans now expect protection if these horrible excesses were followed by others — against the Church or the 'reactionaries' or the 'plutocrats'? Everyone quietly determined the category in which he would be included as soon as the Nazi politicians found it necessary to open the exhaust valve again, in order to let off some of their own irritation or ease the pressure of general discontent.

The specter of terrorism appeared more threatening than ever; and that was precisely what Hitler, master of dual effects that he was, had wanted. In the first place he had delivered a mortal blow to the German Jews. The world was so stunned by the initial shock that it had neither time nor the desire to trace the hundreds of thousands of 'little' individual tragedies that followed in the trail of this act of barbarism. On the other hand, the cowed middle class stared at the Nazi monster like a rabbit at a snake. A general psychosis had been created, under which the populace was reduced to absolute submission; and this effect was valuable to the Nazis. The class was doomed, but for the present it had its uses and would be made to serve.

Although I kept my ears open, I know of only two cases of outright protest. When some of Schacht's employees were called upon to take part in the pogrom, Schacht seized the occasion to make a vigorous statement against the atrocities. There was no place in the Reichsbank for the kind of thugs who participated in such work, he declared. Naturally, the propaganda ministry took this very much amiss, but no one dared to punish this obstinate minister.

The other man who took a stand was Helldorf. During the riots he had been absent from Berlin. Immediately after his return he called a conference of all police officers and berated them for their passivity — even though under orders. To the dismay of all the Nazis he announced that if he had been present he would have ordered his police to shoot the rioters and looters. It was a remarkably courageous statement for a chief of police and high officer of the SA to make. Precisely because of Helldorf's position it was particularly dangerous for him to condemn the official Party line.

Both examples demonstrate to what extent it was still possible in 1938 for a man to voice his opinions. Not a single minister, undersecretary, or general would have been sent to concentration camp for calling things by their right name; any concerted protest might well have led to a revolt of the decent men — if only those whose high office conferred on them the obligation to act had shown a little more courage. Because the Neuraths, Schwerins, Seldtes, Dorpmuellers, Raeders, Keitels, and Brauchitsches — to name only this group of top men — could not muster up the courage, they sank deeper and deeper into the pit of guilt; and at the same time they brought upon millions of innocent human beings, who were waiting for them to lead and to be examples, the terrible lot that has befallen Europe.

THE MARCH MADNESS

WE PRESSED HALDER TO ACT. Oster assembled a collection of documents which he hoped would arouse the chief of the general staff. Canaris missed no opportunity to put in his word. Beck also kept after Halder. Former Under-Secretary Planck and the former Am-

bassador von Hassell added their pressure. Finally Goerdeler pro-
cured an interview with Halder which turned out rather well. Halder,
however, put off making any definite assurances. Evidently he was
still frightened by the memory of Munich.

In the middle of January, 1939, I met him at a social gathering
in Schacht's home. Toward the end of the evening I deliberately
placed myself in his way. He tried to avoid serious conversation, but
I refused to collaborate. Casually I mentioned that I thought it was
time I paid him another visit. 'Hadn't we better wait two or three
months more?' he asked with his schoolmasterly smile.

The allusion was clear to me. Halder was also thinking about the
'March madness.' That was the cynical name with which initiates had
baptized the coming adventure. Hitler wanted to obliterate his 'defeat' at Munich. The conqueror would not be content with the Sudetenland, important as this territory was strategically. Only by possessing all of Bohemia would he control the portal to the southeast.
That was why Hitler had been aiming at Prague from the very beginning.

The fact that Halder wanted to wait two or three months was
significant. The stress was on the word 'wait.' Evidently he no longer
thought very much of the prospects of a conspiracy such as we had
planned for the Munich crisis. Inwardly he was already looking forward to further concessions on the part of the Western Powers. At
the time we could not understand that, but he was probably better
informed than we were. He was in constant contact with Under-
Secretary von Weizsaecker,[1] who had probably whispered that the
diplomatic negotiations over the technical execution of the Munich
agreements were lagging. The Western Powers were decidedly half-
hearted in their stand.

The 'March madness' was maneuvered with diabolical cunning.
Sir Nevile Henderson, the British ambassador, it seemed, was flab-

---

[1] Weizsaecker was a diplomat of the old school who was conducting these
negotiations with the British and French ambassadors. As so often, Hitler employed
a 'moderate' to deal with foreign powers. This was one of the Nazi leader's favorite
devices for camouflaging his real intentions.

bergasted, and he was not the only one. No one had noticed anything, although Himmler's agents had been agitating in Bohemia for months. In order to give the highest possible polish to the theatricals, Goering was sent abroad for a vacation shortly before the campaign opened. He promenaded on the Italian Riviera and expressed complete amazement at the invasion of Czechoslovakia.

This time there were no Germans desperately eager to come 'home to the Reich.' Instead, the Slovaks strove just as desperately to break away from the Prague government. Since 1918 they had been frequently irritated by the unwise Czech policy of centralism; but it took that great hero of liberty, Adolf Hitler, to convince them that they were too proud a nation to abide any longer under the yoke of the Czechs. Within a few days they received the divine command to set up an independent state, and forthwith they appealed to Europe's patron saint for help.

The policies of the Czechs had not been too intelligent. They had overreached themselves, in both internal and foreign politics, in the state that they had created in 1918; and not even in 1933 did they realize the demands of the hour. They never took the precaution of trying to cure internal causes of disruption; they took it for granted that their highly extolled alliances would stand a test of force. Nevertheless, every bit of the moral indignation that Goebbels now trumpeted to the world was sheer melodramatics.

In order to stage the affair in the best blood-and-thunder manner, the act of predation opened with a typical gangster scene. The Nazis had selected as president of the new Slovak state a respectable Catholic cleric who did not at once realize what part had been assigned to him. But haste was necessary: consequently, the Nazis started the 'liberation' by simply kidnaping the hesitant old gentleman. That was the only way they could speed his elevation to his new dignity.

Tiso was none too eager to flee to the shelter of Hitler's arms; he had a premonition of evil; but before he could think twice about it, the men in black had laid hands on him. They 'conducted' him to the nearest open field, and before he realized it a military plane was taking him to Berlin. Had our sense of humor not been crushed by our alarm over the coming European catastrophe, we might have been amused by the scene of the somewhat senile rural priest landing at Tempelhof Airport to be greeted by a band and a parade of Himmler's black-uniformed guards.

Tiso had the consolation of not being the sole celebrity to be received by a presentation of arms and a blare of national anthems. A few hours later a second head of state put in his appearance. There was a slight change of plot this time: Hacha was not a future president still unaware of his good fortune, but a former one who was about to sign his political death sentence.

Hacha, president of the shrunken Czech state, was a chronically ill old man who had replaced Benes after Munich. Toward evening on March 14, 1939, he entered the capital of Germany, accompanied by his foreign minister. He had been informed pleasantly that he was to conduct extremely important diplomatic negotiations. Unfortunately, the negotiations were of a character the poor innocent had not expected.

First the Czech president and foreign minister were made to wait until one o'clock in the morning. Certain preparations had to be completed on the border of Czechoslovakia before the conversations could take place. Hitler's armored divisions invaded the remains of Czechoslovakia without a declaration of war and without even the courtesy of an ultimatum. Since all connections between Prague government headquarters and the Czech president had been cut off — for 'technical reasons' — no one in Prague knew whether or not some binding agreement had been reached. Consequently, the signal for resistance was withheld.

The diplomatic action did not begin until the military *Blitz* had obviously succeeded. Then the victim was solemnly conducted into the marble halls of the Wilhelmstrasse. There the dictator awaited him. Foaming at the mouth, Hitler poured upon the unfortunate man a torrent of words coarser and more brutal than anything Napoleon had ever spoken in his well-known theatrical scenes. Without allowing his guest to say a word, Hitler laid, or rather threw, a document on the table. The hapless Czech president read through it. It contained his own and his nation's abdication.

The conqueror did not take the time to wait for the pitiable old man's reaction. Uttering fierce threats, he rushed out of the room and entered his automobile, to speed behind his troops which were advancing on Prague. Goering took over the 'negotiations' with Hacha. Goering's skill at handling people was manifested by the fact that Hacha fainted around three o'clock in the morning. Then he was ready; he signed the document.

'I told him I should be sorry to have to bomb such a lovely city as Prague. I had no orders for that, nor had we come to any decision about it, but I thought that by making such a remark I might speed the settlement of the whole affair; and I was right.' Such was Goering's description of the scene before the Nuremberg court. A simpler and more expressive portrayal would be hard to find.

With sterling generosity, the Nazis permitted Hacha to return home with all the honors due to the head of a state. However, when he reached Prague he had to put up with a change in residence. The uninvited liberators had made themselves at home in the historic halls of the Burg at Prague. Soon afterward they announced their first ordinances. The ingenious Nazi vocabulary was enriched by a new synonym. In addition to *Anschluss* (the annexation of Austria) and *Rueckgliederung* (the 'reincorporation' of the Sudetenland into the Reich), there was now a new technical term: 'Protectorate.' 'Government-general' was to come a few months later.

The previous fall the Poles had been only too eager to stab the troubled Czechs in the back. Once again the vultures came flocking. This time Hungary gathered its share of the booty. Riding on a splendid white horse — making a remarkable shot for the illustrated journals — Admiral Horthy, regent of Hungary, entered the Carpatho-Ukraine. Up to 1919 this territory had been under Hungarian administration. Consequently, the present annexation was to be considered another step in Hitler's 'peaceful' revision of the treaties of 1918 and 1919. Moreover, none of the involved states protested. The Czechs were not asked. The Poles were beside themselves with joy; they had long wanted a common frontier with Hungary. The

Russians breathed more easily because the germ center of an Ukrainian autonomist movement was being wiped out. The only one who might have cried out about it, King Carol of Rumania, preferred to make the best of the new realities, rather than to hang upon the insubstantial guarantees of the Western Powers.

Once more Hitler appeared in the guise of the harsh but just arbiter, who had made adjustments in the southeastern storm center of Europe which all the bordering states either welcomed or at least accepted in silence. His tactics consisted in threatening some, throwing a few crumbs to others from the abundance of his own loot, and consoling the rest with promises for next time. They need not worry; his quota of peaceful adjustments — that is to say, further extortions and robberies — was not yet exhausted.

From Hitler's point of view it was wonderfully clever, but how shocking it is that as late as the spring of 1939 there were European states ready to abet this transparent trickery! That fact was a sad demonstration that what unity had existed on our continent had been wrecked by a hundred different self-seeking nationalisms. Europe was not only occupied by force; the countries of Europe abandoned their strongest positions in advance — on the ideological front.

Now that the most prominent of the Nazis or Quislings have paid the penalty they deserved, we may admit this openly. Europe was handed over to the destroyer not only by his own agents and by traitors. It was by these incomprehensible collective actions on the part of whole nations that psychological breaches were opened to let in the tide of Nazi aggression.

An even cruder act of treachery was committed by Freiherr von Neurath. The oily diplomat chose this dramatic moment in world history to place himself at the dictator's disposal. From Hitler's hand Neurath accepted the post of Reich protector for Bohemia and Moravia. Everyone knew in advance what excuses he would offer for this utterly unprincipled conduct. It was the old story: he wanted to 'prevent worse things.'

In reality he augmented the evils. It did not matter that now and then he may have moderated the Black Terror. The former foreign minister, who had been so brusquely deprived of his office in February, 1938, and appointed to the 'empty' office of president of a privy council, must have realized what services Hitler required of him. He, with his bourgeois reputation, had been appointed in order to impress the undying legion of the gullible throughout the world. Neurath's respectable and well-mannered gestures were intended to temper the world-wide storm of indignation.

There cannot be any doubt that Neurath saw through this plan. Nevertheless, he collaborated in one of the most cynical acts of violence in history, and thereby deceived millions of Germans of good faith. If a 'decent,' 'respectable' minister lent his hand to it, must there not be some deeper considerations behind the surface indecency? Did that not mean that the Western Powers were secretly spurring on the eastward march? Such was the effect upon the Germans of Neurath's action. The rest of the world, on the other hand, began at least to wonder whether there were *any* Germans who still possessed a sense of decency and justice.

The case of Neurath is typical of the fate of the Wilhelmine bourgeoisie. The Neuraths, Papens, Schwerins, Meissners, Guertners, Keitels, Raeders, and Brauchitsches never fought manfully. Even when they appeared to oppose Hitler, their stand was never very convincing. Shadowy figures, they made a sad showing on the stage of history. Adolf Hitler, the psychologist of nihilism, took these compliant tools out of their bourgeois isolation whenever he was preparing to deliver a particularly vicious blow to their own kind.

The examples are numberless: Meissner on June 30, 1934, forcing the dying Hindenburg to send a shameful telegram of congratulation to Hitler; Papen hastening to Vienna to calm the alarmed bourgeoisie after the murder of Dollfuss, the Austrian chancellor; Guertner signing one amnesty decree after another and thereby condoning the 'excessive zeal' of the Brown thugs; Raeder zealously applauding as his Fuehrer explained to the bourgeois world why he had sent the former U-boat captain, Pastor Niemoeller, to a concentration camp. Whenever the Revolution stamped across another segment of the

bourgeois world or delivered another blow to liberal ideology, these
bemedaled notables, with their sonorous names and reassuring coun-
tenances, were on the spot to give their sanction to it all.

First and foremost, of course, these wretches were hanging themselves as individuals; but it will not do to dismiss them as isolated
phenomena. They cannot be separated from that Wilhelmine class
from which they originated. They wanted both to share in the re-
wards and to escape the penalties. It was the combination of bourgeois impotence and conceit which led them to build up Hitler. Later
on, Hitler exploited these same attributes in his various stabs at
psychological and political hegemony — first in Germany and then
in Europe.

To the alarmed world the invasion of Czechoslovakia supplied conclusive proof that it was not possible to live at peace with Hitler. The
various collections of diplomatic documents of the time corroborate
this. Even Henderson, the British ambassador, became aware at last
of the failure of his mission.

No accounts have, as yet, emphasized sufficiently the fearful psychological effect of this event upon the German people. When the
foreign Powers once again went no farther than a verbal protest or
an indignant note — when neither a breaking of diplomatic relations,
nor economic sanctions, nor a military demonstration took place —
informed Germans were struck dumb and the man in the street stammered shamefacedly: 'Hitler is lucky; Hitler knows better.'

The successful invasion of Czechoslovakia conferred on Hitler the
aura of infallibility. What could rational argument or angry vituperation do against a man who was so obviously Fortune's favorite son?
With contempt or pity the opportunists of all shades looked down upon
us, the grumblers and gripers. Now we had had our lesson! It was
clear at last that the vacillating generals, obeying their timid intellects,
would have got nowhere; whereas the Fuehrer's inspired intuitions
had achieved a miracle.

In 1933 the German people had raised Hitler to power. For six
years they had cravenly borne it while he applied terror, assassination,

and lying to establish his tyranny; but what ultimately made Hitler irresistible was the incomprehensible shilly-shallying of the countries that later opposed him in war. Thereafter the German people suffered everything that happened to them in blindness and utter apathy. From that point on, the attitude of the German intellectuals, or rather unintellectuals, remained stationary, whether they were called upon to cheer triumphs or to stand up under defeats. They simply accepted whatever came, for they felt that they were powerless.

CONVERSATIONS ABROAD

OUR GROUP OF CLOSE FRIENDS had watched the approach of this Prague coup in a state of intense nervousness. Most of us had given up hope before the invasion took place and had accepted the inevitable. If I remember rightly, Oster was one of these; probably Canaris's realistic view had filtered down to him. Schacht behaved from the very beginning as if he expected only good to come of the crisis. (I was always inclined to think he had adopted the fashion of wearing stiff high collars in order more easily to present an inscrutable appearance to the outside world.) But those who knew him well could read the traces of the war of nerves by the sores that appeared on either side of his lower lip; he had a nervous habit of scratching the side of his chin when he was worried. It was obvious to his close friends that his equanimity was pure façade.

Goerdeler remained as optimistic as ever. According to him, the British and French must by now have realized how they had been bluffed during the Munich crisis; they must also be aware that Hitler was no better prepared for a military adventure this spring, let alone for a two-front war, than he had been earlier. For my part, I took Goerdeler's side in arguments and concealed my premonitions of evil. I always felt, during the years of alternation between hope and disillusionment, that his attitude was the correct one, although it might not have been the wisest. This problem of attitude is related to the psychological phenomenon of collective guilt. I cannot prove it, but it seems to me that at certain times frank skepticism or forthright pessimism amount to diabolically concrete forces. In extraordinary situations, during revolutions or world crises, it seems to me that expressions of personal opinion amount to more than mere suppositions. I think they have a real bearing, for all their apparent evanescence, on the march of events. A kind of secret alliance of defeatists is formed, and their conspiracy of passivity, complacency, cowardice, or fatalism is no less powerful than the open conspiracy of the fanatics who requisition for their own purposes all the discontent, adventurousness, unrestraint, and ferocity that exists in the mental atmosphere.

We had decided to hold a meeting in Switzerland after the 'March madness.' We wanted to establish closer connections with the British and French, and it no longer seemed advisable to do this in Berlin. Schacht had business in Basle in any case. I was glad of the opportunity to complete my notes on the Fritsch crisis. Goerdeler intended to stay around Berlin until the end of the Czech crisis; then he planned to follow us as soon as possible.

It was, incidentally, not altogether without danger for us to meet in Switzerland. Whenever I crossed the border, either way, my heart thumped. Both the sojourn in freedom and the return to tyranny were, by their very starkness, a kind of relief. But the frontier was incalculable. What interpretation would the border police put upon the journey? How could one be sure that spies or indiscreet persons in the foreign country had not placed one's life in danger?

During those critical days Schacht and I had not the inner peace to enjoy our environment. Whether we walked restlessly in the lovely Maggia Valley or looked down upon the blue waters of Lago Maggiore, we were tormented always by the same question: Will he or won't he 'pull it off'?

A few days after our arrival a weary voice spoke to us on the telephone. Giving his name as Schulze or Lehmann or something of the sort, Goerdeler informed us that he had arranged an important conference in Geneva on the morrow. He insisted that we must come at once.

Schacht and I took the train, and for the sake of speed, we took the route through the Simplon Pass, although we were aware that in so doing we should probably attract the attention of the Italian secret police. We knew that their detective work was more skillful and thorough than that of our own Gestapo. The Gestapo's spy system abroad was a bother, but it was so crude and obvious that it was easier to shake off and therefore less dangerous.

We met in Ouchy, which seemed to us a little safer than the home of the League of Nations. Goerdeler brought with him his intermediary, a person with considerable influence in London and Paris political circles. The question for us was how far we dared go with this emissary in revealing our anxieties and offering our suggestions. We knew that we could no longer give such definite assurances as we had been able to give during the crisis of the fall of 1938. We could no longer promise that a firm stand by the Western Powers would set off a revolt of the generals. That chance had been lost. The prime task now was not to force a revolt, but to prevent a war. Did not the Western Powers see where their backing down would bring them? Retreating would not help them at all, we said. Sooner or later they would have to oppose Hitler's aggression, and until they did, they would be getting a whole series of weekend surprises.

In retrospect it may be objected that such warnings were superfluous; the invasion of Czechoslovakia had already produced a fundamental change in the attitude of the Western Powers; but at the time we went to Switzerland this was not nearly so apparent — and perhaps in fact it was not so. In spite of all the Nazi betrayals, there were to be a good many Englishmen and Frenchmen during the following months who showed themselves in favor of further appeasement. 'Why die for Danzig?' was already present in the germ in many people's minds.

The worst of it was that no one could say whether Hitler would bide his time for a year or two or whether he was already preparing for a new blow. If he practiced a little patience, the appeasers would once more win credence: the appeasers — and those who wanted to do business with Hitler. It may sound in bad taste for me, as a German, to speak of this, but I must remark that many stockholders in all countries in the world profited splendidly — and gratefully — by Hitler's 'peace.'

On the other hand, in our conversation with the foreign emissary we had to stress as strongly as possible that Hitler must be, from now on, the victim of his own previous actions. Whether it took place today or tomorrow, he could no longer halt his onrush toward Danzig. It was clear to us, moreover, that Danzig was no end in itself, but merely a way-station. From Danzig the march led directly to Warsaw, but there, too, Hitler would not be able to stop; he would have to go on until he reached the oil fields of Rumania and the grainlands of the Ukraine. We felt absolutely certain that sometime and somewhere the Nazi revolutionary armies would collide both with the forces of the Western Powers and with those of the Russians.

It was inevitable that Hitler must repeat the pattern of Napoleon. By threatening the very lives of the world's Great Powers he was forcing an alliance between them and the nations he had subjugated or would subjugate. It had in the end to come to armed conflict. The responsible statesmen of the world must not deceive themselves. The longer they gave ground before this satanic trouble-maker, the bloodier the final accounting would be. The intensity of German rearmament, which in those very months was proceeding on a colossal scale, was sufficient proof of that.

Goerdeler and Schacht were fully agreed on this estimate of the situation, but they differed sharply over what we should tell the British and the French. Both men were too unlike in character ever to agree fully. Goerdeler did not like Schacht's iridescent brilliance and vivacity. Schacht, for his part, could not endure Goerdeler's insistency, loquacity, and obdurateness. A synthesis of their characters would probably have begotten the best imaginable antagonist to Hitler. As it was, the two men, each of whom was indispensable in his own way, were constantly rubbing one another the wrong way. At the same time their political differences caused splits within their circles of friends, which overlapped to a great extent.

Our conversation at Ouchy was a typical example of these discordances. The perceptive Schacht suggested that it would not do merely to warn the Western Powers against Hitler's war-mongering. He also wanted to point out the danger of the theory, popular at the time, that sooner or later the Nazi economy would break down of itself simply because the normal procedures of financing and obtaining raw materials had been abandoned in favor of novel and wholly reckless methods.

Goerdeler objected to this. Goerdeler's great strength was his logic; his weakness was his astonishing lack of sensitivity to imponderables. Every six months for years he had been prophesying a dreadful economic collapse, and always inflation was just around the corner. In every respect Goerdeler was right. The Nazi economy could no longer edge back from its precarious footholds. Nevertheless, the breath-taking climb up the mountain continued, and it would take some time before the whole Party slipped and tumbled to a crash at the bottom — if there were a bottom.

Goerdeler never saw the tiny projections and narrow passes which would enable the Nazis to climb higher and higher. Bankrupt as they were, money meant nothing to them. Certainly they were not the least worried about the rate at which they were 'mining' the whole economy, using up irreplaceable labor force and capital goods. Unmindful of this, Goerdeler thought, even in March, 1938, that he must continue to assert that the Colossus with feet of clay would soon collapse. Just let Western Powers remain firm the next time, he announced, and Hitler would be done for because he simply could not carry out his next military adventure.

Obviously, both men were working toward the same end. They wanted to prevent war, or at least an extension and prolongation of the war, by a demonstration of concentrated force and firm resolution on the part of the Western Powers. They wanted the German people, and especially the generals, to realize that at last the Nazi bluff was over and that now things were becoming deadly earnest. Hitler could be fended off from world war only by an unsheathed sword. Schacht wanted to make his point by painting the picture as black as possible, by showing the Western Powers not only what perils they would encounter in the future, but what terrible risks they were already running. Goerdeler hoped to achieve the same goal by minimizing the difficulties the Western Powers would encounter in opposing Hitler.

Who was right? In retrospect we must, of course, agree with Schacht because he was warning against deceptive illusions. Goerdeler might defend his thesis to this day by arguing that, at that time, none of us had the right to say anything which would have defeatist overtones, for there were only too many statesmen in London and Paris who would have concluded — if we had emphasized the strength of the Nazis — that it would be best not to incense the lion, but rather to lure him toward the eastern steppes.

Our intermediary decided to transmit Goerdeler's version to the British and French. Throughout all the pre-war years gloomy prognoses for the Nazis were much in demand abroad, and those who maintained that the Third Reich could withstand a crisis for a long time to come were by preference decried as semi-Nazis.

Daladier at least received a report of this conference — which is how I happen to know what version the intermediary passed on. The French premier kindly preserved the record in his secret files, so that it was found by the *Abwehr* after the occupation of Paris. Had not Oster spirited away this incriminating document, we should have paid dearly in 1941 for our expedition to Switzerland two years before.

One of the most contested questions among us during the years of the Nazi régime was that of caution. Some were so busy taking precautions that they got around to nothing else. Others aroused panic all around them by their choice of dubious confidants. Goerdeler's bluntness resulted in the loss of his most important contacts. Schacht offended his associates just as often; his subtlety got on their nerves. Finding the proper balance between recklessness and exaggerated caution is one of the prime tasks — and burdens — of any underground activity.

We made still another attempt to get in touch with the Western Powers. Schacht had been friendly for years with the British banker, Montagu Norman. A meeting between them was arranged, and

Schacht had two long conversations with Norman in Basle. He described to him the conditions inside Germany, beginning with the concentration camps and ending with the complex problem of the generals. Prime Minister Chamberlain could scarcely have wished for a more authentic report on the situation in Germany.

I had expressly asked Schacht to go into detail. I was possessed by an *idée fixe,* namely, that radicalism such as we were experiencing would never stay within the borders of Germany. The Nazification of the army must necessarily lead to an adventure across the borders. If the Gestapo reign of terror were not stopped in time, war was inevitable, I thought; nor did it matter how many concessions the foreign Powers cast into the maw of the revolutionary Moloch. The foreign Powers, therefore, had to be convinced that they were not dealing with advocates of peaceful evolution, but with uninhibited revolutionaries. To demonstrate this, it was absolutely necessary to publicize all those atrocities which the Gestapo tyranny included under the concept of 'due process of law.'

Schacht was very loath to admit the validity of this argument. For years he nourished the delusion that at least some temporary agreement, if not a permanent peace, could be concluded with the forces of revolution. It had taken numerous unpleasant experiences to make him relinquish this notion. He, therefore, seemed the person best suited to warn Chamberlain, who derived from the same capitalistic sphere as Schacht himself, against the policy of compromise and appeasement.

But — was Downing Street at that time willing to hear such 'atrocity stories' about the Nazi system?

At the Nuremberg Trials all the leading defendants, led by Goering, the founder of the Gestapo, and Kaltenbrunner, its last chief, swore that they had not only been innocent but ignorant as well of the atrocities. When I testified at the trial — at the request of the defendants Schacht and Frick — I took the liberty of admitting, in the name of our oppositional group at least, that we had known about all the horrors — that, in fact, these had been the chief reason for our taking action. There was something I might have added to that state-

ment: the full truth is that there were a good many more persons outside Germany who also knew, persons who felt themselves responsible
for the fate of Germany and Europe.

For years my experience was that people abroad simply refused to
believe the full extent of SS crimes. There was a tremendous wave of
indignation when, after the Nazi collapse, documentary proofs were
offered in the newsreels and the newspapers. My German fellow
countrymen are mistaken if they think that the world knew all along
and that this sudden outburst of horror was merely whipped up by
a vengeful propaganda campaign on the part of the victors. The
world never did know how far-reaching the horror was. On the other
hand, there were also millions of terrorized Germans who decided
that so much vileness and bestiality was flatly impossible. To some
extent they still do not believe it.

The atrocities that were concealed from a great many Germans and
from the majority of humanity were definitely known to the governments of all civilized countries. Perhaps not all the foreign diplomats
in Germany observed the facts, but during all the horrible years there
were plenty of courageous and trustworthy Germans who conveyed
detailed and indisputable reports to the foreign governments — either
by smuggling them directly abroad or into the foreign diplomatic
missions.

These informers were not always welcomed with open arms. They
disturbed the equilibrium of our European appeasers.

Montagu Norman was only one of the many intermediaries we approached. The least we were hoping for at the time was the establishment of a permanent contact between our group and the British
government. Not even that was attained. Chamberlain sent a message
to us that Schacht was politically without influence; therefore, he felt
that he must continue to deal directly with Hitler. We, of course, knew
perfectly well that Schacht and all the other members of the Opposition were without influence. What we were trying to do was precisely to regain our influence. As I look back today at the history of
the war, it still seems incomprehensible to me that London did not

wish to build up this contact just in the event that the worse came to the worst. Even if the British did not want to collaborate with their well-wishers in peacetime, they should have remembered the potential political and strategic importance of having informants in the enemy camp in case of war.

It must be noted that the British were not simply rejecting Schacht as a person; that we could have understood; but others were treated as coolly. In fact they were not even honored by an official reply. In time interesting tales will be published about some of the desperate efforts that we made during those months of sharpening crisis. For the present it is important, as a step toward neutralizing some of the poison in the atmosphere of Europe, to mention that not all Germans kept their mouths shut.

At no time before or after did individuals fight as they did in the summer of 1939 to avert the coming disaster. There was, for example, the German ambassador, von Hassell (later to be one of the victims of July 20, 1944), who had a cordial relationship with the British ambassador, Sir Nevile Henderson. The more inexorably war neared, the more often von Hassell paid clandestine visits to the British Embassy. Many other unknown or overcautious persons, who did not dare to share their secrets with anyone in Germany, made similar attempts to tell their tale at foreign embassies.

After all, not every German economist or professor who traveled abroad during that period was a member of the fifth column. There were many among them who were good Europeans. Some, unfortunately the majority, lost their balance and were swept away by the wave of Nazi nationalism. Others were frightened by what they found abroad. Their practiced eyes saw clearly the outlines of the coming catastrophe when they observed that most people outside Germany still considered National Socialism a question of internal politics with which they had no right to interfere — an experiment from which they might even learn! As late as 1939 it was still being said abroad that Hitler had achieved 'undeniable successes' — the banishment of unemployment and the establishment of 'order.'

Just before it became apparent that Hitler was consolidating his war position, we transmitted clear and urgent warnings to London. Already the first scent of the Russo-German Pact was in the air. Nevertheless, this attempt to thwart Hitler's truly diabolic game also failed. Today Sir Robert Vansittart devotes a great deal of energy to condemning the Germans *in toto*. He might at that time have prevented terrible evils by the expenditure of far less energy — if only he had taken seriously all the whispered tips passed on to him by Germans.

Instead, this permanent under-secretary of the British foreign office felt it incumbent upon him to soothe the alarmists. The British knew just what was going on, he assured us; they would anticipate Hitler and conclude an agreement with the Russians in good time. We were naturally relieved to hear these consoling words. This time, apparently, the game was being played with consummate skill and the dictator was being lured into that domestic and diplomatic *débâcle* for which we had so long been hoping.

But Sir Robert Vansittart was bluffing. Unfortunately, he was not bluffing Hitler. He was deceiving the German Opposition.

FINAL EFFORTS INSIDE GERMANY

IN ADDITION TO OUR EFFORTS to establish contacts outside Germany, we worked harder than ever at home during the summer of 1939. Fortunately, since May the British government had permitted no doubt as to where England would stand in case of an armed conflict between Germany and Poland. That announcement made many people look and listen. There was not a general to be found who thought the people would support a revolt in the face of Hitler's recent triumphs, but most of them were now resolved to resist any future adventures which involved the risk of war. The conflict during those months did not center around the question of whether Germany could venture a war. Not even Hitler, Himmler, or Ribbentrop admitted the possibility of such an outcome. They, too, argued that the

Western Powers would end by submitting to armed occupation of Danzig.

With every means at our command, we tried to influence the top army leadership. If Brauchitsch, Halder, and Keitel could be convinced that the Western Powers were now resolved to stand firm, the Nazi assault upon world peace might still be prevented. We had already given up hope of getting any co-operation from Admiral Raeder.

The spokesman for our group during this period was General George Thomas. As head of the *Wehrwirtschaftsamt* (the economic staff of the army) he occupied a key position in the army high command. An acknowledged expert in all questions relating to the totalitarian 'defense economy,' he had had frequent disagreements with Hitler in practical matters, but Hitler had permitted him to retain his post.

Thomas had got himself in trouble as early as 1933, after his return from a tour of duty through Russia. Profoundly impressed by the vastness of the Russian spaces, the vigor of the Russian population, the advanced state of Russia's industry, and her potential self-sufficiency in raw materials and agricultural products, he had advocated a continuance of Russo-German co-operation; but Hitler knew better; he was not going to be taken in by Potemkin villages, like his naïve army officers. Bolshevism, Hitler asserted, was incapable of establishing any constructive organization.

A few years afterward Thomas had again fallen into disfavor because he condemned as a fatal error Ribbentrop's policy toward Japan. Long-standing friendly relationships existed between the German army and the government of Generalissimo Chiang Kai-shek. This friendship was kept alive by the presence of Generals Seeckt and Falkenhausen in China. In 1933, China and Germany concluded a long-term agreement for the exchange of raw materials against military equipment. A few weeks after the signing — General von Reichenau was in China at the time to present the Chinese generalissimo with a gift from Hitler — the treaty was disowned. When Thomas protested against this outright breach of faith, Hitler harshly informed him that scruples had no place in politics; treaties were made to be broken.

Thomas had also had irritating run-ins with Blomberg. These disputes grew out of Thomas's collaboration with Schacht, with whom he worked all the more intensively from 1937 on, when both men saw signs that indicated tremendous increases in the expenditures on rearmament. Incredible as it sounds, even the chief of the *Wehrwirtschaftsamt* was not aware of all the contracts that had been let. He obtained virtually no information from the air force or the navy, and the army provided him with only fragmentary information. Each section of the armed forces concealed the extent of its armaments from the others.

Hitler approved of this procedure. He did not want any co-ordinating authority to be able to survey the total situation. He preferred conflicts and rivalries because he thought they would speed the tempo of rearmament. Moreover, this situation enabled him to keep his minister of economics in the dark. This appeared to him important, because Schacht had consented to engage in his rather daring methods of financing only to provide funds for defensive armaments.

During the first three years the contracts that had been let necessarily remained restricted to such a defensive program. The productive capacity was insufficient to do any more. The picture changed, however, after the inauguration of the Second Four-Year Plan in September, 1936. From that point on, the predatory exploitation of financial and raw material resources commenced at such a rate that only a successful war could possibly pay for it.

Schacht, employing General Thomas as an intermediary, solicited War Minister von Blomberg to join with him in persuading Hitler to set reasonable limits to the armaments program. Blomberg's reply ran as follows:

> I don't want to have you again get me into the embarrassing situation where the Fuehrer will have to say to me: 'Herr von Blomberg, I have conferred a great task upon you — the reconstruction of the *Wehrmacht*. Do not trouble yourself about financial or economic or any other questions; I have selected other men to take care of

them. . . .' All this criticizing and worrying of yours doesn't interest me, Herr Schacht, and I wish you would keep away from the clique that is always caviling. . . . You have no responsibility and I have no responsibility when we carry out the Fuehrer's orders. That is precisely where his greatness lies — that he has taken all the responsibility upon himself alone. . . . The Fuehrer sees a good deal farther than all of us put together.

Too little attention has been paid to Blomberg's pernicious rôle in the early years of the Nazi dictatorship. The prepossessing field marshal was one of those who was considered 'decent,' because, to outward appearances, he kept himself aloof from the disorderly deeds of the Nazis. Moreover, he had the questionable good fortune to get involved in his private scandal before the consequences of his behavior had become obvious to all. For Blomberg had tutored all his higher-ranking officers to submit unconditionally to the usurper's will.

There was a direct line of descent from the attitude of Field Marshal von Blomberg to that of General Jodl, who even at Nuremberg was obviously still in awe of the tyrant.

I assure the court [Jodl said at the Nuremberg trials] that Hitler made a sharp division between political and military affairs. It was absolutely impossible to get into a discussion with Hitler. Hitler always made decisions without hesitation, and it made absolutely no difference whether they were right or wrong. Under no circumstances was it possible to argue with Hitler. Hitler was a master at secrecy and deliberate deception of people. His skill at trickery was particularly remarkable. . . . It might have been possible to avoid a great deal of harm if the generals had been able to inform Hitler fully of what was happening. For us soldiers, life in Hitler's headquarters was pure martyrdom. It was not a military but a civilian headquarters in which the officers were treated merely as guests, and for the most part as unwelcome guests.

Jodl called the Fuehrer's headquarters 'a cross between a concentration camp and a monastery.' He did not feel at all comfortable there. He would never forget, he testified, the insults and invectives to which he was subjected by Hitler. For example, in August, 1942, he had openly discussed with the Fuehrer a crisis in army operations. Never in his life, he said, had he witnessed such rage as Hitler then showed. After this scene Hitler never again invited Jodl to dine with him. An SS officer was ordered to be present at every conversation he had with Hitler thereafter. Hitler also refused to shake hands with him or even to address him directly.

Blomberg in 1936 and Jodl in 1946 had the same magic formula which exonerated them from making any decisions of their own: their 'duty of military obedience.' A conception of duty which places all responsibility upon an immediate superior is no more nor less than cynically disguised irresponsibility; and such irresponsibility is no more nor less than irreparable historical — and this time also criminal — guilt.

Thanks to his high position, Thomas was in a particularly favorable position to be the spokesman of our group during the critical weeks before the outbreak of the war. After his liberation from concentration camp, he wrote the following lines on this subject:

> When it became clearly apparent in the summer of 1939 that Hitler was provoking trouble with the Poles in order to give the German people a pretext for his aggression, numerous men approached me with the request that I do everything possible to prevent this war which we felt certain would spread into a world war. The prime advocates of this proposal were Minister Popitz, Doctor Goerdeler, General Beck, Ambassador von Hassell, Doctor Schacht, Under-Secretary Planck, General Oster, Herr Gisevius, and Director-General Wittke. In a number of earnest conferences we decided that everything possible must be done to prevent the outbreak of war and to spare the German people a new carnage. During this period I wrote a brief memorandum which showed clearly that Hitler's plans for conquest must lead to a world war, that this war would become a long war of attrition, and that Germany lacked the raw materials and food supplies to endure such a war without powerful allies. A lost war would mean the ruin of Germany, I wrote, and therefore the war must not come.

I read this memorandum to Keitel some fourteen days before the outbreak of the Polish war. Keitel interrupted me during my reading and stated that Hitler would never lead Germany into a world war. There was no danger of that, he said; Hitler knew for certain that the French were a degenerate, pacifistic nation, that the British were much too decadent to come forth with real aid to Poland, and that America would never again send a single man to Europe to pull the chestnuts out of the fire for England, let alone for Poland. I objected that everyone who really knew the foreign situation held altogether different views. To this Keitel replied sharply that I had apparently been infected by the pacifistic crew who refused to see Hitler's greatness.

On the Sunday before the beginning of the Polish campaign, I again visited Keitel and handed him graphically illustrated statistical evidence on the military-economic potentials of Germany and of the other World Powers. These statistics demonstrated clearly the tremendous military-economic superiority of the Western Powers and the tribulation we would face.

The following day Keitel informed me that he had shown these surveys to Hitler. Hitler, he said, had declared that he by no means shared my anxiety over the danger of a world war, especially since he had now got the Soviet Union on his side. The agreement with Russia, Hitler had said, was the greatest political feat that had been performed by German statesmen in decades. I never did find out whether Hitler, under the influence of Ribbentrop, really did still believe that England would not intervene in the Polish war, or whether even at that time Keitel wished to deceive me.

We in our circle had conferred carefully over Thomas's memoranda. The difficulty for us was not in foreseeing the outbreak of a second world war. The main problem was to find a language that had some prospect of being understood. It was not our intention to construct alibis for ourselves or to assemble evidence which in the future could be used to prosecute Keitel or Hitler. We wanted to stop them short, to force them to revise a decision which — we suspected rather than knew — Hitler would never have taken if he had properly appreciated the diplomatic realities.

There was no point at all in approaching Hitler with humanitarian arguments. Had Thomas argued that he was against any war as a matter of principle, it might have gone hard with him. At best Hitler would once again have let fall a sneering remark about the pacifistic generals. We were again trying to talk in Hitler's own language, or at least in the language of Keitel, Brauchitsch, and Halder. We therefore criticized the notion that a coup in Poland would have no serious consequences and depicted the danger of a long war of attrition. This gave us a chance to place the emphasis on the field in which Thomas was an acknowledged expert — the comparison between the war potentials of Germany and of the Western Powers.

Ludwig Beck now also tried to intervene. He had been quite content so long as he heard from us that his successor, Halder, appeared to be following in his footsteps. Now, for the first time since the Fritsch crisis, he addressed himself directly to Brauchitsch. Beck had completely broken relations with the commander-in-chief of the army. He considered Brauchitsch wholly corrupt and a traitor to the tradition of German army officers; but now, in this hour of extreme danger, he put these emotional considerations aside and wrote a letter to him.

The tone of the letter was such that the normal mind could imagine only two possible reactions to it. Either Brauchitsch would feel that the ideas expressed in this letter were an offense to his loyalty to the Nazi system — in which case he must hand the letter over to the Gestapo — or else he would be struck by the force of the factual arguments and the moral appeal — in which case he must act; but he found a third way out — he said nothing and did nothing.

Beck also wrote to Halder and asked the chief of staff to come to see him. Halder obeyed the summons of his former superior. Beck and Halder had a long conversation. It is easier to talk with someone who disagrees than it is to influence someone on your own side who balks only at drawing the conclusions which must flow out of your point of view. On all matters of principle Halder agreed that Beck was right. Certainly the Gestapo dictatorship was unendurable; certainly a second world war would mean the end of Germany; certainly Hitler must be deposed or there would be no peace for Germany and Europe. On the other hand — and there followed a hundred tactical ifs and buts. The border in the East was unreasonable, Halder maintained; Danzig was, after all, a German city; the British would give Germany a free hand in the East, and Hitler would never permit a world war.

How could Beck convince Halder that it was not at all a question of Danzig? How could he prove that there really would be a world war? How could he convince him of the intangible but vital fact that in wartime soldiers are governed by 'patriotic' motives, by psychological attitudes toward their leader which are different from their attitudes toward a tyrant in peacetime? How, that is, could Beck dispute Halder's prime theory: that the proper psychological moment for a *coup d'état* was not now but a few months hence?

The two men argued on different planes. When they parted, they shook hands for the last time. Beck had found Halder wanting neither in understanding nor patriotism nor a sense of his class tradition. He simply lacked the will.

During those days, when the crisis was approaching its climax, Witzleben telephoned Oster and asked whether I could visit him. At the beginning of the year, Witzleben had been promoted to a colonel-general and transferred from Berlin to the command of an army group in the West. This promotion was proof of how highly his military abilities were appreciated. Witzleben, in his headquarters at Frankfurt-am-Main, thought wistfully of the time when he was not in command of several armies, but had at his disposal in Berlin the one or two divisions which might be able to occupy the chancellery.

In the army hierarchy Witzleben now held one of the three or four highest posts after Brauchitsch. It was only after the outbreak of the war that he was demoted somewhat, for Rundstedt, Leeb, and Bock took over the command of the three army groups. In spite of his high position, however, Witzleben had no idea what was happening in political circles. He did not know whether Hitler really intended to march into Poland or whether it was all another bluff. That was why he had asked Oster to send me.

On August 20, 1939, I took the train to Frankfurt. I found Witzleben sitting with his wife in his study and listening to a British radio broadcast. The BBC was the only reliable source of information accessible to these men who would soon be ordering hundreds of thousands of soldiers into the field of battle. Oster had been optimistic. 'You'll see,' he had said to me, 'the old fellow has had an inspiration; he has something up his sleeve'; but after a few words it became apparent that the general merely wanted information and conversation; he was seeking a sympathetic person with whom he could talk from the heart and pour out his indignation.

A few days previously Brauchitsch and Halder had passed by on an inspection tour of the West. Witzleben had taken it for granted that his commander-in-chief would inform him about the political situation. Instead, Brauchitsch had shut out all possibility of conversation even before they exchanged greetings. 'Today I can discuss only official matters with you,' he had said hurriedly. This had infuriated Witzleben. Halder, his accomplice of former days, had also evaded having any conversation with him. It was really extraordinary behavior, for Witzleben's desire to be informed on the political situation was quite valid, even from the point of view of the Nazis. If the Western Powers did declare war and if the French aided their Polish allies by launching a diversionary offensive, Witzleben's troops would receive the first blow.

It was precisely for this reason that the subject could not be discussed. Hitler and these two generals who were under the spell of his estimate of foreign politics were staking everything on the chance that Gamelin would postpone action in order to see whether and how long the Poles could resist. Therefore, Brauchitsch and Halder had massed almost the entire army in the East, in order to crush the Poles with a few heavy blows. The Siegfried Line, meanwhile, was so thinly occupied that only the most important fortifications were manned at all. 'If the French strike, they'll break through,' Witzleben said to me.

I told Witzleben about the forthcoming conversation between Beck and Halder, which at that time was just being arranged. I agreed to return in four days to let him know whether Beck, Canaris, and Oster thought it would be worth while for him to come to Berlin. We had in mind the possibility that Witzleben, if possible accompanied by Canaris, Thomas, and General Stuelpnagel, might suddenly confront Halder, remind him of his former promises, and compel him if necessary to use force against Brauchitsch.

On Sunday night I left Frankfurt. In Berlin I reserved a sleeper ticket for Tuesday evening; but a few hours after my arrival in Berlin, Witzleben telephoned Oster that my journey would not be necessary.

On the following day Hitler spoke to his generals at Berchtesgaden.

HITLER COOKS A STEW

I WONDER whether the record of that speech which Hitler delivered at Berchtesgaden on August 22, 1939, will ever be found. Its first portion took two hours. Then there was an intermission: a luxurious dinner with caviar; and then two hours more of speech. If it should be found, it would provide later historians with a profound insight into Hitler's quality of diabolic persuasiveness.

It was forbidden to make any copies of the speech before the briefing — for that was what it was. Canaris, who knew this fact, managed to sit in a corner where he could not be seen and take down the speech word for word. The very next day he read the most important passages to us. He was still utterly horrified. His voice trembled as he read. Canaris was acutely aware that he had been witness to a monstrous scene. We all agreed that this document of a time of delirium must be preserved for posterity. Another copy was, therefore, made from Canaris's entry in his journal, and Oster placed this copy in his collection of documents.

Three versions of this crucial speech were laid before the Nuremberg Court. Later on, apparently, others of the audience had written down a few of the more striking sentences from memory, but these notes remained fragmentary. Nevertheless, they suffice to indicate the

broad outline of the speech. We can find in these notes all the arguments with which Hitler tried to sway his listeners, all the twisted
logic that he employed.

A favorite name for Hitler was 'the great simplifier.' This was
apt; in spite of the verbosity and clumsiness of his thought and
language, he really possessed an astonishing ability for summarizing
complicated matters into brief formulas. What has been frequently
overlooked, however, was the sheer impudence of his system, the
manner in which the cunning demagogue first forced his audience
onto ground where such simplifications were psychologically ac-
ceptable.

In mass meetings he wearied his audience by a boring torrent of
words, until they wanted 'action' of any kind and were willing to pay
the price for such diversion — the price being that they would refrain
from inquiring too closely into the validity of his rhetorical propositions. Only then did he begin slashing away with trenchant phrases at
the imaginary target or the convenient straw man. By means of some
political sensation, some scandal, or some wholly fantastic hypothesis
he would completely disconcert his 'reasonable' ministers, generals, or
captains of industry. In their bewilderment they would try to stick
close to the 'facts'; and then Hitler would produce his magic formula
to rescue everyone from his helpless confusion. The formula was by
this time virtually self-evident; like all great things it was impres-
sively simple. Only someone who would dare to commit *lèse majesté*,
who would dare to question the hypnotic orator's specious premise,
could resist Hitler's 'logic.'

This speech at Berchtesgaden was a case in point. At that time it
would have gone ill indeed with the German citizen who whispered
the faintest aspersion against the nobility of Hitler's allies. Hitler
himself brutally revealed all to the generals. Mussolini, with whom
the Fuehrer admittedly felt a certain congeniality, got off rather
easily; but he was, Hitler alleged, dangerously menaced by the court
clique. Any day he might be overthrown, and then there would be
trouble with Italy. The Emperor of Japan was a weak vessel. He
might well be compared with the last Russian czar, his attitude being

so hazy and his ultimate fate so inevitable. Franco, too, who was not a direct partner in the Axis but whose 'neutrality' was indispensable, was a doomed statesman because he had not had the spunk to establish a single totalitarian Party. In short, since all the other dictators were on the down grade, there remained only one great and uncontested 'leader'; and since in five or ten years this one would no longer be as hale and enterprising as — Providence be thanked — he now was, the last, the very last gamble must be risked at once.

But, Hitler continued, was there really any risk at all? Certainly not. Once again, woe to the ordinary German who talked out of turn about Nazi economic policy. It was therefore all the more dramatic when Hitler revealed to the generals Germany's terrible predicament in regard to foreign exchange and raw materials. Consequently, there was really no question about it: Germany had nothing to lose and everything to win. The coming events would be, in essence, a grand lottery for Germany. Since the Nazi players had already gambled away all their smaller stakes, they would have to open up their principal purse.

In the final analysis, Hitler argued, success was the decisive criterion of the wisdom of a policy; and was he not prepared at this very moment to offer them an incomparable success — one, to be sure, that was highly questionable morally and extremely temporary politically — but indisputably a tremendous triumph? Had he not concluded a pact with the Russians?

A few months before, Canaris had returned gloomily from the chancellery. I still recall his downcast expression as he took Oster and me to his room and informed us that he had just become acquainted with the worst possible side of the dictator. Bad news had come from London. The British intended to conclude a guaranty treaty with the Poles. Canaris had spoken to the Fuehrer and informed him that any further steps toward the East would mean war. Thereupon Hitler had flown into a passion. With features distorted by fury, he had stormed up and down his room, pounded his fists on the marble table-top, and spewed forth a series of savage imprecations. Then, his eyes flashing with an uncanny light, he had growled the threat: 'I'll cook them a stew that they'll choke on.'

At the time we took this as a sign of hysteria and as sheer boastful-ness. Canaris alone disagreed with us; he had been too deeply im-pressed by the scene to dismiss it lightly. Then Hitler had cooked his stew, after all! The front lines were more tangled than ever. The vision of Hitler and Stalin walking arm in arm was too much, even for our unpolitical generals. A good many of them were quite pleased with the effect Hitler's surprise pact had produced. Since they them-selves had been thunderstruck, they assumed that the rest of the world had also been shocked into insensibility. Other generals were indig-nant beyond words; but one thing was clear — once more the master of craftiness had turned the trick. His rear was protected, the danger of a second world war had been banished, and Poland had been divided before the first shot was fired.

I have never attempted to gainsay the German war guilt, but pre-cisely because of that, it is necessary to emphasize the historic fact that the Moscow Pact first made it possible for the Nazis to take the leap from daring conjectures and evil plans to their final cynical decision. Even a Hitler would not have dared to start the war in August, 1939, if he had been unable to localize it beforehand and protect his rear by means of the pact. He never would have presented his plans for the invasion of Poland with such cynical frankness to his generals, to the German people, and to Europe if he had not been able to spoon them out a sample of his piquant 'stew' at the same time.

The glory does not belong exclusively to the dictator. It would be grossly underestimating the intelligence and farsightedness of Stalin to assert that he did not know what was involved. Anyone who has the slightest doubt about that need merely read the Russo-German secret treaty.

Hitler's war buried among the ruins of Europe that materialist philosophy of history which speaks of the inevitability of war under capitalism. This war was engendered, to be exact, by an anti-capitalist war guilt. Where were the capitalists, including the German capital-ists, when the Fascist and Communist Internationales joined forces to create a new 'order' under the sign of socialism and collectivism?

The 'have-nots' declared war on the 'plutocrats' and 'exploiters.' Fundamentally, what took place on a gigantic scale in 1939 was a repetition of the misguided policy of 1932, when the Communists joined the Nazis to destroy by votes and by strikes the hated bourgeois order.

Whatever the rôles of capitalistic or anti-capitalistic war guilt, the materialist conception must be shelved because to our horror — and, God grant, to our ultimate salvation — we have all learned a fearful lesson: that even in this technical age of ours the power and energy of a single individual can wield tremendous influence. Neither greedy masses nor unleashed matter nor an inscrutable destiny conjured this war into being. It originated in the will of a single individual, who drew to himself the destructive impulses of many other individual personalities; and it was through the propaganda of such individuals that the Fascists and Communists of all countries adopted that ambivalent attitude which so thoroughly and tragically confused the world's political situation at the outbreak of the war.

WAR

HITLER gave himself one day of rest after his success with the generals. On August 24 he hurried to Berlin. That same afternoon the air cavalcade which had taken Ribbentrop to Moscow landed at Tempelhof. Beaming with satisfaction, the foreign minister went to the chancellery to receive the fervent thanks of his Fuehrer.

Not since the conclusion of the Anglo-German Naval Agreement had the Fuehrer heaped such fulsome praise on Ribbentrop as he did today. For lack of any other patents of nobility, Hitler exalted his foreign minister to the rank of a 'second Bismarck.' This appellation was a shrewd formulation combining both business and pleasure. In the first place it honored the former champagne salesman, who was always ripe for flattery. In the second place it contrived to clarify the Fuehrer's own position. Time and again tactless after-dinner speakers had compared Hitler with the founder of the German Reich, thereby removing him from his solitary heights to the plane of ordinary human values. Hitler wanted no comparisons; he wanted to be 'unique.'

Naturally, Ribbentrop had only favorable news to report. He had been received in the most charming manner possible. His Russian hosts had behaved in a far more civilized manner than had been thought possible. Stalin had been so outstandingly friendly that from then on he ranked directly after Hitler on the list of dictatorial peers. The Nazi orators were still careful to emphasize the distance between the Vozhd and the Fuehrer, but from now on Stalin always took precedence over the Duce. From now on there were only two great centers of world politics: Berlin and Moscow.

The Duce had to wait until he was asked, or at least informed; but since it would be bad taste to break off the old friendship for the new one too brusquely, Hitler decided to let Rome in on the Moscow decisions. At the same time he informed the Duce of his intention to issue marching orders on the morning of the twenty-fifth. Late that evening Ambassador von Mackensen transmitted to Mussolini the news that had up to then been conscientiously concealed from the Italian dictator.

On the morning of that historic twenty-fifth of August, everything was in readiness. The military preparations were complete. Ambassador von Mackensen telegraphed the Duce's congratulations on the conclusion of the Moscow Pact. All that Hitler was waiting for were reports on the helpless fury of the Western Powers at the pact with the Russians.

Hitler felt absolutely certain that there would be tremendous confusion in Paris and London. He was so confident, in fact, that he asked Dietrich, the Reich press chief, to show him the reports dealing with the cabinet crises. The surprised press chief did not understand what the Fuehrer meant. 'The resignation of the British and French governments, of course,' Hitler complacently informed him. He was sure that no democratic government could survive so fearful a defeat as the one he had inflicted upon Britain and France by wrecking their own negotiations with the Soviet Union.

He was astonished when Dietrich showed him a transcription of Chamberlain's final declaration. Chamberlain left a loophole for a peaceful settlement. On the other hand, he made a strong statement that England would stand by her obligations to Poland.

Visibly disturbed, Hitler asked Sir Nevile Henderson, the British ambassador, to call on him at one-thirty. There now remained only one course: he would have to immobilize British diplomacy for the next few days, during which he carried out his lightning war, by dangling a tremendously tempting offer. He would give the British everything, anything they desired, even a guaranty of their empire, if only they would keep still this once more and permit him to correct the 'Macedonian conditions' in the East.

It is not worth while studying this offer, which was never meant seriously. Even before Henderson's car had left the chancellery grounds, Hitler (it was then two-thirty) issued the final order to his military chief adjutant, Colonel Schmundt. The invasion of Poland was to begin the following morning at five o'clock.

For the sake of parity, the French ambassador was also to be the recipient of a few kind words. He was asked to come to the chancellery at five-thirty. Meanwhile, however, an uninvited guest made his appearance. Ambassador Attolico made an urgent request for an audience, which Hitler unsuspectingly granted. When Attolico came at three o'clock, he handed Hitler a short note. It was barely two pages long, but it spoke volumes. To his great regret the Duce found himself compelled to inform Hitler of Italy's complete unpreparedness for war. This, Mussolini declared hypocritically, 'was one of the most tragic moments' of his life, but he had to inform his friend and ally that there was only a three weeks' supply of gasoline for the Italian air force, not much more for the army, and that even worse conditions prevailed with regard to other necessary matériel. The fleet alone was amply supplied. Naturally, Mussolini solemnly assured Hitler, these terrible conditions which had just been discovered would be promptly remedied, but until measures could be taken, Italy would be completely dependent upon German supplies.

Seldom had an ambassador ever been dismissed as ungraciously as

was Attolico. Hitler foamed with rage. Only that morning the hypocritical Roman had telegraphed his congratulations! Obviously this
disastrous shortage of raw materials could not have become known in
the few short hours since the telegram was sent.

What had happened was soon revealed. Around four o'clock Hitler
received information from London which had apparently been transmitted to Rome a few hours before. The news was that the same
evening an Anglo-Polish treaty of alliance was to be published. Undoubtedly it was this report which had induced Mussolini to reverse
his stand. This was not surprising, since up to now Hitler had
consoled the Duce with repeated assurances that the war against
Poland would remain an isolated campaign.

Did not this new development also represent a severe blow to the
Fuehrer himself? Did it not mean the collapse of his policy of localiz-
ing the war? For once again Germany was being threatened by a
two-front war, that dreaded spector of 1914-18 which the dictator had
all along claimed to have banished. All along, that claim had been
his major argument with the hesitant generals.

Once again, as so often in his life, Hitler began to waver. At this
climactic point of the crisis the usual nervous breakdown took place.
When Ambassador Coulondre entered the chancellery at five-thirty,
however, he was met by a chancellor who was still able to reiterate the
same old saws. Hitler made exactly the same statements to the French
ambassador that he had made to Henderson a few hours before.
Nevertheless, the Fuehrer was sick with doubt. The torrent of his
speech had not gone on for as long as usual, and consequently had
not yet reached the final stage of frenzy, when Hitler unexpectedly
rose and politely indicated that the audience was over. Coulondre tried
to say a few words, but the dictator quickly put an end to the somewhat one-sided conversation. 'I have, as you know, made an agreement
with Moscow which is, I may say, concrete and not theoretical. . . .
I believe I shall win. You believe you will win. . . . I repeat once
more, it greatly depresses me to be forced to assume that we have
come so far. Please tell Monsieur Daladier that I have said this. . . .
I am even ready to believe that men like Polish Foreign Minister Beck

are moderates; but they are no longer masters of the situation. . . . The thought that I may have to fight against your country depresses me greatly, but that does not depend on me. Please inform Monsieur Daladier of this.'

'I could no longer prolong the interview and therefore took my leave after these final words of Hitler's,' Coulondre reported to his foreign minister. He could find no explanation for Hitler's sudden haste.

It was quite understandable, however. Immediately after the ambassador left, Hitler again sent for his chief adjutant (it was now six-fifteen) and ordered the military operation, which was already under way, to be called off at once.

The reader can imagine the state of fearful suspense in which my small group of friends and I found ourselves. Our mood, however, was tinged with fatalism; we no longer doubted that the marching orders would be issued. To our minds the die had already been cast on August 23, when the Moscow Pact was signed.

Although we had virtually abandoned hope, Schacht and I waited throughout the day, firmly resolved that the moment the command was given we would try one last desperate step. Twice Schacht tried to see Halder or Brauchitsch. Both times he was refused. Everything was still hanging in the balance, they declared; there would be no point to a conversation.

The evasions these generals adopted were truly grotesque. If they had fooled themselves but once, during the latter part of August, 1939, I should not revive these sad memories, but they repeated the same pattern every time from then on, before every new invasion, before every new act of madness. Each time these responsible leaders of the army refused to take action against plans which already lay on their desks on the ground that they had not yet received the 'final' order. Like men hypnotized, they stared at the impending menace, but once the order arrived which they had so tremulously awaited — once it came, they sighed with relief, for then they felt themselves freed from all pangs of conscience; then inscrutable Fate had snatched away the opportunity to make a decision; then their manifest duty as unpolitical soldiers was to obey.

Just before the twenty-fifth of August, neither Brauchitsch nor Halder wanted to talk with us. They were only waiting for the time when they could post a sign on the entrance to their headquarters: CIVILIANS KEEP OUT. We were determined, however, not to let them off so easily. The moment they turned their weapons against the external foe, we wanted to point a pistol at their own breasts.

Schacht and I had arranged with Thomas and Oster that during the waiting period between the issuance of marching orders and the first act of war we would go to headquarters and confront Halder. The guards wouldn't be likely to bar the way to the minister of the Reich, we reckoned, and once we reached the chief of staff, Schacht would call his attention to the unconstitutionality of a declaration of war without consultation of the cabinet. We then were going to demand that Halder and Brauchitsch place at Schacht's disposal the troops necessary to preserve the rights of the cabinet — or else to arrest us. If he chose the latter course we would, however, feel relieved of any obligation to preserve silence on the various subjects we had discussed with those gentlemen during recent years.

Around four o'clock word reached the *Abwehr* that the order to advance had been given. Admiral Canaris's key position by no means entitled him to any priority in receiving news of important decisions. Even before the war began, the counter-intelligence service was provided with very little intelligence indeed. Had not Oster long before built up his own secret service, it is probable that we should have learned nothing at all about the marching order that was first issued and then revoked. As it was, we were able to keep an hour or two behind events. It was, therefore, around five o'clock when I called on Schacht with my latest information: that Hitler had set the machinery of war into motion.

We at once got into Schacht's car. First we hunted up Thomas, and found him at last — unexpectedly — at his home. Thomas thought that we should be able to see Halder, who was at headquarters in Zossen, south of Berlin, only by using guile. It seemed to him that we should need Canaris's help.

Shortly after seven o'clock the three of us met again near the Bendlerstrasse. We had long had a habit of meeting in the Hildebrandstrasse, a near-by side street, since parked cars in the Bendlerstrasse might attract attention, and the Gestapo could easily check up on the owners of the cars through the license numbers. Thomas went up to see Canaris. Schacht and I waited in the car.

After a painful wait of more than half an hour, we saw Oster instead of Thomas approaching us. Half-grinning, half-shaking his head, Oster strolled toward us. With exasperating equanimity, he got into the car with us, ordered the chauffeur to cruise around the neighborhood, closed the windows of the car, and then burst into hearty laughter. 'That's what happens when a corporal tries to conduct a war,' he said. A silence followed. Neither Schacht nor I was especially delighted at being administered world-shaking news by droplets; but Oster insisted on savoring the pleasure of recounting the events of the afternoon at leisure, and it took quite a while before he came to the point: that the war orders had been rescinded.

'Well, what now?' I asked. 'Have Halder and Brauchitsch agreed to strike now?' Oster looked at me in frank astonishment. His reaction has remained as one of my most vivid memories of that exciting day. His surprise arose from his familiarity with my temperament. He was aware that I was always pressing, always trying to anticipate future events, and now for once he thought that I was straggling hopelessly behind something that had already happened. Now that this had happened, why in the world should Brauchitsch and Halder revolt either this evening, or tomorrow, or during the next few days? A supreme commander who rescinded so clear-cut a command, who changed his mind on the question of war and peace from one moment to the next, was finished. 'The Fuehrer is done for,' Oster said. For him, our desperate plans for a *Putsch* were outdated. It was now merely a question of time and manner: How could this unmasked impostor be removed with the least trouble and the most elegance?

A great many of the other generals must have had similar thoughts that evening. Since I have always considered the psychological developments by far the most significant aspects of these past twelve years, I want to stress Oster's reaction. Since 1933, Oster had fought against the Gestapo criminals. Of all the officers he had been most resolute and uncompromising in his determination to overthrow the Nazi government; and it was this man who under the fresh impression of Hitler's reversal now thought that his goal had already been achieved. Consequently, Oster was no longer interested in pondering what should be done with Hitler. Instead, he talked with unwonted verbosity of the German military machine's impressive achievement in recalling a widely ramified military action which had already been in progress for some hours.

I recall that afterward Schacht and I had dinner together. Like all rich men who have acquired their own fortune, the minister did not have expensive tastes. Since our first meeting I had always enjoyed watching him squirm while I ordered the dinner with that luxuriousness which only the non-plutocrat can afford. Schacht had no liking for this frank testimony of how wealthy I thought him, and he did his best to evade such expensive rendezvous; but today he did not refuse to pay the check for both of us. There was a rather wry expression on his face, but I persuaded him that the check had its good side — the other side, to be exact, on which we wrote a memento of that truly 'historic' evening.

I could scarcely wait to get to the offices of the OKW the following morning. Oster's good-humor was, if possible, even more pronounced. Everything had worked out well. A harmless skirmish had taken place at a bridge on the Polish frontier; but no attention was paid to this actual border incident precisely because dozens of similar clashes had been falsely reported during the previous war of nerves; the world was overjoyed so long as the war had not really begun.

On the other hand, the Poles would have been wise to have protested loudly. Parachute troops had occupied Jablonka Pass, an important strategic position. The deployment plans provided that the Germans should seize this pass before the enemy had been alarmed by the general advance. Incredible as it sounds, in the midst of the so-called peace this pass remained in the possession of the parachute troops for an entire week. The incident should have served to warn the European public during that deceptive week of quiet that the 'lightning' had already struck, that the *Blitz* had been launched.

Canaris, too, reflected the general sense of satisfaction. 'Well, what do you say?' he greeted me jubilantly. 'He'll never recover from this blow. . . . Peace has been saved for the next twenty years. . . .'

I have no reason to boast of my answer, because it was simply an expression of that *idée fixe* of mine that Hitler would suffer a nervous breakdown every single time, before each of his decisions. Therefore, I was saying nothing new when I replied: 'Only if we act now. Otherwise Himmler and Ribbentrop will make their influence felt again and in a week we'll be back in the same situation.'

Even stronger than his sharp perception of political realities was Canaris's intuitive sense for intangibles. Seldom have I known anyone with so keen a feeling for the direction of events. Usually he was so taken up with the intangible realities that he never brought himself to the point of action; but on that August 26 both his intuition and his intellect played him false. I am quite certain that he was pretending neither to me nor to himself. The 'out of the question' with which he dismissed my remark was quite genuine. He really believed that peace had been saved for the next twenty years. It was the one false estimate of a situation that I ever heard from his lips.

The days before August 25 had been fearfully nerve-racking; the day itself had witnessed a dramatic succession of ups and downs. By contrast, the following six days passed in an even, an apathetic tempo — and the irrevocable disaster took place on August 31 with equal lack of drama.

No one was thinking of war any more. Everyone was convinced that a week of negotiations was about to begin. As it was, the greatest surprise of the outbreak of war was that Hitler deserted his habit of five years' standing. This time it was no sudden weekend blow. It was on a perfectly ordinary Friday that Hitler took arms against a sea of troubles, and the fateful decision had been made on a Thursday.

If any war were started without the sound of trumpets and drums, without the jubilant cheering of enthusiastic masses, it was this one. In the life of nations as in the lives of individuals, the first reactions may well be more genuine and trustworthy than all subsequent emotional outbursts and rationalizations. While Hitler's address to the Reichstag was blaring from loudspeakers on every corner of the city, I drove through the streets to observe the reaction. I saw no sign of cheering masses. Most people were not even listening to the speech; it almost seemed as if they were trying hard to shut their ears. Here and there I saw small groups standing silently, nervously, with faraway expressions. These people were not so dulled to disaster as similar groups are today as they queue up among the ruins to receive a few scant items of food, but they were far more frightened, far more inwardly disturbed. As soon as the speech was over, they scattered in all directions without waiting to hear the singing of the national anthem.

The night before, all the fearful rumors had suddenly assumed reality. The conscripts were ordered to report with scarcely any fuss. The military Moloch took a hint from the manner in which the Gestapo swallowed up its victims; it stretched out its tentacles for the reservists in the darkness of night. Thus protest demonstrations by despairing women and children were avoided. When Berlin awoke in the morning, the droning motors of bombing planes announced that the day had been dedicated to Mars — and not only to the god of war, but to the Draconian laws of war. (The planes were allegedly on their way to the front; actually they were conducting purely propaganda flights.)

Late in the afternoon on August 31, Oster called me excitedly. In spite of his circumlocutions, I understood very well the message he wanted to convey. I drove at once to the OKW. Taking two steps at a time, I raced up the flight of stairs into the *Abwehr* section of the building. When I reached the second story, I saw Canaris and a number of high officers descending from the next floor. I tried to get out of their way, since in public we pretended not to know one another, but Canaris had caught sight of me. He let his companions go on ahead and drew me into a dimly lit corridor. The admiral grasped my arm firmly, but he did not look straight at me. His eyes were staring absently down at the floor, and yet there was something fiercely penetrating about that look of his, as if he were boring a hole down to the foundations of the building.

'Well, what do you say now?'

I had no reply ready.

In a voice choked with tears, Canaris supplied the answer himself: 'This means the end of Germany.'

2

Toward the Catastrophe
September, 1939, to July, 1944

THE FIRST 'FEELERS'

A T THE NUREMBERG TRIALS it was asserted that Goering had
made a last desperate attempt to save peace during the three days
that intervened between Hitler's invasion of Poland and the Anglo-
French declaration of war. The question was examined with minute
care, but it was clear then and it is clear now that a world conflagration could have been avoided only by Hitler's withdrawal from the
Polish adventure. That is all that need concern the historians in regard
to those three days.

On the other hand, psychologists will find much interesting material
in the secret history of those three days. Who could have dreamed
what is now proved fact — that up to the last moment Hitler refused
to believe that the British would declare war? Who would have
imagined the terrible state of depression that the news of the British
declaration produced in the chancellery? 'What are we going to do
now?' For the clairvoyant, the man who behaved with the 'sureness
of a somnambulist,' was completedy stunned, and his uneasiness was
communicated to his entire entourage. Everyone around him was confused and numbed.

On the eighteenth day the Russian troops — 'in order to safeguard
the complete neutrality of Soviet Russia' — invaded eastern Poland.
That, of course, decided the fate of the country. As a matter of fact,

the Poles fought much more bravely than they at first seemed to have done. In the light of the feeble resistance offered by some of the countries that were later invaded, the Polish stand was admirable indeed. Had their valor been fully appreciated, who can say that the liberty of Europe might not have been won then and there? But for that a similar performance on the part of the Western Powers was necessary. The fact that it was not forthcoming, in spite of all the Allied promises, is a second reason for not overestimating the German accomplishment in that first campaign; for the victory that Hitler won there was nothing but gambler's luck.

We know that Hitler staked everything on the belief that the British and the French would not advance. Neither his clairvoyance nor his superior strategy, but simply and solely the incompetence of the West provided him at that fateful moment with an antagonist — perhaps collaborator would be the better word — of the temper of Gamelin. Gamelin was precisely the type of opposing commander that the dictator needed; a general of the old school, dragged down by memories of the wearing, endless battles of 1918. Gamelin feared nothing more than an attempt to break through heavily fortified lines of defense. He was the type of European who had remained untouched by a dynamic epoch; who detested risks and wanted only to wait; who was dead-set against recognizing that it might be necessary to take the offensive in order to defend peace.

Because Gamelin refused to risk a fight, Hitler won his gamble. We Germans have no right to cite the military and political sins of the other side as excuses for ourselves; but for all Europeans the clear recognition of their onetime reluctance to fight can be transformed into a source of creative power, just as the honest admission of their guilt can redeem the Germans.

Had Halder waited for Gamelin to break through? Did he resign himself to the inevitable only when the 'setback' did not occur?

Poland lay shattered; the Warsaw victory parade was over; and now Hitler's generals were overcome by fear. Was it absolutely necessary for the war to go on to the end — or was some compromise still

possible? Outwardly Germany appeared to be standing tense and
firm, taking a deep breath before plunging headlong into the un-
plumbed abysses of a great war. In reality fearful confusion reigned
in all authoritative quarters.

Hitler brooded and tormented himself. He instinctively felt that he
himself must take the active rôle, but he knew that the decision involved total war, irrevocable, all-destructive war. Once he gave the
signal, the only remaining alternatives would be victory or ruin. He
remembered very well what had happened in 1918, when the human
and material resources of America came to the rescue of the hard-
pressed Allies. Germany must not again be outstripped by time. Because he felt this pressure of time, he conceived the idea of striking
an unexpected blow, violating the neutral countries and trying for a
surprise triumph on the widest possible front. Who can say how often
his restless mind had already traveled that blood-stained military
route that led from Holland into the Belgian flank and from there
straight across France to the Pyrenees?

Although Hitler dreamed of an incomparable triumph, his generals
were alarmed. They knew how perilous that road was. In October
and November, 1939, they still had inhibitions about entrusting their
personal lives and their country's destiny to the unbalanced visions of
'the greatest military leader of all time.' They were still afraid both
of what would take place if the revolutionary Fuehrer won and what
would happen if he lost. At last they had come face to face with the
question of whether an outright overthrow of the government would
not be cheaper than the otherwise inevitable carnage.

A savage struggle began — between the unhappy generals and their
Fuehrer; between the worried civilians and the military demi-gods;
between the generals' own doubts and irresolution and their longing
for glory. For weeks the decision hung by a thread. More than once
it appeared that the outcome of the war would be decided, not on the
battlefield, but among the cliques of conspirators in the *Oberkommando der Wehrmacht.*

At that time our group of friends put out the first tentative feelers
to determine whether and how we could act in unison with the

'enemy.' I use the word 'unison' deliberately because I want to avoid any misunderstanding. In these first peace feelers, as in all others, we never wanted to produce a victorious peace for Hitler or for Nazism. We knew if Hitler survived any peace that was concluded, the practical result would be a stabilization of his system and a justification of his unscrupulous foreign policy.

We were aiming at something entirely different, but for the present we had to discover whether it would be at all possible to deal with the Allies. We wanted to take precautions against the new 'stab-in-the-back' legend to the extent that the opposing armies would not fall upon Germany at the moment we opened our civil war. Above all, we wanted to prove to the wavering generals that there was another recourse besides plunging blindly ahead, that it would be possible to put an end to the war honorably — although we would undoubtedly have to make the concessions that the Allies would justly demand in order to guarantee that they would not be dragged into another military adventure within a few years.

Our previous experience had shown that all pleas to the generals were vain as soon as Hitler set a fixed date on which the armies were to march. Then, they held, it was no longer time to be concocting seditious plans. Therefore, we had to anticipate Hitler. We must so fortify the opposition among the generals that the intuitive Hitler would not dare to set the critical date. To do this we had to show Brauchitsch and Halder that there were tangible chances for peace if they would precipitate the occasion by refusing to obey Hitler's order to take the offensive.

Once more Oster took this responsibility upon himself. With the outbreak of the war he had been promoted and had become one of the four department heads within the *Abwehr*. Within an intelligence service many things can be managed so that they escape the eyes even of so ubiquitous an espionage organization as the Gestapo. Oster proved this during his first weeks in his new post by cautiously establishing certain foreign ties. Doctor Joseph Mueller took his first trip to the Vatican. The inquiries he made there and the answers he received gave us the right to assure Halder and Brauchitsch that all

bonds had not been severed and that there were still understanding
people on the enemy side who were willing to collaborate toward an
honest liquidation of the Nazi system.

But was it not likely that the generals would reply that they knew
nothing officially about such offers? At last we decided to take a
carefully considered step. Our generals would certainly pay attention
if the President of the United States intervened and personally
guaranteed that a just peace would be concluded with a denazified
Germany. Therefore, Schacht sent a letter to America in the hope
that the recipient, Frazer, former president of the Bank of International Trade, would bring it to the attention of President Roosevelt.

What we had in mind was to restrain Hitler until the opposing
forces could gather strength. At the same time we planned on more
than action by the generals. Since it seemed to us more and more
dubious that they would ever act, we had decided to strike at the
critical point of Nazi rule: the temper of the people. Up to the very
last year of the war, Hitler was singularly tremulous about the psychological reactions of the masses. It was a curious phenomenon, con-
trasting strongly with his usual brutality. Did he know intuitively
not only that he affected the masses suggestively, but that he was also
borne along by the popular mood?

The dictator's caution in this respect went so far that until shortly
before July 20, 1944, he could not bring himself to proclaim total
war; he did not go even so far as the British had gone long since. Up
to the last months of the war the principal exponents of the popular
temper, the women, were not drafted. It was out of the same concern
for safeguarding this source of mystic strength that he ordered the
Party propaganda system to spread all sorts of peace rumors in the
fall of 1939.

We thought we could trap the Nazis in the net of their own peace
talk. We would seize their slogans; we would, so to speak, try to
extract some truth out of the propagandist lies. The Nazis at the time
were mysteriously hinting that Hitler was engaged in vital diplomatic negotiations, that things were not half so bad as they seemed,
and that the war declaration was merely a matter of form. What we

wanted was to launch a real peace offensive. In short, we wanted to point out to the Germans which persons were merely pretending and which were actually ready to negotiate.

Before the Polish invasion the dictator had tricked his generals by proffering an 'ironclad' guaranty that the war would not spread. It was clear, now that the Western Powers had not taken the invasion of Poland lying down, that any further action would ignite the world conflagration. All that was needed now was three or four months of public discussion in which Hitler would be forced to declare himself. Otherwise the 'phony' war would do us no good. Unless it were accompanied by a propaganda offensive its effect would necessarily boomerang: because the Germans would no longer take the war seriously their concern about peace would lapse. The German people must be told that they were letting themselves into a life-and-death struggle. The Nazis' 'divisive' propaganda must be counteracted. The ideal person to do this was the President of the United States. He was still considered non-partisan, and his name was highly respected in Germany in spite of — or perhaps because of — the Nazi slanders against him.

Roosevelt had, of course, already made several sincere appeals without eliciting any response but a mocking echo. It was perhaps asking too much to request him to mediate once more. He might well make the obvious objection that first the Germans themselves ought to bring about some fundamental changes. It was to this that Schacht was alluding when he wrote:

> My feeling is that gaining time will help a great deal at the present moment. . . . There are people who think it might be too early to discuss plans before certain conditions have taken place. I am starting from another point. My feeling is that the earlier discussions should be opened, the earlier it will be to influence the development of certain existing conditions.[1]

I smuggled this letter to Switzerland; Oster arranged a trip for me especially for this purpose. Unfortunately, it was all in vain. No

[1] In English in the original.

reply came from across the Atlantic. Inwardly, Roosevelt had already made his decision. He had resolved to burn the Nazi canker out, root and stalk. Consequently, there was only one course left open to him. Gradually he drifted farther and farther from the rôle of mediator, until at last he was able to throw the decisive power of America openly into the scales.

THREE CRITICAL WEEKS

DURING THE LATTER PART OF OCTOBER, while I was in Zurich, I received a telegram recalling me to Berlin. Somewhat reluctantly I took the next train to the capital. By then I was all too familiar with those alarms which at first awakened high hopes and ended in depressing disillusionments. My premonitions were correct; Schacht and Oster were already regretting having sent the telegram. For a time, they told me, it had appeared that something was in the air. Hitler had flown to Berchtesgaden a few days before to retire into his usual brooding silence. Then he had surprised the drowsing generals with a revised plan of campaign. By mid-November at the latest he wanted to begin the offensive in the West, but no more had come of this than a brief shock. Upon the urgent representations of Brauchitsch and Halder the dictator had given ground. For some days now he had communicated with no one. Apparently he was ready to renounce this latest notion; consequently, any chance for a *Putsch* also had to be postponed.

A thousand rumors were flying around Berlin, but it still appeared utterly fantastic that Hitler should launch an attack against the Western Powers. It would be much more sensible for him to wait on the defensive behind the Siegfried Line. A brutal invasion of Belgium and Holland seemed equally inconceivable. In time we became accustomed to such violations of neutrality, but in 1939 our conception of international law had not yet been blunted, so that even the generals were tormented by scruples.

On October 30 the spell was broken. We learned that Hitler had finally resolved to strike and had set November 12 as the date for the offensive. For us this news initiated a period of intense activity. We were determined to exert all the strength we had; to implore, argue, and cajole.

During this period I made some notes which I concealed inside of some innocent-looking atlases. I hid them so well that later on I was no longer able to find some of the notes. Others may have become a bit mixed up. I can, therefore, offer no more than rather inadequate recollections of a vital period in world history.

In a sense this casual diary may be said to reflect only the under-currents, for it deals with the mental distraction and the condition of incessant civil war of nerves, rather than with the drama of political and strategical decisions that were made — or rather not made — at the time. In the first place, it makes clear how hotly contested the great turning-point of the war actually was. In the second place, it is clear that the internal situation in Germany in the fall of 1939 and the spring of 1940 was basically different from what it was conceived to be by those in the enemy and neutral camps. Thirdly, it proves once more that in times of historic upheavals the fate of nations depends not so much upon the resolution or the daring of the great brigands as it does upon the irresoluteness and cowardice of those who are called — but not chosen — to defend freedom.

October 31, 1939

OSTER, his assistant von Dohnanyi, and I went to see Thomas in the morning to discuss what we could do to prevent the imminent disaster. The general thought the military-political situation hopeless. He was certain that sooner or later any offensive would bog down, either immediately at the bridges over the Rhine and Meuse or in the mud of Flanders. His armament program had not provided for lengthy battles of attrition.

On the other hand, there did not seem to be any openings for us. Halder would no longer see Oster. Beck was also out of the running.

Canaris had resigned himself to the worst. All the generals who had any say were scattered over various sectors of the front. By the time all of them could be consulted and their various views co-ordinated, the critical date — November 12 — would be upon us.

We discussed Halder's setback theory and the problem of the junior officers. Thomas reluctantly admitted that the young officers were in a pernicious state of mind. Their confidence in Hitler's leadership had been tremendously fortified by those first victories and by the absence of any threats from the West. Now they were eager for new heroic feats. This was a critical factor that we could not afford to overlook.

Thomas declared his readiness to mediate between us and Halder once more. We agreed to draw up a memorandum for him to present to Halder, once more summarizing all the political arguments against launching an offensive.

I warned Thomas that Halder would surely reject the idea of a *coup d'état.* Instead, he would probably return to his suggestion that Hitler be assassinated, for that digression enabled him to evade open discussion of a revolt. I advised Thomas not to reject this suggestion at the outset, but at least to listen in order to find out what Halder had on his mind.

The amazed horror this suggestion evoked afforded me a certain satisfaction. I was pleased to find a general who could not believe his chief of staff capable of such ideas. Even Oster, who remembered perfectly well the scene to which I was alluding, thought it out of the question that Halder would mention again those peculiar plans he had broached in the summer of 1938.

November 1

IN THE MORNING Dohnanyi visited me at home so that we could discuss the memorandum without disturbance. The memorandum was not hard to compose. We showed why an offensive in the West must constitute a politically irrevocable mistake. The deliberate violations of the neutral countries would discredit the generals forever. We showed, on the basis of Joseph Mueller's first reports from the Vatican, that the Allies were willing to consider the question of peace. Thus we cut off a possible line of retreat for Halder. Point by point we exposed Goebbels's 'divisive' propaganda.

By that afternoon it appeared that I had missed the mark. There was good news from Zossen. Oster's secret intelligence service reported great excitement at the headquarters. There were unmistakable signs of that extreme tension that always prevailed shortly before important actions. Perhaps our efforts to influence Halder would prove superfluous; perhaps he had already decided to 'act.'

November 2

THOMAS went to see Halder in the morning. The chief of staff became candid and talkative. He used the most energetic phrases and let fall meaningful hints. In conclusion he returned to his idea of assassination and spoke at length about it. This solution still seemed to him the most practicable. He was absolutely resolved to give no occasion for another stab-in-the-back legend.

In the afternoon Halder ordered Oster to come to see him at headquarters. The conversation between the two officers could not have been clearer or more open. Halder at once requested Oster to reconstruct and if necessary to supplement his preliminary studies of the previous year. Not a word was said about assassination; the entire discussion centered around revolt. As soon as Hitler gave the final order for the offensive in the West, Halder would start a *Putsch*.

At Halder's request, Oster spoke with General von Stuelpnagel, the chief of staff's deputy. Chief Quartermaster-General Stuelpnagel was no less frank. He gave Oster full details and even mentioned the name of the general whose panzer corps was to take care of the most urgent tasks in Berlin. This concrete naming of names reassured us, for it showed they had already got past the contemplative stage.

Late at night I met Oster, who told me how profoundly impressed he had been by his conversation with Halder, and how moved by their parting. When Halder accompanied him to the door and shook hands with him, Oster had expressed the heartfelt wish that the general would come to a 'strong and noble resolution.' There had been tears in the chief of staff's eyes, Oster reported.

November 3

LIEUTENANT-COLONEL GROSSKURTH, one of Halder's closest associates and also a confidant of Oster, joyfully informed us that the time had come at last. Halder had instructed him to warn Beck and Goerdeler to hold themselves in readiness from November 5 on. Grosskurth reported that all the details were being carefully worked out at Zossen. Officers were making extremely careful studies of the chancellery blueprints, looking for possible underground exits.

November 5

INTENSIVE ACTIVITY. Once more the atmosphere was feverish like that before Munich in 1938. I rushed back and forth between OKW, police headquarters, the ministry of the interior, Beck, Goerdeler, Schacht, Helldorf, Nebe, and a number of other places and persons.

Brauchitsch and Halder flew to the West in the morning. Allegedly on an inspection tour, they intended to discuss practical procedures with the most important generals. Their plan was to wait for Hitler's command to launch the offensive and then to refuse to transmit the order to their subordinates. For them to do this effectively, the collaboration of the army group commanders was essential. The best part of it was that these commanders were precisely the ones who, conscious of the difficulties, strongly objected to an autumn offensive. Therefore, they would be glad for Brauchitsch and Halder to provide an example, enabling them, as it were, to mutiny on orders from above.

The next day Brauchitsch was slated to report to Hitler. The final decision was to be made then.

Goerdeler, as usual, was already composing his premature lists of ministers. Beck had to admonish him in a friendly fashion to keep a grip on himself, but since Halder had communicated officially with him, Goerdeler felt his optimism perfectly justified. Popitz, Planck, and Hassell were also getting ready for the great event. Schacht was skeptical as usual. 'Just you watch,' he said. 'Hitler will smell a rat and will not announce any decision at all tomorrow.'

November 5

GENERAL WAGNER, quartermaster-general IV, visited Schacht, employing the pretext that he wished to discuss currency problems that would crop up in Belgium after occupation. Without beating about the bush, he stated that he had come on orders from his chief. The chief of staff sent his greetings to Schacht and wished to remind the minister of their conversations of last summer. Halder requested Schacht to hold himself in readiness.

We were, of course, as ready as we should ever be. All of us were fearfully tense and eager. But we had become slightly uneasy, for as yet — it was now evening — we had heard nothing specific about the conference between Brauchitsch and Hitler. Had the decision been postponed again?

I sat up with Goerdeler until late at night. He refused to admit any doubts and was already deep in his plans for the future. He had everything worked out so clearly and convincingly and apparently unemotionally that one was carried along by his faith.

November 6

OVERNIGHT our obscure premonitions had come true. At Zossen everybody was in the throes of a general nervous crisis. Perhaps this is putting it too moderately; it was more like a state of panicked confusion. What in Heaven's name had happened now?

Later

WE FOUND OUT, although it was no simple matter. Whenever responsible generals were taking the 'road back,' they covered their tracks with remarkable adroitness. It took Oster's informants precious hours to find out details; special couriers had been speeding back and forth between Zossen and Berlin. After all, Oster and Grosskurth themselves could not be continually on the go. Now and then they had to sit in their offices and pretend to be attending to their duties. Canaris was particularly insistent upon such burdensome formalities; he did not want Oster to show his distraction too ostentatiously.

Yesterday the expected conference between Brauchitsch and Hitler had taken place. There was a sharp clash when the general expressed his fears about the offensive. All his strategical arguments were repulsed; Hitler did not even listen to his political arguments. At last the commander-in-chief of the army brought up one of his heavy guns — which he should not have done. Brauchitsch declared to Hitler that the morale among the troops was so poor that they could not risk such a daring enterprise.

That was the last straw. Hitler worked up the usual fit of rage. He must have bellowed fearfully at Brauchitsch. Finally he ordered him to supply immediate proofs for his shameless assertion. That evening urgent telegrams were sent out to the army commanders. Now they were all sitting in a sweat, wondering how on the one hand to prove poor morale and on the other hand not to offend Hitler.

The entire conversation lasted only twenty minutes. But this concentrated dose was more effective than the usual palaver that, in the past, would go on for hours. Brauchitsch suffered a real nervous breakdown; and of course Halder, too, was soon bawling like a baby. That man Halder! We might have known!

General von Stuelpnagel was carried away by the panic. He sent for Lieutenant-Colonel Grosskurth and excitedly ordered him to destroy all the dangerous papers — by which he did not mean the plans for the offensive in the West. Halder was in a panic about all those promises he had given and lists he had received — material on which for a few days we had so naïvely based our hopes.

To make the let-down complete, we heard from Zossen a few hours later that a date had been set for the entire headquarters to transfer to operational headquarters in the West. Halder was to leave on the eighth, Brauchitsch on the ninth of November. We knew only too well what that meant. Once those heroes at headquarters embarked on their special train, all prospect for any kind of decision would be gone for good.

This afternoon there was a certain relaxation. Apparently the generals had reconsidered more calmly. At any rate, they suddenly recalled that they had a specific reason for wanting to revolt: they had intended to forestall a military disaster.

Brauchitsch recovered to the extent that he frankly admitted he had permitted Hitler to take him by surprise. He still felt that the offensive would be fatal and ought to be prevented at all costs. But how? When Halder asked Brauchitsch this question in the presence of a third officer, the commander-in-chief shrugged. 'I myself shall do nothing, but I will not oppose anyone who does do something. . . .'

Apparently that was permission enough for the chief of staff. In his name Grosskurth transmitted to the chief of German counter-intelligence the urgent request that Canaris have Hitler assassinated. If that condition were fulfilled, he, Halder, would be willing to take 'action.'

Canaris's angry refusal to listen to more was perfectly understandable. It was one thing for Halder to discuss plans which he was ready to carry out himself; it was quite another thing when he passed on such indiscreet commissions to his subordinates. Canaris was so infuriated that it was impossible for Oster or for me to intervene.

The admiral sent word to the chief of staff that if he, Halder, wished to discuss such grave political measures, he ought to do it in person. He demanded that Halder take the responsibility in a manly fashion, and added that before he would consider assassination every possibility for an open military revolt would have to be exhausted.

In the afternoon Canaris had an interview with the Fuehrer. He returned in a very downcast mood. Hitler had personally dictated that troops of the *Abwehr* dressed in Dutch and Belgian uniforms were to be secretly landed to stand guard and prevent bridges from being blown up. Such gangster methods, otherwise known as Hitler's military 'dodges,' had not been customary in the German army. Three months before I had first heard from Nebe how the expected Polish 'attack' on German troops was arranged. The Gestapo was going to send newsreel operators to the spot at the precise moment to film the scene. A few days after this brilliant idea had been hit on, the Gestapo requested the *Abwehr* to supply some Polish uniforms for 'purposes of study.' I had passed Nebe's information on to Canaris, and the admiral protested to Brauchitsch. The result was a slight change in plans. Instead of 'attacking' German troops, the disguised Gestapo criminals merely made a raid on the radio station at Gleiwitz.

Now this shameful abuse of foreign uniforms was to be repeated on a greater scale. Canaris was very much disturbed. He asked us whether he ought to resign, but this question was largely a matter of form; he often asked it in order to have us confirm his indispensability; for what would we do if his protection were no longer available?

The offensive, Canaris informed us, would begin as scheduled, on the morning of November 12 at seven-fifteen.

I then went to see Oster and asked him whether he thought we should make one last attempt to influence the generals at the Zossen headquarters. Would it not be a good idea for us to revive our old plans, which had taken as their starting-point a fictional Goering-Himmler uprising? What I proposed was easier than ever to carry out precisely because of all the confusion. The soldiers would certainly not have objected to disarming the *Waffen-SS* and clamping down on the Gestapo. The invented claim would have the advantage of being in its essence close to the truth. Moreover, the grapevine was already replete with rumors about the measures that Hitler allegedly or actually intended to take on the home front while the army was busy with its war.

Late at night Oster went to Zossen, taking with him a number of hastily drafted proclamations which he intended to show to his intimates at headquarters. Oster's friends approved the idea at once. The allegation of an SS uprising was far more congenial to the military mentality than the proposal that Hitler be declared insane. Oster's journey to Zossen proved worth while from another point of view. A few hours before, he was informed, Halder had sighed heavily and declared that he wanted to take action, but was powerless without Witzleben's backing. That was enough for Oster; he decided at once that Witzleben must come to Zossen. But Witzleben was now an army commander in the West. Someone would have to see him and explain it all to him. Oster and I were the only ones available.

November 7

BEFORE WE LEFT we visited Thomas. We described what had happened the day before, showed him my drafts of proclamations, and discussed what proposals we would make to Witzleben. Thomas supplemented Oster's account of the mood at Zossen. He too thought that nothing could be done without Witzleben. Halder would listen to him; the colonel-general possessed the authority of rank and age which we unfortunately lacked.

Because of the blackout we did not get farther than Frankfurt-am-Main. I did not tell Oster until after we had started that I had packed my bags. If Witzleben did not give an absolutely affirmative answer, I intended to stay in Germany just long enough to visit Kluge in Cologne. Then I was going to Zurich.

November 8

EARLY IN THE MORNING we continued on to Kreuznach. At ten o'clock, the mist was still so dense that we could scarcely see our way in the streets. We could not have desired a more vivid demonstration of what madness it was to launch a mechanized offensive in such weather. For some time we had to wait in Kreuznach. This was annoying, for Oster had wanted to be back in Berlin that same day, but Witzleben's health had not been too good of late, and he was using the opportunity of his stay in Kreuznach to take the waters. Our first impression upon seeing the general was not at all a happy one. Physically at least he appeared in need of rest, and not in readiness for action. Psychically as well, Witzleben was rather low. He no longer believed the order for the offensive could be canceled, and he considered the chances for the success of the enterprise virtually zero. His troops, of course, faced the Maginot Line directly, but even farther north, on the unfortified front where the invasion was to take place, the generals in command of the panzer divisions and Reichenau in particular were warning against the operation. The autumn mud would make the use of tanks almost impossible.

Witzleben did not believe there was any chance at all to influence Brauchitsch and Halder. The two were hopeless cases now, he said. He had recently seen them on their inspection tour of the West and Brauchitsch had impressed him as being in a particularly wretched state of mind. Imagine, the commander-in-chief of the army had confided to Witzleben that he no longer felt personally safe! 'Heydrich is after me,' he had said. When Witzleben retorted, 'Why don't you arrest him?' Brauchitsch had not answered.

While we were talking with Witzleben, the colonel-general received an urgent telephone message. The transfer of headquarters to Giessen had been postponed seventy-two hours, and the offensive was being put off for the same length of time. Hitler probably considered it wiser to let a decent interval pass between the pacific proposals of the Dutch and Belgian monarchs and his invasion of their countries.

It required lengthy persuasion before Witzleben could be induced to override his misgivings and visit Halder — and then only on condition that his group commander, von Leeb, consented. He asked Oster to prepare the ground with Leeb's chief of staff, who he said was one of those 'on the right side.'

We returned to Frankfurt, where Oster paid a call on the colonel in the group command staff who was supposed to be 'on the right side.' After a while he returned gloomily. As soon as the colonel had heard of our intentions, he became frightened out of his wits and could not be calmed until Oster supplied him with a pretext for evading our request.

It was clear to me that the time had come for me to leave for

Switzerland. We parted late at night; Oster intended to return to Berlin early in the morning and I wanted to catch up on lost sleep.

November 9

CONTRARY TO OUR AGREEMENT, Oster woke me early. While I rubbed my eyes, I heard him saying through the haze of sleep: 'Hans, they tried to do for our Emil yesterday.'

I was suddenly electrified and was wide awake at once. Oster summarized for me what he had read in the morning newspapers. Yesterday had been the day for the traditional Nazi memorial meeting in the Hofbraeuhaus at Munich. Hitler had made his customary oration. Not five minutes after he left the room a bomb had exploded with a tremendous noise and brought the room down on the heads of the guests. There were seven dead and sixty-three injured.

Oster, with his usual unemotionalism, considered this brief summary sufficient and started off. I barely had time to call out to him my friendly advice that now the only thing to do was to arrest Himmler as the terrorist. I was so annoyed at his haste to return to Berlin that I angrily called out that now I should certainly go to Switzerland, but my vexation was quickly dissipated and I reconsidered. Evidently some group close to ours had decided to strike of its own accord. The Gestapo would certainly not fail to settle accounts.

By evening I was in the capital. There were no Gestapo men watching the exit from the railroad terminal; there were no cordons in the streets; and the people in the city did not seem especially excited or tense. In fact, there was not the slightest sign that anything extraordinary had happened. I was pleased, for it confirmed my assertion that even an unsuccessful assassination would not necessarily result in bloody retaliation by the Gestapo, as our anxious bourgeois habitually claimed whenever they issued warnings against uprisings and 'unconsidered individual actions.'

November 10

HELLDORF sent his chauffeur to fetch me in his car. I felt tremendously excited; I thought I should now hear incredible tales. Instead, the Berlin chief of police asked me whether I had any idea who the assassins were. He knew not one whit more than had already appeared in the newspapers.

I was unable to get in touch with Nebe. Undoubtedly he had been ordered to Munich to assist in the detective work. I therefore had to subsist on mere guesses and outlined to Helldorf the conclusions I had come to during my railroad journey of the day before. Helldorf was in complete agreement with me. My spontaneous exclamation to Oster, which had been my first reaction, had imperceptibly become organized in my mind: Himmler, and preferably Goering as well, must be arrested at once as the chief suspects. Who could say how many hours still remained to us if we wanted to forestall a counter-blow by the SS?

Oster, whose nerves were on edge, had all sorts of unpleasant news. An army officer had already been arrested. Admiral Canaris was badly worried and had warned him to exercise more caution. I made the insolent remark that our caution would only land us in Himmler's dungeons. Then I informed my friend that I was going to write a letter to Halder.

I set to work dictating at once and did not finish until noon. What I wrote was a kind of miniature criminological study of the Munich affair, based on the sparse information in the newspapers. I stressed three facts. In the first place, Himmler and Goering had not been present at the meeting. In the past they had always attended this 'historic' demonstration. In the second place, it was obvious that something had been amiss from the start. According to everyone who had heard the radio broadcast, Hitler had abruptly ended his speech. He had cut it short while still in the first phase of his rhetorical pattern, so that perfectly unsuspecting and politically innocent people had wondered at this truncation. They wondered all the more when they read of the bomb plot in the morning newspapers.

The third consideration carried the most weight. All of us had spent so much time reflecting on the possibilities of assassination that we knew only too well how difficult it was to place a bomb correctly. Halder certainly should appreciate that. Apparently the Munich bomb had been installed very skillfully. The time fuse ticked away inside the column directly back of the speaker's platform. Was it conceivable that so complicated an installation could have been carried out with impunity under the watchful eyes of the Gestapo?

I explained in detail that all the information that had been published so far was on the face of it implausible. In addition, the reactions of Gestapo and chancellery, or rather the lack of any 'lightning-like' revelations, suggested that something was amiss. It seemed more than incredible that Hitler should have stood under a bomb which exploded five minutes after he left the hall. It seemed far more likely that 'Providence' had tipped him off in advance. In that case the agents of Providence must have been members of his intimate circle. Communists or other 'enemies of state' could scarcely have informed him of the favor he was about to receive.

The long and short of it was that I showed Halder exactly what reasons made it imperative that the army do something to 'protect' the chief of state. The least the Munich bombing proved was that the SS was not competent to guarantee Hitler's safety. Consequently, the soldiers ought to leap into the breach. Halder would have no difficulty guessing what kind of 'protective custody' I had in mind.

While I was dictating this memorandum, Oster came in and with a meaningful glance handed me a dispatch that had just been brought in. According to a radioed report from the frontier station of Loerrach, a certain Herr Elser of Munich, a carpenter by trade, had been arrested on the night of November 8-9 while attempting illegal entry into Switzerland. The arrested man was suspected of complicity in the Munich bomb plot because a photograph had been found on his person showing an interior view of the Hofbraeukeller, with one of the columns marked by a cross.

Oster shook his head. 'There we have Lubbe Number 2' was all he said. Then he returned to his desk. I myself was too occupied with my dictation to waste words in unnecessary conversation. Offhand, this punctual arrest seemed to me more stupid than was customary even for the Gestapo.

In addition to my criminological memorandum, I wrote a personal letter to Halder. I made it brief and to the point. Almost exactly two years before, I said, I had sent such a memorandum to his predecessor, Ludwig Beck. At that time, too, my hypotheses had appeared quite daring at first reading, but in the course of the investigation of the Fritsch case my suspicions had been fully confirmed. This time it might well turn out the same way. Therefore, I begged to suggest that the chief of staff read the appended memorandum very carefully.

Around six o'clock the letter and the enclosure were sent to Zossen by special courier — with the knowledge and consent of Canaris.

By evening the confusion reached its climax with the sudden announcement that the offensive had been completely suspended. I went to see Beck, Schacht, and Helldorf in quick succession. Then I had a strained talk with Goerdeler. For some inexplicable reason that optimist seemed to think that everything looked rosy.

November 11

I BEGAN my day's peregrinations by visiting Helldorf, because overnight I had decided that it was time we found out something definite about the Munich bombing. Otherwise we would scarcely know how to forestall Hitler's or Himmler's plans.

There appeared to be no doubt that the bomb had been the work of a group. This group could have consisted of Communists, clericals, discontented Nazi Party members or 'reactionaries,' daring officers or SS men acting on Himmler's — or possibly even on Hitler's — orders. In each case the reaction from the chancellery would be different. Therefore, I suggested to Helldorf that he go to see Goering and inform the field marshal that he was gravely concerned about police protection for the Fuehrer in Berlin. It seemed likely that Goering would make some slip which would provide us with invaluable information.

Helldorf leaped at this idea. He telephoned Koerner, Goering's under-secretary, to ask that an audience be arranged. Meanwhile, there was nothing to do but wait for some echo of my letter to Halder.

I did not have to wait long, and the reply was absurdly unequivocal. Grosskurth had personally handed my letter to the chief of staff. As soon as Halder heard that it was from me, he showed unmistakable annoyance. Mistrustfully, he inquired whether Grosskurth knew me well. Then he declared, 'I intend to tear up this letter immediately.' He then made a number of unpleasant allusions to Oster. He was going too far, Halder said; he ought to be warned.

This total defection on the part of Halder increased our curiosity about what had really happened at Munich. Meanwhile, the chancellery kept us guessing. The offensive which had been canceled was now, it was said, slated for November 19.

I was now all for beating a final retreat. If these generals were willing to put up with this undignified game of turning on and turning off the offensive, if they themselves had not the least idea what they really wanted, there was no hope at all and we had better give up sticking our necks out. I put it as crudely as that to Oster. My remarks took hold the better because Canaris had at last had enough of the whole business. I had to admit that the admiral had been right all along in his estimation of the characters of Halder, Raeder, Keitel, and Brauchitsch. Probably his crushing judgment of the other important generals was equally valid. In any case, Canaris forbade Oster to engage in any further 'putschist' activities.

The chief of staff wished Oster to know that he had heard about his trip to the Western Front. He had also heard that Oster had 'traveled around' and that he had even carried manuscripts with him. Oster was a singularly good-natured person, but this time he too lost patience. He became furiously indignant and sent a rude and angry message to Halder.

At bottom we were glad that the air was cleared at last. On the other hand, the impudence of that man Halder was really incredible. First, he kept agitating everyone around him, so that his associates thought he would certainly start a revolt any moment. Then he exploited Oster's zeal, so that Oster supplied him with incriminating material and got himself into all sorts of perilous situations. Then he conspired with a great many other friends and sent them indiscreet messages. Then he ordered Canaris to arrange an assassination. Then he became terrified of his own boldness, and brooded about whether, under the complicated structure of military hierarchy, he could deliver an unnecessary and insulting warning to Oster. . . .

November 12. Pause.

November 13

THE NEW WEEK began on a humorous note. Yesterday at noon Grosskurth spied my letter — allegedly torn up at once — lying on Halder's desk. The chief of staff noticed his subordinate's glance resting on the manuscript. Discomfited, he apparently felt called upon to admit that he had read my exposition with interest and believed that it was correct. He had shown it to Brauchitsch, he said, and the commander-in-chief had also agreed.

In the afternoon Stuelpnagel telephoned Oster and asked him to come to see him. Oster refused to go to Zossen. What was the use?

November 14

STUELPNAGEL again called Oster and declared that he must speak to him; it was a matter of the greatest urgency. Hesitantly, Oster yielded. After all, one could never know whether those generals at Zossen might not have been struck by a revelation from above during the night. He had a good excuse for going; at the urging of Goering the offensive had been postponed once more, this time to November 22. The reason given was bad weather. When I called on Oster in the afternoon, I found him alternating between laughter and outbursts of fury. All Stuelpnagel had wanted was to pass on to him Halder's order that Oster burn all his papers.

November 15

MUCH ADO ABOUT NOTHING. Telephone calls, conferences, crisscross rides about the city. Helldorf was going to try again to get an interview with Goering. It was curious, to say the least, that Goering should ignore the Berlin police chief's proposal and should not even receive him.

November 16

AT HEADQUARTERS in Zossen the generals seemed to be spinning in a whirligig. To introduce a note of novelty into their daily embarrassment, these great strategists had now hit on the idea of getting the backing of the big industrialists. In any case, on November 15 Hugo Stinnes was asked by Halder to prepare for a talk with Brauchitsch.

It was still not certain that the offensive would 'finally' take place on the twenty-second — the decision was to be made today. Canaris told me that now all of Holland instead of merely the Maestricht corner was to be occupied.

The admiral could merely shake his head in wonderment. He could not understand how Brauchitsch, Halder, and the other staff generals could consent to an adventure which all the experts were certain would fail. If the Dutch blew up their bridges in time — and it seemed hardly likely that they would not — the tank advance would not even get started. This would give the Belgians at least a chance to offer effective resistance. Gaining time meant everything to the other side, for Gamelin would not wait idly by, but would march into Belgium at once.

Canaris thought that the inevitable outcome would be Halder's pet setback. Once more the admiral lamented at length what a misfortune this war was. I could scarcely endure to listen, so black a picture did he paint. As I left, I asked him to tell me once more quite honestly — leaving aside all professional pessimism — whether he really believed that this famous setback would actually take place. At that he laughed loudly. Disaster was as certain as death this time, he said.

Then his whole mood abruptly changed. He began philosophizing about how terrible it was that he in his position could still laugh over such a matter. I exploited this mood of softened melancholy to give

him a piece of advice that had been on my mind for some time. More
and more it seemed to me that the continual postponements of the
offensive could be attributed to Goering, who was not at all anxious
for the war to begin. When he could get no further with pretexts
about bad flying weather, he might, if the circumstances were right,
try that violent overthrow of Hitler which the generals did not have
the courage to attempt. I implored Canaris to keep on the alert and,
in case Hitler suddenly vanished from the scene, to use all his influence
to insure that the *Wehrmacht* did not swear a new oath to Nazi
Number 2. But Canaris merely answered despondently: 'Take my
word for it, that is exactly what will happen.'

November 17

OSTER was able to obtain a report on the conversation between
Brauchitsch and Hugo Stinnes. That incident represented the nadir of
our experiences with field marshals and aspirant field marshals.

Halder, it seemed, had brought the industrialist in to see Brauchitsch
at once. The two men had had a perfectly private *tête-à-tête*. At
times the astonished Stinnes had the impression that the commander-
in-chief of the German army considered him his father confessor.
Apparently Brauchitsch felt a strong urge to pour out his heart. He
considered the impending offensive pure madness. The undertaking
could only fail, he asserted, and the consequence would probably be
not a new 1918, but rather the end of the German Reich that
Bismarck had built up. He, Brauchitsch, had completely broken with
the Fuehrer. 'The situation is such that at any moment he might arrest
me or I him. But what can I do? None of my generals will talk to
me. . . . Will they follow me? I don't know what to do. Perhaps we
shall never see each other again in this life.'

Brauchitsch had given Stinnes the impression of a completely
broken man. Understandably enough, the industrialist was thoroughly
shocked.

This conversation was highly significant to us, too. On the one
hand, we were, of course, outraged. To think that such a creature

called himself the commander-in-chief of the army; that such a man could send hundreds of thousands of soldiers to their deaths! On the other hand, it seemed impossible that the situation could continue as it was. Perhaps this total nervous collapse of Brauchitsch offered us a chance. Might it not be a good idea to have a few more 'civilians' — say Goerdeler, Hassell, or Popitz — hammer away at Brauchitsch? Wasn't it possible that the man was simply waiting for someone to take him under his arms, prop him up, and push him along? Perhaps Beck ought to make one last attempt, not so much in an official capacity but rather as one man to another. However, Beck was not willing to subject himself to another rebuff. We had to admit that we were at the end of our rope.

At least another of Halder's pronunciamentos made it easier to resign ourselves to defeat. We heard that at the end of a lengthy monologue the chief of the general staff had sighed audibly and re-marked that he was happy to have arrived at a definite decision at last: he was going to do nothing at all. No comment is necessary. However, I might add that at the same time Halder had complained that he had scarcely been able to endure listening to Hitler's last speech. Dreadful to relate, he said, he had had to keep his radio on — because he did not trust his adjutant.

November 18

THE OFFENSIVE was postponed again, but it was absolutely and posi-tively to take place on November 26.

So much for my 'journal.' Thoroughly disgusted, I betook myself to the peaceful mountains of Switzerland. I no more expected the offensive to take place than a *Putsch* by the generals. Somehow I knew that that continuance of the war was being postponed until spring — and that thereby Hitler was saved.

During that November of 1939 the usurper skated by disaster three times. The first was when he rushed out of the Munich beer hall five minutes before the bomb exploded. The second was when he wore out the generals, who had at last summoned up the energy to act, by repeatedly postponing the offensive. Finally he had let his 'Providence' persuade him to wait. In the chaotic conditions I have described a sudden concrete order to launch the offensive might, after all, have evoked an uprising of the generals — certainly not a planned action, but some unpredictable, unforeseeable act of desperate self-defense. Even if this had not taken place, the unpopular offensive, if it had been launched six crucial months too soon, would certainly have meant the military end of Hitler.

In November, 1939, Hitler did not yet possess those 'secret weapons' with which in May, 1940, he surprised the Dutch and Belgians and, in fact, the general staffs of the rest of the world. In November, 1939, a dense autumnal fog covered the muddy and impassable fields of the Western Front. In November, 1939, above all, the 'phony' war had not yet gained much ground for the Nazis. The French soldiers had not yet gone through that enervating wait in and behind the Maginot Line while the Nazi loudspeakers blasted them with well-calculated defeatist propaganda.

November, 1939 — what tremendous potentialities still existed at that time for Germany, for Europe, for the whole world! But the time was not yet ripe for Hitler's downfall. First the destiny of Europe's North and West had to be fulfilled. Even then the stormy waves of the Revolution would surge on and on, southward to the Mediterranean, eastward almost to the Nile, until at last they mingled with the blood-stained stream of the Volga, until they broke against the myth-ridden mountainous wall of the Caucasus and at last gradually ebbed to nothing upon the endless reaches of the Russian steppes.

THE ZITHER PLAYER

MUCH OF THE SECRET HISTORY of the Third Reich remains to be revealed. In the brief period since the collapse we have had time only to skim through the many documents of that history. Our brief glimpse, however, has served to establish one remarkable fact: that Nazi reality was far more sober, far more banal, than the rumor-peddlers in all countries were willing to believe. Fundamentally, there are not too many secrets to come to light.

For example, how numerous were the alleged attempts at assassination that were 'reliably' reported? Again and again attacks on prominent Nazis — Himmler, Ley, Goering, Hitler most of all — were rumored. When all these tales came to nothing, the outside world found a simple explanation: there were no assassins; there was no opposition; eighty million Germans were submitting passively to tyranny.

Today we know that there were in fact very few attempts at assassination, but, on the other hand, that the resistance to Hitler was incomparably stronger than outsiders assumed. Are these two facts contradictory? Surely it is hard to comprehend how millions of Germans could see a terrible catastrophe gathering to overwhelm them and yet do nothing to stave it off; but have we not witnessed similar paralysis of will and inability to react in earlier times and under other systems of terror? At most we can say that in our mass age the sum of suffering has been raised to a higher power, and that in collective living individuals' sensitiveness to psychic and physical demands upon them has been dulled. The same mystery of submissiveness is illustrated by the four or five million murdered Jews who for years could have had no doubts as to their fate and who yet, even on the final march to death, did not attempt to take a few of their murderers with them into the next world. There is the even clearer example of the twelve million foreign laborers who lived in the Third Reich during the last years of the war. Virtually unguarded, or at any rate numerically and in united strength far surpassing their guards, they did not rise up until after the collapse. Night after night explosives were secretly dropped over Germany by planes for the use of this strongest of all fifth columns. The only one who made use of them was a German: Stauffenberg.

No one would wish to assert that all of these millions were

cowardly or lacking in resolution. That is not it. Rather, they simply did not have the opportunity to attempt an assassination. True enough, Hitler often drove more or less unprotected through crowds of people without being attacked; but spontaneous assassinations are very rare in history, and dictators prefer to make their public appearances a surprise. Whenever the Nazi leaders made a previously announced appearance, the measures taken for their protection were on a tremendous scale.

Since the end of the war, we have had many descriptions by 'insiders' of the protective cordon that even an army officer resolved on assassination would have to penetrate. After the war began, no civilians had any chance to come into Hitler's presence, except the highest state functionaries — who were Nazis. It was even more difficult to obtain an effective explosive. When these hurdles had been overcome, there still remained the indispensable political preparations; for what was the good of a successful assassination if afterward Goering or Himmler should take over — and of course launch a merciless purge and an intensified reign of terror?

An assassination without a simultaneous *Putsch* would be senseless. Responsible political men could not go in for anything of the sort. Therefore, it was not by chance that on November 8, 1939, a solitary fanatic and not an oppositional group ventured the great gamble.

The last mention I have made of this attack was Oster's informing me on November 9, 1939, of the incredible announcement that 'Lubbe Number 2' had been arrested. For days afterward we heard nothing at all. This intensified our suspicions. Ordinarily the Gestapo was very quick to supply 'explanations.' There were always some Jews, Bolshevists, reactionaries, priests, or other 'enemies of state' on hand when the Black hangmen needed to get themselves out of an embarrassing situation. Whether they organized their incidents themselves or waited for some pretext, the SS was never at a loss about striking back hard and fast.

Why was nothing happening this time? Did the SS intend to make particularly careful preparations for its counter-blow against the Opposition? We breathed easier when the newspapers reported that

Nebe had been appointed to head the investigating committee. Now we should find out what was going on. Moreover, it was ground for feeling a good deal safer, since Nebe either would make the investigation come to nought if any danger threatened us or deliberately lead it into a false track. On the other hand, we wondered a good deal about this appointment. It was highly unusual for the Gestapo to be barred from an investigation that was obviously a matter of highest politics. There must be cogent reasons for this.

Once again we had to wait patiently for days. No more exciting arrests were announced. The Gestapo maintained impenetrable silence. The most startling aspect of the affair was that even Goebbels, so ready with tongue and pen, refrained from making any threats at all.

When the results of the investigation were at last published, we burst into laughter. We would not have credited even the Nazi propagandists with such crude lies. Every line of the account seemed to prove that the Nazis were so upset by the truth that they had by mistake taken an overdose of their usual mendacity. It seemed obvious to us that Himmler or some other active Nazi of the group of 'old fighters' had been virtually convicted.

The very manner in which the news was presented stamped it as a fabrication of the propaganda ministry. All the newspapers were required to publish the sensational news on the first page and with every sentence in the same order. Two columns were placed side by side. In the first was the picture of 'Lubbe Number 2,' along with the details of how he had installed the bomb. His alleged employer was also unmasked: Otto Strasser, who was then living in Switzerland. In the adjacent column the arrest of two high functionaries of the British secret service was also reported. In the early morning hours of November 9, Colonels Best and Stevens had been lured to the German-Dutch border near Venlo, on the pretext that they were to meet members of the German Opposition. The two British colonels had then been kidnaped. A Dutch intelligence officer who had served as intermediary had been killed in the course of the kidnaping. The Dutch government was demanding the return of his body. Hitler now boasted to his generals that he had proved that the Dutch were violating their neutrality by collaborating with the British.

This search for a pretext for violating Dutch neutrality was, in fact, one of the chief reasons for the staging of this incident. Not even Goebbels dared to assert that there was any connection between the attempted assassination and the presence of the two British agents. The correlation was too improbable; the British would certainly not have met anyone to discuss the prospects of assassination if they had just instigated an unsuccessful attempt, but the appearance of the two stories in adjoining columns suggested to the innocent newspaper reader that an inner connection between them did exist.

As soon as Nebe returned from Munich, I asked him whether any-one in the chancellery or the Gestapo believed his detective story. His reply astonished me. Naturally, he said, neither Otto Strasser nor the British colonels had anything to do with the attack. 'Lubbe Number 2' was the actual assassin. Self-taught in planting bombs, he could well boast of having achieved a masterpiece.

At first the Gestapo had jealously tried to prevent any interference in the investigation by Nebe. As early as the morning of November 9, Heydrich had determined the plotters — not by name, of course, but roughly speaking. Himmler presented his Fuehrer with a list of forty — exactly forty — Bavarian legitimists whom he wished to have shot at once as agents and accomplices, in order to set a terrible ex-ample; but to Heydrich's and Himmler's alarm, Hitler had refused to approve any mass executions. Instead, he had demanded a more convincing explanation, and when, after three days, the investigation continued to revolve around these forty legitimists, the Fuehrer had bluntly ordered the criminal police to work on the case.

Nebe told me that his first reaction had not been different from ours. He too had suspected that the conspirators were to be found in the *Oberkommando der Wehrmacht,* but his first glance at the evi-dence had relieved his mind considerably. It was quite obvious that the bomb, of which fragments remained, had not come from a military arsenal; unquestionably it had been put together by some private person. He quickly found another cause for satisfaction. Hundreds of confidential denunciations and affidavits had been turned in — and all of them accused Munich 'old fighters' or the SS.

Nebe had also discounted the report of the capture of our 'Lubbe Number 2.' Consequently, he let several days go by before paying any attention to the arrested man. Other clues had seemed to him far more promising. It was not until quite late in his investigation that he interrogated Elser. Then he concluded that Elser had in fact attempted the assassination. He claimed to have done it all alone. There was every reason to doubt this assertion. Nevertheless, the detectives finally were convinced that it was true. Elser's description of the construction and installation of the bomb was correct in every point. Moreover, from the psychological point of view Nebe found his story entirely credible. Here was a fanatical Communist who had resolved to kill the tyrant and who had done what numberless other determined enemies of Hitler had not been able to do: that is, he had found an answer to the crucial preliminary question of how precisely to calculate the right moment. A native of Munich, Elser had reflected that once a year Hitler always stood at the same spot at the same hour and always for the same length of time. This took place on the occasion of his traditional address in the Buergerbraeukeller on the evening of November 8. This reasoning was perhaps the assassin's finest achievement.

The most amazing feature of the bomb was the time fuse, which could be set ten days ahead of time. This was something that even experts had not yet accomplished. Otherwise, it was a rather primitive infernal machine. Nevertheless, its success indicated that even such old-fashioned *objets d'art* can produce, when well placed, tremendous explosive effects. After the explosion the hall was a shambles.

Still the question remained, Where and how to place the bomb? Elser found a place that was both effective and easy to work on unobserved — a column directly behind the speakers' desk. Under the guise of innocent beer-drinking, he utilized the quiet hours before closing time to drill his holes. Ten days before — that is, at a time when the police were not yet guarding the building — he concealed himself in the place one evening and within a few night hours completed the installation of the bomb.

Immediately afterward, Elser wanted to flee to Switzerland. His plan was to arrive early enough so that he could confide to someone his world-shaking secret. Naturally no one would believe him, but afterward no one would be able to deny that he was the author. It was for this reason that he equipped himself with the postcard picture of the beer hall with the marked column, the card that was afterward found on his person. But when he arrived at the border, he turned back. Shaken by doubts, he rode back to Munich, went to the Buerger-braeukeller once more and applied his ear to the column. He was relieved to hear his apparatus still faintly ticking. Unfortunately he had lost so much time that it was not until the night of November 8 that he was able to attempt his illegal crossing of the border.

Once captured, 'Lubbe Number 2' had to fight as bitterly for his fame as sole author of the attempt as had his predecessor Marinus. Himmler and Heydrich were infuriated. How dare anyone claim that one man alone had created so much noise and disturbance? Impossible!

But they finally had to admit reluctantly that this Communist had been, if not the sole assassin, at least one of the chief agents. This destroyed their case against the forty Bavarian legitimists. Another story had to be invented into which the figure of this simple fanatical worker might credibly be fitted. The police had determined that the time fuse had been constructed out of an alarm clock of Swiss origin, and Elser had intended to flee to Switzerland. Both facts pointed to Otto Strasser, that bitter enemy of Hitler, to whose group the assassin might well belong ideologically. A month of torture began for the confessed assassin in the attempt to squeeze out of him a story he was simply unable to tell.

Himmler, jealous for his reputation as a bloodhound, refused to publish anything so slender and incredible as the authentic account. Similarly, Goebbels as a concocter of fairy tales trembled for his fame. The propaganda minister indignantly rejected Nebe's final report, even with the Gestapo addition of a mythical case against Otto Strasser. Undoubtedly to their own extreme surprise, the two British colonels found themselves linked with the Munich plot. Perhaps the English were not altogether unhappy about the charge.

The two colonels were not sent to a prisoner-of-war camp for officers. Instead, they were locked up in a concentration camp and for two full years in solitary cells they wore heavy chains day and night. The gentleman-criminal who had kidnaped them and was now 'caring for' them was a man who managed to look like a wide-eyed innocent with disarming good manners. As with so many of these gangsters, the man's utter vileness is demonstrated more vividly by some 'triviality' than by dozens of greater crimes. In their tormenting loneliness the two prisoners longed for news from their families. Their kidnaper expressed his regrets. Sympathetically, he gave Colonel Stevens his 'word of honor' that everything had been done to establish contact, but unfortunately all the letters had been in vain. 'You see' — he snapped his briefcase open — 'here I have four letters for your comrade Colonel Best, but there hasn't been any mail at all for you.' Then he went to see Best, a few cells farther down the row. Again the same kindly look, the same word of honor, the same snapping open of the briefcase — only this time he showed the prisoner five letters for his comrade Colonel Stevens.

The name of this cavalier, who founded his career by abusing the confidence of two British officers and making them victims of his private taste for refined sadism, soon became well known indeed. It was Schellenberg.

Elser was never tried, nor was he executed out of hand. Instead, he was taken to Dachau as a private prisoner of the Fuehrer. He was placed in the wing that housed the other guests of honor at Dachau, among them Martin Niemoeller and — later on — Best and Stevens as well. An SS guard stood constantly before the door of Elser's cell. Remarkably enough, he was no longer tortured. He had two rooms for himself, in one of which a cabinet-maker's shop was set up so that this inventive fellow could work on new ideas. Another pleasure that was permitted him was his zither, on which he played mournful songs.

Naturally, he soon became a legendary and mysterious figure. Why had he been allowed to live? The inhabitants of Dachau soon concluded that the zither player had planted his bomb on orders from

Himmler and Hitler or from one of the pair. This seemed to be the only explanation for his curious immunity; but would Himmler have permitted a man to live if that man had been a tool of his on such an assignment? Or, if the incident had been prearranged, would Hitler have stood under a ticking time fuse which might easily have made the bomb go off a few minutes too early? If it had been done on orders, where was the follow-up? Himmler had not used the bombing as a basis for a Gestapo round-up, nor had Hitler twisted it to his own purpose. As we have seen, two weeks later the proposed offensive was definitely postponed until much later.

The original explanation holds: Elser had independently tried to play the part of Providence: not only tried, but succeeded; for every unsuccessful assassination produces an effect diametrically opposed to its intention; and this attack, too, constituted a gain for Hitler. Once again Providence had saved him. He himself believed it. In the midst of his speech, he declared, an inner voice had repeatedly told him: 'Get out! Get out!' For a few minutes he had tried to shout down this voice; then he had obeyed it. Abruptly, he had broken off his address.

The generals and a large part of the populace were now no less ready to believe in this Providence of his. Six dead and sixty-three severely injured — in truth only a miracle had saved the Fuehrer.

So tangled were the obsessive ideas to which Hitler was subject that it is quite possible that he condemned Elser to his shadow existence because he seriously imagined that anyone who had prepared an assassination with so much imagination and skill must be capable of producing an ingenious invention. More likely the superstitious Hitler felt, on the basis of some astrological oracle, that his own life was inseparably linked with the destiny of 'his' assassin, so that he must not condemn him to death prematurely. There seems to be no other explanation for the special treatment that was accorded Elser in the very last days of the Third Reich, for later on, a secret order was found in Dachau 'from the very highest authority' that Elser was to be killed — and reported as 'a victim of an air attack.'

When the Gestapo men killed on their own account or on direct orders from Himmler, they did not require such complicated instructions, and Hitler's orders for the liquidation of unwanted persons were not usually phrased in so tactful a manner. When the last notes of the Nazi *Goetterdaemerung* were sounding and the curtains were falling thunderously on the last moments of the Nazi thousand years, Hitler suddenly recalled the existence of 'the zither player'; and fearfully, as if possessed by a sudden and inexplicable shame, this murderer of millions attempted to conceal his execution of an assassin who had long since been forgotten by the world public.

THE OPPOSITION

THE WINTER OF 1939-40 has gone down in the history of the war under the name of the 'phony war,' the *drôle de guerre,* as the French so piquantly called it. Would the mockers have chosen that appellation if they had had the gift of seeing into the future?

The malignant deceptiveness of that winter consisted precisely in the fact that nothing happened. Once more the revolutionary philosophy of the 'as if,' that perennial philosophy of our thousand years, took its toll. Because the terrors did not fall at once, because the insatiable revolutionaries paused to take a deep breath before they plunged into new violence, all our worried contemporaries sighed with relief and decided that now the worst was over and everything would turn out well. In the recent past they had not perceived the clash of arms in the midst of peace; now they were completely unable to comprehend this uncanny calm before the storm of 'real' war.

'General Time' was on Hitler's side in this first stage of the war. True, the Western Powers were arming; but they did not plug the gap at Sedan and they continued to barricade themselves psychologically as well as physically behind the Maginot Line. They refused to seize the initiative from the dictator, although the war in Finland was suggestive enough to make them reflect on the positive and negative importance of the Norwegian bases.

Hitler's actions, to be sure, also lagged. Obviously he was infected by his generals' skepticism. He continued to dream of great victories, but the conception that before midsummer he would have subjugated all of France and would possess jumping-off bases on the Channel may well have seemed bold even to him. Certainly he had not thought out all the political and strategic consequences of such an outcome. Otherwise he would have regeared his war machinery; he would have begun by the spring of 1940 at the latest what was already too late in the fall of 1940: the assemblage of every available ship, barge, and raft for the great leap which Napoleon had failed to take.

There was only one group that profited by this 'strange' winter. The military bureaucracy in all the belligerent countries and even in the neutral lands began to seize the whole life of those countries in the grip of its coercive administration. Military censorship, military justice, military laws, and so-called military necessities became the canon binding upon all and sundry, and the uniformed bureaucrats became, from then on, more and more inexorable and arbitrary. It was not only the extension of total war to the civil population, but also, and in fact above all, this extreme military schematization and mechanization that climaxed the dreadful process of 'leveling' which has been the most prominent mark of our revolutionary epoch.

It is remarkable how slowly all of us — men all too accustomed to the excesses of this machine age — realized the power that a military machine can exert, the despotic tendency inherent in it, and the cold-bloodedness with which it operates. The fact that its gears and pinions were composed of men of flesh and blood did not make it any the less mindless and soulless. Quite the contrary. The technical limits of all precision machinery can be nicely calculated, but here the imagination and the intellect of millions of individual particles labored incessantly upon this anonymous 'thing' to discover and close up every gap, every avenue of escape, from the grip of the military machine.

At first many persons thought that such excesses on the part of the military, such arrogant self-assurance and insensitivity, were possible only within the framework of the Prussian military caste; but it soon turned out that other nations were to suffer the same development. In a sense we Germans had in our misfortunes the saving grace that two bureaucracies rivaled one another. Because the Party and the state or the *Waffen-SS* and the *Wehrmacht* were fighting a constant underground battle, each side attempted to put forward the milder face.

The explanation for this mechanized zeal cannot be found in viciousness or in individual exploitation of unexpected power. This stubborn adherence to the new idol, 'orders,' emerged quite naturally from the very stuff of war; and it is significant that at the end of the war a military tribunal had to struggle to define where, in this circular distribution of authority from top to bottom and from bottom to top, the responsibility begins and ceases, and who is most answerable — he who gives the order or he who carries it out.

May humanity be spared any more wars! But if this wish should prove illusory, then may sensible men in all lands at least take timely precautions to make sure that next time the military machinery does not become even more all-encompassing, so much so that it atomizes human society before even the first atom bomb is dropped. Only those who have come in contact with a military machine — it is sufficient to have touched the invisible and impenetrable nimbus that surrounds it like a protective layer — can judge what it means to practice opposition or obstruction.

The German Opposition was hard hit by this change from 'ordinary' Gestapo terror to the inflexible severity of military laws. In 1933 and 1934 the unions and political party organizations had been shattered. For years thereafter no tightly knit opposition groups had been formed — at least none that could be considered well-defined centers of resistance. Basically, there existed only individual oppositionists around whom groups of like-minded people formed. It was only after the alarming events of 1938 that the resistance front began to form anew. It grew at first in a hesitant fashion on a local scale; groups with the same point of view rarely submitted to a central leadership and even more rarely sought contact with other resistance groups; but just about the time these promising beginnings had progressed to the point where a gradual merging of these various circles and groups could be hoped for, the psychological and material changes of wartime threatened to undo all that had been accomplished.

The Opposition had to consider its stand in the new situation. A man might have fought bitterly against Hitler's insane war policy, but now the war was there. How was he to react toward it? As an oppositionist? As a patriot? As a European? Or as none of these, but quite simply as a soldier whose business it was to obey orders?

Let us not forget that totalitarianism and opposition are two mutually exclusive political ideas. In a democracy it is possible to practice opposition, but dictatorship permits no antagonists; it does not even put up with the lukewarm and the skeptical. Whoever is not for it is against it. Oppositionists must keep silent, or they must decide on underground activity.

Underground resistance and opposition are again two different matters. Opposition is struggle against an existing régime; it is an attempt to bring about a shift in course or a change in personnel, without directly overthrowing a system. The Opposition, therefore, recommends a more prudent policy, offers reasoned advice, tries to reform by appeals to the common sense of the rulers and attempts to win the favor of the voters; but the oppositionist under a totalitarian system must not try to reform at all. His good advice would only help the tyranny; any intelligent recommendation would support the reign of terror.

Perhaps the penance for a nation that through folly or trickery has become subject to a dictatorship is precisely that it is left only with the alternative of exchanging tyranny for the yoke of the conquered. Or else the people of the nation must take upon their conscience the tremendous burden of devoting all their imagination and zeal to the purely destructive activities of underground work.

In such ambivalent situations the tempter approaches, and his shrewd arguments sound very good indeed. People say to themselves that they must not try to play God; the Lord knows what he intends to do. People who express themselves less piously say that now everyone is in the same boat. Others assert that in wartime a good citizen can do only one thing: patriotically fulfill all his obligations to the government, whether or not he likes that government.

This latter objection must be taken more seriously than people outside Germany, especially the German exiles, have done. The question could have been settled with relative ease had the attitude of obedience and loyalty arisen only out of fear of the Draconian wartime laws; for there is no excuse for a nation whose leaders have criminally started a war; at whatever cost the nation must refuse to abet the guilt of its leaders. If the prime question, however, appears to be, what consequences will a lost war have? — then oppositionists may well ask themselves whether there ought not to be a limit to their opposition and obstruction. Should they not co-operate with their government — even at the risk of preserving the reign of terror — in order to keep not only their own country, but the community of nations from the consequences of a disastrous collapse? What good European today will not regret the fact that when the Third Reich came to an end all state power ceased to exist in Germany, so that the victor powers found no valid authorities at all to serve them in the difficult task of occupation?

There was an additional element that grew in importance the longer the war lasted. The air attacks reinforced the people's sense of belonging to a community for good or ill. The bombs fell alike upon the just and the unjust. This instructive example on the home front led logically to the conclusion that this time the outraged enemy would be 'tougher' than he had been in 1918. Twenty-five years before, the Germans had been firmly convinced that they were not guilty of the outbreak of world war, but with this war of Hitler's they could no longer evade their war guilt. Moreover, every day new and unique crimes were being committed. Perhaps the populace was not aware of the full extent of these, but enough reports trickled through the wall of silence to create a tremendous sense of guilt, and this guilt influenced all decisions.

With every new crime the Nazis deliberately cut off their lines of retreat. During the days of victory the corrupt sub-leaders boasted cynically of their diabolic system of involving themselves and others in so much guilt that there could be no turning back, only a colder and more ruthless pursuit of the war to its end.

The non-participants, those who really fought the Nazis and who demonstrably had done none of the killing, felt equally implicated. The 'collective guilt' which is nowadays so indignantly repudiated was not invented by any armchair psychologists. The decent people of Germany were aware of it and suffered from it, and some, precisely because of this sense that they were fatally involved in guilt, advanced the thesis that only Hitler and Himmler were in a position to keep the avengers off German soil. The desire to stand together with one's fellows in times of distress cannot be condemned out of hand as immoral. It springs from a universal natural impulse, and we should not dismiss as trifling this phenomenon of the guiltless turning guilty because of their sense of shared responsibility.

Another fundamental difference between oppositional methods in a democratic and a totalitarian state must be noted. In a democracy the Opposition can and in fact must work openly. Under totalitarianism it is only possible to obstruct and oppose if one is in some manner 'on the inside.' But how far can a man participate in a hated system without selling his soul? The more the Opposition came to recognize that the Nazi rulers could be defeated only by their own methods, the harder it was for them to solve the problem of conscience. It became more difficult for them to avoid objective as well as subjective guilt. Undoubtedly many paid too dear a price for the sake of having one or both feet 'inside,' and many others were unjustly accused of opportunism.

I recall my first encounter with von Hassell shortly after his dismissal in 1938. I congratulated him for having successfully got himself kicked out; for it was well known that highly placed officials found it virtually impossible to resign when they wanted to. It took a great deal of skill to espy an opportunity to jump off the bandwagon. Even when one did break away, the dictator's whims were wholly unpredictable. Hitler often availed himself of an official's temporary unemployment to promote the man, to entrust him with a special commission, or to extort a public declaration of loyalty from him.

Hassell gave me a look of surprise. He could not understand that I really meant my congratulations. Then he advanced a thesis that gave me much to think about for years afterward. An oppositionist under a dictatorship must defend his official post with tooth and claw, he said, and if dismissed he must strive to get into the government again. Even an unpretentious post on the inside, Hassell urged, afforded an opportunity for exerting influence.

Goerdeler, too, had much the same view and repeatedly tried to get 'on the inside' again. He had all the more reason for wanting this, since his constant traveling inside Germany and abroad was possible only if he enjoyed some official or semi-official protection.

The foolish talk of So-and-So's being 'paid' by Hitler is evidence of the grotesque misunderstandings of the Opposition's true situation. Running through the list of the dead of July 20, I find that almost all of them were 'inside' and 'paid.' Were the officers and officials who wanted to overthrow the Nazis to abandon the key positions they had acquired with such difficulty and maintained so tenaciously, merely in order to give possible moralistic critics no grounds for complaint? Or should they not rather take the stand that the money they received — from the state treasury, not from Hitler — was paid gladly by millions of taxpayers, who paid their taxes without wanting to subsidize Nazism, and who, though they might be prosperous business men or wage-earners, did not feel themselves inwardly corrupted by Hitler?

As far as I myself was concerned, I made the attempt in 1936 — on an irrational and sentimental basis — to escape this 'being paid by Hitler' by transferring to the 'free' business world; but in 1937 a special federal law forbade officials to leave the civil service — another point that is passed over by critics. Thus, in the early part of 1939, I had to return to my former bondage; but even in retrospect I do not feel troubled in my conscience for having rejoined the class of salaried state employees.

The potentialities for effective opposition were directly proportionate to an individual's inclusion or exclusion from the Nazi governmental machine. Why else was it that the principal figures in the history of 'putsches' from 1938 to 1944 were military officers, government officials, or industrial leaders, while the Left never participated, not even in an unsuccessful partial action? The organizations of Left and Right and Center had been destroyed by the end of 1934; but politically and socially, the members of the Center and the Right were closer to the generals and the high government officials; and that was what counted, once the chance for an uprising from below had been lost.

The Resistance in the occupied countries had a clear task to perform: to get rid of the foreign conqueror. On this basis it was possible for the most diverse political and ideological groups to unite — although their unity did not outlast the war. In Germany no such clear issue existed, nor could it exist.

Communists, Social Democrats, liberals, conservatives, and Christians, all drew their own conclusions from the experiences of past and present. They were agreed mostly on the negative plank: that Nazism must go; but their positive aims were diametrically opposed. Some wanted socialism; others considered it the root of all evil. Some affirmed collectivism; others believed that we were already so deeply immersed in collectivism that we must do everything possible at least to ameliorate its ill effects. Some desired a centralized Germany, others a federal union. All were concerned with the question of educating the youth, but what a diversity of opinion there was on the problem, for example, of Christianity in the schools!

How, in such a situation, could there arise an Opposition leader, an 'anti-Fuehrer' who would tower above all and unite the dissenting groups? How could there be any common lines of activity when the various groups could not even agree on the methods to pursue in their negative struggle? Running directly across all the oppositional groups from Right to Left was a dividing line between those who wanted immediate action and those who thought that honest opponents of Nazism must wait patiently, exercising great alertness but even greater restraint. The latter were convinced that those activists who were pressing for a *Putsch* or an assassination might well prove to be conscious or unconscious pacemakers for a new and even more dangerous type of nationalism.

Consequently, any attempt to classify the German Opposition must necessarily fail. Basically, there were only oppositionists. Each of these more or less strong personalities had a group of friends who agreed with him. Each of them sought to extend his influence and therefore tried to establish contact with other groups and circles. This resulted in those many intersecting and tangential lines which so confused the picture. None of these men could possibly appeal directly to the masses. Never were they able to issue common slogans. So long as the reign of terror raged, they could do no more than prepare a shadow coalition of men of good will. For the rest, these upright men, though filled with the great urge to take their stand publicly, had to bear up under a heavy mental burden for which the Bible provides permission, but at the cost of inner peace: that is to say, they had to be as 'wise as serpents.'

OPPOSITIONAL CIRCLES

IF I REMEMBER RIGHTLY, it was in November, 1939, that Wilhelm Leuschner, the leader of the Social Democrats, and Jakob Kaiser, the leading personality of the former Christian Union heads, put out their first cautious feelers to the *Oberkommando der Wehrmacht* and got in touch with the *Abwehr* groups. These two were perhaps the only ones — outside of Oster — who could claim to represent sharply defined circles.

In contrast to groups, which gathered around single strong personalities, I shall speak of circles only in connection with someone who had at his disposal a broad network of functionaries and who was technically in a position to maintain contact with these men. Leuschner and Kaiser, and for a long time Oster as well, had the good fortune and skill to conceal their shadow organizations from the eyes of the Gestapo until July 20, 1944.

Wilhelm Leuschner had formerly been minister of the interior in Hesse. In 1933 he was sent to concentration camp. After his release he decided not to emigrate, but to continue the struggle from inside

Germany. After some groping he founded a small business, not without assistance from certain 'capitalists,' men who had been his opponents in political life, but who were convinced of the need for a Social Democratic Opposition. His purchasing organization was splendidly adapted for camouflaging political work. Leuschner was a careful politician; his nickname 'Uncle' indicated that some of his friends thought he could have used a little more passion and firmness. On the other hand, he was a very clever tactician and fully realized that in underground work it would not do to butt one's head against the wall. There were dozens of personal and political idiosyncrasies that had to be tolerated in order to prevent needless friction, for the ultimate outcome of internal dissension was unpleasant attention from the alert Gestapo. In retrospect we may well say that the Black bloodhounds almost never had any success so long as a group held together in a disciplined fashion. It was only when intrigues were being woven or something else was 'out of tune' that the discords were picked up by the microphones in the Prinz Albrechtstrasse, which were peculiarly sensitive to every note of disharmony.

It is to Leuschner's credit that he put by all personal ambitions and gave Goerdeler the precedence as soon as he came to know him better. A number of Leuschner's Party friends criticized this as a weakness in him, and some of them tried to outwit him. They succeeded only in harming themselves and the common front. Leuschner's retiring behavior cannot be ascribed to any 'wait-and-see' policy, of which he has recently been accused. Rather, he recognized the conclusive importance of the military in any uprising, and he was selfless enough to respect and honor Goerdeler's position as the real instigator of a generals' *Putsch*.

Jakob Kaiser perseveringly reorganized the Christian Unions, without, however, forgetting the functions that accrued to him as a former Reichstag deputy of the Center. (Since the end of the Hitler régime he has again become prominent in parliamentary affairs.) Like Leuschner, with whom he had come to a broad agreement on matters of future social policy, Kaiser refused to be seduced from his allegiance to Goerdeler.

Oster, too, had formed a circle around himself, although he was so utterly without personal ambitions that he never sought the position of a leader; but he utilized the potentialities of the *Abwehr* so cannily that he was able to establish a whole network of confidential agents. His strength consisted in the fact that most people were ignorant of the extent of his influence. This unpretentious man was not fond of good notices especially in the grapevine press of the Opposition. He pursued his undeviating path, just as he had secretly marked it out for himself years earlier, and every day he had to cut his way anew through the tangle of oppositional problems or suspicions. Never did he participate in political negotiations. He deliberately avoided all so-called preliminary conferences in which good intentions or daring plans were often talked threadbare and which always ended merely in the prayer for *the* general to come to the rescue. The goal Oster had set for himself was to find that general and to place his apparatus at his disposal.

In fact, probably no oppositional approaches to generals were made except under Oster's guidance. Perhaps it might have been better if he had made use of or extended these connections on his own behalf; but this ran contrary to his nature. Accustomed to take a subordinate rôle, he left the military connections to Beck and political affairs to Goerdeler. Once he had arranged a conference for these men, he concentrated on his own work. 'You must understand that my secondary occupation happens to be that of chief of staff in the *Abwehr*,' he used to say to me as he sat at his desk writing out his instructions. He preferred to give orders in writing in order to save himself superfluous conversations; but while he worked, he would keep his ears cocked to note any news or incidents. He had worked very hard to consolidate his position. He would have risked all he had achieved if he had ever permitted any flaw in the daily conduct of his official work.

It was Canaris's great achievement to raise this virtually unknown major to the position of power which Oster held as a colonel and major-general during the war. Again and again the admiral extended his protecting hand over this controversial officer whose waiting room sometimes resembled a pigeon coop, filled as it was with mysterious persons — civilians among them! — for Oster seemed to be organizing an intelligence service of his own within the counter-intelligence service, although, as chief of the organizational division, he presumably should not have kept any agents of his own; and this aroused suspicion. Nowhere does professional jealousy produce so much inquisitive gossip as in an intelligence service. Not only the Nazified zealots, of whom there were a great many in the *Abwehr,* but quite respectable, unpolitical, and even opposition-minded officers endangered Oster's life by gossiping about the number of irons he evidently had in the fire.

Protection by a patron is never sufficient to cover a man. Under tense circumstances — which occur daily in underground work — the protégé must be able to demonstrate his competence. Oster did just this. Neither the personal and professional temptations inherent in military intelligence work nor the inescapable trickery of underground activity had any adverse effect upon his character. The onlooker sensed that this difficult and devious subsidiary occupation left the man quite untainted. Cheerfully he began and ended his day's work. Irritating circumstances could not confuse him; disappointments did not make him lose heart. He remained firm within himself, and this firmness sprang from his unshakable trust in God.

'To our last breath we all remain upstanding men, as we were taught to be from childhood and in our soldierly discipline. Come what may, we fear only the wrath of God that will fall upon us if we are not clean and decent and do not do our duty.' These were the words he wrote to his son from prison on his last birthday, and these were the principles he followed all his life.

How did Oster make use of his key position? One of the most important of his activities was to install his own confidential agents in the most diverse positions. These men did not necessarily have to be in on the conspiracy. It was sufficient if he knew he could depend on them in a crisis. This requirement alone made the choice of agents extremely difficult, for the officers assigned to the *Abwehr* were selected by the army personnel office, which considered qualifications from a viewpoint somewhat different from Oster's.

Aside from Nebe, who was eternally on the alert, Oster was almost always the first to hear about it when someone was threatened by the Gestapo, whether the person was a friend or stranger. Showing apparent abstraction, he would listen attentively to all conversations about new 'cases.' Now and then — of course merely out of curiosity — he would inquire about particulars or involve the officers in charge of the matter in an innocuous conversation. Oster managed to encircle the German Opposition with a cordon of silence. Naturally he was not always successful. With deep bitterness he often had to look on helplessly while the Gestapo and, alas, even his own *Abwehr*, seized some unfortunate, but in general he succeeded for years on an astonishing scale. Even today many persons do not know that they owe their lives to him.

This was by no means all he did. A secret-service organization naturally is equipped with a great many steel safes. Oster became the archivist of the Opposition. The collection of documents that we had started back in 1933 swelled to considerable proportions with the passage of time. Almost daily Oster sent his loyal chauffeur, Jakobs, to Beck with a secret portfolio containing foreign newspapers or the latest military news or reports on Gestapo crimes. At the same time he operated as a kind of secret post office. He sent countless letters to the front or abroad, successfully evading the Gestapo censorship. In this regard he was especially glad when he could be helpful to the churches. The journey that Joseph Mueller made to the Vatican gave Oster great satisfaction. The work of Doctor Schoenfeld and Dietrich Bonhoeffer with the ecumenical movement in Geneva would not have been possible without his assistance.

But all that he did was done silently. Although he was one of the best-informed officers in the OKW, although even field marshals in their hunger for information sent emissaries to him, he preferred to play dumb. Only his very closest friends were aware of his underground activities. Toward the end he no longer spoke at all about his negotiations with the generals. This prompted many persons who were constantly seeking news about prospective 'putsches' to declare that he was tired and resigned. The high-strung intellectuals within the Opposition who were concerned only with 'politics' began to doubt his wisdom. I recall that on the afternoon of July 20, 1944, Beck, who badly missed this most loyal and best of assistants, talked to me about all this foolish gossip. Probably it was precisely his exaggerated selflessness that brought Oster into ill repute among the dashing young colonels of the Opposition, Beck said. 'Now his greatest virtue, his ability to keep his mouth shut, is costing him his reputation.'

To some extent Oster deliberately strove to remain colorless to the eyes of those outside of his immediate circle. He depersonalized himself; he made an effort to impress people as an emotionless and matter-of-fact administrator. He once described to me in one sentence his own conception of his function within the Resistance Movement. He was standing at his desk looking down pensively at the four or five telephones whose secret circuits connected him with the most diverse authorities. 'This is what I am,' he said. 'I facilitate communications for everyone everywhere.' Nevertheless, he was far more than a human switchboard, and his work went beyond those telephone conversations in which he repeatedly gave brusque warnings to generals and field marshals in their distant headquarters. He was the driving force, not merely the technician, of the Opposition. How wonderfully he had worked for us became clear to everyone when he was at last driven from office.

For the sake of his task, Oster renounced the chances for commands at the front with their possibilities of very swift promotion. This does not mean that he was not a soldier in heart and mind, and a soldier in the best sense of the word. He suffered greatly from the moral and professional collapse of his class. His alienation from the generals went so far toward the last that even on important occasions he could scarcely be persuaded to wear his uniform. He always wore his unpretentious civilian outfit, no matter how much Canaris protested — and Canaris had an extremely formalistic point of view about such matters. Nevertheless, he had a profound sense of what an officer's honor should be; it existed for him, although it had no connection with the stars and decorations of our other brass hats. There was no contradiction between his rejection of the uniform and the statement that I made at the Nuremberg Trials with my eyes on Keitel and Jodl: 'In the midst of a German inflation in field marshals and generals that utterly devaluated those titles, Oster was really — a general.'

The so-called Oster circle was treated inside the *Abwehr* with suspicion and often with open hostility. The other officers spoke contemptuously of the 'civilians,' by which they meant not so much the external matter of dress (since most of Oster's men were in military service) as the manner in which we worked together with a challenging disregard for epaulets and stripes.

Nevertheless, there were a large number of officers in the circle, among them such outstanding military men as Lahousen. Although Lahousen did not count himself a member of the innermost Oster Circle, it was he who supplied the explosives needed for the attempt on Hitler's life. Hansen was one of the oldest oppositionists within the *Abwehr*. Until the maelstrom of July 20 swallowed him up, he held to a clear, undeviating line. When Canaris was forced to leave, Hansen succeeded for almost a year in guiding the remnants of the badly shaken organization with such adroitness that the Gestapo, which had had a failure of nerve, was prompted to let it alone.

Lieutenant-Colonel Heinz and Colonels Count Rudolf Marogna-Redwitz and Rudolf Schrader returned to military service when the reserve officers were reactivated. The war brought in naval Captain Liedig, Captain Gehre, and Count Ulrich von Schwerin. Heinz played an important part as a wise adviser and aide up to the very last. Unfortunately, he never got a chance to participate in a more active fashion, although he had temporarily taken command of a section of the Brandenburg sabotage regiment in the hope that he would be able to use it in the *Putsch*. Oster carefully installed Schrader as an *Abwehr* officer in headquarters where his zeal and energy found excellent application. He gathered information, performed courier service, and practiced espionage against his own counter-espionage organization. After the failure of the *Putsch* on July 20, he made the courageous decision to commit suicide rather than endanger his friends.

Count Marogna, an old Austrian officer, was stubbornly shielded by Oster in his position as chief of the *Abwehr* branch in Vienna, although Marogna was engaged in a perpetual guerrilla war with the Gestapo. He too was murdered after July 20. Some day, when the history of the Austrian liberation movement is written, his name will take one of the first places. There will be many witnesses in the countries of southeastern Europe to testify to the devotion which this splendid man, a true European, lavished upon the cause.

The chief provost marshal of the army, Ministerial Director Doctor Sack, was more or less the connecting link between the military men and the civilians. In spite of his high military rank he remained a civilian to the core who never departed from simple decency in spite of all the pomp, the clicking of heels, and the barking of orders that surrounded him. Inexorable in his judgments, unrelenting even toward friends, Doctor Sack worked under tremendous difficulties — for he was Keitel's subordinate. He had to find the mean between the requirements of the Opposition and the general dissolution of moral concepts. This mean was often extremely elusive, for quite frequently criminals or freebooters alleged that they were oppositionists in order to profit by the general social decay. Sack was able to ward off intervention of the Gestapo in a large number of cases by quickly instituting a 'severe' investigation by a court-martial and then winding up the affair after his own fashion. Some charges he was able to quash at once.

Among the civilians I mention in first place *Reichsgerichtsrat* (supreme court justice) Doctor von Dohnanyi, who from the beginning of the war was Oster's closest associate. An unusually clever man, he had scarcely passed his majority when he took the leap from *Oberregierungsrat* in the ministry of justice to his position in the supreme court. As personal assistant to Minister of Justice Guertner he persuaded the minister to intervene in a vast number of cases. With his inflexible sense of justice and his fervor, he repeatedly took over the reins from his phlegmatic chief. During the Fritsch crisis he joined up with Oster, and from then on he was part and parcel of the history of that circle. Dohnanyi became the judicial expert of the *Abwehr* in all cases where something had to be 'fixed.' It was he who undertook the drafting of secret political reports, applying to them the clarity of intelligence and diction that characterized all his work. Dohnanyi had a share in every protest on the part of Canaris, every aid rendered by the *Abwehr*, every illegal action on the part of the Oster circle during those years.

I need say nothing about Dietrich Bonhoeffer, the brother-in-law of Dohnanyi. His name has gone down in the history of the militant Church. Bonhoeffer contrived, from his vantage-point in the *Abwehr* branch at Munich, to provide Joseph Mueller with effective protection.

Before 1933 Joseph Mueller had been one of the leaders of the Bavarian People's Party. A praiseworthy exception, he had vehemently resisted the general capitulation to the Nazis of the bourgeois parties in his area. Very soon he began to engage in underground work. The beginning of the war brought him in contact with Oster, who entrusted him with using his connections in the Vatican to broach conversations on the possibilities of peace. Mueller accomplished his task with remarkable adroitness, and this cleverness stood him in good stead after 1943, when he had to justify his activities to the Gestapo. He withstood interrogations in such a manner that the Nazis decided that he was one of their most valuable hostages, whom they hoped to use in some kind of exchange. Together with other prominent prisoners, he was liberated in South Tyrol.

Were I to name all the gallant opponents of the Nazis, the list would run on and on. But I must give a special place to Elisabeth and Theodor Struenck.

I had been friendly with the couple for a long time. Toward the end of 1937 I introduced them to Oster. From that time on, they were part of his intimate circle. When the war broke out, Oster installed Struenck, who was at the time director of a large insurance firm in Frankfurt-am-Main, in the *Abwehr* headquarters. In view of Struenck's low military rank — he entered the service as a lieutenant of the reserve and died a captain — it was difficult to find an occupation for him that was commensurate with his abilities. He had a strong and self-willed personality and did not wish to idle away his time. In the *Abwehr*, as throughout the OKW, there was a swarm of colonels and naval captains whose arrogance was all the more bound-

less for their possessing no other qualifications outside of their insignia
of rank. Finding a place for Lieutenant Struenck was all the more
difficult because his work in the *Abwehr* was in reality to be merely
his subsidiary occupation; his main task was to perform special missions for Oster. Oster worked out an adequate solution which his
successor Hansen was to perpetuate, so that Struenck was able to
hold his position and play his important rôle of intermediary up to
the last few days before the *Putsch* of July 20, 1944.

The Struencks had rented a modest little apartment in Berlin which
remained listed under the name and telephone number of their landlord. It was definitely known to be unobserved and was therefore a
splendid meeting-place in the center of the city for members of the
Opposition. It is unfortunate that Frau Struenck was not able to keep
a guest-book; it would be something she could exhibit with pride
today, for a great many men of the Opposition met in her apartment.
It was there that the first meeting between Goerdeler and Stauffenberg
took place. In fact the Struencks' apartment in Nuernbergerstrasse 31
was virtually Goerdeler's headquarters whenever he stayed in Berlin.
Sometimes he visited there three times a day. He was fond of discussing the strenuous and only too often depressing negotiations he
conducted and he liked to forge new plans among his close friends.
The Struencks were not only patient listeners, but candid advisers and
counselors as well. I should judge that there was scarcely a single
letter or memorandum that Goerdeler wrote during those years,
scarcely a single conference in which he engaged, or a single tour
of investigation that he undertook, which were not thoroughly discussed before and after with the Struencks.

After a while it became customary for every friend of the household
to bring along his friends. The result was that things were at times
rather lively in the tiny two-room apartment. It was quite a feat to
prevent the various visitors from encountering one another. This
tactic, upon which Nebe repeatedly insisted, was a precaution against
the possibility of Gestapo espionage. Later events were to prove its
fatal importance, at least in respect to many other persons. Struenck
himself could not be saved. The Nazis treated his brave wife more

viciously than they had the wives of any of the other conspirators of July 20, but she was rescued just before they were about to put her to death. Struenck himself traveled the last bitter road together with Oster and Canaris; he died fearlessly in his faith, a good comrade, a true friend.

GROUPS AND INDIVIDUALS

THE SCHULZE-BOYSEN GROUP cannot be called a circle, although nearly a hundred men affiliated to it went to their deaths and the group had established an extensive espionage network. The discovery by the Gestapo of the numerous secret radio transmitters they had set up developed into the biggest espionage trial of the war. The organization was guided by convinced Communists and worked for the Russian secret service.

The Schulze-Boysens, both husband and wife, were fanatical Communists who knew exactly for whom they were working. This was not true of most of the persons on the list of victims. The majority of them were adherents of the Left, but they had no suspicion that they were members of a Communist organization guided from Moscow; they first learned about these connections in court. Schulze-Boysen occupied a key position in the air ministry. Thus he had a large number of acquaintances with whom he could continually exchange oppositional information. It took some time before we were able to find out most — not all — of the particulars about this tragic case and ascertain which members belonged to the inner Communist circle, which ones merely wanted to give expression to their oppositional sentiments, and which were dragged into a fatal situation through lack of caution.

Hitler was extraordinarily agitated by this espionage case. For years the Nazis had been engaged in a spy-hunt because it seemed apparent from radio messages that were picked up that there must be Russian spies inside German headquarters, and somewhere near

the very top. Everyone suspected everyone else, until sheer chance
exposed the real spies. Then it was Goering's turn to rage. He had
long since retired from active conduct of the war to spend his time
at Karinhall with his banquets and his collection of paintings; but this
scandal dealt a severe blow to the reputation for special reliability
that his air ministry had cultivated. Therefore, he was sedulous in
his backing of Hitler when the Fuehrer refused to confirm the Reich
military tribunal's verdict condemning 'only' fifty persons to death.
Goering and Hitler insisted upon another forty-five death sentences,
mainly for the wives of the chief defendants. When the presiding
judge of the court refused to assent to this improvement on justice,
he was forced to resign, but since anything was possible in the Third
Reich, the judge who had just been dismissed for being overlenient
was given the post of chief military prosecutor. In this capacity the
first important case that he conducted — not too benevolently — was
that of Oster and his comrades.

Another group that did not comprise a circle according to our strict
definition consisted of members of the churches. Everyone knows
how many fighters and patient oppositionists there were in the ranks
of the churches, but nothing would have suited the Nazis better than
to convict important representatives of the Catholic or the Protestant
churches of political conspiracy. It is important to note this in order
to understand the complex problem of the Opposition in a totalitarian
state. Good churchgoers had to be, or to become, convinced oppositionists. Their loyalty to their churches forced them into this intellectual position; but this effect of the Churches was precisely the
reason for cheating the Gestapo of its desired pretext for annihilating
these centers of resistance. On the other hand, the bishops and other
leaders of the churches must not compromise themselves by political
concessions. It was very difficult indeed to find the proper course
between these dilemmas; and we regret to note that a good many
church leaders contented themselves with the far too worldly solution
of steering an intact organization and bureaucracy through the turbulent waves.

Men like Ambassador Ulrich von Hassell, Freiherr von Hammerstein (the former commander-in-chief of the army who retired in 1934), Nikolaus von Halem, and even Niemoeller cannot be assigned to any circle. Either out of stubbornness or deliberate intent these anti-Nazis remained independent.

In 1939, Hammerstein had considered arresting Hitler when the Fuehrer made a visit to the Western Front. Before the plan could be carried out, his intuitive master deprived him of his military command. From then until his premature death in 1942, the recalled general issued warning after warning. When Hitler plunged into the Russian adventure, the former commander-in-chief made the terrifying prophecy: 'Of the army that is now marching against Russia not a single man will come back.' We know now what hecatombs of human lives were to follow those first hundreds of thousands whom 'the greatest general of all times' sent marching to their deaths on June 22, 1941. But who among the generals was willing to listen?

Hassell was highly esteemed by Beck and by almost everyone else in the Opposition. With his trenchant humor, his diplomatic finesse, and his unshakable political principles, he was one of the most distinguished figures of the German Opposition Movement. He devoted his diplomatic talents to mediating among individuals of extremely diverse temperaments and opinions.

Nikolaus von Halem, in a sense a bohemian in the Opposition, was a man whose ingenuity was more marked than his genius; but he possessed a superb mind and was the best kind of cosmopolitan European. In his restlessness he drifted from one circle and group to the next. Everywhere, he sought an assassin who would kill Hitler — until at last he found the wrong one: Beppo Roemer. Arrested in 1942 together with Legation Councilor von Mumm, von Halem went to his death after July 20, 1944, with magnificent courage.

Around Popitz, the Prussian minister of finance, there gathered a group of men who were striving toward the same goal. In 1933, Popitz had offered his services to the Nazis, which was an astonishing act for a man who had served as under-secretary under Hilferding, the Social Democratic minister of finance. For years Popitz maintained that the only way to keep some curbs on the Revolution was to play off Goering against Hitler and Himmler. In order to make the sybarite of Karinhall amenable, Popitz used the Prussian state treasury to bribe Goering heavily, but by 1938 he realized where the Nazi express was headed. From then on his oppositional attitude solidified more and more. In the end he became one of the extremists. His application for membership in the Opposition, however, met with strong objections. Popitz's case seemed to be far more crass than the 'ambiguous' case of Schacht. Although his intelligence was prized and although his profound acquaintance with the machinery of state was almost indispensable, he had shared too long in building up the Nazi dictatorship to be readily accepted. I myself was one of those who vetoed him most strongly, but when I at last met the man personally, I was deeply impressed by his manifest sincerity. He suffered greatly from the catastrophe that had befallen Germany and Europe, and in a sense he tried personally to atone for it. Year after year his pleas to generals and civilians, his struggles to win them over, became more anguished and more affecting. He may well have felt his death on the gallows as a release.

If it is to become a principle of international law that men who make the mistake of contributing toward totalitarianism can never turn back (the totalitarians hang them as traitors; the other side condemn them as accomplices), some may be deterred; but such a principle would profit chiefly the statesmen of disaster like Hitler. If such politicians should succeed again in involving their followers, associates, or fellow travelers in guilt, they would be able to confront those they had tricked with an ultimatum: henceforth there was only one way to redeem themselves internationally — to drag other nations down with them or — to *win* a war.

Professor Peter Jessen, who was a close friend of Popitz, also came out of the Nazi Movement — and split with it all the more emphatically. He was a member of the activistic wing of the Opposition.

Under-Secretary Erwin Planck, the brilliant son of the famous physicist, had moved from the army to his office in the chancellery under the chancellorships of Bruening and Schleicher. From 1933 on, he unswervingly opposed the Nazi system. In 1942 he abandoned all hopes of a *Putsch,* but this did not save him from the gallows.

Attorney Carl Langbehn, who chanced to be personally acquainted with Himmler, also wanted to play off the Gestapo against Hitler. He and Popitz worked together on this dangerous ruse. Himmler said neither yes nor no; he played along until after July 20. Then he struck savagely.

There was another group in the foreign office. The strongest and most resolute personality in this group was the later ambassador, Erich Kordt. Kordt was one of the few early advocates of assassinating Hitler. He was in the fortunate position of being admitted to the secret parleys in the chancellery, and as early as 1939 he offered to set off the bomb. At that time it was not feasible to procure the necessary explosives for him behind the backs of the generals. In 1941, Ribbentrop more or less exiled Kordt by shipping him off to Tokio.

The names of the legation councilors, Hans Berndt von Haeften and Adam von Trott zu Solz, are very well known. When the war broke out, Trott was sent off to a diplomatic post in East Asia. On the way there and back he formed many important ties. Until 1944 he served as an emissary of the cultural department, in which capacity he was able to travel frequently to Switzerland and Sweden. He never missed an opportunity to put out feelers. But his real oppositionist activity began when he became a member of the Kreissau circle, which I am about to discuss. Albrecht von Kessel had the good luck to be in the Vatican on July 20; otherwise he would have met the same fate as his friends.

There is one more — among so many — whom I must mention: Otto Kiep, the former consul-general in New York, who was condemned to death in June, 1944, and was executed a few months later, together with that courageous woman, Elisabeth von Thadden.

From about 1941 on, the Kreissau circle was concerned with establishing a program for future domestic and foreign policy. Its approach to these problems was essentially a socialistic one. Strictly speaking, it was no circle but a group, composed of men of relatively the same age who were bound by ties of friendship, but who represented the most diverse political views. These men tried to establish bases for a common socialistic policy. The fruit of their labors was preserved in memoranda which, when published, will testify to the number of progressive and truly European-minded men who were waiting for the hour of liberation.

Publication of their conclusions will prove something else. It will demonstrate how many principles which may be branded as idealistic were accepted as a matter of course by those who had passed through the purgatory of Nazi rule. Very few had any patience with a change of personnel or an amelioration of existing practices — which would mean, of course, simply an improved totalitarianism. The rejection of nationalism and imperialism was fairly general; so also was the desire for a federated Germany. The Socialists, on the basis of their collectivist doctrine, did not want to go so far in decentralization as the conservatives and liberals. The Socialists considered it essential that governmental direction of the economy and social policy be retained; the others desired a thoroughgoing relaxation of all controls.

Goerdeler, Leuschner, and Jakob Kaiser were not members of this Kreissau circle. At the risk of being condemned as too 'old' and too 'reactionary,' the three forbore to consider premature experiments. Goerdeler in particular was given short shrift by the 'youths' — an attitude which was to have a fateful effect upon the preparations for and the execution of the *Putsch* of July 20.

The name Kreissau circle derived from the meetings that were held on the Silesian country estate of Count Helmuth von Moltke, who was not only the host but the intellectual chief of the circle. Von Moltke had many personal and professional ties with the Anglo-Saxon countries. During the war he served as an administrative official in the foreign branch of the *Abwehr* and dealt with questions of international law. A clever, thoughtful, energetic man who was worthy of his great forbear, he was probably 'the most vigorous militant among the socialistic conservatives,' to quote Emil Henk's depiction of the 'Tragedy of July 20.' 'But as a politician his fiery days were over,' Henk continues. This lack of fire made it easier for Moltke to hold undeviatingly to the line he considered correct and to pursue with tranquil persistence his preparations for the period after the inevitable collapse. On the other hand, it prevented him from understanding fully the point of view of the 'activists.'

It is essential to note this. For von Moltke's great significance lay in his being the most prominent advocate of inaction — and one whose purity of motive could not be doubted. All his zeal and all his imagination were devoted, on principle, to what would come after the fall of the Nazis. Profoundly skeptical of any action on the part of the military, Moltke had in mind something like a 'directed defeat.'

Because of Moltke's personality and political weight, his leadership was trusted by many oppositionists who were not at all prone to fold their hands in their laps and who, in another situation, might have enlisted their minds and wills under the banner of those who favored 'action' rather than 'politics.' The most vigorous advocate of this latter line was Goerdeler, who certainly could not be considered an unpolitical man. But in politics men can ill afford to let their opponents plunge ahead into disasters. Once the situation is out of hand, chaos devours even the best-laid plans of the men who are holding themselves in readiness to take over the inheritance.

Beck, in truth, stood above all the parties. Consequently, there were no dissenting voices at all when, in the winter of 1939, he was appointed head of the *fronde*. This nomination was the result of Oster's urging. It had become clear since the outbreak of the war that any attempt to overthrow the régime would be doomed from the outset unless the problem of the future head of the state were solved to the satisfaction of the army. The military and civil executive power could be conferred only on someone whom the soldiers would acknowledge as a leader. Beck was the only general with an unimpaired reputation, the only general who had voluntarily resigned. No one among the military men could surpass him in personal or soldierly capacity.

In the past year it had become a kind of mania within the Opposition to hunt for *the* general. Everyone beat the bushes, and wherever someone had a cousin who knew an officer on the staff of an army commander, word of this 'connection' was passed on in whispers, to the accompaniment of mysterious and significant winks. Complete nonentities were puffed up into noble tyrannicides, and in every case infinite trouble ensued first to pierce the secrecy and discover what legendary general was being referred to and then to determine the extent of his resolution or the actual force of soldiers he commanded. This sort of unnecessary but mandatory detective work could be done only by an informed military man like Beck. It was above all necessary to reassure the few generals who were really in on the conspiracy, for they were likely to be frightened off when all sorts of well-meaning persons spoke to them about their alleged or actual plans.

Carl Friedrich Goerdeler also cannot be assigned to any one circle. He chose his numerous friends and collaborators without regard to their group allegiances. The particular task he had set himself was to unite the most variegated individualities, temperaments, and theories under a common banner. Of his indefatigability, his courage, his zeal, I have spoken frequently, but his chief merit was that he rationalized the Opposition. With a truly admirable one-sidedness he refused to see the things that divided oppositionists; he saw only human beings who were striving toward the same goal of eliminating Hitler. He straightway tried to bring these people together.

Naturally he was keenly aware that the Opposition had to have a program for government, and he had in fact masterfully succeeded in uniting his grand coalition upon such a program. This accomplishment was largely due to the wisdom with which he limited his aims. He was convinced that everything that did not have to be settled during the first days and weeks after the establishment of a post-Hitler government could be safely left to the discretion of the new order. Indeed, a new government would not acquire significance and permanency unless these problems could be discussed with full freedom. What Goerdeler tried with all his might to avoid was the coup within a coup — confronting the public with the accomplished fact of definite reforms as soon as the overthrow of Hitler succeeded. No matter how justified such reforms might be, he felt that they would violate the democratic character of the future régime.

In this respect, then, Goerdeler did not engage in 'politics,' although he was overbrimming with ideas and proposals of his own. To him all conferences had but one item on the agenda. First the Nazis must be overthrown; then it would be time to think of governing. Consequently, he endeavored to divert the thoughts of the men with whom he negotiated from the dispute about persons and programs and impress them instead with the need for action. His letters and memoranda referred incessantly to what was to be *done*. For the sake of action he traveled constantly. For the sake of action he occasionally took the risk of passing on his prognoses and information, in order to stimulate the hesitant.

He was often suspected of being too free with secrets, and undoubtedly the Goerdeler critics were often right. Nevertheless, he found himself, as time wore on, forced more and more into an unenviable, even a tragic rôle. It was not that people became tired of his 'harassing,' as they called it. Rather it was that the stragglers in the Opposition Movement balked at giving him the respect which was due him as an established leader. In the underground as anywhere else a man can outlive his usefulness. When the knell sounds, he can be pushed aside by the bold throng of his followers, not because he has become too old, but simply because he stands too high in the seniority list of active rebels.

The greatest tragedy for Goerdeler consisted in the fact that he, with his temperament, his energy, his eagerness, with his eternal invocation of action, was himself never in a position to act. He always had to wait for others; he always had to urge others; his was the painful task of challenging others to risk their lives on an act that he himself could not attempt. For how could he personally carry out a *Putsch*? For a civilian to prove to a general that there did exist a possibility for revolt, that it was merely a question of his having the courage to risk his own life, was an extremely embarrassing affair when one was disqualified from going ahead and providing a good example. There was no reason to assume that the sentinels of the three protective cordons around Hitler's headquarters or the SS guards outside — and inside — the Fuehrer's conference room would admit a civilian simply on his assurance that the briefcase in his hand contained matter of the greatest importance.

Consequently, Goerdeler had to wait and wait, until it was too late and he himself was no longer an actor, scarcely a coadjutor, but was dragged down by others into the maelstrom. After July 20, he fled like a hunted animal for a full month — and what 'flight' means in such cases can be understood only by those who have experienced the terrible physical and mental strain of being pursued incessantly. Then he was arrested in West Prussia. Who will be the first to cast stones at him for what followed? For the technical experts in torture and drugs extracted far more information from him than this thoroughly decent man would ever have given out had he been in full possession of his senses. Resistance to interrogation from the first to the third degree is not primarily a matter of character. It is essentially a question of physical constitution.

If Goerdeler can be blamed for anything, it is at most the fact that he unquestionably spoke to more people and informed more people about the conspiracy than, afterward, proved needful. We frequently had bitter disputes about this matter. I had been thoroughly convinced by Oster's example and by Nebe's constant warnings and had made it a point of pride in underground work to make as few personal contacts as possible and not even to confide in those whose agreement with our principles was beyond doubt and whose friendship was gladdening and encouraging. Goerdeler felt that he himself had to be an exception to this general rule. He felt that, quite apart from all questions of conspiracy, he was so much the drummer and politician of the Movement that he had to obtain a personal impression of all the leading figures behind the rebellion — leading in the broadest sense. Someone, he maintained, had to have a comprehensive view of the whole situation.

In February, 1945, Goerdeler died a pious and dignified death. His fame will remain as the man who, throughout the whole frightful time of Hitler's war, achieved the stature of the most indefatigable and undaunted warrior for religion, justice, and humanity.

I cannot conclude my remarks on the Opposition without considering a man to whom I was very close. I find myself constantly wondering whether, of all the diverse personalities that I met in the course of those twelve years, he was not after all the wisest. Certainly Wilhelm Canaris was one of the profoundest and most perplexing personalities among the oppositionists. More significant than any sketch which I could offer is that of General Lahousen, written after he was taken prisoner. His portrait of Canaris ought not to molder away in some dusty archives. I quote it here:

Any attempt to get to the bottom of Canaris's personality will probably always remain no more than an attempt. I am undertaking it here only because it is necessary to illuminate the background of many events that would otherwise remain incomprehensible.

Many people will deny my ability to judge Canaris objectively. They are both right and wrong. For I was too close to Canaris to achieve that objectivity in judging his complicated personality which only distance from a person can assure. On the other hand, precisely because of my close relationship with him and because I was one of his confidants within the Opposition circle of the OKW, I had the opportunity to gain insights into his complex mind which were inevitably withheld from many outsiders.

Canaris was the most difficult superior I have encountered in my thirty-year career as a soldier. Contradictory in his instructions, given to whims, and not always just, always mysterious, he had nevertheless developed intellectual and, above all, human qualities which raised him far above the military rubber stamps and marionettes that most of his colleagues and superiors were. He never struck me, Austrian that I am, as the typical German military man; rather he seemed a cosmopolitan in the uniform of a German admiral.

As one who shared his secret plans I know that Canaris played a double game; in the existing situation he could not help doing that. Nevertheless, I can scarcely say where the limits of that game lay. In general, in all that Canaris did or, as the case might be, omitted to do, it was very difficult to define the limits or to recognize a clear and undeviating line. The rôle he played was conditioned, in this respect as in all others, by his peculiar personality. He hated violence in itself. Therefore, he was repelled by the war. And therefore, he hated Hitler and the Nazi system. The weapons he used against that system were intellect, influence, cunning, above all, his 'double game.'

Canaris was not at all a technical expert in his work; rather he was a great dilettante. The underground circle that he had gathered around himself was as colorful and heterogeneous as his own personality. Men of all classes and professions, people whose horizons were broad and narrow, idealists and political adventurers, sober rationalists and imaginative mystics, conservative noblemen and Freemasons, theosophists, half-Jews or Jews, German and non-German anti-fascists, men and women — all of them united only in their underground resistance to Hitler and his system. This circle was by no means directed by secret orders. Rather, it was an intellectual association which Canaris constantly influenced by slight or direct hints and which he guided by active intervention only in rare cases. Only a few initiates received concrete instructions, and even these were not always perfectly clear.

Canaris's urge to travel was literally a mania with him. Like Ahasuerus fleeing from himself and other men, he journeyed from town to town, everywhere spreading unrest and disorder in the Nazi system. Some of his intimates would then always have to put in order the things that Canaris had jumbled as might an overgrown child his toys. This they had to do in order not to endanger him and themselves. Their reward was rarely gratitude; it was usually an irritated reproach. Yet at many other times Canaris would take care of situations with exemplary clarity and without equivocation — with the same clarity and directness with which he (and to my mind he was the only one) sensed and predicted the actual course of this latest world-wide catastrophe.

His diary is impregnated with this fundamental understanding of the impending disaster. Those notes of his constitute, I think, an essential contemporary contribution to the history of this war's origins and are especially valuable as an exposé of its character as an aggressive war. All the chief actors are to be found in this document, and the subsidiary figures as well. We meet the men who bore the main responsibility, the knowing and the unknowing, the guilty and the innocent and the mere henchmen, those who profited by and those who were robbed by the Nazi system. Only one character is absent: Canaris himself. He does cite his words, his opinions, and his actions; but ordinarily he presents only one half, perhaps one third, of himself. The rest remains hidden.

Canaris rarely estimated men by their accomplishments or their character. Sympathy and antipathy were the guiding factors in his view of men — these and a number of curious complexes deriving from his exaggerated love for animals. 'Anyone who does not love dogs I judge out of hand to be an evil man,' he once said.

I was one of his closest intimates. An intimate, but not a friend, as some ignorant people have maintained. Whether the conclusions that Canaris drew from his knowledge of affairs were correct or incorrect, I do not know. But that he did draw conclusions I do know, and he was willing to follow those conclusions to their ultimate consequences. Canaris was not the man to oppose boldly and openly something that seemed wrong or bad to him. Nor do I know whether such conduct would have produced any meaningful result in the situation that then existed. He fought with the weapons with which his Creator had endowed him: his extremely flexible intelligence, his lively imagination, and his gift for cunning. But he fought against Hitler!

I lived with this confused, iridescent personality in every conceivable situation. Never did I witness in Canaris a trace of crudity or brutality, neither in thought nor in action. On the contrary, I have witnessed only sudden revelations of his deep-seated humanity, and somehow I was always greatly affected by each such revelation. I shall never forget his complete psychological breakdown under the impression of smoking and devastated Belgrade, where the stench of unburied corpses still lingered. And at such moments Canaris was not dissimulating.

It was his awareness of this and similar acts of violence and brutality which hardened his resolve to do everything in his power to prevent a victory of the Nazi system. I do not know what other motives may have influenced Canaris or what other aims he may have had. But I am certain that a knowledge of good and evil based on purely human considerations was the chief mainspring of his actions.

From about 1942 on, the admiral was inwardly a completely broken and distrait man. The hopelessness of his struggle and a premonition of his personal fate had left their mark upon him out-

wardly as well. At the end Canaris probably stumbled and fell—
over Canaris. But in a time of incredible horrors he always remained,
in contrast to many persons around him, decent and thoroughly
human.

Of the admiral's instrument, the *Abwehr,* one might choose to say
a great deal or very little. A great deal if one wished to write about
the secret history of the war. In such case it would be necessary to
enter a field far broader than that of German military espionage and
counter-espionage; a narrower span would falsify the picture. Perhaps it is still too early for that, but very little need be said beyond the
statement that work in the *Abwehr* proceeded along quite normal and
ordinary lines. A number of investigators of the victorious Powers
are nowadays extremely astonished to learn how badly they overestimated this organization around which mercenary sensational jour-
nalists wove the most incredible legends. Actually, the *Abwehr* func-
tioned well in small matters and very badly in large.

That, to be sure, must be accounted the merit of its chief. Now
and then, among the heaped-up pebbles of daily reports from agents,
a gold nugget gleamed, but there were always busy hands ready to
bury the nugget at once in the useless pile of 'reliable' news from
'informed sources.' Canaris would then demonstrate his remarkable
talents, on the one hand, by praising the ambitious prospectors for
their zeal and, on the other hand, by offering them his expert help:
no, they must not dig there but here; what they had found was a
piece of false gold, but they must be close; was not this other glit-
tering fragment of glass in reality a precious gem? He was an artist
in reducing a vital report by his intelligence service to such a trifle
that it vanished amid the mass of false information; or else he slashed
away at the material his agents brought him until in the end they
gaped in confusion and wondered how they could possibly have
stumbled on such a false trail. In every case he intuitively found the
right course, and always, of course, he played his part of a keen and
industrious chief of counter-intelligence. Everyone around him felt
that he held firm opinions and definite intentions, and everyone

reckoned that he would be better off not to get too much involved with this mysterious man.

Thus the *Abwehr* became his own personal instrument, upon whose keyboard he played with sovereign grace. He passionately hated not only Hitler and Himmler, but the entire Nazi system as a political phenomenon, but there cannot be any doubt that far more could have been achieved by full employment of the *Abwehr*. Canaris tolerated the seditious activities of the Oster circle by deliberately refusing to take cognizance of them. Except for a brief aberration of some twelve hours, he never wanted an assassination. He was particularly emphatic in his disapproval of any contact or collaboration with the enemy in the war. If I were to attempt to describe the nature of the man's activity — which sprang from a well-thought-out philosophy of life and a deep religious faith — I would say that his sole aim was to 'prevent.' Never did he want to play an active part in determining the fate of Germany and the world. To his mind, what could not be prevented was fated to happen as it did happen — even if it meant disaster for Germany and for himself personally.

'Passive leadership accompanied by the appearance of extremest activity' — that was the watchword he gave his associates to guide them in their official duties. He was everywhere and nowhere at once. Everywhere, in that he traveled to and fro, at home and abroad and to the front, always leaving a whirl of confusion behind him. No-where, in that, when the situation grew dangerous or the Fuehrer's headquarters was threatening to ask unpleasant questions, Canaris was never around. Even Hitler employed the much-traveled admiral, whom he saw personally no more than once every two or three months, to carry out extremely important secret foreign missions.

The manner in which Canaris carried out these missions can be indicated by a single example. At the apex of the Nazi successes a plan for conquering Gibraltar was drawn up. Canaris was assigned the task of softening up Franco's foreign minister, Jordana. He flew to Spain, accompanied by General Lahousen, and even before the audience was held he dictated to his general a secret report on Jordana's flat refusal of any assistance by Spain. Afterward he was somewhat disquieted when the foreign minister expressed himself in far more compliant terms than those Canaris had put into his mouth.

Prevention! As a result of the Nuremberg Trials the skill with which Canaris prevented the murders of Generals Giraud and Weygand has become public knowledge. When Hitler censured him for letting these men escape, Canaris cleverly made use of the assassination of Heydrich to shift all the blame to the Black hangman. In the spring of 1943, when Oster heard of the scheme for kidnaping both the King of Italy and the Pope, in order to prevent the fall of Mussolini, he made a brief telephone call to Canaris and hinted at what he had learned. The admiral at once emplaned from the Crimea to Berlin, and from there flew on to Venice to warn his Italian colleagues.

Similarly, many carefully planned acts of sabotage against the enemy were suddenly revealed as technically impracticable; Canaris saw to it that they failed for inexplicable reasons. On countless occasions assistance was given to Jews, Christians, or citizens of enemy countries who were threatened by death; such work was part of the regular 'official' activity of the *Abwehr*. Canaris approved these instructions and concealed them from the Gestapo. This last was often the most difficult part of such enterprises. It is hard to say whether Canaris instituted or composed those courageous memoranda in which the diabolic intentions of the SS in occupied territories were revealed beforehand or their cruel practices proved afterward by documentary evidence. What is essential is that he was responsible whenever such 'undesired' proofs were laid before Keitel, Brauchitsch, Halder, Raeder, or anyone else whose conscience he felt needed stirring.

One might imagine that only a particularly robust personality would be capable of such a dangerous double game as Canaris played for an entire decade. In reality, this small, frail, and somewhat timid man was a vibrating bundle of nerves. Extremely well read, oversensitive, 'sicklied o'er with the pale cast of thought,' Canaris was an 'outsider' in every respect. In bearing and manner of work he was the most unmilitary of persons. To be sure, he could at times be harsh, so that the 'little Greek' as he was called enjoyed the respect of everyone. (Although his family had been settled in Germany since the seventeenth century — his father was the manager of a Westphalian mine — his Levantine origins were so marked that his nickname was virtually inevitable.)

Canaris had a natural bent for leading his opponents astray. He could recite the Nazi verses so convincingly that even the greatest skeptics temporarily no longer dared to question the genuineness of his claims. As one of the leading Gestapo officials exclaimed in angry candor to one of the few survivors of the July 20 *Putsch*: 'That Canaris fooled everyone, Heydrich, Himmler, Keitel, Ribbentrop, and even the Fuehrer.'

Canaris, however, would never go far enough. The fact that he did not remains, to my mind, the great weakness in his philosophy and his way of life. On the other hand, he was not of the passive school. He did things; he did a great deal; and he ventured something that was even more valuable than life: his honor as it would be judged by those who could not comprehend his attitude.

'What do they say about me abroad?' How often he asked me this question! I might almost say he put the question to me as a challenge, but with trembling voice, as if he expected my reply to be a verdict which I had neither the will nor the right to pronounce.

'Your game will soon have to come out in the open,' I used to say to him at such earnest moments. I meant by that to persuade him to rebel openly; that was what so many expected of him precisely because he had stamped himself outwardly as a devout functionary of the Nazi system.

His game did indeed come out in the open, but in another and more tragic sense. By murdering him his executioners themselves freed him from the Nazi embrace. Death the reconciler intervened and clarified on a higher plane the many ambiguities which he would never have been able to resolve fully in life.

FRUITLESS PEACE FEELERS,
USELESS WARNINGS

ONCE THE WINTER MONTHS were past and the spring of 1940 smiled
upon the land, the Opposition stirred again.

It is not by chance that the Ides of March and the Eighteenth
Brumaire (November 9) are the classical days for crises in revolutionary epochs. When the sap is rising and new life throbs, the
spirit of enterprise mounts. Similarly, it flickers up one last time
before the long winter sleep descends. I recall only one case in which
plans for revolt took concrete form in the hot summer months. That
was in July, 1944. We know the result.

All the reflections in which we had engaged during November
were revived that spring. No one knew what interpretation to put
upon the *drôle de guerre*. Some thought it had been merely a necessary winter pause. Others claimed to know better; it had all been a
matter of histrionics, they asserted. After a decent interval in which
both parties had played 'Let's pretend' with remarkable stagecraft,
they would now sit down at the conference table and negotiate.

This spreading of peace rumors from time to time was a favorite
trick of the Nazis. Such rumors encouraged the populace, which was
very unenthusiastic about the war. On the other hand, they aroused
considerable uneasiness among the Western Powers. Thus the Pied
Piper of Hamelin attained his end. With skirling pipes of peace he
led his people from one campaign to the next, while at the same time
he aroused in his enemies such apprehension that their own coalition
would break up that they stopped considering the possibility of a pact
with the German *fronde*.

Among our circle of friends no one doubted that Hitler would
venture an offensive in the West. We, therefore, had to hurry if we
wanted to prove to the generals that a possibility for peace with
honor still existed. Beck decided to continue along the lines of the
conversations that Joseph Mueller had begun in the Vatican in the fall
of 1939. Mueller enjoyed such confidence in Rome that the reliability

of his information would not be questioned. Thus the doubts of the British would be allayed, and on the other hand, Halder and Brauchitsch could not question the sincerity of the British negotiator — which they could have done in any other case, for if the Pope were intervening personally, the two generals could no longer fall back upon such an evasion.

The German Opposition was not a government competent to offer a binding signature to treaties or agreements. It, therefore, redounds greatly to the honor of the Pope that he, for the sake of European peace, put aside all misgivings and volunteered his services as a mediator. The conversations covered a wide range; there were repeated questions and inquiries referred back to sources at home. The details are no longer important in the light of the five years of war that followed, but the result cannot be overstressed. Provided, of course, that the Nazi system was thoroughly and completely eliminated, an arrangement was still possible!

At Beck's instigation a detailed final report was prepared. Toward the end of March, General Thomas handed this report to the chief of the general staff; but now, in the midst of war, Halder did not dare take the course which he (together with Witzleben) had been prepared to take in 1938 — going over his chief's head if necessary. He made his decision contingent on Brauchitsch's approval and Brauchitsch refused to act. Not only that, but he indignantly threatened to have Thomas and Oster arrested.

Thus failed the last impressive attempt to prevent the extension of the war and to persuade the top leadership of the *Wehrmacht* to take action. Brauchitsch and Halder had their choice, and they made it. They chose Hitler — and world war.

This is the proper place to interlard a few words on the other peace negotiations that were conducted by the Opposition.

Throughout the war there was incessant talk abroad of alleged peace feelers by an Opposition resolved on revolt. Many travelers from Germany — only those who possessed 'good connections' received visas, after all — hinted darkly about a legendary field marshal or an even more legendary group of conspirators. Most of these amateur diplomats hoped to elicit a favorable reaction to stimulate the forces of resistance at home in Germany. These advocates of a 'Dutch wedding,' who claimed to have the agreement of the one partner in order to win the consent of the other, were quite numerous in the innermost circles of the Opposition. They hoped to bring about a marriage of convenience — in this case a *Putsch* by the skeptical generals.

Unfortunately, their zeal did more harm than good. The enemy secret services were so swamped with reports from 'reliable' sources that they no longer knew whom to believe. Indeed, the task of intelligence on the other side was complicated by the fact that some of these peace rumors were spread by agents of the *Sicherheitsdienst* (Heydrich's organization) or the *Abwehr,* in order to test the enemy's firmness, or by Gestapo spies who hoped to get on the trail of the Opposition. In order totally to confuse the situation, a good many of the oppositionists who spread such reports were of the type who at home either rejected any thought of revolt or declared stoutly that a *Putsch* would be premature. Since all of these conversations naturally awakened certain hopes on the other side, the disappointment abroad was all the greater afterward. In the end various people had cried wolf so many times, had announced revolts and named dates so often, that the very existence of an Opposition to Hitler was no longer believed.

In reality there were very few authorized peace feelers. Naturally Goerdeler, von Hassell, Count Moltke, and Trott zu Solz — to name only these few — had kept up their old ties with highly placed personages abroad and had endeavored to make new connections, partly in order to obtain information and partly to pass on what they themselves knew. Every chance had to be exploited to create understanding abroad for the difficulties the Opposition faced and to prevent all ties from being broken off. Beck, however, constantly warned against our going too far. He was absolutely against giving any definite assurance which would necessarily discredit the Opposition if no *Putsch* was forthcoming. Therefore, he narrowed his negotiations down to those few situations which seriously presented a chance for an uprising. There were only five such occasions during the war: in November, 1939, in the spring of 1940, in the early part of 1943 after the disasters at Stalingrad and Tunis, at the end of 1943, and in July, 1944.

Certainly there is no validity to the argument that the Opposition wanted to overthrow Hitler, but that the *Putsch* was repeatedly hindered because statesmen abroad were not ready to come to an agreement. Up to January, 1943, when the Casablanca formula of 'unconditional surrender' was propounded, any such formulation was flatly incorrect and served only to further the lie that the Allies were prolonging the war. It may be that a few encouraging words from abroad would have helped the Germans to come to their senses, but even this is not absolutely certain, for during 1940, 1941, and 1942 the German diplomats in neutral capitals — the oppositionist diplomats as well, unfortunately — wrote continual messages home about the splendid chances for an arrangement with England. They merely served as a stimulant to Hitler and the Nazis, while at the same time our vacillating generals sighed with relief because now they could let the situation 'mature' for another six months — by which they meant that they would wait for the British to 'soften' or until they had attained by conquest a more favorable position for negotiation.

The conversations that Dietrich Bonhoeffer had with the Bishop of Chichester in Stockholm in May, 1942, were intended to offset any false impression produced by the negotiations in the Vatican. The idea was to show that the Opposition involved other than purely Catholic circles. There was, however, no intention of breaking off the connections that had been established through the Vatican; Bonhoeffer's proposals were co-ordinated with those of Joseph Mueller. At that time we could not give the Allies any definite assurances of a *Putsch* because the three field marshals who were the prospective *Putsch* leaders had been eliminated. Mannstein wanted to conquer Sebastopol first; Kluge was wavering as he always did; and Witzleben, who sincerely wanted to overthrow Hitler, was in Paris at the time — a commander who had no soldiers to command.

As is well known, the British government was not interested in the Bishop of Chichester's communications. After having overcome tremendous difficulties to arrange Bonhoeffer's trip, we were deeply disappointed by this inflexible refusal to consider negotiation. The zenith of Hitler's successes was past; his armies were rushing toward their first obvious disaster. Should it not have been time for the Allies to prepare for a psychological counter-offensive, in close collaboration with the German *fronde*? Such an offensive should certainly have begun after the shock of Stalingrad — and begun with a more generous gesture than the formula of 'unconditional surrender.'

Let us return, however, to Halder's and Brauchitsch's fateful refusal to act against Hitler. For most of the world, though not for German 'insiders,' one of the greatest revelations of the Nuremberg Trials was that our generals' guilt was not what it had been thought to be. In place of the charge of having planned aggressive war, the charge had to be that they let themselves be forced into it step by step, first into their intoxicating triumphs and then into their shameful defeats.

Such was the case with their Viking expedition to Norway. As in all the military adventures up to the end of 1941, the generals and admirals expected an outright failure. The success of this coup depended on too many reckless calculations; it seemed impossible that all the factors would divide out evenly. For example, some of the slow, heavy whaling vessels in whose holds entire regiments could be concealed required two weeks to make the crossing. It could scarcely be assumed that the extensive ship movements in the ports would escape the attention of British air reconnaissance or of the secret service. The experts declared that the British fleet would certainly be on hand to intercept the German transports sailing for Bergen, Trondheim, and Narvik. Today, knowing as we do what actually happened, it is hard to re-envision the dismay of the generals at learning early in 1940 of Hitler's plan for the Norwegian invasion. By that time the generals were inclined to acknowledge that their Fuehrer was politically infallible, but they continued to make fun of him as a 'corporal' and were highly unwilling to yield the field of military strategy to him.

Consequently, a failure of the Norwegian expedition would undeniably constitute the 'setback' that Halder had talked of so often. On the other hand, its success would do for Hitler's military prestige what the bloodless conquest of Prague had done for his political renown. The fate of Holland and Belgium hung upon the outcome of this northern campaign — as indeed the whole question of whether the war was to be extended.

For the first time during the war, the question arose in our circle of friends of transmitting military information. During the Polish war we had not needed to worry about this matter. The campaign was transparent, and indeed there was nothing that could be done about it. Now the situation was fundamentally different. The end of tyranny was within reach if — yes, if the other side knew what was to happen and what was at stake.

Some of us laughed aloud at the suggestion that Hitler's preparations could possibly be unknown to the British. Others refused to accept, personally, the rôle of destiny. If the British muffed this unique chance, they simply could not be helped, these friends maintained. Still others pointed out that British intervention based on our information would cost the lives of thousands of German sailors and soldiers. A minority in our circle took precisely the opposite view. Did we have the right to consider only the German casualties deriving from such an invasion?

No agreement was reached. In any event the actual number of persons who were in a position to transmit warnings to the British was extremely small; and some of these did resolve to obey the commands of conscience and 'betray' their fatherland. At that historic hour, however, the Norwegians had their quislings; the British contented themselves with laying a few mines — after the Nazi transport fleet had passed the danger zone.

There are still some worrisome souls among the Germans who will not admit that such warnings were issued, because they want to prevent the creation of a new 'stab-in-the-back' legend. The answer for such people is that the legend of 1918 was based on an historical lie;

that these warnings by German oppositionists, on the other hand, are historical facts. In the long run truth cannot be suppressed, and in this case it also ought not to be. It is important and necessary to demonstrate that during Hitler's war there were Germans who endeavored to turn the evil tide of events.

In any case, every one of these warnings was in vain. In 1940, Hitler was able to exploit his victories to the full. No one can possibly claim that the war was lost for the Germans because of such vain warnings. On the other hand, for those who seek more adequate explanations than that afforded by branding sixty million people guilty, is it not significant that the usurper was able to fascinate the entire world with the succession of his triumphs? There was no power inside Germany — but none outside Germany either — that was able to stop him. Not only the Germans, but the rest of the world as well, were hypnotized by the wizard's baleful eye, and it took some time before the spell was broken.

After the Norwegian triumph, of course, there were no longer any generals who would have dared to mutiny. The *fronde* made desperate, utterly desperate, attempts to do something, for its members had a premonition of the fate that would inevitably befall Germany and Europe if Hitler were permitted to attack in the West; but it was no longer possible to make any moral appeal to the generals and their answer to military arguments was always the same: 'It's working.'

But would it really 'work'? First the bridges over the Meuse and the Rhine, as well as Fort Ebenemael near Liége, would have to be taken by a coup. If the tanks and their supporting infantry columns did not cross the bridges at the very beginning, the break-through into the fields of Flanders would be blocked and Hitler's surprise tactics would fail. Practically, this meant that the success or failure of the offensive would be decided in the first twenty-four hours. Hitler had devoted all his thought and imagination throughout the winter to this *Blitz* and to the notorious secret weapons — the gliders that were to land on the top of Fort Ebenemael, the parachute troops that were to secure those strategically important bridges far behind the front, and the sabotage troops in Dutch uniforms which were supposed to operate at dawn on the day of the offensive and prevent the destruction of the bridges.

Once again the question arose as to whether we ought not to reveal these secret weapons. There were some among us who thought it no longer necessary, since a courier plane bound for Cologne from Munich and carrying essential deployment plans, including instructions for the parachute troops, had made a forced landing in Mechlin, Belgium; but the Belgians had assumed that the forced landing was a refined deception. As if they and the Dutch had not received enough information to prove that the danger was by no means over and that extreme alertness was imperative!

It was tremendously important at that time to convince Hitler or at least the generals of the tenuousness of their hopes that the key strategic positions would fall into their hands intact. Actually, they would believe in this only if the Dutch blew up their bridges before the invasion. Unquestionably that was an expensive undertaking. Nevertheless, it did not seem too high a price for them to pay if thereby the Dutch prevented an invasion of their country. If that had been done, the *Blitz* would have been started somewhere else, presumably directly against the Maginot Line — for the plans called for an offensive through Holland only if those bridges could be taken. Such a shift would have involved extensive dislocation of troop deployments and a complete revision of the timetable, and it certainly seemed more than doubtful that the hesitant generals would then have gone ahead. A thrust against the unprotected flank followed by the alluring war of movement was one thing; the prospect of long battles of attrition such as had been fought during the First World War was quite another.

All the Opposition's messages to the Dutch to forestall Hitler fell on deaf ears. Never fear, they would be on the alert; that was the reply we received. They needed only to press a button in order to blow up a bridge. Moreover, they were fully aware of the recent theft of Dutch police uniforms — the matter had even been mentioned in the newspapers; and none of the many travelers who were passing constantly back and forth between Germany and Holland could have failed to notice that whole armies were on the move along the Rhine. Seldom had the German Opposition received such self-assured and reassuring statements as during those last few weeks before the storm broke.

At that time conscientious oppositionists took great risks in order to convey warnings to the threatened neutrals. I shall mention but one case, one that created a great stir inside the *Abwehr*. At a certain neutral town the Belgian Embassy was receiving constant warnings of the impending invasion. With astonishing naïveté, the Belgian ambassador telegraphed a long report to his government, the greater part of which consisted of his arguments for discounting these warnings. His information, he said, came from a high German military source, for which reason it was probably intended as a deceptive maneuver, for otherwise the informer must be a — traitor.

This telegram, like so many others, was decoded. There was a great scandal. The *Abwehr* set feverishly to work — trying to cover up. I did my best to get in on the investigation, so that I could guide it into proper channels. Some day, perhaps, I shall write a special account of all the indiscretions — each one endangering someone's life — which were uncovered in the course of this investigation. It seemed that certain statesmen and certain countries simply did not want to be helped.

On the evening of May 9 a last urgent warning was issued. For the duration of the war the infuriated Hitler was to keep after the *Abwehr* and the Gestapo with demands that they find out who the 'traitor' or 'traitors' had been.

The events were afterward reconstructed in minute detail. It appeared that an hour after the final order was issued, the Dutch military attaché at the embassy in Berlin, Lieutenant-Colonel Sas, had word that the invasion was to start at four in the morning. Evidently he passed his information on to the Dutch army leadership, for two hours later — over the regular telephone lines! — he received a call from the Dutch secret service chief in The Hague. The chief simply could not believe that Mrs. Sas would actually have to go to the hospital and that the 'dental operation' was really going to be performed at four in the morning. He asked whether Sas had 'consulted several doctors.'

According to the sober stenographic record of the telephone-tapping department, the military attaché had brusquely replied that it was so, that all the doctors were agreed, and that the operation would undoubtedly take place early that morning, but that he could not understand how they could have the bad taste to trouble him over the telephone at such a moment as this.

Six hours later, Hitler's panzer armies rolled across the intact Dutch bridges, and the surprise assault upon Fort Ebenemael also went through without a hitch. The rest followed inevitably.

On June 14 Paris fell. Can we remember our feelings? The very thought was inconceivable. At first the Germans responded timidly and with a touch of embarrassment to the news of the victory. They, too, could not really believe that Paris had been taken; or rather, they hardly dared admit — what was already inevitable — that now Hitler could no longer be stopped; that now there was no one to block the onrush of the Revolution; that now there were no longer any limits.

I shall never forget those days after the fall of Paris. There was no sign of rejoicing, no trace of jubilation. One would have thought that they, the totalitarians rather than the democrats, had received terrible hammer-blows. The propaganda ministry had to put forth great effort to shake out of their mental paralysis these *Herrenmenschen* who were overwhelmed by their own victory. But then, as if only this prompting had been needed, as if overnight invisible defenses had been torn down, the choked tumult of victory suddenly poured out over Germany with tremendous vehemence. Madly intoxicated, these children of fortune pounced upon their new treasures; they divided up the goods and the lands of Europe. The doubters were put in stocks; the triumphant dictator was canonized; the Revolution went mad.

A few weeks later, Hitler held a session of his Reichstag. In the hall all the Nazi Party dignitaries crowded together. The jubilant wave of brown surged up to the platforms where, gray row upon gray row, each gray uniform splashed with the red of the coat-flap, the victorious generals sat and received decorations and honors from their 'greatest general of all time.' New generals of the army, new colonel-generals, twelve field marshals and a Reich marshal — Goering's title, newly invented for the occasion. Twelve field marshals! It was enough to take one's breath away. Afterward the people tried to console themselves with a joke: 'They're cheaper by the dozen.'

What were they to console themselves for? Clearly, for the conclusion of a campaign which, as everyone felt, was only a beginning. For a victory would not be succeeded by peace, but by incessant new campaigns.

On the rare occasions thereafter that the field marshals were to be seen, they seemed to be clinging desperately to their marshal's staffs; for they themselves knew best what the people did not suspect: that they were no more than the chief technicians for a usurper intoxicated with his own power, for a tyrant who was ruthlessly killing off the flower of his own people in order to satisfy his insatiate zest for destruction.

WASTED YEARS

I AM FORCED TO SUMMARIZE briefly the interval between the offensive in the West and the dramatic events of July 20, 1944 — not because there is too little, but because there is too much to say. The full story of the ebb and flow of events during that dramatic time, and especially the tale of the many missed opportunities, cannot be told until the other side has also revealed its secrets. Therefore, I shall point out only a few of the themes in the tapestry of events, those few motifs which run through all the shifting scenes and constitute the fate of our *fronde*.

The fall of 1940 brought about a significant change for me personally. In the autumn of 1938, my furlough to private industry was rescinded. After considerable trouble I succeeded in obtaining a transfer to the Potsdam administration. Thus I remained within arm's reach of my friends in Berlin. It soon turned out that this was not enough. The obvious thing to do, it seemed, was to find a place for me in the *Abwehr,* but for this a clean bill of health from the Gestapo was necessary, and I could scarcely expect that. Without more ado, Oster filled out a printed induction form in my name, calling me up to service in the *Abwehr.* Naturally, this forged document did not offer a permanent solution, but we were counting on the régime's being overthrown within the next few months, and there was no other way to have me on the spot in Berlin. There was a considerable risk involved for me under the stringent military laws, and Canaris and Oster tried to lessen this risk by sending me off to Switzerland during quiet periods. This could be done without attracting attention, since the *Abwehr* had authority to issue its own passports which did not have to be checked by the Gestapo.

With the fall of Paris, our oppositionist hopes were smashed. We now had to reckon on a much longer term of Nazi rule. Moreover, we now more than ever needed some kind of base abroad. Canaris, therefore, took advantage of the fact that the victorious *Wehrmacht* was at this time riding high. He appointed me to fill a post in the consulate-general at Zurich which was at the disposal of his counter-intelligence service. It was only some time later that the Gestapo found out what had happened, and then, for 'diplomatic' reasons, it was more difficult to have me recalled than it would have been had I been employed in the *Wehrmacht* headquarters.

This solution by no means legalized my position inside the *Abwehr.* I had refused to take any constructive part in the internal work of the *Abwehr,* but it was so organized that neither the admiral nor his chief of staff was empowered to make special assignments. Only the section heads of counter-espionage or information could cover up such an off-color affair. Thus it constantly cost us a tremendous amount of trouble to find new and urgent missions for me, investigations and approaches to persons of importance, and each of these missions had to be patently so delicate and complicated that my information could not be committed to paper, but had to be reported to the admiral or to Oster in person. Only by such pretense could my frequent trips back and forth between Berlin and Zurich be justified.

Even then the difficulties remained. The previous *Abwehr* chief in
Berne had to be deposed and a new and more tolerant officer located
who would already find me there busy with my special assignment.
Unfortunately, the gallant colonel asked all sorts of indiscreet questions and finally requested my recall. Whereupon he was promptly
relieved of his post. Since he was demanding not only my head,
but that of his military superiors, Canaris and Oster, his own was just
as much imperiled under military law unless he really could provide
proof of treason. With these considerations urged upon him, he
agreed to a decent compromise. It was not long before the colonel
began to doubt his own reason and was relieved when he was summarily dismissed from the *Abwehr* and sent off to a psychiatric retreat.

We had even more trouble with his successor. This officer started
out in a somewhat more promising manner than his predecessor; after
half a year he began to spy upon me, and in another half-year he had
prepared a very annoying — and moreover erroneous — indictment
of high treason against me; but by this time it was the spring of 1943,
when Oster's fall and the subsequent dismissal of Canaris in any case
put an end to this ambiguous situation.

The fall of 1940 provided perhaps the greatest test for all of us.
We soon learned that the invasion of England had been called off
after the first maneuver, but Hitler began threatening to loose aerial
warfare over England — which meant, in due time, over Germany
also. We heard grotesque details from insiders in the air ministry —
that, for instance, there was no possible protection against the fearful
destructiveness of German bombs.

With truly wonderful persistence the *Luftwaffe* won victory after
victory — on paper, to which Canaris soberly opposed the reports of
his own agents. One time Liverpool was razed to the ground overnight. For days afterward sparks flew — not over England, but between the *Abwehr* and the *Luftwaffe* command. Finally Goering was
forced to abate his claim to that of having ignited a cleverly arranged
camouflage set.

There were analogous troubles with those annoying British fighter planes. Thanks to the mathematical precision which distinguished all of Hitler's military calculations, an exact date could be set by which these nuisances would be wiped out. The British production figures were accurately known; the reports by our pilots of planes shot down were accepted *verbatim,* but the German pilots had placed their adding machines on a war footing to an even greater extent than had their English rivals. Every morning the number of remaining enemy fighter planes was announced: 200, 150, 100, 80, 20. When the sum reached minus 100, the cruel game was stopped, not by Canaris but by Goering. His *Blitz* had finally worn itself out with reports of victories.

At that time, when the thought of an air offensive upon Germany still seemed inconceivable, a remarkably large number of Germans suffered severe mental pangs at the thought of these bombings of English cities and English civilians. They felt thoroughly ashamed of this rage of destructiveness on the part of their leaders. The Opposition was entirely unified in its moral condemnation of the bombings and in its shame at the strident trumpetings of victory.

The events that followed, however, created widespread confusion — when, for example, Rumania, Bulgaria, and Hungary joined the Axis in quick succession, or when the British did not exploit the Greek victory over the Italians. If they could not profit by it militarily, why at least did they not make political capital of it? Generally speaking, the other side never profited sufficiently by the instability of Italy. Time and again Italy, which did not want war and was winning no victories, was on the point of breaking away from the Nazis; time and again she was pushed back into her rôle — which from a propagandist point of view was of tremendous importance — of the loyal and faithful ally.

The shock the British felt in 1941 could have been no greater than ours when Hitler's daring venture in Crete succeeded. For months afterward, of course, there was no possibility of talking revolt to the generals. Similar psychological devastation was wrought by Rommel's campaigns up and down the breadth of Africa. We depended not so much upon Rommel's reports as upon certain radio messages from enemy headquarters which provided all the information Rom-

mel needed — that Hitler's luck was holding out once again. Beck
was a lone voice crying in the wilderness — striking some as foolish,
others as tragic — when he repeatedly warned every general he could
engage in conversation that glorious victories counted for nothing;
only solid successes that could decide the war mattered.

Even more detrimental to the Opposition were the reports of victories in the Far East. With Singapore in the hands of the Japanese,
it was impossible even to talk with the generals.

To go back a bit, it is scarcely necessary for me to stress that every
possible opportunity was seized to warn the generals against the war
with Russia, but the *fronde* had been too often proved wrong by the
course of events. The generals refused to believe the prophecies of the
Becks and Hammersteins. This time they reckoned falsely. The people of Germany and the world were fed with incredible figures on the
prisoners and booty seized, but by the end of July and the early part
of August, 1941, Mars had already girded himself for his final de-
sertion to the opposing side. During the next twenty months our
armies advanced thousands of kilometers into the vast spaces of
Russia; and yet Beck was right. Some six weeks after the beginning
of the Russian campaign, when the central army group ground to a
halt, Beck proclaimed that the turning-point in the war had come.
After that halt they were merely advancing headlong into winter
without any real hope that they could reach the winter quarters in
Moscow for which they were longing. Halder and Brauchitsch must
have realized this. More criminal than all their strategic errors was
the cynicism with which these two 'commanders' obediently took their
orders and drove their soldiers on and on, well knowing that no
preparations had been made for a winter campaign and that the snow
and cold would claim frightful sacrifices.

During those weeks there arose in our minds a new conception of
how the inevitable defeat might take place. At the risk that we may
be mocked for having cherished illusions for so long, I want nevertheless to report this frankly. Up to that time we had conceived of the
defeat as taking the form of a gradual undermining of the strength of

Germany, either by starvation or by bombings. We had thought that
once the Germans recognized that it was hopeless to carry on the war,
they would voluntarily abandon the struggle. The form such a
capitulation would take, we thought, would probaly be a *Putsch* by
the generals — when it was too late, of course. We had never discussed the possibility that the German armies might be utterly beaten
on the field of battle; but in October, 1941, Nebe returned to Berlin
after having exercised a brief command at the front, and with absolute
assurance he maintained: 'We will not gradually lose our precedence;
this time we will suffer an undisguised military defeat.'

The conception of our *Wehrmacht* beaten in the field, of whole
armies in flight and of dozens of generals surrendering at once — even
oppositionists once found that hard to grasp.

Every day that the Russian war lasted, the crimes that were committed behind the fronts grew more and more fearful. The atrocities
committed by the SD police against Jews, captured commissars, and
guerrillas had no parallel in the whole bloody history of the Gestapo
tyranny. For a time it might be possible to cover up this terrible
shame and guilt, but that could not be done forever. Too many people
knew or suspected what was going on. Among the oppositionists
more and more men came to the conclusion that the war simply must
not — not any longer — be lost to the Russians. At worst it must be
won together with them.

Thus new confusion ensued. Many oppositionists made a virtue of
necessity. They discovered that, fundamentally, they had always been
against the plutocracies, against the unimaginative, aged Western
Powers. And they concluded that the only way to evolve away from
the Nazi régime was along totalitarian and collectivist lines. Paint
the brown gray again and let the gray be merged with the old revolutionary red. No sooner was Hitler's spell broken than the old
daemonic forces circumscribed us once more, and again many thinking people saw no way out of the vicious circle.

The sum of all this was that, under the pressure of victory, the
Opposition could not move. For two and a half fateful years nothing

happened. I do not mean to imply that we sat idle with our hands in our laps. Far from it. Nerve-racking rushings back and forth from one conference to the next, agitated journeys, excessive hopes or wild calculations that bore the distinct mark of helplessness, became our daily fate. The first preparations for an assassination of Hitler took place during this period. Even Canaris at one time relented on the question of assassination to the extent of locking Lahousen and me in his private office for a conversation on the matter. On Struenck's recommendation Oster called a well-known marksman into the *Abwehr* and gave him a 'furlough' which the man did not employ by going fishing. Popitz in his despair involved himself in his dangerous game with Himmler, while Doctor von Dohnanyi at times hoped he would be able to draw Wolf, chief group leader of the SS, into the conspiracy. Nevertheless, neither an assassination nor a *Putsch* took place. There was always something to interfere, some objection, some new plan, someone's decision to wait. When we tried to advance, we ran into a rubber wall.

Typical of our efforts at that time was a madcap adventure of Goerdeler's, his trip to Smolensk. There Kluge had his headquarters; his aides were General von Tresckow and the latter's son-in-law, Fabian von Schlabrendorff, whom we had contrived to install in the staff of the army group when he was a first lieutenant. Schlabrendorff had been in touch with Oster since 1938. In July, 1942, he offered to arrange a conference for Goerdeler with Kluge and Tresckow. Goerdeler immediately set about making preparations for a long journey. The Bosch firm that employed him had, it appeared, economic interests of the greatest importance in the Smolensk forest, and these had to be seen to without delay. Oster provided the various passes necessary for this trip.

Goerdeler was fortunate. Kluge saw him and talked with him several times. The field marshal was understanding and definite agreements were reached. What was more important, Goerdeler won over General Tresckow. Tresckow was one of the few officers who had been sympathetic to Nazism as early as 1933. A Pomeranian gentleman farmer, a Prussian to the core, and a talented military man, he had for years seen only the sides of National Socialism that were naturally appealing to a soldier: the discipline, the reassertion of Germany's right to arm, the revisions of the Versailles Treaty. While his comrades had at first been skeptical or opposed, only later to go over to the triumphant Hitler with all flags flying, Tresckow went through a reverse development. Probably he was not fully aroused until he had witnessed the horrors in Poland or the atrocities of the war in Russia. In any case, Goerdeler came just at the right time and succeeded in drawing this general, who inwardly had long since broken with Hitler, into active participation in our conspiracy. Tresckow adhered to the cause with the energy and clarity of purpose that was so characteristic of him until he committed suicide on the morning after July 20, 1944. It was particularly unfortunate that this officer, who really knew how to go the limit, was not in the Bendlerstrasse on that dramatic day, but was far away on the Eastern Front.

Schlabrendorff was soon introduced to Beck, and it was he who assured continual co-ordination among Tresckow, Oster, Goerdeler, and Beck. However, neither he nor Tresckow succeeded in holding Kluge in line. As soon as Goerdeler left Smolensk, the marshal began to worry. In a letter to Beck he criticized the 'surprise-assault' nature of Goerdeler's visit and said he wished to avoid possible 'misunderstandings.'

Goerdeler had joyfully reported his success to Beck, without understanding our tactful hints that it was always necessary to be skeptical about Kluge's promises. When Kluge's letter was shown to him, he was reduced to a state of utter despair. Then everyone jumped on him for being 'premature' and 'pressing,' for never being able to wait for the proper moment. In this little segment of history the whole tragedy of Goerdeler's fate as an oppositionist was contained.

Before anything could really be done, the outlines of military defeat had to be clearly apparent. In the middle of December, 1942, Oster called me to Berlin. The news I heard was startling indeed. Not even the neutral press or the newspapers in the belligerent countries had wind of it as yet, but Beck insisted that a tremendous disaster was in the making. On his military map he drew a circle around a city — Stalingrad.

There still remained the possibility that Hitler could give the order to retreat in time. The iron ring around the Sixth Army was not yet closed. All rational military strategy demanded retreat — and just for that reason Beck did not expect it. Hitler, by making his megalomaniac speech in the Sportspalast, in which he had declared that Stalingrad would be taken at all costs, had cut off all retreat for some five hundred thousand men. Hitler's prestige was worth whole armies to him — especially in a case where the city under siege bore the name of his detested adversary.

Beck arranged that as soon as the fate of the Sixth Army was sealed, I should return to Berlin again — and for good, we assumed.

In the spring of 1942, Oster had won over General Olbricht, the man who from now on directed the technical headquarters of our conspiracy. In the OKW, Olbricht held the office of chief of the *Allgemeine Heeresamt* (the general army office). As such — and this was of prime importance — he was the permanent deputy of the commander-in-chief of the home army. He held a real key position, one that was even more important than Oster's, for he not only saw and heard a great deal, but had the power of command over active troops. Practically speaking, the entire organism of the home army was at his fingertips and — at least for a few hours — he could issue orders to it. Moreover, if necessary he could arrange the transference of reserve troops to the front in such a way that they would be at our disposal for purposes of a *Putsch*. Olbricht was not a man for revolutionary action; he was equipped to be what he now was, an administrative head. Therefore, he confined himself to doing all the preparatory work and to covering up our tracks — an achievement for which this devoted man will always be remembered with gratitude, in spite of all his later mistakes.

Olbricht informed Oster and Beck that he was willing to provide a refuge for me in his office; I would enter under an assumed name, of course. On January 12, 1943, I came to Berlin. The Stalingrad *débâcle* was already in progress. Day and night we thought of the thousands of individual tragedies that must be taking place in the icy winter cold along the Volga. Each of the few planes that came out of the encircled army brought new messages of despair. Nevertheless, it was simply impossible to imagine that Hitler, blind with fury though he was, should want to sacrifice half a million men to his prestige. Nor was it possible to get used to the idea that hundreds of thousands of men would be sent to imprisonment in Siberia.

What about the generals? We expected that dozens of them would now have to commit suicide, since they had not had the courage to defy the orders of an insane dictator and to save the lives of the soldiers under their charge either by withdrawing from the ring in time or by surrendering before the slaughter mounted to such incredible proportions. Would one or two cowards among them personally surrender . . . ? Unthinkable! When the announcement of their surrender by the dozen came, the main assignment of the intelligence service was to determine whether the Russians were making a false claim!

Olbricht locked me in a room so that I would not be disturbed while I drafted the necessary preliminary measures, and, since accidents always happen when they are least desired, one day the key broke off in the lock and Olbricht had to go to a great deal of trouble to free me — thus making me the object of the curiosity of suspicious adjutants, stenographers, and so on.

We found that in one important respect nothing had changed since 1938. There were still no instructions providing for a military state of emergency. Similarly, there was no information on the distribution of SS bases throughout the Reich. The Gestapo — for reasons of secrecy, of course — had kept all such knowledge to itself. Finally, however, one ingenious soul devised a solution. He persuaded the police vice squad to make a map for him of newly established brothels. Wherever the SS was established in force, such institutions for their physical well-being had been set up. By this roundabout method we obtained an accurate picture of the SS bases.

Without support from the uniformed police and the criminal police a *Putsch* could not be carried out, but conditions in the police force had changed alarmingly since 1938. Many of the police officers had been eliminated. Many had deserted to the Nazis, out of opportunism or the consciousness that they, too, were involved in the general guilt that the Nazis had brought down upon Germany.

Our *Putsch* was based on evading as far as possible the problem of the soldier's oath to Hitler. Most of the generals still did not dare to take that hurdle without flinching. They knew that at the end of 1941 Hitler had appropriated arbitrarily the title of Supreme Commander of the Army. Somewhat later he had also taken over the functions of a commander-in-chief in the East — because he feared that too much power in the hands of a few marshals might prove dangerous to him. Our plan was to take advantage of this. The moment the Stalingrad disaster was complete, the marshals in the East were to act. They would not renounce their oath to Hitler as head of the state or as their supreme commander, but simply refuse to obey him in his capacity of commander-in-chief in the East. This was to serve as a pretext for Witzleben, as commander-in-chief in the West, to break with Hitler — still on a purely military basis. In the ensuing confusion Beck would take over in order to restore a unitary military command. Then, employing Olbricht's well-prepared home army, we could carry out a 'legal' *Putsch*.

The whole plan was obviously a purely theoretical creation, but if it soothed the consciences of those marshals who were confirmed in their habit of receiving orders from above, it would do very well. A prerequisite, of course, was that Kluge should join the action, and for him to join there was another necessary precondition: that Paulus should not silently commit suicide, but link his departure from the military stage with a proclamation to the army and the people.

It was at this point that our calculations went astray. Paulus did not commit suicide, nor did he attempt to convert the disaster that had befallen him and his soldiers into a beacon light for the nation. As a reward for his senseless sacrifice of hundreds of thousands of brave soldiers, he hurriedly had the title of field marshal conferred upon himself. Then this man, who had composed so many orders of the day enjoining the troops to hold out to the last, calmly led his generals into Russian captivity. The shock of this behavior drove

Mannstein back into Hitler's arms. Mannstein had in any case a guilty conscience because he had neither ordered Paulus to retreat in time nor committed his reserves in an attempt to break the encirclement.

There remained one marshal, Kluge. Depressed, but allegedly still resolute, Kluge went to a decisive conference at the Fuehrer's eastern headquarters. We suspected the worst from the fact that he was still willing even to talk with Hitler.

I can still envision the thin tape which contained the message from the chief of army communications, General Fellgiebel, who had installed a secret direct wire to Olbricht's office especially for this purpose. Slowly the teletype ticked off the message. Kluge, too, had capitulated. The Fuehrer had made a few strategic concessions, had given him permission to 'straighten the line' here and there, and this had 'convinced' Kluge that he had to 'try it' once more with Hitler.

SEVERE SETBACKS

LATER, IT WAS ASSERTED that this Stalingrad *Putsch* had been crippled at the last moment by the Casablanca formula of 'unconditional surrender.' This story is an attempt to relieve the generals of the blame for missing a unique opportunity. In those dramatic days, however, the Casablanca formula — debatable as it was from both the political and the propagandist points of view — did not in any way influence the chief persons concerned.

In the first place, that formula was not widely published until the very last days of January, and the grave psychological effect it was to have upon many groups within the Opposition was not fully realized until some time later. On the contrary, at first many oppositionists thought that 'unconditional surrender' might be the only terms in which to talk to the German generals. It was necessary, many believed, to show our generals a clenched fist, so that they would at last understand that their plight too was growing serious. In the second place, dozens of generals had provided sufficient proof that as a class they were not averse to unconditional surrender once they recognized clearly that they were defeated in the field, for dozens of them had surrendered to the Russians. The question for them was, of course, solely whether they recognized defeat. A sense of honor they no longer possessed; it had long since been blunted by the practices of Hitler and Himmler.

At the time we did not abandon hope, in spite of Kluge's defection. Another shock, the mass surrender in Tunis, had been foreshadowed months before. We hoped that we should be able to make use of this opportunity. Unfortunately, we assumed that the Anglo-American forces would take the leap across to Sicily immediately thereafter. At the time virtually no German troops were stationed on that island. It was only during the following two months that Hitler constructed his new defensive front — while the Allies were marking time. Therefore, we waited in vain — as Badoglio probably waited with us.

A great many details must still be published to fill out the story of those critical months, for it was then that the future was sealed, the fact that the war would be protracted to the point of total destruction. If only the event that took place on July 24, 1943 — the fall of Mussolini — had taken place two months earlier! If only the event had not been dismissed with the bitter and malicious phrase that the Italians would be left 'to stew in their own juice'!

Even when such hammer-blows crashed down upon the Opposition, Beck and Goerdeler were not swayed from the determination that Hitler must be overthrown. Every day brought new and more terrible casualties. The bombings mounted night after night. Little imagination was required to predict the frightful devastation which we can see today. But could a revolt now be expected of any of the generals? Scarcely. That much was clear by February, 1943. Consequently, at that time Beck gave his consent to assassination, which until then he as well as Goerdeler had rejected for religious and political reasons.

Fabian von Schlabrendorff (in his book *Offiziere gegen Hitler*) has given us a detailed account of the attempt that he and General von Tresckow made to assassinate Hitler. At the end of February, Olbricht told Schlabrendorff: 'We are ready. The "ignition" can be turned on.' Then Canaris (who once more suspected more than he wished to admit), Dohnanyi, and Lahousen flew to Smolensk for an *Abwehr* conference. Upon Oster's request Lahousen took from his Berlin supplies particularly 'good material' — explosives, that is — for his subordinate in Smolensk, Colonel von Gersdorff.

Tresckow and Schlabrendorff checked their bomb dozens of times; but it was all for nothing. Hitler's guardian devil on that March 13 would not let the tiny percussion-cap function. The bomb that had been smuggled into the Fuehrer's plane never did explode.

In his study of July 20, which we have already quoted, Emil Henk reports that at the end of 1942 the leading Socialists came to a decision 'to prevent the *Putsch* in the spring and to set the date finally for the weeks after the successful invasion of Europe by the Allies, not before.' We are grateful to Henk for this information, for it proves that the authoritative men among the Social Democrats were opposed to any action even at that time. This will serve as an example of all the tensions that pervaded the Opposition.

On the other hand, the facts I have just recounted prove how mistaken is Henk's assertion that Beck was informed of the Socialists' decision by Count Moltke who 'convinced' him that he must stand aside from any *Putsch* or attempt at assassination. Quite the contrary: Beck became increasingly active. He even wrote to Mannstein one last time, although such begging letters were altogether distasteful to him. Mannstein's reply was worthier of a subaltern than of a field marshal possessing his intelligence, and it was also insincere and untrue. 'After all,' he wrote, 'a war is not lost until one gives it up for lost.'

Not all the Social Democrats agreed with the position of their Kreissau wing. Leuschner continued to support Goerdeler's 'harassing.' The destruction was growing to such monstrous proportions that he felt oppositionists could not afford the luxury of letting the situation mature. Goerdeler's letter to Olbricht of May 17, 1943, was basically addressed not only to the general, but to the Kreissau group as well:

> Again and again I have considered this view that we must first wait for the psychologically correct moment.

If by that is meant the time when events themselves will compel action, then that time will be synonymous with the beginning of total collapse. Any action taken will be too late to be exploited politically. In the meantime irreplaceable cultural monuments and our most important centers of economic life will have become rubble-heaps and the military leaders will have sacrificed many precious human lives. Therefore, we may not wait for the 'psychologically correct' time to arrive; it must be brought about by adroit leadership. For certainly we agree that leadership is legitimate only for those who have acted correctly and with foresight. For the sake of the future of our country I should not wish the intelligentsia, a class which has evolved over centuries, to be excluded from that leadership, nor, for the same reason, should the experienced leading minds among our soldiers be left out.

Stalingrad and Tunis are defeats so grave that German history has not had their like since Jena and Auerstaedt. In both cases the German people were told that cogent reasons required the sacrifice of whole armies. We know that this is untrue; for soldiers and statesmen can defend the necessity of sacrifices only when they can guarantee a success in other realms that outweighs the sacrifices. The truth is that incompetent and conscienceless leadership is alone responsible; good leadership would have avoided both those tragedies and thus obtained at least a somewhat more favorable military and political situation.

The number of civilians of all nations, men, women, and children, who have been killed on orders before and during this war, including the Russian prisoners, far exceeds one million. The manner in which they were put to death is monstrous; in these killings there has been no trace of chivalry, humanity, or even the most primitive standards of decency among savage tribes. Yet the German people are falsely informed that the Russian Bolshevists are the ones who are continually committing monstrous crimes against innocent people.

Facts can be added to the list almost without number. I have stressed only these two matters because they are elementary examples of the moral pollution of the German people. These facts, together with the fact of a general corruption unexampled in German history and the fact that justice has been annihilated, afford every incentive for creating the 'psychologically' correct moment. Undoubtedly the great majority of the German people, and almost the entire working class, know today that this war cannot end well.

In the face of this realization the patience of the people seems inexplicable; but this phenomenon is solely due to the fact that terror and secrecy shield the lies and the crimes. The people will show their true feelings at once when they see that the terror is being halted, the corruption annihilated, and candor and truth presented them, instead of secrecy and lies. In that hour all Germans will be brought to their senses, the good ones as well as the bad; all Germans will renounce and condemn the actions which only yesterday they tolerated because those actions were kept secret; for the decent Germans will see their responsibility and the bad Germans will once more become aware of the existence of decency.

If we can find no other way, I am ready to do everything possible to arrange a conclusive personal conversation with Hitler. I would tell him what must be said, in particular that the vital interests of his nation demand his resignation.

I do not say that such a conversation, if it can be brought about, must necessarily end badly. Surprises are possible, though not probable; but the risk must be taken. However, I do not think it presumptuous of me to demand assurance that my step would be followed by immediate action.

The political preparations for this step have been made. I urgently request you, my dear General, once more to examine the question of whether the obstacles in the way of the requisite technical measures cannot be overcome. I ask you also to consider thoroughly the procedure I have proposed and to give me the opportunity, after my return, for a quiet discussion with you of the situation and the possibilities.

The proposed conference did not come off. It was not until November, when the avalanche could scarcely be stopped any longer, that Beck, Goerdeler, and Tresckow met in Olbricht's home. Kluge, too, was on hand. In July, Goerdeler had once more made a written offer to Kluge in the following letter:

In the face of this obvious national misfortune to which we have been brought by an insane leadership that despises divine and human laws, I presume to direct one last plea to you. You may be assured that it will be the last. The hour has now come when we must finally decide our own personal destinies as well. There is one path that conscience clearly points out; there is another, more comfortable one. Perils may lie along the former path, but it is honorable; the latter leads to a bitter end and terrible repentance. Do you know any means whereby, in the face of the frightful and ever-increasing destruction of German cities, a victory can be won? Do you know any means whereby Russia can be repulsed from Europe and the United States and the British Empire can be forced to desist from these bombings and make peace? That is the political and military question with which we are confronted. . . . If such a victory is not possible, then continuance of the war is an outright crime, for a nation can never end its life heroically; it is always under the compulsion to go on living.

I have once again determined, and I will take the responsibility for this statement, that a possibility still exists for us to conclude peace on a favorable basis if we Germans make of ourselves a people with whom it is once again possible to deal. It is obvious that no statesman in the world can negotiate with criminals and fools, because none would recklessly entrust the fate of his nation to the hands of fools. Our own conscience can tell us that. Naturally, then, it is more difficult now than it was a year ago to transform the possibilities into realities; and the possibilities can be exploited only if our statesmen have a little time in which to maneuver, and not if, as in 1918, they are overnight confronted with military collapse. If this prerequisite, which depends on the military forces, is fulfilled, we would be able through negotiation to put a stop to the war in the air at once, and gradually to slow down the military actions on land. Today anyone who can proclaim to the German people that the bombings are ended will have the people behind him and no one will dare to raise his voice against him or lay a finger on him. That is the situation, that and no other.

I shall not trouble you any longer. I ask only one reply from you and I shall know what it means if you refuse to answer me.

In July, Kluge had remained silent. Goerdeler's feelings can easily be imagined when, in November, the marshal cordially held out his hand and said: 'You were right.'

Thus the year 1943 was a year of disasters for the Opposition. Everything failed — first the projects for a *Putsch* and then several attempts at assassination. For there was more than one. That dauntless lieutenant-colonel, Schrader, and General Stieff, who joined the *fronde* toward the end of 1943, also made attempts. At one occasion Hitler called off a meeting; at another the explosives went off by spontaneous combustion. This latter incident produced a piquant situation. As *Abwehr* chief at the Fuehrer's headquarters, Schrader himself conducted the investigation of the explosion, and it cost him a great deal of trouble to lead it into false channels and finally drop it.

Toward the end of the year, Mierendorff was killed in an enemy air attack. With him was lost the strongest and most ardent personality among the Social Democrats. A few weeks later Count von Moltke was struck: the Gestapo arrested him early in 1944. Thus the Kreissau circle lost its leader. What that meant we were to learn during the days before July 20. Moltke's balance and moderation undoubtedly had prevented many careless and improvised actions.

The worst blow, however, was the destruction of the Oster circle, which took place in April, 1943. As early as the winter of 1942 we had heard from Nebe that the Gestapo was preparing to strike; but Himmler still did not dare. An attack on the *Abwehr* would stir up too much dust.

Brigade Leader Schellenberg, however, was urging action. As chief of the political intelligence service he had kept an especially suspicious eye on the bustle surrounding Oster. In addition, Schellenberg was impelled by pure rivalry. For a long time he had aimed at becoming head of a unified political and military intelligence service, and unfortunately he was the cleverest of the department heads in the *Reichssicherheitshauptamt*.[1] He saw through the camouflage of exclusively 'military' intelligence work with which Oster's 'special deputies' in Sweden, Spain, Switzerland, or the Vatican disguised their

[1] Through this 'main security office' Himmler controlled the entire police forces of the Reich. The criminal police, which Nebe headed, was subordinate to the *Reichssicherheitshauptamt*. Helldorf's police forces, the uniformed *Ordnungspolizei*, were directly subordinate to the ministry of the interior, which at this time was also headed by Himmler. (*The translators.*)

'seditious' conversations. Indeed, Schellenberg saw more closely than
the Gestapists, whom we succeeded in persistently deceiving up to
July 20, 1944.

It was very nerve-racking to hear Nebe's accounts of the pertinacity
of this evil genius, and, as if everything were conspiring against us,
Schellenberg secured a first-rate 'pretext.' A Bavarian industrialist, a
member of the *Abwehr* in Munich, had wormed his way into the
confidence of Doctor von Dohnanyi and had offered his services in
political work. In a mutual exchange of opinions the industrialist had
learned more than necessary. Arrested for smuggling foreign exchange, he had tried to use his knowledge to extort protection from
Canaris. When Canaris indignantly refused, the man had testified to
what he knew. Thus, the Gestapo, among other things, found out
about Joseph Mueller's and Dietrich Bonhoeffer's negotiations. The
report sounded so sensational that at first the Gestapo chiefs, Kaltenbrunner and Mueller — Gestapo Mueller, as he was called — refused
to believe it.

Naturally the gentlemen of the Prinz Albrechtstrasse knew very well
that 'something was wrong' with Oster, but even they could not
imagine so much high treason all at once. At any rate, they deemed
it too dangerous to call a spade a spade, for it was quite clear that
in such a situation Canaris would have to defend himself by every
conceivable means. If the denunciation were only half true, the
Canaris-Oster group could only end on the gallows. Himmler, with
his typical cowardice, therefore circled his victim for months. Telephone-tapping, opening of letters, shadowing, were continuous, but
we were now on our guard: the Black gangsters could not get the
'final' proofs.

The agents of the *Sicherheitshauptamt* were very well aware that
they would learn nothing by surprise raids on dwellings or by initial
interrogations, and even in this relatively late year of 1943 they
would not have been able to put over a coup that would last for
longer than twenty-four hours. Then the machinery of military justice
would have intervened, for the military alone could conduct investigations of the *Abwehr*. The SS would be robbed of its prey. With Sack

running the investigation, he would have insured that there would have been a great to-do that came to nothing, and in such tempestuous times actions that misfired tended to boomerang against their initiators. Himmler did not want to run that risk. Therefore, the SS leaders conferred for months before they at last found the proper 'twist.'

They uncovered a vast and scandalous story of fraud. Jews in danger had been aided by being smuggled into Switzerland as *Abwehr* 'agents.' In addition, considerable sums in foreign exchange had been paid out to them to compensate them for the loss of their German property. The technical basis for this had not been too far-fetched; 'agents' could not, after all, be sent across the border without funds. The difficulty was that the Gestapo had not for a moment believed this tall tale, although Canaris personally argued the matter out with Kaltenbrunner. Of the fourteen Jews who had by this means escaped death, no more than two or three could possibly be considered to have the qualifications of espionage agents. So far as the others were concerned, the charitable motive was all too unmistakable. With their characteristic bravado, the Gestapists now asserted that these 'agents' had been employed by the *Abwehr* in smuggling foreign exchange for the personal profit of members, and unfortunately they uncovered a number of personal missteps by a leading member of the *Abwehr* — who had no connection at all with the Oster circle or with the rescue of the Jews. With their usual adeptness at coloring the truth, however, the Gestapists stirred the two 'cases' together into such an impenetrable mixture that any unsuspecting observer would have to agree that these wholly 'unpolitical' and purely 'criminal' charges must certainly be investigated by the appropriate authorities. At any rate, no uninitiated person would be inclined to stop such proceedings once they had been instituted.

People who are conducting a risky underground conspiracy can afford to become involved in rescue work only to a very limited extent, no matter how well camouflaged such work may be. Naturally there had been no trace of fraud in this matter. Every imaginable safeguard had been taken to make sure that the funds for the agents were deposited with some neutral institution, but fraud was not the issue.

Even before the investigation began, the Gestapo knew what the outcome would be, as they cynically admitted a few days afterward. Unfortunately, they attained their end completely. They now had a safe and simple pretext for making initial arrests. Then, in the course of the interrogations — quite by chance, of course — they would shift from the criminal to the political problem.

The plan was diabolically clever, but it was still necessary to obtain the consent of Hitler and Keitel to the initiation of an indictment. Calculating cleverly, the men in black hid behind Goering. They knew that Goering wanted revenge for the discovery of the 'Red conspiracy' in the air ministry. What was more obvious than to discover the existence of a 'Christian conspiracy' in the OKW? They would prove collaboration with the Vatican and Geneva! Goering persuaded Hitler to appoint for the investigation of the *Abwehr* that tried-and-true grand inquisitor who had just handed down his ninety-fifth death sentence as 'Special Commissioner with the Reich Military Tribunal.' This man, Chief Provost Officer Roeder, a thoroughly vicious scoundrel, requested the Gestapo to assign a number of agents to him. Thus 'legal' military proceedings were instituted. There was no connection with 'politics,' no connection with the Gestapo.

On April 5 the long-awaited blow was struck. One of the first to be arrested was Doctor von Dohnanyi. As bad luck would have it, there was an incident when he was arrested. When Roeder, accompanied by Canaris, appeared in Oster's office and requested his presence at the arrest of his subordinate, Oster refused to let them pass into Dohnanyi's room, which adjoined his. If Roeder wanted to arrest someone, he said, then let him arrest him, not his subordinate, for whose official activities he took the full responsibility. Humanly speaking, this was beautifully courageous; politically, it was unwise and, moreover, quite impossible, since the order for arrest referred, not to official activities, but allegedly to Dohnanyi's private affairs. Oster had to yield. All that remained of his gesture was an atmosphere of extreme irritation, which was discharged in the scene that followed.

The day before, Canaris had warned Dohnanyi and had made sure that his private safe was 'in order.' The admiral could, therefore, not be reproached for admitting Roeder to Dohnanyi's office without announcing him. Nevertheless, Dohnanyi was apparently caught by surprise. While Roeder was searching the safe, Dohnanyi excitedly whispered several times to Oster, who was standing by his desk: 'Those papers, those papers!' Oster went through moments of mental torment. Should he ignore these pleas, or play the part of a correct superior and order his collaborator to be quiet? Or should he not try his best to take possession of the papers which lay on the desk? Dohnanyi would never have made so rash a suggestion unless the papers in question were matters of life and death. Oster chose the second course — and the Gestapo official who was assisting Roeder observed him.

A few hours later Oster was relieved of his post, and because of the bit of byplay that had accompanied their discovery, the 'important papers' acquired even greater importance. One of them was a letter from Dietrich Bonhoeffer asking for the release of seven 'indispensable' Protestant pastors from military service. Even before the 'political' side of the investigation had begun, the Gestapo had in its hands the first evidence for the Christian conspiracy. One of the leading members of the *Bekenntnisskirche*,[1] Dietrich Bonhoeffer, whom the Gestapo had forbidden to speak or travel, was revealed as an agent of the *Abwehr* in Rome, Geneva, and Sweden. In addition, Oster was virtually convicted of releasing clergymen from military service under false pretenses. According to the latest 'legal' practice, the punishment for such manipulation of the draft machinery was death.

There is not space to go into the details of what followed; I must restrict my account to the tragic circumstances of Oster's fall, for it is both significant and grotesque that the Gestapo needed this 'pretext' in order to overthrow its most dangerous adversary.

As I look back on my experiences in the Third Reich, those two days when I was interrogated by Roeder, under constant threats of

---

[1] An organization of ministers who upheld freedom of worship and maintained that religious allegiances took precedence over national allegiance. Literally, 'Confessional Church.' (*The translators.*)

arrest, still seem to me the most exciting. It was with great hesitation that I obeyed his summons to testify, but my remaining away would have badly incriminated Oster. My feeling about the situation did not betray me. All was not yet lost. For a full day I listened, a doubting Thomas, to the questions and recriminations that Roeder put to me with the spiteful smile of one who knew more than he cared to say. On the afternoon of the second day, when I was called upon to take the oath, I suddenly refused to testify. To the utter amazement of Roeder, I asserted that Field Marshal Keitel had just forbidden me to testify on such 'political' matters which concerned only 'internal conditions in the service.' The interrogation had to be broken off for an hour while they checked up on this assertion of mine, and that was the last I ever saw of Roeder.

I made good use of that hour by hurrying off to Chief Magistrate Sack. I shall never forget his invaluable help; he intervened at once and secured a twenty-four-hour postponement of the warrant for my arrest. In great haste I dictated a detailed complaint in which I demonstrated that the questions Roeder had put to me were directed against neither Dohnanyi, Oster, nor Canaris, but in reality against Field Marshal Keitel in his capacity as supreme chief of the *Abwehr*. I will not attempt to decide whether this argument was quite cogent. In any event it produced the effect I intended upon the chief of the OKW. Keitel intervened in his capacity as titular head of the Reich military tribunal. A few days later Roeder was promoted. He could not have gone higher or farther; he flew, quite literally, to Salonika as chief provost marshal of an air fleet. A new examining magistrate was appointed and the proceedings dragged on for more than a year.

However, I did not wait for this outcome. By taking a very devious route and by crossing the frontier at a small border station, I made my way back to Switzerland. I received a number of official or friendly invitations to return to Germany. When I did not respond to those overtures, I was asked to come to France. The chief of the Berne *Abwehr* had made an additional charge of high treason against me.

When Canaris heard of this, he tried for the last time to use his influence. In spite of my vigorous attempt to dissuade him from getting involved in a lost cause, he came to Berne. When I proved to him that Bureau F of the *Abwehr* had sent its spies into my apartment, he immediately recalled the agent who was behind all this; but, contradictory, as he always was, he demanded that I do something for him in return; he wanted me finally to renounce all activity.

My whole temperament and all my political views made it impossible for me to agree with the reasoning he outlined in our last conversation; and yet today, when I reflect on the disaster that befell Germany and Europe, I cannot refrain from thinking that a wise man correctly interpreted to me the signs of those chaotic times.

THE NEW DYNAMISM

A FEW WEEKS LATER Canaris had been removed and the *Abwehr* broken up. The greater part of the organization, in particular the counter-espionage section, was incorporated into the Gestapo. Only the strictly military intelligence service retained a degree of independence — within the framework of Kaltenbrunner's *Sicherheitshauptamt* — until July 20, 1944.

Earlier precautions now bore fruit, for Colonel Hansen became head of this remnant of the *Abwehr*. Hansen used this rump *Abwehr* to steer a large number of friends through the perils of the Underground. During this period Doctor Struenck became, more and more, Hansen's political adviser. He repeatedly sent Struenck to Switzerland, so that even I was not completely cut off. At that time there were fresh sensations in the foreign press every few months when one diplomat or another deserted the Nazis. Hitler and Ribbentrop had no liking for this sort of thing, and Himmler, too, believed that unnecessary publicity should be avoided. For almost a year Hansen succeeded in convincing his new superiors that he was making the most strenuous efforts to get me back to Germany without a scandal.

Hansen went a step farther. In order to restore permanent contact with the Berlin *fronde,* he installed Eduard Waetjen as consul in the

Zurich consulate-general. Waetjen, a confirmed antagonist of the
Nazi system, had been in close touch with the *Abwehr* circle for years,
as well as with Count von Moltke and his friends. He had relatives in
America and had often traveled to that country, so that we placed
great hopes in his appointment. July 20, 1944, put an end to his
'consular' activities, but in that short time we succeeded, after carefully conferring with Beck and Goerdeler, in transmitting a vitally important message to the Americans through Waetjen.

In March, 1944, Beck concluded that we must once more determine
whether there existed any possibility of an understanding between the
Opposition and the Western Powers. In the meanwhile Germany's
military situation had deteriorated to such an extent that there could
no longer be the slightest doubt of an impending Allied military victory. It would certainly be ridiculous for any Germans again to speak
of an army 'unbeaten in the field.' It therefore seemed all the more
senseless for the war to be prolonged to the point of total destruction.
Many of the leading generals began to realize that they must at last
break with Hitler and his system. But the military disaster had not
yet reached such proportions that they could decide to surrender unconditionally. Had not the time come now to pave the way psychologically for a cessation of the war by persuading the Allies to drop
the rigid Casablanca formula, or at least to moderate it somewhat by
a generous interpretation? Beck desired clarity: Did the Allies
still want a constructive solution of the chaos in Germany — that is
to say, a dissolution of the Nazi system by co-operation with the
German *fronde*? Or were they themselves by now no longer able to
relax the imperatives imposed by their alliances and by ideological
and strategical considerations?

The best way to direct these questions to the political chiefs in the
opposing camp appeared to be through Allen S. Dulles, who worked
at the American Embassy in Berne. Toward the end of 1942, Dulles
had come to Switzerland as head of the Office of Strategic Services
(OSS), and since then he had made his impress not only upon the
American intelligence service, but upon all the other Allied intelligence services in Europe. In spite of our many efforts, it had hitherto

proved impossible to maintain permanent political contact with the enemy. There had been only occasional meetings because the Allies restricted themselves largely to pure espionage. Naturally no serious conversations could be conducted on such a basis. The British above all stuck to the old-fashioned scheme in which the 'enemy' was considered solely as an object of espionage. It was saddening to observe how this point of view hindered them from drawing any political advantage from the existence of a German Underground.

Dulles was the first intelligence officer who had the courage to extend his activities to the political aspects of the war. With his keen mind and his broad knowledge of European problems, with which he had been familiar since the First World War and the peace negotiations in Versailles, Dulles concluded that it was time to think intensively about the political end of the bloody struggle. Therefore, he tried to establish contact with all the Resistance groups in Europe. His bureau on the Herrengasse in Berne grew in time into a virtual center of the European Resistance. Not only Germans, but Austrians, Hungarians, Italians, Rumanians, and Finns, not to mention the citizens of occupied countries, met there. Everyone breathed easier; at last a man had been found with whom it was possible to discuss the contradictory complex of problems emerging from Hitler's war.

Dulles was assisted by Gero von Gaevernitz. A German-American who had been living in Switzerland since the outbreak of the war and who was amazingly well informed on German conditions, von Gaevernitz worked indefatigably to make important contacts. This was not always the easiest thing in the world; it required a great deal of understanding; even more perseverance; and most of all — discretion. With the end of the war approaching, everyone wanted to be in touch with him. To make the proper choices, to shake off burdensome curiosity-seekers, to outwit the Nazi spies who found this spot a rich new hunting-ground, and at the same time to pursue ardently all foci of opposition to the Nazis — these difficult tasks must have given Gaevernitz and his chief quite an exciting time.

The Dulles bureau was particularly troubled by the flourishing guild of professional spies, the traders in espionage materials, who

would visit the agents of the *Abwehr* or the SD in the morning, the
secret service in the afternoon, and the Dulles office on the Herrengasse in the evening, offering to each their carefully prepared and
sensational reports. The mysterious Dulles not only kept the German
counter-espionage agents busy; he proved a difficult customer for these
professional spies because he was so tactless as to check up on their
information. A good many humorous memoirs could be written about
the manner in which Dulles, by his character and his multifarious
activities, 'Americanized' the peaceful idyll of the secret services in
Switzerland.

To a large extent Anglo-American policy was governed by the fear
that any unilateral conversations with the German Opposition might
ultimately lead, through maladroitness, indiscretion, or deliberate
intent, to an agreement between the Nazis and the Bolshevists. From
our conversations with Dulles, Waetjen and I were more aware of this
than were our friends in Berlin. Consequently, we decided to lay our
cards on the table.

We informed the Allied representative that the German *fronde*
was now going to attempt assassination, and we gave him details about
the generals and civilians who were ready to strike at the Nazis. We
also discussed earnestly the demand, raised by so many Allied statesmen, that this time all Germany must be occupied by the Allied
Powers. Whether or not this demand was politically correct, one
thing seemed quite clear to us: if the invasion did not lead definitely
to the military defeat of Germany by September, 1944, the war would
be protracted until the spring of 1945 and a wholly new situation
would be created. We did not, of course, know when the invasion
would take place, or even whether there was to be one at all, but we
felt that whatever psychological value a conquest of Berlin in open
battle would have, it could never outweigh the inevitable increasing
devastation in Germany — and Europe! — which would follow from
prolongation of the war.

This last peace feeler of ours had been authorized by Beck, and unquestionably Dulles transmitted it to his superiors and laid the proper

stress upon it. Unfortunately, we received no positive reply. The terrible conflict had to run its course.

Goerdeler retained his hope that some political arrangement would be attainable after we had succeeded in overthrowing the Nazis. Beck held a more skeptical view; but he, too, though he recognized the necessity of asking for an armistice as soon as possible, never planned his first act as chief of state in the new German régime to be the sending of an emissary to Eisenhower's headquarters in order to negotiate immediate surrender.

It is quite possible that some persons in the group of younger military leaders — though not Hansen and not Stauffenberg, who looked toward a reconciliation with Russia — might have harbored their own plans behind the backs of the political leaders of the *fronde.* This is quite likely in view of the general political confusion which was the chief characteristic of the preparations for the July *Putsch.*

These political problems bring me directly to the most important development of the year 1943. The fall of Oster and the destruction of his network was an event of far-reaching consequence for the entire Opposition. As always happened after such rude blows by the Gestapo, the psychological shock produced paralysis. A kind of conspiratorial vacuum was created until, toward the fall of the year, the gap was filled — and a new dynamism came into being.

Colonel in the General Staff Count Klaus von Stauffenberg, who now came so powerfully and commandingly to the fore and established a new cell of resistance in the OKW, was very different indeed from Oster. In the account of the events of July 20 there will be ample occasion to elaborate on the nature of this man and on his place in the history of the National Socialist Revolution. Here I shall speak less of him personally than of what I have called the new dynamism.

Up to this time the military men had made no claim to leadership inside the *fronde.* In his oppositional activity Beck felt and behaved as a civilian. Oster had renounced all political ambitions. Canaris refused to play any part in the activistic conspiracy. Thomas had withdrawn in disillusionment in 1942. Witzleben deliberately kept out of all non-military affairs. The recent convert, Tresckow, submitted to Goerdeler's political leadership. Such purely military men as Stuelpnagel and Olbricht were entirely colorless politically. In short, the oppositional officers had confined themselves to the technical functions which were naturally theirs — and indeed these functions were highly responsible and important. But Stauffenberg introduced a basic change into this situation. He and his 'officers against Hitler' suddenly began to claim, if not the right to political leadership, at least the prerogative of sharing in the political decisions. A man of intractable will, contradictory in many things, Stauffenberg was clear and purposeful in one respect: he did not want Hitler to drag the fatally imperiled army down with him in his own destruction. A soldier to the core, the salvation of his fatherland was equivalent in Stauffenberg's mind to the salvation of the *Wehrmacht*.

Some authors have attempted to show that Stauffenberg went over to the Opposition primarily out of Christian motives. Unquestionably he was a deeply religious Christian, but these Christian elements in his make-up were not what motivated him to commit assassination; if that had been so, he would not have needed to wait until July, 1944. Rather we might point out the religious qualms which inclined him to waver; up to the last moment he doubted whether he ought to commit assassination. Nor, as others have held, was Stauffenberg as a South German revolting against the domination of the Prussian type. The National Socialist leaders, and Hitler in particular, have abundantly proved that the South Germans who adopted Prussianism usually developed into super-Prussians. Stauffenberg was above all a passionate soldier who saw everything from the standpoint of his profession, and for this reason it took the military disaster to shock him into the Opposition.

In this he was by no means alone. He was representative of the military leaders of the Opposition of July 20. It is not at all by chance that a tightly knit group of officers, all firmly resolved to direct events, first coalesced in 1942, and grew in number and determination with each successive defeat. Generals von Tresckow,

Olbricht, and Fellgiebel began it; in 1943 they were joined by Count
Stauffenberg and Colonel Merz von Quirnheim; toward the end of
that year by General Stieff and still later by Quartermaster-General
Wagner and General Lindemann; finally Kluge and Colonel-General
Hoeppner fell in line; and last of all came Marshal Rommel. These
generals, either because of their strength of numbers, their key positions for a revolt, or because of the recognition that the fate of their
class was at stake, began to feel an increasing sense of unity. It was
they who on July 20, 1944, set the tone of the conspiracy and of its
technical execution. Men like Beck, Witzleben, and Oster were
crowded out more and more, when they were not actually lied to.

In addition to this structural change within the Opposition there
began, from the middle of 1943 on, another development that might
even be considered more important. The powerful influence of
military — and militaristic! — men probably could have been held
within bounds after a successful *Putsch* by a united civilian oppositionist group. But the chance for such inter-civilian unity was destroyed when, under the impression produced by the Russian victories
and the Anglo-American air bombings, significant sections of the
military and civilian Opposition formed an ideological and political
merger.

From 1943 on, there arose out of the chaos within Germany a kind
of militant socialism which attempted to tame the National Socialist
torrent and divert it into a new bed, once more in accord with the
temper of the times. Could there any longer be an understanding with
the West, this socialistic group demanded? The West refused to take
cognizance of the Opposition; with its bombings it seemed to be trying to bring all Germans together in collective anguish. Was not a
new agreement with the East the only possible recourse? A significant
group of the 'younger' men, whose politics ran diagonally from Left
to Right, so that they can really be classed neither as Left nor Right
but rather as adherents of a peculiar new line, theorized about the potentialities implicit in the wave of fraternization between the foreign
forced laborers and the German working masses. As it happened, no

such wave of fraternization between the foreign forced laborers and the working masses had occurred.

As early as January, 1943, Trott zu Solz, when visiting Geneva, had made a statement to the effect that this social-revolutionary turn toward the East on the part of the Opposition had already been completed. His remarks were intended for the ears of the British. For my part, I always feared that such commentary would simply intensify the determination of the Allies to let this German crater burn itself out thoroughly.

There is no doubt, however, that Trott voiced what his closest friends were thinking. The fiction of a social-revolutionary fraternization between the German and the foreign laboring masses lent a tremendous impetus to the already thriving Stauffenberg circle. In April, 1943, on the occasion of Trott's last stay in Switzerland, I discussed these matters with him. I was frankly shocked to find how radically this diplomat, whose fundamental attitude had been a 'Western' one, had made his choice for the East — or rather, had completed psychologically his rejection of the West. For this deeply disillusioned man was no longer concerned with the desire for political equilibrium; he no longer felt any interest in what in normal times is called political rationality. Carried along by a new and surging tide, he let himself be driven by a new, or, if you will, the old revolutionary dynamism.

Throughout the history of the Nazi Revolution, Moscow always exercised a remarkable subterranean influence. In 1932, when the Communists by their tactics helped the Nazis to take power; in 1939, when the Moscow Pact finally freed Hitler for his war — in every case the decisive impetus, the solution, the salvation, came from the East. What in 1944 could have led the 'dynamic' Opposition to believe that a pact with Bolshevism would lead to a result other than that the totalitarian Revolution — without Hitler, perhaps, but with General von Seydlitz's Moscow League of Officers — would take another gigantic leap forward and into the abyss?

It is only against this political background that two facts are comprehensible. After the unsuccessful ventures at the end of December, 1943, Stauffenberg withdrew from all action for months. It is hardly credible that this long period presented no opportunity for an assassination. Convinced that the front in the East would remain stable, Stauffenberg and his circle wanted 'to give Hitler a last chance.' What they meant by that was the repulse of the Allied invasion of France, for until the summer they had all firmly believed that the invasion would either fail or come to a halt near the coast. Naturally it was not that they wanted Hitler to have this success to his credit. If the 'plutocrats' were dealt a bloody defeat there, the chances for an agreement with Russia would be heightened.

Logically enough, the immediate circle around Stauffenberg sought an alliance with the extreme Left, the Communists. The initiator of these proposals was Administrative President Count Fritz von der Schulenberg. The son of a well-known general of the First World War, Schulenberg had toyed with Communistic ideas when he was a *Korps* student at Goettingen. From intellectual socialism he had later moved over to National Socialism. In the Opposition once more from 1938 on, it was he who converted Stauffenberg and who remained closest to him to the last. Schulenberg was unquestionably the most active officer in the circle and he vigorously opposed the candidacy of the 'reactionary' Goerdeler for chancellor after the overthrow of Hitler. Instead of Goerdeler, Schulenberg nominated the former Social Democratic military expert in the Reichstag, Leber.

From that time on, the Opposition was split wide open. For it was not a question of Goerdeler or Leber as individuals, but rather of two diametrically opposite political lines and ideological aims. This underground struggle for power characterized the first half of 1944, although the majority of the oppositionists knew scarcely anything about this conflict and continued to believe there was a unified leadership. Even Beck, Goerdeler, and Leuschner did not learn of the tragic consequences of this conspiracy within a conspiracy until it was too late. I shall cite the report of Emil Henk, the Social Democrat, about this incident:

As so often, an unexpected event wrecked all the plans again. At the end of June members of the Kreissau circle had begun a series of conferences with the so-called CC (Central Committee of the Communist Party of Germany). . . .

Beforehand, there had been lively disputes within the circle about this step. . . . For years the rule had been: 'Collaboration with the Communists only after X day.' ('X' day had always meant the day Hitler fell.) Reichwein and Leber urged that this rule now be abandoned, but no one else shared their view. Leuschner knew nothing of these events or designs. Had he known, he would have done everything in his power to prevent the meetings; afterward he protested bitterly about his having been kept in the dark. In any case, Leber and Reichwein went to the first conference with the leading Communists. . . .

In the course of the discussion the Communists expressed the desire to be put in touch with the active military Opposition. Such a request was flabbergasting, for cross-contacts between groups were very rare in the underground and were only allowed after long acquaintance and the most careful check-ups on the persons involved. . . . At a second conference, which Reichwein attended alone, all the participants were arrested. It turned out that one of the three men of the CC was a Gestapo spy!

This took place in the first week in July, 1944. A wave of arrests commenced and Leber too fell into the hands of the Gestapo. . . . Leber was well known to be a stalwart; he would preserve silence. But in this most important of hours, the secret was out and the Opposition could no longer afford to lose time. If they were to keep the initiative, the oppositionists would have to act before the agreed time. In addition, Stauffenberg knew both Leber and Reichwein very well and respected both men highly. He felt that the assassination would lose much validity unless these two men could be rescued. The most important members of the Opposition were therefore once more tremendously pressed for time, and thus compelled to improvise.

From then on, everything happened with a rush. Stauffenberg's justified fear that the Gestapo would soon uncover the entire conspiracy influenced all decisions. Nevertheless, it would be wrong to attribute the failure of July 20 to pressure of time or the necessity for improvisation. There was enough time for reflection and careful action. After all the previous preparations, two weeks should really have been sufficient. It was not time that was lacking, but inner clarity and resolution. It was the ideological and political conflict over the 'true' meaning of the German Revolution, the question of whether it was to be carried on, 'completed,' or utterly swept away, that hampered the chief actors.

The dramatic course of the tragedy which was about to befall the Opposition was governed by ambivalent emotions and divided minds. Before the *Putsch* began, an inexorable text was writ large above that catastrophe: *too late.*

3

Too Late—July 20, 1944

PRELUDE

I NEED MERELY GLANCE through my appointment calendar for the last weeks of June and the beginning of July, 1944, to confirm once again the condition of nervous tension which was mine throughout that period. I traveled back and forth throughout Switzerland, stopping now in Berne, now in Geneva, now in Zurich, with a few scattered days in between for walking tours in the mountains. When would the thunder and lightning break? Would the generals let pass this very last chance to act?

The disaster on the Eastern Front could no longer be covered up. The Russians had ripped a great hole through the army group in the center, and their victorious armies were advancing without pause into this gap. Dozens of generals, cut off from their communications, were surrendering their troops virtually without a fight. It seemed evident that the military collapse was so drastic precisely because it was also a moral breakdown.

The situation in the West was no better. The invasion was still in its first stages; the decisive break-through had not yet taken place. But the very fact of the success of the invasion could not be explained away. The Hitler-Rommel strategy had failed; the German army was unable to force the enemy into a wearing battle of position in Normandy. It was evident that the dikes would soon give, and then there would remain no more inane excuses for those vacillating generals who insisted that the *Putsch* must wait until the invasion was

490

beaten back or at least contained so that, coupling it with the Bolshe-vist threat from the east, they would have a basis for negotiations with the Anglo-Americans.

July 9

I WAS VACATIONING in the mountains when I at last received a long-awaited telephone call. Struenck was back in Switzerland. It was exactly a month since I had sent him to Germany with my messages to Beck and Hansen. The fact that he returned at all was a good sign. If Hansen had taken my letter amiss, he would not have sent Struenck with an answer. The situation, of course, had deteriorated tremen-dously in the meantime. The message I had sent a month ago was even more timely now. I had written that an opportunity for negotia-tion with the Allies no longer existed and that there was no longer any sense in preliminary discussions; it was now time to act.

The urgency of Struenck's telephone call misled me into thinking that the critical moment had come at last. Instead, he barely took time to shake hands with me before he assailed me with warnings that I was in terrible danger and must go into hiding at once. A particularly embarrassing indiscretion had occurred and Schellenberg had made a great fuss about it. Nebe and Hansen had been ques-tioned by Kaltenbrunner and by the Gestapo officer, Mueller, whom we called Gestapo Mueller to distinguish him from our own Joseph Mueller. Then Himmler had ordered that I be brought back to Germany by hook or crook. Since they knew that I would not come voluntarily, they decided to call me to the colors so that I could be defamed as an army deserter. Then they would try to kidnap me. Struenck reminded me of the cases of the two unfortunates in Madrid who had been dragged into the embassy and shipped over the border inside a trunk, labeled as diplomatic baggage.

Hansen's request that I should be suddenly taken ill seemed to me quite reasonable. Hitherto he had skillfully covered up my refusal to return, but if I did not obey an induction order, Colonel Hansen would undoubtedly be held responsible. We were prepared, and had a physician ready to certify that I was undergoing an operation for appendicitis or that I had just broken a leg.

'Aren't they ready yet?' I asked, cutting short this interminable discussion of personal affairs. There were really more important matters to talk about.

'Yes and no,' Struenck replied precisely. 'The assassination is supposed to take place any day now, but you know how often we have been strung along with promises. Even Hansen is doubtful that Stauffenberg will actually do it.'

'Does he at least want to?' I asked.

'He is said to want to,' Struenck replied in the same non-committal manner. 'But part of the Stauffenberg group has religious scruples.'

Struenck was weary and resigned. I could see that after so many failures he did not want to encourage premature hopes either in himself or in me. But since he had brought with him concrete requests from Beck, Goerdeler, and Hansen, I quickly realized that the affair had progressed beyond the stage of mere theorizing. Their doubts no longer revolved around the question of the validity of assassination. What concerned them now was the fear that someone might lose his nerve, or that it would prove impossible to get at Hitler, or that the Gestapo would strike at them a few minutes beforehand.

Waetjen, who joined us, shared my impression. He and I sat up late at night talking and assuring each other again and again that this time it really looked like business. Too bad I could not go to Berlin, but our comrades in Berlin had expressly forbidden that.

July 10

OVERNIGHT I decided that it would be absolute madness for me to stay away from Berlin. For years I had hoped for the great event — and now that the assassination was about to come off, was I to watch it from afar in Zurich? Every fiber of my being revolted against this paltry safety. I made up my mind to go after all. Himmler was no longer counting on my coming to Germany voluntarily. Consequently,

I should be able to manage the critical crossing of the frontier. In Berlin I could disappear at once.

Before I set out, there were a number of technical preparations that had to be completed quickly. I thought it wise to prepare myself for a rather lengthy stay this time, and for possible complications.

First I hurried off to the consulate-general. There my appearance aroused considerable surprise. The consul was even more surprised when I explained to him the purpose of my visit. But I assured him that in this case there was no need to fear Berlin's disapprobation. After all, I said, Himmler would certainly not object to my returning to Germany.

The consul saw the light; he gave me the visa.

Then I carried out a few errands, put my papers in order, and in the afternoon Waetjen and I took care of a number of technical problems that Hansen had committed to us. I left behind with Waetjen a lengthy memorandum for Dulles, which was to be given to him after my departure. I considered myself duty-bound to give Dulles a sketch of the European and German situation to which my friends and I looked forward if the *Putsch* succeeded.

July 11

IN BERNE, Waetjen and Struenck rode to the embassy. Struenck was traveling as a courier; he too had to give Bureau F a specious explanation of the purposes of his journey, so that no one's suspicions would be aroused.

Meanwhile, I went to the federal building to call on the chief of the Swiss police department, Doctor Rothmund, who for months had handled with encouraging benevolence Struenck's requests for visitor visas. He was understanding and helpful this time, too, when I asked him to make out a return visa for me without going through the formality of inquiry at the German Embassy.

Then I rejoined Struenck and Waetjen. Apparently Struenck's frequent reappearances in Switzerland at such short intervals had excited no suspicion at all.

It is hard to escape a mood of depression when one is setting out on an adventure whose end may be bad indeed. During the hour's ride between Berne and the border at Basle we could not manage to cheer up. It was as if we felt a need to suffer a little in advance, before we took the short step from the peaceful idyll of Switzerland into the uncertainties of Naziland.

The passport formalities were completed without any trouble at all. Struenck, bearing his courier's visa, was treated with proper respect. Since I was in his company and was able to show a diplomatic passport, it did not occur to the officials to look into their list of wanted men. If they did not get the idea later on and telephone ahead of me, I should be able to sleep peacefully all the way to Berlin. From the platform I saw a German railroad train for the first time in a whole year. It was shocking to see how neglected the cars looked. They were covered with grime; there was not a trace of paint left; the windows were smashed.

Frau Struenck was waiting for us in Weil. I found her as lively as ever, although she was startled and frightened by my unexpected appearance on the train.

With the aid of a little coffee concentrate and a few of those wrapperless Swiss cigars, I convinced the conductor that he must arrange a sleeper compartment for me. Two sips of cherry brandy were enough to persuade him that he need not make me surrender my passport. Why give extra work to the Gestapo agents that accompanied every train? With a sigh of relief we shut ourselves up in Struenck's compartment and celebrated our reunion. High above us in the darkness the enemy bombers were probably hurtling along with their load of death and destruction.

In Karlsruhe I saw how much the sum of destruction had mounted during the past few months. Soon these twisted iron girders protruding out of ruins, these wrecked railroad stations and the vista of more ruin would become familiar sights again. But the first impression was tremendously powerful. It was necessary to return to Germany from afar to see how inexorably the whole land was progressing toward utter annihilation. Soon, I felt, Germany would be a single burnt-out crater, on the model of these thousands of smaller craters that lined the railroad track.

July 12

THE STRUENCKS were going to be met in Berlin. I myself did not think it safe to arrive there by this train. Therefore, I left the train at Potsdam, rushed through the underground passage to the commuters' platform and had the good luck to catch a train that was just leaving.

At Wannsee I changed trains. The route passed through the neighborhood where I had lived. Sorrowfully, I looked down the smashed street on which lay our bombed-out house. It was not until a full year later that I was to look about in that blackened hole in the ground. There, scattered, soaked by rain, partly torn, or in pieces, lay a few things that were really more valuable to me than all that the bombs and the pillagers had taken away: a few family photographs, the last mementoes of people and of times that will never come again.

In Zehlendorf I got out and walked the few hundred yards to Helldorf's home. Once this street had been a splendid boulevard lined with mansions. Now ruins gaped on either side. It was with difficulty that I found the house, which had recently received a direct hit. The police chief was now living in a hotel in the city; a few servants were still using the concrete shelter of his former home. This was rather upsetting. My plan had been to ask Helldorf to put me up. The Gestapo certainly would not have been likely to look for me in the home of the Berlin chief of police.

None of the coin telephones were in working order. Through a patrolman I telephoned the Count over the official police wires. Foolishly, Helldorf did not recognize my voice, and since I did not want to give my name there was a good deal of fussing back and forth until he finally caught on to the identity of his caller. Then he said I ought to come to see him at once. When I asked in a roundabout manner whether his office was the most suitable place for us to meet, he replied, with that cheek that was always so charming in him, that at the moment I could be safe with him from unwelcome bombings.

He was not able to send a car for me. Not even the Berlin chief of police had that much gasoline at his disposal any more. I had to take the subway, which was just as well because it gave me the opportunity to gather some impression of Berlin and the Berlin populace. Because of the continual night attacks, all the people were overtired; they fell asleep standing up. Accustomed to the normal, rested look on faces in Switzerland, I saw what human havoc had been wrought upon these people. And yet the shift from total war to total destruction had just started.

Alexanderplatz was a ghastly scene of wreckage. But the bombs seemed often to have spared the strongholds of the tyrants. In the midst of this smoke-blackened and razed area rose the remains of the police headquarters; what was left of the building still sufficed to shelter the most important offices.

In Helldorf's anteroom I found familiar faces. These police officers who had grown old in the service were former patrolmen who had been transferred to office work when they were nearing the end of their period of service. They were fine men, honest, devoted to duty, very decent. How were they to defend themselves when, one morning, they were informed of an order by which they had been transferred into the SS? Or what could they do upon being suddenly ordered to serve in the 'fighting police troops'? 'Combating guerrillas' was the ostensible function of this force; in reality it was assigned to murder Jews or patriots. What course remained open to them? Could they desert to the Russians, who were not especially benevolent toward members of Himmler's SS? Could they openly refuse to obey orders, which in the most favorable case meant concentration camp? Could they attempt to vanish amid the internal confusion of Germany, which meant that they might be picked up by Himmler's henchmen at any time and that their families would suffer as hostages? In condemning the horrors wrought by Himmler's police we ought not to forget the fate of these unfortunate men who, as a consequence of pursuing a decent profession, had voluntarily been enmeshed by the Nazi machinery and were now being ground between the millstones of the Revolution.

Helldorf was not at all surprised to see me. Had I guessed, he asked, that the assassination planned for yesterday would be called off? At the last moment Goering and Himmler had not appeared, and Stauffenberg had been unwilling to take responsibility for the assassination unless there was a good chance of killing Goering and Himmler as well. This was the first I had heard that 'the day' had been yesterday.

Then Helldorf gave me the details. Basically it was the old plan. After the assault, General Olbricht would call Helldorf to the OKW headquarters and declare the Berlin police subject to the orders of the *Wehrmacht*. Helldorf would then use this as a pretext for calling his police officers together and paralyzing the police apparatus for the next few critical hours. The regular police would resume their functions — under military supervision — only after the panzer troops had surrounded all the crucial buildings. Nebe was informed about the entire plan and had made the necessary preparations for handling the criminal police.

Helldorf reported all this to me in the most casual of tones, as if he were discussing the next air-raid drill. I noticed at once, however, that he seemed to be not sure of himself. His lackadaisical tone worried me. Sure enough, he finally got around to saying that I must not deceive myself; the old crew was no longer around and he didn't really have confidence in the young men.

I asked whom he meant.

'The whole clique,' he replied.

'Olbricht? Beck?'

No, he trusted both those men fully. But he was never able to see them; Stauffenberg barred everyone. And although Stauffenberg's emissary, Schulenberg, kept assuring him that everything was prepared perfectly, Helldorf could not shake off his hunch that something was amiss.

Count Fritz von Schulenberg had for a long time been assistant police chief under Helldorf. Helldorf complained that Schulenberg always gave the same answers; it was impossible to find out anything from him. Now, he had the impression that Schulenberg was not so much concealing something from him as lacking the necessary clarity on all points. Up to the present moment not a single directive on police measures had been laid before him.

Helldorf said that he had not been able to get in touch with Stauffenberg at all. Stauffenberg had behaved like a sphinx, and had not even admitted openly that he intended to set off the bomb. Helldorf felt that so much wariness was a bit insulting, especially in view of the rôle that had been assigned to him as Berlin police chief. I had better talk with Nebe, he suggested. Nebe was even more pessimistic than he and had repeatedly proposed withdrawing entirely from the whole affair.

Helldorf said all this without a trace of malice or excitability. Involuntarily I wondered whether he were already so dulled by the past that he could no longer summon up the inner strength to participate energetically. But perhaps his calm and impassive manner at this critical juncture was rather the product of his curious temperament, of that remarkable compound of reckless *Landsknecht* and nonchalant aristocrat that I had so often observed in him. Once things began to happen he would surely be on the spot.

Helldorf stretched his gasoline to take me to Struenck's in his car. From Alexanderplatz to Heerstrasse is a considerable distance. Now and then I asked him to make a détour down some of the worst-devastated streets. Had anyone told me that the bombs would be raining down on these ruins for eight months more, that the bombings would be followed by days of street-fighting, and that at the end of it all three million human beings would creep out of the rubble and try to pursue their usual occupations, I think I should have laughed at the grotesqueness of such a thought.

Helldorf told me some astonishing things about the persistence of normality. Almost as soon as the 'all clear' was sounded, the clean-up squads set to work, and within a few hours the trains were running again. Long interruptions were rare. Mail was still delivered on the minute. As yet there had been no trouble about the distribution of food. In short, the gears were clashing, but the war machinery, both its technical and human aspects, continued to run.

I asked Helldorf about morale. He said that everyone was longing for the war to end; that no one would fight for the Nazis on the barricades; the general sense of weariness was overwhelming. Nevertheless, there were no signs of revolt. The terror of the bombings forged men together. In rescue work there was no time for men to ask one another who was for and who against the Nazis. In the general hopelessness people clung to the single fanatical will they could see, and unfortunately Goebbels was the personification of that will. It was disgusting to see it, Helldorf continued, but whenever that spiteful dwarf appeared, people still thronged to see him and felt beatified to receive an autograph or a handshake from him.

Helldorf was not trying to annoy me. He was firmly convinced that the *Putsch* was both essential and possible. He warned me, however, against the error of imagining that the masses would act on their own account. They would, he said, certainly never do anything at all without a signal from above. How often I had argued this point with German and foreign friends in the past years! The matter came up whenever they confided to me their 'reliable information' about impending mass action — strikes or local uprisings. For the most part they insisted that I could not understand such matters because I was not sufficiently Left and had no contact with working-class circles.

One of the most remarkable phenomena of the war years, moreover, was the creation not only of a collective frenzy of jubilation, but a collective sense of misery as well. In calculating the inner strength of a government based on terror, one must take into account the tremendous efforts that frightened men will put forth, not out of enthusiasm, desire for victory, or blind submission, but quite simply out of hopelessness and despair.

The Struencks' new home was on a small side street in the West End. Schacht owned a villa there. When he was banished to the country, he had rented it out, keeping only two rooms in the cellar for storing his furniture. After the Struencks were bombed out, Schacht had placed these cellar rooms at their disposal. I had never known how comfortably a cellar could be arranged. It seemed to be sealed against the outside world, and concealed from it as well. These cellar walls were, at any rate, microphone-proof.

Hansen had sent word that he intended to come to see me toward evening. Nebe would not be free to see me until the next day.

After lunch I wanted to go to see Beck at once. Aside from other considerations, I wanted to shield myself against Hansen's taking my disobedience in bad part. After all, the *Abwehr* was a military organization. He was my chief, and he had expressly ordered me not to come to Berlin. I didn't want him to take it into his head to give me orders 'officially.' I thought I would block that possibility by meeting him from the first on the plane of rebellion; there we had a different scale of rank.

The ride out to Lichterfelde was time-consuming under the existing conditions. It was nearly four o'clock when I arrived at the Goethestrasse. All the houses around had been destroyed; Beck's little place alone had been spared by the bombs.

The doorbell, of course, did not work. I had to pound energetically on the door before the housekeeper came. She looked suspiciously at me and said that Beck was not at home. I told her to say that Herr Doctor Lange was calling, and followed her. This alias was not particularly ingenious, since my friends generally referred to me as 'der Lange.'[1] Nevertheless, I said it with so credible a ring that it was weeks before the Gestapo found out who Doctor Lange really was.

The general looked up in amazement from his desk. He was as glad to see me as I was to see him. 'Well, at last!' he exclaimed. He said he had been expecting me for days. Stauffenberg had frequently assured him that I would be there in time.

Beck was having his Wednesday at home that day; it was the only opportunity he had to meet Popitz and Hassell without attracting attention. Nothing would be happening before Saturday, he told me; therefore, we arranged to meet again on the following afternoon, when he would have more time. For all his customary caution, Beck was optimistic this time, but he warned me that we must not expect too much afterward. In the East the situation was very bad; the center

---

[1] Lange means 'tall,' and is also a common name in German.

army group no longer existed. If they had the presence of mind, the Russians could advance far across the Vistula. In the West the front was being held for the time being, but Kluge had already sent word that there might be a break-through within a fortnight; in Rommel's opinion within at most three weeks. For the first time Kluge of his own accord was demanding action.

Beck asked me to get in touch with Stauffenberg as quickly as possible. Stauffenberg had helped him tremendously during the past few months, he said. He had borne the entire burden of practical preparations. After the elimination of Oster, his had been the only wholehearted work to be carried on in the OKW.

By six o'clock I was back at the Struencks'. There I met Walter Cramer, our loyal and energetic comrade who had never compromised since 1933. General manager of one of the largest Leipzig textile firms, he had for years been assisting Goerdeler wherever he could. He had hidden many important documents in the files of his factory, had made many a trip abroad for Goerdeler, and had been helpful to me too in many ways.

A year ago the Gestapo had deprived Cramer of his passport, so that he was no longer able to travel abroad. He was constantly watched. Now he was going to visit his daughter in Vienna for a few days. He was never to get there; the Gestapo picked him up on the way. As I bade good-bye to this white-haired man, I tried to register emphatic optimism. But it was in vain. From the way he shook hands with me I suspected that he thought this would be a last parting.

It seems to me that for years Cramer had lived with a premonition of how frightfully they would torture him to death. Did he also guess, this cultivated business man spoiled by luxury, who had reached an age when he was certainly no longer any too strong — did he also guess how he would rise above himself during his suffering? Did he suspect that some day the few survivors of the prison near the Lehrter railroad station would mention his name with admiration whenever they recalled those days of horror?

Goerdeler came. We had agreed to surprise him. When 'Doctor Blank' telephoned to ask whether he could call about his insurance policy, Struenck had given him no hint that a visitor would be present. From the cellar window we heard and saw him walk toward the building with his energetic, elastic step. The Struencks received him in the kitchen. Then he appeared suddenly at the door. He reeled back, thinking for a moment that his eyes, adapted to the bright sunlight outside, were deceiving him in this dimly lit cellar. I heard him murmur a long-drawn-out 'Gisevius!' Had not the years of struggle brought us so close together, I think this welcome alone would have been enough to make me vow fidelity to him for the rest of my life.

Frau Struenck had made coffee. For Goerdeler, rushing as he did from conference to conference, a cup or two of good coffee was wonderfully refreshing. At first we talked about purely family affairs. This was one of the pleasantest aspects of our small group. For a long time now we had not confined ourselves to the political plane alone. We had come to cherish one another on a human basis and to share each other's domestic joys and sorrows.

I quickly noticed that, although Goerdeler held himself erect as ever, he had grown weary and older. There was a melancholy droop around the corners of his mouth. Even the indomitable Goerdeler no longer radiated his old optimism; somehow he too was at the end of his rope. I could not forbear speaking to him about it.

'Yes,' he said, with an expressive, resigned gesture, 'this past year has really not been easy. The way the generals have managed it, we will have to drink the cup to the dregs.'

'But now?'

He replied with a shrug. A year ago he would have poured out a torrent of hopes and plans. 'Apparently it is going to be done at last, but . . . ' Again he shrugged wearily.

I asked how he got along with Stauffenberg. To my amazement he replied that he had seen Stauffenberg no more than two or three times. All other negotiations had been conducted through Beck. 'But Beck thinks a good deal of him, and he certainly is a very courageous and energetic man,' Goerdeler added evasively.

'But how have you got along with him?' I insisted.

Goerdeler tilted his head back and stared at the ceiling — a frequent gesture with him. 'Well, you know,' he replied, 'if he were not young and I were not much older, I would not be able to stand the way he cuts me off short. But as it is . . .'

And then he broke out and confessed all the disappointment and worries that had been consuming him for the past few months. Until recently, he recounted, the division of labor had been strictly adhered to. The military men were to deal with the technical strategy of the *Putsch*; the civilians were supposed to take care of everything connected with politics, for they consciously wanted to avoid the faintest semblance of a military *Putsch*. A real overthrow of the Nazis was conceivable only if the entire civilian Resistance Front, from Right to Left, collaborated. The military officers had completely discredited themselves on the moral plane. Beck was one of the frankest advocates of this position; that was precisely why he had entrusted Goerdeler with all the political preparations.

Stauffenberg, however, would not adhere to this agreement. Goerdeler reported that since their first meeting Stauffenberg had insisted on taking over the political as well as the technical direction. The young colonel could not and would not deny his origins in authoritarian National Socialism. What he had in mind was the salvation of Germany by military men who could break with corruption and maladministration, who would provide an orderly military government and would inspire the people to make one last great effort. Reduced to a formula, he wanted the nation to remain soldierly and become socialistic. Only in this way, he thought, could Germany escape the deadly peril from East and West and fight her way through to a tolerable peace.

Goerdeler, too, did not count on immediate capitulation. Yet he thought the enemy would be inclined to end the war, once a fundamental change in the German régime had taken place. But the views of Goerdeler and Stauffenberg differed fundamentally. Goerdeler's deepest and sincerest convictions led him to desire a democracy. Therefore, he was working for a grand coalition of all non-totalitarians, which meant all the forces of Resistance from the Social Democrats to the conservatives. Stauffenberg wanted a military dictatorship of 'true National Socialists.' Now that the Nazi leadership had failed and Hitler had been exposed as the bungling strategist he was, the soldiers were to spring into the breach and save the lost cause. Stauffenberg wanted to retain all the totalitarian, militaristic, and socialistic elements of National Socialism.

No wonder Stauffenberg avoided Goerdeler and even took an open stand against him. Not without bitterness Goerdeler told me that the colonel had tried to persuade even Leuschner and Jakob Kaiser to oppose him, Goerdeler, for chancellor. Both men had refused. Then Stauffenberg had found a new candidate in the former Social Democratic Reichstag deputy, Leber. Presumably a man of the Left and former specialist for his Party fraction on military affairs, a secret love for the object of his constant criticism had led Leber into the circle around young Colonel Stauffenberg. Leber had instructed Stauffenberg to base himself primarily on the forces of the militant Left, and to make sure beforehand that he had the Communists on his side.

Goerdeler had no objection if the Communists honestly wanted to take their place in the front ranks of the forces for defense and reconstruction. But he did refuse to endanger our project by needless preliminary conferences. After all the indiscretions that had taken place in the past, Goerdeler had this time preserved absolute silence. Aside from Leuschner, Letterhaus, and Kaiser, not even the candidates for ministries had been informed.

And now the thing that had always been feared had happened at last. Stauffenberg had continued his political conferences. The day before yesterday his intermediaries, Leber and Professor Reichwein, together with three leading Communists, had been arrested, just as they were on the point of arranging a meeting between Stauffenberg and the Communists. Goerdeler did not yet know that one of the three Communists had been a Gestapo spy, but he was outraged. What would happen if one of those men made any revelations and put the Gestapo on the track of Stauffenberg?

'Take my word for it, what I said to Stauffenberg as I left him after our first meeting is true as ever. "I want to warn you against playing the part of a political military man," I said, "or you'll end as Schleicher did." ' [1]

Goerdeler did not believe that the Western Powers would adhere to their demand for unconditional surrender. If the army succeeded in halting the Russians, he felt sure that the British at least would reconsider. It would deny the whole meaning of their fight against Hitler's attempt to achieve hegemony over Europe if they permitted the vast Russian Empire to overrun Europe.

I disagreed with Goerdeler about this. The war had already gone too far, I felt; the Allies also could not turn back. On the other hand, I thought that the question of which Power occupied Germany, and in what manner, was of vital importance. Despite the agreements made at Teheran and Yalta concerning the zones of occupation, there was the possibility that the Anglo-Saxons would be the first to reach the line running through Koenigsberg, Prague, Vienna, and Budapest.

Goerdeler felt that my view was far too pessimistic.

We talked about personalities. The list of ministers was by and large the old one. Besides Goerdeler as chancellor, Leuschner (Social Democrat) was to be vice-chancellor. The ministry of economics was assigned to Lejeune-Jung (Conservative); of culture, Bolz (Center); finance, Losser (National-Liberal); labor, Letterhaus. On the insistence of Stauffenberg, Leber would receive the ministry of the interior and Olbricht the war ministry.

The foreign ministry was in dispute. So far Hassell had been the only candidate. But Goerdeler now asked me to influence Beck in favor of Count von der Schulenberg, the former ambassador to Moscow. Schulenberg had hazarded the hope that he might be able to reach an agreement with Stalin. At any rate, he could not be considered anti-Russian. During the past year, he had got in touch with Kluge, while the latter was still on the Eastern Front. He proposed

---

[1] General Kurt von Schleicher, war minister under the Weimar Republic and chancellor for eight weeks before he was succeeded by Hitler, was one of the first victims of the blood purge of June 30, 1934. (*The translators.*)

that Kluge smuggle him through the Russian lines as a secret negotiator. Kluge was willing — but when the ambassador asked the
concrete question whether, if any agreement were forthcoming, he
would be able to give Stalin his word of honor that Hitler would be
overthrown, the field marshal had backed down — as usual.

Goerdeler wanted me to be his assistant secretary in the chancellery. Temporarily, he thought, I could administer the police force
also, or rather the 'Reich Commissariat for Purgation and Restoration
of Public Order,'[1] as we now wanted to call it. Since that office had
been intended for me since 1938, I asked him to settle this question
with Beck, who had requested me for his chief assistant.

Goerdeler unfortunately had to leave for Frankfurt-am-Main, where
he had an urgent appointment. Living in Leipzig as he did, it was not
practicable for him to remain in Berlin all the time — especially since
every journey now had to be approved by some public authority. For
a long time it had been necessary for him to disguise his political
conferences as business affairs. We finally parted at the Potsdamer-
platz station.

Since I was in the center of the city, I walked the few steps over
to the Hotel Excelsior, where Helldorf lived. As I was passing, I
glanced at the Prinz Albrechtstrasse. The Gestapo building was still
standing, although the bombs had created much havoc in the whole
vicinity.

Helldorf said he had met Olbricht and had arranged for Nebe to
go to the Bendlerstrasse at eleven o'clock tomorrow so that Olbricht
could show him the plans for the police preparations. Since Helldorf's
own car was not in, he telephoned around the neighborhood for half
an hour, but could find no car that could be placed at the disposal of
police headquarters. Here was another instance of the mounting
shortages. Only the Gestapo officials still received their old allotment
of gasoline. All the other police authorities were restricted to a
fraction of their needs.

---

[1]*Reichskommissariat zur Saeuberung und Wiederherstellung der oeffentlichen
Ordnung. Saeuberung* implies both 'purge' in the political sense and 'purification'
in the moral sense. (*The translators.*)

I rode back by subway. The Struencks were already beginning to worry about me. They informed me that Olbricht and Stauffenberg were planning to come to see me later. Naturally I felt very curious about this meeting with Stauffenberg. Since he had appeared in Berlin after I had fled, I knew him only by hearsay. The descriptions given by various people were so contradictory that I had been unable to obtain any clear conception of him.

It was past midnight before we heard loud footsteps resounding through the cellar. Hansen could easily find the way in the darkness; he felt quite at home at the Struencks' place. Then there was a knock, and the powerful frames of the two colonels appeared in the doorway. Stauffenberg was, if anything, even bigger than Hansen. At least his broad, vigorous body gave that impression. He held out his left hand; his right arm had been terribly wounded. There was a black patch over his eye, too, and in the course of the conversation he frequently lifted this patch to dab the eye with a wad of cotton.

The appearance of the man was not inspiring. It was easy to divine the psychology of so energetic and talented an officer who suddenly found himself crippled. I sensed at once that this unfortunate man must renounce the hope of attracting masses of people to his cause. His effectiveness must henceforth be confined to small groups. It was as if a pitiless destiny had deliberately planned to thrust him into the rôle of a conspirator.

With a brief greeting, Stauffenberg dropped into one of the wooden chairs. He pulled open the jacket of his uniform and demanded rather than asked Frau Struenck, who was somewhat taken aback, to prepare a cup of coffee. It had been a hot day for him, he sighed, and with his hand he wiped the perspiration from his forehead, brushing it back into his tangle of hair.

I don't know whether Stauffenberg had always showed his ruder side. But now, consciously or unconsciously, he was trying to overcompensate for the inferiority feelings engendered by his mutilation. As he sat there with his arms dangling limply and his legs in their heavy top-boots sprawled out in front of him, I marveled at the vast difference between this Stauffenberg and the disciple of Stefan

George whom I had imagined. I tried to see the connection between this unquestionably forceful but rather boorish person and the verses of the aristocratic poet.

Stauffenberg's voice made an interesting contrast to his massive build. There was a hoarse softness about that voice; a voice such as the 'Iron Chancellor' must have had. I would never have taken this young colonel for the model of the traditional officer, nor for a credible representative of that younger generation which had already been inwardly alienated from the Nazis. Undoubtedly this Stauffenberg was a swashbuckler who knew what he wanted; but he struck me as rather typical of the 'new' class of general staff officers: the kind of man best suited to Hitler's purposes — or to purposes of assassination.

Frau Struenck left us to prepare the coffee and to chat with Hansen's chauffeur, whom we did not want to hear our conversation.

Hansen exclaimed cordially, 'I knew you would come.' It required a certain generosity of spirit on his part to accept tacitly my breach of military formalities. In this respect he was pleasingly different from most of his colleagues, who enjoyed giving orders to civilians.

Stauffenberg took over the conversation almost at once. In curiously circumlocutory phrases he said to me that I probably knew how grave the situation was. As chief of staff to the commander of the home army he wanted me to 'inform' him about phases of the situation with which he was not acquainted. I came from Switzerland where all sorts of information was available. Would I give him my impressions?

Goerdeler need not have tipped me off beforehand. Here was the true 'political military man.' Here was a professional soldier who was being drawn willy-nilly into the complex problems of a revolutionary era and was making his first groping steps in politics. He made the mistake common to a fundamentally unpolitical person when he essays being diplomatic; he considered complicated and even tortuous speaking to be a kind of higher diplomacy.

I willingly expounded my view of the radical shift that had taken place in the past few months. Since the invasion, I said, there could no longer be any turning back for the Anglo-Saxons. It was quite possible to argue about the specific meaning of 'unconditional surrender,' but to my mind we could no longer avoid total occupation with all the consequences implicit in that. The only matter for discussion was whether the final act would be brought about from within or without, and whether the army — now at least — would muster up its courage for internal action.

While I talked, Stauffenberg had stared at the floor, a meaningful smile on his face. I did not know whether he was trying to express disapproval or whether he intended to confide a special secret to me.

'Isn't it altogether too late for the West?' he interjected. With that he launched into an endless divagation in which he attempted to show that I was a hopeless 'Westerner.'

The long and short of it was: What could I hope to gain by coming to an agreement with the Western Powers, whether before or after the collapse? Didn't I know that the central army group had ceased to count for anything? Within a few weeks Stalin would be standing before Berlin. The decision in the East had already been reached; therefore, all political activity had to be directed toward the East.

Hansen cast a significant look at me. In the first place, I had said not a word that might indicate I was in favor of a one-sided 'Western' policy. I had spoken only of 'unconditional surrender' and of the fact that it was already 'too late' — and that these factors must influence all our thoughts on foreign policy. In the second place, Stauffenberg, of course, knew about the numerous messages that Beck and Goerdeler had sent to Switzerland requesting that if possible we come to a preliminary accord with the Anglo-Americans. Why this sudden polemic against the West?

If, however, Stauffenberg had formulated his opinion with any clarity there would have been a basis for discussion. But the above summary is only an approximation of what he said, for he contradicted himself in the same breath; after each statement he added that he did not want me to misunderstand him, that he had not really decided the matter in his own mind, and was for this reason simply taking the rôle of an *advocatus diaboli*. From the vehemence with which he developed his ideas, I clearly perceived that he had long since made his choice, but that he was not yet sure how he could justify his change of heart to Beck or Goerdeler.

Finally I lost patience and told him that I should now like to hear his real opinion. It was no use, however, for Stauffenberg did not say outright that an arrangement with the Russians was possible. Instead, he pictured the situation on the Eastern Front as being so black that any reasonable man would give up all hope. We began disputing whether the Russians really would conquer Berlin within a few weeks. Stauffenberg backed his assertion with a technical knowledge that I, of course, could not counter. He took my one halfway-cogent argument — that up to now all military prognoses had proved false — as a personal insult. Actually I was referring to the field marshals and not to him. I was prudent enough not to remind him of how positive he had been at the beginning of the year that the situation on the Eastern Front was stable and that the invasion of Europe by the Western Powers would be a reckless and at best a time-consuming enterprise.

The more involved the conversation became, the more I tried to approach the man from the human side. After all, we were comrades who were working toward the same goal. For all the differences of opinion among us, I wanted him to feel that we applauded his courage.

'How do you know whether I will set off the bomb at all?' he suddenly burst out, after we had spent some time talking over the technical details of the assassination. I retorted, 'Why else have you come here?' And the subject was dropped.

That evening I certainly had the impression that before me was a man who would go the limit. But in the light of what followed, I must, in retrospect, ask myself whether this mysterious posturing, this bent for dialectic, this talking around the subject and playing the devil's advocate — whether this behavior did not have its origin in a basic lack of clarity, if not confusion. Stauffenberg was motivated by the impulsive passions of the disillusioned military man whose eyes had been opened by the defeat of German arms. And now, with an exaggerated sense of his mission, he thought he had to be everything at once: soldier, politician, tyrannicide, savior of his fatherland. Political life during revolutions is fantastically equivocal. On the one hand stood this soldierly revolutionary who in the final analysis was fighting for the continuation of Nazi-militaristic 'legality'; on the other hand stood the anti-revolutionary civilians militantly striving to achieve something new.

Stauffenberg insisted that the problem of purging was to be attacked with extreme caution. Naturally he had no objection to administering just punishment to the Nazi and Gestapo murderers, but he would not tolerate a verdict of guilty being passed against the top generals for 'political' reasons; that is, he would not condemn Brauchitsch and Halder for their well-known cowardice or the field marshals for their characterless attitude toward Hitler's invasions.

I objected that only a broad, self-inflicted purge on our part could convince the Allies that a fundamental change and not a merely tactical shift was taking place. Stauffenberg would not agree. How could he hope to save the reputation of the army for the future if once it were revealed with what recklessness and smallness of mind the army leaders had allowed our nation to plunge into the calamity of war?

I was somewhat taken aback by the candor with which Stauffenberg announced that my book, with its description of the Fritsch crisis and its attacks on the generals, would have to be banned. By this time it was already growing light. We had to break up. Perhaps our nerves were overstrained. At any rate, we quarreled almost at the last moment.

I asked Stauffenberg to give my regards to Olbricht and to tell him that I would be ready to see him any time he wished. Stauffenberg became terribly agitated. I knew the Gestapo was after me, he told me hotly; I must not let myself be seen or everything would be endangered. I had, of course, not the slightest intention of being rash, and I therefore assured him that aside from Beck, Goerdeler, Nebe, and Helldorf, I did not expect to talk to anyone.

'Not even Oster!' he retorted in a tone of command. His manner was so sharp, so peremptory, that I could not help replying with equal sharpness that if Oster should show up in Berlin, I would see him the moment he arrived.

Oster had been banished to the country. Naturally I was not so mad as to send him a telegram informing him of my arrival or of our plans, but I was infuriated by this exclusion of a man who had laid the foundation for all the work which Stauffenberg was now doing. In a flash I saw how this bit of byplay really illuminated the whole psychological situation. Oster was the officer who had fought most clear-headedly, most resolutely, most indomitably against the Brown tyranny — and had fought it longest. There was a vast gulf between his mentality and that of Stauffenberg, who had shifted to the rebel side only after Stalingrad. These two army men were representatives of two different worlds.

Hansen warned that they had better go now, but I wished I knew what he had been thinking all evening. During the conversation he had turned frequently to look searchingly at Stauffenberg, then at me; then for a while he had stared in embarrassment at the floor. Was he merely being courteous to Struenck, as our host, or was he reluctant to show me openly that he was displeased with me?

Now, just as they were leaving, I saw that he wanted to speak to me. As soon as he felt sure his comrade was not observing him, he turned back and gripped my arms with both his hands. I could feel his fingers digging into my flesh. Agitatedly, he whispered to me: 'We absolutely must talk. I'll come tomorrow morning to see you.'

This still did not tell me what he really thought, but before I could ask, he gave me a long, meaningful look and spoke two sentences which I shall always remember as the final word on the history of July 20. I shall never forget the tone of voice in which he spoke, the gestures that accompanied his words.

'It all strikes me as so playful,' he said. 'It . . . can't . . . be . . . done . . . this . . . way.'

July 13

THERE WAS NOT MUCH TIME left for sleeping; first we had to air out the smoke-filled cellar. Early in the morning there was a radio signal. I knew nothing about the newly invented radar, which gave the position of approaching bombers, and therefore I did not understand the haste with which the Struencks packed their belongings, for the sirens had not yet begun howling. We put our belongings into the adjoining bunker and waited outside in the garden to see what would happen.

This was the first daylight attack I was experiencing. A year ago the nonchalance with which those great flights of bombers flew across all of Germany to Berlin would have been inconceivable. Now no one thought anything of it, or of the fact that fighter planes no longer rose to combat them and that the flak was pretty ineffectual. People accepted the inevitable apathetically and sighed with relief if the attack proved mild. A 'mild' attack meant, of course, that the quota of bombs rained down on some other quarter of the vast area of Berlin.

It was all over in an hour. Although the attack had been directed against the center of the city, I noticed on my way to Alexanderplatz that normal business activity continued in spite of fires and blockaded streets. When I asked the police officers in Helldorf's waiting room what had happened, they had to dig out their reports before they could give me a list of the larger fires and the more serious bomb damage. 'Nothing special,' I was told. They were so dulled to destruction that they took notice of it only when a serious traffic obstruction was created or when a government building was hit. To one who had come from an oasis of peace, this equanimity, or rather this lack of ability to react, was altogether uncanny. How could people who no longer had any emotions left be willing and able to break with the hard-won habits of daily life in order to participate in a rebellion or even in a riot?

Helldorf was not at all surprised by my impressions. He had not volunteered his opinion forcibly the day before, he said, because he had not wanted to influence my initial impression. But he simply could not arrive at any precise and unambiguous relationship with Stauffenberg. As he had told me, it was the same with Schulenberg. Before 1933, Schulenberg had been one of those intellectual Socialists who gathered around Otto Strasser and the East Prussian *Gauleiter*, Erich Koch. The difference between Stauffenberg, Helldorf, and Schulenberg — all three of them counts — was that Helldorf had come to the Nazi Movement as a primitive, I might almost say an unpolitical revolutionary. The other two had been attracted primarily by a political ideology. Therefore, it was possible for Helldorf to throw everything overboard at once: Hitler, the Party, the entire system. Stauffenberg, Schulenberg, and their clique wanted to drop no more ballast than was absolutely necessary; then they would paint the ship of state a military gray and set it afloat again.

Nebe came. We greeted each other warmly. As if we were right in the middle of one of our old discussions, he poured forth his usual plaint against the generals. 'Take my word for it, they'll never get anything done. Everything will go wrong this time too.'

I soon found what the excitement was about. According to pre-arrangement Nebe had gone to the Bendlerstrasse at eleven o'clock. This in itself took some courage on his part. When he got to Olbricht's waiting room, an adjutant at once took him in hand and, as befitted an SS general, led him directly to his superior, who politely inquired what he wanted.

Nebe did not know Olbricht by sight. Fortunately, he noticed that the officer to whom he was speaking wore three stars. So far as Nebe knew, Olbricht was not yet a colonel-general. Therefore, Nebe was cautious and said he had come at Helldorf's request in regard to certain police officers whom Helldorf wished released from military duty. The officer replied that he had better discuss such questions of detail with General Olbricht. He had been led in to see — Colonel-General Fromm!

This, of course, was just the sort of thing that would happen to the cautious Nebe. Olbricht had merely laughed about the incident and had then introduced Nebe to one of his junior officers, who was to show him the plans for the police action. Nebe was put out by this as well. 'Those generals are always ready to call in help, but they themselves like to keep away from dangerous conferences,' he growled.

What had made him absolutely furious was the fact that the maps of the city which he was shown had seemed very familiar to him. Incredible as it sounds, they were our own maps from the time of Stalingrad. Nebe himself had made notes on them. The only hitch was that in the meantime a vast number of the buildings indicated on the maps had been converted into heaps of rubble, and many other dislocations had occurred.

Helldorf came in excitedly. The acting *Gauleiter* of Berlin had just paid him a visit and had poured out his heart about the terrible reactionary generals. But at least, he had said, the *Grossdeutschland* battalion of guards had been entrusted to a sensible commander who was a National Socialist of unquestionable loyalty: Major Roemer. Stauffenberg was counting upon this same Major Roemer to conduct the action during the first — and therefore the most important — few hours, until the panzer troops moved up. This was too much for Helldorf. He asked me to arrange an audience with Beck for him. I was more than willing. To my mind, the assistance of the police force would be the decisive factor in the *Putsch.* It seemed to me that Stauffenberg was staking everything on the opposite card. He was relying completely on his bomb and on the military forces.

Helldorf drove me back to the Struencks'. Hansen was already waiting there. He was overtired, for he had had to take Stauffenberg home. On the way they had quarreled furiously. They had continued their argument in the car — much too long and much too loudly, so that the chauffeur would be able to testify to a great deal. Hansen and especially the Struencks were to pay dearly for that indiscretion.

During lunch Hansen told me all that was troubling him. He still admired Stauffenberg for his superb talents as a military man, for his noble manner, his gift for organization, his culture. On many evenings Stauffenberg had recited Stefan George's poems for hours at a time. His deep religious feeling also marked him as many notches above the average of his colleagues; but it was impossible to discuss politics with him.

Nowadays Stauffenberg no longer seemed to be the same man, Hansen said. Of late he had been secretive, subject to whims, tyrannical, and noticeably nervous. Was all this solely a result of the tremendous psychic pressure upon him since he had resolved upon the assassination? Hansen did not think so. Formerly he had been a man without nerves. The great change in him had come with his terrible wound.

Hansen said that it was possible to talk with Stauffenberg alone, but that he felt himself an alien in the 'debating club' that Stauffenberg had recently gathered around himself. Hansen was a talented, uncomplicated professional officer. It was quite natural that he would not know how to handle this curious mixture of 'putschist' and theoretician. Everything was too vague and misty, he felt; there was a lack of inner discipline. What with all the profound debates on the moral justification of assassination and on the salvation that would come from socialism or from the East, it became impossible to discuss with Stauffenberg and his circle the technical details of a *Putsch*. At once they became evasive. Somehow, they took it all too lightly.

Hansen mentioned again what he had said the night before and tried to explain to me what he meant by 'playful.' He did not deny the firmness of Stauffenberg's resolution. What was missing was a basic conception of the gravity of the undertaking. He informed me that Stauffenberg had been playing hide-and-seek with me. A few weeks before he had counted upon playing off the West against the East; now he was imagining a joint victorious march of the German and Red armies against the plutocracies. It was an open question whether the recent military disaster had not accelerated this radical reorientation.

I had to hurry off, in order not to keep Beck waiting. In Lichterfelde I made a slight détour in order to examine Beck's house from all sides for possible lurking watchers. The immediate vicinity of the Goethestrasse had been so shattered by bombs that it would have been difficult for spies to find any inconspicuous post.

When I mentioned this to Beck, he smiled slyly. The watch had been given up last November, he informed me. A bomb had struck the house adjoining his. He had spent the night helping to extinguish the fire, and in the early hours of the morning he had invited his neighbor in for a glass of brandy. The neighbor had drunk his health and congratulated him — for the corner room of the ruined building had been requisitioned by the Gestapo so that they could watch and photograph his visitors.

As he had so often done before, Beck had drawn up extensive notes in preparation for our conference. He could not give up this habit, although he must have known how dearly he would have to pay for such scribblings if the Gestapo should make a sudden raid. But he was and remained the model of a chief of the general staff. He never said a word too much or too little, and he was fond of thinking in writing. Because of this habit, he did not hurdle any of the more obvious steps. Although there was really scarcely any need for us to discuss the matter, he led off with the question of whether we should undertake an assassination and why at the present moment it was morally, politically, and militarily imperative.

For Beck also the prime factor was the situation in the East. Once more I heard a description of the disaster that had befallen the army group of the center. The situation of the northern army group was even more perilous, he said. There a new Stalingrad was in the making. Hitler had refused to withdraw the two hundred and fifty thousand men — and his obstinacy appeared all the more grotesque because these armies were urgently needed on the border of East Prussia. According to Beck's information, it would prove impossible, in the long run, to continue supplying those troops by sea or by air. And there were not enough forces available to relieve them by an offensive. If the Russians were cunning, they would draw a powerful ring around the troops in the north and then avoid further battles there while advancing across the Vistula. This latest absurdity of Hitler's amateur strategy had evoked a revolt in the general staff. Zeitzler, the chief, had suffered a nervous breakdown and was at the moment hospitalized. This abandonment of an entire army group had had the effect of preparing many of the generals at headquarters for an uprising against Hitler.

In the West the invasion had succeeded. A number of unforeseen pieces of good luck had helped the Anglo-Americans. In spite of the ban on furloughs, Rommel had secretly flown home for a birthday celebration. By the time he reached the front again, hours had passed. More precious hours were lost because Keitel had not dared to wake Hitler, a late sleeper, too early; and Hitler had undertaken sole command of the mobile defense corps.

Kluge, who had just succeeded Rundstedt, sent word by special courier that Hitler had deceived him as to the true situation. He had been given false figures on the forces at his disposal. No wonder he urged a speedy revolt. Falkenhausen, after his dismissal from the post of military commander in Belgium, had remained in Brussels to await events and to work for us at Kluge's headquarters.

Beck traced anew the course of events which I had been able to follow only somewhat vaguely from Zurich. After the failure of the previous December, the idea of an assassination had been postponed for months. Even the Stauffenberg circle had been willing to give Hitler a last chance to beat back the invasion and then initiate peace negotiations.

Now, Beck believed, it was too late. He stressed his conviction that Germany was beaten; total occupation could not be prevented, he said, and the fate of the army was sealed. Under the conditions of the present collapse, only a German Badoglio could resolve the situation, and he, Beck, was probably the one general who was still respected both abroad and by the troops at home. For that reason he was willing to take over the thankless task and help see to it that the inevitable bitter pill was swallowed with a certain amount of dignity and respect.

Naturally Beck asked me whether I thought any chance still existed for an agreement with the Western Powers. He found it unfortunate that we were unable at least to discuss the matter with them. In contrast to Goerdeler, I believed that we should have difficulty in persuading the Allies to recognize at all a Reich government capable of functioning. In his circumspect manner Beck summed it up: he could not exclude this pessimistic possibility, but we must try to get whatever we could out of Goerdeler's optimism and zest.

We now turned to a discussion of the technique of the *Putsch*. Not much had changed. The opportunity for Stauffenberg to commit the assassination would come at a conference in Hitler's headquarters. It was still an open question where Hitler would be at the time — whether in East Prussia, at Berghof, or in Munich. Olbricht had arranged matters so that a number of important orders would have to be reported orally to Hitler. This would be done during the usual morning conference, which was ordinarily attended by a variable number of high officers. There was the chance that some innocent person might also be killed.

No matter where the bomb exploded, the headquarters' communications center would be blown up immediately afterward. The communications chief, General Fellgiebel, was in charge of this. This would insure that the headquarters would be cut off from the outside world for several hours, so that the initial action could not be thwarted by counter-orders.

As soon as the code word 'Walkuere' was given, the troops stationed around Berlin would start moving. For the first three hours, however, only the guards regiment would be at our disposal, because giving the alarm, issuing live munitions, and getting the troops going would be time-consuming. These three 'stagnant' hours represented the real danger to us. During that period the Gestapo could get set to strike back. Therefore, it was especially important for us, with Helldorf's co-operation, to paralyze the Berlin police. According to our information, no significant number of *Waffen-SS* troops were stationed in the Reich capital.

The attempt would be made to draw Colonel-General Fromm over to our side, since this would greatly facilitate the progress of the *Putsch*. Olbricht thought it quite likely that Fromm would accede to a *fait accompli.* If he did not, Colonel-General Hoeppner would replace him. Before I had the slightest chance to protest, Beck assured me that his opinion of Hoeppner had not altered in any way. He still considered him an intolerable opportunist. After all the disappointments we had had with Hoeppner in the past years, Beck did not intend to let him hold any office for more than three days. But Stauffenberg and Olbricht felt that they needed Hoeppner as a counterpoise to Guderian.

Hoeppner had been with us in the conspiracy of 1938. He had also been one of the revolting panzer generals in November, 1939. But in the spring of 1940, when the soil of Flanders was no longer a muddy swamp and decorations, laurels, and military glory could be

won so easily there, Hoeppner was unable to resist the allure. He did
not even object to the Russian campaign. Occasionally, however,
under the influence of alcohol, he had boasted to his intimates of the
plans he had harbored back in 1938.

Fate caught up with Hoeppner before Moscow. The greatest general of the ages was dissatisfied with him. A simple telegram was
sent, and the colonel-general found himself out of the army and on
his way home. Back in Berlin, Hoeppner spent a few days protesting.
He insisted that his legal position be clarified. Had he been degraded
to the rank of an ordinary cavalryman? Had he been completely
expelled from the army? Who was going to pay his pension? And
how big was the pension?

The jurists in the OKW racked their brains. Our immortally generous Fuehrer found the solution. Hoeppner was and remained expelled from the *Wehrmacht,* but he was compensated by continuing
to draw his pay; he was also permitted to retain occupancy in his
official mansion.

Witzleben would take general command of all the armed forces and
direct command of the army as well. Witzleben was waiting near
Zossen, where the major part of army headquarters was stationed.
Quartermaster-General Wagner, who was at last co-operating unreservedly, was making the fullest preparations at Zossen. The *Luft-waffe* had been so terribly shattered that we no longer needed to fear
it. Doenitz's cruisers were at the bottom of the sea, and he could
hardly hasten to the aid of his Fuehrer in Berlin with submarines and
destroyers.

Since Beck would become head of the state, he would thereby be
the supreme commander of the *Wehrmacht.* He had no intention,
however, of interfering with Witzleben's and especially with Olbricht's
and Stauffenberg's work. He did not want to create confusion and obliterate responsibilities *à la* Hitler by interference from above in questions of detail.

He had an excellent plan for preserving the civilian character of the
coup d'état. Just as the troops were subordinate to him as chief of
state, so he would also place the police directly under his authority

during the early period. Thus, during the emergency, he would be able to co-ordinate *Wehrmacht* and police. In order to facilitate this co-ordination, he would insist that I remain as his immediate assistant with the title of 'Reich Minister to the Chief of State.' This provided me with an opening for discussing the events of the night before. I described the long conversation with Stauffenberg and let Beck know how worried I was. He thought these political digressions on the part of a young colonel should not be taken too seriously. During the past half-year he had come to respect Stauffenberg highly, he said, as the sole activist among the soldiers. He, too, had noticed Stauffenberg's temporary uncertainty and nervousness, but considering the tremendous risk he was about to take, that was hardly surprising. We should let him be, thought Beck; we had no right to try to change his plans beforehand. Once the assassination succeeded, he, Beck, would possess the necessary power of command. Then he would know how to handle the situation, and he did not doubt Stauffenberg's loyalty; he felt sure the colonel would consent wholeheartedly to his decisions. This sounded clear and reassuring. Nevertheless, Beck said he would talk to Stauffenberg about the stupidity of Nebe's being led into Fromm's office and about the outmoded maps of the city. And he would also have to look into Helldorf's warning against Major Roemer.

I hastened back to the Struencks', to find Nebe waiting for me. The past year had left its traces on Nebe; it had tried his nerves more than all the other war years. He described the present attitude of the Nazi leaders in the face of the mounting disasters. Himmler was wavering between his slavish submissiveness toward Hitler and his natural shrewdness which warned him that evil days were coming. Nebe was sure that Himmler knew nothing of our preparations. He was counting on the general fear of the Russians and on the formula of unconditional surrender, which played right into his hands. Because he correctly judged the majority of the generals, he considered the domestic situation at the moment less tense than it had been many times in the past, when the powerful pressure from outside was lacking.

Goering had lost all standing, Nebe said. The failure of the *Luftwaffe* during the invasion had been the final mark against him. For this reason we need no longer worry about his attitude during the *Putsch*. On the other hand, Nebe pointed out that a fundamental change had taken place in the popular attitude toward Himmler. Much as he was feared as a hangman, he was also looked to as the only man amid all the confusion who still had power behind him. The people were in terror of the twelve million foreign workers who were virtually overrunning Germany. They also feared grave disruptions in supplies to the cities should an uprising take place. Scarcely anyone could conceive of a change in the system without the participation of Himmler. For this reason Nebe proposed that we drop our old plan of attributing the assassination to Himmler. For by now anyone who undertook to kill Hitler would be so popular that we should merely be contributing to Himmler's prestige. However, the chief consideration was the first reaction among the troops, and for them Himmler was the hated Gestapist.

The administrative apparatus was already extensively disorganized, Nebe informed me, so that resistance from the provincial satraps was improbable. He nevertheless was thoroughly pessimistic. 'You'll see, nothing will come of it again,' he said gloomily. At the very least, he thought, he himself would be killed in the course of the *Putsch*. The assassination was to take place between twelve noon and two. Every afternoon around two o'clock the department heads of the *Sicherheitshauptamt* — Mueller, Schellenberg, Ohlendorf, and Nebe — had lunch with their chief, Kaltenbrunner, in the Prinz Albrechtstrasse building. Usually this was a welcome opportunity for Nebe to keep his ears open. But on the *Putsch* day — just two days away now — he would prefer, he said, to stay away. However, that would be too dangerous; if something went wrong, they might draw conclusions about the reasons for his absence.

I consoled him with the assurance that by two o'clock it would all be over and the guards regiment would have rolled up to the Prinz Albrechtstrasse. Nebe shook his head. The news would undoubtedly burst in on them during their lunch, he averred. And he pictured the scene: how annoying it would be for him to be shot down at the last moment, and in the company of such high-ranking SS gangsters as these.

July 14

A QUIET DAY. This was just as well, for on the morrow we should have need of steady nerves. I saw Beck briefly. He had talked with Stauffenberg, who had refused to take any heed of Helldorf's warning against Major Roemer. In any event, they had a gallant stand-in for every commander. Each of these men, at the slightest sign of refusal to obey orders, would shoot down the unco-operative officer and take over the command himself.

Stauffenberg had also denied Nebe's statement that the maps of Berlin were outmoded. Schulenberg had examined them carefully, he said. Perhaps Nebe had been shown the wrong maps by mistake. Beck had let the matter drop. It was already too late for argument or reproof, he said. We could only hope that everything would turn out well. Stauffenberg, he said, had been extremely nervous. Tomorrow was the great trial. They had even decided to give the signal, 'Walkuere,' at eleven o'clock — before the crucial Hitler conference — in order to shorten the three 'stagnant' hours.

Saturday, July 15

GOERDELER arrived at the Struencks' promptly at eleven o'clock, and we went by subway to Beck's home in Lichterfelde. For the first time in many years the reticent Beck emerged from his shell to greet us with unwonted cordiality. 'How good that you're here. This waiting alone is unendurable.'

For a while we talked half-heartedly. In order to divert our minds from thoughts of what must now be happening at Hitler's headquarters, Beck took out a pad of notes and asked me about a large number of persons. He had made a long list of prospects for subordinate posts. To me it seemed highly objectionable to be endangering needlessly people who would not count at all until two or three days 'afterward.' In making plans for uprisings, rebels should concern themselves only with ministers, under-secretaries, and the governing heads of provinces. The names of such persons could easily be memorized. Any other lists of names were, to my mind, idle speculation and — in case of failure — virtually warrants for arrest. We were soon to have bloody proof of this thesis.

Waiting became more and more of a torment. At two o'clock lunch began at the Fuehrer's headquarters. The bomb was supposed to explode between twelve and one. What had happened? Had it been called off again? Then, certainly, we ought to have heard by now. I don't know how often each of us looked at his watch. Our mood became more and more depressed. We fumbled about for something to say to each other, but our minds were not on our conversation.

All afternoon we waited, talking intermittently. By six o'clock we could no longer stand it. By then it was virtually impossible that any news from the Bendlerstrasse would be good news. We decided we might just as well not permit the Gestapo to catch all three of us at once. Heavy-heartedly, we took our leave of Beck. In order not to attract attention, I went first. Goerdeler would meet me at the near-by public telephone. Meanwhile, I would try to get in touch with Helldorf.

Remarkably enough, the public telephone in front of the post office was still in working order, and I succeeded in getting Helldorf. Without waiting for me to ask a camouflaged question, he said, with provoking cheekiness, 'You know, of course, that the celebration did not take place?' When I said I had not known, he decided it would be better not to continue the conversation over the telephone. He would drop in at the Struencks' in the evening.

At any rate, the Gestapo apparently had not yet been called in. For a moment Goerdeler and I considered whether we ought not to run back to Beck's and tell him. But a bus was just coming along and we automatically boarded it. We assumed that Beck would soon find out. Had we known that he would have to wait until midnight, we unquestionably would have turned back in order to relieve him of his suspense, now doubly hard to bear because he was alone.

Helldorf arrived at the Struencks' soon after we had finished a morose supper. At one o'clock he had driven over to the Bendlerstrasse, as had been agreed. There he met Olbricht and Hoeppner and the Stauffenberg group, all assembled in the adjutants' room. They did not have to wait long for the prearranged telephone call from the Fuehrer's headquarters. Everyone stood around the telephone as Lieutenant von Haeften answered the call. Stauffenberg was at the other end of the line. The lieutenant replied apparently to a question from Stauffenberg; in a clear, unhesitant voice von Haeften gave his instructions. Then he hung up and informed the others that Stauffenberg had stated in a disguised fashion that Goering and Himmler were not present and had asked whether he should go ahead anyway. Haeften had at once said yes on his own authority. Although Helldorf approved of this decision, he thought Olbricht and Hoeppner were quite right in their indignation at the way the answer had been given over their heads.

A quarter of an hour later, Stauffenberg called again. When he had returned to the meeting, everyone had been on the point of leaving and Hitler had just rushed away. As Helldorf described it, Olbricht had appeared visibly relieved. At once he had locked the papers relating to the *Putsch* in his safe and had good-humoredly remarked that at least they could enjoy a quiet weekend. This bit of humor may have been a natural reaction to the tremendous nervous tension. Nevertheless, it was somehow symptomatic.

Helldorf insisted that if we had witnessed the scene we would undoubtedly have concurred with his opinion — that next time as well the affair would not come off properly. He could not, he said, rationalize his feeling, but a revolt could not be successfully carried out if it were to be undertaken in such an easy-going manner.

Had Providence once more saved Hitler by impelling him to leave the meeting in time? It can be taken that way, for after receiving an affirmative answer, Stauffenberg had gone back to set off his bomb. There was something inexplicable about this, however. Why had Stauffenberg felt any need to get confirmation by telephone? Last

Wednesday the action had been called off because Goering and
Himmler were unexpectedly missing. There could be no surprise
about it this time. Either they were present or not present, and presumably Stauffenberg had decided on his course of action in either
case. We did not know what decision he and his friends had framed
for these eventualities, but they must have decided something. Why,
then, had it been necessary for Stauffenberg to make a telephone call
which would inevitably be answered as the lieutenant had in fact im-
pulsively answered it? This dangerous as well as superfluous telephone call indicated that Stauffenberg had somewhat lost his head.
Consequently, the melancholy conclusion was forced on us that Hitler
had been saved not so much by a beneficent Providence as by Stauffenberg's psychological inhibitions. It seemed highly unlikely that he
would succeed a third time where he had funked twice before.

Perhaps this failure today was a sign from above that we had to
look for other ways and means. I suggested once more the 'Western'
solution, which we had repeatedly discussed in Switzerland. By that
I meant that we would abandon the attempt at assassination and a
Putsch in Berlin in favor of a unilateral action in the West. If Kluge
and Rommel had crossed their psychological Rubicon, then let them
refuse to obey Hitler and make an offer for a separate armistice to
Eisenhower. Practically this would mean that the front in the West
would be broken and the Anglo-American troops would pour across
the Siegfried Line into Germany, meeting very little or no resistance.
At the very least they would reach Berlin before the Russians. That,
to be sure, had implications even deeper than 'unconditional surrender.' We should have to reckon with open civil war, and the
legend of the stab in the back would once more create trouble. But
how much destruction we could save this way!

But would Kluge co-operate? And how could we get to see him?
Struenck reassured us on that point. Hansen had informed him
several days ago that his official plane was prepared to take off for
Kluge's headquarters at a moment's notice. Hansen had even taken
the precaution of manufacturing an urgent pretext for visiting the
general. These preparations, Struenck told me, were chiefly for my
benefit, in case it proved necessary for me to disappear in a hurry.

We would confront Kluge with a simple alternative; if he wasn't going to act, he would have to arrest us at once. We also intended to inform him that we were quite ready to provide the Gestapo with all the information it required about his and Rommel's constructive proposals in the past.

Admittedly, this would be an act of desperation. But was there any other way to accomplish anything with those generals? They themselves had long since thrown overboard every ounce of old-fashioned chivalry.

The sirens howled. Helldorf rushed out to his car. He wanted to get to his shelter office in the center of the city before the bombs fell. Afterward we sat up together for a long time. Goerdeler wanted to leave early in the morning for Leipzig, in order to bid good-bye to his family. Whatever came, it was clear that this time the die was cast. Fate would permit no more evasions; we had advanced too far. The *fronde* could not go on forever fleeing from its own decisions.

At such times Goerdeler liked to discuss everything anew. Just as his whole mind had for years revolved around one central point, so his conversation turned endlessly in a circle.

At last weariness overwhelmed us. The Struencks fixed a small room for the two of us. Around two in the morning we collapsed into bed. For a while we talked in whispers. Goerdeler urged me to see Beck early in the morning and win him over to our side — that is, persuade him to accept the 'Western' solution.

After but two or three hours' sleep the alarm clock clanged. Goerdeler wanted to take the seven-o'clock train. To make sure of getting a place on it, he had to be on the platform at least an hour beforehand.

I heard him rise heavily. Half asleep, I shook hands with him. 'Well, then, till Tuesday.'

How gracious is Fate, in kindly concealing it from us when we are seeing our friends for the last time on this earth. Had I known what was to come, I would have sprung to my feet; I would not have released his hand until our eyes had met and contrived to express all the unspoken feelings, all the comradeship that cannot be put into words. As it was, I watched sleepily in the uncertain light of dawn while a dear and unforgettable friend walked softly out of the door and vanished — forever.

July 16

IN THE AFTERNOON I went to see Beck. The marks of his long vigil of the day before were still upon him. Waiting alone for six hours after we left must have tried him sorely. He informed me that Stauffenberg was coming to see him that evening, to explain personally what had taken place. I told him about the decision Goerdeler and I had come to — that we now favored an immediate adoption of the 'Western' solution. He did not reject the suggestion outright. But he would not take a position on the question until he had heard Stauffenberg's report.

July 17

THE ENEMY BOMBERS took care that we did not sleep too late in the morning. Helldorf had telephoned. Between two air-raid alarms I made my way to Alexanderplatz.

Over Sunday, it appeared, the police chief had had an attack of nerves. He wanted to know whether Beck agreed to the 'Western' solution. His disappointment was marked when I told him that Beck had not yet decided. While I was there, Kaltenbrunner telephoned. Helldorf let me listen in on another receiver. I was not yet acquainted with that famous Gestapist and was therefore interested in hearing his voice. To my surprise, it was not an unpleasant voice at all, much calmer and more distinct than the run of Nazi ranters. Of course, Kaltenbrunner imitated the typical Hitlerian accent; all the Party leaders who were able to reproduce the South German dialect did that.

The subject of the telephone conversation was a complaint of Helldorf's which to my knowledge he had already lodged the last time I saw him, a year before. Helldorf was police chief of Berlin and was also a *Polizeifuehrer,* which gave him an even higher rank

Nevertheless, on the basis of a reorganization within the ministry of the interior, control over the local *Ordnungspolizei* and the *Staatspolizei* was taken from him. The net result was that Helldorf was left in command merely of the detective force and parts of the traffic police force. But since the ordinary mortal could never find his way through this snarl of interlocking responsibilities, Helldorf was generally thought to command the real police power in Berlin. He had decided that he would no longer put up with this situation. Twice he had offered his resignation. Once he had gone to the front to escape the intolerable situation of being held responsible while possessing so little power. At last he had appealed to Goebbels in the latter's capacity of Berlin *Gauleiter* and Reich defense commissioner. That had worked. The ambitious little Goebbels was extremely jealous of his rights, and even Black Heinrich was unwilling to risk a brush with so accomplished a slanderer.

Himmler had, therefore, ordered a reconciliation with Helldorf, and Kaltenbrunner was now asking him to come to a conference in the Prinz Albrechtstrasse on Friday. The whole manner of his invitation, the fact that on the one hand he was in no hurry and that on the other he was soft-soaping Helldorf, indicated that he harbored no suspicions. That, at least, was a consolation.

Helldorf wanted to meet Hansen. It is hard to imagine how difficult it was to bring together men who were, after all, pulling on the same rope. Each one was jealous of his 'connections.' The many mutual refusals to meet were always, of course, justified on grounds of camouflage — in the end we should be so occupied in covering our tracks that we would forget what we were planning to do.

I telephoned Frau Struenck to ask whether I might bring along a guest. She was used to such troubles, and without asking any questions simply said yes. When we reached the cellar, I could not refrain from laughing. In addition to Hansen another unexpected guest was there — Doctor Hans Koch, an old friend and comrade. It was quite an achievement for Frau Struenck to have found provisions for one permanent guest and three unannounced visitors who were not backward at table.

Hansen was indignant about the kind of 'politics' the Stauffenberg clique was practicing. Alongside of Goerdeler's cabinet, which he detested, Stauffenberg wanted to install military administrators with full powers of control, who would 'establish order' during the first weeks. Nine months later, I found proof of this interpretation of Hansen's. One of the few survivors of the intimate group around Stauffenberg published an account which employed almost Hansen's exact words about this *Putsch* within a *Putsch*. 'In case the uprising should succeed, military administrators were to be appointed at once for the various Reich ministries. . . .'

Hansen shared Helldorf's conclusion about the scene in the Bendlerstrasse that morning. Neither could say why he felt it so clearly, but both men believed that the affair would turn out badly. Both broke out that I had not put the matter of the 'Western' solution strongly enough to Beck, and said that I must insist on it. Hansen expressly offered to put his plane at my disposal. He could guarantee my safe delivery to Kluge's headquarters.

Through the cellar window we saw a pair of high black boots trudge by. Struenck rushed out. In a moment he returned, red-faced. Nebe was outside, he said, and extremely excited. He would not come in and said that he had to speak to me privately. I went outside, and Nebe drew me into the darkest part of the cellar proper. Breathlessly he informed me that at lunch that afternoon the Gestapo chiefs had decided to issue an order for the arrest of Goerdeler.

The situation was not quite so bad as it sounded. It seemed that a certain retired colonel who had talked too carelessly had been arrested and had confessed under torture that Goerdeler had repeatedly been mentioned as a candidate to succeed Hitler. The colonel, a stouthearted old soldier who had been living on pension for a long time, was well known for his loquacity. We had always avoided him for that very reason, so that he could not have betrayed any real plans for revolt. He was merely a kind and decent old gossip — just the type the Gestapo men made a habit of picking up. They never seemed to catch any of the real plotters.

Nebe assured me that neither Kaltenbrunner nor Mueller had mentioned or hinted at Beck or any of the rest of us. This was some good luck amid bad; at least we knew that the Gestapists were as yet unaware of our conspiracy; but Goerdeler would have to remain under cover.

With difficulty I persuaded Nebe to come in. He was always like that; he had to be reassured repeatedly and coaxed out of the initial shock. Everyone was disturbed by his news. Helldorf, hard-boiled as he was, remarked that the Gestapo was beginning to make things hot for us. It would only be a question of days, he said, before the Gestapo drew their circles tighter and tighter and finally closed in on our cellar. As he sketched these circles on the table with professional calm and showed their ever-narrowing radii, we began to feel distinctly ill at ease. We would have to hurry.

Hansen lent me his car so that I could report to Beck. Sooner or later, I thought, the frequent appearance of a man so conspicuously tall as myself must attract attention, even in a quiet by-street like the Goethestrasse. Involuntarily, an order for the arrest of a comrade produces a peculiar psychosis: I suddenly decided that I had been extremely unwise these past few days with my reckless bustling around town as far as Alexanderplatz.

First, I listened to Beck's news. I didn't want to inhibit him by telling him my bad news at once. Even so, his description of his meeting with Stauffenberg was by no means encouraging. Stauffenberg blamed his friend and contemporary, General Stieff. This talented officer was one of Hitler's youngest generals, who had behind him a brilliant career in the general staff. For the past six months he had been one of the main activists in Stauffenberg's group. For months the bomb had been locked in his safe, awaiting its great hour. According to Stauffenberg's description, Stieff had suddenly lost his nerve on Saturday. While Stauffenberg was telephoning the Bendlerstrasse, Stieff had taken the briefcase with its deadly contents and carried it out of the room. That was all very well. But this account did not answer our pressing question of why it had been necessary for Stauffenberg to make that telephone call. Stauffenberg had again reassured Beck about Major Roemer, but Beck nevertheless intended to talk to Olbricht about the man.

The preliminary alarm on Saturday had had the effect we feared. Both Fromm and Keitel had heard about the measure and made further inquiries. Olbricht had assured both of them that he had issued the watchword 'Walkuere' as a mere drill measure. But obviously such a 'drill' could not be repeated twice within five days. Next time the unfortunate period of three 'stagnant' hours would have to remain unabridged.

From the way Beck spoke, it was clear that he was still counting on the assassination, while my thoughts were occupied completely with the 'Western' solution. I informed him of Hansen's offer to supply us with a plane and suggested that we start for Kluge's headquarters directly after Goerdeler arrived in the morning.

Beck reacted strongly to this suggestion. We must leave to him the final decision on the question of assassination or capitulation of the Western armies. Stauffenberg had given him his word of honor yesterday that this coming Thursday he would explode his bomb, come what may. In sheer loyalty to Stauffenberg, he had to let the colonel have this last chance.

I asked him whether, after all that had happened, he could still really believe that the assassination would succeed. His reply was disconcerting. He told me that he considered it highly questionable that the *Putsch* would be successful. Still, if Stauffenberg did set off his bomb, we could in all probability count on Hitler's liquidation, and this positive factor outweighed all other possible mishaps. An unsuccessful *Putsch* with a dead Hitler would be better than a partially successful uprising in which that master of the black arts would be alive to lead the other side in a civil war.

Beck explained this decision with such gravity that I could not help realizing how much inner struggle it had cost him. If we gave the signal for a civil war, it would be said that in our country's darkest hour we had stayed the hand of the tyrannicide.

Emotionally, I disagreed; rationally, I had to admit that Beck was right. There was no help for it; we would have to summon up the nervous strength to wait for Thursday, July 20. Afterward we were free. If nothing happened, Beck pledged himself to try the 'Western' solution. 'But mind you,' he said to me, 'Kluge will not take the hurdle either. At the last moment he'll back down.'

I told Beck about the order for the arrest of Goerdeler, but also reassured him that the rest of us were at the moment not implicated. We agreed that Goerdeler must hide out at once, but be accessible within a few hours. Beck provided me with a messenger to send to Goerdeler: Captain Kaiser, an old schoolfellow of Beck's.

July 18

I SAW BECK AGAIN, and this time told him what I thought the trouble was. He must, I said, take over the leadership of the action — especially the military leadership. His fair-minded and retiring attitude — that he would not take the position of chief of state until the assassination succeeded — was not sufficient. Military men expected clear-cut commands.

Beck listened patiently to my argument. What else was there for him to do, he asked, but to sit here on his sofa and wait until the time came? 'I am to be chief of state,' he said; 'I am to become the military supreme commander; everyone assures me of his confidence in me, and in the final analysis the responsibility is already mine. Yet I am still a civilian; I cannot issue a single order and must be grateful if my advice is taken.'

Was he right? My whole feeling about the matter ran counter to his. His theory was that a good general must refrain — unlike the amateur Hitler — from losing himself in details or interfering with the technical execution of orders to subordinates. This might be all very well in the auditorium of a military academy, but uprisings could not be conducted according to the textbooks. They shattered the normal canons of subordination and command; they required arbitrary decisions, boldness, courage; they needed leaders rather than thinkers.

Beck took my arm. With an imploring gesture he continued: 'You must know what a bundle of nerves Stauffenberg is. He has already threatened twice not to set off the bomb. . . .'

There we had it! What good were the most intelligent commands if the initiation of the *Putsch* depended on the free will, or rather the unpredictable character, of one man who was resolved, precisely because of his own tremendous stake, to gamble everything on his own card?

At the Struencks' the telephone had been ringing all morning. They had taken care not to answer it. They had a fairly good idea who would be telephoning so persistently. When it rang again during lunch, we sent the maid to answer it. Of course it was 'Doctor Blank.'

Struenck went to the telephone and manifested his inflexibility when Blank announced that he was coming to pay a visit. Absolutely not; the insurance policy was already 'in the works'; there was nothing more to discuss. There was no need for Doctor Blank to worry about it any longer; with all these air alarms it would be best for him to stay close to the safety of his shelter.

Goerdeler did not give up easily. He still wanted to propose a vital change in the policy; there were certain additional points that had to be discussed. Above all, he wanted to speak with the other business partner. Struenck had to give in and hand the telephone to me. Although I declared once more that the project had been thoroughly discussed, that it was a waste of energy to argue the matter out over the telephone, and that I was in any case bound by a decision of the directors, Blank insisted on the proposals he had made Saturday night. He absolutely must speak to me about that, he said.

I have always felt that fear brings on dangers. On the other hand, it would be wrong to behave with exaggerated carelessness. Our friend ought to have been happy that he had received warning in time and that he had a safe hiding-place for the next few days. Any more discussion could only lead to trouble. Therefore, I put an end to the useless argument with unmistakable firmness. For compelling reasons the directors could not alter their decision, I said. We must bow to their attitude. In any case, Doctor Blank could count on receiving additional information in the immediate future.

July 19

I SAW BECK briefly in the morning. There was nothing more to discuss. We could only hope that tomorrow the torment of waiting would be over. Since the Saturday experience had indicated the need for caution, Beck suggested that I stay with Helldorf while waiting for the signal and then accompany him to the Bendlerstrasse. We shook hands for the last time before the fateful day. He gave me a meaningful look and said: 'I shall have two revolvers in my pocket. . . .'

In the evening Helldorf and Nebe dropped in. We wanted to talk over once more all the police measures that would have to be taken. It was clear that they would do their part. Helldorf realized that his long term of office under the Nazis had compromised him too thoroughly. Within a few days after the *Putsch* he would have to resign. I respected his acumen and assured him that we would know how to acknowledge the manner in which he had co-operated with us for so many years.

After we had again discussed for the thousandth time all the personalities and immediate orders to be issued, our conversation turned toward the general course of the action. We resolved not to agitate ourselves any more. At this point there was nothing we could change; everything would have to proceed along its predestined course.

I protested vigorously when Nebe expressed pessimism about the explosive effect of Stauffenberg's bomb. It was true, of course, that since the mass bombing attacks had been launched, every layman could cite the most astonishing peculiarities about bombs. There were stories of bomb-hits that had knocked down whole blocks of houses and left plaster casts in the very center of the explosion without so much as a chip. Helldorf described vividly how a thin curtain had protected all the objects in his study from the air pressure when a bomb burst directly in front of his home.

But what was the use of such speculation? It could only bring bad luck, I felt. Nebe and Helldorf both laughed when I brusquely cut short their musings about what guardian devil might shield Hitler on the morrow.

JULY 20, 1944

I AWOKE TO THE KEEN CONSCIOUSNESS of the importance of this day.

The bombers did not appear. If they were decent, they would show up between twelve and two. Then the military action could begin while the Gestapo men were huddling in their air-raid shelters.

Even this early in the morning the heat was unbearable. The Struencks accompanied me to the railroad station. A certain solemnity in their manner made me recollect how much was at stake.

Around eleven o'clock I reached Helldorf's office. The police chief sighed with relief when I appeared. Soon Count Bismarck joined us. For the most part we mused dully or complained to one another about the heat.

Shortly after twelve the sergeant on duty reported that a major was outside with a message from General Olbricht. Helldorf and I were electrified. The major entered, a small man, ghastly pale, obviously nervous. To judge by his face he could not have been older than thirty. In one hand he clutched a black briefcase as if it contained a treasure in diamonds. His other hand he raised stiffly in the Nazi greeting; then he appeared to realize that he might at least omit the 'Heil Hitler.' With a suspicious glance at Count Bismarck and me, he asked Helldorf whether he might speak to him privately.

Helldorf could not refrain from smiling. He inspected this messenger of the fates who seemed overwhelmed by his historic rôle and said jovially, 'Come, now, let's have it.'

The young major did not dare talk. Helldorf had to assure him that we knew all about it and that he need not fear to speak openly.

Now, we thought, we would hear the great news. Instead, a very different bomb burst. The major stated that he was a member of the staff of the district command. General Olbricht had given him the city maps with the marked buildings which were to be occupied today. He was instructed to discuss the rest with Helldorf.

The map of the city that the young major unfolded with trembling hands seemed strangely familiar to me. Sure enough, it was the one we had used at the time of Stalingrad, the one Olbricht had recently had his adjutant show to Nebe, and which, we had afterward been assured, must have been brought out by mistake. A little study soon corroborated Nebe's statement that it had not even been corrected for recent bombings or evacuations.

The major wanted to know what help could be expected from the police. Helldorf replied that it had been agreed that the police would be completely restrained during the first few hours and would not begin to act until after the lightning occupation of all important buildings by the *Wehrmacht* had been completed.

Olbricht's emissary could not understand this. Would he at least have at his disposal Nebe's detectives to undertake the necessary arrests? He was informed that these men, too, could be used only after the occupation of the government buildings. The officer objected. The soldiers were merely supposed to surround the building; Nebe's detectives were to take care of everything else.

With exemplary calm Helldorf corrected these misapprehensions. But correction did not help much at this critical hour. Therefore, I asked whether it would not be possible for the police to go ahead and do what apparently was expected of them. Helldorf said he could not let his men act until the *Wehrmacht* had actually completed the seizure of power. He suggested that the major would do best to follow out the scheme outlined in Olbricht's plans and to surround all the buildings indicated on the map in their proper order. Undoubtedly headquarters would then issue the commands for further action.

I rather think the major left not much wiser than when he had come. As he took his leave with exemplary military precision, I indulged in some private reflections on the scene. In the machinery of a total war that conscripted fifteen-year-old children, such young majors might have their place, but whether they were of the stuff of which uprisings were made, the next few hours would prove.

'A likely prospect' — that was Helldorf's succinct commentary on this little intermezzo.

The clock was already approaching one. Our wait would soon be over; for whether it was the oppressive heat and humidity or our enforced inactivity, time dragged unconscionably.

As I stood looking out of Helldorf's window down upon the wreckage of Alexanderplatz, upon the weary, gaunt people who moved slowly amid the ruins, I realized fully what was at stake now, perhaps this very second. Were death and destruction to continue to rain from the sky? Would there be no end to the blood-letting on both sides in East and West? Or was the explosion of a bomb at this moment ushering in a change in the course of history?

Enough of these thoughts. We had better wait without thinking. It would be time soon enough.

From one o'clock on, Helldorf had kept urging me every five minutes to telephone Nebe. Perhaps he would have heard something. I had already arranged with Nebe, however, that he would call the moment he heard anything at all. If I made an unnecessary call, he would take alarm. That was how he always reacted.

As the hands of the clock moved around toward two, the suspense became unbearable. Was it possible that Nebe, with his excessive caution, would leave his office without telephoning beforehand? At five minutes to two, I made up my mind and called him on the phone. He pretended to be in exceptionally good humor. When I asked whether we could not see him for a few minutes, he said he was unfortunately too busy at the moment. Something strange had happened in East Prussia and he had to give instructions to two detectives who were to leave with Kaltenbrunner in half an hour and fly to the Fuehrer's headquarters in order to conduct the initial investigation.

Had the bomb already exploded? That seemed to be the import of Nebe's message. But the communications center was to have been blown up at the same time. Had some message, nevertheless, leaked through? Why was Kaltenbrunner already going into action? Were our men trying to lure him into a trap in East Prussia? I could make nothing of Nebe's words or of his tone of voice.

Naturally, I could not ask questions. Therefore I urged Nebe to come. I absolutely had to see him at once, I said. At first he would not consent. But when I insisted, 'Where are you?' he asked.

'Right near you,' I replied. 'In the restaurant — you know, the one where we recently met with that mutual acquaintance of ours.'

Nebe said he would come right over.

Helldorf and Bismarck were as mystified as I was. For if the assassination had taken place, *Wehrmacht* headquarters would undoubtedly know about it, whether it had succeeded or failed. And it seemed utterly out of the question that Olbricht would let us wait unnecessarily for even a minute.

At two o'clock Helldorf was scheduled for a meeting with the chief of his detective force. At three o'clock there was a conference at his office with the staff of the Party district. He had to pretend to have some official business today, and if the Berlin Party leaders were 'by chance' all gathered together in his office, so much the better. We should not have to conduct a search in order to arrest them.

Helldorf asked Bismarck and me to wait in an adjoining room while he conferred with the chief of his detectives. As soon as Nebe came, he said, he would interrupt the conference for a moment and come in. But Nebe did not come. It was nearly three when Helldorf returned to the room where we were waiting in an agony of suspense. He was more nervous than annoyed. 'We've had a bad break,' he said. 'My switchboard reported that Nebe was calling. Naturally, I thought he was waiting outside and sent word to him that the chief of the detective force was with me at the moment and that he should join you in my waiting room in the meanwhile. The sergeant delivered this message. Now I've just found out that Nebe called from outside. He was waiting in the Hotel Excelsior.'

Such an idiotic misunderstanding could occur only on a day like this! Because I had mentioned a restaurant, Nebe had thought I meant Helldorf's hotel, which was also near his office. When he did not find us there and telephoned, he had apparently taken the message that the chief of the detective force was there as a concealed warning not to come to police headquarters.

I tried to reach Nebe at his office, but by then he was at lunch in the Prinz Albrechtstrasse.

At four o'clock Helldorf at last rushed excitedly into our room. 'It's starting!' he exclaimed. Olbricht had just telephoned him to hold himself in readiness; there would be an important message within half an hour.

This time, at least, we did not have to wait the full half-hour. Before four-thirty Helldorf reappeared. 'Gentlemen, we're off!' he exclaimed triumphantly. 'Olbricht has just given me an official order to report at the Bendlerstrasse: he says the Fuehrer is dead, a state of siege has been proclaimed, and he has urgent orders to deliver to me in the name of Colonel-General Fromm.'

Helldorf said this with a completely credible imitation of surprise. His energetic manner bore witness to his full appreciation of the significance of this moment. Obviously he was already imagining the scene in which he would persuade his police officers that they must remain inactive for the time being.

During our ride in Helldorf's limousine, I involuntarily imagined that every pedestrian past whom we flitted must be able to sense the vibrations of our nerves. But the people of Berlin slouched along in the sultry heat, weary and dull to all that went on outside their immediate and pathetic concerns. We were sobered and disappointed when even the Bendlerstrasse presented a deserted appearance. Not the slightest change had taken place, even at the entrance to the OKW.

It seemed perfectly natural to me that the guards admitted Helldorf in his uniform of a police general. But I was slightly disquieted by the fact that they did not even check up on me, a civilian.

Only that part of *Wehrmacht* headquarters which had always contained the offices of Fromm and Olbricht was still standing. We rushed up the stairs and were led into Olbricht's waiting room directly, without being announced beforehand; but those few steps from the outer door to the office were enough for us to absorb the atmosphere of this headquarters of the *Putsch.* Not only Olbricht's but Stauffenberg's office was located here. Here — not far from Fromm's rooms — the crucial orders were being written, the secret telephone calls received. We felt at once: now we were 'inside.'

The general was standing quite a distance behind his desk as we entered. He came toward us, and we met somewhere in the middle of the big room. Even as we were crossing the room, however, I saw something that for the moment made me doubt my eyes. Those two officers standing at one side of the desk were — Stauffenberg, and Lieutenant von Haeften who had accompanied and assisted him today. How could they possibly be here? They could not have been shot from East Prussia in a rocket. If they had come by plane, the assassination must have taken place hours ago. How did this fit in with Nebe's hint over the telephone? Were we limping along three and a half irretrievable hours behind the Gestapo? These and a thousand other thoughts were quickly swept aside by the overwhelming perception: Now you are about to shake the hand that struck down the tyrant.

Stauffenberg's appearance was impressive. Tall and slender, he stood breathless and bathed in perspiration. Somehow the massiveness of the man had been reduced; he seemed more spiritualized, lighter. There was a smile of victory on his face; he radiated the triumph of a test successfully completed.

Beck came toward us. We greeted one another with a silent, deeply felt clasp of the hands. What could be said at such a moment?

Olbricht was the first to speak. As if he had learned a text by heart, he informed Helldorf in the tone of a military command that the Fuehrer had been the victim of assassination that afternoon. The *Wehrmacht* had taken over the direction of the government; a state of siege was being proclaimed. The Berlin police were hereby subordinated directly to the *Oberkommando der Wehrmacht* and he, Helldorf, was to carry out at once the necessary measures.

Olbricht's voice quivered with excitement. Nevertheless, I had the feeling that there was nothing original about this. It did not sound like a proclamation of a great change; rather, it seemed like pure declamation, a histrionic accomplishment. The very theatricality of it restored me to reality. Of course — the battle was not yet won, the Gestapo nest not yet cleaned out. . . .

Helldorf played along. He made a brief military bow and started to leave in order to convoke the meeting of his officers, but before he was out of the door, Beck's quiet, firm voice reached out to him. The former chief of the general staff spoke more loudly than usual: 'One moment, Olbricht. In all loyalty we must inform the chief of police that according to certain reports from headquarters Hitler may not be dead. We must now decide clearly how . . .'

Olbricht did not let him finish. Excitedly he exclaimed, 'Keitel is lying! Keitel is lying! . . .'

Stauffenberg laughed triumphantly. Haeften did not join him.

Beck raised his hand in dissent. 'No, no, no . . .'

But Olbricht obviously wanted the discussion to wait until Helldorf was gone. Again he interrupted and repeated, 'Keitel is lying! Keitel is lying!'

Helldorf, Bismarck, and I looked at one another in utter consternation. All at once the fiction was being torn to shreds. Suddenly we were confronted with the brutal reality of the *Putsch*.

Beck would not be put off. 'Olbricht, it doesn't matter whether Keitel is lying. What is important is that Helldorf must know what the other side has asserted about the failure of the assassination, and we must also be prepared for a similar announcement over the radio. What will we say then?'

Olbricht referred to Stauffenberg's conclusive report. Stauffenberg stated in confirmation that the bomb had exploded and that there had been a darting flame such as was produced by the bursting of a fifteen-centimeter shell. No one could have come out of the explosion alive, he said. At the very least, Hitler must have been critically wounded.

In growing agitation Olbricht insisted that he knew what a liar Keitel was.

Beck had no intention of casting any doubt upon Stauffenberg's report. Nor did he assume that Hitler would speak on the radio within the next few hours — although he did mention this as a possibility.

'Olbricht,' he said, 'a clear watchword must be issued. What will Helldorf say, what will you tell the other officers, if Keitel, Himmler, and Goebbels declare that Hitler is alive?'

Beck continued. He made a brief, explicit summary of the situation. He asked the others to keep their solidarity with him. 'For me this man is dead. That is the basis of my further activity. Indisputable proof that Hitler — and not his double — is still alive cannot possibly come from headquarters for hours. By then the action in Berlin must be completed.'

No one contradicted him. Helldorf hurried away to return to his office.

Colonel-General Hoeppner came into the room to fetch his suitcase, which he had left with Olbricht. Two years ago Hoeppner had been deprived of the right to wear a uniform; now he wanted to dress up for his part.

Olbricht declared that it was high time to confront Colonel-General Fromm with an ultimatum. He wanted to do this before Fromm was alarmed by telephone calls of inquiry. The orders for the imposition of a state of siege were being sent out over the teletype in Fromm's name. Stauffenberg went with Olbricht to see Fromm. Then I impolitely suggested to Bismarck, the administrative president of Potsdam, that there must be urgent business awaiting him at the government building in Potsdam. Bismarck left.

Now Beck and I were alone. I asked him bluntly how it was that Stauffenberg was back so soon? Why had they waited so long? Beck responded to my questions with a typical gesture: he shook his head repeatedly and struck his forehead with the palm of his hand. He was obviously none too optimistic. Then he took my arm reassuringly. 'Don't ask too many questions,' he said. 'You can see how excited they all are. We can no longer change anything — we can only hope that all will go well . . .' He still assumed that something had gone wrong at headquarters, so that the word of the assassination had not come through in time and Stauffenberg had brought it when he returned. It is sad that in the few hours of life that were left to him he was not spared the tragic knowledge that they had deliberately deceived him.

Around twelve o'clock Stauffenberg had arrived at headquarters in Rastenburg to participate in the conference with the Fuehrer. This usually took place in an underground shelter, and the explosive force of the bomb had been calculated for such a concrete-walled room. But on this day Hitler — was it the heat or one of his intuitive whims? — had ordered a change of meeting-place just before the session. The conference took place in a wooden barracks.

Stauffenberg delivered his report. The briefcase with its deadly contents stood right under the table over which Hitler was leaning to study the maps. The mechanism of the bomb could be started by a slight pressure of his foot. Toward one o'clock the opportunity seemed favorable. Stauffenberg had himself called out of the room, allegedly to answer a telephone call, and as he left he activated the detonating mechanism. He and Haeften were scarcely a hundred yards away when they observed the dart of flame from the explosion. There was a thunderous noise and a number of persons were hurled through the air and out of the barracks; the thin walls had permitted the air pressure to escape. Unquestionably the explosion had not been as effective as it would have been inside the concrete walls of the shelter.

The two men were satisfied, however, by what they had seen and sprang into their waiting car. In the panic they succeeded in making their way unhindered to the airport; but while their plane was hurtling toward Berlin, something totally unexpected took place at *Wehrmacht* headquarters in the Bendlerstrasse. A few minutes after the explosion General Fellgiebel telephoned Olbricht, as agreed, and gave the cue. But the blowing-up of the communications center, which had also been planned, did not take place.

Colonel-General Fromm was receiving a military report when, shortly after two o'clock, Olbricht stormed into his office. He said he had something of such vital importance to communicate that he must speak to Fromm privately. Fromm interrupted the report. Olbricht curtly informed his chief that Hitler had just been the victim of an assassination. How did he know? He had been informed by General Fellgiebel, who had just telephoned personally from headquarters. Olbricht proposed that under the circumstances Fromm should issue to the various deputy headquarters in charge of the reserve forces the code word for internal disorders: 'Walkuere.' Thereby the state power would temporarily pass into the hands of the *Wehrmacht*.

Fromm was astonished, but not quite convinced. Under the circumstances he did the natural thing: he telephoned the Fuehrer's headquarters to check up. *And the Rastenburg communications center had not been blown up.* Olbricht, feeling perfectly sure of himself, listened in on another telephone. To his shocked surprise, the Fuehrer's headquarters responded to the call. Worse yet, Keitel answered the telephone. And still worse, Keitel denied that anything had happened to Hitler. The text of the telephone call has been preserved. It ran as follows:

> *Fromm:* 'What in the world is going on at headquarters? Here in Berlin the wildest rumors are afloat.'
>
> *Keitel:* 'What is supposed to be going on? Everything is all right.'
>
> *Fromm:* 'I have just received a report that the Fuehrer was killed by assassination.'
>
> *Keitel:* 'Nonsense. There was an attempted assassination, but fortunately it failed. The Fuehrer is alive and received only superficial injuries. Where, by the way, is the chief of your staff, Colonel Stauffenberg?'
>
> *Fromm:* 'Stauffenberg is not here yet.'

Not one word of indignation about the assassination. Not even an obvious inquiry as to what had taken place and whether anyone else was killed. Not a word about what either intended to do. Fromm wanted only to listen, Keitel to cover up. As soon as Fromm hung up, two generals sighed with relief. Thank God, it had turned out well once more. Well? Certainly — they need not make a decision.

Fromm informed Olbricht that in view of this situation there seemed to be no occasion to issue the code word for internal disorder. Obviously confused by the telephone call, Olbricht returned to his office to confer with the Stauffenberg group. Colonel-General Hoeppner was also present. But good counsel was scarce — at least here.

At the time if they had at least called Beck or sent for Helldorf, Nebe, and myself, we undoubtedly would have declared unanimously

that the only course was to go ahead with the *Putsch*. But not even
Beck was informed, let alone us 'civilians.' The leaderless and therefore mindless Stauffenberg group agreed with Olbricht's decision that
in the face of so complicated a situation it would be best to wait
until Stauffenberg's return, and meanwhile to do nothing at all.

We can imagine Stauffenberg's horrified dismay when he arrived
at the Rangsdorf airport around four o'clock and heard that nothing
had happened yet. In an understandable outburst of indignation, he
ordered the *Putsch* to begin at once.

But as I have said, neither Beck nor I yet knew anything about all
this. For this reason we were ignorant of the background of the scene
that now took place with Fromm.

Olbricht and Stauffenberg informed the commander-in-chief of the
home army that Hitler was indeed dead and that Stauffenberg could
personally confirm his decease. The text of this scene is taken from
the war crime indictment against Fromm:

> *Fromm:* 'It is impossible; Keitel assured me that it was not so.'
>
> *Stauffenberg:* 'Field Marshal Keitel is lying as usual. I myself saw
> Hitler being carried out dead.'
>
> *Olbricht:* 'In view of this situation we have issued the code word
> for internal unrest to the commanding generals.'
>
> *Fromm* (springing to his feet and pounding his fist on the desk):
> 'That is sheer disobedience! What do you mean by "we"? Who gave
> the order?'
>
> *Olbricht:* 'My chief of staff, Colonel Merz von Quirnheim.'
>
> *Fromm:* 'Send Colonel Merz in here at once.'
>
> *Merz von Quirnheim enters.* He admits to having issued the code
> word to the commanding generals without Fromm's permission.
>
> *Fromm:* 'You are under arrest. We shall see about further action.'
>
> *Colonel Stauffenberg* stands and declares icily: 'General Fromm, I
> myself detonated the bomb during the conference in Hitler's head-
> quarters. There was an explosion like that of a fifteen-centimeter
> shell. No one who was in that room can still be living.'
>
> *Fromm:* 'Count Stauffenberg, the assassination failed. You must
> shoot yourself at once.'
>
> *Stauffenberg:* 'I shall do nothing of the kind.'

Olbricht: 'General Fromm, the moment for action has come. If we do not strike now, our country will be ruined forever.'

Fromm: 'Does that mean that you, too, are taking part in this *coup d'état,* Olbricht?'

Olbricht: 'Yes, sir. But I am not a member of the group that will take over the government of Germany.'

Fromm: 'I hereby declare all three of you arrested.'

Olbricht: 'You cannot arrest us. You do not realize who holds the power. We arrest you!'

Somehow, the whole truth about the *Putsch* was expressed by this interview. 'What do you mean by "We"?' The question was quite justified. And the answer was not: 'I.' Had Merz, on Stauffenberg's orders, presented Olbricht with a *fait accompli,* just as they were now trying to do with Fromm?

In any case, there ensued an angry scuffle — though it did not come to much more than indignant words and a violent waving of hands. All four were equally relieved when Fromm, amid empty protests, permitted them to intern him in the adjoining room.

Olbricht and Stauffenberg returned to the office in which Beck and I were pacing back and forth. Both were exhausted as they informed us of the 'skirmish' they had just been through. Stauffenberg had no time to go into lengthy reflections on Fromm's behavior. Activity halted whenever he did not stand behind it with his organizational talent and impulsiveness. He left us quickly, and looked in only now and then to say a word or to search for something in Olbricht's safe.

Beck and I remained alone — the only civilians among all these uniformed men. It was rather depressing to sit and feel wholly deserted, while all around us history was being made. As if we were schoolboys who had misbehaved, we were being punished by having to sit passively for three hours. We talked to one another in whispers, as if the Gestapo were still listening.

Beck was prompted to call out: 'By the way, Olbricht, what measures have been taken to assure our safety in this building?'

Without rising from his desk, Olbricht replied that the doors had been shut and the guards had received orders to admit no one. Unfortunately, there were no more than the usual guards available. As Beck knew, the troops were just starting out.

Beck asked in his quiet, firm fashion: 'Olbricht, what instructions have the guards been given? Whose orders do they obey?'

'Mine.'

'What will the guards do if the Gestapo should suddenly appear?'

Olbricht shrugged. Nevertheless, he left his desk and approached us.

'Olbricht, will the guards shoot?'

'Dinna ken . . .'

Olbricht was the last person to be impolite, nor was he inclined to bluff his way out of rotten situations. For that reason it was easy to sense the insincerity and uncertainty in his reply.

For a moment Beck was silent. Then he repeated, quietly, calmly, but with great emphasis: 'Olbricht, will those soldiers stand to the death for you?'

'Dinna ken . . .'

With amazing equanimity, but with the same friendly urgency, Beck said: 'Olbricht, when Fritsch was here it would have been different.'

Olbricht flushed and shrugged in embarrassment.

'Olbricht, the soldiers would have stood to the death for Fritsch . . .'

I asked Beck whether he ought not to do something. He tried to quench my impatience. 'Go easy, easy, easy.' A general must keep his nerve, he said again. Now it was up to Hoeppner, Olbricht, Stauffenberg, and Witzleben to do their part. He did not intend to confuse them by unnecessary interference.

I admired his self-discipline. His behavior was perfectly reasonable — but emotionally I objected violently to it. I told him about our experience with the young major who had brought us the outmoded maps at noon.

'A number of things seem to be going wrong today,' he remarked dryly.

Olbricht returned, accompanied by Hoeppner. Colonel-General Fromm had asked him for permission to go home. He offered his word of honor to remain quiet and undertake no action against us. Olbricht and Hoeppner recommended that he be allowed to go. Beck was obviously impressed by their recommendation. He disliked Fromm intensely, but if Hoeppner and Olbricht were willing to take the responsibility . . .

I intervened hotly. The best Fromm deserved was to be shot, I said angrily.

Just at this moment Stauffenberg joined us. Olbricht pointed out that Fromm had always been fair. If he gave his word of honor he would keep it.

'What does a word of honor mean?' I retorted. I reminded them that Stauffenberg himself had broken his word of honor; a few months ago he had given Fromm his word of honor not to take any action against Hitler. Consequently, Fromm in his turn would not feel obliged to keep his. In fact, having not decided for us, he must necessarily act against us.

I had not had the slightest intention of insulting Stauffenberg, but he took my parallel as a personal affront. He started to explain — as if I needed explanation — what patriotic motives had led him to feel that his word of honor was no longer binding.

Beck ordered that Fromm be kept in custody.

Since we were all together and all slightly irritated, I thought this was as good an opportunity as any to say all at once what had to be said. Therefore, I suggested that we ought to discuss what police measures were to be taken. At least an hour had passed since Helldorf had left us. It was time he and Nebe received further instructions. In my excitement I may have asked too many questions or too precise ones. I wanted to know what buildings were being surrounded, what was being done about the radio, above all whether, among the immediate tasks allocated to the *Grossdeutschland* battalion of guards, the storming of the Gestapo building and the shooting of Goebbels had been included.

I did not notice how angry Stauffenberg was becoming until Beck plucked soothingly at the colonel's arm and with great friendliness asked the three of us to leave him alone with Stauffenberg for a moment; he wished to confer privately with the colonel.

Olbricht and Hoeppner went off into Fromm's rooms, which were one flight up. I stayed in Olbricht's waiting room. My wait was interrupted by the exchange of a few words with Count Fritz Schulenberg and Count Yorck. Then I saw Stauffenberg hurry past the door. I went in to see Beck again. But I had no opportunity to talk to him, for as I entered, Olbricht rushed into the room, somewhat out of breath because he had been called down from upstairs, and somewhat at a loss because Keitel wanted to talk with him on the telephone. Olbricht wanted Beck to advise him whether or not to accept the call.

Beck thought there was little point to answering Keitel; I vehemently insisted there was. Perhaps it was a chance to worm out of him some information about Hitler. Such a conversation could do no harm, at any rate. Olbricht decided to take the call. There was a business of switching and cross-switching before the connection was transferred from Fromm's waiting room to Olbricht's office. By the time this was over, Keitel had abandoned the attempt and hung up.

Olbricht had to rush away again. Hoeppner had just run into a furious dispute with the acting military district commander of Berlin who was unwilling to co-operate. This prompted Beck to ask me where Witzleben was. So far as I knew, he was on the way to Zossen. He had received the code word while on an estate near Luebben and was now going to Zossen to take command there. Beck was dissatisfied with this. As commander of all three divisions of the *Wehrmacht* (army, navy, and air force), Witzleben ought to be in Berlin, he said.

By this time Olbricht was back, seething with indignation. Beck must come up to Hoeppner's office at once, he said. General Kortzfleisch was insisting that Hitler was not dead, and for this reason he refused to declare a state of siege in Berlin. He had come to talk to Fromm. Instead, Hoeppner had received him, but Kortzfleisch still wanted to see Fromm. Perhaps it would help if Beck talked to him. In any event, Olbricht had a stand-in ready to take the place of Kortzfleisch as commander in Berlin.

'You see,' Beck remarked to me as he was going out. 'I was right. Witzleben ought to be here.'

I sat down on the sofa in the waiting room again. From minute to minute the bustle appeared to increase. Adjutants came and went. The telephones rang continually. Suddenly thumping footsteps sounded in the corridor. The door flew open and an SS *Standarten-fuehrer* (equivalent to a colonel) of the typical butcher type appeared in the doorway. A more vivid, more typical SS hangman could scarcely be imagined. This creature clicked his heels with a report like a pistol-shot, raised his hand in the 'German' greeting and growled loudly, 'Heil Hitler.'

For a second the thought flashed through my mind: Have they come already? But the hangman merely asked politely whether he might speak to Colonel von Stauffenberg. 'On orders of the chief of the Reich security office,' he added self-importantly.

The two men greeted each other curtly and formally. Then Stauffenberg invited his strange guest into his office. I had heard the man boom out his name. He was *Standartenfuehrer* Pfiffrather, one of the worst of the Gestapo crew who was now in charge of the counter-espionage organization, the *Abwehr,* which had been placed under the Gestapo after it was withdrawn from Canaris. I was amazed at the boldness of the man at venturing into the lions' den. Evidently the Reich security office — that is, the Gestapo — was still groping in the dark. Otherwise they would not have sent one of their prominent men to the Bendlerstrasse.

After a while Stauffenberg returned. Pfiffrather had wanted to question him about his obvious hurry to fly back from the Fuehrer's headquarters. Stauffenberg's reply had been to lock the fellow up.

For a moment I was speechless. Then I said: 'Stauffenberg, why didn't you shoot that murderer at once?'

His turn would come, the colonel remarked, and started off.

'Stauffenberg, how can you leave this man here to watch everything that's going on? Just imagine if he should make a break later on.'

Now it was Stauffenberg's turn to be speechless. By the angry glow in his eyes I realized how many doubts he must have read into this advice of mine that such burdensome witnesses ought to be summarily put out of the way.

'Stauffenberg, we cannot wait passively for these full three hours. We must do something. If you don't want to shoot that fellow, let us form an officers' troop and drive over to the Prinz Albrechtstrasse. We must eliminate Mueller and Goebbels.

Stauffenberg would listen to proposals for action. The troops hadn't arrived yet, as I well knew, he said. Nevertheless, he had himself thought of an officers' troop. He would talk to Colonel Jaeger. Jaeger was a well-known daredevil whom we had long considered the natural leader for such shock-troop actions. How fortunate that he was here!

Beck returned. I had never yet seen him so angry. He described the scene that had taken place in Hoeppner's room. General Kortz-fleisch had refused to co-operate on the grounds of his oath to Hitler. Beck repeated his indignant reply to me: 'How dare you talk of oaths? Hitler has broken his oath to the constitution and his vows to the people a hundred times over. How dare you refer to your oath of loyalty to such a perjurer!'

Argument, however, had accomplished nothing. Kortzfleisch was now providing company for Fromm and Pfiffrather.

I was called to the telephone. Who knew I was here?

Helldorf's adjutant was waiting at the street entrance. He asked me to come down; the guards would not let him in. I hurried downstairs. Helldorf wanted to know what was going on. I told the adjutant that the action was beginning and that Helldorf would have to be patient, since unfortunately I knew no more than he. The adjutant was none too satisfied with the meager information. His chief was beginning to grow impatient, he said. Couldn't I return with him to Helldorf; undoubtedly Helldorf would want to discuss things with me.

This suggestion seemed sensible. I had nothing to do upstairs in any event and could easily be back within three quarters of an hour. I left word with Olbricht's adjutant and departed.

It was around six o'clock when I entered Helldorf's office. Nebe was with him. Both men were drinking coffee.

It was not easy for me to perform the mental shift from the turbulence of the Bendlerstrasse to this compound of peaceful idyll and challenging skepticism. Instead of asking any questions, Helldorf contented himself with a long-drawn-out, 'What now?' Nebe gave me a look that seemed to say: 'My poor friend, I myself don't think you're crazy, of course, but you can't deny that you've just come from an insane asylum.'

I, too, of course, was not satisfied with all that was taking place at *Wehrmacht* headquarters. But for the present the tank troops were just moving up; they could not arrive before half-past seven. I pointed out — with perhaps a touch of hypocritical equanimity — that we were still passing through that period of three 'stagnant' hours in which, as we had always known, nothing special could happen.

Helldorf refused to concede this. That might be true of *Wehrmacht* headquarters, but it was not true for him at police headquarters. In the two hours that had passed since Olbricht's instructions to him, nothing, absolutely nothing, had happened. According to plan, he had frozen his entire police apparatus; but not a single representative of the military had come to see him. Helldorf pointed out that General von Haase should long since have sent for him or come to see him or sent a liaison officer to him.

Moreover, where was Major Roemer's battalion of guards, who did not need three hours to reach Berlin and who were supposed to take care of the most essential immediate tasks? I could not make any rebuttal to this challenge, but I tried to explain it as a result of the confusion in the military district command.

I asked Nebe about conditions in the Prinz Albrechtstrasse. So far as he knew, up to half-past five the Gestapo knew nothing at all about the beginning of the *Putsch* and was not even certain that Stauffenberg had set off the bomb. A few minutes ago Helldorf had spoken with Group Leader Mueller. Mueller had brashly told him that there seemed to be a military *Putsch* in progress; there were troops around the Wilhelmstrasse and the Prinz Albrechtstrasse, but the Fuehrer was on the alert and a statement would be issued over the radio. SS reinforcements were on the march from outside Berlin.

As I re-entered the *Wehrmacht* building on the Bendlerstrasse, I encountered Olbricht on the stairs. 'Beck wants to see you,' he said to me, 'but there can't be such a hurry about it. Come to my office for a minute. I want to discuss something with you privately.'

He informed me that while I was gone the radio statement about the failure of the assassination had been issued. No details were given and not a word had been said about the probable assassin. But, the general said, he no longer had the slightest doubt that Hitler was still alive. Colonel von Hayessen had also telephoned to confirm the fact. Hitler was having tea with Mussolini in the Fuehrer's pavilion; the Italian dictator had chosen just this day to pay an unexpected visit.

I waited eagerly to hear what Olbricht wanted to discuss with me. He had certainly not invited me in simply to give me information. Finally it came out. 'My dear Gisevius — just for the sake of discussion I wanted to hear your opinion . . .' Pause. 'But of course . . .' Another pause. 'Of course — we can't call it off and deny it at this point, can we?'

Somehow, the manner in which Olbricht asked me this question drained all anger out of me. 'No,' I said, 'you're quite right; we can't really call it off or deny it any more.' Hadn't Beck wanted to see me? I excused myself.

I went upstairs to Fromm's spacious office. Beck caught sight of me and rushed toward me. According to a number of telephone calls, Hitler was about to speak on the radio. Was I prepared to make a radio statement for our side? I was amazed. Up to this moment the program had called for General Lindemann to read the first statement. If it seemed inadvisable to have a general initiate matters, then certainly the proper candidates were Goerdeler or Beck. But Beck would not hear of it. The situation had been fundamentally changed, he said, by the report that Hitler was still alive. Goerdeler was not here. He himself must stay around.

An evil premonition told me that perhaps this radio address would be all that the public would ever hear about the events of this day. I should be foolish to miss this opportunity to leave at least one visiting card.

I asked where the original proclamation was. General Lindemann, it seemed, had the only copy in his keeping — and Lindemann was nowhere to be found. He had been there earlier in the afternoon, but had not been seen for hours. I made my private conjectures about this mysterious disappearance and sat down in a corner of Fromm's office to write out a few sentences. Actually, I did not want to make any sort of outline. If I did eventually speak, it would be too good an opportunity to extemporize. Such a speech had to evolve out of the inspiration of the moment; it ought to sound like a rallying-cry, not like a newspaper editorial.

Fromm's office was separated only by a sliding door from that of his chief of staff, Stauffenberg. There was a constant bustling back and forth between these two rooms. One moment the telephone on Fromm's desk would ring, then one of the two telephones on Stauffenberg's desk. Each time Stauffenberg rushed back and forth the twenty steps from the one telephone to the other. Everyone was asking for him — understandably. For the generals in the provinces scarcely knew Hoeppner, and the switchboard operators had been instructed to say that Fromm was not in.

Everyone listened to every conversation. Sooner or later there would have to be important messages from the provinces, and we could really do with a little good news. At our end of the wire Stauffenberg incessantly repeated the same refrain: 'Keitel is lying ... Don't believe Keitel ... Hitler is dead ... Yes, he is definitely dead ... Yes, here the action is in full swing ... '

The questions he was being asked could easily be imagined. What was interesting was the variety of tones in which Stauffenberg responded. One moment his voice was firm and commanding, the next friendly and persuasive, the next imploring. 'You must hold firm ... See to it that your chief doesn't weaken ... Hayessen, I'm depending on you ... Please, don't disappoint me ... We must hold firm ... We must hold firm ... ' Stauffenberg was the only one in control of the situation, the only one who knew what he wanted.

Beck, too, was impressed by Stauffenberg's conduct. In reality, however, our thoughts were on something else entirely: on the feeling we had, baseless, perhaps, but persistent, that the other officers were not holding firm. Hoeppner in particular depressed us by his obvious misery. Beck sat beside me watching the agitated bustle and repeating what he had said so often during these past few days. 'A good general must be able to wait.' All that he could do was to inquire about the progress of the *Putsch* in Zossen. Where was Witzleben? I stopped asking this question, because the mere mention of it so upset Beck. The latest news was that Witzleben had left Zossen and was on his way to Berlin.

General Wagner, whom Beck had telephoned twice and who was responsible for the co-operation of the headquarters at Zossen, would no longer answer the telephone.

Now and then Stauffenberg stopped for a moment in our corner. According to the count, everything was proceeding splendidly. The tanks were on the way. They would reach the center of the city by half-past seven at the latest. Then the main action could begin, blow upon blow. This sounded reassuring because the hands of the clock were rapidly approaching half-past seven. As yet we had received no disturbing reports about Gestapo or *Waffen-SS* activity. We seemed to have the head start. Nevertheless, I could not shake off the tormenting feeling that we ought not wait so long.

When I had a chance to talk privately to Stauffenberg for a moment, I said urgently: 'Stauffenberg, too little is happening. Goebbels and Mueller are still alive.' I offered to accompany any group of officers that he would form into a shock troop. After the failure of the blow against Hitler, it would be a good idea to choose some other victims; with Goebbels and Mueller dead, the other side would be temporarily paralyzed and our side would be encouraged.

At first Stauffenberg would not agree. As soon as the tanks arrived, the program of arrests would begin. The most important buildings would be surrounded by a cordon; no one would escape. I pointed out that the question was not one of escape, but of psychological benefit. Apparently I convinced him by stressing this psychological aspect of the matter. He ran off to look for Colonel Jaeger; Jaeger would form a shock troop of officers, he said.

Had he not been seeking Jaeger an hour ago?

Beck came over to me to ask whether my radio address was ready. He might have seen that I had been writing nothing; most of the time I had been talking either with him or others; but how could I convince my formal-minded friend who was so fond of the written word that in certain situations it was necessary to depend on extemporaneous speech? He, when he saw that he could not persuade me to write out a draft of my speech, insisted that at least we must discuss it point by point. In clear, cogent sentences, he explained what he thought should be said. The basic idea was of the simplest: that it did not matter at all whether Hitler was dead or still living. A 'leader' whose immediate entourage included those who opposed him to the extent of attempting assassination must be considered morally dead. From this starting-point all the rest fell naturally into line, no matter what radio statements emanated from Goebbels.

A sensation. Paris was telephoning. Up to now none of the commands from the front or from the occupied territories had reported. Beck hurried to the telephone to talk personally with Stuelpnagel. It was a refreshing conversation; we who were listening felt for once that the general on the other end was not trying to dodge the issue. Stuelpnagel reported that he had taken all the appropriate measures. The responsible SS leaders were under arrest. The troops were responding to his orders without demur. What about Kluge? Stuelpnagel advised Beck to talk with him directly.

Stuelpnagel succeeded in switching the call to the Western headquarters, which was situated near Paris. We all stood tensely around Beck as he spoke to Kluge in comradely, persuasive, firm tones. He described the measures that had been taken in Berlin, called upon the marshal not to vacillate at a time that was, psychologically, so critical.

I felt that Beck was not pressing him toward an unequivocal answer. I therefore whispered to him: 'Make it clear to Kluge that he can no longer back down.' He nodded agreement and handed the second receiver to me.

'Kluge, I now ask you clearly: Do you approve of this action of ours and do you place yourself under my orders?'

Kluge stammered a few phrases that were apparently the outburst of a tormented soul. It was impossible to make anything of them; yes was no and no was yes.

'Kluge, in order to remove the slightest doubt, I want to remind you of our last conversations and agreements. I ask again: Do you place yourself unconditionally under my orders?'

Kluge remembered all the conversations, but the failure of the assassination had created an unexpected situation, he said. He would have to confer with his staff. He would call back in half an hour.

'Kluge!' Beck exclaimed to me as he hung up. 'There you have him!'

Colonel-General Fromm contrived to divert us from our gloomy thoughts. He sent one of the officers who was guarding him to inform us that he was hungry; wouldn't we permit him to go home? His offer of his word of honor still stood. In the present state of affairs, everyone agreed that Fromm must not be released, but one after the other, Beck, Olbricht, Hoeppner, and Stauffenberg, asserted that they wanted to treat him in a perfectly honorable fashion. They would have a bottle of wine and sandwiches sent in to him from the officers' canteen.

The guards telephoned up to us that Witzleben had arrived at last. He entered, holding his cap in one hand and waving his marshal's staff with the other in a casual reply to the greetings of the other officers, who were standing at attention. His face was beet-red. I did not need to hear his first words to know what he was thinking.

Stauffenberg went up to the marshal and saluted. 'A fine mess, this,' Witzleben growled at him.

Then he caught sight of Beck, toward whom the field marshal always — and this was a credit to him — observed our rebel scale of ranks. 'Reporting for duty, sir,' he said.

But even this was spoken in a surly tone. I was the only one he bothered to shake hands with. Then he took Beck's arm, crossed the wide room to Fromm's desk, and an excited debate began. After a few minutes Beck signaled to Stauffenberg, who was standing with our group like a drenched poodle, to join them. A few minutes later Stauffenberg fetched Ulrich Schwerin, who of late had been the intermediary between Witzleben and the Stauffenberg group.

Although we were standing too far away to make out a word, it was evident that Witzleben was sharply reproaching the two officers. Beck seemed to be trying to intervene in their favor. Witzleben would not listen and continued to address Stauffenberg excitedly.

I sat down again in my favorite corner, and here I was soon joined by Doctor Sack, who stood more or less in the middle between us, the civilians, and the military men. Sack was annoyed because he had been called openly on the telephone and asked to come, although the *Putsch* had not yet succeeded and there was nothing for him to do. He would soon pay on the gallows for the haste with which he had been invited to stand around in the Bendlerstrasse.

The conference at Fromm's desk lasted at least half an hour. Once, as I looked in through the sliding doors, I heard Olbricht and Hoeppner quarreling loudly. Hoeppner's voice sounded tearful, Olbricht's angry. Our eyes met — and Olbricht called me in. Certain snatches of conversation remain in our memories for the rest of our lives.

'Ask Gisevius.'

'No, no, if it's such a risk, one oughtn't to take the gamble.'

'There's a risk in every *coup d'état*.'

'Yes, but one must have a ninety per cent probability that the *Putsch* will turn out well.'

'Nonsense, you'll never have a ninety per cent probability. Fifty-one per cent is enough.'

'No, fifty-one per cent is too little. Let's say eighty at least.'

'Eighty? How do you expect to get eighty?'

'There you are, not even eighty! Then you can't go ahead and try a *Putsch* . . .'

Olbricht asked me my opinion. I looked at them in utter amazement.

Colonel Merz von Quirnheim came in to say that Helldorf had tele-phoned; he wanted 'the gentleman who was with him before' to come at once. He had something very important to communicate. Merz said that Helldorf had sounded extremely excited. I could well imagine what he wanted and I had not the slightest desire to listen to his complaints and reproaches. The outcome of the conference be-tween Beck and Witzleben was far more important. Neither Olbricht nor Hoeppner would hear of my declining to answer. Both urged me that it was tremendously important to find out what Helldorf's news was. Certainly nothing would happen in the next half-hour.

I thought, however, that the great decision was closer than that, and since I was sure that Helldorf merely wanted to complain, I in-sisted that I could not leave now. Schulenberg came over and also began urging that I go. This made me all the more obstinate. I opened the sliding door wide enough for Beck to see me signal, so that he could indicate whether or not he wanted me to come in, but he waved me away. Evidently he wanted no additional witnesses to the heated debate.

Olbricht had spied this bit of byplay. Now he insisted that I go.

By chance, Count Stauffenberg left the group in the other room for a moment. He came to get something from his desk. As he was on the way back, however, Olbricht blocked his way and told him that Helldorf had an important message for me, but that I insisted on staying to be ready to work with Beck and Witzleben.

Stauffenberg confirmed Olbricht's assertion that I would not be needed in the next half-hour. I objected that I had had trouble getting into the building a while ago and that by now I certainly could not pass through the street blockades.

Stauffenberg ran back to his desk and handed me a pass. It was printed on heavy brown linen paper and signed by Stauffenberg per-sonally. As I took this piece of paper from him, I reflected that at least something had been well prepared. This document really looked impressive.

There seemed to be no choice for me; they even provided me with an ordnance officer who was to rustle up an automobile — no small undertaking — and see me through the street cordons.

Downstairs I had to wait a full quarter of an hour. The lieutenant ran from place to place, trying to find a car. Finally he drove up with a small private car. I was just about to get in when I saw Olbricht's face at the window above. 'Are you still there?' he called out to me, and asked me to come up for a moment; he had something important to tell me. I raced up the stairs two at a time. Olbricht saved me the trouble of climbing the whole way. With radiant face he called down to me: 'I just wanted to tell you that we've just had good news. The guards regiment is marching up to protect us. Tell Helldorf about it, please.' Olbricht's joy was unmistakable. We waved to one another again as I started down the stairs.

As we drove up to the first intersection, a troop of heavily armed soldiers came marching toward us. I could not refrain from waving gladly to them. How much more hopeful the atmosphere in the Bendlerstrasse would soon be, now that these men had arrived!

At the Brandenburg Gate we encountered our first disillusionment. A heavily armed double guard stopped us. These two warriors, with their self-important expressions, their steel helmets, submachine guns, and harsh voices, were almost sufficient to remind us that a *Putsch* was in progress. I took out my handsome pass. But, incredibly enough, we were not permitted to drive through the Brandenburg Gate. We had to take the roundabout route by way of the Canal.

As I glanced into side streets on the way, two things struck me. Down one street I saw several blocks of buildings surrounded. Every twenty yards I glimpsed one of those awe-inspiring warriors holding a submachine gun. But a few streets farther on, I saw another such troop of soldiers forming ranks and marching away from the scene.

What was going on?

At Alexanderplatz I did not drive directly up to Helldorf's entrance. I left the car some distance away and slipped into the building from the rear. My precautions were not justified. Not a single Gestapo man was watching the police headquarters. Helldorf's 'freeze' order was being carried out to perfection. I was greatly disappointed, however, not to find the count in his office. He was in his air-raid shelter office on Karlsplatz.

A complicated business of telephoning ensued, because I did not want to compromise Helldorf by giving my name, and the men in the office were unwilling to connect me even with his adjutant unless I said who I was. At last I persuaded them to let me talk to the adjutant, who agreed to come for me.

I returned to the lieutenant, who was waiting below. The matter of those troops who seemed to be withdrawing was worrying me. I might be mistaken, but it would be better to inform Olbricht of my observations. And while beating about in unexplored territory, it is well not to carry any incriminating documents. Therefore, I divested myself of my note pad, which contained the notes for my undelivered radio address. I instructed the lieutenant to keep it for me until I returned. He then drove off and I waited in the deserted Alexanderplatz.

At last Helldorf's adjutant came and drove me quickly to the shelter. There was a misunderstanding and I had to wait for a while; the officers on duty informed me that the count was having an important conference with an SS general. I fidgeted for ten minutes until the SS general turned out to be Nebe.

I was still unsuspecting when I entered the room. The glances of both men told me at once: it was all over. Helldorf manifested a calm about it all that was possible only for a person who had been a passionate gambler all his life. For with all respect for the fact that he ended his life on the gallows, I cannot falsify the drama of that moment by attributing to him the serenity of a devoted idealist who feels that his life and death are dependent upon the will of a higher power.

Nebe's eyes were mournful, profoundly melancholy, I scarcely want to say reproachful. There was, of course, an element of sorrowful reproach in his eyes; but at the same time there was a touch of compensatory satisfaction that he had been right after all.

Helldorf was sensible enough not to torment me with suspense. His account was derived from the fragmentary information that he and Nebe had been able to piece together. It seemed that the *Grossdeutschland* guards battalion had been alarmed and the commander,

Major Roemer, had been ordered to arrest Goebbels. Goebbels promptly telephoned the Fuehrer's headquarters and Hitler personally talked to Roemer and conferred upon him full powers to crush the *Putsch*. At this very moment Roemer was marching to the Bendlerstrasse to arrest the 'putschists.' Himmler was reported to be en route to Berlin by plane.

When Helldorf told me this, he assumed treachery on the part of Major Roemer, against whom he had warned us so many times. We did not know that the major had at first been ready to carry out the order given to him simply because it was an order.

But an insane chance would have it that, the night before, a Nazi morale officer had delivered a lecture to the guards regiment and on this very afternoon had been invited by Roemer to have a drink with him before leaving. When word of the imposition of the state of siege arrived, this Nazi propagandist happened to be with Roemer. The lieutenant, in civilian life an official of the propaganda ministry, pleaded with Roemer to wait a few minutes until he checked up with Goebbels personally to make sure that Hitler was dead. Why act prematurely, he demanded, when there was a direct telephone wire to the Fuehrer's headquarters?

If . . . if only the order had not come over the teletype; if only one of the many generals standing idle around the Bendlerstrasse had appeared in person to give the order to this thirty-year-old major who at the moment was the most important troop commander in Germany . . .

As it was, Roemer yielded. He agreed to a half-hour delay. Goebbels summoned the major at once. Roemer hesitated; Goebbels was not his superior officer. But finally skepticism won out. Where was the Fuehrer?

For once Goebbels refrained from loquacity. He handed the telephone to Roemer — and on the other end of the wire was Hitler himself.

'Do you recognize me, Major Roemer? Do you recognize my voice?'

'*Jawohl, mein Fuehrer.*'

Thousands of majors had never exchanged a word with Hitler. But as chance would have it, Roemer, one of the youngest officers, had been in Hitler's presence only a few weeks before to receive the oak leaf cluster to the chevalier cross from the Fuehrer's hand.

So Hitler was alive! And now this Fuehrer whom Providence had again spared was conferring upon the little major full power over field marshals and generals, over the commanders of the troops that were moving up on Berlin. The Fuehrer was making him responsible for the protection of the capital, for the safety of the Third Reich . . .

Intuitively, Hitler contrived to enlist the young soldier so cleverly that there was no chance of his defection. Hitler imposed so many responsibilities upon him, so many independent actions, that he had no time for superfluous thought. He was ordered to march to the Bendlerstrasse, to make the approaching companies turn back, to see to the safety of the ministries . . .

Three quarters of a year later the young major, who had since been promoted to a colonel, committed suicide.

It was fortunate that Helldorf had only prosaic facts to impart to me, not this hair-raising melodrama. His monotonous report, touched with incisive sarcasm and grim humor, was far more affecting than the most imaginatively tragic sketch would have been. His description of events so confused me that I asked one of the most foolish questions that ever passed my lips during my years in the Third Reich: whether we could not intercept Himmler. Would it not be possible to meet him with Helldorf's or Nebe's police officers and shoot down the arch-hangman?

Quite justifiably Helldorf and Nebe repudiated this proposal. When the field marshals had muffed and the generals no longer had any power to command their majors, no policeman could avail.

Nebe dragged me back into reality again. All this time he had allegedly been conducting reconnaissance in Berlin or in police headquarters. Now he must return to his inferno to inform the Cerberus that all the hell-hounds were still properly chained.

I began to feel uncomfortable. At this moment everyone had his place of refuge: Helldorf would go to his police generals; Nebe would fall into the arms of the Gestapists. But where was I to go? A curious sense of pride took possession of me. I declared that I would now return to the Bendlerstrasse.

Helldorf dryly remarked that I was out of my mind.

'But what are we to do now? You? Nebe? Myself?'

Helldorf's reply was elementary and disarming. I can still see him standing before me, his expression certainly not that of an idealist and his language not at all appropriate to the gravity of the moment. And yet his tone and his jauntiness were just right; they could no longer save the situation, but they might still save a life. 'Now only sheer impudence can help us,' he said. 'We will deny everything. We'll pretend that nothing happened.'

Nebe seconded Helldorf. He himself felt reassured that he had played his game with the Gestapists so adeptly that up to the present moment they had no suspicion of him.

I objected. 'Helldorf, you may be able to invent a thousand alibis; Nebe, you can tell the most incredible fairy tales; but how is Government Councilor Gisevius — who at the moment is supposed to be performing his duties as vice-consul at the consulate-general in Switzerland — to explain his presence in the Bendlerstrasse or police headquarters today?'

Helldorf looked at me as if he thought I had lost the last remnants of my reason. 'It's simple enough,' he said calmly. 'Naturally you have to disappear.'

Nebe rushed off; Group Leader Mueller must not be permitted to grow suspicious. Helldorf also had to leave in a hurry. I literally plucked at his coat-tails. I needed a car, I said. I could have one, Helldorf said; but I ought not to use it too long.

'No, I'll go no farther than the Bendlerstrasse.'

Helldorf stopped short. He turned around to face me once more. 'You're out of your mind.'

'Helldorf, I am addressing you now as a count . . .'

Helldorf looked at me with an expression almost pitying. Or was he surprised that for the first time I was speaking to him in such a personal vein?

'Helldorf, I ask you as a man of honor: Wouldn't you be thoroughly disgusted with me if I did not return to Beck in the Bendlerstrasse?'

I shall never forget the reply I received from this count, this notable of the Nazi Revolution, because it helped me to overcome many conscientious scruples. In the most vulgar manner imaginable Helldorf answered: 'I should say not. Don't kid yourself, Gisevius. For years these generals have shit all over us. They promised us everything; they've kept not one of their promises. What happened today was right in line with the rest — more of their shit.'

I looked inquiringly at Helldorf. I still wondered what I should do, and I was hoping for advice. But Helldorf continued on the same mental track. He merely repeated: 'It was all shit, all shit . . .'

I found a small police car downstairs and ordered the chauffeur: 'To the Bendlerstrasse.'

I sat in the car staring dully into space. With part of my consciousness I noticed, as we turned into Unter den Linden, that on all sides troops were marching away. The Wilhelmstrasse was quite free of soldiers; there was no sign of any cordon. In another part of my mind, which seemed to operate quite independently of the observations that my eyes were recording, I was repeating again and again the same foolish, weary refrain: 'These generals don't even know how to rebel and now you're riding to suicide . . .'

At the Brandenburg Gate I was startled out of my musings. Two martial fellows just like the ones I had met before would not let us through, not even after I showed them my handsome pass. The way to the Bendlerstrasse was blocked. Why? They were not able to say.

I instructed the chauffeur to take the roundabout route. We drove to the Victory Column. On the way I repeated my refrain incessantly: 'I am riding to suicide, I am riding to suicide . . .'

The more often I repeated it, the more ridiculous I began to seem to myself. One could commit suicide, but one could hardly ride to suicide. My reason intervened and my sense of humor returned. I imagined the astonished expression on Major Roemer's face if I should appear in the Bendlerstrasse vehemently demanding admission to the doomed circle there.

As we were about to turn left at the Victory Column in order to proceed to *Wehrmacht* headquarters, two more messengers of destiny stopped us. Again we were not permitted to go on. The sentinels gaped at Stauffenberg's flourishing signature, but they still refused to permit me to continue my ride to suicide.

The chauffeur shifted gears. I shifted plans.

Perhaps Fate would have it that I must deliver my radio address before departing this life. Since there was nothing else to do but to plunge ahead, I directed the chauffeur to drive out to the radio station, which was situated in Charlottenburg, a considerable distance from where we now were.

The farther we drove, the more senseless my situation seemed to me. What did I really have in common with these generals? Was I now to die for them? But no, I did not really have it in mind to die for them. A sense of loyalty made it necessary for me not to desert Beck in his disappointment. Was Beck a general? Just as much and as little a one as Oster. Was Oster a general? Yes and no. Of course he was a general. And yet I could very well understand why he disliked donning his uniform.

As the car left the scene of the drama farther behind, my own situation began to strike me as less dramatic. Suddenly the thought flashed through my mind: You've wanted for a long time to know what an unsuccessful *Putsch* is like; you've really never been able to imagine it. You know an old major who is said to have participated in an unsuccessful *Putsch,* but you've never asked him to tell you why that *Putsch* failed. You weren't interested; it struck you as ancient history.

I recalled the Kapp *Putsch.* I thought of all the grotesque details that had once made it seem so ludicrous. Was it really so ludicrous? Was not any unsuccessful *Putsch* ludicrous? What about the successful ones? Perhaps all uprisings were ludicrous. What could have been more ludicrous than the Eighteenth Brumaire, that textbook model of the successful *Putsch*? I recalled how Napoleon, the great genius, had been anything but a hero on that mad day; it was his reckless brother who virtually pushed him into fame.

We turned into the street on which the radio station was situated. I was very tense, but a glance was enough. There were no military guards, no police protecting the building. As far as the radio station was concerned, the *Putsch* had ended before it began.

At this point my chauffeur suddenly informed me that he could drive me no farther; he would have to hurry back. *Sic transit gloria mundi.* A moment ago I had been the guest of the police chief of the Reich capital and of a police general of the Reich security office. Now this chauffeur refused to transport me any longer. Sadly I watched the vehicle disappear. No doubt that this was the last police automobile I should ride in as a 'free' man in the Third Reich. Next time I was given a free ride, the destination would be Gestapo headquarters on the Prinz Albrechtstrasse.

Fortunately, I was now only a short distance from the Reichskanzlerplatz, which was quite near to the Struencks' cellar apartment. As I passed a tall picket fence, I tossed over it the fragments of my handsome pass signed by Colonel Count Klaus von Stauffenberg, of the general staff.

The Struencks received me with the tact appropriate for beaten rebels. They asked no questions; my silence was eloquent enough. Obviously they were happy to see me return at all. They had spent the morning and the afternoon in the same torment of waiting as myself. They had to listen to the dreadful radio report. To heighten the piquancy of the situation, they had had the company of one of the future ministers of the new government, Wirmer, the prospective minister of justice, who as yet had no idea of the honor reserved for him. He had received a letter from Goerdeler and had dropped in to see them about it. While having coffee with them, he was surprised by the announcement of the attempted assassination.

I had a hasty bite to eat. Then I repaid their hospitality with an unadorned recital of the facts. But the closer I came to the end of my tale, the more troubled I became. I explained to my friends that I could not possibly leave Beck alone at such a moment as this. Undoubtedly he had long since left for Zossen. Witzleben would have taken Beck with him on his return to the headquarters, and even a Major Roemer would not have barred the way of a field marshal.

In retrospect this line of thought sounds utterly confused. But at the moment I could imagine the end as taking place in no other way: the final battle, I thought, would certainly be fought at Zossen. There, under the command of General Wagner, were enough general staff officers to put up a good fight. Therefore, I wanted to go to Zossen to be with Beck. Beck — not Olbricht, not Stauffenberg, not any of the others, but Beck the 'civilian' seemed to me the most tragic figure of the afternoon. Beck was a man — among so many who were mean-spirited.

Actually, Beck's fate had long since been sealed, and that of the others as well. Witzleben alone, who had gone home in a rage, had to wait until early the next morning.

Shortly after eight o'clock the guards battalion, whose arrival Olbricht had so happily announced, surrounded the *Wehrmacht* headquarters. But there were no arrests. Roemer contented himself with taking the rebels under his 'protection.' Apparently neither Olbricht nor Stauffenberg nor Merz von Quirnheim, nor any of the others, took the obvious step of talking to the major. Had they asked questions, had they personally inquired what had come of the action in the propaganda ministry, they would have found that they were caught in their own 'protective custody.' Then, by exercise of their authority and their persuasive powers, they might after all have drawn the troops over to their side or at least negotiated a free withdrawal to Zossen. At least they would have been able to load their revolvers . . .

Instead, for a full hour and a half they did not even realize what was going on. 'Orders are orders'; their guard had come, the panzer troops were rolling up; no one was disturbing them; the telephones continued to ring incessantly — what should they distrust?

The *Putsch* continued — a phantom *Putsch*.

At ten o'clock sharp commands suddenly rang out. The guards battalion was being withdrawn. A number of the neutral 'putschists' — those officers who had gone along with the revolt in the afternoon and then had got cold feet and had been seeking an escape for hours — understood at once: the SS must be moving up: and they realized that the punishment of the Black hangman would fall upon the just and the unjust alike.

Lieutenant-Colonel von der Heyden, one of these half-hearted rebels, recognized that only one thing could save him and his like-minded fellows. Quickly a group was formed. 'Treason!' they cried. They rushed into Stauffenberg's room, and Heyden shot the colonel; but none of these officers could shoot straight today. Stauffenberg was only wounded. Trailing a stream of blood, he ran upstairs to Beck.

Stauffenberg's friends, who were in the room when he was shot, stood around in utter consternation. Not one of them reached for his gun. Or rather one did — the one who described this scene to us — but he found himself too inhibited to shoot; and the trigger-happy SS men were already approaching to put an end to such poaching in their special field.

Upstairs, Stauffenberg arrived just in time to be in at the finish. Fromm, now 'liberated,' hastened into his office. 'Well, gentlemen,' he declared, 'now I am going to do to you what you wanted to do to me this afternoon.'

What was that? Was he going to lock the rebels in the adjoining room and feed them sandwiches and wine until the storm blew over?

Fromm knew well that such things are done only by men who feel too sure of themselves, who still toy with their fate when the issue is in deadly earnest. He could not afford such sentimental gestures; his own head was at stake. He swung his revolver threateningly. Harshly he barked at the conspirators: 'Lay down your weapons.'

'None of us had any weapons,' said Colonel-General Hoeppner in describing this final scene. I shall continue to quote from his account:

> *Beck:* 'I have a pistol here, but I should like to keep it for my private use.'
>
> *Fromm:* 'Very well, do so. But at once.'
>
> Beck took the pistol and loaded it. Fromm warned Beck not to point it at him. Then Beck said a few words: 'At this moment I am thinking of earlier days.'
>
> *Fromm, interrupting:* 'We do not wish to go into that now. Will you kindly go ahead!'
>
> Beck said a few more words, put the gun to his head, and shot.

The bullet struck the top of his head. Beck, reeling: 'Did it fire properly?'

Fromm: 'Help the old fellow.'

Two officers who were standing on Beck's left went up to him.

Fromm: 'Take away his gun.'

Beck: 'No, no, I want to keep it.'

Fromm: 'Take the gun away from him; he hasn't the strength.'

While the two officers busied themselves with Beck, Fromm turned to Olbricht, Stauffenberg, Merz, and Haeften. 'And you, gentlemen, if there is anything you want to put in writing, you still have a few moments.'

Olbricht: 'I should like to write.'

Fromm: 'Come over to the round table here, where you always sat opposite me.'

Olbricht wrote. Fromm went out.

Five minutes later Fromm returned.

Fromm: 'Are you finished, gentlemen? Please hurry, so that it will not be too hard for the others. Now, then, in the name of the Fuehrer a court-martial, called by myself, has taken place. The court-martial has condemned four men to death: Colonel of the General Staff Merz von Quirnheim, General of Infantry Olbricht, this colonel whose name I will no longer mention, and this lieutenant.' He meant Stauffenberg and Haeften.

Fromm gave the order to a lieutenant standing by: 'Take a few men and execute this sentence downstairs in the yard at once.'

The four were led away.

Fromm turned to Beck again. 'Well, what about it?'

Beck, half-dazed, managed to answer: 'Give me another pistol.'

One of the men standing by handed a gun to him.

Fromm: 'Very well, you have time for a second shot.'

Fromm walked to the door and pointed to Hoeppner. 'Lead him away.'

At that moment a shot rang out.

This was the sum and substance of Hoeppner's account to the People's Court. We can spare ourselves the interjected remarks of Freisler, the president of the court.

Or can we not?

The sound film tells no lies, and this entire court scene was filmed and exhibited. Somehow Hoeppner's further description must be included, his account of how he had objected to his court-martial sentence and had demanded that he be given a chance to be heard. He could 'justify' himself, he had said; he was 'not a *Schweinehund*.'

'You are not a *Schweinehund*?'

Freisler stretched in his judge's seat and spitefully barked at the defendant: 'Well, then, if you don't want to be a *Schweinehund*, tell us what zoological class you consider to be your proper category?'

Hoeppner hesitated briefly. With the sound camera grinding away, Freisler pursued his point.

'Well, what are you?'

'An ass.'

Outside the building four salvos boomed.

Olbricht, Merz von Quirnheim, and Haeften died silently. Stauffenberg's last utterance sounded upon the command to fire. 'Long live the eternal Germany!' he shouted.

Within the building the small group of arrested men thought the walls would crash from the vibration of the thunderous roar below: 'Our Fuehrer, Adolf Hitler — *Sieg Heil! Sieg Heil! Sieg Heil! . . .*'

About an hour later a large personnel truck circled a near-by cemetery. The driver, an army sergeant, found the gate locked. He learned that the sexton of the church a short distance from the cemetery had the key. The sergeant awakened the sexton from his sleep. There were five bodies in his truck, he said. He had been officially ordered to bury them quietly in this cemetery. The incident must remain absolutely secret, and no one was to know afterward where the grave was situated.

The distracted sexton opened the cemetery gate. He helped to carry the bodies inside the cemetery wall. The sergeant began digging at once. He would have to dig a big grave, he said; thirty more bodies were to follow. The sexton was terrified. He ran to the nearest policeman. Two patrolmen accompanied him back to the cemetery. By the light of their pocket torches they examined the bodies: one general, two colonels, a lieutenant, a civilian.

The precinct chief was sent for. Five puzzled men stood around five still-bleeding bodies and conferred. They finally decided it would be best not to do too much thinking. Orders were orders. All five of them began digging. In the morning the precinct chief would make a written report. For a while they kept a death-watch. They were waiting for the remaining thirty bodies; but these did not come, and no one dared to inquire at the headquarters where so many horrors were taking place that night.

The grave was closed. Quietly this curious assemblage of grave-diggers slunk away.

At dawn the sexton was startled out of his bed again. The SS wanted 'their' bodies back: the identification office had to take a few photographs, and then the five dead men were sent off to the crematorium.

Dully, we sat around the radio in the Struencks' apartment. For an hour there had been repeated announcements that Hitler would speak. Again and again the broadcast had been postponed. Consequently, we clung to the faint hope that it was all a fraud, that he was dead after all. If that were the case, who could say that the revolt would not be revived and spread out from Zossen into the rest of the country?

Long after midnight it came at last. The music stopped abruptly. Hans Fritzsche came to the microphone and announced: 'The Fuehrer speaks.'

We cast questioning glances at one another. Would it really be he? The first few sentences were enough to remove our doubts. It was Hitler — his voice, his coarse speech, the typical Hitlerian vocabulary which was aped by the thousand little Hitlers, but which yet had its own inimitable sound when it came from his own lips. It was Hitler all right, from the inevitable 'in the first place' to the equally inevitable 'exterminate.'

If I speak to you today, I do so for two special reasons. In the first place, so that you may hear my voice and know that I myself am sound and uninjured; and in the second place, so that you may also hear the particulars about a crime that is without peer in German history.

An extremely small clique of ambitious, conscienceless, and criminal and stupid officers forged a plot to eliminate me and, along with me, to exterminate the staff of officers in actual command of the German *Wehrmacht*. The bomb, which was planted by Colonel Count von Stauffenberg, burst two yards from my right side. It severely injured several of my colleagues; one of them has died. I myself am wholly unhurt. . . .

The clique of usurpers is, as you may well imagine, very small. It has nothing to do with the German armed forces and above all nothing to do with the German army either. It is an extremely small band of criminal elements who are now being mercilessly exterminated. . . .

I am convinced that with the liquidation of these very small cliques of traitors and conspirators, we are at last creating at home in the rear the atmosphere that the fighters at the front need. . . .

This time an accounting will be given such as we National Socialists are wont to give. . . .

I wish especially to greet you, my old comrades in the struggle, for it has once more been granted me to escape a fate which holds no terrors for me personally, but which would have brought terror down upon the heads of the German people. I see in this another sign from Providence that I must and therefore shall continue my work.

March music.

On such an occasion Goering, of course, could not hold his peace. We were revolted by his hypocritical sentimentality.

Comrades of the *Luftwaffe!* An inconceivably base attempt at the murder of our Fuehrer was committed today by Colonel Count von Stauffenberg on the orders of a miserable clique of one-time generals who, because of their wretched and cowardly conduct of the war, were driven from their posts. The Fuehrer was saved as by a miracle.

These criminals are now attempting to usurp power and to sow confusion among the troops by issuing false orders. . . .

Officers and soldiers, no matter what their rank, and civilians who support these criminals in any manner or who approach you to win support for their wretched undertaking, are to be seized and shot at once. Those of you who are called to help exterminate these traitors must act with utter ruthlessness.

These are the same miserable creatures who have tried to betray and sabotage the front.

Officers who participate in this crime cut themselves off from their nation, from the *Wehrmacht,* from all soldierly honor, from fealty to their oath. Their annihilation will give us new strength.

The *Luftwaffe* counters this treachery with its sworn loyalty to and fervent love for the Fuehrer and its ruthless devotion to victory.

Long live our Fuehrer whom Almighty God so visibly blessed on this day!

Again a blaring military march. Then it was Doenitz's turn. The supreme commander of the naval forces surpassed himself in superlatives:

Men of the Navy! Holy wrath and immeasurable rage fill our hearts at the criminal assault which was intended to take the life of our beloved Fuehrer. Providence wished to have it otherwise; Providence guarded and protected the Fuehrer; thus Providence did not desert our German Fatherland in its fated hour.

An insanely small clique of generals, who have nothing in common with our brave army, were so cowardly and faithless as to instigate this attempt at murder, thus committing the basest sort of treason to the Fuehrer and the German people. For these scoundrels are no more than the agents of our enemies, whom they serve with their characterless, craven, and perverse cleverness. In actuality their stupidity is boundless. . . .

We will stop these traitors in their tracks. The navy stands true to its oath in tested loyalty to the Fuehrer, absolute in its devotion and readiness to battle. . . .

It will ruthlessly annihilate anyone who is unmasked as a traitor. Long live our Fuehrer, Adolf Hitler!

The *Putsch* was over.

4

Escape to the Future

SHALL I DENY that I slept poorly that night? Many and variegated were the scenes that whirled before my eyes as I lay dozing: generals, officers, police, civilians, the Bendlerstrasse and Alexanderplatz, an assassin, a radio voice — and how many victims? I felt that the walls of the cellar were about to collapse around me, so oppressed was I by the memory of all the hopes, fears, and disappointments that had engrossed us in our talks within these four walls during the past few days and hours.

The following morning I was impelled to leave the house some time before seven o'clock. I did not breathe easily until I found myself safely inside an overcrowded commuters' train. While standing, I surreptitiously bent my knees — a gymnastic exercise that is quite exhausting after a time. I began cursing all the women who had tried to persuade me that it was wonderful to be so tall. 'Don't attract attention' — that is the first command for adventurers who dwell under a system of terror. It is unwise, or at least indiscreet, in revolutionary times to tower a head above one's fellow men.

My goal was Berlin West, where I knew someone whom I had more than once had occasion to help. Recently, when he heard about my being bombed out, he had offered to put me up for the night at his home. But times had changed. When he saw me walking through his garden so early in the morning, he turned pale. He barely had the composure to stammer a greeting; then he at once assured me that his house was oh, so unfortunately overcrowded with guests. Evidently he had a radio.

576

In such cases it is better to accept the situation with good grace. I drank a cup of coffee and accepted his recommendation that I go to see a neutral diplomat who lived near-by. My friend said he would send another foreign diplomat there, one in whom I placed high hopes. I did not know the gentleman personally, but not long before I had had the opportunity to assist him in a situation that was highly embarrassing for him personally and for his country.

Diplomats hear about everything, and so my host also knew about the events of the day before. Nevertheless, he permitted me to wait in his home until late that afternoon, when he brought with him his colleague whom I wanted to see. The latter's memory needed some jogging before he recalled that it was not some 'group' but I, in person, who had given him that needed tip. Then he proved to me that he had the most cogent diplomatic reasons for being cautious. I understood quite well — but earlier, when he had accepted my help with a thousand assurances of gratefulness, he had not turned my messenger away on the ground that he could not violate his country's neutrality.

Both diplomats greedily absorbed my account of the previous day's events. Since Hans Fritzsche had just announced on the radio that only 'half a dozen' generals and officers had participated in the *Putsch,* I wished at least to give some publicity to the fact that Field Marshal von Witzleben had been one of the rebels. For all I knew the Nazis might attempt to smother this embarrassing fact in silence.

Then I accepted the diplomat's friendly offer to take me part of my way in his car. I had arranged with the Struencks that we would leave messages and information for one another at the home of our friend, Hans Koch. Since my host was headed for the golf course, Koch's home was on his route. Perhaps Koch would be able to put me up.

I left the diplomat's car at an underpass, and for the next ten minutes I went at a jog-trot. I was in the neighborhood of my former home, which at this particular time, I thought, would undoubtedly exercise a certain attraction for the Gestapo.

There was good news for me at Koch's. The Struencks, thank God, had not been picked up, and Koch's reaction was reassuring. He was a rather timid man, circumspect and not overfond of wild ventures, but when he saw me he did not even start back in dismay. I have always felt a particular respect for men on whom nature has conferred a considerable degree of caution — or let us frankly say, timidity — and who nevertheless voluntarily perform acts of great courage. That is a mode of behavior that shows up most vividly under systems of terror.

Hans Koch sheltered me. We arranged an alibi for him in case I should be captured: that I had just arrived from Zurich that morning and had asked him to put me up temporarily since my own home had been destroyed. I did not intend to abuse his hospitality for long.

Weariness soon overwhelmed me. That night I slept splendidly. I forgot everything.

The following morning Frau Koch telephoned the Struencks from a public telephone. Everything appeared to be all right. I sat down with a book on theology to distract my mind. As a matter of fact, I felt that calmness that comes over people who with the best will in the world can no longer think of anything at all to do. For what could I do? Was I to take the next train to the vicinity of the Swiss frontier? During those days there were three separate police authorities checking up on railroad passengers. The military police were looking for deserters, the criminal police for shirking laborers or escaping prisoners of war, and the Gestapo for traitors. Later on perhaps Colonel Hansen would be able to help me, or perhaps some other friend in the *Abwehr,* or perhaps Nebe.

In order not to endanger Koch unnecessarily, I met the Struencks at a crowded suburban station where we hoped to be lost in the throng. Frau Struenck had meanwhile spoken with Nebe. He had stopped quickly at some street-corner and she had got into his car. Apparently the Gestapo still did not suspect either him or Helldorf. In general, Nebe had said, the Gestapists were not at all certain how they should proceed. They were still shivering from the shock. They felt themselves seriously compromised, for they had been taken by surprise everywhere. In Paris they had put up a particularly poor showing; all the SS leaders had let themselves be arrested without offering the slightest resistance. Himmler and Goebbels would have preferred to cover up this scandal. After all, there was no chance of another *Putsch,* and it seemed to them pointless to let the general public know how widely ramified the conspiracy had been. Kaltenbrunner and Mueller, however, were hot for revenge, but Hitler had not yet made his decision; they still did not know how literally to interpret his threat to 'exterminate' the rebels.

Nebe sent word to me that I must on no account travel anywhere by railroad. Remarkably enough, he had not heard my name mentioned by any of the Gestapists as yet. I had to wait for almost ten months before I solved this mystery.

By sheer chance the Gestapo was diverted from my trail for three days which were of inestimable value to me. It seemed that Consistorialist Eugen Gerstenmaier, who for years had been an outspoken opponent of the Confessional Church, had in recent years become a member of the Kreissau circle of the Opposition, and, as it happened, he arrived in Berlin after an absence of a month on the morning of July 20. Hearing the radio report of the unsuccessful attempt at assassination, he had gone to the Bendlerstrasse, arriving there a few minutes after I had left the building. (It was he who later recounted to me the manner of Beck's death.) For once the Gestapists who were invading the building did something that was highly sensible from the point of view of police work. Before they occupied the building, they asked the doormen and the soldiers in the courtyard whom they had seen inside. All answered unanimously that there had been only army officers except for one civilian who had come and gone frequently.

While making their very first arrests in Olbricht's waiting room, they found this 'one civilian' — Herr Gerstenmaier. It helped him not at all to insist that he had just arrived in Berlin that morning and had come to the Bendlerstrasse late in the evening. The SS men beat him all the harder for his 'lying.' Then, on the fifth day, they suddenly let him alone; and he, too, had to wait ten months before he found out

who it was that competed for his distinction — a distinction for which
he had had to pay by enduring so many beatings — of being the sole
civilian in the Bendlerstrasse during the *Putsch*. This stout-hearted
church official had some moments of altogether un-Christian bitterness in May, 1945, when I explained to him why the Gestapists had
suddenly, after five days, taken his word for it. The flight of Nebe
and myself clarified the situation for them.

That came about in the following manner.

Up to Sunday, July 23, everything still seemed to be going well.
That morning I had become intensely curious about Helldorf. Boldly
I went into the nearest police station — certainly the last place the
Gestapo would look for me — and declared it was urgent that I talk
to the chief of police over the internal police telephone system. I put
over my bluff, and fortunately Helldorf understood at once who the
caller was who wanted to discuss the next air-raid drill with him. He
asked me to come to his private home at four o'clock — that is, to
the ruins that remained of his home.

Since it was Sunday, the streets were almost deserted, nor did I
encounter any Gestapo patrols; but in front of Helldorf's door, in an
attitude of studied nonchalance, stood his chauffeur who bore the
lovely name of Kelch (chalice). The man was deliberately looking
away from me, and he held a white handkerchief in his hand. Since
he was being so ostentatious about not seeing me, I thought it a signal
to continue on my way as fast as I could; but when I surreptitiously
looked back, he beckoned to me as if to say that the coast was clear
and that I must hurry. Never had I exchanged a word with this man
about our *Putsch* — and yet, how many such stout-hearted Kelches
must have been secretly in on the conspiracy during all those years.

Helldorf pretended to be perfectly at ease. Nevertheless, I could see
by every one of his gestures that he felt dreadfully insecure. Significantly enough, he asked me whether I had heard any details about who
was dead and who had been arrested. That was precisely what I had
been hoping to hear from him. When I looked my astonishment, he
assured me that since our last meeting on the evening of July 20 he
had learned nothing, in spite of a number of telephone conversations

with Kaltenbrunner and Goebbels. All he knew was of that nocturnal scene at the cemetery, a story he had learned from one of his precinct captains.

Nevertheless, Helldorf put on a good show of assurance. He brushed his hand over his handsome uniform, showed me his chevalier cross, which he had received only a few weeks before, and declared that the system was too shaky for them to dare to take the police chief of the Reich capital to the gallows. We discussed once more our mutual alibis. Then I left.

Near the Grunewald station I met Struenck. He was much more agitated than he had been the day before. He felt that he had to get away. But where to? Colonel Hansen had not yet been heard from, and we felt that we could not leave him in the lurch. If Struenck, his military subordinate, fled prematurely, Hansen would be incriminated. As Struenck left me, I suddenly saw Ambassador Ulrich von Hassell. He seemed to be hurrying like someone who wants to catch a train, and yet I could tell that in reality he was in no haste; but his head was bent in such a curious fashion. It was as if he were trying to hide from some terrible danger that was pursuing him. I involuntarily felt: There goes someone who has death at his heels.

I called out to him in a low voice. He started in fright, then we walked up and down for a while, so that I could tell him about the details of the *Putsch* — the uprising for which he had longed all these many years. He, too, had heard about its failure only over the radio.

As we talked, his posture changed; he stood upright again, as he always had in the past, and showed once more the same impressive bearing and inner strength I had always known him to possess. But the picture of Hassell as he walked, brooding and trying to escape from himself, will always remain with me as one of my most vivid impressions of the days after July 20. Perhaps his complicity would not be discovered by the Gestapo. In that case he must not draw suspicion upon himself by an ill-considered flight. I have already described how I prepared an alibi for my friends. But this alibi would not do for anyone who lived in Germany. How could Hassell — or anyone else — buy his own salvation at the possible cost of the lives of friends and their families?

The real terror of those times is something that cannot be expressed in abstractions, but only in images. Thus, whenever I think of the abstract problem of 'flight under total terror,' the image of Hassell rises before my mind's eye. His was the tragic situation of hundreds of thousands (and not only after July 20!); his was the fate of famous and unknown men, of Jews and Christians. The fact simply was that in certain situations there was nothing to do at all. No amount of courage, skill, or force of will could help. Many men simply had to wait for the hangman to come. They could not risk doing anything at all, for fear of endangering their fellows!

That Sunday at the Fuehrer's headquarters the choice was made between prudence and revenge. Kaltenbrunner and his bloodhound, Mueller, won out. Hitler ordered a clean sweep to be made of the Opposition.

On Monday morning Hansen was arrested. He was recalled by telegram from the bedside of his sick wife. Allegedly the matter was one connected with his official duties. He decided to continue in his rôle of the unsuspecting innocent, and in fact he was received with all due honors at the Gestapo headquarters in the Prinz Albrecht-strasse. In Kaltenbrunner's waiting room, however, the Gestapo thugs were waiting for him. He was handcuffed and his feet were chained, and these fetters were not removed until he was led to the gallows.

Helldorf received a similar friendly invitation from Kaltenbrunner. Again the visitor was received with full honors, and again the Gestapists fell upon the man when his back was turned. Like Hansen, Helldorf bravely kept silent under torture for long days. Their heroism gave the Struencks and myself a head start of about a week.

Nebe now realized that he would have to make haste. Kaltenbrunner, who still did not have a clear view of the extent of our conspiracy, laughingly remarked to him that word was going around that he, Nebe, had been seen frequently in Helldorf's company. 'If that's the case I'll have to arrest you too,' he added.

Nebe did not ask to hear that remark repeated. Returning to his office, he tossed into his car the box containing a civilian suit that he had long had ready and declared that he had to leave on an urgent official mission; he would be gone until the following night. But then came the hitch: the SS man at the gasoline pump, from whom Nebe had always received the fuel for these urgent official missions, refused to issue supplementary cans of gasoline to him. He had strict orders from above that no more than twelve gallons of gasoline should be issued without special permits.

Toward evening Struenck knocked excitedly on our door. He scarcely gave me time to pack my few belongings; then he dragged me along to the next corner, where Nebe's car was waiting. Our small amount of gasoline set narrow limits. We had to eliminate the obvious persons at once because it would have been too easy to trace us. Under a system of total terror a large circle of acquaintances is a luxury that conspirators cannot afford. As long as everything goes well, that is an advantage. The fewer persons one knows, the less there are to betray one later on, under torture, but when it is necessary to flee, one becomes conscious of the disadvantages of such caution, for suddenly the small group of friends and acquaintances are all on the same blacklist. It becomes quite a problem to find someone whom one knows well enough to ask for refuge and who is at the same time not suspect.

I recalled that Hans Asmussen, one of the leaders of the Confessional Church, had spoken to me years ago about a pastor in the provinces who would be able to hide me with his peasants if need be. While Nebe and Struenck drove off to pick up Frau Struenck, I looked up another pastor I knew and obtained the address and a note of introduction.

It was late at night when we finally left the city. Our destination was a village about sixty miles beyond Potsdam. Finding our way in the blackout was extremely difficult. Again and again we had to get out of the car to check the roads. Above us the bombers roared to drop their cargoes on Berlin. We sent up to them our pious wishes that they might score a direct hit on the Prinz Albrechtstrasse.

En route we were stopped dozens of times by police patrols or militia units. Fortunately, Nebe's uniform of an SS group leader still merited respect, but I was given a good lesson on how limited were the chances for escape by automobile in wartime. Who had sufficient gasoline? Who had permission to travel beyond the narrowest local limits? Who would be permitted to take unknown passengers in his car? Only a high-ranking leader of the SS could meet all such requirements, and by tomorrow noon at the latest, by which time the warrant would have been wirelessed and telegraphed throughout the country, even Nebe's precious papers would be valueless . . .

In a dictatorship even the so-called 'big shots' could be reduced overnight to insignificance. In the face of omnipotent terror, everything is fictional. That was why so many had hastened to hide behind the saving mask — a title, a membership book in the Nazi Party, a uniform; that was why so few people dared to go along without such camouflage, even long after they had with horror recognized the true nature of the Nazi criminals — and of themselves.

We must not make the error of thinking that all those who eat the bread of dictatorship are evil from the first; but they must necessarily become evil. Other systems of government, including democracy, may have their faults; but so long as they permit the possibility of free choice between good and evil, defects can be remedied and the crooked made straight. The curse of a system of terror is that there is no turning back; neither in the large realm of policies nor the 'smaller' realm of everyday human relationships is it possible for men to retrace their steps.

It was past midnight when we knocked on the door of the parsonage. Frau Struenck had some difficulty persuading the pastor that we were neither robbers nor Gestapo officers, but people who needed help. But we had no luck. In his whole parish he no longer knew anyone who would be willing to run such a risk. The people in the villages were no longer by themselves. Everywhere bombed-out refugees were being quartered, and all of them were intensely suspicious of one another. Every prefect or gendarme was required to report immediately the presence of unannounced visitors, and in wartime men fit for military service were not usually seen playing cards at a village tavern.

'I implore you for the sake of my wife and children not to come here again,' the pastor had called after us as we left. He had already had more than one run-in with the Gestapo. He had, however, mentioned to us a remote village. His colleague there would certainly be able to help us, he thought. Only recently he had hidden a number of Jews.

Over deserted back roads we made our way toward the village. It was already dawn when we knocked again. The pastor and his wife were friendly and invited us into their tiny little parsonage. Yes, of course, he had concealed a number of Jews. But naturally he could not endanger them for our sakes.

We ourselves realized that this splendid man had done what he could — indeed, had outdone himself. We were really at a loss now. We still had half a gallon of gasoline. What should we do with the car? Finally we decided to hide the car in the dense underbrush of a forest. Then we returned to the parsonage. On the way, Nebe demonstrated to me the correct technique for concealing our trail from bloodhounds. In this at least we were successful, for two days later, when the car was found and a grand search was organized, dozens of police dogs passed by the parsonage without pausing.

In the laundry-room we burned Nebe's uniform. For another twenty-four hours we wandered around this vicinity. Then hunger and closed doors convinced us that it was all in vain. Finally I insisted on my old thesis, that in such dangerous times there is only one relatively safe refuge — in the lions' den.

The ride back to Berlin was sheer torment. For we had to change trains five times. I felt immensely relieved when we at last reached the center of Berlin.

The Struencks went their own ways. We had made arrangements for keeping in touch with one another. At first Nebe and I tried our luck together, but after a few hours we realized that two was too many: we also would have to separate.

As we were walking through the streets of Berlin West in search of a mutual acquaintance, Nebe and I suddenly felt ourselves observed by persons in a car parked near-by. Quickly we vanished into the entrance of a building. Fortunately the spies were interested only in their own special task. They were watching the chief provost marshal of the army, Doctor Sack, who lived there. Sack came home a moment later. Not suspecting that it was by pure chance that we had encountered him here, he assumed we had come to meet him. I shall never forget the tense warning spoken by this noble man: 'Clear out; I am under observation; the Gestapo is at my heels.'

The scene was one that is possible only in revolutionary times and that an outsider will scarcely understand. Here was the chief of military justice, the man who at the moment was entrusted with the judicial investigation of the events of July 20, giving a warning to two fugitives, while outside the spies set to watch him were waiting. Moreover, Sack continued in his position for at least another week! Then the ring had closed so tightly around him that it left space only for a cell in the Prinz Albrechtstrasse. There he sat close by his fellow fighters and fellow sufferers whom he had protected and to some extent prosecuted. Together with them he died courageously the death of a believing Christian.

On August 30 Struenck was picked up. Twenty days later his brave wife was taken. A full five months more passed before the Gestapo ferreted out Nebe in his hiding-place. A few days later, when they raided my last hiding-place (they threw a cordon around several street blocks and several dozens of them swarmed into the house), they found that the bird had flown. My rescuers had forestalled them by a few days.

I am loath to recount the details of this game of hide-and-seek. Those who have had luck ought not to boast about it. I say 'luck' because I cannot dare speak of skill or intelligence; I was aided at dramatic moments by too many strange chances and coincidences. The lucky ones must be grateful for their luck and must look upon their furlough from death as imposing a mission upon them: to speak of the struggles and sufferings of their dead friends.

I shall mention only three examples. The brave man who concealed Nebe was killed, his family was arrested and his property was confiscated. My friend, Otto Huebner, the insurance man, who was a real 'plutocrat' and might have escaped to the safety of some Bavarian village, lost his life in the very last days of the Nazi régime because he had sheltered two fleeing French officers. And on my account more than a dozen men and women were thrown into the Gestapo cellars because they had really or allegedly hidden me. I thank God that 'only' one of them had to sacrifice his life, my faithful friend and helper Hans Koch.

But of what importance are these personal difficulties compared to the torture of those who suffered in the Gestapo cellar? For day and night, even when they ate, even when they walked to the scaffold, they were fettered hand and foot. They were not fed so well or treated so carefully as the Nuremberg war criminals. Their cell doors always stood open; two SS men stared continually at them. Their food was insufficient for living and too much for dying. . . . But it is not possible to describe the kind of 'interrogation' that was practiced in the Prinz Albrechtstrasse. We do know one thing, however, from the records that were found and from the accounts of the few survivors: those martyred men heroically kept silence.

When the storm was over, some persons in their initial flurry leveled the accusation that this one or that one had talked too much, but, as I have said earlier in connection with Goerdeler, resistance to interrogation, or to the chemical preparations that were mixed with the prisoners' food, is not primarily a matter of character but of physical constitution. Some resisted, some talked, and some — made mistakes.

Since I was spared by the kindness of destiny from 'softening up' or from making such 'mistakes,' I have the right to give myself as an example. Every day that I continued to 'enjoy' my freedom, I considered anew the burning question: What will you say if the police come this minute? The longer I remained at liberty and the more I heard of others who had already been tried, the more opportunities

I had to judge what the Gestapo knew and what it did not know, and the more simple my situation appeared to me. After about four months I said to myself: Now they know everything. Consequently, I may as well die with dignity. I would openly hurl defiance into their faces. Yes, I would say, I thought so and so, those men were my friends, these were my deeds.

When everything was over, I was shocked that I had ever had such thoughts. I learned how many of my friends had preserved their secrets unto death. Goerdeler and Schlabrendorff sat in adjoining cells, but in the presence of the Gestapists they did not admit to knowing one another. The 1943 plans for assassination were never revealed. Oster, Struenck, and Canaris sat in adjoining cells — and yet the Gestapo never learned how far their collaboration had gone. Almost the entire *fronde* were gathered in cells within a few yards of one another, and yet, up to the very last, the Gestapo tortured 'only a few' to death and never grasped the full extent of the conspiracy. What would have happened if at the end of 1944 or the beginning of 1945 I had joined this company of martyrs who were heroically concealing the truth and if I had 'bravely' and 'honestly' confessed the truth? Perhaps my court record would read more nobly today than the statements of the others in which the defendants portrayed their friends, if not themselves, as hundred-per-cent Nazis and patriots. It may be argued that in the end almost all were executed, but I should nevertheless have been the one who provided the final evidence the Gestapo needed, the final pretext they desired, for incredible as it may seem, even in 1945 murder was still being done 'legally.' Even while millions of Jews were being killed without any judicial proceedings, Freisler, the president of the revolutionary tribunal, insisted upon having 'proofs' or a 'confession.'

It is tragic, indeed, to suffer martyrdom without having said a last word of self-justification, but how terrible a torment of conscience would it have been to know, as one mounted the scaffold, that a hasty word had meant the deaths of friends or relations!

Afterward Frau Struenck told me that immediately following her arrest she was mockingly informed that I had long been in the hands of the Gestapo. To prove it to her and to make it easier for her to confess, she was read pages of statements that I had allegedly made on the subject of our joint treasonous activities. This stratagem restored Frau Struenck's composure, for she knew definitely that I was still at liberty. What would have happened if, months later, I had been read the confessions of Goerdeler, Oster, Canaris, Struenck, or Nebe? In truth, perhaps the greatest perversion of human nature that takes place under a system of terror is that more character is needed, more courage required, to lie than to confess the truth.

Not only did those men and women keep their secrets bravely; they died even more bravely. Both men and women went to the scaffold with a bearing and courage for which no tribute is too high. I know that for many the end was certainly not the worst, not so tormenting as the interrogations, not so wearing as the waiting. When the hoarse, harsh cry came: 'Number 27, finish him off, quick, quick . . .' there may have been some to whom it meant release.

Nevertheless, it could not be easy to die amid the mocking laughter of Gestapo men.

In mid-October I sent word to Hans Koch from my hiding-place that I thought the coast was clear and could responsibly ask him to pay me a visit. He came the following night. I was happy to see him again and to find him looking well. But before I could say a word about this, he took my hand and said: 'Forgive me; please don't say anything; I've simply been too cowardly to come . . .'

What could I say to him? My friend was the father of five children. In 1934 he had been thrown into the Gestapo cellar for the first time because he attempted to save a Jew's property. Then he had courageously defended Niemoeller at his trial. In hundreds of cases he had quietly contributed his help, and always he had gone his own straight way. Without quavering he had concealed me during the first days after July 20. And now he was apologizing because he had, out of a perfectly reasonable sense of caution, kept away for a few months. To such behavior this man, who for years had been oppressed by premonitions of a violent death, gave the name of 'cowardice.'

Moreover, Koch had not been inactive during this time. He had gathered a great deal of information, although in times of terror mere curiosity can prove fatal and is certainly unwise when a man has something to conceal. Koch had nevertheless found out that for weeks after Struenck's arrest the Gestapo had posted five men in Struenck's house and garden in case I should turn up there. They were still paying visits to the place at regular intervals.

Hans Koch also had news of my sister. In mid-August the Gestapo had located her in the country. Since then she had vanished without a trace. Apparently one hostage was not enough for them. I had succeeded in getting my mother safely into Switzerland before it was too late. Determined to have their revenge, they sent a special plane to arrest a cousin of mine who was at the moment fighting on the Baltic front. 'Arrest of kin,' this was called; it was the latest Gestapo accomplishment. Until the day the American army in South Tyrol liberated my sister, together with other 'prominent' persons — Léon Blum, Schuschnigg, Martin Niemoeller, the family of Goerdeler, and many, many others of almost every nation — no one had any idea where these unfortunates were. They were not permitted to send to their relations any indication that they were still alive. They themselves were not even allowed to know where they were being kept. It created a sensation among them one day when they found a name engraved on the underside of a chair in their quarters — the name: Buchenwald Concentration Camp.

Was torment of the prisoners the only motive? Not at all. On the one hand, the Nazis wanted to hold hostages for the future, so that they could buy themselves free. On the other hand, they deliberately spread the word that all relations of traitors were being executed. They knew very well the panicky terror this would create among all those who had ever had oppositional ideas. Everyone has the moral right to risk his own life, but can he justify himself before God and man if he also hazards the lives of his wife and children?

The rest of what Koch had to tell was equally crushing. Almost all our friends were under arrest, but Koch had a horrible story to tell about them. Many of these men, especially the prominent ones, were still alive. Condemned to death by Nazi justice and long ago hanged according to the reports of the grapevine or of official sources, they were still dragging out a shadow existence in the Gestapo cellars. The technicians of torture and drugs still hoped to squeeze some more information out of their living corpses . . .

Around the time of Koch's visit some good news came from Switzerland for me personally. Help was on the way. I had friends there — and friends helped. A 'book' given to intermediaries was to serve as a confirmation to me that I could trust the messenger. A week passed — two, three, four. Then at last it came. I read every page over twice, three times, to see whether the text contained some hidden message; I tore open the binding; I guessed and puzzled and reasoned; but I learned nothing beyond what the accompanying written note had told me, that a further message would be forthcoming 'shortly.'

'Shortly.' I have sworn eternal enmity with that word. At first I smiled with the knowingness of an old hand at conspiracy. Splendid! Now they have determined that the coast is clear and that I am still here, I thought. Tomorrow they'll certainly send their promised additional message. 'Shortly.'

Next day I waited till darkness fell. Of course, how could I have been so foolish as to expect them at once? They must have spent the day making sure that the house was not surrounded by the Gestapo. I gave them two days more. I suddenly had an inspiration. 'Shortly' must certainly mean the next change in the phase of the moon. How could I expect them to come for me during nights such as these when the moon was so bright that I, tall as I was, would easily be recognized against the bright background of snow?

The moonless nights approached closer and closer, and they passed; but for all my looking out of the window and satisfying myself as to the blackness of the night, nothing came of the promised 'shortly.' Again imagination came to my rescue. How could I have made such a mistake? I asked myself. In order for us to find our way through underbrush and swamps to the border, some natural light was needed. Not, of course, bright sunlight, but on the contrary the full moon that so many lyric poets have justly praised. The message had been smuggled to me at the time of the last full moon. When the next came . . .

The moon swelled; then it began to diminish again; and 'shortly' was still not yet. Twice more I waited for the dark of the moon, twice more for the full moon. In vain.

Meanwhile Christmas came. What a fool I had been! I told myself. Shouldn't I have realized from the first that they would have chosen the peace of Christmas Eve for my rescue? On that night even the Gestapo patrols stayed at home. Which would it be — Christmas Eve or Christmas Night?

When these last illusions proved false, I decided now that I definitely knew what 'shortly' must mean. One thing was clear, I thought, and that was that half a year of hiding had utterly dulled my mind. After all, my rescuers would have realized that all the customs officials and border guards in the world would want to drink to the New Year. Undoubtedly 'shortly' must mean New Year's Eve.

By the middle of January I gave up hoping. Something must have gone wrong. Well, what did it matter; the rescue probably would not have worked successfully anyway. Nature, too, went on strike. For a week I lay in bed with a severe case of grippe. I ran a dangerously high fever. Was it that I knew intuitively that Nebe had just been arrested and that the search for me was being renewed with fresh intensity? Or was I disturbed by an official announcement that after January 21 there would be no more trains for civilian passengers and all travelers would have to obtain special permits from the police?

On Saturday, January 20, Koch intended to visit me. But he did not turn up. Around eight o'clock in the evening I had a sudden attack of nervousness. It was pitch-dark outside, and so I ventured out and ran to a coin telephone. My friend did not answer. He had gone out a few hours ago, an unknown voice informed me. I imagined that the person who answered must have been some tenant in his house.

Then he must be on his way to see me, I thought. I hastened back in order not to miss him, and I did not have long to wait, for soon the bell rang. But it was not Koch. The woman who had brought me the 'book' months ago — I will call her Miss 'Shortly' — stood at the door and breathlessly asked me whether everything was all right. When I said yes, she vanished into the darkness.

Dramatic! But what did this strange visit mean?

A few moments later there was another ring. I rushed outside, only to hear a blacked-out automobile driving away.

But there was a fat envelope in the mailbox. The first thing that fell into my hand was a thick metal badge — the well-known badge of executive officers of the Gestapo. Then I unfolded an official German passport with a picture of myself. I found that my name was Hoffmann and that I was a high-ranking functionary of the Gestapo. There was a special pass and a letter from Gestapo headquarters instructing all officials of the government and the Nazi Party to assist me in my secret mission to Switzerland.

My jubilation was mingled with a little alarm. It had been a point of pride with me that none of the many offices in which I had worked in the Third Reich possessed any picture of me. I knew that the Gestapo had been compelled to work with an old passport picture dating from 1932. They had even sent a 'good friend' to visit my mother in her peaceful room in Zurich in order to secure a picture. Only a few weeks before they had at last found a photograph — not a passport photo, but an almost full-length portrait, and this very portrait now looked at me out of the passport. My friends had done an artistic job of reducing its size, but for that very reason it was all the more likely to attract attention. The Gestapo passport office generally used the ordinary type of police photograph, showing only the head and shoulders.

Moreover, there was no railroad ticket. I hoped Hans Koch would obtain one for me. Still he did not come. Finally I went to the telephone again. This time I was more tenacious. When the unknown voice informed me that he was 'away on a trip,' I asked for Frau Koch. Although it was just before the time for an air-raid alarm, she had gone out. I asked for the oldest daughter. She also was not there. Then I knew what had happened.

There was nothing for me to do but to buy the ticket myself. I thought it would be better to get it at night than in broad daylight on the morrow. Unfortunately, it was too late for me to walk all the way to the railroad station. For good or ill I would have to venture the subway. The worst of that was that the subway stations and trains were illuminated, but there was no help for it. At the railroad terminal the ticket agent looked critically at my pass, and then he handed me my ticket.

I stood for a while in front of the blacked-out station wondering whether I ought to return to my hideout at all. How long would Koch resist the torture? Had he made agreements with his wife and daughter beforehand on what they would say? Many months later I learned that all three of them had heroically refused to talk, but the Gestapo placed in Frau Koch's cell a woman spy who alleged that she was about to be released and offered to help in any way she could. Frau Koch was convinced of her sincerity, and in order to warn me she gave the woman my address. In the meantime I had made good my escape.

Those last hours seemed an eternity to me. The train was scheduled to leave at six P.M. I would have to be at the station by five at the latest in order to get a seat. That meant that I would have to leave my hideout in broad daylight.

Nevertheless, I reached the railroad terminal safely. There was a double platform; on one side stood my own train, which was bound for Stuttgart, and on the other side the Vienna Express. On the other side of the platform I saw a line of SS guards and a host of SS officers and adjutants. As I found out a little later, Kaltenbrunner was taking a trip to his native Austria. Perhaps that was my salvation. Everyone's attention was concentrated upon this Gestapo chief and no one regarded his subordinate, 'Doctor Hoffmann.'

I wanted to jump right into the first car and disappear amid the crowd, but it was impossible. Probably the train had been jammed for hours with people who wanted to take advantage of this last opportunity for civilian travel.

In despair I walked up front to the locomotive. I thought of bribing the engineer to give me a place. Just then I heard furious outburst of cursing and screeching from the dense crowd around the baggage car. The conductor and the baggage-master were trying to get into their baggage car, but the crowd had stormed it and filled it to overflowing. The two railroad officials stood on the platform gesticulating wildly. In front of them was a huge crowd of people who also wanted to get in.

The saving idea flashed through my mind. Pure chance had thrust me into my life's adventure in 1933, when I suddenly found myself a member of the newly established Gestapo. Since I had witnessed the beginnings of that noble institution, I ought to help its unpopularity along a bit, now that it was in its death-throes.

I took out my Gestapo badge. With a few vigorous thrusts of arms and elbows I worked my way through the shouting, pushing throng and in a moment had reached the two excited officials. 'Gestapo!' I barked. And I offered to help them clear the car.

And I did clear it.

I proved, however, to be a very mild-mannered Gestapist. As soon as I had worked my way into the car and had reached the conductor's seat, my officious zeal suddenly faded. Behind me the crowd poured into the car again. I myself sat down and took two small children on my knee — hiding my face behind them. I paid no attention when I heard the two railroad officials despairingly call out for the police officer who had just promised to help them. Let them find me in this mob!

At last the train was ready to depart. Slowly it began to move, and the bombers, too, spared us this time. We emerged safely from the city, and the trip went much faster than I had expected. We were only twelve hours late!

There were a few more agitating intermezzos. As we left the bombed areas behind, the conductor regained control of his baggage car. I had several run-ins with him because, peculiar Gestapo man that I was, I absolutely refused to go forward where a special compartment was reserved for government officials.

My destination was the little border station of St. Margrethen. But instead the train was routed to Constance. Perhaps this was lucky for me. I went on foot to the tiny border crossing in Kreuzlingen.

Hungry, thirsty, and exhausted by my illness and the strain of the journey, I entered the little waiting room of the frontier post on January 23, 1945, at six o'clock in the morning. The two officials, the Gestapo man and the customs officer, rubbed their eyes sleepily. It was rare for them to have travelers at such an early hour, particularly a traveler from Berlin and a high functionary of the Gestapo. Chills ran down my spine as they stood looking searchingly at me.

Certainly my physical and sartorial appearance had not improved in the past six months. I had worn my suit continuously since July 20, and it badly needed a pressing. My light spring coat was dirty and torn. I had given my own hat to Nebe when we parted. However, I had 'borrowed' another from someone during the railroad journey. It did not fit too well, but at least it covered my thick head of hair, which was fortunate. When for a whole year you have been your own barber and have had to snip away at your hair with a nail scissors, your hair is not likely to be cut according to the correct, close-cropped SS pattern. My fleece-lined high shoes looked none too appropriate to my thin summer suit, but I had had to wear them because my other shoes were so worn that they would have done little credit to a Gestapo agent. In short, my appearance was not one to inspire confidence.

Perhaps it was for that very reason that they let me cross the border. They may have assumed that I had been carefully costumed for this particular expedition, so that, once across the border, I would be able to work as a member of the Fifth Column. They opened the border gate. I raised my arm limply in response to their greeting, for the two of them stood stiffly to see me out of the Gestapo's Germany.

And then I was free!

What was I to do now? If I reported myself to the Swiss frontier police as a political refugee, I would probably have been quarantined for several days and afterward interned. Therefore, I again drew out my forged passport. It had certainly been fabricated well. The Swiss officials looked crossly at this Doctor Hoffmann who wanted to go to the German Embassy, but they let him pass.

I rushed to a telephone. My friends were overjoyed, for I was days overdue and they had already given me up for lost.

A few hours later I reached Zurich. Eddi Waetjen was there to meet me at the station, and in his excitement and joy he kissed not me but my mother. Then Gero von Gaevernitz joined us. He was too modest to listen to my thanks for all his efforts. Instead he told me the story of my 'shortly.'

Allen Dulles had quickly obtained from his superiors permission to help me. Thereupon Gero had personally gone to the London office of the OSS. My friends in the German Embassy in Berne had supplied him with several models of passports. By October my papers were ready. But the OSS was careful. An important stamp had not been printed clearly, and if they were going to assist the Gestapo in issuing passports, they were determined to have the documents correct to the last dot over the last 'i'; and so the passport had been sent back to London. In order to speed matters, it had been given to an Allied official who was flying to London. At the Paris airport the American military police had asked him whether he had any written matter with him. The man had innocently said yes and taken out my Gestapo passport.

I understood that this little incident produced something of a delay!

When the passport was ultimately returned to Berne, they still had to make sure of their courier connection with Berlin. The Hamburg publisher, Henry Goverts, had undertaken this most difficult and most courageous part of the task. Twice he went to Constance to meet the messenger, who was to smuggle the forged passport over the border, and twice he missed him.

But at last the rendezvous was made. With this dangerous paper in his pocket, Goverts entered his hotel in Constance. He intended to return to Hamburg and then go on to Berlin to deliver the papers to me. Had he done so, he would have arrived too late. But again chance came to my rescue.

In the hotel lobby Goverts encountered an acquaintance who inquisitively asked what Goverts was doing there. This man knew that Goverts traveled about as a liaison officer for the *Abwehr* —for he was the new chief of the *Abwehr*, the notorious SS General Schellenberg. The shock of this encounter made Goverts decide to get rid of his perilous papers at once. He took the fastest train to Berlin, and thus arrived just in time.

Gero and Eddi ran through a hasty summary of this story. Then I went straight to the barber's. The barber proved to be an amateur detective. He glanced expertly at my hair and informed me that I had just come from Germany. He said no more, but his manner told me the state of my hair had convinced him that Germany was at last collapsing.

In the evening I called on Allen Dulles in the Herrengasse in Berne. The servant led me to the club room that was so familiar to me. I settled into the handsome red easy-chair by the fireplace where we had so often chatted. I felt as if my pilgrimage through the Nazi millennium was over at last. I was deeply moved, profoundly grateful. I thought of my friends, of the dead, of the living.

Allen came in. I held out both hands.

'Thank you,' I said. And for a long time I could say no more.

At last I began to talk. I recounted my experiences of the past six months. And the more I talked, the less oppressed my heart felt. I stopped thinking of the bitter end and began to hope for a new and better beginning.

EPILOGUE

Epilogue

Now that my story is finished, I must ask my readers to pause for a moment's reflection. No one can accuse me of having written a book containing facile apologies for Germany. Indeed, many of my German countrymen have accused me of disloyalty; they say that I should never have revealed my knowledge of so many shameful lacks and defects. In reply to them I have written a different final chapter for the German edition of this book, a chapter entitled *On Guilt*.

But I should also like to clear up all doubts in the minds of my readers abroad. Unfortunately, the phrase 'collective guilt' has been abused with evil intent and ill results in recent years. Generalizations are never salutary. Often their effect is the opposite of the intended one, for after a time the pendulum swings in the other direction — and again swings too far. Then it is said that everything is relative, everything is destined; what could we 'little people' do to stop the daemonic forces? And in fact the killing, the pillaging, the cynicism, were so monstrous that we often ask whether real men were capable of these things or whether altogether inhuman forces were not behind them. Not the individual criminals but the extent of their crimes assume, to our horrified eyes, superhuman proportions. Nevertheless, at the present moment nothing would be more dangerous than to blur over the personal responsibility — and therefore the guilt — of every individual.

This is not a matter of pharasaical sitting in judgment; what we are aiming at is a vital and generally valid political lesson, and for this reason we are in duty bound not to conceal or cover up what went on in Germany during the past twelve years. Above all, we must understand the inherent logic of events; we must see why things had to happen — and to end — as they did. Today the Germans can no

longer recognize themselves. The Nazi epoch seems to them a confused nightmare which they try irritably to shake off in order to clear
the mind for a fresh day's work. Best of all, they would like to forget
the whole diabolic business. Is it really sheer hypocrisy when they
advance a thousand-and-one reasons to 'explain' all the incomprehensible facts?

We ought to consider carefully and not satisfy ourselves with the
simple answer that the Germans were or are a nation of devils. The
self-enslavement of sixty or eighty million people remains an historic
phenomenon of tremendous importance, and in the age of the atomic
bomb it is a phenomenon that must be disquieting for all non-
Germans as well. It is incontrovertible that there existed in Germany
a class of moral and honorable men of the highest quality. The
obvious question is: How could such men permit themselves to be
overrun by the Nazi usurpers without offering resistance? Is the
civilization of all other nations impregnably fortified against similar
outbreaks of imminent evil?

It was with this in mind that I attempted to arrange the history of
1933 to 1938 around certain psychological turning-points. I wanted
to show how the Nazi catastrophe began, because the guilt that later
emerged can be understood only against the background of a slow —
and often initially unperceived — growth of complicity.

The Reichstag fire, the thirtieth of June, and the Fritsch crisis were
plain signposts along the precipitous road to revolutionary totality.
Each event provided in itself a clear, definite set of facts. To be entirely candid, however, we must admit that, in spite of the clarity of
the facts, there remain elements that are mysterious, opaque, and bewildering for foreign observers as well. A small group of men on
top appeared guilty or responsible, and below them were millions who
either were unsuspecting or without influence. In the beginning the
latter did not at all perceive what responsibility they were being forced
to share. Their real guilt began when they did recognize the crimes
being committed in their name, and neglected to oppose them; that
is to say, their duty to oppose the régime really began at a stage when
effective opposition had become immeasurably more difficult.

From the middle of 1938 on, the direction in which things were headed became terrifyingly clear even to those far removed from the centers of government. From month to month the outline of things to come grew more and more distinct. It was clear that 'this man Hitler' wanted 'his' war. The history of all revolutions was being repeated: first terror raged at home; then an adventure abroad was embarked upon. By that time, however, too many people were already caught in their own trap. Is it not altogether uncanny the way these ministers, economists, scholars, and bishops, and above all the hesitant generals, acted again and again against their better judgment? With open eyes they let themselves be dragged down into a general and a personal disaster.

These psychological or political considerations must not divert us from the question of guilt. Rather, they should lead us to consider that question more profoundly and more honestly. Naturally no serious-minded person can pronounce all Germans guilty in the criminal sense. We have seen how careful the Nuremberg judges were, even with so prominent a group of persons as the members of the Reich government. But when such a calamity descends upon a civilized nation, and when for twelve years that nation is incapable of throwing off the shame that burdens it, it goes against the sound ethical instinct of people to cast all the blame upon a clique of leaders, no matter whether that clique is numbered in the dozens, the hundreds, or the thousands. When such a disaster takes place, there must have been something wrong with those who were led or misled.

What is that thing? One of the vital lessons that we must learn from the German disaster is the ease with which a people can be sucked down into the morass of inaction; let them as individuals fall prey to overcleverness, opportunism, or cowardliness and they are irrevocably lost. In this mass epoch it is by no means a settled thing that acts alone make for guilt. Passive acceptance, intellectual subservience, or, in religious terms, failure to pray against the evil, may constitute a kind of silent support for authoritarian rule. Once the system of terror has been installed, however, there is only one course remaining to each individual and to all individuals collectively: to fight the terrorists with the same courage and tenacity, with the same willingness to take risks, that they employ in wartime under 'orders' when they fight against the 'enemy.'

There are some Germans who mistakenly examine the history of the Nazi Revolution in search of 'daemonic forces' or other alibis. Everyone knows that terrorism and Gestapo methods existed in other places — and still exist. No one will attempt to deny that others were also guilty — and still are. In the final analysis there were millions of unteachable persons throughout the world who made a pact with the forces of Revolution and only came to their senses when the Revolution swallowed them alive. These provisos may assert many psychological or political truths; they may serve to warn the rest of the world against hasty or one-sided condemnation; but they do not excuse the Germans.

I have not, in this book, had the intention of clapping myself or my friends on the shoulder and saying: 'At least we did what we could.' The 'success' of our oppositional efforts proves that we should have done much more. So far as my dead friends are concerned, I should be dishonoring the memory of their sacrifices were I to assert that in all their actions they behaved without hesitation and without error. Of myself I can only say that every page of this book has given me cause to reflect on how frequently I thought wrongly or acted wrongly. I know that I am responsible for these mistakes, and that is why, out of my experience with twelve years of Nazism, I cannot help maintaining that German guilt does exist; it is a reality. It cannot be cast off upon a collective group, so that each individual need bear only a millionth part of the weight of guilt. All of us, and not alone the Nazis, strayed into dangerous, evil ways. We were guilty of failure to understand, of willful blindness, of misguided obedience, of paltry compromising, of exaggerated caution or of persistent shirking of the logical conclusions. In these turbulent times only those who courageously face the fact of personal guilt will be saved from going astray again in the future.

Nowadays — in practice if not in words — fatalism is the fashion. People wait for orders from above, or take refuge by invoking political necessity; or they ask: What can one individual do to oppose the course of 'destiny'? It is precisely because I do literally believe in daemonic evil forces that I do not wish to amalgamate two elements which should be kept strictly apart in any factual report on the Nazi régime. Without doubt there existed the incomprehensible and irrational element, the eruptiveness, the temper of the times, or whatever else we choose to call it; but there is also no doubt that on the other hand there existed the distinctly concrete reaction of responsible men to demands or necessities.

We must once more clearly delimit responsibilities, and what persons have more right to lead the way in such an endeavor than those who died fighting, not against any 'destiny,' but for their sincerest convictions? Few ages have produced so many martyrs as ours, and in time to come countless Germans will also be included in the roll of honor of those who perished for freedom and a better future. It is my duty, at the end of this book, to pay this tribute to my dead friends.

This homage is directed, not alone to those whose story I tell in this book; if it were I should tremble to think of how many names I have omitted. The world feels a justified sense of outrage at what happened in Germany and because of Germany during those terrible years of tyranny. Let us not forget, however, that long before the first foreigner was murdered by the SS killers, hundreds of thousands of Germans had died. Let us leave to those whose ashes have been scattered at least their undefiled faith in a better world. Let us leave to them their last despairing hope that the world would be startled out of its slumber by their lonely cries of agony and would not wait for the thunder of Hitler's cannon.

THE END

Glossary

Abwehr: The counter-espionage service of the German armed forces.

alter Kaempfer: Old fighter; a Nazi who was with Hitler in the days when the Nazi Party was small and struggling.

Amt: Office, authority, bureau.

Anschluss: The annexation of Austria.

Bekenntnisskirche: 'Confessional Church' — an organization of Protestant ministers who claimed the precedence of religious allegiance over allegiance to the state.

Bendlerstrasse: The street in Berlin where the ministry of war was located. Used as a synonym for ministry of war or high command of the armed forces.

Fuehrerstaat: Leader state; a state in which the will of the leader is the highest law.

Gauleiter: District leader of the National Socialist Party.

Gestapo: Abbreviation for *Geheime Staatspolizei* — secret state police. Formally, the Gestapo existed only in Prussia, but all the police forces established under the Nazis were generally known as Gestapo.

Gleichschaltung: Co-ordination; bringing into line with Nazi policies.

Gruppenfuehrer: Group leader; a rank in the SA and SS equivalent to that of a major-general in the army.

Herrenmensch: A member of the 'master race.'

Karinhall: Goering's palatial home.

Korps: Reactionary student fraternities.

Maerzgefallene: 'Those who fell in March' — the name given to the converts who flocked to join the Nazi Party in March, 1933.

Obergruppenfuehrer: Chief group leader; a rank in the SA and SS equivalent to that of a general in the army.

Oberkommando der Wehrmacht (OKW): The high command of the armed forces.

Ordensburg: School for the training of Nazi leaders.

Prinz Albrechtstrasse: The street in Berlin where the Gestapo headquarters was located. Used as a synonym for Gestapo.

Raubbau: Reckless exploitation of natural resources; mining the soil.

Reichsbanner: Veterans' organization.

Reichsleiter: Members of the executive committee of the Nazi Party.

Reichssicherheitshauptamt: Reich security office: headquarters of the SS police forces.

Reichswehr: The German army until 1933.

SA: Sturmabteilung, the storm troops.

Schloss: The famous Royal Palace in Berlin.

SD: Sicherheitsdienst, security service; Heydrich's special police force within the SS.

Stahlhelm: Conservative veterans' organization.

SS: Schutzstaffel, the élite guard; originally a branch of the SA, used principally as an auxiliary police force.

Voelkischer Beobachter: Hitler's newspaper.

Volksdeutsche: A German by race who is a foreign citizen.

Volksgenosse: 'Racial comrade' — the Nazi variant of the Communist 'comrade.'

Waffen-SS: The SS-in-arms, a branch of the SS which constituted a separate army along with the regular German army.

Wehrmacht: The German armed forces; this term replaced *Reichswehr* after Hitler came to power.

Wehrwirtschaft: An economy geared for war.

Wehrwirtschaftsamt: The economic staff of the army.

Wilhelmstrasse: The street in Berlin where the chancellery was situated Used as a synonym for the chancellery or the German government.

Index

(With identifications of the principal characters)

of England condemned by, 459; caution, discussed, 348; emigration, discussed, 329-330; Gestapo leary of prominent members of, 190-191; hunt for *the* general, 435-436; international law and, 432; military information given Allies by, 451-453; military laws and, 413-419; military members, politics of, 483-485; peace negotiations of, 447-450; and a popular Opposition movement, 216; any *Putsch* must be well prepared, 298; resign or 'stay-in,' a problem, 282-283, 296-298, 416-418; technique of meeting one another, 236; tensions within, 469; vacations, proper use of, 133; and vicious circle, 270-271

1938: coup d'état preparations, 306-317; warns British, 319; intelligence activities, 323-324; position after Munich, 328

1939: contacts with British and French, 344-352; warning to London, 351-352; efforts inside Germany, 352-361, 369-373; attempts to contact British and French, 378-382; and Nazi peace propaganda, 380-381

1940: and Pope, 447; warns Dutch, 453-454; German victories and, 458-459

1941: warns generals against war with Russia, 460; new conception of defeat of Germany, 460-461; effect of atrocities committed against Russia on, 461

1942: first assassination plans, 462

1943: Stalingrad *Putsch,* 466-467; and Tunis, 468; a year of disaster, 473

1944: and Western Powers, 480

July, 1944: new dynamism, 483-486; Communists contacted, 487-488; annihilated after, 191, 582. See *also Coup d'état, 1938; November, 1939, crisis; Putsch, July 20, 1944*

Optimism, of people, 177-178

Ordensburgen, 213, 317

Ordnungspolizei, 529. See *also* Police

Oster circle, 419, 425-429, 473-478

Oster, Major General Hans — Chief of Staff of the *Abwehr;* Oppositionist —

sketch of, 142-144, 421-425; aids Gisevius, 457; office of, center of Opposition's intelligence, 324; in prison, 588; saves Gisevius, Schacht, and Goerdeler, 348; and Stauffenberg, compared, 511-512

anti-Gestapo: assists Gisevius to make contacts in Bendlerstrasse, 144; on *June 30,* 162; aids fight against Gestapo, 186

Fritsch-Blomberg crisis: on Blomberg, 234, 235; calls in Blomberg's adjutant, 236-237; gets Blomberg's resignation, 241; and Beck-Schacht resignation talks, 280-282

coup d'état, 1938: talks with Halder, 283-286, 296; talks with Witzleben, 304-305; gives documents to Gisevius, 317

Czechoslovakia to Poland: and Czechoslovakian invasion, 335, 343; and Poland, 361, 370-372, 374

November, 1938, crisis: foreign contacts, 379-380; crisis, 382-386, 388-395, 397-398, 400; threatened by Brauchitsch, 447

1941 to dismissal from Abwehr: has a marksman join *Abwehr,* 462; wins over Olbricht, 464; Lahousen and, 469; at Dohnanyi's arrest, 476-477; relieved of his post, 477

Panef, Henry — alias of one of the three Bulgarian Communists suspected of starting the Reichstag fire. See Georgi Dimitroff; Blagoy Poppoff; Vassil Taneff

Papen, Franz von — one-time Chancellor of Germany; Vice-Chancellor under Hitler — Diels and, 40; consents to Hitler's dissolving the Reichstag, 83; collecting evidence, 85-86; Nationalist Bloc of, last enemy of Nazis, 123; Marburg speech, 126-127; on *June 30, 1934,* 151; and Dollfuss murder, 341

Pardons, for Nazi crimes, 105. See *also* Amnesty decrees

Paris, fall of, German reaction, 455-456